George Grote

# A history of greece from the earliest period to the close of the generation contemporary with Alexander the Great

George Grote

**A history of greece from the earliest period to the close of the generation contemporary with Alexander the Great**

ISBN/EAN: 9783742803092

Manufactured in Europe, USA, Canada, Australia, Japa

Cover: Foto ©ninafisch / pixelio.de

Manufactured and distributed by brebook publishing software (www.brebook.com)

George Grote

**A history of greece from the earliest period to the close of the generation contemporary with Alexander the Great**

A

# HISTORY OF GREECE;

FROM THE

EARLIEST PERIOD TO THE CLOSE OF THE GENERATION
CONTEMPORARY WITH ALEXANDER THE GREAT.

By GEORGE GROTE, F.R.S.,

D.C.L. OXON. AND LL.D. CAMB.,
VICE-CHANCELLOR OF THE UNIVERSITY OF LONDON.

*A NEW EDITION.*

IN TWELVE VOLUMES.—VOL. IX.

WITH PORTRAIT AND PLANS

LONDON:
JOHN MURRAY, ALBEMARLE STREET.
ALPHONS DÜRR, LEIPZIG.
1870.

# CONTENTS OF VOLUME IX.

## PART II.—CONTINUATION OF HISTORICAL GREECE.

### CHAPTER LXXII.

GREECE UNDER THE LACEDAEMONIAN EMPIRE.

| | Page |
|---|---|
| Sequel of Grecian affairs generally—resumed | 1 |
| Spartan empire—how and when it commenced | ib. |
| Oppression and suffering of Athens under the Thirty | 2 |
| Alteration of Grecian feeling towards Athens—the Thirty are put down and the democracy restored | 3 |
| The Knights or Horsemen, the richest proprietors at Athens, were the great supporters of the Thirty in their tyranny | ib. |
| The state of Athens, under the Thirty, is a sample of that which occurred in a large number of other Grecian cities, at the commencement of the Spartan empire | 4 |
| Great power of Lysander—he establishes in most of the cities Dekarchies, along with a Spartan harmost | ib. |
| Intimidation exercised everywhere by Lysander in favour of his own partisans | 5 |
| Oppressive action of these Dekarchies | 6 |
| In some points, probably worse than the Thirty at Athens | 8 |
| Bad conduct of the Spartan harmosts—harsh as well as corrupt. No justice to be obtained against them at Sparta | 9 |
| Contrast of the actual empire of Sparta, with the promises of freedom which she had previously held out | 10 |
| Numerous promises of general autonomy made by Sparta—by the Spartan general Brasidas especially | 12 |
| Gradual change in the language and plans of Sparta towards the close of the Peloponnesian war | 14 |
| Language of Brasidas contrasted with the acts of Lysander | 15 |
| Extreme suddenness and completeness of the victory of Ægospotami left Lysander almost omnipotent | ib. |
| The Dekarchies became partly modified by the jealousy at Sparta against Lysander. The Harmosts lasted much longer | 17 |
| The Thirty at Athens were put | |

## CHAPTER LXXII.—continued.

| | Page |
|---|---|
| down by the Athenians themselves, not by any reformatory interference of Sparta | 19 |
| The empire of Sparta much worse and more oppressive than that of Athens | 19 |
| Imperial Athens deprived her subject-allies of their autonomy, but was guilty of little or no oppression | 20 |
| Imperial Sparta did this and much worse—her harmosts and decemvirs are more complained of than the fact of her empire | 21 |
| This is the more to be regretted, as Sparta had now an admirable opportunity for organizing a good and stable confederacy throughout Greece | 22 |
| Sparta might have recognized the confederacy of Delos, which might now have been made to work well | 23 |
| Insupportable arrogance of Lysander—bitter complaints against him as well as against the Dekarchies | 24 |
| Lysander offends Pharnabazus, who procures his recall. His disgust and temporary expatriation | 25 |
| Surrender of the Asiatic Greeks to Persia, according to the treaty concluded with Sparta | 26 |
| Their condition is affected by the position and ambitious schemes of Cyrus, whose protection they seek against Tissaphernês | 27 |
| After the death of Cyrus, Tissaphernês returns as victor and satrap to the coast of Asia Minor | 28 |
| Alarm of the Asiatic Greeks, who send to ask aid from Sparta. The Spartans send Thimbron with an army to | |

| | Page |
|---|---|
| Asia. His ill-success and recall—he is superseded by Derkyllidas | 22 |
| Conduct of the Cyreians loose as to pillage | ib. |
| Derkyllidas makes a truce with Tissaphernês, and attacks Pharnabazus in the Troad and Æolis | 30 |
| Distribution of the Persian empire: relation of king, satrap, subsatrap | ib. |
| Mania, widow of Zênis, holds the subsatrapy of Æolis under Pharnabazus. Her regular payment and vigorous government | 31 |
| Military force, personal conquests, and large treasures, of Mania | 32 |
| Assassination of Mania, and of her son, by her son-in-law Meidias, who solicits the satrapy from Pharnabazus, but is indignantly refused | ib. |
| Invasion and conquest of Æolis by Derkyllidas, who gets possession of the person of Meidias | 33 |
| Derkyllidas acquires and liberates Skepsis and Gergis, deposing Meidias, and seizing the treasures of Mania | 34 |
| Derkyllidas concludes a truce with Pharnabazus, and takes winter quarters in Bithynia | 36 |
| Command of Derkyllidas—satisfaction of Sparta with the improved conduct of the Cyreians | 38 |
| Derkyllidas crosses into Europe, and employs his troops in fortifying the Chersonesus against the Thracians | ib. |
| He captures and garrisons Aternæus | 40 |
| He makes war upon Tissaphernês and Pharnabazus, upon the Mæander | 41 |

## CONTENTS OF VOLUME IX.

### CHAPTER LXXII.—*continued.*

| | Page |
|---|---|
| Timidity of Tissaphernês—he concludes a truce with Derkyllidas | 42 |
| Derkyllidas is superseded by Agesilaus | 43 |
| Alienation towards Sparta had grown up among her allies in Central Greece | ib. |
| Great energy imparted to Spartan action by Lysander immediately after the victory of Ægospotami; an energy very unusual with Sparta | ib. |
| The Spartans had kept all the advantages of victory to themselves—their allies were allowed nothing | 44 |
| Great power of the Spartans—they take revenge upon those who had displeased them—their invasion of Elis | 45 |
| The Spartan king Agis invades the Eleian territory. He retires from it immediately in consequence of an earthquake | 46 |
| Second invasion of Elis by Agis—he marches through Triphylia and Olympia: victorious march with much booty | 47 |
| Insurrection of the oligarchical party in Elis—they are put down | ib. |
| The Eleians are obliged to submit to hard terms of peace | 48 |
| Sparta refuses to restore the Pisatans to the Olympic presidency | 50 |
| Triumphant position of Sparta—she expels the Messenians from Peloponnesus and its neighbourhood | ib. |

### CHAPTER LXXIII.

AGESILAUS KING OF SPARTA.—THE CORINTHIAN WAR.

| | Page |
|---|---|
| Triumphant position of Sparta at the close of the war—introduction of a large sum of gold and silver by Lysander—opposed by some of the Ephors | 52 |
| The introduction of money was only one among a large train of corrupting circumstances which then became operative on Sparta | 53 |
| Contrast between Sparta in 432 B.C., and Sparta after 404 B.C. | 54 |
| Increase of peculation, inequality, and discontent at Sparta | 55 |
| Testimonies of Isokratês and Xenophon to the change of character and habits at Sparta | 58 |
| Power of Lysander—his arrogance and ambitious projects—flattery lavished upon him by sophists and poets | 58 |
| Real position of the kings at Sparta | 60 |
| His intrigues to make himself king at Sparta—he tries in vain to move the oracles in his favour—scheme laid for the production of sacred documents, as yet lying hidden, by a son of Apollo | 62 |
| His aim at the kingship fails—nevertheless he still retains prodigious influence at Sparta | 63 |
| Death of Agis king of Sparta—doubts as to the legitimacy of his son Leotychidês. Agesilaus, seconded by Lysander, aspires to the throne | 64 |

## CHAPTER LXXIII. *continued.*

| | Page |
|---|---|
| Character of Agesilaus | 61 |
| Conflicting pretensions of Agesilaus and Leotychides | 66 |
| Objection taken against Agesilaus on the ground of his lameness—oracle produced by Diopeithes—eluded by the interpretation of Lysander | 67 |
| Agesilaus is preferred as king—suspicions which always remained attached to Lysander's interpretation | 68 |
| Popular conduct of Agesilaus—he conciliates the Ephors—his great influence at Sparta—his energy, combined with unscrupulous partisanship | ib. |
| Dangerous conspiracy at Sparta—terror-striking sacrifices | 70 |
| Character and position of the chief conspirator Kinadon—state of parties at Sparta—increasing number of malcontents | ib. |
| Police of the Ephors—information laid before them | 72 |
| Wide-spread discontent reckoned upon by the conspirators | 73 |
| Alarm of the Ephors—their manœuvres for apprehending Kinadon privately | ib. |
| Kinadon is seized, interrogated, and executed—his accomplices are arrested, and the conspiracy broken up | 74 |
| Dangerous discontent indicated at Sparta | 76 |
| Proceedings of Derkyllidas and Pharnabazus in Asia | 77 |
| Persian preparations for reviving the maritime war against Sparta—renewed activity of Konon | 78 |
| Agesilaus is sent with a land-force to Asia, accompanied by Lysander | ib. |
| Large plans of Agesilaus, for conquest in the interior of Asia | 80 |

| | Page |
|---|---|
| General willingness of the Spartan allies to serve in the expedition, but refusal from Thebes, Corinth, and Athens | 80 |
| Agesilaus compares himself with Agamemnon—goes to sacrifice at Aulis—is contemptuously hindered by the Thebans | ib. |
| Arrival of Agesilaus at Ephesus—he concludes a fresh armistice with Tissaphernes | 81 |
| Arrogant behaviour and overweening ascendency of Lysander—offensive to the army and to Agesilaus | 82 |
| Agesilaus humbles and degrades Lysander, who asks to be sent away | ib. |
| Lysander is sent to command at the Hellespont—his valuable service there | 83 |
| Tissaphernes breaks the truce with Agesilaus, who makes war upon him and Pharnabazus—he retires for the purpose of organising a force of cavalry | 84 |
| Agesilaus indifferent to money for himself, but eager in enriching his friends | 85 |
| His humanity towards captives and deserted children | 86 |
| Spartan side of his character—exposure of naked prisoners—different practice of Asiatics and Greeks | 87 |
| Efforts of Agesilaus to train his army, and to procure cavalry | 89 |
| Agesilaus renews the war against Tissaphernes, and gains a victory near Sardis | 90 |
| Artaxerxes causes Tissaphernes to be put to death and superseded by Tithraustes | 91 |
| Negotiations between the new satrap and Agesilaus—the |

## CONTENTS OF VOLUME IX.

### CHAPTER LXXIII.—continued.

| | Page |
|---|---|
| satraps in Asia Minor hostile to each other | 92 |
| Commencement of action at sea against Sparta—the Athenian Konon, assisted by Persian ships and money, commands a fleet of eighty sail on the coast of Karia | 93 |
| Rhodes revolts from the Spartan empire—Konon captures an Egyptian corn-fleet at Rhodes | ib. |
| Anxiety of the Lacedæmonians —Agesilaus is appointed to command at sea as well as on land | 94 |
| Severity of the Lacedæmonians towards the Rhodian Dorians—contrast of the former treatment of the same men by Athens | ib. |
| Sentiment of a multitude compared with that of individuals | 96 |
| Efforts of Agesilaus to augment the fleet—he names Peisander admiral | 97 |
| Operations of Agesilaus against Pharnabazus | 97 |
| He lays waste the residence of the satrap, and surprises his camp — offence given to Spithridatês | 98 |
| Personal conference between Agesilaus and Pharnabazus | 100 |
| Friendship established between Agesilaus and the son of Pharnabazus — character of Agesilaus | 102 |
| Promising position and large preparations for Asiatic land-warfare, of Agesilaus—he is recalled with his army to Peloponnesus | 103 |
| Efforts and proceedings of Konon in command of the Persian fleet—his personal visit to the Persian court | ib. |
| Pharnabazus is named admiral jointly with Konon | 105 |
| Battle of Knidus—complete defeat of the Lacedæmonian fleet—death of Peisander the admiral | 106 |

### CHAPTER LXXIV.

#### FROM THE BATTLE OF KNIDUS TO THE REBUILDING OF THE LONG WALLS OF ATHENS.

| | | | Page |
|---|---|---|---|
| War in Central Greece against Sparta—called the Corinthian war | | | 108 |
| Relations of Sparta with the neighbouring states and with her allies after the accession of Agesilaus. Discontent among the allies | | | ib. |
| Great power of Sparta, stretching even to Northern Greece —state of Herakleia | | | 109 |
| Growing disposition in Greece to hostility against Sparta, when she becomes engaged in the war against Persia | | | ib. |
| The Satrap Tithraustês sends an envoy with money into Greece, to light up war against Sparta—his success at Thebes, Corinth, and Argos | | | 110 |
| The Persian money did not create hostility against Sparta, but merely brought out hostile tendencies pro-existing. Philo-Laconian sentiment of Xenophon | | | 111 |
| War between Sparta and Thebes—the Bœotian war | | | 113 |
| Active operations of Sparta against Bœotia—Lysander is sent to act from Herakleia on the northward—Pausanias | | | |

## CHAPTER LXXIV.—*continued.*

| | Page |
|---|---|
| conducts an army from Peloponnesus | 114 |
| The Thebans apply to Athens for aid—remarkable proof of the altered sentiment in Greece | 115 |
| Speech of the Theban envoy at Athens | ib. |
| Political feeling at Athens— good effects of the amnesty after the expulsion of the Thirty | 116 |
| Unanimous vote of the Athenians to assist Thebes against Sparta | 117 |
| State of the Bœotian confederacy—Orchomenus revolts and joins Lysander, who invades Bœotia with his army and attacks Haliartus | 118 |
| Lysander is repulsed and slain before Haliartus | ib. |
| Pausanias arrives in Bœotia after the death of Lysander —Thrasybulus and an Athenian army come to the aid of the Thebans | 119 |
| Pausanias evacuates Bœotia, on receiving the dead bodies of Lysander and the rest for burial | 120 |
| Anger against Pausanias at Sparta; he escapes into voluntary exile; he is condemned in his absence | 121 |
| Condemnation of Pausanias not deserved | ib. |
| Sparta not less unjust in condemning unsuccessful generals than Athens | 123 |
| Character of Lysander—his mischievous influence, as well for Sparta, as for Greece generally | ib. |
| His plans to make himself king at Sparta—discourse of the sophist Kleon | 124 |
| Encouragement to the enemies of Sparta, from the death of Lysander—alliance against her between Thebes, Athens, Corinth, and Argos—the Eubœans and others join the alliance | 125 |
| Increased importance of Thebes —she now rises to the rank of a primary power—the Theban leader Ismenias | ib. |
| Successful operations of Ismenias to the north of Bœotia—capture of Herakleia from Sparta | 126 |
| Synod of anti-Spartan allies at Corinth—their confident hopes—the Lacedæmonians send to recall Agesilaus from Asia | 127 |
| Large muster near Corinth of Spartans and Peloponnesians on one side, of anti-Spartan allies on the other | 127 |
| Boldness of the language against Sparta—speech of the Corinthian Timolaus | ib. |
| The anti-Spartan allies take up a defensive position near Corinth—advance of the Lacedæmonians to attack them | 129 |
| Battle of Corinth—victory of the Lacedæmonians in their part of the battle; their allies in the other parts being worsted | 130 |
| Lacedæmonian ascendency within Peloponnesus is secured, but no farther result gained | 132 |
| Agesilaus—his vexation on being recalled from Asia— his large plans of Asiatic conquest | 133 |
| Regret of the Asiatic allies when he quits Asia—he leaves Euxenus in Asia with 4000 men | 134 |
| Agesilaus crosses the Hellespont and marches homeward through Thrace, Macedonia, and Thessaly | 135 |

## CHAPTER LXXIV.—continued.

| | Page |
|---|---|
| Agesilaus and his army on the northern frontier of Bœotia—eclipse of the sun—news of the naval defeat at Knidus | 135 |
| Bœotians and their allies mustered at Koroneia | ib. |
| Battle of Koroneia—Agesilaus with most of his army is victorious; while the Thebans on their side are also victorious | 137 |
| Terrible combat between the Thebans and Spartans: on the whole the result is favourable to the Thebans | 138 |
| Victory of Agesilaus, not without severe wounds—yet not very decisive—his conduct after the battle | 139 |
| Army of Agesilaus withdraws from Bœotia—he goes to the Pythian games—sails homeward across the Corinthian Gulf—his honourable reception at Sparta | 141 |
| Results of the battles of Corinth and Koroneia. Sparta had gained nothing by the former, and had rather lost by the latter | ib. |
| Reverses of Sparta after the defeat of Knidus. Loss of the insular empire of Sparta. Nearly all her maritime allies revolt to join Pharnabazus and Konon | 142 |
| Abydos holds faithfully to Sparta, under Derkyllidas | 143 |
| Derkyllidas holds both Abydos and the Chersonesus opposite, in spite of Pharnabazus—anger of the latter | 144 |
| Pharnabazus and Konon sail with their fleet to Peloponnesus and to Corinth | 145 |
| Assistance and encouragement given by Pharnabazus to the allies at Corinth—remarkable fact of a Persian satrap and fleet at Corinth | 146 |
| Pharnabazus leaves the fleet with Konon in the Saronic Gulf, and aids him with money to rebuild the Long Walls of Athens | ib. |
| Konon rebuilds the Long Walls—hearty cooperation of the allies | 147 |
| Great importance of this restoration—how much it depended upon accident | 148 |
| Maintenance of the lines of Corinth against Sparta, was one essential condition to the power of rebuilding the Long Walls. The lines were not maintained longer than the ensuing year | 149 |

## CHAPTER LXXV.

### FROM THE REBUILDING OF THE LONG WALLS OF ATHENS TO THE PEACE OF ANTALKIDAS.

| | Page |
|---|---|
| Large plans of Konon—organization of a mercenary force at Corinth | 150 |
| Naval conflicts of the Corinthians and Lacedæmonians, in the Corinthian Gulf | 151 |
| Land-warfare—the Lacedæmonians established at Sikyon—the anti-Spartan allies occupying the lines of Corinth from sea to sea | 151 |
| Sufferings of the Corinthians from the war being carried on in their territory. Many Co- | |

## CHAPTER LXXV.—*continued.*

rinthian proprietors become
averse to the war ............ 151
Growth and manifestation of
the philo-Laconian party in
Corinth. Oligarchical form
of the government left open
nothing but an appeal to force 153
The Corinthian Government
forestal the conspiracy by a
coup d'état ................ 154
Numerous persons of the philo-
Laconian party are banished;
nevertheless Pasimelus the
leader is spared, and remains
at Corinth ................ 157
Intimate political union and
consolidation between Corinth and Argos ............ ib.
Pasimelus admits the Lacedæmonians within the Long
Walls of Corinth. Battle
within those walls .......... 158
The Lacedæmonians are victorious—severe loss of the
Argeians .................. 159
The Lacedæmonians pull down
a portion of the Long Walls
between Corinth and La-
chæum, so as to open a free
passage across. They capture
Krommyon and Sidus .... 160
Effective warfare carried on by
the light troops under Iphikratês at Corinth—military
genius and improvements of
Iphikratês ................ ib.
The Athenians restore the Long
Walls between Corinth and
Lechæum—expedition of the
Spartan king Agesilaus, who,
in concert with Teleutias, retakes the Long Walls and
captures Lechæum ........ 163
Alarm of Athens and Thebes
at the capture of the Long
Walls of Corinth. Propositions sent to Sparta to solicit
peace. The discussions come
to no result ................ 166

Advantages derived by the Corinthians from possession of
Peiræum. At the instigation
of the exiles, Agesilaus
marches forth with an army
to attack it ................ 168
Isthmian festival — Agesilaus
disturbs the celebration. The
Corinthian exiles, under his
protection, celebrate it; then,
when he is gone, the Corinthians from the city, and
perform the ceremony over
again ...................... 169
Agesilaus attacks Peiræum,
which he captures, together
with the Heræum, many
prisoners, and much booty .. 170
Triumphant position of Agesilaus. Danger of Corinth. The
Thebans send fresh envoys
to solicit peace—contemptuously treated by Agesilaus 172
Sudden arrival of bad news,
which spoils the triumph .. ib.
Destruction of a Lacedæmonian
mora by the light troops under
Iphikratês ................ 173
Daring and well-planned manœuvres of Iphikratês ...... 174
Few of the mora escape to Lechæum .................... 175
The Lacedæmonians bury the
bodies of the slain, under
truce asked and obtained.
Trophy erected by Iphikratês 176
Great effect produced upon the
Grecian mind by this event.
Peculiar feelings of Spartans:
pride of the relatives of the
slain ...................... 177
Mortification of Agesilaus—he
marches up to the walls of
Corinth and defies Iphikratês
—he then goes back humiliated to Sparta ............ 178
Success of Iphikratês—he retakes Krommyon, Sidus, and
Peiræum — Corinth remains

## CHAPTER LXXV.—continued.

| | Page | | Page |
|---|---|---|---|
| pretty well undisturbed by enemies. The Athenians recall Iphikrates | 178 | Tiribazus cannot prevail with the Persian court, which still continues hostile to Sparta. | |
| Expedition of Agesilaus against Akarnania—successful, after some delay—the Akarnanians submit, and enrol themselves in the Lacedæmonian confederacy | ib. | Struthas is sent down to act against the Lacedæmonians in Ionia | 188 |
| The Lacedæmonians under Agesipolis invade Argos | 181 | Victory of Struthas over Thimbron and the Lacedæmonian army. Thimbron is slain | ib. |
| Manœuvre of the Argeians respecting the season of the holy truce. Agesipolis consults the oracles at Olympia and Delphi | ib. | Diphridas is sent to succeed Thimbron | 189 |
| Earthquake in Argos after the invasion of Agesipolis—he disregards it | 182 | Lacedæmonian fleet at Rhodes —intestine disputes in the island | ib. |
| He marches up near to Argos—much plunder taken—he retires | ib. | The Athenians send aid to Evagoras at Cyprus. Fidelity with which they adhered to him, though his alliance had now become inconvenient | 191 |
| Transactions in Asia—efforts of Sparta to detach the Great King from Athens | 184 | Thrasybulus is sent with a fleet from Athens to the Asiatic coast—his acquisitions in the Hellespont and Bosphorus | 192 |
| The Spartan Antalkidas is sent as envoy to Tiribazus. Konon and other envoys sent also, from Athens and the anti-Spartan allies | ib. | Victory of Thrasybulus in Lesbos—he levies contributions along the Asiatic coast—he is slain near Aspendus | ib. |
| Antalkidas offers to surrender the Asiatic Greeks, and demands universal autonomy throughout the Grecian world—the anti-Spartan allies refuse to accede to those terms | 185 | Character of Thrasybulus | 193 |
| | | Agyrrhius succeeds Thrasybulus—Rhodes still holds out against the Lacedæmonians | 194 |
| Hostility of Sparta to all the partial confederacies of Greece, now first proclaimed under the name of universal autonomy | ib. | Anaxibius is sent to command at the Hellespont in place of Derkyllidas—his vigorous proceedings—he deprives Athens of the tolls of the strait | 195 |
| Antalkidas gains the favour of Tiribazus, who espouses privately the cause of Sparta, though the propositions for peace fail. Tiribazus seizes Konon—Konon's career is now closed, either by death or imprisonment | 187 | The Athenians send Iphikrates with his peltasts and a fleet to the Hellespont. His stratagem to surprise Anaxibius | 193 |
| | | Defeat and death of Anaxibius | ib. |
| | | The Athenians are again masters of the Hellespont and the strait dues | 198 |
| | | The island of Ægina—its past history | ib. |
| | | The Æginetans are constrained by Sparta into war with Athens. The Lacedæmonian | |

## CHAPTER LXXV.—*continued.*

admiral Teleutias at Ægina. He is superseded by Hierax. His remarkable popularity among the seamen .. .. .. 198

Hierax proceeds to Rhodes, leaving Gorgôpas at Ægina. Passage of the Lacedæmonian Antalkidas to Asia .. .. .. 200

Gorgôpas is surprised in Ægina, defeated, and slain, by the Athenian Chabrias; who goes to assist Evagoras in Cyprus 201

The Lacedæmonian seamen at Ægina unpaid and discontented. Teleutias is sent thither to conciliate them .. 202

Sudden and successful attack of Teleutias upon the Peiræus 203

Unprepared and unguarded condition of Peiræus—Teleutias gains rich plunder, and sails away in safety .. .. .. .. ib.

He is enabled to pay his seamen — activity of the fleet—great loss inflicted upon Athenian commerce .. .. .. .. .. 204

Financial condition of Athens. The Theôrikon .. .. .. .. 205

Direct property-taxes .. .. .. 206

Antalkidas goes up with Tiribazus to Susa—his success at the Persian court—he brings down the terms of peace asked for by Sparta, ratified by the Great King, to be enforced by Sparta in his name .. .. 210

Antalkidas in command of the Lacedæmonian and Syracusan fleets in the Hellespont, with Persian aid. His successes against the Athenians .. .. 211

Distress and discouragement of Athens—anxiety of the anti-Spartan allies for peace .. ib.

Tiribazus summons them all to Sardis, to hear the convention which had been sent down by the Great King .. .. .. 212

Terms of the convention, called the peace of Antalkidas .. ib.

Congress at Sparta for acceptance or rejection. All parties accept. The Thebans at first accept under reserve for the Bœotian cities .. .. ib.

Agesilaus refuses to allow the Theban reserve, and requires unconditional acceptance. His eagerness, from hatred of Thebes, to get into a war with them single-handed. The Thebans are obliged to accept unconditionally .. .. .. 213

Agesilaus forces the Corinthians to send away their Argeian auxiliaries. The philo-Argeian Corinthians go into exile: the philo-Laconian Corinthians are restored .. .. 214

## CHAPTER LXXVI.

### FROM THE PEACE OF ANTALKIDAS DOWN TO THE SUBJUGATION OF OLYNTHUS BY SPARTA.

Peace or convention of Antalkidas. Its import and character. Separate partnership between Sparta and Persia 215

Degradation in the form of the convention—a fiat drawn up, issued, and enforced, by Persia upon Greece .. .. .. 216

Gradual loss of Pan-hellenic dignity, and increased sub-

## CHAPTER LXXVI.—continued.

mission towards Persia as a means of purchasing Persian help—on the part of Sparta .. 219
Her first application before the Peloponnesian war; subsequent applications .. .. ib.
Active partnership between Sparta and Persia against Athens, after the Athenian catastrophe at Syracuse. Athens is ready to follow her example .. .. .. .. 220
How Sparta became hostile to Persia after the battle of Ægospotami. The Persian force aids Athens against her, and breaks up her maritime empire .. .. .. .. .. 221
No excuse for the subservience of Sparta to the Persians— she was probably afraid of a revived Athenian empire .. 222
Hellenism betrayed to the enemy, first, by Sparta, next by the other leading states. Evidence that Hellenic independence was not destined to last much longer .. .. 224
Promise of universal autonomy —popular to the Grecian ear —how carried out .. .. ib.
The Spartans never intended to grant, nor ever really granted, general autonomy. They used the promise as a means of increased power to themselves .. .. .. .. .. 225
Immediate point made against Corinth and Thebes—isolation of Athens .. .. .. .. 226
Persian affairs—unavailing efforts of the Great King to reconquer Egypt .. .. .. 227
Evagoras, despot of Salamis in Cyprus .. .. .. .. .. 228
Descent of Evagoras—condition of the Island of Cyprus.. .. ib.
Greek princes of Salamis are dispossessed by a Phœnician dynasty .. .. .. .. .. 230
Evagoras, dethrones the Phœnician, and becomes despot of Salamis .. .. .. .. .. ib.
Able and beneficent government of Evagoras .. .. .. 231
His anxiety to revive Hellenism in Cyprus—he looks to the aid of Athens .. .. .. .. 232
Relations of Evagoras with Athens during the closing years of the Peloponnesian war .. .. .. .. .. .. 233
Evagoras at war with the Persians—he receives aid both from Athens and from Egypt —he is at first very successful, so as even to capture Tyre 234
Struggle of Evagoras against the whole force of the Persian empire after the peace of Antalkidas .. .. .. .. 235
Evagoras, after a ten years' war, is reduced, but obtains an honourable peace, mainly owing to the dispute between the two satraps jointly commanding .. .. .. .. 236
Assassination of Evagoras, as well as of his son Pnytagoras, by an eunuch slave of Nikokreon .. .. .. .. .. 238
Nikoklês, son of Evagoras, becomes despot of Salamis 238
Condition of the Asiatic Greeks after being transferred to Persia—much changed for the worse. Exposure of the Ionian islands also .. .. 240
Great power gained by Sparta through the peace of Antalkidas. She becomes practically mistress of Corinth, and the Corinthian isthmus. Miso-Theban tendencies of Sparta—especially of Agesilaus .. .. .. .. .. 242
Sparta organized anti-Theban

## CHAPTER LXXVI.—continued.

| | Page | | Page |
|---|---|---|---|
| oligarchies in the Bœotian cities, with a Spartan harmost in several. Most of the cities seem to have been favourable to Thebes, though Orchomenus and Thespiæ were adverse | 242 | Intervention, committed by Sparta towards her various allies | 255 |
| The Spartans restore Platæa. Former conduct of Sparta towards Platæa | 244 | Return of the philo-Laconian exiles in the various cities, as partisans for the purposes of Sparta—case of Phlius | 256 |
| Motives of Sparta in restoring Platæa. A politic step, as likely to sever Thebes from Athens | 248 | Competition of Athens with Sparta for ascendency at sea. Athens gains ground, and gets together some rudiments of a maritime confederacy | ib. |
| Platæa becomes a dependency and outpost of Sparta. Main object of Sparta to prevent the reconstitution of the Bœotian federation | ib. | Ideas entertained by some of the Spartan leaders, of acting against the Persians for the rescue of the Asiatic Greeks. — Panegyrical Discourse of Isokratês | 258 |
| Spartan policy at this time directed by the partisan spirit of Agesilaus, opposed by his colleague Agesipolis | 243 | State of Macedonia and Chalkidikê—growth of Macedonian power during the last years of the Peloponnesian war | 259 |
| Oppressive behaviour of the Spartans towards Mantineia. They require the walls of the city to be demolished | 249 | Perdikkas and Archelaus— energy and ability of the latter | ib. |
| Agesipolis blockades the city, and forces it to surrender, by damming up the river Ophis. The Mantineians are forced to break up their city into villages | 250 | Contrast of Macedonia and Athens | 261 |
| | | Succeeding Macedonian kings —Orestês, Aeropus, Pausanias, Amyntas. Assassination frequent | 262 |
| Democratical leaders of Mantineia—owed their lives to the mediation of the exiled king Pausanias | 251 | Amyntas is expelled from Macedonia by the Illyrians —he makes over much of the sea-coast to the Olynthian confederacy | ib. |
| Mantineia is pulled down and distributed into five villages | 252 | Chalkidians of Olynthus—they take into their protection the Macedonian cities on the coast, when Amyntas runs away before the Illyrians. Commencement of the Olynthian confederacy | 264 |
| High-handed despotism of Sparta towards Mantineia— signal partiality of Xenophon | ib. | |
| Mischievous influence of Sparta during this period of her ascendency, in decomposing the Grecian world into the smallest fragments | 254 | |
| The treatment of Mantineia was only one among a series of other acts of oppressive | | Equal and liberal principles on which the confederacy was framed from the beginning. Accepted willingly by the Macedonian and Græco-Macedonian cities | 265 |

## CHAPTER LXXVI.—continued.

The Olynthians extend their confederacy among the Grecian cities in Chalkidic Thrace—their liberal procedure—several cities join—others cling to their own autonomy, but are afraid of open resistance .. .. .. .. 266

Akanthus and Apollonia resist the proposition. Olynthus menaces. They then solicit Spartan intervention against her .. .. .. .. .. .. 267

Speech of Kleigenês the Akanthian envoy at Sparta .. .. ib.

Envoys from Amyntas at Sparta 269

The Lacedæmonians and their allies vote aid to the Akanthians against Olynthus . 271

Anxiety of the Akanthians for instant intervention. The Spartan Eudamidas is sent against Olynthus at once, with such force as could be got ready. He checks the career of the Olynthians . 272

Phœbidas, brother of Eudamidas, remains behind to collect fresh force, and march to join his brother in Thrace. He passes through the Theban territory and near Thebes 273

Conspiracy of Leontiadês and the philo-Laconian party in Thebes, to betray the town and citadel to Phœbidas .. ib.

The opposing leaders—Leontiadês and Ismenias—were both Polemarchs. Leontiadês contrives the plot and introduces Phœbidas into the Kadmeia .. .. .. .. .. 274

Leontiadês overawes the Senate, and arrests Ismenias; Pelopidas and the leading friends of Ismenias go into exile .. .. .. .. .. 275

Phœbidas in the Kadmeia—terror and submission at Thebes 276

Mixed feelings at Sparta—great importance of the acquisition to Spartan interests .. .. ib.

Displeasure at Sparta more pretended than real, against Phœbidas: Agesilaus defends him .. .. .. .. .. .. 277

Leontiadês at Sparta—his humble protestations and assurances—the Ephors decide that they will retain the Kadmeia, but at the same time fine Phœbidas .. .. .. ib.

The Lacedæmonians cause Ismenias to be tried and put to death. Iniquity of this proceeding .. .. .. . 278

Vigorous action of the Spartans against Olynthus—Teleutias is sent there with a large force, including a considerable Theban contingent. Derdas cooperates with him . 279

Strenuous resistance of the Olynthians — excellence of their cavalry .. .. .. . 280

Teleutias being at first unsuccessful, and having become overconfident, sustains a terrible defeat from the Olynthians under the walls of their city ib.

Agesipolis is sent to Olynthus from Sparta with a reinforcement. He dies of a fever . 281

Polybiadês succeeds Agesipolis as commander—he reduces Olynthus to submission—extinction of the Olynthian federation. Olynthus and the other cities are enrolled as allies of Sparta .. .. .. 282

Great mischief done by Sparta to Greece by thus crushing Olynthus .. .. .. .. ib.

Intervention of Sparta with the government of Phlius. The Phliasian government fa-

## CHAPTER LXXVI.—*continued.*

voured by Agesipolis, persecuted by Agesilaus .. .. .. 284
Agesilaus marches an army against Phlius—reduces the town by blockade, after a long resistance. The Lacedæmonians occupy the acropolis, naming a Council of One Hundred as governors 289

## CHAPTER LXXVII.

**FROM THE SUBJUGATION OF OLYNTHUS BY THE LACEDÆMONIANS DOWN TO THE CONGRESS AT SPARTA, AND PARTIAL PEACE, IN 371 B.C.**

Great ascendency of Sparta on land in 379 B.C. .. .. .. .. 240
Sparta is now feared as the great despot of Greece—her confederacy with the Persian king, and with Dionysius of Syracuse .. .. .. .. .. *ib.*
Strong complaint of the rhetor Lysias, expressed at the Olympic festival of 384 B.C. .. .. 292
Demonstration against the Syracusan despot Dionysius, at that festival .. .. .. .. 293
Panegyrical oration of Isokrates .. .. .. .. .. .. .. 292
Censure upon Sparta pronounced by the philo-Laconian Xenophon .. .. .. .. 293
His manner of marking the point of transition in his history—from Spartan glory to Spartan disgrace .. .. 294
Thebes under Leontiades and the philo-Spartan oligarchy, with the Spartan garrison in the Kadmeia—oppressive and tyrannical government .. .. *ib.*
Discontent at Thebes, though under compression. Theban exiles at Athens .. .. .. 295
The Theban exiles at Athens, after waiting some time in hopes of a rising at Thebes, resolve to begin a movement themselves .. .. .. .. 297
Pelopidas takes the lead—he, with Mellon and five other exiles, undertakes the task of destroying the rulers of Thebes. Cooperation of Phyllidas the secretary, and Charon at Thebes .. .. .. 297
Plans of Phyllidas for admitting the conspirators into Thebes and the government-house—he invites the polemarchs to a banquet .. .. 298
The scheme very nearly frustrated—accident which prevented Childon from delivering his message .. .. .. 299
Pelopidas and Mellon get secretly into Thebes, and conceal themselves in the house of Charon. Sudden summons sent by the polemarchs to Charon. Charon places his son in the hands of Pelopidas as a hostage—warning to the polemarchs from Athens—they leave it unread .. .. 300
Phyllidas brings the conspirators, in female attire, into the room where the polemarchs are banqueting — Archias, Philippus, and Kabeirichus are assassinated .. .. .. 301
Leontiades and Hypates are slain in their houses .. .. 302
Phyllidas opens the prison, and sets free the prisoners. Epameinondas and many other citizens appear in arms .. 303
Universal joy among the cit-

## CHAPTER LXXVII.—*continued.*

Scene on the ensuing morning, when the event was known. General assembly in the market-place — Pelopidas, Mellon, and Charon are named the first Bœotarchs .......... 304
Aid to the conspirators from private sympathisers in Attica. Alarm of the Spartans in the Kadmeia—they send for reinforcements .......... *ib.*
Pelopidas and the Thebans prepare to storm the Kadmeia — the Lacedæmonian garrison capitulate and are dismissed — several of the oligarchical Thebans are put to death in trying to go away along with them. The harmost who surrendered the Kadmeia is put to death by the Spartans .. 305
Powerful sensation produced by this incident throughout the Grecian world .......... 308
It alters the balance of power, and the tenure of Spartan empire .............. 310
Indignation in Sparta at the revolution of Thebes—a Spartan army sent forth at once, under King Kleombrotus. He retires from Bœotia without achieving anything ...... *ib.*
Kleombrotus passes by the Athenian frontier—alarm at Athens—condemnation of the two Athenian generals who had favoured the enterprise of Pelopidas ........ 311
Attempt of Sphodrias from Thespiæ to surprise the Peiræus by a night-march. He fails .............. 314
Different constructions put upon this attempt and upon the character of Sphodrias .. *ib.*
Alarm and wrath produced at Athens by the attempt of Sphodrias. The Lacedæmonian envoys at Athens seized, but dismissed ........ 316
Trial of Sphodrias at Sparta. He is acquitted, greatly through the private favour and sympathies of Agesilaus *ib.*
Comparison of Spartan with Athenian procedure ..... 317
The Athenians declare war against Sparta, and contract alliance with Thebes .... 318
Exertions of Athens to form a new maritime confederacy, like the Confederacy of Delos. Thebes enrolls herself as a member .............. 319
Athens sends round envoys to the islands in the Ægean. Liberal principles on which the new confederacy is formed. The Athenians formally renounce all pretensions to their lost properties out of Attica, and engage to abstain from future Kleruchies ............ *ib.*
Envoys sent round by Athens —Chabrias, Timotheus, Kallistratus .............. 321
Service of Iphikratês in Thrace after the peace of Antalkidas. He marries the daughter of the Thracian prince Kotys, and acquires possession of a Thracian sea-port, Drys .. 321
Timotheus and Kallistratus— their great success in winning the islanders into confederacy with Athens ........ 323
Synod of the new confederates assembled at Athens—votes for war on a large scale .. 328
Members of the confederacy were at first willing and harmonious—a fleet is equipped 329
New property-tax imposed at Athens. The Solonian census *ib.*
The Solonian census retained in the main, though with

## CHAPTER LXXVII.—*continued.*

modifications, at the restoration under the archonship of Eukleidês in 403 B.C. .. .. 330

Archonship of Nausinikus in 378 B.C.— New census and schedule then introduced, of all citizens worth 52 minæ and upwards, distributed into classes, and entered for a fraction of their total property; each class for a different fraction .. .. .. .. 331

All metics, worth more than 25 minæ, were registered in the schedule; all in one class, each man for one-sixth of his property. Aggregate schedule .. .. .. .. .. 332

The Symmories — containing the 1200 wealthiest citizens —the 300 wealthiest, leaders of the Symmories .. .. .. 333

Citizens not wealthy enough to be included in the Symmories, yet still entered in the schedule and liable to property-tax. Purpose of the Symmories—extension of the principle to the trierarchy .. 334

Enthusiasm at Thebes in defence of the new government and against Sparta. Military training—the Sacred Band .. 335

Epaminondas .. .. .. .. .. 336
His previous character and training—musical and intellectual, as well as gymnastic. Conversation with philosophers, Sokratic as well as Pythagorean .. .. .. .. 337

His eloquence—his unambitious disposition—gentleness of his political resentments .. .. 340

Conduct of Epaminondas at the Theban revolution of 379 B.C.— he acquires influence, through Pelopidas, in the military organization of the city .. .. .. .. .. .. 341

Agesilaus marches to attack Thebes with the full force of the Spartan confederacy— good system of defence adopted by Thebes - aid from Athens under Chabrias .. .. 342

Agesilaus retires, leaving Phœbidas in command at Thespiæ —desultory warfare of Phœbidas against Thebes—he is defeated and slain. Increase of the Theban strength in Bœotia, against the philo-Spartan oligarchies in the Bœotian cities .. .. .. .. 343

Second expedition of Agesilaus into Bœotia—he gains no decisive advantage. The Thebans acquire greater and greater strength. Agesilaus retires—he is disabled by a hurt in the leg .. .. .. .. 345

Kleombrotus conducts the Spartan force to invade Bœotia— he is stopped by Mount Kithæron, being unable to get over the passes—he retires without reaching Bœotia .. *ib.*

Resolution of Sparta to equip a large fleet, under the admiral Pollis. The Athenians send out a fleet under Chabrias—victory of Chabrias at sea near Naxos. Recollection of the battle of Arginusæ .. 346

Extension of the Athenian maritime confederacy. In consequence of the victory of Naxos 347

Circumnavigation of Peloponnesus by Timotheus with an Athenian fleet—his victory over the Lacedæmonian fleet —his success in extending the Athenian confederacy—his just dealing .. .. .. .. .. 348

Financial difficulties of Athens 349
She becomes jealous of the growing strength of Thebes—

## CHAPTER LXXVII.—continued.

| | Page |
|---|---|
| steady and victorious progress of Thebes in Bœotia | 350 |
| Victory of Pelopidas at Tegyra over the Lacedæmonians | 351 |
| The Thebans expel the Lacedæmonians out of all Bœotia, except Orchomenus—they reorganise the Bœotian federation | ib. |
| They invade Phokis—Kleombrotus is sent thither with an army for defence—Athens makes a separate peace with the Lacedæmonians | 352 |
| Demand made upon the Lacedæmonians from Thessaly, for aid to Pharsalus | 354 |
| Polydamas of Pharsalus applies to Sparta for aid against Pheræ | ib. |
| Jason of Pheræ—his energetic character and formidable power | 355 |
| It is prudent dealing with Polydamas | 356 |
| The Lacedæmonians find themselves unable to spare any aid for Thessaly—they dismiss Polydamas with a refusal. He comes to terms with Jason, who becomes Tagus of Thessaly | ib. |
| Evidence of the decline of Spartan power during the last eight years | 357 |
| Peace between Athens and Sparta—broken off almost immediately. The Lacedæmonians declare war again, and resume their plans upon Zakynthus and Korkyra | 358 |
| Lacedæmonian armament under Mnasippus, collected from all the confederates, invades Korkyra | 359 |
| Mnasippus besieges the city—high cultivation of the adjoining lands | ib. |
| The Korkyræans blocked up in the city—supplies intercepted—want begins—no hope of safety except in aid from Athens. Reinforcement arrives from Athens—large Athenian fleet preparing under Timotheus | 360 |
| Mnasippus becomes careless and insolent from over-confidence—he offends his mercenaries—the Korkyræans make a successful sally—Mnasippus is defeated and slain—the city supplied with provisions | 361 |
| Approach of the Athenian reinforcement—Hypermenes, successor of Mnasippus, conveys away the armament, leaving his sick and much property behind | 362 |
| Tardy arrival of the Athenian fleet—it is commanded not by Timotheus, but by Iphikrates—causes of the delay—preliminary voyage of Timotheus, very long protracted | 363 |
| Discontent at Athens, in consequence of the absence of Timotheus—distress of the armament assembled at Kalauria—Iphikrates and Kallistratus accuse Timotheus. Iphikrates named admiral in his place | 364 |
| Return of Timotheus—an accusation is entered against him, but trial is postponed until the return of Iphikrates from Korkyra | 366 |
| Rapid and energetic movements of Iphikrates towards Korkyra—his excellent management of the voyage. On reaching Kephallenia, he learns the flight of the Lacedæmonians from Korkyra | ib. |
| He goes on to Korkyra, and captures by surprise the ten Syracusan triremes sent by Dionysius to the aid of Sparta | 367 |
| Iphikrates in want of money—he sends home Kallistratus to | |

b 2

## CHAPTER LXXVII.—continued.

Athens—he finds work for his seamen at Korkyra—he obtains funds by service in Akarnania .......... 368

Favourable tone of public opinion at Athens, in consequence of the success of Korkyra—the trial of Timotheus went off easily—Jason and Alketas come to support him—his accuser is condemned to death ...... 370

Timotheus had been guilty of delay, not justifiable under the circumstances—though acquitted, his reputation suffered—he accepts command under Persia ........ 371

Discouragement of Sparta in consequence of her defeat at Korkyra, and of the triumphant position of Iphikratês. They are farther dismayed by earthquakes and other divine signs—Helikê and Bura are destroyed by an earthquake 374

The Spartans again send Antalkidas to Persia, to sue for a fresh intervention—the Persian satraps send down an order that the Grecian belligerents shall make up their differences ...... ib.

Athens disposed towards peace 375

Athens had ceased to be afraid of Sparta, and had become again jealous of Thebes . ib.

Equivocal position of the restored Plataea, now that the Lacedaemonians had been expelled from Boeotia. The Plataeans try to persuade Athens to incorporate them with Attica .......... 376

The Thebans forestal this negotiation by seizing Plataea, and expelling the inhabitants, who again take refuge at Athens .......... 377

Strong feeling excited in Athens against the Thebans, on account of their dealings with Plataea and Thespiae. The Plataic discourse of Isokratês 379

Increased tendency of the Athenians towards peace with Sparta—Athens and the Athenian confederacy give notice to Thebes. General congress for peace at Sparta........ 381

Speeches of the Athenian envoys Kallias, Autoklês, Kallistratus .............. 382

Kallistratus and his policy ... ib.

He proposes that Sparta and Athens shall divide between them the headship of Greece—Sparta on land, Athens at sea—recognising general autonomy .............. 383

Peace is concluded. Autonomy of each city to be recognised: Sparta to withdraw her harmosts and garrisons...... 384

Oaths exchanged. Sparta takes the oath for herself and her allies. Athens takes it for herself: her allies take it after her successively .... ib.

The oath proposed to the Thebans. Epaminondas, the Theban envoy, insists upon taking the oath in the name of the Boeotian federation . ib.

Agesilaus and the Spartans require that he shall take it for Thebes alone ........ 385

Daring and emphatic speeches delivered by Epaminondas in the congress—protesting against the overweening pretensions of Sparta. He claims recognition of the ancient institutions of Boeotia, with Thebes as president of the federation .............. ib.

Indignation of the Spartans, and especially of Agesilaus

## CHAPTER LXXVII.—continued.

– brief questions exchanged
—Thebes is excluded from
the treaty .. .. .. .. .. 386
General peace sworn, including
Athens, Sparta, and the rest
—Thebes alone is excluded 388
Advantageous position of
Athens—prudence in her to
make peace now .. .. .. 388
Terms of the peace—compulsory and indefensible confederacies are renounced—
voluntary alliances alone
maintained .. .. .. .. 389
Real point in debate between
Agesilaus and Epaminondas 390

## CHAPTER LXXVIII.

### BATTLE OF LEUKTRA AND ITS CONSEQUENCES.

Measures for executing the
stipulations made at the congress of Sparta .. .. .. .. 392
Violent impulse of the Spartans
against Thebes .. .. .. .. ib.
King Kleombrotus is ordered
to march into Bœotia, out of
Phokis .. .. .. .. .. .. 393
He forces the defences of Bœotia, and encamps at Leuktra 394
Epaminondas and the Thebans
at Leuktra—discouragement
in the army .. .. .. .. .. 395
New order of battle adopted
by Epaminondas .. .. .. 396
Confidence of the Spartans and
of Kleombrotus .. .. .. .. 397
Battle of Leuktra .. .. .. 398
Defeat of the Spartans and
death of Kleombrotus .. .. 399
Faint adherence of the Spartan
allies .. .. .. .. .. .. ib.
Spartan camp after the defeat
—confession of defeat by
sending to solicit the burial-truce .. .. .. .. .. .. 400
Great surprise, and immense
alteration of feeling, produced throughout Greece by
the Theban victory .. .. .. 401
Effect of the news at Sparta—
heroic self-command .. .. 404
Difference of Athens and
Sparta—Athens, equal in active energy .. .. .. .. .. 405
Reinforcements sent from Sparta 406
Proceedings in Bœotia after
the battle of Leuktra. The
Theban victory not well
received at Athens .. .. .. ib.
Jason of Pheræ arrives at Leuktra—the Spartan army retires
from Bœotia under capitulation .. .. .. .. .. .. 407
Treatment of the defeated citizens on reaching Sparta—
suspension of the law .. .. 410
Lowered estimation of Sparta
in Greece—prestige of military superiority lost .. .. 411
Extension of the power of
Thebes. Treatment of Orchomenus and Thespiæ .. .. 412
Power and ambition of Jason 413
Plans of Jason—Pythian festival .. .. .. .. .. .. .. ib.
Assassination of Jason at
Pheræ .. .. .. .. .. .. 414
Relief to Thebes by the death
of Jason—satisfaction in
Greece .. .. .. .. .. .. 415
Proceedings in Peloponnesus
after the defeat of Leuktra.
Expulsion of the Spartan
harmosts and dekarchies .. 416
Skytalism at Argos—violent
intestine feud .. .. .. .. 417
Discouragement and helplessness of Sparta .. .. .. .. 419
Athens places herself at the

## CHAPTER LXXVIII.—continued.

| | Page |
|---|---|
| head of a new Peloponnesian land confederacy | 419 |
| Accusation preferred in the Amphiktyonic assembly, by Thebes against Sparta | 420 |
| The Spartans are condemned to a fine—importance of this fact as an indication | 421 |
| Proceedings in Arcadia | 422 |
| Re-establishment of the city of Mantineia by its own citizens | 423 |
| Humiliating refusal experienced by Agesilaus from the Mantineians—keenly painful to a Spartan | 424 |
| Feeling against Agesilaus at Sparta | 425 |
| Impulse among the Arcadians towards Pan-Arcadian union. Opposition from Orchomenus and Tegea | 426 |
| Revolution at Tegea—the philo-Spartan party are put down or expelled. Tegea becomes anti-Spartan, and favourable to the Pan-Arcadian union | 427 |
| Pan-Arcadian union is formed | 428 |
| March of Agesilaus against Mantineia. Evidence of lowered sentiment in Sparta | 429 |
| Application by the Arcadians to Athens for aid against Sparta; it is refused: they then apply to the Thebans | 431 |
| Proceedings and views of Epaminondas since the battle of Leuktra | ib. |
| Plans of Epaminondas for restoring the Messenians in Peloponnesus | 432 |
| Also, for consolidating the Arcadians against Sparta | 433 |
| Epaminondas and the Theban army arrive in Arcadia. Great allied force assembled there. The allies entreat him to invade Laconia | 434 |
| Reluctance of Epaminondas to | |

| | Page |
|---|---|
| invade Laconia — reasonable grounds for it | 435 |
| He marches into Laconia—four lines of invasion | ib. |
| He crosses the Eurotas and approaches close to Sparta | 436 |
| Alarm at Sparta—arrival of various allies to her aid by sea | 437 |
| Discontent in Laconia among the Periœki and Helots—danger to Sparta from that cause | 438 |
| Vigilant defence of Sparta by Agesilaus | 439 |
| Violent emotion of the Spartans, especially the women. Partial attack upon Sparta by Epaminondas | 440 |
| He retires without attempting to storm Sparta: ravages Laconia down to Gythium. He returns into Arcadia | 441 |
| Great effect of this invasion upon Grecian opinion—Epaminondas is exalted, and Sparta farther lowered | 442 |
| Foundation of the Arcadian Megalopolis | ib. |
| Foundation of Messênê | 444 |
| Abstraction of Western Laconia from Sparta | 445 |
| Great diminution thereby of her power, wealth, and estimation | 446 |
| Periœki and Helots established as freemen along with the Messenians on the Lacedæmonian border | 447 |
| The details of this reorganising process unhappily unknown | 449 |
| Megalopolis—the Pan-Arcadian Ten Thousand | 450 |
| Epaminondas and his army evacuate Peloponnesus | 451 |
| The Spartans solicit aid from Athens—language of their envoys, as well as those from Corinth and Phlius, at Athens | 453 |

## CHAPTER LXXVIII.—*continued.*

| | Page | | Page |
|---|---|---|---|
| Reception of the envoys—the Athenians grant the prayer | 454 | army to the Isthmus | 456 |
| Vote passed to aid Sparta—Iphikrates is named general | 455 | Trial of Epaminondas at Thebes for retaining his command beyond the legal time—his honourable and easy acquittal | 458 |
| March of Iphikrates and his | | | |

# HISTORY OF GREECE.

## PART II.
CONTINUATION OF HISTORICAL GREECE.

### CHAPTER LXXII.
GREECE UNDER THE LACEDÆMONIAN EMPIRE.

THE three preceding Chapters have been devoted exclusively to the narrative of the Expedition and Retreat immortalized by Xenophon, occupying the two years intervening between about April 401 B.C. and June 399 B.C. That event, replete as it is with interest and pregnant with important consequences, stands apart from the general sequence of Grecian affairs—which sequence I now resume.

It will be recollected that as soon as Xenophon with his Ten Thousand warriors descended from the rugged mountains between Armenia and the Euxine to the hospitable shelter of Trapezus, and began to lay their plans for returning to Central Greece—they found themselves within the Lacedæmonian empire, unable to advance a step without consulting Lacedæmonian dictation, and obliged, when they reached the Bosphorus, to endure without redress the harsh and treacherous usage of the Spartan officers Anaxibius and Aristarchus. *Sequel of Grecian affairs generally—resumed.*

Of that empire the first origin has been already set forth. It began with the decisive victory of Ægospotami in the Hellespont (September or October 405 B.C.), where the Lacedæmonian Lysander, without the loss of a man, got possession of the entire Athenian fleet and a large portion of their crews—with the exception of eight or nine *Spartan empire—how and when it commenced.*

VOL. IX. B

triremes with which the Athenian admiral Konon effected his escape to Euagoras at Cyprus. The whole power of Athens was thus annihilated. Nothing remained for the Lacedæmonians to master except the city itself and Peiræus; a consummation certain to happen, and actually brought to pass in April 404 B.C., when Lysander entered Athens in triumph, dismantled Peiræus, and demolished a large portion of the Long Walls. With the exception of Athens herself—whose citizens deferred the moment of subjection by a heroic, though unavailing, struggle against the horrors of famine—and of Samos—no other Grecian city offered any resistance to Lysander after the battle of Ægospotami; which in fact not only took away from Athens her whole naval force, but transferred it all over to him, and rendered him admiral of a larger Grecian fleet than had ever been seen together since the battle of Salamis.

Oppression and suffering of Athens under the Thirty.

I have recounted, in my sixty-fifth chapter, the sixteen months of bitter suffering undergone by Athens immediately after her surrender. The loss of her fleet and power was aggravated by an extremity of internal oppression. Her oligarchical party and her exiles, returning after having served with the enemy against her, extorted from the public assembly, under the dictation of Lysander who attended it in person, the appointment of an omnipotent Council of Thirty, for the ostensible purpose of framing a new constitution. These Thirty rulers—among whom Kritias was the most violent, and Theramenês (seemingly) the most moderate, or at least the soonest satiated—perpetrated cruelty and spoliation on the largest scale, being protected against all resistance by a Lacedæmonian harmost and garrison established in the acropolis. Besides numbers of citizens put to death, so many others were driven into exile with the loss of their property, that Thebes and the neighbouring cities became crowded with them. After about eight months of unopposed tyranny, the Thirty found themselves for the first time attacked by Thrasybulus at the head of a small party of these exiles coming out of Bœotia. His bravery and good conduct—combined with the enormities of the Thirty, which became continually more nefarious, and to which even numerous oligarchical citizens, as well as Theramenês himself, successively became victims—enabled him soon to strengthen himself, to seize the Peiræus and to carry on a civil war which ultimately put down the tyrants.

These latter were obliged to invoke the aid of a new Lacedæmonian force. And had that force still continued at the disposal of Lysander, all resistance on the part of Athens would have been unavailing. But fortunately for the Athenians, the last few months had wrought material change in the dispositions both of the allies of Sparta and of many among her leading men. The allies, especially Thebes and Corinth, not only relented in their hatred and fear of Athens, now that she had lost her power—but even sympathised with her suffering exiles, and became disgusted with the self-willed encroachments of Sparta; while the Spartan king Pausanias, together with some of the Ephors, were also jealous of the arbitrary and oppressive conduct of Lysander. Instead of conducting the Lacedæmonian force to uphold at all price the Lysandrian oligarchy, Pausanias appeared rather as an equitable mediator to terminate the civil war. He refused to concur in any measure for obstructing the natural tendency towards a revival of the democracy. It was in this manner that Athens, rescued from that sanguinary and rapacious *régime* which has passed into history under the name of the Thirty Tyrants, was enabled to re-appear as a humble and dependent member of the Spartan alliance—with nothing but the recollection of her former power, yet with her democracy again in vigorous and tutelary action for internal government. The just and gentle bearing of her democratical citizens, and the absence of reactionary antipathies, after such cruel ill-treatment—are among the most honourable features in her history.

Alteration of Grecian feeling towards Athens—the Thirty are put down and the democracy restored.

The reader will find in preceding chapters, what I can only rapidly glance at here, the details of that system of bloodshed, spoliation, extinction of free speech and even of intellectual teaching, efforts to implicate innocent citizens as agents in judicial assassination, &c.—which stained the year of Anarchy (as it was termed in Athenian annals[1]) immediately following the surrender of the city. These details depend on evidence perfectly satisfactory; for they are conveyed to

The Knights or Horsemen, the richest proprietors at Athens, were the great supporters of the Thirty in their tyranny.

[1] Xen. Hellen. ii. 8. 1.

us chiefly by Xenophon, whose sympathies are decidedly oligarchical. From him too we obtain another fact, not less pregnant with instruction; that the Knights or Horsemen, the body of richest proprietors at Athens, were the mainstay of the Thirty from first to last, notwithstanding all the enormities of their career.

*The state of Athens under the Thirty, is a sample of that which occurred in a large number of other Grecian cities, at the commencement of the Spartan empire.*
We learn from these dark, but well-attested details, to appreciate the auspices under which that period of history called the Lacedæmonian Empire was inaugurated. Such phænomena were by no means confined within the walls of Athens. On the contrary, the year of Anarchy (using that term in the sense in which it was employed by the Athenians) arising out of the same combination of causes and agents, was common to a very large proportion of the cities throughout Greece. The Lacedæmonian admiral Lysander, during his first year of naval command, had organised in most of the allied cities factious combinations of some of the principal citizens, corresponding with himself personally. By their efforts in their respective cities, he was enabled to prosecute the war vigourously; and he repaid them, partly by seconding as much as he could their injustices in their respective cities —partly by promising to strengthen their hands still farther, as soon as victory should be made sure.[1] This policy, while it served as a stimulus against the common enemy, contributed still more directly to aggrandise Lysander himself; creating for him an ascendency of his own, and imposing upon him personal obligations towards adherents, apart from what was required by the interests of Sparta.

*Great power of Lysander—he establishes in most of the cities Dekarchies, along with a Spartan harmost.*
The victory of Ægospotami, complete and decisive beyond all expectations either of friend or foe, enabled him to discharge these obligations with interest. All Greece at once made submission to the Lacedæmonians,[2] except Athens and Samos—and these two only held out a few months. It was now the first business of the victorious commander to remunerate his adherents, and to take permanent security for Spartan dominion as well as for his own. In the greater number of cities, he

---

[1] Plutarch, Lysand. c. 5.    [2] Xen. Hellen. ii. 2, 6.

established an oligarchy of Ten citizens, or a Dekarchy,[1] composed of his own partisans; while he at the same time planted in each a Lacedæmonian harmost or governor, with a garrison, to uphold the new oligarchy. The Dekarchy of Ten Lysandrian partisans, with the Lacedæmonian harmost to sustain them, became the general scheme of Hellenic government throughout the Ægean, from Eubœa to the Thracian coast towns, and from Miletus to Byzantium. Lysander sailed round in person with his victorious fleet to Byzantium and Chalkêdon, to the cities of Lesbos, to Thasos, and other places; while he sent Eteonikus to Thrace for the purpose of thus recasting the governments everywhere. Not merely those cities which had hitherto been on the Athenian side, but also those which had acted as allies of Sparta, were subjected to the same intestine revolution and the same foreign constraint.[2] Everywhere the new Lysandrian Dekarchy superseded the previous governments, whether oligarchical or democratical.

At Thasus, as well as in other places, this revolution was not accomplished without much bloodshed as well as treacherous stratagem; nor did Lysander himself scruple to enforce, personally and by his own presence, the execution and expulsion of suspected citizens.[3] In many places, however, simple terrorism probably sufficed. The

Intimidation exercised everywhere by Lysander in favour of his own partisans.

---

[1] These Councils of Ten, organised by Lysander, are sometimes called *Dekarchies*—sometimes *Dekadarchies*. I use the former word by preference; since the word *Dekadarch* is also employed by Xenophon in another and very different sense—as meaning an officer who commands a *Dekad*.

[2] Plutarch, Lysand. c. 13.

Καταλύων δὲ τοὺς δήμους καὶ τὰς ἄλλας πολιτείας, ἕνα μὲν ἁρμοστὴν ἑκάστῃ Λακεδαιμόνιον κατέλιπε, ἕνα δὲ ἄρχοντας ἐκ τῶν ὑπ' αὐτοῦ συγκεκροτημένων κατὰ πόλιν ἑταιρειῶν. Καὶ ταῦτα πράττων ὁμοίως ἔν τε ταῖς πολεμίαις καὶ ταῖς συμμάχοις γεγενημέναις πόλεσι, παρέπλει σχολαίως τρόπον τινὰ κατασκευαζόμενος ἑαυτῷ τὴν τῆς

Ἑλλάδος ἡγεμονίαν. Compare Xen. Hellen. ii. 3, 2-5; Diodor. xiii. 3, 10, 13.

[3] Plutarch, Lysand. c. 18. πολλοὺς παραγινομένους αὐτὸς ἐργάτης καὶ συνεπιβάλλων τοῖς τῶν φίλων ἐχθροῖς, οὐκ ἐπιεικὲς ἐδίδου τοῖς Ἕλλησι δεῖγμα τῆς Λακεδαιμονίων ἀρχῆς, &c.

Ib. c. 14. Καὶ τῶν μὲν ἄλλων πόλεων ὁμαλῶς ἁπασῶν κατέλυε τὰς πολιτείας καὶ καθίστη διακοσμίας· κολλῶν μὲν ἐν ἑκάστῃ σφαττομένων, πολλῶν δὲ φευγόντων, &c.

About the massacre at Thasus, see Cornelius Nepos, Lysand. c. 2; Polyæn. l. **, 4. Compare Plutarch, Lysand. c. 19; and see Vol. VIII. Ch. lxv. p. 19 of this History.

new Lysandrian Ten overawed resistance and procured recognition of their usurpation, by the menace of inviting the victorious admiral with his fleet of 200 sail, and by the simple arrival of the Lacedæmonian harmost. Not only was each town obliged to provide a fortified citadel and maintenance for this governor with his garrison, but a scheme of tribute, amounting to 1000 talents annually, was imposed for the future, and assessed rateably upon each city by Lysander.[1]

**Oppressive action of these Dekarchies.** In what spirit these new Dekarchies would govern, consisting as they did of picked oligarchical partisans distinguished for audacity and ambition[2]—who, to all the unscrupulous lust of power which characterised Lysander himself, added a thirst for personal gain, from which he was exempt, and were now about to reimburse themselves for services already rendered to him—the general analogy of Grecian history would sufficiently teach us, though we were without special details. But in reference to this point, we have not merely general analogy to guide us; we have farther the parallel case of the Thirty at Athens, the particulars of whose rule are well known and have already been alluded to. These Thirty, with the exception of the difference of number, were to all intents and purposes a Lysandrian Dekarchy; created by the same originating force, placed under the like circumstances, and animated by the like spirit and interests. Every subject town would produce its Kritias and Theramenês, and its body of wealthy citizens like the Knights or Horsemen at Athens to abet their oppressions, under Lacedæmonian patronage and the covering guard of the Lacedæmonian harmost. Moreover, Kritias, with all his vices, was likely to be better rather than worse, as compared with his oligarchical parallel in any other less cultivated city. He was a man of letters and philosophy, accustomed to the conversation of Sokratês, and to the discussion of ethical and social questions. We may say the same of the Knights or horsemen at Athens. Undoubtedly they had been better educated, and had been exposed to more liberalising and improving in-

[1] Diodor. xiv. 10. Compare Isokratês, Or. iv. (Panegyr.) s. 151; Xen. Hellen. iv. 8, 1.
[2] Plutarch, Lysand. c. 13. τοῦ Λυσάνδρου τῶν ὀλίγων τοῖς θρασυτάτοις καὶ φιλονεικοτάτοις τὰς πόλεις ἐγχειρίζοντος.

fluences, than the corresponding class elsewhere. If then these Knights at Athens had no shame in serving as accomplices to the Thirty throughout all their enormities, we need not fear to presume that other cities would furnish a body of wealthy men yet more unscrupulous, and a leader at least as sanguinary, rapacious, and full of antipathies, as Kritias. As at Athens, so elsewhere; the Dekarchs would begin by putting to death notorious political opponents, under the name of "the wicked men;"[1] they would next proceed to deal in the same manner with men of known probity and courage, likely to take a lead in resisting oppression.[2] Their career of blood would continue—in spite of remonstrances from more moderate persons among their own number, like Theramenês—until they contrived some stratagem for disarming the citizens, which would enable them to gratify both their antipathies and their rapacity, by victims still more numerous—many of such victims being wealthy men, selected for purposes of pure spoliation.[3] They would next dispatch by force any obtrusive monitor from their own number, like Theramenês; probably with far less ceremony than accompanied the perpetration of this crime at Athens, where we may trace the effect of those judicial forms and habits to which the Athenian public had been habituated—overruled indeed, yet still not forgotten. There would hardly remain any fresh enormity still to commit, over and above the multiplied executions, except to banish from the city all but their own immediate partisans, and to reward these latter with choice estates confiscated from the victims.[4] If called upon to excuse such tyranny, the leader of a Dekarchy would have sufficient invention to employ the plea of Kritias—that all changes of government were unavoidably death-dealing, and that nothing less than such stringent measures would suffice to maintain his city in suitable dependence upon Sparta.[5]

[1] Xen. Hellen. II. 3, 13.
... ἐκεῖνον Λύσανδρον φρουροὺς σφίσι ξυμπράξαι ἐλθεῖν, ἕως δὴ τοὺς πονηροὺς ἐκκοδὼν ποιησάμενοι κατασρήσαιντο τὴν πολιτείαν, &c.
[2] Xen. Hellen. II. 3, 14. Τῶν δὲ φρουρῶν τούτου (the harmost) ξυμπέμποντος αὐτοῖς, οὓς ἐβούλοντο, ξυνελάμβανον οὐκέτι τοὺς πονηροὺς καὶ ὀλίγου ἀξίους, ἀλλ' ἤδη οὓς ἐνό-

μιζον ἥκιστα μὲν παρωθουμένους ἀνέχεσθαι, ἀντιπράττειν δέ τι ἐπιχειροῦντας πλείστους τοὺς ξυνεθέλοντας λαμβάνειν.
[3] Xen. Hellen. II. 3, 21.
[4] Xen. Hellen. II. 4, 1.
[5] Xen. Hellen. II. 3, 24-32. Καὶ εἰσι μὲν δήπου πόσαι μεταβολαὶ πολιτειῶν θανατηφόροι, &c.

Of course, it is not my purpose to affirm that in any other city, precisely the same phænomena took place as those which occurred in Athens. But we are nevertheless perfectly warranted in regarding the history of the Athenian Thirty as a fair sample, from whence to derive our idea of those Lysandrian Dekarchies which now overspread the Grecian world. Doubtless each had its own peculiar march: some were less tyrannical; but perhaps some even more tyrannical, regard being had to the size of the city. And in point of fact, Isokratês, who speaks with indignant horror of these Dekarchies, while he denounces those features which they had in common with the Triakontarchy at Athens—extrajudicial murders, spoliations, and banishments—notices one enormity besides, which we do not find in the latter—violent outrages upon boys and women.[1] Nothing of this kind is ascribed to Kritias[2] and his companions; and it is a considerable proof of the restraining force of Athenian manners, that men who inflicted so much evil in gratification of other violent impulses, should have stopped short here. The Decemvirs named by Lysander, like the Decemvir Appius Claudius at Rome, would find themselves armed with power to satiate their lusts as well as their antipathies, and would not be more likely to set bounds to the former than to the latter. Lysander, in all the overweening insolence of victory, while rewarding his most devoted partisans with an exaltation comprising every sort of licence and tyranny, stained the dependent cities with countless murders, perpetrated on private as well as

*marginal notes:* In some points, probably worse than the Thirty at Athens.

---

[1] Isokratês, Orat. iv. (Panegyr.) s. 187-189 (c. 82).

He has been speaking, at some length, and in terms of energetic denunciation, against the enormities of the Dekarchies. He concludes by saying—Φυγάς δὲ καὶ στάσεις καὶ νόμων συγχύσεις καὶ πολιτειῶν μεταβολάς, ἔτι δὲ παίδων ὕβρεις καὶ γυναικῶν αἰσχύνας καὶ χρημάτων ἁρπαγάς, τίς ἂν δύναιτο διεξελθεῖν; πλὴν τοσοῦτον εἰπεῖν ἔχω καθ' ἁπάντων, ὅτι τὰ μὲν ἐφ' ἡμῶν δεινά ῥᾳδίως ἄν τις ἐνὶ ψηφίσματι διέλυσε, τὰς δὲ σφαγὰς καὶ τὰς ἀνομίας τὰς ἐπὶ τούτων γενομένας οὐδεὶς ἂν ἰάσασθαι δύναιτο.

See also, of the same author, Isokratês, Orat. v. (Philipp.) s. 110; Orat. viii. (De Pace) s. 119-124; Or. xii. (Panath.) s. 54, 60, 106.

[2] We may infer that if Xenophon had heard anything of the sort respecting Kritias, he would hardly have been averse to mention it; when we read what he says (Memorab. I. 2, 29). Compare a curious passage about Kritias in Dion. Chrysostom. Or. xxi. p. 270.

## OPPRESSION OF THE TEN.

on public grounds.[1] No individual Greek had ever before wielded so prodigious a power of enriching friends or destroying enemies, in this universal reorganisation of Greece;[2] nor was there ever any power more deplorably abused.

It was thus that the Lacedæmonian empire imposed upon each of the subject cities a double oppression;[3] the native Decemvirs, and the foreign Harmost; each abetting the other, and forming together an aggravated pressure upon the citizens, from which scarce any escape was left. The Thirty at Athens paid the greatest possible court to the harmost Kallibius,[4] and put to death individual Athenians offensive to him, in order to purchase his cooperation in their own violences. The few details which we possess respecting these harmosts (who continued throughout the insular and maritime cities for about ten years, until the battle of Knidus, or as long as the maritime empire of Sparta lasted—but in various continental dependencies considerably longer, that is, until the defeat of Leuktra in 371 B.C.) are all for the most part discreditable. We have seen in the last chapter the description given even by the philo-Laconian Xenophon, of the harsh and treacherous manner in which they acted towards the returning Cyreian soldiers,

*Had occasion;[3] the native Decemvirs, and the foreign Harmost; each abetting the other, and forming together an aggravated pressure upon the citizens, from which scarce any escape was left. The Thirty at Athens paid the greatest possible court to the harmost Kallibius,[4] and put to death individual Athenians offensive to him, in order to purchase his cooperation in their own violences.* — Spartan harmosts— harsh as well as corrupt. No justice to be obtained against them at Sparta.

---

[1] Plutarch, Lysand. c. 19. Ἦν δὲ καὶ τῶν ἄλλων ἐν ταῖς πόλεσι δημοτικῶν φόνος οὐκ ἀριθμητός, ἅτε δὴ μὴ κατ' ἰδίας μόνον αἰτίας αὐτοῦ κτείνοντος, ἀλλὰ πολλαῖς μὲν ἔχθραις, πολλαῖς δὲ πλεονεξίαις, τῶν ἑκασταχόθι φίλων χαριζομένου τὰ τοιαῦτα καὶ συνεργοῦντος: also Pausanias, vii. 10, 1; ix. 32, 6.

[2] Plutarch, Agesilaus, c. 7.

[3] See the speech of the Theban envoys at Athens, about eight years after the surrender of Athens (Xen. Hellen. III. 5, 13).
... Οὐδὲ γὰρ φυγεῖν ἐξῆν (Plutarch, Lysand. c. 19).

[4] Xen. Hellen. ii. 3, 13. τὸν μὲν Καλλίβιον ἐθεράπευον ἀδοξ θεραπείᾳ, ὡς πάντα ἐκεῖνοι, ἃ πράττοιεν, &c. (Plutarch, Lysand. c. 15).

The Thirty seem to have outdone Lysander himself. A young Athenian of rank, distinguished as a victor in the pankratium, Autolykus,—having been insulted by Kallibius, resented it, tripped him up, and threw him down. Lysander, on being appealed to, justified Autolykus, and censured Kallibius, telling him that he did not know how to govern freemen. The Thirty however afterwards put Autolykus to death, as a means of courting Kallibius (Plutarch, Lysand. c. 15). Pausanias mentions Eteonikus (not Kallibius) as the person who struck Autolykus; but he ascribes the same decision to Lysander (ix. 32, 3).

combined with their corrupt subservience to Pharnabazus. We learn from him that it depended upon the fiat of a Lacedæmonian harmost whether these soldiers should be proclaimed enemies and excluded for ever from their native cities; and Kleander, the harmost of Byzantium, who at first threatened them with this treatment, was only induced by the most unlimited submission, combined with very delicate management, to withdraw his menace. The cruel proceedings of Anaxibius and Aristarchus, who went so far as to sell 400 of these soldiers into slavery, has been recounted a few pages above. Nothing can be more arbitrary or reckless than their proceedings. If they could behave thus towards a body of Greek soldiers full of acquired glory, effective either as friends or as enemies, and having generals capable of prosecuting their collective interests and making their complaints heard—what protection would a private citizen of any subject city, Byzantium or Perinthus, be likely to enjoy against their oppression?

Contrast of the actual empire of Sparta, with the promises of freedom which she had previously held out.

The story of Aristodemus, the harmost of Oreus in Eubœa, evinces that no justice could be obtained against any of their enormities from the Ephors at Sparta. That harmost, among many other acts of brutal violence, seized a beautiful youth, son of a free citizen at Oreus, out of the palæstra—carried him off—and after vainly endeavouring to overcome his resistance, put him to death. The father of the youth went to Sparta, made known the atrocities, and appealed to the Ephors and Senate for redress. But a deaf ear was turned to his complaints, and in anguish of mind he slew himself. Indeed we know that these Spartan authorities would grant no redress, not merely against harmosts, but even against private Spartan citizens, who had been guilty of gross crime out of their own country. A Bœotian near Leuktra, named Skedasus, preferred complaint that two Spartans, on their way from Delphi, after having been hospitably entertained in his house, had first violated, and afterwards killed, his two daughters; but even for so flagitious an outrage as this, no redress could be obtained.[1] Doubtless,

[1] Plutarch, Amator. Narration. p. 773; Plutarch, Pelopidas, c. 20. In Diodorus (xv. 54) and Pausanias (ix. 13, 8), the damsels thus outraged are stated to have slain themselves. Compare another story in Xenoph. Hellen. v. 4, 56, 57.

when a powerful foreign ally, like the Persian satrap Pharnabazus,[1] complained to the Ephors of the conduct of a Lacedæmonian harmost or admiral, his representations would receive attention: and we learn that the Ephors were thus induced not merely to recall Lysander from the Hellespont, but to put to death another officer, Thorax, for corrupt appropriation of money. But for a private citizen in any subject city, the superintending authority of Sparta would be not merely remote but deaf and immovable, so as to afford him no protection whatever, and to leave him altogether at the mercy of the harmost. It seems too that the rigour of Spartan training, and peculiarity of habits, rendered individual Lacedæmonians on foreign service more self-willed, more incapable of entering into the customs or feelings of others, and more liable to degenerate when set free from the strict watch of home—than other Greeks generally.[2]

Taking all these causes of evil together—the Dekarchies, the Harmosts, and the overwhelming dictatorship of Lysander—and construing other parts of the Grecian world by the analogy of Athens under the Thirty—we shall be warranted in affirming that the first years of the Spartan Empire, which followed upon the victory of Ægospotami, were years of all-pervading tyranny, and multifarious intestine calamity, such as Greece had never before endured. The hardships of war, severe in many ways, were now at an end, but they were replaced by a state of suffering not the less difficult to bear because it was called peace. And what made the suffering yet more intolerable was, that it was a bitter disappointment and a flagrant violation of promises proclaimed, repeatedly and explicitly, by the Lacedæmonians themselves.

[1] Plutarch, Lysand. c. 19.
[2] This seems to have been the impression not merely of the enemies of Sparta, but even of the Spartan authorities themselves. Compare two remarkable passages of Thucydidês, i. 77, and L 86. Ἄριστα γάρ (says the Athenian envoy at Sparta) τά τε καθ' ὑμᾶς αὐτοὺς νόμιμα τοῖς ἄλλοις ἔχετε, καὶ προσέτι εἰς ἕκαστος ἐξιὼν οὔτε τούτοις χρῆται, οὐδ' οἷς ἡ ἄλλη Ἑλλάς

νομίζει.
After the recall of the regent Pausanias and of Dorkis from the Hellespont (in 477 B.C.), the Lacedæmonians refuse to send out any successor, φοβούμενοι μὴ σφίσιν οἱ ἐξιόντες χείρους γίγνωνται, ὅπερ καὶ ἐν τῷ Παυσανίᾳ ἐνεῖδον, &c. (L 95).
Compare Plutarch, Apophtheg. Laconic. p. 220 F.

For more than thirty years preceding—from times earlier than the commencement of the Peloponnesian War—the Spartans had professed to interfere only for the purpose of liberating Greece, and of putting down the usurped ascendency of Athens. All the allies of Sparta had been invited into strenuous action—all those of Athens had been urged to revolt—under the soul-stirring cry of "Freedom to Greece." The earliest incitements addressed by the Corinthians to Sparta in 432 B.C., immediately after the Korkyræan dispute, called upon her to stand forward in fulfilment of her recognised function as "Liberator of Greece," and denounced her as guilty of connivance with Athens if she held back.[1] Athens was branded as the "despot city;" which had already absorbed the independence of many Greeks, and menaced that of all the rest. The last formal requisition borne by the Lacedæmonian envoys to Athens in the winter immediately preceding the war, ran thus—"If you desire the continuance of peace with Sparta, restore to the Greeks their autonomy."[2] When Archidamus king of Sparta approached at the head of his army to besiege Platæa, the Platæans laid claim to autonomy as having been solemnly guaranteed to them by King Pausanias after the great victory near their town. Upon which Archidamus replied—"Your demand is just: we are prepared to confirm *your* autonomy—but we call upon you to aid us in securing the like for those other Greeks who have been enslaved by Athens. This is the sole purpose of our great present effort."[3] . And the banner of general enfranchisement, which the Lacedæmonians thus held up at the outset of the war, enlisted in their cause encouraging sympathy and good wishes throughout Greece.[4]

[1] Thucyd. I. 69. οὐ γάρ ὁ βουλόμενος, ἀλλ' ὁ δυνάμενος μὲν κωλῦσαι, περιορῶν δὲ, ἀληθέστερον αὐτὸ δρᾷ, εἴπερ καὶ τὴν ἀξίωσιν τῆς ἀρετῆς ὡς ἐλευθερῶν τὴν Ἑλλάδα φέρεται.
To the like purpose the second speech of the Corinthian envoys at Sparta, c. 122-124—μὴ μέλλετε Ποτιδαιάταις τε τοιοῖσδε τιμωρίαν. ... καὶ τῶν ἄλλων μετελθεῖν τὴν ἐλευθερίαν, &c.
[2] Thucyd. I. 139. Compare Isokrates, Or. iv. Panegyr. c. 34. s.

140; Or. v. (Philipp.) s. 121; Or. xiv. (Plataic.) s. 42.
[3] Thucyd. ii. 72. Παρασκευὴ δὲ τόσηδε καὶ πόλεμος γεγένηται αὐτῶν ἕνεκα καὶ τῶν ἄλλων ἐλευθερώσεως.
Read also the speech of the Theban orator, in reply to the Platæans, after the capture of the town by the Lacedæmonians (iii. 63).
[4] Thucyd. ii. 8. ἡ δὲ εὔνοια παρὰ πολὺ ἐποίει τῶν ἀνθρώπων μᾶλλον ἐς τοὺς Λακεδαιμονίους, ἄλλως τε

But the most striking illustration by far, of the seductive promises held out by the Lacedæmonians, was afforded by the conduct of Brasidas in Thrace, when he first came into the neighbourhood of the Athenian allies during the eighth year of the war (424 B.C.). In his memorable discourse addressed to the public assembly at Akanthus, he takes the greatest pains to satisfy them that he came only for the purpose of realising the promise of enfranchisement proclaimed by the Lacedæmonians at the beginning of the war.[1] Having expected, when acting in such a cause, nothing less than a hearty welcome, he is astonished to find their gates closed against him. "I am come (said he) not to injure, but to liberate the Greeks; after binding the Lacedæmonian authorities by the most solemn oaths, that all whom I may bring over shall be dealt with as autonomous allies. We do not wish to obtain you as allies either by force or fraud, but to act as your allies at a time when you are enslaved by the Athenians. You ought not to suspect my purposes, in the face of these solemn assurances; least of all ought any man to hold back through apprehension of private enmities, and through fear lest I should put the city into the hands of a few chosen partisans. I am not come to identify myself with local faction: I am not the man to offer you an unreal liberty by breaking down your established constitution, for the purpose of enslaving either the Many to the Few, or the Few to the Many. That would be more intolerable even than foreign dominion; and we Lacedæmonians should incur nothing but reproach, instead of reaping thanks and honour for our trouble. We should draw upon ourselves those very censures, upon the strength

*Numerous promises of general autonomy made by Sparta—by the Spartan general Brasidas, especially.*

καὶ προσιόντων ὅτι τὴν Ἑλλάδα ἐλευθεροῦσιν. See also iii. 13, 14—the speech of the envoys from the revolted Mitylenê, to the Lacedæmonians.

The Lacedæmonian admiral Alkidas with his fleet is announced as crossing over the Ægean to Ionia for the purpose of "liberating Greece;" accordingly, the Samian exiles remonstrate with him for killing his prisoners, as in contradiction with that object (iii. 32)—ἔλεγον οὐ καλῶς τὴν Ἑλλάδα ἐλευθεροῦν αὐτόν, εἰ ἄνδρας διαφθείρει, &c.

[1] Thucyd. iv. 85. Ἡ μὲν ἔκπεμψίς μου καὶ τῆς στρατιᾶς ὑπὸ Λακεδαιμονίων, ὦ Ἀκάνθιοι, γεγένηται τὴν αἰτίαν ἀπαληθεύουσα ἣν ἀρχόμενοι τοῦ πολέμου προείπομεν, Ἀθηναίοις ἐλευθεροῦντες τὴν Ἑλλάδα πολεμήσειν.

of which we are trying to put down Athens; and that too in aggravated measure, worse than those who have never made honourable professions; since to men in high position, specious trick is more disgraceful than open violence.— If (continued Brasidas) in spite of my assurances, you still withhold from me your cooperation, I shall think myself authorised to constrain you by force. We should not be warranted in forcing freedom on any unwilling parties, except with a view to some common good. But as we seek not empire for ourselves—as we struggle only to put down the empire of others—as we offer autonomy to each and all—so we should do wrong to the majority if we allowed you to persist in your opposition."[1]

*Gradual change in the language and plans of Sparta towards the close of the Peloponnesian War.*

Like the allied sovereigns of Europe in 1813, who, requiring the most strenuous efforts on the part of the people to contend against the Emperor Napoleon, promised free constitutions, yet granted nothing after the victory had been assured—the Lacedæmonians thus held out the most emphatic and repeated assurances of general autonomy in order to enlist allies against Athens; disavowing, even ostentatiously, any aim at empire for themselves. It is true, that after the great catastrophe before Syracuse, when the ruin of Athens appeared imminent, and when the alliance with the Persian satraps against her was first brought to pass, the Lacedæmonians began to think more of empire,[2] and less of Gre-

[1] Thucyd. iv. 85. Αὐτός τε οὐκ ἐπὶ κακῷ, ἐπ' ἐλευθερώσει δὲ τῶν Ἑλλήνων παρελήλυθα, ὅρκοις τε Λακεδαιμονίων καταλαβὼν τὰ τέλη τοῖς μεγίστοις, ἦ μὴν οὓς ἂν ἔγωγε προσαγάγωμαι ξυμμάχους ἔσεσθαι αὐτονόμους.... Καὶ εἰ τις ἰδίᾳ τινὰ δεδιὼς ἄρα, μὴ ἐγώ τισι προσθῶ τὴν πόλιν, ἀπρόθυμός ἐστι, κἀντῶν μάλιστα πιστευσάτω. Οὐ γὰρ ξυστασιάσων ἥκω, οὐδὲ ἀσαφῆ τὴν ἐλευθερίαν νομίζω ἐπιφέρειν, εἰ τὸ πάτριον παρεὶς, τὸ πλέον τοῖς ὀλίγοις, ἢ τὸ ἔλασσον τοῖς πᾶσι, δουλώσαιμι. Χαλεπωτέρα γὰρ ἂν τῆς ἀλλοφύλου ἀρχῆς εἴη, καὶ ἡμῖν τοῖς Λακεδαιμονίοις οὐκ ἂν ἀντὶ πόνων χάρις καθίσταιτο, ἀντὶ δὲ τιμῆς καὶ δόξης αἰτία μᾶλλον εἰς τε τοὺς Ἀθηναίους ἐγκλήματι καταπολεμοῦμεν, αὐτοὶ ἂν φαινοίμεθα ἐχθίονα ἢ ὁ μὴ ὑποδείξας ἀρετήν κατακτώμενοι.

[2] Thucyd. iv. 87. Οὐδὲ ἐπιθυμοῦμεν οἱ Λακεδαιμόνιοι μὴ κοινοῦ τινος ἀγαθοῦ αἰτίᾳ τοὺς μὴ βουλομένους ἐλευθεροῦν. Οὐδ' αὖ ἀρχῆς ἐφιέμεθα, παῦσαι δὲ μᾶλλον ἑτέρους σπεύδοντες τοὺς πλείους ἂν ἀδικοῖμεν, εἰ ξύμπασιν αὐτονομίαν ἐπιφέροντες ὑμᾶς τοὺς ἐναντιουμένους περιίδοιμεν. Compare Isokratês, Or. iv. (Panegyr.) s. 140, 141.

[3] Feelings of the Lacedæmonians during the winter immediately succeeding the great Syracusan

cian freedom; which indeed, so far as concerned the Greeks on the continent of Asia, was surrendered to Persia. Nevertheless the old watchword still continued. It was still currently believed, though less studiously professed, that the destruction of the Athenian empire was aimed at as a means to the liberation of Greece.[1]

The victory of Ægospotami with its consequences cruelly undeceived every one. The language of Brasidas, sanctioned by the solemn oaths of the Lacedæmonian Ephors, in 424 B.C.—and the proceedings of the Lacedæmonian Lysander in 405-404 B.C., the commencing hour of Spartan omnipotence—stand in such literal and flagrant contradiction, that we might almost imagine the former to have foreseen the possibility of such a successor, and to have tried to disgrace and disarm him beforehand. The Dekarchies of Lysander realised that precise ascendency of a few chosen partisans which Brasidas repudiates as an abomination worse than foreign dominion; while the harmosts and garrison, installed in the dependent cities along with the native Decemvirs, planted the second variety of mischief as well as the first, each aggravating the other. Had the nobleminded Kallikratidas gained a victory at Arginusæ, and lived to close the war, he would probably have tried, with more or less of success, to make some approach to the promises of Brasidas. But it was the double misfortune of Greece, first that the closing victory was gained by such an admiral as Lysander, the most unscrupulous of all power-seekers, partly for his country, and still more for himself—next, that the victory was so decisive, sudden, and imposing, as to leave no enemy standing, or in a position to insist upon terms. The fiat of Lysander, acting in the name of Sparta, became omnipotent, not merely over enemies, but over allies; and to a certain degree even over the Spartan authorities themselves. There was no present necessity for conciliating allies—still less for acting up to former engagements; so that nothing remained to oppose the naturally ambitious inspirations of the Spartan Ephors, who allowed the ad-

*Margin notes: Language of Brasidas contrasted with the acts of Lysander. Extreme suddenness and completeness of the victory of Ægospotami left Lysander almost omnipotent.*

catastrophé (Thuc. viii. 2)—καὶ λὼς ἠτήσασθαι καθελόντες Ἀττικοὺς (the Athenians) αὑτοὶ τῆς πάσης 'Ελλάδος ἤδη ἀσφα-    [1] Compare Thucyd. viii. 46, 3; viii. 46, 3.

miral to carry out the details in his own way. But former assurances, though Sparta was in a condition to disregard them, were not forgotten by others; and the recollection of them imparted additional bitterness to the oppressions of the Decemvirs and Harmosts.[1] In perfect consist-

[1] This is emphatically set forth in a fragment of Theopompus preserved by Theodorus Metochita, and printed at the end of the collection of the Fragments of Theopompus the historian, both by Wichers and by M. Didot. Both these editors however insert it only as Fragmentum Spurium, on the authority of Plutarch (Lysander, c. 19), who quotes the same sentiment from the comic writer Theopompus. But the passage of Theodorus Metochita presents the express words Θεόπομπος ὁ ἱστορικός. We have therefore his distinct affirmation against that of Plutarch; and the question is, which of the two we are to believe. As far as the sense of the fragment is concerned, I should be disposed to refer it to the historian Theopompus. But the authority of Plutarch is earlier and better than that of Theodorus Metochita: moreover, the apparent traces of comic senarii have been recognised in the Fragment by Meineke (Fragm. Com. Græc. ii. p. 819). The Fragment is thus presented by Theodorus Metochita (Fragm. Theopomp. 344, ed. Didot).

Θεόπομπος ὁ ἱστορικὸς ἀπεικώκτων εἰς τοὺς Λακεδαιμονίους, εἴκαζεν αὐτοὺς ταῖς φαύλαις κανηλίαιν, αἳ τοῖς χρωμένοις ἐγχέουσαι τὴν ἀρχὴν οἶνον ἡδύν τε καὶ εὔχρηστον σοφιστικῶς ἐπὶ τῇ λήψει τοῦ ἀργυρίου, μεθύστερον φαυλὸν τινα καὶ ἐκτροπίαν καὶ ὀξίνην κατακρινῶσι καὶ παρέχουσαι· καὶ τοὺς Λακεδαιμονίους τοίνυν ἔλεγε, τὸν αὐτὸν ἐκείνοις τρόπον, ἐν τῷ κατὰ τῶν Ἀθηναίων πολέμῳ, τὴν ἀρχὴν ἡδίστῳ πόματι τῆς ἐπ' Ἀθηναίων ἐλευθερίας καὶ προγράμματι

καὶ κηρύγματι τοὺς Ἕλληνας δεκάσαντας, ὕστερον αἱρετώτατα σφίσιν ἐγχέαι καὶ ἀηδέστατα κράματα βιοτῆς ἐκποδόνου καὶ χρήσεως πραγμάτων ἀλγεινῶν, πάνυ τοι κατατυραννοῦντας τὰς πόλεις δυναρχίαις καὶ ἁρμοσταῖς βαρυτάτοις, καὶ πραττομένους, ἃ δυσχερὲς εἶναι σφόδρα καὶ ἀνύποιστον φέρειν, καὶ ἀκαττινόναι. Plutarch, ascribing the statement to the comic Theopompus, affirms him to be silly (ἔοικε ληρεῖν) in saying that the Lacedæmonian empire began by being sweet and pleasant, and afterwards was corrupted and turned into bitterness and oppression: whereas the fact was, that it was bitterness and oppression from the very first. Now if we read the above citation from Theodorus, we shall see that Theopompus did not really put forth that assertion which Plutarch contradicts as silly and untrue. What Theopompus stated was, that first the Lacedæmonians, during the war against Athens, tempted the Greeks with a most delicious draught and programme and proclamation of freedom from the rule of Athens—and that they afterwards poured in the most bitter and repulsive mixtures of hard oppression and tyranny, &c. The sweet draught is asserted to consist—not, as Plutarch supposes, in the first taste of the actual Lacedæmonian empire after the war, but—in the seductive promises of freedom held out by them to the allies during the war. Plutarch's charge of ἔοικε ληρεῖν has thus no foundation. I have written δεκάσαντας which stands in Didot's

ency[1] with her misrule throughout Eastern Greece, too, Sparta identified herself with the energetic tyranny of Dionysius at Syracuse, assisting both to erect and to uphold it; a contradiction to her former maxims of action which would have astounded the historian Herodotus.

The empire of Sparta, thus constituted at the end of 405 B.C., maintained itself in full grandeur for somewhat above ten years, until the naval battle of Knidus[2] in 394 B.C. That defeat destroyed her fleet and maritime ascendency, yet left her in undiminished power on land, which she still maintained until her defeat by the Thebans[3] at Leuktra in 371 B.C. Throughout all this time, it was her established system to keep up Spartan harmosts and garrisons in the dependent cities on the continent as well as in the islands. Even the Chians, who had been her most active allies during the last eight years of the war, were compelled to submit to this hardship; besides having all their fleet taken away from them.[4] But the native Dekarchies, though at first established by Lysander universally throughout the maritime dependencies, did not last as a system so long as the Harmosts. Composed as they were to a great degree of the personal nominees and confederates of Lysander, they suffered in part by the reactionary jealousy which in time made itself felt against his overweening ascendency. After continuing for some time, they lost the countenance of the Spartan Ephors, who proclaimed permission to the cities (we do not precisely know when) to resume their preexisting governments.[5] Some of the Dekarchies thus be-

*The Dekarchies became partly modified by the jealousy at Sparta against Lysander. The Harmosts lasted much longer.*

Fragment, because it struck me that this correction was required to construe the passage.

[1] Isokrates, Or. iv. (Panegyr.) s. 145; Or. viii. (de Pace) s. 122; Diodor. xiv. 10·44; xv. 23. Compare Herodot. v. 92; Thucyd. i. 18; Isokrates, Or. iv. (Panegyr.) s. 144.

[2] Isokrates, Panathen. s. 61. Σπαρτιᾶται μὲν γὰρ ἔτη δέκα μόλις ἐπιστάτησαν αὐτῶν, ἡμεῖς δὲ πέντε καὶ ἑξήκοντα συνεχῶς κατέσχομεν τὴν ἀρχήν. I do not hold myself bound to make out the exactness of the chronology of Isokrates. But here we may remark that his "hardly ten years," as a term, though less than the truth by some months if we may take the battle of Ægospotami as the beginning, is very near the truth if we take the surrender of Athens as the beginning, down to the battle of Knidus.

[3] Pausanias, viii. 52, 2; ix. 6, 1.
[4] Diodor. xiv. 84; Isokrates, Orat. viii. (de Pace) s. 121.
[5] Xen. Hellen. iii. 4, 2. Lysander accompanied King

came dissolved, or modified in various ways, but several probably still continued to subsist, if they had force enough to maintain themselves; for it does not appear that the Ephors ever systematically put them down as Lysander had systematically set them up.

*The Thirty at Athens were put down by the Athenians themselves, not by any reformatory interference of Sparta.*

The government of the Thirty at Athens would never have been overthrown, if the oppressed Athenians had been obliged to rely on a tutelary interference of the Spartan Ephors to help them in overthrowing it. I have already shown that this nefarious oligarchy came to its end by the unassisted efforts of Thrasybulus and the Athenian democrats themselves. It is true indeed that the arrogance and selfishness of Sparta and of Lysander had alienated the Thebans, Corinthians, Megarians, and other neighbouring allies, and induced them to sympathise with the Athenian exiles against the atrocities of the Thirty—but those neighbours never rendered any positive or serious aid. The inordinate personal ambition of Lysander had also offended King Pausanias and the Spartan Ephors, so that they too became indifferent to the Thirty, who were his creatures. But this merely deprived the Thirty of that foreign support which Lysander, had he still continued in the ascendent, would have extended to them in full measure. It was not the positive cause of their downfall. That crisis was brought about altogether by the energy of Thrasybulus and his companions, who manifested such force and determination as could not have been put down without an extraordinary display of Spartan military power; a display not entirely safe when the sympathies of the chief allies were with the other side—and at any rate adverse to the inclinations of Pausanias.

As it was with the Thirty at Athens, so it probably was also with the Dekarchies in the dependent cities. The

Agesilaus (when the latter was going to his Asiatic command in 396 B.C.). His purpose was—ὅπως τὰς δικαρχίας τὰς κατασταθείσας ὑπ᾽ ἐκείνου ἐν ταῖς πόλεσιν, ἐκπεπτωκυίας δὲ διὰ τοὺς ἐφόρους, οἳ τὰς πατρίους πολιτείας παρήγγειλαν, πάλιν καταστήσειε μετ᾽ Ἀγησιλάου.

It shows the careless construction of Xenophon's Hellenica, or perhaps his reluctance to set forth the discreditable points of the Lacedæmonian rule, that this is the first mention which he makes (and that too, indirectly) of the Dekarchies, nine years after they had been first set up by Lysander.

Spartan Ephors took no steps to put them down; but where the resistance of the citizens was strenuous enough to overthrow them, no Spartan intervention came to prop them up; and the Harmost perhaps received orders not to consider his authority as indissolubly linked with theirs. The native forces of each dependent city being thus left to find their own level, the Decemvirs, once installed, would doubtless maintain themselves in a great number; while in other cases they would be overthrown—or perhaps would contrive to perpetuate their dominion by compromise and alliance with other oligarchical sections. This confused and unsettled state of the Dekarchies—some still existing, others half-existing, others again defunct—prevailed in 396 B.C., when Lysander accompanied Agesilaus into Asia, in the full hope that he should have influence enough to reorganise them all.[1] We must recollect that no other dependent city would possess the same means of offering energetic resistance to its local Decemvirs, as Athens offered to the Thirty; and that the insular Grecian cities were not only feeble individually, but naturally helpless against the lords of the sea.[2]

Such then was the result throughout Greece when that long war, which had been undertaken in the name of universal autonomy was terminated by the battle of Ægospotami. In place of imperial Athens was substituted, not the promised autonomy, but yet more imperial Sparta. An awful picture is given by the philo-Laconian Xenophon, in 399 B.C., of the ascendency exercised throughout all the Grecian cities, not merely by the Ephors and the public officers, but even by the private citizens, of Sparta. "The Lacedæmonians (says he in addressing the Cyreian army)

*The empire of Sparta much worse and more oppressive than that of Athens.*

---

[1] Compare the two passages of Xenophon's Hellenica, iii. 4, 7; iii. 5, 13.

Ἅτε συντεταραγμένων ἐν ταῖς πόλεσι τῶν πολιτειῶν, καὶ οὔτε δημοκρατίας ἔτι οὔσης, ὥσπερ ἐπ' Ἀθηναίων, οὔτε δεκαρχίας, ὥσπερ ἐπὶ Λυσάνδρου.

But that some of these Dekarchies still continued, we know from the subsequent passage. The Theban envoys say to the public assembly at Athens, respecting the Spartans,—

Ἀλλὰ μὴν καὶ οὓς ὑμῶν ἀπέστησαν φανεροί εἰσιν ἐξηπατηκότες· ἀντὶ γὰρ τῶν ἁρμοστῶν τυραννοῦνται, καὶ ὑπὸ δέκα ἀνδρῶν, οὓς Λύσανδρος κατέστησεν ἐν ἑκάστῃ πόλει—where the Decemvirs are noted as still subsisting, in 395 B.C. See also Xen. Agesilaus, i. 37.

[2] Xen. Hellen. iii. 5, 15.

are now the presidents of Greece; and even any single private Lacedæmonian can accomplish what he pleases."¹ "All the cities (he says in another place) then obeyed whatever order they might receive from a Lacedæmonian citizen."² Not merely was the general ascendency thus omnipresent and irresistible, but it was enforced with a stringency of detail, and darkened by a thousand accompaniments of tyranny and individual abuse, such as had never been known under the much-decried empire of Athens.

We have more than one picture of the Athenian empire in speeches made by hostile orators who had every motive to work up the strongest antipathies in the bosoms of their audience against it. We have the addresses of the Corinthian envoys at Sparta when stimulating the Spartan allies to the Peloponnesian War³—that of the envoys from Mitylênê delivered at Olympia to the Spartan confederates, when the city had revolted from Athens and stood in pressing need of support —the discourse of Brasidas in the public assembly at Akanthus—and more than one speech also from Hermokratês, impressing upon his Sicilian countrymen hatred as well as fear of Athens.⁴ Whoever reads these discourses, will see that they dwell almost exclusively on the great political wrong inherent in the very fact of her empire, robbing so many Grecian communities of their legitimate autonomy, over and above the tribute imposed. That Athens had thus already enslaved many cities, and was only watching for opportunities to enslave many more, is the theme upon which they expatiate. But of practical grievances —of cruelty, oppression, spoliation, multiplied exiles, &c., of high-handed wrong committed by individual Athenians—not one word is spoken. Had there been the smallest pretext for introducing such inflammatory topics, how much more impressive would have been the appeal of

*Marginal note:* Imperial Athens deprived her subject-allies of their autonomy, but was guilty of little or no oppression.

---

¹ Xen. Anab. vi. 6, 12. Εἰσὶ μὲν γὰρ ἤδη ἐγγὺς αἱ Ἑλληνίδες πόλεις· (this was spoken at Kalpê in Bithynia) τῆς δὲ Ἑλλάδος Λακεδαιμόνιοι προεστήκασιν ἱκανοὶ δέ εἰσι καὶ εἷς ἕκαστος Λακεδαιμονίων ἐν ταῖς πόλεσιν ὅτι βούλονται διαπράττεσθαι.

² Xen. Hellen. iii. 1, 5. Πᾶσαι γὰρ τότε αἱ πόλεις ἐπείθοντο, ὅ,τι Λακεδαιμόνιος ἀνὴρ ἐπιτάττοι.

³ Thucyd. I. 68-120.

⁴ Thucyd. iii. 9; iv. 59-85; vi. 76.

Brasidas to the sympathies of the Akanthians! How vehement would have been the denunciations of the Mitylenæan envoys, in place of the tame and almost apologetic language which we now read in Thucydidês! Athens extinguished the autonomy of her subject-allies, and punished revolters with severity, sometimes even with cruelty. But as to other points of wrong, the silence of accusers, such as those just noticed, counts as a powerful exculpation.

The case is altered when we come to the period succeeding the battle of Ægospotami. Here indeed also, we find the Spartan empire complained of (as the Athenian empire had been before), in contrast with that state of autonomy to which each city laid claim, and which Sparta not merely promised to ensure, but set forth as her only ground of war. Yet this is not the prominent grievance—other topics stand more emphatically forward. The Decemvirs and the Harmosts (some of the latter being Helots), the standing instruments of Spartan empire, are felt as more sorely painful than the empire itself; as the language held by Brasidas at Akanthus admits them to be beforehand. At the time when Athens was a subject city under Sparta, governed by the Lysandrian Thirty and by the Lacedæmonian harmost in the acropolis—the sense of indignity arising from the fact of subjection was absorbed in the still more terrible suffering arising from the enormities of those individual rulers whom the imperial state had set up. Now Athens set up no local rulers—no native Ten or native Thirty—no resident Athenian harmosts or garrisons. This was of itself an unspeakable exemption, when compared with the condition of cities subject, not only to the Spartan empire, but also under that empire to native Decemvirs like Kritias, and Spartan harmosts like Aristarchus or Aristodêmus. A city subject to Athens had to bear definite burdens enforced by its own government, which was liable in case of default or delinquency to be tried before the popular Athenian Dikastery. But this same Dikastery (as I have shown in a former volume, and as is distinctly stated by Thucydidês[1]) was the harbour of refuge to each subject city; not less against individual Athenian wrong-doers than against mis-

*Imperial Sparta did this and much worse—her Harmosts and Decemvirs are more complained of than the fact of her empire.*

---
[1] See the remarkable speech of Phrynichus in Thucyd. viii. 48, 5, which I have before referred to.

conduct from other cities. Those who complained of the hardship suffered by a subject city, from the obligation of bringing causes to be tried in the Dikastery of Athens— even if we take the case as they state it, and overlook the unfairness of omitting those numerous instances wherein the city was thus enabled to avert or redress wrong done to its own citizens—would have complained both more loudly and with greater justice of an ever-present Athenian harmost; especially if there were co-existent a native government of Ten oligarchs, exchanging with him guilty connivances, like the partnership of the Thirty at Athens with the Lacedæmonian harmost Kallibius.[1]

*This is the more to be regretted, as Sparta had now an admirable opportunity for organising a good and stable confederacy throughout Greece.*
In no one point can it be shown that the substitution of Spartan empire in place of Athenian was a gain, either for the subject cities or for Greece generally; while in many points, it was a great and serious aggravation of suffering. And this abuse of power is the more deeply to be regretted, as Sparta enjoyed after the battle of Ægospotami a precious opportunity—such as Athens had never had, and such as never again recurred —of reorganising the Grecian world on wise principles, and with a view to Pan-hellenic stability and harmony. It is not her greatest sin to have refused to grant universal autonomy. She had indeed promised it; but we might pardon a departure from specific performance, had she exchanged the boon for one far greater, which it was within her reasonable power, at the end of 405 B.C., to confer. That universal town autonomy, towards which the Grecian instinct tended, though immeasurably better than universal subjection, was yet accompanied by much internal discord, and by the still more formidable evil of helplessness against any efficient foreign enemy. To ensure to the Hellenic world external safety as well as internal concord, it was not a new empire which was wanted, but a new political combination on equitable and comprehensive principles; divesting each town of a portion of its autonomy, and creating a common authority, responsible to all, for certain definite controlling purposes. If ever a tolerable federative system would have been

[1] Xen. Hellen. II. 3, 14. Compare the analogous case of Thebes, after the Lacedæmonians had got possession of the Kadmeia (v. 2, 34-36).

practicable in Greece, it was after the battle of Ægospotami. The Athenian empire—which, with all its defects, I believe to have been much better for the subject-cities than universal autonomy would have been—had already removed many difficulties, and shown that combined and systematic action of the maritime Grecian world was no impossibility. Sparta might now have substituted herself for Athens, not as heir to the imperial power, but as president and executive agent of a new Confederacy of Delos —reviving the equal, comprehensive, and liberal principles on which that confederacy had first been organised.

It is true that sixty years before, the constituent members of the original synod at Delos had shown themselves insensible to its value. As soon as the pressing alarm from Persia had passed over, some had discontinued sending deputies, others had disobeyed requisitions, others again had bought off their obligations, and forfeited their rights as autonomous and voting members, by pecuniary bargain with Athens; {Sparta might have reorganised the confederacy of Delos, which might now have been made to work well.} who being obliged by the duties of her presidency to enforce obedience to the Synod against all reluctant members, made successively many enemies, and was gradually converted, almost without her own seeking, from President into Emperor, as the only means of obviating the total dissolution of the Confederacy.

But though such untoward circumstances had happened before, it does not follow that they would now have happened again, assuming the same experiment to have been retried by Sparta, with manifest sincerity of purpose and tolerable wisdom. The Grecian world, especially the maritime portion of it, had passed through trials not less painful than instructive, during this important interval. Nor does it seem rash to suppose, that the bulk of its members might now have been disposed to perform steady confederate duties, at the call and under the presidency of Sparta, had she really attempted to reorganize a liberal confederacy, treating every city as autonomous and equal, except in so far as each was bound to obey the resolutions of the general synod. However impracticable such a scheme may appear, we must recollect that even Utopian schemes have their transient moments, if not of certain success, at least of commencement not merely possible but promising. And my belief is, that had Kallikratidas, with his ardent Pan-hellenic sentiment and force of moral resolution, been the final victor over imperial Athens, he would not have let the moment of pride and omnipotence pass over without essaying some noble project like that sketched above.

It is to be remembered that Athens had never had the power of organizing any such generous Pan-hellenic combination. She had become depopularized in the legitimate execution of her trust, as president of the Confederacy of Delos, against refractory members.[1] She had been obliged to choose between breaking up the Confederacy, and keeping it together under the strong compression of an imperial chief. But Sparta had not yet become depopularized. She now stood without competitor as leader of the Grecian world, and might at that moment have reasonably hoped to carry the members of it along with her to any liberal and Pan-hellenic organization, had she attempted it with proper earnestness. Unfortunately she took the opposite course, under the influence of Lysander; founding a new empire far more oppressive and odious than that of Athens, with few of the advantages, and none of the excuses, attached to the latter. As she soon became even more unpopular than Athens, *her* moment of high tide, for beneficent Pan-hellenic combination, passed away also—never to return.

*Insupportable arrogance of Lysander—bitter complaints against him, as well as against the Dekarchies.*

Having thus brought all the maritime Greeks under her empire, with a tribute of more than 1000 talents imposed upon them—and continuing to be chief of her landed alliance in Central Greece, which now included Athens as a simple unit—Sparta was the all-pervading imperial power in Greece.[2] Her new empire was organized by the victorious Lysander; but with so much arrogance, and so much personal ambition to govern all Greece by means of nominees of his own, Decemvirs and Harmosts—that he raised numerous rivals and enemies, as well at Sparta itself as elsewhere. The

---

[1] Such is the justification offered by the Athenian envoy at Sparta, immediately before the Peloponnesian War (Thucyd. I. 75, 76). And it is borne out in the main by the narrative of Thucydides himself (I. 99).

[2] Xen. Hellen. III. 1, 3. πάσης τῆς Ἑλλάδος προστάτιν, &c.

## ARROGANCE OF LYSANDER.

jealousy entertained by King Pausanias, the offended feelings of Thebes and Corinth, and the manner in which these new phænomena brought about (in spite of the opposition of Lysander) the admission of Athens as a revived democracy into the Lacedæmonian confederacy—has been already related.

In the early months of 403 B.C., Lysander was partly at home, partly in Attica, exerting himself to sustain the falling oligarchy of Athens against the increasing force of Thrasybulus and the Athenian exiles in Peiræus. In this purpose he was directly thwarted by the opposing views of King Pausanias, and three out of the five Ephors.[1] But though the Ephors thus checked Lysander in regard to Athens, they softened the humiliation by sending him abroad to a fresh command on the Asiatic coast and the Hellespont; a step which had the farther advantage of putting asunder two such marked rivals as he and Pausanias had now become. That which Lysander had tried in vain to do at Athens, he was doubtless better able to do in Asia, where he had neither Pausanias nor the Ephors along with him. He could lend effective aid to the Dekarchies and Harmosts in the Asiatic cities, against any internal opposition with which they might be threatened. Bitter were the complaints which reached Sparta, both against him and against his ruling partisans. At length the Ephors were prevailed upon to disavow the Dekarchies, and to proclaim that they would not hinder the cities from resuming their former governments at pleasure.[2]

But all the crying oppressions set forth in the complaints of the maritime cities would have been insufficient to procure the recall of Lysander from his command in the Hellespont, had not Pharnabazus joined his remonstrances to the rest. These last representations so strengthened the enemies of Lysander at Sparta, that a peremptory order was sent to recall him. Constrained to obey, he came back to Sparta, but the comparative disgrace, and the loss of that boundless power which he had enjoyed on his command, was so insupportable to him, that he obtained permission to go on a pilgrimage to the temple of Zeus Ammon in Libya, under

*Lysander offends Pharnabazus, who procures his recall. His disgust and temporary expatriation.*

[1] Xen. Hellen. II. 4, 28–30.   [2] Xen. Hellen. III. 4, 2.

the plea that he had a vow to discharge.¹ He appears also to have visited the temples of Delphi and Dodona,² with secret ambitious projects which will be mentioned presently. This politic withdrawal softened the jealousy against him, so that we shall find him, after a year or two re-established in great influence and ascendency. He was sent as Spartan envoy, at what precise moment we do not know, to Syracuse, where he lent countenance and aid to the recently established despotism of Dionysius.³

The position of the Asiatic Greeks, along the coast of Ionia, Æolis, and the Hellespont, became very peculiar after the triumph of Sparta at Ægospotami. I have already recounted how, immediately after the great Athenian catastrophe before Syracuse, the Persian king had renewed his grasp upon those cities, from which the vigorous hand of Athens had kept him excluded for more than fifty years: how Sparta, bidding

*Surrender of the Asiatic Greeks to Persia, according to the treaty concluded with Sparta.*

---

¹ Plutarch, Lysand. c. 19, 20, 21.

The facts, which Plutarch states respecting Lysander, cannot be reconciled with the chronology which he adopts. He represents the recall of Lysander at the instance of Pharnabazus, with all the facts which preceded it, as having occurred prior to the reconstitution of the Athenian democracy, which event we know to have taken place in the summer of 403 B.C.

Lysander captured Samos in the latter half of 404 B.C., after the surrender of Athens. After the capture of Samos, he came home in triumph, in the autumn of 404 B.C. (Xen. Hellen. III. 2, 7). He was at home, or serving in Attica, in the beginning of 403 B.C. (Xen. Hellen. II. 4, 30).

Now when Lysander came home at the end of 404 B.C., it was his triumphant return; it was not a recall provoked by complaints of Pharnabazus. Yet there can have been no other return before the restoration of the democracy at Athens.

The recall of Lysander must have been the termination, not of this command, but of a subsequent command. Moreover, it seems to me necessary, in order to make room for the facts stated respecting Lysander as well as about the Dekarchies, that we should suppose him to have been again sent out (after his quarrel with Pausanias in Attica) in 403 B.C., to command in Asia. This is nowhere positively stated, but I find nothing to contradict it, and I see no other way of making room for the facts stated about Lysander.

It is to be noted that Diodorus has a decided error in chronology as to the date of the restoration of the Athenian democracy. He places it in 401 B.C. (Diod. xiv. 53), two years later than its real date, which is 403 B.C.; thus lengthening by two years the interval between the surrender of Athens and the reestablishment of the democracy. Plutarch also seems to have conceived that interval as much longer than it really was.

² Plutarch, Lysand. c. 25.

³ Plutarch, Lysander, c. 2.

for his aid, had consented by three formal conventions to
surrender them to him, while her commissioner Lichas even
reproved the Milesians for their aversion to this bargain:
how Athens also, in the days of her weakness, competing
for the same advantage, had expressed her willingness to
pay the same price for it.¹ After the battle of Ægospotami,
this convention was carried into effect; though seemingly
not without disputes between the satrap Pharnabazus on
one side, and Lysander and Derkyllidas on the other.²
The latter was Lacedæmonian harmost at Abydos, which
town, so important as a station on the Hellespont, the
Lacedæmonians seem still to have retained. But Pharnabazus and his subordinates acquired more complete command of the Hellespontine Æolis and of the Troad than
ever they had enjoyed before, both along the coast and in
the interior.³

Another element however soon became operative.
The condition of the Greek cities on the coast
of Ionia, though according to Persian regulations
they belonged to the satrapy of Tissaphernês,
was now materially determined,—first, by the
competing claims of Cyrus, who wished to take
them away from him, and tried to get such
transfer ordered at court—next, by the aspirations of that young prince to the Persian throne.
As Cyrus rested his hope of success on Grecian
cooperation, it was highly important to him to
render himself popular among the Greeks, especially on
his own side of the Ægean. Partly his own manifestations
of just and conciliatory temper, partly the bad name and
known perfidy of Tissaphernês, induced the Grecian cities
with one accord to revolt from the latter. All threw themselves into the arms of Cyrus, except Miletus, where Tissaphernês interposed in time, slew the leaders of the intended
revolt, and banished many of their partisans. Cyrus,
receiving the exiles with distinguished favour, levied an
army to besiege Miletus and procure their restoration;
while he at the same time threw strong Grecian garrisons
into the other cities to protect them against attack.⁴

*Their con-
dition is af-
fected by
the position
and ambi-
tious
schemes of
Cyrus,
whose pro-
tection they
seek
against Tis-
saphernês.*

¹ Thucyd. viii. 6, 18—37, 58—58,  Xen. Hellen. iii. 1, 9.
84.  ² Xen. Hellen. iii. 1, 13.
² Plutarch, Lysander, c. 19, 20;  ⁴ Xen. Anab. i. 1, 8.

This local quarrel was however soon merged in the
more comprehensive dispute respecting the
Persian succession. Both parties were found
on the field of Kunaxa; Cyrus with the Greek
soldiers and Milesian exiles on one side—Tissaphernês on the other. How that attempt,
upon which so much hinged in the future history
both of Asia Minor and of Greece, terminated
—I have already recounted. Probably the impression
brought back by the Lacedæmonian fleet which left Cyrus
on the coast of Syria, after he had surmounted the most
difficult country without any resistance, was highly favourable to his success. So much the more painful would be
the disappointment among the Ionian Greeks when the
news of his death was afterwards brought: so much the
greater their alarm, when Tissaphernês, having relinquished
the pursuit of the Ten Thousand Greeks at the moment
when they entered the mountains of Karduchia, came
down as victor to the seaboard; more powerful than ever
—rewarded[1] by the Great King, for the services which he
had rendered against Cyrus, with all the territory which
had been governed by the latter, as well as with the title
of commander-in-chief over all the neighbouring satraps—
and prepared not only to reconquer, but to punish, the
revolted maritime cities. He began by attacking Kymê;[2]
ravaging the territory, with great loss to the citizens, and
exacting from them a still larger contribution, when the
approach of winter rendered it inconvenient to besiege
their city.

In such state of apprehension, these cities sent to
Sparta, as the great imperial power of Greece, to entreat
her protection against the aggravated slavery impending
over them.[3] The Lacedæmonians had nothing farther to
expect from the king of Persia, with whom they had already broken the peace by lending aid to Cyrus. Moreover
the fame of the Ten Thousand Greeks, who were now coming
home along the Euxine towards Byzantium, had become
diffused throughout Greece, inspiring signal contempt for
Persian military efficiency, and hopes of enrichment by
war against the Asiatic satraps. Accordingly, the Spartan Ephors were induced to comply with the petition of

[1] Xen. Anab. ii. 3, 19; ii. 4, 8;  [2] Diodor. xiv. 35.
Xen. Hellen. iii. 1, 3; iii. 5, 13.   [3] Diodor. ut sup.

their Asiatic countrymen, and to send over to Asia Thimbron at the head of a considerable force: 2000 Neodamodes (or Helots who had been enfranchised), and 4000 Peloponnesian heavy-armed, accompanied by 300 Athenian horsemen, out of the number of those who had been adherents of the Thirty, four years before; an aid granted by Athens at the special request of Thimbron. Arriving in Asia during the winter of 400-399 B.C., Thimbron was reinforced in the spring of 399 B.C. by the Cyreian army, who were brought across from Thrace as described in my last chapter, and taken into Lacedæmonian pay. With this large force he became more than a match for the satraps, even on the plains where they could employ their numerous cavalry. The petty Grecian princes of Pergamus and Teuthrania, holding that territory by ancient grants from Xerxes to their ancestors, joined their troops to his, contributing much to enrich Xenophon at the moment of his departure from the Cyreians. Yet Thimbron achieved nothing worthy of so large an army. He not only miscarried in the siege of Larissa, but was even unable to maintain order among his own soldiers, who pillaged indiscriminately both friends and foes.[1] Such loud complaints were transmitted to Sparta of his irregularities and inefficiency, that the Ephors first sent him an order to march into Karia where Tissaphernês resided,—and next, before that order was executed, dispatched Derkyllidas to supersede him; seemingly in the winter 399-398 B.C. Thimbron on returning to Sparta was fined and banished.[2]

*B.C. 400-899. Alarm of the Asiatic Greeks, who send to ask aid from Sparta. The Spartans send Thimbron with an army to Asia. His ill-success and recall—he is superseded by Derkyllidas.*

It is highly probable that the Cyreian soldiers, though excellent in the field, yet having been disappointed of reward for the prodigious toils which they had gone through in their long march, and having been kept on short allowance in Thrace, as well as cheated by Seuthês—were greedy, unscrupulous, and hard to be restrained, in the matter of pillage; especially as Xenophon, their most influential general, had now left them. Their conduct greatly improved under Derkyllidas. And though such improvement was

*Conduct of the Cyreians loose as to pillage.*

[1] Xen. Hellen. iii. 1, 5—8; Xen. Anab. vii. 8, 8—16.  [2] Xen. Hellen. iii. 1 8; Diodor. xiv. 68.

doubtless owing partly to the superiority of the latter over Thimbron, yet it seems also partly ascribable to the fact that Xenophon, after a few months of residence at Athens, accompanied him to Asia, and resumed the command of his old comrades.[1]

**Derkyllidas makes a truce with Tissaphernês, and attacks Pharnabazus in the Troad and Æolis.**

Derkyllidas was a man of so much resource and cunning, as to have acquired the surname of Sisyphus.[2] He had served throughout all the concluding years of the war, and had been Harmost at Abydus during the naval command of Lysander, who condemned him, on the complaint of Pharnabazus, to the disgrace of public exposure with his shield on his arm:[3] this was (I presume) a disgrace, because an officer of rank always had his shield carried for him by an attendant, except in the actual encounter of battle. Having never forgiven Pharnabazus for thus dishonouring him, Derkyllidas now took advantage of a misunderstanding between the satrap and Tissaphernês, to make a truce with the latter, and conduct his army, 8000 strong, into the territory of the former.[4] The mountainous region of Ida generally known as the Troad —inhabited by a population of Æolic Greeks (who had gradually Hellenized the indigenous inhabitants), and therefore known as the Æolis of Pharnabazus—was laid open to him by a recent event, important in itself as well as instructive to read.

**Distribution of the Persian empire; relation of king, satrap, subsatrap.**

The entire Persian empire was parcelled into so many satrapies; each satrap being bound to send a fixed amount of annual tribute, and to hold a certain amount of military force ready, for the court at Susa. Provided he was punctual in fulfilling these obligations, little inquiry was made as to his other proceedings, unless in the

---

[1] There is no positive testimony to this; yet such is my belief, as I have stated at the close of the last chapter. It is certain that Xenophon was serving under Agesilaus in Asia three years after this time; the only matter left for conjecture is, at what precise moment he went out the second time. The marked improvement in the Cyreian soldiers, is one reason for the statement in the text; another reason is, the great detail with which the military operations of Derkyllidas are described, rendering it probable that the narrative is from an eye-witness.

[2] Xen. Hellen. iii. 1, 8; Ephorus ap. Athenæ. xi. p. 500.

[3] Xen. Hellen. iii. 1, 9. ἐστάθη τὴν ἀσπίδα ἔχων.

[4] Xen. Hellen. iii. 1, 10; iii. 2, 28.

rare case of his maltreating some individual Persian of high rank. In like manner, it appears, each satrapy was divided into sub-satrapies or districts; each of these held by a deputy, who paid to the satrap a fixed tribute and maintained for him a certain military force—having liberty to govern in other respects as he pleased. Besides the tribute, however, presents of undefined amount were of constant occurrence, both from the satrap to the king, and from the deputy to the satrap. Nevertheless, enough was extorted from the people (we need hardly add), to leave an ample profit both to the one and to the other.[1]

This region called Æolis had been entrusted by Pharnabazus to a native of Dardanus named Zênis, who, after holding the post for some time and giving full satisfaction, died of illness, leaving a widow with a son and daughter still minors. The satrap was on the point of giving the district to another person, when Mania, the widow of Zênis, herself a native of Dardanus, preferred her petition to be allowed to succeed her husband. Visiting Pharnabazus with money in hand, sufficient not only to satisfy himself, but also to gain over his mistresses and his ministers?—she said to him—"My husband was faithful to you, and paid his tribute so regularly as to obtain your thanks. If I serve you no worse than he, why should you name any other deputy? If I fail in giving you satisfaction, you can always remove me, and give the place to another." Pharnabazus granted her petition, and had no cause to repent it. Mania was regular in her payment of tribute—frequent in bringing him presents—and splendid, beyond any of his other deputies, in her manner of receiving him whenever he visited the district.

*Mania, widow of Zênis, holds the sub-satrapy of Æolis under Pharnabazus. Her regular payment and vigorous government.*

Her chief residence was at Skêpsis, Gergis, and Kebrên—inland towns, strong both by position and by fortifi-

---

[1] See the description of the satrapy of Cyrus (Xenoph. Anab. i. 9, 19, 21, 22). In the main, this division and subdivision of the entire empire into revenue-districts, each held by a nominee responsible for payment of the rent or tribute, to the government or to some higher officer of the government—is the system prevalent throughout a large portion of Asia to the present day.

[2] Xen. Hellen. iii. 1, 10. Ἀναζτάξασα τὸν στόλον, καὶ χρήματα λαβοῦσα, ὥστε καὶ αὐτῷ Φαρναβάζῳ δοῦναι, καὶ ταῖς παλλακίσιν αὐτοῦ χαρίσασθαι καὶ τοῖς δυναμένοις μάλιστα παρὰ Φαρναβάζῳ, ἐπορεύετο.

cation, amidst the mountainous region once belonging to the Teukri Gergithes. It was here too that she kept her treasures, which, partly left by her husband, partly accumulated by herself, had gradually reached an enormous sum. But her district also reached down to the coast, comprising among other towns the classical name of Ilium, and probably her own native city the neighbouring Dardanus. She maintained, besides, a large military force of Grecian mercenaries in regular pay and excellent condition, which she employed both as garrison for each of her dependent towns, and as means for conquest in the neighbourhood. She had thus reduced the maritime towns of Larissa, Hamaxitus, and Kolônæ, in the southern part of the Troad; commanding her troops in person, sitting in her chariot to witness the attack, and rewarding everyone who distinguished himself. Moreover, when Pharnabazus undertook an expedition against the predatory Mysians or Pisidians, she accompanied him, and her military force formed so much the best part of his army, that he paid her the highest compliments, and sometimes condescended to ask her advice.[1] So, when Xerxes invaded Greece, Artemisia queen of Halikarnassus not only furnished ships among the best-appointed in his fleet, and fought bravely at Salamis, but also, when he chose to call a council, stood alone in daring to give him sound opinions contrary to his own leanings; opinions which, fortunately for the Grecian world, he could bring himself only to tolerate, not to follow.[2]

*Military force, personal conquests, and large treasures of Mania.*

Under an energetic woman like Mania, thus victorious and well-provided, Æolis was the most defensible part of the satrapy of Pharnabazus, and might probably have defied Derkyllidas, had not a domestic traitor put an end to her life. Her son-in-law, Meidias, a Greek of Skêpsis, with whom she lived on terms of intimate confidence —"though she was scrupulously mistrustful of everyone else, as it is proper for a despot to be"[3] —was so inflamed by his own ambition and by the suggestions of evil counsellors, who told him

*Assassination of Mania, and of her son, by her son-in-law Meidias, who solicits the satrapy from Pharnabazus, but is indignantly refused.*

[1] Xen. Hellen. iii. 1, 15.
[2] Herod. viii. 69.
[3] Such is the emphatic language of Xenophon (Hellen. iii. 1, 14)— Μειδίας, θυγατρὸς ἀνὴρ αὐτῆς ὤν, ἀναπτερωθεὶς ὑπό τινων, ὡς αἰσχρὸν εἴη, γυναῖκα μὲν ἄρχειν, αὐτὸν δ' ἰδιώτην εἶναι, τοὺς μὲν ἄλλους

it was a shame that a woman should thus be ruler while he was only a private man, that he strangled her in her chamber. Following up his nefarious scheme, he also assassinated her son, a beautiful youth of seventeen. He succeeded in getting possession of the three strongest places in the district, Kebrên, Skêpsis, and Gergis, together with the accumulated treasure of Mania. But the commanders in the other towns refused obedience to his summons, until they should receive orders from Pharnabazus. To that satrap Meidias instantly sent envoys, bearing ample presents, with a petition that the satrap would grant to him the district which had been enjoyed by Mania. Pharnabazus, repudiating the presents, sent an indignant reply to Meidias—"Keep them until I come to seize them—and to seize you also along with them. I would not consent to live, if I were not to avenge the death of Mania."[1]

At that critical moment, prior to the coming of the satrap, Derkyllidas presented himself with his army, and found Æolis almost defenceless. The three recent conquests of Mania—Larissa, Hamaxitus, and Kolônæ—surrendered to him as soon as he appeared; while the garrisons of Ilium and some other places, who had taken special service under Mania, and found themselves worse off now that they had lost her, accepted his invitation to renounce Persian dependence, declare themselves allies of Sparta, and hold their cities for him. He thus became master of most part of the district; with the exception of Kebrên, Skêpsis, and Gergis, which he was anxious to secure before the arrival of Pharnabazus. On arriving before Kebrên, however, in spite of this necessity for haste, he remained inactive for four days,[2] because the sacrifices were unpropitious; while

*Invasion and conquest of Æolis by Derkyllidas, who gets possession of the places of Meidias.*

μάλα φυλαττομένης αὐτῆς, ὥσπερ ἐν τυραννίδι προσῆκει, ἀπείργῳ δὲ πιστευούσης καὶ δοκαζομένης, ὥσπερ ἐν γυνὴ γαμβρὸν ἀσπάζοιτο,—εἰσελθὼν ἀποσφίζει αὐτὴν λέγεται.

For the illustration of this habitual insecurity in which the Grecian despot lived, see the dialogue of Xenophon called Hieron (i. 12; ii. 8—10; vii. 10). He particularly dwells upon the multitude of family crimes which stained the houses of the Grecian despots, murders by fathers, sons, brothers, wives, &c. (iii. 5).

[1] Xen. Hellen. iii. 1, 18.
[2] Xen. Hellen. iii. 1, 15; Diodor. xiv. 38.

The reader will remark here how Xenophon shapes the narrative in such a manner as to inculcate the

a rash subordinate officer, hazarding an unwarranted attack during this interval, was repulsed and wounded. The sacrifices at length became favourable, and Derkyllidas was rewarded for his patience. The garrison, affected by the example of those at Ilium and the other towns, disobeyed their commander, who tried to earn the satrap's favour by holding out and assuring to him this very strong place. Sending out heralds to proclaim that they would go with Greeks and not with Persians, they admitted the Lacedæmonians at once within the gates. Having thus fortunately captured, and duly secured, this important town, Derkyllidas marched against Skêpsis and Gergis, the former of which was held by Meidias himself; who, dreading the arrival of Pharnabazus, and mistrusting the citizens within, thought it best to open negotiations with Derkyllidas. He sent to solicit a conference, demanding hostages for his safety. When he came forth from the town, and demanded from the Lacedæmonian commander, on what terms alliance would be granted to him, the latter replied—"On condition that the citizens shall be left free and autonomous;" at the same time marching on, without waiting either for acquiescence or refusal, straight up to the gates of the town. Meidias, taken by surprise, in the power of the assailants, and aware that the citizens were unfriendly to him, was obliged to give orders that the gate should be opened; so that Derkyllidas found himself by this rapid manœuvre, in possession of the strongest place in the district without either loss or delay; to the great delight of the Skepsians themselves.[1]

*Derkyllidas acquires and liberates Skêpsis and Gergis, deposing Meidias, and seizing the treasures of Mania.*

Derkyllidas, having ascended the acropolis of Skêpsis to offer a sacrifice of thanks to Athênê, the great patron goddess of Ilium and most of the Teukrian towns—caused the garrison of Meidias to evacuate the town forthwith, and consigned it to the citizens themselves, exhorting them to conduct their political affairs as became Greeks and freemen. This proceeding, which reminds us of Brasidas in contrast with Lysander, was not less

pious duty in a general of obeying the warnings furnished by the sacrifice—either for action or for inaction. I have already noticed (in my preceding chapters) how often he does this in the Anabasis. Such an inference is never (I believe) to be found suggested in Thucydidês.

[1] Xen. Hellen. iii. 1, 20—23.

politic than generous; since Derkyllidas could hardly hope to hold an inland town in the midst of the Persian satrapy except by the attachments of the citizens themselves. He then marched away to Gergis, still conducting along with him Meidias, who urgently entreated to be allowed to retain that town, the last of his remaining fortresses. Without giving any decided answer, Derkyllidas took him by his side, and marched with him at the head of his army, arrayed only in double file, so as to carry the appearance of peace, to the foot of the lofty towers of Gergis. The garrison on the walls, seeing Meidias along with him, allowed him to approach without discharging a single missile. "Now, Meidias (said he), order the gates to be opened, and show me the way in, to the temple of Athênê, in order that I may there offer sacrifice." Again, Meidias was forced, from fear of being at once seized as a prisoner, to give the order; and the Lacedæmonian forces found themselves in possession of the town. Derkyllidas, distributing his troops round the walls, in order to make sure of his conquest, ascended to the acropolis to offer his intended sacrifice; after which he proceeded to dictate the fate of Meidias, whom he divested of his character of prince and of his military force—incorporating the latter in the Lacedæmonian army. He then called upon Meidias to specify all his paternal property, and restored to him the whole of what he claimed as such, though the bystanders protested against the statement given in as a flagrant exaggeration. But he laid hands on all the property, and all the treasures of Mania—and caused her house, which Meidias had taken for himself, to be put under seal—as lawful prey; since Mania had belonged to Pharnabazus,[1] against whom the Lacedæmonians

[1] Xen. Hellen. iii, 1, 26. Εἶxί μοι, ἔφη, Μανία δὲ τίνος ἦν; Οἱ δὲ πάντες εἶπον, ὅτι Φαρναβάζου. Οὐκοῦν καὶ τὰ ἐκείνης, ἔφη, Φαρναβάζου; Μάλιστα, ἔφασαν. Ἡμέτερ' ἂν εἴη, ἔφη, ἐπεὶ κρατοῦμεν· πολέμιος γὰρ ἡμῖν Φαρνάβαζος.
Two points are remarkable here.
1. The manner in which Mania, the administratrix of a large district, with a prodigious treasure and a large army in pay, is treated as belonging to Pharnabazus—as the servant or slave of Pharnabazus.

2. The distinction here taken between public property and private property, in reference to the laws of war and the rights of the conqueror. Derkyllidas lays claim to that which had belonged to Mania (or to Pharnabazus); but not to that which had belonged to Meidias.

According to the modern rules of international law, this distinction is one allowed and respected, everywhere except at sea. But in the ancient world, it by no means

were making war. On coming out after examining and
verifying the contents of the house, he said to his officers,
"Now, my friends, we have here already worked out pay
for the whole army, 8000 men, for near a year. Whatever
we acquire besides, shall come to you also." He well knew
the favourable effect which this intelligence would produce
upon the temper, as well as upon the discipline, of the army
—especially upon the Cyreians, who had tasted the discomfort of irregular pay and poverty.

"And where am I to live?" asked Meidias, who found
himself turned out of the house of Mania. "In your rightful place of abode, to be sure (replied Derkyllidas); in your
native town Skêpsis, and in your paternal house."[1] What
became of the assassin afterwards, we do not hear. But
it is satisfactory to find that he did not reap the anticipated
reward of his crime; the fruits of which were, an important
advantage to Derkyllidas and his army,—and a still more
important blessing to the Greek cities which had been
governed by Mania—enfranchisement and autonomy.

B.C. 399.
Derkyllidas
concludes a
truce with
Pharnaba-
zus, and
takes
winter
quarters in
Bithynia.

This rapid, easy, and skilfully-managed exploit—the
capture of nine towns in eight days—is all
which Xenophon mentions as achieved by
Derkyllidas during the summer. Having
acquired pay for so many months, perhaps the
soldiers may have been disposed to rest until it
was spent. But as winter approached, it became
necessary to find winter quarters, without incurring the reproach which had fallen upon Thimbron of consuming the substance of allies. Fearing however that if he changed his position, Pharnabazus would
employ the numerous Persian cavalry to harass the Grecian
cities, he tendered a truce, which the latter willingly
accepted. For the occupation of Æolis by the Lacedæmonian general was a sort of watch-post (like Dekeleia to
Athens), exposing the whole of Phrygia near the Propontis
(in which was Daskylium the residence of Pharnabazus)
to constant attack.[2] Derkyllidas accordingly only marched

stood out so clearly or prominently; and the observance of it here
deserves notice.

[1] Xen. Hellen. iii. 1, 23.
Thus finishes the interesting
narrative about Mania, Meidias,
and Derkyllidas. The abundance

of detail, and the dramatic manner,
in which Xenophon has worked it
out, impress me with a belief
that he was actually present at the
scene.

[2] Xen. Hellen. iii. 2, 1. νομίζων

through Phrygia, to take up his winter quarters in Bithynia, the north-western corner of Asia Minor, between the Propontis and the Euxine; the same territory through which Xenophon and the Ten Thousand had marched, on their road from Kalpê to Chalkêdon. He procured abundant provisions and booty, slaves as well as cattle, by plundering the Bithynian villages; not without occasional losses on his own side, by the carelessness of marauding parties.[1]

One of these losses was of considerable magnitude. Derkyllidas had obtained from Seuthês in European Thrace (the same prince of whom Xenophon had had so much reason to complain) a reinforcement of 300 cavalry and 200 peltasts—Odrysian Thracians. These Odrysians established themselves in a separate camp, nearly two miles and a half from Derkyllidas, which they surrounded with a palisade about man's height. Being indefatigable plunderers, they prevailed upon Derkyllidas to send them a guard of 200 hoplites, for the purpose of guarding their separate camp with the booty accumulated within it. Presently the camp became richly stocked, especially with Bithynian captives. The hostile Bithynians however watching their opportunity when the Odrysians were out marauding, suddenly attacked at daybreak the 200 Grecian hoplites in the camp. Shooting at them over the palisado with darts and arrows, they killed and wounded some, while the Greeks with their spears were utterly helpless, and could only reach their enemies by pulling up the palisade and charging out upon them. But the light-armed assailants, easily evading the charge of warriors with shield and spear, turned round upon them when they began to retire, and slew several before they could get back. In each successive sally, the same phænomena recurred, until at length all the Greeks were overpowered and slain, except fifteen of them, who charged through the Bithynians in the first sally, and marched onward to join Derkyllidas, instead of returning with their comrades to the palisade. Derkyllidas lost no time in sending a reinforcement; which however came too late and found only the naked bodies of

τὴν Ἀλοκὴθα ἐπιστατειχίσθαι τῷ ἑαυτοῦ and significant, in Grecian warfare.
οἰκίστι Φρυγή.
The word ἐπιτειχίζων is capital  [1] Xen. Hellen. III. 2, 2—5.

the slain. The victorious Bithynians carried away all their own captives.[1]

At the beginning of spring the Spartan general returned to Lampsakus, where he found Arakus and two other Spartans just arrived out as commissioners sent by the Ephors. Arakus came with instructions to prolong the command of Derkyllidas for another year; as well as to communicate the satisfaction of the Ephors with the Cyreian army, in consequence of the great improvement in their conduct, compared with the year of Thimbron. He accordingly assembled the soldiers, and addressed them in a mingled strain of praise and admonition; expressing his hope that they would continue the forbearance which they had now begun to practise towards all Asiatic allies. The commander of the Cyreians (probably Xenophon himself), in his reply, availed himself of the occasion to pay a compliment to Derkyllidas. "We (said he) are the same men now as we were in the previous year; but we are under a different general: you need not look farther for the explanation."[2] Without denying the superiority of Derkyllidas over his predecessor, we may remark that the abundant wealth of Mania, thrown into his hands by accident (though he showed great ability in turning the accident to account), was an auxiliary circumstance, not less unexpected than weighty, for ensuring the good behaviour of the soldiers.

*Command of Derkyllidas—satisfaction of Sparta with the improved conduct of the Cyreians.*

It was among the farther instructions of Arakus to visit all the principal Asiatic Greeks, and report their condition at Sparta; and Derkyllidas was pleased to see them entering on this survey at a moment when they would find the cities in undisturbed peace and tranquillity.[3] So long as the truce continued both with Tissaphernês and Pharnabazus, these cities were secure from aggression and paid no tribute; the land-force

*Derkyllidas crosses into Europe, and employs his troops in fortifying the Chersonesus against the Thracians.*

---

[1] Xen. Hellen. iii. 2, 4.
[2] Xen. Hellen. iii. 2, 6, 7.
Morus supposes (I think, with much probability) that ὁ τῶν Κυρείων προσηγνεκὼς here means Xenophon himself.
He could not with propriety advert to the fact that he himself had not been with the army during the year of Thimbron.
[3] Xen. Hellen. iii. 2, 9. Ἔπεμψεν αὐτοὺς δὲ' Ἐφέσου διὰ τῶν Ἑλληνίδων πόλεων, ἡδόμενος ὅτι ἔμελλον ὄψεσθαι τὰς πόλεις ἐν εἰρήνῃ εὐδαι-

of Derkyllidas affording to them a protection¹ analogous to that which had been conferred by Athens and her powerful fleet, during the interval between the formation of the Confederacy of Delos and the Athenian catastrophe at Syracuse. At the same time, during the truce, the army had neither occupation nor subsistence. To keep it together and near at hand, yet without living at the cost of friends, was the problem.

It was accordingly with great satisfaction that Derkyllidas noticed an intimation accidentally dropped by Arakus. Some envoys (the latter said) were now at Sparta from the Thracian Chersonesus (the long tongue of land bordering westward on the Hellespont), soliciting aid against their marauding Thracian neighbours. That fertile peninsula, first hellenised a century and a half before by the Athenian Miltiadês, had been a favourite resort for Athenian citizens, many of whom had acquired property there during the naval power of Athens. The battle of Ægospotami dispossessed and drove home these proprietors, at the same time depriving the peninsula of its protection against the Thracians. It now contained eleven distinct cities, of which Sestos was the most important; and its inhabitants combined to send envoys to Sparta, entreating the Ephors to dispatch a force for the purpose of building a wall across the isthmus from Kardia to Paktyê; in recompense for which (they said) there was fertile land enough open to as many settlers as chose to come, with coast and harbours for export close at hand. Miltiadês, on first going out to the Chersonese, had secured it by constructing a cross wall on the same spot, which had since become neglected during the period of Persian supremacy; Periklês had afterwards sent fresh colonists, and caused the wall to be

μονικῶς διαγούσας. I cannot but think that we ought here to read ἀπ' Ἐφέσου not ἀπ' Ἐφέσου; or else ἀπὸ Λαμψάκου.

It was at Lampsakus that this interview and conversation between Derkyllidas and the commissioners took place. The commissioners were to be sent from Lampsakus to Ephesus through the Grecian cities.

The expression ἐν εἰρήνῃ εὐδαι- μονικῶς διαγούσας has reference to the foreign relations of the cities and to their exemption from annoyance by Persian arms— without implying any internal freedom or good condition. There were Lacedæmonian harmosts in most of them, and Dekarchies half broken up or modified in many: see the subsequent passages (III. 2, 20; III. 4, 7; iv. 8, 1).

¹ Compare Xen. Hellen. iv. 2, 5.

repaired. But it seems to have been unnecessary while the Athenian empire was in full vigour—since the Thracian princes had been generally either conciliated, or kept off, by Athens, even without any such bulwark.[1] Informed that the request of the Chersonesites had been favourably listened to at Sparta, Derkyllidas resolved to execute their project with his own army. Having prolonged his truce with Pharnabazus, he crossed the Hellespont into Europe, and employed his army during the whole summer in constructing this cross wall, about 4¼ miles in length. The work was distributed in portions to different sections of the army, competition being excited by rewards for the most rapid and workmanlike execution; while the Chersonesites were glad to provide pay and subsistence for the army, during an operation which provided security for all the eleven cities, and gave additional value to their lands and harbours. Numerous settlers seem to have now come in, under Lacedæmonian auspices—who were again disturbed, wholly or partially, when the Lacedæmonian maritime empire was broken up a few years afterwards.[2]

On returning to Asia in the autumn, after the completion of this work which had kept his army usefully employed and amply provided during six months, Derkyllidas undertook the siege of Alarneus, a strong post (on the continental coast eastward of Mitylênê) occupied by some Chian exiles, whom the Lacedæmonian admiral Kratesippidas had lent corrupt aid in expelling from their native island a few years before.[3] These men, living by predatory expeditions against Chios and Ionia, were so well supplied with provisions that it cost Derkyllidas a blockade of eight months before he could reduce it. He placed in it a strong garrison well supplied, that it might serve him as a retreat in case of need—under an Achæan named Drako, whose name remained long terrible from his ravages on the neighbouring plain of Mysia.[4]

B.C. 395-397. He captures and garrisons Alarneus.

Derkyllidas next proceeded to Ephesus, where orders presently reached him from the Ephors, directing him to

[1] Herodot. vi. 86; Plutarch, Perikles, c. 19; 'Isokratês, Or. v. (Philipp.) s. 7.
[2] Xen. Hellen. iii. 2, 10; iv. 8, 5.
Diodor. xiv. 38.
[3] Didor. xiii. 65.
[4] Xen. Hellen. iii. 2, 11; Isokratês, Or. iv. (Panegyr.) s. 167.

march into Karia and attack Tissaphernês. The temporary truce which had hitherto provisionally kept off Persian soldiers and tribute-gatherers from the Asiatic Greeks, was now renounced by mutual consent. These Greeks had sent envoys to Sparta, assuring the Ephors that Tissaphernês would be constrained to renounce formally the sovereign rights of Persia, and grant to them full autonomy, if his residence in Karia were vigorously attacked. Accordingly Derkyllidas marched southward across the Mæander into Karia, while the Lacedæmonian fleet under Pharax cooperated along the shore. At the same time, Tissaphernês on his side had received reinforcements from Susa, together with the appointment of generalissimo over all the Persian force in Asia Minor; upon which Pharnabazus (who had gone up to court in the interval to concert more vigorous means of prosecuting the war, but had now returned[1]) joined him in Karia, prepared to commence vigorous operations for the expulsion of Derkyllidas and his army. Having properly garrisoned the strong places, the two satraps crossed the Mæander, at the head of a powerful Grecian and Karian force, with numerous Persian cavalry, to attack the Ionian cities. As soon as he heard this news, Derkyllidas came back with his army from Karia to cover the towns menaced. Having recrossed the Mæander, he was marching with his army in disorder, not suspecting the enemy to be near, when on a sudden he came upon their scouts, planted on some sepulchral monuments in the road. He too sent some scouts up to the neighbouring monuments and towers, who apprised him that the two satraps, with their joint force in good order, were planted here to intercept him. He immediately gave orders for his hoplites to form in battle array of eight deep, with the peltasts, and his handful of horsemen, on each flank. But such was the alarm caused among his troops by this surprise, that none could be relied upon except the Cyreians and the Peloponnesians. Of the insular and Ionian hoplites, from Priênê and other cities, some actually hid their arms in the thick standing corn, and fled; others, who took their places in the line, manifested dispositions which left little hope that they would stand a charge; so that the Persians had the opportunity

[1] Diodor. xiv. 39.

of fighting a battle not merely with superiority of number, but also with advantage of position and circumstances. Pharnabazus was anxious to attack without delay. But Tissaphernês, who recollected well the valour of the Cyreian troops, and concluded that all the remaining Greeks were like them, forbade it; sending forward heralds to demand a conference. As they approached, Derkyllidas, surrounding himself with a body-guard of the finest and the best-equipped soldiers,[1] advanced to the front of the line to meet them; saying that he for his part was prepared to fight—but since a conference was demanded, he had no objection to grant it, provided hostages were exchanged. This having been assented to, and a place named for conference on the ensuing day, both armies were simultaneously withdrawn; the Persians to Trallês, the Greeks to Leukophrys, celebrated for its temple of Artemis Leukophryne.[2]

*Timidity of Tissaphernês—he concludes a truce with Derkyllidas.*

This backwardness on the part of Tissaphernês, even at a time when he was encouraged by a brother satrap braver than himself, occasioned to the Persians the loss of a very promising moment, and rescued the Grecian army out of a position of much peril. It helps to explain to us the escape of the Cyreians, and the manner in which they were allowed to cross rivers and pass over the most difficult ground without any serious opposition; while at the same time it tended to confirm in the Greek mind the same impressions of Persian imbecility as that escape so forcibly suggested.

The conference, as might be expected, ended in nothing. Derkyllidas required on behalf of the Asiatic Greeks complete autonomy—exemption from Persian interference and tribute; while the two satraps on their side insisted that the Lacedæmonian army should be withdrawn from Asia, and the Lacedæmonian harmosts from all the Greco-Asiatic cities. An armistice was concluded, to allow time for reference to the authorities at home; thus replacing matters

---

[1] Xen. Hellen. III. 2, 18.
In the Anabasis (ii. 3, 5) Xenophon mentions the like care on the part of Klearchus, to have the best-armed and most imposing soldiers around him, when he went to his interview with Tissaphernês. Xenophon gladly avails himself of the opportunity, to pay an indirect compliment to the Cyreian army.

[2] Xen. Hellen. III. 2, 19; Diodor. xiv. 39.

in the condition in which they had been at the beginning of the year.[1] 

Shortly after the conclusion of this truce, king of Sparta arrived with a large force, and the war in all respects began to assume larger proportions—of which more in the next chapter.

*Agesilaus Derkyllidas is superseded by Agesilaus.*

But it was not in Asia alone that Sparta had been engaged in war. The prostration of the Athenian power had removed that common bond of hatred and alarm which attached the allies to her headship: while her subsequent conduct had given positive offence, and had even excited against herself the same fear of unmeasured imperial ambition which had before run so powerfully against Athens. She had appropriated to herself nearly the whole of the Athenian maritime empire, with a tribute scarcely inferior, if at all inferior, in amount. How far the total of 1000 talents was actually realised during each successive year, we are not in a condition to say; but such was the assessment imposed and the scheme laid down by Sparta for her maritime dependencies—enforced too by omnipresent instruments of rapacity and oppression, decemvirs and harmosts, such as Athens had never paralleled. When we add to this great maritime empire the prodigious ascendency on land which Sparta had enjoyed before, we shall find a total of material power far superior to that which Athens had enjoyed, even in her day of greatest exaltation, prior to the truce of 445 B.C.

*Alienation towards Sparta had grown up among her allies in Central Greece.*

This was not all. From the general dullness of character pervading Spartan citizens, the full resources of the state were hardly ever put forth. Her habitual shortcomings at the moment of action are keenly criticised by her own friends, in contrast with the ardour and forwardness which animated her enemies. But at and after the battle of Ægospotami, the entire management of Spartan foreign affairs was found in the hands of Lysander; a man not only exempt from the inertia usual in his countrymen, but of the most unwearied activity and grasping ambition, as well for his country as for himself. Under his direction

*Great energy imparted to Spartan action by Lysander immediately after the victory of Ægospotami; an energy very unusual with Sparta.*

[1] Xen. Hellen. iii. 2, 20.

the immense advantages which Sparta enjoyed from her new position were at once systematised and turned to the fullest account. Now there was enough in the new ascendency of Sparta, had it been ever so modestly handled, to spread apprehension through the Grecian world. But apprehension became redoubled, when it was seen that her ascendency was organized and likely to be worked by her most aggressive leader for the purposes of an insatiable ambition. Fortunately for the Grecian world, indeed, the power of Sparta did not long continue to be thus absolutely wielded by Lysander, whose arrogance and overweening position raised enemies against him at home. Yet the first impressions received by the allies respecting Spartan empire, were derived from his proceedings and his plans of dominion, manifested with ostentatious insolence; and such impressions continued, even after the influence of Lysander himself had been much abated by the counter-working rivalry of Pausanias and others.

While Sparta separately had thus gained so much by the close of the war, not one of her allies had received the smallest remuneration or compensation, except such as might be considered to be involved in the destruction of a formidable enemy. Even the pecuniary result or residue which Lysander had brought home with him (470 talents remaining out of the advances made by Cyrus), together with the booty acquired at Dekeleia, was all detained by the Lacedæmonians themselves. Thebes and Corinth indeed presented demands, in which the other allies did not (probably durst not) join, to be allowed to share. But though all the efforts and sufferings of the war had fallen upon these allies no less than upon Sparta, the demands were refused, and almost resented as insults.[1] Hence there arose among the allies not merely a fear of the grasping dominion, but a hatred of the monopolising rapacity, of Sparta. Of this new feeling an early manifestation, alike glaring and important, was made by the Thebans and Corinthians, when they refused to join Pausanias in his march against Thrasybulus and the Athenian exiles in Peiræus[2]—less than a year after the surrender of Athens, the enemy whom these two cities had hated with

*The Spartans had kept all the advantages of victory to themselves— their allies were allowed nothing.*

[1] Xen. Hellen. iii. 5, 5; Plutarch, Lysand. c. 27; Justin. v. 10.
[2] Xen. Hellen. ii. 4, 30.

such extreme bitterness down to the very moment of surrender. Even Arcadians and Achæans, too, habitually obedient as they were to Lacedæmon, keenly felt the different way in which she treated them, as compared with the previous years of war, when she had been forced to keep alive their zeal against the common enemy.[1]

The Lacedæmonians were however strong enough not merely to despise this growing alienation of their allies, but even to take revenge upon such of the Peloponnesians as had incurred their displeasure. Among these stood conspicuous the Eleians; now under a government called democratical, of which the leading man was Thrasydæus—a man who had lent considerable aid in 404 B.C. to Thrasybulus and the Athenian exiles in Peiræus. The Eleians in the year 420 B.C., had been engaged in a controversy with Sparta —had employed their privileges as administrators of the Olympic festival to exclude her from attendance on that occasion—and had subsequently been in arms against her along with Argos and Mantineia. To these grounds of quarrel, now of rather ancient date, had been added afterwards, a refusal to furnish aid in the war against Athens since the resumption of hostilities in 414 B.C., and a recent exclusion of King Agis, who had come in person to offer sacrifice and consult the oracle of Zeus Olympius; such exclusion being grounded on the fact that he was about to pray for victory in the war then pending against Athens, contrary to the ancient canon of the Olympic temple, which admitted no sacrifice or consultation respecting hostilities of Greek against Greek.[2] These were considered by

*B.C. 402. Great power of the Spartans—they take revenge upon those who had displeased them—their invasion of Elis.*

[1] Xen. Hellen. III. 5, 12. Κορινθίους δὲ καὶ Ἀρκάδας καὶ Ἀχαιούς τε φῶμεν; οἱ ἐν μὲν τῷ πρὸς ὑμᾶς (it is the Theban envoys who are addressing the public assembly at Athens) πολέμῳ μάλα λιπαρούμενοι ὑπ' ἐκείνων (the Lacedæmonians), πάντων καὶ πόνων καὶ κινδύνων καὶ δαπανημάτων μετείχον· ἐπεὶ δ' ἔπραξαν ἃ ἐβούλοντο οἱ Λακεδαιμόνιοι, ποίας ἢ ἀρχῆς ἢ τιμῆς ἢ πολῶν χρημάτων μεταδεδώκασιν αὐτοῖς; ἀλλὰ τοὺς μὲν εἵλωτας ἁρμοστὰς καθιστάναι ἀξιοῦσι, τῶν δὲ

συμμάχων ἐλευθέρων ὄντων, ἐπεὶ εὐτύχησαν, δεσπόται ἀναπεφήνασιν.

[2] Xen. Hellen. III. 2, 21. Τούτων δ' ὕστερον, καὶ Ἀγίδος πεμφθέντος θῦσαι τῷ Διὶ κατὰ μαντεῖον τινὸς, ἐκώλυον οἱ Ἠλεῖοι, μὴ προσεύχεσθαι νίκην πολέμου, λέγοντες, ὡς καὶ τὸ ἀρχαῖον εἴη οὕτω νόμιμον, μὴ χρηστηριάζεσθαι τοὺς Ἕλληνας ἐφ' Ἑλλήνων πολέμῳ· ὥστε ἄθυτος ἀπῆλθεν.

This canon seems not unnatural, for one of the greatest Pan-hellenic temples and establishments. Yet

Sparta as affronts, and the season was now favourable for resenting them, as well as for chastising and humbling Elis.[1] Accordingly Sparta sent an embassy, requiring the Eleians to make good the unpaid arrears of the quota assessed upon them for the cost of the war against Athens; and farther—to relinquish their authority over their dependent townships or Periœki, leaving the latter autonomous.[2] Of these dependencies there were several, no one very considerable individually, in the region called Triphylia, south of the river Alpheus, and north of the Neda. One of them was Lepreum, the autonomy of which the Lacedæmonians had vindicated against Elis in 420 B.C., though during the subsequent period it had again become subject.

B.C. 402. The Spartan king Agis invades the Eleian territory. He retires from it immediately in consequence of an earthquake.

The Eleians refused compliance with the demand thus sent, alleging that their dependent cities were held by the right of conquest. They even retorted upon the Lacedæmonians the charge of enslaving Greeks;[3] upon which Agis marched with an army to invade their territory, entering it from the north side where it joined Achaia. Hardly had he crossed the frontier river Larissus and begun his ravages, when an earthquake occurred. Such an event, usually construed in Greece as a divine warning, acted on this occasion so strongly on the religious susceptibilities of Agis,

---

it was not constantly observed at Olympia (compare another example —Xen. Hellen. iv. 7, 2); nor yet at Delphi, which was not less Pan-hellenic than Olympia (see Thucyd. i. 118). We are therefore led to imagine that it was a cason which the Eleians invoked only when they were prompted by some special sentiment or aversion.

[1] Xen. Hellan. III. 2, 23. Ἐκ τούτων οὖν πάντων ὀργιζομένοις, ἔδοξε τοῖς ἐφόροις καὶ τῇ ἐκκλησίᾳ, σωφρονίσαι αὐτούς.

[2] Diodorus (xiv. 17) mentions this demand for the arrears; which appears very probable. It is not directly noticed by Xenophon, who however mentions (see the passage cited in the note of page preceding) the general assessment levied by Sparta upon all her Peloponnesian allies during the war.

[3] Diodor. xiv. 17.

Diodorus introduces in these transactions King Pausanias, not King Agis, as the acting person.

Pausanias states (III. 8, 2) that the Eleians, in returning a negative answer to the requisition of Sparta, added that they would enfranchise their Periœki, when they saw Sparta enfranchise her own. This answer appears to me highly improbable, under the existing circumstances of Sparta and her relations to the other Grecian states. Allusion to the relations between Sparta and her Periœki was a novelty, even in 371 B.C.,

that he not only withdrew from the Eleian territory, but disbanded his army. His retreat gave so much additional courage to the Eleians, that they sent envoys and tried to establish alliances among those cities which they knew to be alienated from Sparta. Not even Thebes and Corinth, however, could be induced to assist them; nor did they obtain any other aid except 1000 men from Ætolia.

In the next summer Agis undertook a second expedition, accompanied on this occasion by all the allies of Sparta; even by the Athenians, now enrolled upon the list. Thebes and Corinth alone stood aloof. On this occasion he approached from the opposite or southern side, that of the territory once called Messenia; passing through Aulon, and crossing the river Neda. He marched through Triphylia to the river Alpheius, which he crossed, and then proceeded to Olympia, where he consummated the sacrifice from which the Eleians had before excluded him. In his march he was joined by the inhabitants of Lepreum, Makistus, and other dependent towns, which now threw off their subjection to Elis. Thus reinforced, Agis proceeded onward towards the city of Elis, through a productive country under flourishing agriculture, enriched by the crowds and sacrifices at the neighbouring Olympic temple, and for a long period unassailed. After attacking, not very vigorously, the half-fortified city—and being repelled by the Ætolian auxiliaries—he marched onward to the harbour called Kyllênê, still plundering the territory. So ample was the stock of slaves, cattle, and rural wealth generally, that his troops not only acquired riches for themselves by plunder, but were also joined by many Arcadian and Achæan volunteers, who crowded in to partake of the golden harvest.[1]

*B.C. 401. Second invasion of Elis by Agis—he marches through Triphylia and Olympia: victorious march, with much booty.*

The opposition or wealthy oligarchical party in Elis availed themselves of this juncture to take arms against the government; hoping to get possession of the city, and to maintain themselves in power by the aid of Sparta. Xenias their leader, a man of immense wealth, with several of his adherents, rushed out armed, and assailed the

*Insurrection of the oligarchical party in Elis—they are put down.*

---

at the congress which preceded the battle of Leuktra.

[1] Xen. Hellen. III. 2, 25, 26; Diodor. xiv. 17.

government-house, in which it appears that Thrasydæus and his colleagues had been banqueting. They slew several persons, and among them one, whom, from great personal resemblance, they mistook for Thrasydæus. The latter was however at that moment intoxicated, and asleep in a separate chamber.[1] They then assembled in arms in the market-place, believing themselves to be masters of the city; while the people, under the like impression that Thrasydæus was dead, were too much dismayed to offer resistance. But presently it became known that he was yet alive; the people crowded to the government-house "like a swarm of bees,"[2] and arrayed themselves for his protection as well as under his guidance. Leading them forth at once to battle, he completely defeated the oligarchical insurgents, and forced them to flee for protection to the Lacedæmonian army.

Agis presently evacuated the Eleian territory, yet not without planting a Lacedæmonian harmost and a garrison, together with Xenias and the oligarchical exiles, at Epitalium, a little way south of the river Alpheius. Occupying this fort (analogous to Dekeleia in Attica), they spread ravage and ruin all around throughout the autumn and winter, to such a degree, that in the early spring, Thrasydæus and the Eleian government were compelled to send to Sparta and solicit peace. They consented to raze the imperfect fortifications of their city, so as to leave it quite open. They farther surrendered their harbour of Kyllênê with their ships of war, and relinquished all authority over the Triphylian townships, as well as over Lasion, which was claimed as an Arcadian town.[3]

*B.C. 400. The Eleians are obliged to submit to hard terms of peace.*

## CHAP. LXXII.  PEACE GRANTED TO ELIS.  49

Though they pressed strenuously their claim to preserve the town of Epeium (between the Arcadian town of Heræa and the Triphylian town of Makistus), on the plea that they had bought it from its previous inhabitants at the price of thirty talents paid down—the Lacedæmonians, pronouncing this to be a compulsory bargain imposed upon weaker parties by force, refused to recognise it. The town was taken away from them, seemingly without any reimbursement of the purchase-money either in part or in whole. On these terms the Eleians were admitted to peace, and enrolled again among the members of the Lacedæmonian confederacy.[1]

---

is something perplexing in Xenophon's description of the Triphylian townships which the Eleians surrendered. First, he does not name Lepreum or Makistus, both of which nevertheless had joined Agis on his invasion, and were the most important places in Triphylia (iii. 2, 25). Next, he names Letrini, Amphidoli, and Marganeis, as Triphylian; which yet were on the north of the Alpheius, and are elsewhere distinguished from Triphylian. I incline to believe that the words in his text, καὶ τὰς Τριφυλίδας πόλεις ἀφεῖναι, must be taken to mean Lepreum and Makistus, perhaps with some other places which we do not know; but that a καὶ after ἀφεῖναι has fallen out of the text, and that the cities, whose names follow, are to be taken as not Triphylian. Phrixa and Epitalium were both south, but only just south, of the Alpheius; they were on the borders of Triphylia —and it seems doubtful whether they were properly Triphylian.

[1] Xen. Hellen. iii. 2, 30; Diodor. xiv. 34; Pausan. iii. 8, 2.

This war between Sparta and Elis reaches over three different years: it began in the first, occupied the whole of the second, and was finished in the third. Which years these three were (out of the seven which separate B.C. 403—395), is a point upon which critics have not been unanimous.

Following the chronology of Diodorus, who places the beginning of the war in 402 B.C., I differ from Mr. Clinton, who places it in 401 B.C. (Fasti Hellen. ad ann.), and from Sievers (Geschichte von Griechenland bis zur Schlacht von Mantinea, p. 282), who places it in 398 B.C.

According to Mr. Clinton's view, the principal year of the war would have been 400 B.C., the year of the Olympic festival. But surely, had such been the fact, the coincidence of war in the country with the Olympic festival, must have raised so many complications, and acted so powerfully on the sentiments of all parties, as to be specifically mentioned. In my judgement, the war was brought to a close in the early part of 400 B.C., before the time of the Olympic festival arrived. Probably the Eleians were anxious, on this very ground, to bring it to a close before the festival did arrive.

Sievers, in his discussion of the point, admits that the date assigned by Diodorus to the Eleian war, squares both with the date which Diodorus gives for the death of

VOL. IX.  E

The time of the Olympic festival seems to have been
now approaching, and the Eleians were probably
the more anxious to obtain peace from Sparta,
as they feared to be deprived of their privilege
as superintendents. The Pisatans—inhabitants
of the district immediately round Olympia—
availed themselves of the Spartan invasion of Elis to petition for restoration of their original privilege, as administrators of the temple of Zeus at Olympia with its great
periodical solemnity—by the dispossession of the Eleians
as usurpers of that privilege. But their request met with
no success. It was true indeed that such right had belonged to the Pisatans, in early days, before the Olympic
festival had acquired its actual Pan-hellenic importance
and grandeur; and that the Eleians had only appropriated
it to themselves after conquering the territory of Pisa.
But taking the festival as it then stood, the Pisatans, mere
villagers without any considerable city, were incompetent
to do justice to it, and would have lowered its dignity in
the eyes of all Greece.

Accordingly, the Lacedæmonians, on this ground, dismissed the claimants, and left the superinten-
dence of the Olympic games still in the hands
of the Eleians.[1]

This triumphant dictation of terms to Elis
placed the Lacedæmonians in a condition of
overruling ascendency throughout Peloponnesus,
such as they had never attained before. To
complete their victory, they rooted out all the

*Sparta refuses to restore the Pisatans to the Olympic presidency.*

*Triumphant position of Sparta— she expels the Messe- nians from Pelopon- nesus and its neigh- bourhood.*

Agis, and with that which Plutarch
states about the duration of the
reign of Agesilaus—better than the
chronology which he himself
(Sievers) prefers. He founds his
conclusion on Xenophon, Hell. III.
2, 21. Τούτων δὲ πραττομένων ἐν τῇ
Ἀσίᾳ ὑπὸ Δερκυλλίδα, Λακεδαιμόνιοι
κατὰ τὸν αὐτὸν χρόνον πάλαι ὀργιζόμενοι τοῖς Ἠλείοις, &c.
This passage is certainly of some
weight; yet I think in the present
case it is not to be pressed with
rigid accuracy as to date. The
whole third Book down to these
very words, has been occupied

entirely with the course of Asiatic
affairs. Not a single proceeding
of the Lacedæmonians in Peloponnesus, since the amnesty at Athens,
has yet been mentioned. The
command of Derkyllidas included
only the last portion of the Asiatic exploits, and Xenophon has
here loosely referred to it as if it
comprehended the whole. Sievers
moreover comprises the whole
Eleian war into one year and a
fraction; an interval, shorter, I
think, than that which is implied
in the statements of Xenophon.

[1] Xen. Hellen. III. 2, 31.

remnants of their ancient enemies the Messenians, some of whom had been planted by the Athenians at Naupaktus, others in the island of Kephallenia. All of this persecuted race were now expelled, in the hour of Lacedæmonian omnipotence, from the neighbourhood of Peloponnesus, and forced to take shelter, some in Sicily, others at Kyrênê.[1] We shall in a future chapter have to commemorate the turn of fortune in their favour.

[1] Diodor. xiv. 84; Pausan. iv. 26, 2.

## CHAPTER LXXIII.

### AGESILAUS KING OF SPARTA.—THE CORINTHIAN WAR.

THE close of the Peloponnesian War, with the victorious organization of the Lacedæmonian empire by Lysander, has already been described as a period carrying with it increased suffering to those towns which had formerly belonged to the Athenian empire, as compared with what they had endured under Athens—and harder dependence, unaccompanied by any species of advantage, even to those Peloponnesians and inland cities which had always been dependent allies of Sparta. To complete the melancholy picture of the Grecian world during these years, we may add (what will be hereafter more fully detailed) that calamities of a still more deplorable character overtook the Sicilian Greeks: first, from the invasion of the Carthaginians, who sacked Himera, Selinus, Agrigentum, Gela, and Kamarina—next from the overruling despotism of Dionysius at Syracuse.

B.C. 404-396.

Triumphant position of Sparta at the close of the war—introduction of a large sum of gold and silver by Lysander—opposed by some of the Ephors.

Sparta alone had been the gainer; and that to a prodigious extent, both in revenue and power. It is from this time, and from the proceedings of Lysander, that various ancient authors dated the commencement of her degeneracy, which they ascribe mainly to her departure from the institutions of Lykurgus by admitting gold and silver money. These metals had before been strictly prohibited; no money being tolerated except heavy pieces of iron, not portable except to a very trifling amount. That such was the ancient institution of Sparta, under which any Spartan having in his possession gold and silver money, was liable, if detected, to punishment, appears certain. How far the regulation may have been in practice evaded, we have no means of determining. Some of the Ephors strenuously opposed the admission of the large sum brought home by Lysander as remnant of what he had received from Cyrus towards the prosecution of the war. They contended that the admission of so much gold and silver into public treasury was a flagrant transgression of the Lykurgean ordinances. But their resistance was unavailing, and the new acquisitions were received; though it still continued to be a penal offence (and was even made a capital offence, if we may trust Plutarch) for any individual to be found with gold and silver in his possession.[1] To enforce such a prohibition, however, even if practicable before, ceased to be practicable so soon as these metals were recognised and tolerated in the possession, and for the purposes, of the government.

There can be no doubt that the introduction of a large sum of coined gold and silver into Sparta was in itself a striking and important phænomenon, when viewed in conjunction with the peculiar customs and discipline of the state. It was likely to raise strong antipathies in the bosom of an old-fashioned Spartan, and probably King Archidamus, had he been alive, would have taken part with the opposing Ephors. But Plutarch and others have criticised it too much as a phænomenon by itself; whereas it was really one characteristic mark and portion of a new assemblage of circumstances, into which Sparta had been gradually arriving during the last years of the war, and which were brought into the most effective action by the decisive success at Ægospotami. The institutions of Lykurgus, though excluding all Spartan citizens, by an unremitting drill and public mess, from trade and industry, from ostentation, and from luxury—did not by any means extinguish in their bosoms the love of money;[2] while they had a positive tendency to exaggerate, rather than to abate, the love of

*The introduction of money was only one among a large train of corrupting circumstances which then became operative on Sparta.*

---

[1] Plutarch, Lysand. c. 17. Compare Xen. Rep. Lacad. vii. 6.

Both Ephors and Theopompus recounted this opposition to the introduction of gold and silver into Sparta, each mentioning the name of one of the Ephors as taking the lead in it.

There was a considerable body of ancient sentiment, and that too among high-minded and intelligent men, which regarded gold and silver as a cause of mischief and corruption, and of which the stanza of Horace (Od. III. 8) is an echo:—

Aurum irrepertum, et sic melius
situm
Cum terra celat, spernere fortior
Quam cogere humanos in usus,
Omne sacrum rapiente dextrâ.

[2] Aristotel. Politic. II. 6, 21.

Ἀποβέβηκε δὲ τοὐναντίον τῷ νομοθέτῃ τοῦ συμφέροντος· τὴν μὲν γὰρ πόλιν πεποίηκεν ἀχρήματον, τοὺς δ' ἰδιώτας φιλοχρηματίους.

power. The Spartan kings Leotychidês and Pleistoanax had both been guilty of receiving bribes; Tissaphernês had found means (during the twentieth year of the Peloponnesian War) to corrupt not merely the Spartan admiral Astyochus, but also nearly all the captains of the Peloponnesian fleet, except the Syracusan Hermokratês; Gylippus, as well as his father Kleandridês, had degraded himself by the like fraud; and Anaxibius at Byzantium was not at all purer. Lysander, enslaved only by his appetite for dominion, and himself a remarkable instance of superiority to pecuniary corruption, was thus not the first to engraft that vice on the minds of his countrymen. But though he found it already diffused among them, he did much to impart to it a still more decided predominance, by the immense increase of opportunities, and enlarged booty for peculation, which his newly-organized Spartan empire furnished. Not merely did he bring home a large residue in gold and silver, but there was a much larger annual tribute imposed by him on the dependent cities, combined with numerous appointments of harmosts to govern the cities. Such appointments presented abundant illicit profits, easy to acquire, and even difficult to avoid, since the decemvirs in each city were eager thus to purchase forbearance or connivance for their own misdeeds. So many new sources of corruption were sufficient to operate most unfavourably on the Spartan character, if not by implanting any fresh vices, at least by stimulating all its inherent bad tendencies.

Contrast between Sparta in 432 B.C., and Sparta after 404 B.C.

To understand the material change thus wrought in it, we have only to contrast the speeches of King Archidamus and of the Corinthians, made in 432 B.C. at the beginning of the Peloponnesian War—with the state of facts at the end of the war, during the eleven years between the victory of Ægospotami and the defeat of Knidus (405-394 B.C.). At the former of the two epochs, Sparta had no tributary subjects, nor any funds in her treasury, while her citizens were very reluctant to pay imposts:[1] about 334 B.C., thirty-seven years after her defeat at Leuktra and her loss of Messenia, Aristotle remarks the like fact, which had then again become true;[2] but during the continuance of

Thucyd. l. 80. ἀλλὰ πολλῷ ἔτι πλέον τούτου (χρημάτων) ἐλλείπομεν, καὶ οὔτε ἐν κοινῷ ἔχομεν, οὔτε ἑτοίμως ἐκ τῶν ἰδίων φέρομεν.
[2] Aristotel. Polit. II. 6, 23. Φαύλως δ' ἔχει καὶ περὶ τὰ κοινὰ χρή-

her empire, between 405 and 394 B.C., she possessed a large public revenue, derived from the tribute of the dependent cities. In 432 B.C., Sparta is not merely cautious but backward; especially averse to any action at a distance from home;[1] in 404 B.C., after the close of the war, she becomes aggressive, intermeddling, and ready for dealing with enemies or making acquisitions remote as well as near.[2] In 432 B.C., her unsocial and exclusive manners against the rest of Greece, with her constant expulsion of other Greeks from her own city, stand prominent among her attributes;[3] while at the end of the war, her foreign relations had acquired such great development as to become the principal matter of attention for her leading citizens as well as for her magistrates; so that the influx of strangers into Sparta, and the efflux of Spartans into other parts of Greece, became constant and inevitable. Hence the strictness of the Lykurgean discipline gave way on many points, and the principal Spartans especially struggled by various shifts to evade its obligations. It was to these leading men that the great prizes fell, enabling them to enrich themselves at the expense either of foreign subjects or of the public treasury, and tending more and more to aggravate that inequality of wealth among the Spartans which Aristotle so emphatically notices in his time;[4] since the smaller citizens had no similar opportunities opened to them, nor any industry of their own, to guard their properties against gradual subdivision and absorption, and to keep them in a permanent state of ability to furnish that contribution to the mess-table, for themselves and their sons, which formed the groundwork of Spartan political franchise. Moreover

Increase of peculation, inequality, and discontent at Sparta.

ματα τοῖς Σπαρτιάταις· οὔτε γάρ ἐν τῷ κοινῷ τῆς πόλεως ἐστιν οὐδέν, πολέμους μεγάλους ἀναγκαζόμενοι φέρειν· εἰσφέρουσί τε κακῶς, &c. Contrast what Plato says in his dialogue of Alkibiadês, L c. 59. p. 122 E. about the great quantity of gold and silver then at Sparta. The dialogue must bear date at some period between 400—371 B.C.

[1] See the speeches of the Corinthian envoys and of King Archidamus at Sparta (Thucyd. i. 70-84;

compare also viii. 24-96).

[2] See the criticism upon Sparta, about 595 B.C. and 872 B.C. (Xenoph. Hellen. III. 5, 11-15; vi. 2, 8-11).

[3] Thucyd. i. 77. Ἅπαντα γάρ τά τε καθ' ὑμᾶς αὐτοὺς νόμιμα τοῖς ἄλλοις ἔχετε, &c. About the ξενηλασίαι of the Spartans—see the speech of Periklês in Thucyd. L 139.

[4] Aristotel. Politic. ii. 6, 18.

the spectacle of such newly-opened lucrative prizes—accessible only to that particular section of influential Spartan families who gradually became known apart from the rest under the title of the Equals or Peers—embittered the discontent of the energetic citizens beneath that privileged position, in such a manner as to menace the tranquillity of the state—as will presently be seen. That sameness of life, habits, attainments, aptitudes, enjoyments, fatigues, and restraints, which the Lykurgean regulations had so long enforced, and still continued to prescribe,—divesting wealth of its principal advantages, and thus keeping up the sentiment of personal equality among the poorer citizens—became more and more eluded by the richer, through the venality as well as the example of Ephors and Senators;[1] while for those who had no means of corruption, it continued unrelaxed, except in so far as many of them fell into a still more degraded condition by the loss of their citizenship.

It is not merely Isokratês,[2] who attests the corruption wrought in the character of the Spartans by the possession of that foreign empire which followed the victory of Ægospotami—but also their earnest panegyrist Xenophon. After having warmly extolled the laws of Lykurgus or the Spartan institutions, he is constrained to admit that his eulogies, though merited by the past, have become lamentably inapplicable to that present which he himself witnessed. "Formerly (says he[3])

*Testimonies of Isokratês and Xenophon to the change of character and habits at Sparta.*

---

[1] Aristot. Politic. ii. 6, 14-16; ii. 7, 3.
[2] Isokrates, de Pace, s. 118—127.
[3] Xen. de Republ. Laced. c. 14.

Οἶδε γάρ πρότερον μὲν Λακεδαιμονίους αἱρουμένους, οἴκοι τὰ μέτρια ἔχοντας ἀλλήλοις συνεῖναι μᾶλλον, ἢ ἁρμόζοντας ἐν ταῖς πόλεσι καὶ κολακευομένους διαφθείρεσθαι. Καὶ πρόσθεν μὲν οἶδα αὐτοὺς φοβουμένους, χρυσίον ἔχοντας φαίνεσθαι· νῦν δ' ἐστιν οὓς καὶ καλλωπιζομένους ἐπὶ τῷ κεκτῆσθαι. Ἐπίσταμαι δὲ καὶ πρόσθεν τούτου ἕνεκα ξενηλασίας γιγνομένας, καὶ ἀποδημεῖν οὐκ ἐξόν, ὅπως μὴ ῥᾳδιουργίας οἱ πολῖται ἀπὸ τῶν ξένων ἐμπίμπλαιντο· νῦν δ'

ἐπίσταμαι τοὺς δοκοῦντας πρώτους εἶναι ἐσπουδακότας ὡς μηδέποτε παύωνται ἁρμόζοντες ἐπὶ ξένης. Καὶ ἦν μέν, ὅτε ἐπεμελοῦντο, ὅπως ἄξιοι εἶεν ἡγεῖσθαι· νῦν δὲ πολὺ μᾶλλον πραγματεύονται, ὅπως ἄρξουσιν, ἢ ὅπως ἄξιοι τούτου ἔσονται. Τοιγαροῦν οἱ Ἕλληνες πρότερον μὲν ἰόντες εἰς Λακεδαίμονα ἐδέοντο αὐτῶν, ἡγεῖσθαι ἐπὶ τοὺς δοκοῦντας ἀδικεῖν· νῦν δὲ πολλοὶ παρακαλοῦσιν ἀλλήλους ἐπὶ τὸ διακωλύειν ἄρξαι πάλιν αὐτούς. Οὐδὲν μέντοι δεῖ θαυμάζειν τούτων τῶν ἐπιψόγων αὐτοῖς γιγνομένων, ἐπειδὴ φανεροί εἰσιν οὔτε τῷ θεῷ πειθόμενοι οὔτε τοῖς Λυκούργου νόμοις.

the Lacedæmonians used to prefer their own society and moderate way of life at home, to appointments as harmosts in foreign towns, with all the flattery and all the corruption attending them. Formerly, they were afraid to be seen with gold in their possession; now, there are some who make even an ostentatious display of it. Formerly, they enforced their (Xenelasy or) expulsion of strangers, and forbade foreign travel, in order that their citizens might not be filled with relaxed habits of life from contact with foreigners; but now, those, who stand first in point of influence among them, study above all things to be in perpetual employment as harmosts abroad. There was a time when they took pains to be worthy of headship; but now they strive much rather to get and keep the command, than to be properly qualified for it. Accordingly the Greeks used in former days to come and solicit, that the Spartans would act as their leaders against wrong-doers; but now they are exhorting each other to concert measures for shutting out Sparta from renewed empire. Nor can we wonder that the Spartans have fallen into this discredit, when they have manifestly renounced obedience both to the Delphian god and to the institutions of Lykurgus."

This criticism (written at some period between 394—371 B.C.) from the strenuous eulogist of Sparta is highly instructive. We know from other evidence how badly the Spartan empire worked for the subject cities: we here learn how badly it worked for the character of the Spartans themselves, and for those internal institutions which even an enemy of Sparta, who detested her foreign policy, still felt constrained to admire.[1] All the vices, here insisted upon by Xenophon, arise from various incidents connected with her empire. The moderate, home-keeping, old-fashioned, backward disposition—of which the

The expression "taking measures to hinder the Lacedæmonians from again exercising empire"—marks this treatise as probably composed some time between their naval defeat at Knidus, and their land-defeat at Leuktra. The former put an end to their maritime empire—the latter excluded them from all possibility of recovering it; but during the interval between the two, such recovery was by no means impossible.

[1] The Athenian envoy at Melos says—Λακεδαιμόνιοι γὰρ πρὸς μὲν σφᾶς αὐτοὺς καὶ τὰ ἐπιχώρια νόμιμα, πλεῖστα ἀρετῇ χρῶνται· πρὸς δὲ τοὺς ἄλλους—ἐπιφανέστατα ὧν ἴσμεν τὰ μὲν ἡδέα καλὰ νομίζουσι, τὰ δὲ ξυμφέροντα δίκαια (Thucyd. v. 105). A judgement, almost exactly the same, is pronounced by Polybius (vi. 48).

Corinthians complain,[1] but for which King Archidamus takes credit, at the beginning of the Peloponnesian War —is found exchanged, at the close of the war, for a spirit of aggression and conquest, for ambition public as well as private, and for emancipation of the great men from the subduing[2] equality of discipline enacted by Lykurgus.

*Power of Lysander—his arrogance and ambitious projects—flattery lavished upon him by sophists and poets.* Agis the son of Archidamus (426—399 B.C.), and Pausanias son of Pleistoanax (408—394 B.C.), were the two kings of Sparta at the end of the war. But Lysander, the admiral or commander of the fleet, was for the time[3] greater than either of the two kings, who had the right of commanding only the troops on land. I have already mentioned how his overweening dictation and insolence offended not only Pausanias, but also several of the Ephors and leading men at Sparta, as well as Pharnabazus the Persian satrap; thus indirectly bringing about the emancipation of Athens from the Thirty, the partial discouragement of the Dekarchies throughout Greece, and the recall of Lysander himself from his command. It was not without reluctance that the conqueror of Athens submitted to descend again to a private station. Amidst the crowd of flatterers who heaped incense on him at the moment of his omnipotence, there were not wanting those who suggested that he was much more worthy to reign than either Agis or Pausanias: that the kings ought

---

[1] Thucyd. i. 68, 70, 71, 84. ἀργυιότροπα ὑμῶν τά ἐπιτηδεύματα—ἄσκνοι πρὸς ὑμᾶς μελλητάς καὶ ἀποδημηταί πρὸς ἐνδημοτάτους; also viii. 24.

[2] Σπάρτην θαμασίμβροτον (Simonides ap. Plutarch. Agesilaum, c. 1).

[3] See an expression of Aristotle (Polit. ii. 6, 22) about the function of admiral among the Lacedæmonians—ἐπὶ γάρ τοῖς βασιλεῦσιν, οὖσι στρατηγοῖς ἀϊδίοις, ἡ ναυαρχία σχεδόν ἑτέρα βασιλεία καθέστηκα.

This reflection,—which Aristotle intimates that he has borrowed from some one else, though without saying from whom—must in all probability have been founded upon the case of Lysander; for never after Lysander, was there any Lacedæmonian admiral enjoying a power which could by possibility be termed exorbitant or dangerous. We know that during the later years of the Peloponnesian War, much censure was cast upon the Lacedæmonian practice of annually changing the admiral (Xen. Hellen. i. 6, 4).

The Lacedæmonians seem to have been impressed with these criticisms, for in the year 396 B.C. (the year before the battle of Knidus) they conferred upon King Agesilaus, who was then commanding the land army in Asia Minor, the command of the fleet also—in order to secure unity of operations. This had never been done before (Xen. Hell. iii. 4, 28).

to be taken, not from the first-born of the lineage of Eurysthenês and Proklês, but by selection out of all the Herakleids, of whom Lysander himself was one;[1] and that the person elected ought to be not merely a descendant of Hêraklês, but a worthy parallel of Hêraklês himself. While pæans were sung to the honour of Lysander at Samos²— while Chœrilus and Antilochus composed poems in his praise—while Antimachus (a poet highly esteemed by Plato) entered into a formal competition of recited epic verses called *Lysandria*, and was surpassed by Nikêratus —there was another warm admirer, a rhetor or sophist of Halikarnassus, named Kleon,³ who wrote a discourse proving that Lysander had well earned the regal dignity—that personal excellence ought to prevail over legitimate descent—and that the crown ought to be laid open to election from the most worthy among the Herakleids. Considering that rhetoric was neither employed nor esteemed at Sparta, we cannot reasonably believe that Lysander really ordered the composition of this discourse as an instrument of execution for projects preconceived by himself, in the same manner as an Athenian prosecutor or defendant before the Dikastery used to arm himself with a speech from Lysias or Demosthenês. Kleon would make his court professionally through such a prose composition, whether the project were first recommended by himself, or currently discussed among a circle of admirers; while Lysander would probably requite the compliment by a reward not less munificent than that which he gave to the indifferent poet Antilochus.⁴ And the composition would be put into the form of an harangue from the admiral to his countrymen, without any definite purpose that it should be ever so delivered. Such hypothesis of a speaker and an audience was frequent with the rhetors in their writings, as we may see in Isokratês—especially in his sixth discourse, called Archidamus.

---

[1] Plutarch, Lysand. c. 24. Perhaps he may have been simply a member of the tribe called Hyllies, who probably called themselves Herakleids. Some affirmed that Lysander wished to cause the kings to be elected out of all the Spartans, not simply out of the Herakleids. This is less probable.
² Duris ap. Athenæum, xv. p. 695.
³ Plutarch, Lysand. c. 19; Plutarch, Agesil. c. 20.
⁴ Plutarch, Lysand. c. 17.

**Real position of the kings at Sparta.**

Either from his own ambition, or from the suggestions of others, Lysander came now to conceive the idea of breaking the succession of the two regal families, and opening for himself a door to reach the crown. His projects have been characterised as revolutionary; but there seems nothing in them which fairly merits the appellation in the sense which that word now bears, if we consider accurately what the Spartan kings were in the year 400 B.C. In this view the associations connected with the title of king, are to a modern reader misleading. The Spartan kings were not kings at all, in any modern sense of the term; not only they were not absolute, but they were not even constitutional kings. They were not sovereigns, nor was any Spartan their subject; every Spartan was the member of a free Grecian community. The Spartan king did not govern; nor did he reign, in the sense of having government carried on in his name and by his delegates. The government of Sparta was carried on by the Ephors, with frequent consultation of the senate, and occasional, though rare appeals, to the public assembly of citizens. The Spartan king was not legally inviolable. He might be, and occasionally was, arrested, tried, and punished for misbehaviour in the discharge of his functions. He was a self-acting person, a great officer of state; enjoying certain definite privileges, and exercising certain military and judicial functions, which passed as an *universitas* by hereditary transmission in his family; but subject to the control of the Ephors as to the way in which he performed these duties.[1] Thus, for example, it was his

---

[1] Aristotle (Polit. v. 1, 5) represents justly the schemes of Lysander as going πρὸς τὸ μέρος τι κινῆσαι τῆς πολιτείας οἷον ἀρχήν τινα καταστῆσαι ἢ δυαλσίν. The Spartan kingship is here regarded as ἀρχή τις—one office of state, among others. But Aristotle regards Lysander as having intended to destroy the kingship—καταλῦσαι τὴν βασιλείαν—which does not appear to have been the fact. The plan of Lysander was to retain the kingship, but to render it elective instead of hereditary. He wished to place the Spartan kingship substantially on the same footing, as that on which the office of the kings or suffetes of Carthage stood; who were not hereditary, nor confined to members of the same family or Gens, but chosen out of the principal families or Gentes. Aristotle, while comparing the βασιλεῖς at Sparta with those at Carthage, as being generally analogous, pronounces in favour of the Carthaginian election as better than the Spartan hereditary transmission (Arist. Polit. ii. 8, 2).

privilege to command the army when sent on foreign service; yet a law was made, requiring him to take deputies along with him, as a council of war without whom nothing was to be done. The Ephors recalled Agesilaus when they thought fit; and they brought Pausanias to trial and punishment, for alleged misconduct in his command.[1] The only way in which the Spartan kings formed part of the sovereign power in the state, or shared in the exercise of government properly so called, was that they had votes *ex officio* in the Senate, and could vote there by proxy when they were not present. In ancient times, very imperfectly known, the Spartan kings seem really to have been sovereigns; the government having then been really carried on by them or by their orders. But in the year 400 B.C., Agis and Pausanias had become nothing more than great and dignified hereditary officers of state, still bearing the old title of their ancestors. To throw open these hereditary functions to all the members of the Herakleid Gens, by election from their number, might be a change better or worse: it was a startling novelty (just as it would have been to propose, that any of the various priesthoods, which were hereditary in particular families, should be made elective), because of the extreme attachment of the Spartans to old and sanctified customs; but it cannot properly be styled revolutionary. The Ephors, the Senate, and the public assembly, might have made such a change in full legal form, without any appeal to violence; the kings might vote against it, but they would have been outvoted. And if the change had been made, the Spartan government would have remained, in form as well as in principle, just what it was before; although the Eurystheneid and Prokleid families would have lost their privileges. It is not meant here to deny that the Spartan kings were men of great importance in the state, especially when (like Agesilaus) they combined with their official station a marked personal energy. But it is not the less true, that the associations, connected with the title of *king* in the modern mind, do not properly apply to them.

To carry his point at Sparta, Lysander was well aware that agencies of an unusual character must be employed. Quitting Sparta soon after his recall, he visited the oracles of Delphi, Dodona, and Zeus Ammon in Libya,[2] in order

[1] Thucyd. v. 63; Xen. Hellen. III. 5. 25; iv. 2, 1.
[2] Diodor. xiv. 13; Cicero, de Divin. i. 43, 96; Corn. Nepos, Lysand. c. 3.

to procure, by persuasion or corruption, injunctions to the
Spartans countenancing his projects. So great
was the general effect of oracular injunctions on
the Spartan mind, that Kleomenês had thus obtained the deposition of King Demaratus,—and
the exiled Pleistoanax, his own return;[1] bribery
having been in both cases the moving impulse.
But Lysander was not equally fortunate. None
of these oracles could be induced, by any offers,
to venture upon so grave a sentence as that of
repealing the established law of succession to
the Spartan throne. It is even said that the
priests of Ammon, not content with refusing his
offers, came over to Sparta to denounce his
proceeding; upon which accusation Lysander was put on
his trial, but acquitted.

The statement that he was thus tried and acquitted,
I think untrue. But his schemes thus far miscarried—and
he was compelled to resort to another stratagem, yet still
appealing to the religious susceptibilities of his countrymen.
There had been born some time before, in one of the cities
of the Euxine, a youth named Silenus, whose mother affirmed that he was the son of Apollo; an assertion which
found extensive credence, notwithstanding various difficulties raised by the sceptics. While making known at
Sparta this new birth of a son to the god, the partisans of
Lysander also spread abroad the news that there existed
sacred manuscripts and inspired records, of great antiquity,
hidden and yet unread, in the custody of the Delphian
priests; not to be touched or consulted until some genuine
son of Apollo should come forward to claim them. With
the connivance of some among the priests, certain oracles
were fabricated agreeable to the views of Lysander. The
plan was concerted that Silenus should present himself at
Delphi, tender the proofs of his divine parentage, and then
claim the inspection of these hidden records; which the
priests, after an apparently rigid scrutiny, were prepared
to grant. Silenus would then read them aloud in the presence of all the spectators; and one would be found among
them, recommending to the Spartans to choose their kings
out of all the best citizens.[2]

[1] Plutarch, Lysand. c. 25, from 66; Thucyd. v. 19.
Ephorus. Compare Herodot. vi. [2] Plutarch, Lysand. c. 26.

So nearly did this project approach to consummation, that Silenus actually presented himself at Delphi, and put in his claim. But one of the confederates either failed in his courage, or broke down, at the critical moment; so that the hidden records still remained hidden. Yet though Lysander was thus compelled to abandon his plan, nothing was made public about it until after his death. It might probably have succeeded, had he found temple-confederates of proper courage and cunning—when we consider the profound and habitual deference of the Spartans to Delphi; upon the sanction of which oracle the Lykurgean institutions themselves were mainly understood to rest. And an occasion presently arose, on which the proposed change might have been tried with unusual facility and pertinence; though Lysander himself, having once miscarried, renounced his enterprise, and employed his influence, which continued unabated, in giving the sceptre to another instead of acquiring it for himself[1]—like Mucian in reference to the Emperor Vespasian.

*His aim at the kingship fails—nevertheless he still retains prodigious influence at Sparta.*

---

[1] Tacit. Histor. i. 10. "Cui expeditius fuerit tradere imperium, quam obtinere."

The general fact of the conspiracy of Lysander to open for himself a way to the throne, appears to rest on very sufficient testimony—that of Ephorus; to whom perhaps the words ρασὶ τινες in Aristotle may allude, where he mentions this conspiracy as having been narrated (Polit. v. 1, 5). But Plutarch, as well as K. O. Müller (Hist. of Dorians, iv. 8, 5) and others, erroneously represent the intrigues with the oracle as being resorted to after Lysander returned from accompanying Agesilaus to Asia; which is certainly impossible, since Lysander accompanied Agesilaus out, in the spring of 396 B.C.—did not return to Greece until the spring of 395 B.C.—and was then employed, with an interval not greater than four or five months, on that expedition against Bœotia wherein he was slain.

The tampering of Lysander with the oracle must undoubtedly have taken place prior to the death of Agis—at some time between 403 B.C. and 399 B.C. The humiliation which he received in 396 B.C. from Agesilaus might indeed have led him to revolve in his mind the renewal of his former plans, but he can have had no time to do anything towards them. Aristotle (Polit. v. 6, 2) alludes to the humiliation of Lysander by the kings as an example of incidents tending to raise disturbance in an aristocratical government; but this humiliation probably alludes to the manner in which he was thwarted in Attica by Pausanias in 403 B.C. —which proceeding is ascribed by Plutarch to both kings, as well as to their jealousy of Lysander (see Plutarch, Lysand. c. 21)—not to the treatment of Lysander by Age-

It was apparently about a year after the campaign in Elis, that King Agis, now an old man, was taken ill at Heræa in Arcadia, and carried back to Sparta, where he shortly afterwards expired. His wife Timæa had given birth to a son named Leotychidês, now a youth about fifteen years of age.[1] But the legitimacy of this youth had always been suspected by Agis, who had pronounced, when the birth of the child was first made known to him, that it could not be his. He had been frightened out of his wife's bed by the shock of an earthquake, which was construed as a warning from Poseidon, and was held to be a prohibition of intercourse for a certain time; during which interval Leotychidês was born. This was one story: another was, that the young prince was the son of Alkibiadês, born during the absence of Agis in his command at Dekeleia. On the other hand, it was alleged that Agis, though originally doubtful of the legitimacy of Leotychidês, had afterwards retracted his suspicions, and fully recognised him; especially, and with peculiar solemnity, during his last illness.[2] As in the case of Demaratus about a century earlier[3]—advantage was taken of these doubts by Agesilaus, the younger brother of Agis, powerfully seconded by Lysander, to exclude Leotychidês, and occupy the throne himself.

Agesilaus was the son of King Archidamus, not by Lampito the mother of Agis, but by a second wife named Eupolia. He was now at the mature age of forty,[4] and having been brought up without any prospect of becoming king—at least until very

*Marginalia:*
B.C. 399. Death of Agis king of Sparta—doubt as to the legitimacy of his son Leotychidês. Agesilaus, seconded by Lysander, aspires to the throne.
Character of Agesilaus.

---

silaus in 396 B.C. The mission of Lysander to the despot Dionysius at Syracuse (Plutarch, Lysand. c. 2) must also have taken place prior to the death of Agis in 399 B.C. whether before or after the failure of the stratagem at Delphi, is uncertain; perhaps after it.

[1] The age of Leotychidês is approximately marked by the date of the presence of Alkibiadês at Sparta 414—413 B.C. The mere rumour, true or false, that this young man was the son of Alkibiadês, may be held sufficient as chronological evidence to certify his age.

[2] Xen. Hellen. lit. 3, 2; Pausanias, iii. 8. 4; Plutarch, Agesilaus, c. 3.

[3] Herodot. v. 66.

[4] I confess I do not understand how Xenophon can affirm, in his Agesilaus, l. 6, 'Αγησίλαος τοίνυν ἔτι μὲν νέος ὢν ἔτυχε τῆς βασιλείας. For he himself says (ii. 28), and it seems well established, that Agesilaus died at the age of above

recent times—had passed through the unmitigated rigour of Spartan drill and training. He was distinguished for all Spartan virtues: exemplary obedience to authority, in the performance of his trying exercises, military as well as civil—emulation, in trying to surpass every competitor—extraordinary courage, energy, as well as facility in enduring hardship—simplicity and frugality in all his personal habits—extreme sensibility to the opinion of his fellow-citizens. Towards his personal friends or adherents, he was remarkable for fervour of attachment, even for unscrupulous partisanship, with a readiness to use all his influence in screening their injustices or shortcomings; while he was comparatively placable and generous in dealing with rivals at home, notwithstanding his eagerness to be first in every sort of competition.[1] His manners were cheerful and popular, and his physiognomy pleasing; though in stature he was not only small but mean, and though he laboured under the additional defect of lameness on one leg,[2] which accounts for his constant refusal to suffer his statue to be taken.[3] He was indifferent to money, and exempt from excess of selfish feeling, except in his passion for superiority and power.

In spite of his rank as brother of Agis, Agesilaus had never yet been tried in any military command, though he had probably served in the army either at Dekeleia or in Asia. Much of his character therefore lay as yet undisclosed. And his popularity may perhaps have been the greater at the moment when the throne became vacant, inasmuch as, having never been put in a position to excite jealousy, he stood distinguished only for accomplishments, efforts, endurances, and punctual obedience, wherein even the poorest citizens were his competitors on equal terms. Nay, so complete was the self-constraint, and the habit of smothering emotions, generated by a Spartan training, that even the cunning Lysander himself did not at this time know him. He and Agesilaus had been early and intimate

80 (Plutarch, Agesil. c. 40); and his death must have been about 360 B.C.

[1] Plutarch, Agesilaus, c. 3—5; Xenoph. Agesil. vii. 8; Plutarch, Apophth. Laconic. p. 212 D.

[2] Plutarch, Agesil. c. 2; Xenoph. Agesil. viii. 1

It appears that the mother of Agesilaus was a very small woman, and that Archidamus had incurred the censure of the Ephors, on that especial ground, for marrying her.

[3] Xenoph. Agesil. xi. 7; Plutarch Agesil. c. 2.

friends,[1] both having been placed as boys in the same herd or troop for the purposes of discipline; a strong illustration of the equalising character of this discipline, since we know that Lysander was of poor parents and condition.[2] He made the mistake of supposing Agesilaus to be of a disposition particularly gentle and manageable; and this was his main inducement for espousing the pretensions of the latter to the throne, after the decease of Agis. Lysander reckoned, if by his means Agesilaus became king, on a great increase of his own influence, and especially on a renewed mission to Asia, if not as ostensible general, at least as real chief under the titular headship of the new king.

*Conflicting pretensions of Agesilaus and Leotychidês.*

Accordingly, when the imposing solemnities which always marked the funeral of a king of Sparta were terminated,[3] and the day arrived for installation of a new king, Agesilaus, under the promptings of Lysander, stood forward to contest the legitimacy and the title of Leotychidês, and to claim the sceptre for himself—a true Herakleid, brother of the late king Agis. In the debate, which probably took place not merely before the Ephors and the Senate but before the assembled citizens besides—Lysander warmly seconded his pretensions. Of this debate unfortunately we are not permitted to know much. We cannot doubt that the mature age and excellent reputation of Agesilaus would count as a great recommendation, when set against an untried youth; and this was probably the real point (since the relationship of both was so near) upon which decision turned;[4] for the legitimacy of Leotychidês was positively asseverated by his mother Timæa,[5] and we do not find that the question of paternity was referred to the Delphian oracle, as in the case of Demaratus.

There was however one circumstance which stood much in the way of Agesilaus—his personal deformity. A lame king of Sparta had never yet been known. And if

---

[1] Plutarch, Agesil. c. 2.
[2] Plutarch, Lysand. c. 2.
[3] Xenoph. Hellen. iii. 3, 1.
[4] Plutarch, Lysand. c. 22; Plutarch, Agesil. c. 3; Xen. Hellen. iii. 3, 2; Xen. Agesil. 1. 5—κρίνασα ἡ πόλις ἀναπληρότερον εἶναι Ἀγησίλαον καὶ τῷ γένει καὶ τῇ ἀρετῇ, &c.
[5] Xen. Hellen. iii. 3, 2. This statement contradicts the tale imputed to Timæa by Doris (Plutarch, Agesil. c. 3; Plutarch, Alkibiad. c. 23).

we turn back more than a century to the occurrence of a similar deformity in one of the Battiad princes at Kyrenê,[1] we see the Kyrenians taking it so deeply to heart, that they sent to ask advice from Delphi, and to invite the Mantineian reformer Demônax. Over and above this sentiment of repugnance, too, the gods had specially forewarned Sparta to beware of "a lame reign." Diopeithês, a prophet and religious adviser of high reputation, advocated the cause of Leotychidês. He produced an ancient oracle, telling Sparta, that "with all her pride she must not suffer a lame reign to impair her stable footing;[2] for if she did so, unexampled suffering and ruinous wars would long beset her." This prophecy had already been once invoked, about eighty years earlier,[3] but with a very different interpretation. To Grecian leaders, like Themistoklês or Lysander, it was an accomplishment of no small value to be able to elude inconvenient texts or intractable religious feelings, by expository ingenuity. And Lysander here raised his voice (as Themistoklês had done on the momentous occasion before the battle of Salamis[4]), to combat the professional expositors; contending that by "a lame reign," the god meant, not a bodily defect in the king—which might not even be congenital, but might arise from some positive hurt—but the reign of any king who was not a genuine descendant of Hêraklês.

*Objection taken against Agesilaus on the ground of his lameness—oracle produced by Diopeithês —eluded by the interpretation of Lysander.*

The influence of Lysander,[5] combined doubtless with

[1] Herodot. iv. 161. Διεδέξατο δὲ τὴν βασιληίην τοῦ 'Αρκεσίλεω ὁ υἱὸς Βάττος, χωλός τε ἐὼν καὶ οὐκ ἀρτίπους. Οἱ δὲ Κυρηναῖοι πρὸς τὴν καταλαβοῦσαν συμφορὴν ἔπεμπον ἐς Δελφοὺς, ἐπειρησομένους ὄντινα τρόπον καταστησάμενοι κάλλιστα ἂν οἰκέοιεν.

[2] Plutarch, Lysand. c. 22; Plutarch, Agesil. c. 3; Pausan. iii. 8, 5.

[3] Diodor. xi. 50.

[4] Herodot. vii. 143.

[5] Xen. Hellen. iii. 3, 3. ὡς οὐκ οἴοιτο, τὸν θεὸν τοῦτο κελεύειν φυλάξασθαι, μή προσπταίσαί τις χω-

λεύσῃ, ἀλλὰ μᾶλλον, μὴ οὐκ ὢν τοῦ γένους βασιλεύσῃ.

Congenital lameness would be regarded as a mark of divine displeasure, and therefore a disqualification from the throne, as in the case of Battus of Kyrênê above noticed. But the words χωλὴ βασιλεία were general enough to cover both the cases—superinduced as well as congenital lameness. It is upon this that Lysander founds his inference—that the god did not mean to allude to bodily lameness at all.

[6] Pausanias, iii. 8, 5; Plutarch,

a preponderance of sentiment already tending towards Agesilaus, caused this effort of interpretative subtlety to be welcomed as convincing, and led to the nomination of the lame candidate as king. There was however a considerable minority, to whom this decision appeared a sin against the gods and a mockery of the oracle. And though the murmurs of such dissentients were kept down by the ability and success of Agesilaus during the first years of his reign, yet when, in his ten last years, calamity and humiliation were poured thickly upon this proud city, the public sentiment came decidedly round to their view. Many a pious Spartan then exclaimed, with feelings of bitter repentance, that the divine word never failed to come true at last,[1] and that Sparta was justly punished for having wilfully shut her eyes to the distinct and merciful warning vouchsafed to her, about the mischiefs of a "lame reign."[2]

*Agesilaus is preferred as king— suspicions which always remained attached to Lysander's interpretation.*

Besides the crown, Agesilaus at the same time acquired the large property left by the late King Agis; an acquisition which enabled him to display his generosity by transferring half of it at once to his maternal relatives—for the most part poor persons.[3] The popularity acquired by this step was still farther increased by his manner of conducting himself towards the Ephors and Senate. Between these magistrates and the kings there was generally a bad understanding. The kings, not having lost the tradition of the plenary power once enjoyed by their ancestors, displayed as much haughty reserve as they dared, towards an authority now become essentially superior to their own.

*Popular conduct of Agesilaus— he conciliates the Ephors— his great influence at Sparta—his energy, combined with unscrupulous partisanship.*

[1] Agesil. c. 3; Plutarch, Lysand. c. 22; Justin. vi. 2.

"Ἴδ᾽ υἷον, ὦ παῖδας, προσίμιζεν ἀφρῳ

Τοῦτος τὸ θεόσρακον ἡμῖν

Τῆς κολαιφάτου προνοίας,

Ὅν Πάκεν, &c.

This is a splendid chorus of the Trachiniæ of Sophoklês (822) proclaiming their sentiments on the awful death of Heraklês, in the tunic of Nessus, which has just been announced as about to happen.

[2] Plutarch. Agesil. c. 30; Plutarch, Compar. Agesil. and Pomp. c. 1. Ἀγησίλαος δὲ τὴν βασιλείαν ἔλαβε λαβεῖν, οὔτι τὰ πρὸς θεοὺς ἄμεμπτος, οὔτε τὰ πρὸς ἀνθρώπους, κρίνας νοθείας Λεωτυχίδην, ὃν υἱὸν αὐτοῦ ἀπέδειξεν ὁ ἀδελφὸς γνήσιον, τὸν δὲ χρησμὸν καταπειρωπευσάμενος τὸν περὶ τῆς χωλότητος. Again, Ib. c. 2. δι᾽ Ἀγησίλαον ἐπεκυρώθη τῷ χρησμῷ Λύσανδρος.

[3] Xen. Agesil. iv. 5; Plutarch, Ages. c. 4.

But Agesilaus—not less from his own pre-established habits, than from anxiety to make up for the defects of his title—adopted a line of conduct studiously opposite. He not only took pains to avoid collision with the Ephors, but showed marked deference both to their orders and to their persons. He rose from his seat whenever they appeared; he conciliated both Ephors and senators by timely presents.[1] By such judicious proceeding, as well as by his exact observance of the laws and customs,[2] he was himself the greatest gainer. Combined with that ability and energy in which he was never deficient, it ensured to him more real power than had ever fallen to the lot of any king of Sparta; power, not merely over the military operations abroad which usually fell to the kings—but also over the policy of the state at home. On the increase and maintenance of that real power, his chief thoughts were concentrated; new dispositions generated by kingship, which had never shown themselves in him before. Despising, like Lysander, both money, luxury, and all the outward show of power—he exhibited, as a king, an ultra-Spartan simplicity, carried almost to affectation, in diet, clothing, and general habits. But like Lysander also, he delighted in the exercise of dominion through the medium of knots or factions of devoted partisans, whom he rarely scrupled to uphold in all their career of injustice and oppression. Though an amiable man, with no disposition to tyranny and still less to plunder, for his own benefit—Agesilaus thus made himself the willing instrument of both, for the benefit of his various coadjutors and friends, whose power and consequence he identified with his own.[3]

At the moment when Agesilaus became king, Sparta was at the maximum of her power, holding nearly all the Grecian towns as subject allies, with or without tribute. She was engaged in the task (as has already been mentioned) of protecting the Asiatic Greeks against the Persian satraps in their neighbourhood. And the most interesting portion of the life of Agesilaus consists in the earnestness with which he espoused, and the vigour and ability with

---

[1] Plutarch, Agesil. c. 4.
[2] Xen. Agesil. vii. 2.
[3] Isokratês, Orat. v. (Philipp.) s. 100; Plutarch, Agesilaus, c. 5, 13-23; Plutarch, Apophthegm. La-
conica, p. 209 F—212 D.
See the incident alluded to by Theopompus ap. Athenæum, xiii. p. 609.

which he conducted, this great Pan-hellenic duty. It will be seen that success in his very promising career was intercepted[1] by his bad factious subservience to partisans, at home and abroad—by his unmeasured thirst for Spartan omnipotence—and his indifference or aversion to any generous scheme of combination with the cities dependent on Sparta.

<small>B.C. 398-397.

Dangerous conspiracy at Sparta— terror-striking sacrifices.</small>

His attention however was first called to a dangerous internal conspiracy with which Sparta was threatened. The "lame reign" was at yet less than twelve months old, when Agesilaus, being engaged in sacrificing at one of the established state solemnities, was apprised by the officiating prophet, that the victims exhibited menacing symptoms, portending a conspiracy of the most formidable character. A second sacrifice gave yet worse promise; and on the third the terrified prophet exclaimed, "Agesilaus, the revelation before us imports that we are actually in the midst of our enemies." They still continued to sacrifice, but victims were now offered to the averting and preserving gods, with prayers that these latter, by tutelary interposition, would keep off the impending peril. At length, after much repetition and great difficulty, favourable victims were obtained; the meaning of which was soon made clear. Five days afterwards, an informer came before the Ephors, communicating the secret, that a dangerous conspiracy was preparing, organised by a citizen named Kinadon.[2]

<small>Character and position of the chief conspirator Kinadon— state of parties at Sparta— increasing number of malcontents.</small>

The conspirator thus named was a Spartan citizen, but not one of that select number called the Equals or the Peers. It has already been mentioned that inequalities had been gradually growing up among qualified citizens of Sparta, tending tacitly to set apart a certain number of them under the name of The Peers, and all the rest under the correlative name of The Inferiors. Besides this, since the qualification of every family lasted only so long as the citizen could furnish a given contribution for himself and his sons to the public mess-table, and since industry of every kind was inconsistent with the rigid personal drilling im-

<small>[1] Isokratês (Orat. v. ut sup.) makes a remark in substance the same.
[2] Xenoph. Hellen. iii. 3, 4.</small>

posed upon all of them—the natural consequence was, that in each generation a certain number of citizens became disfranchised and dropped off. But these disfranchised men did not become Periœki or Helots. They were still citizens, whose qualification, though in abeyance, might be at any time renewed by the munificence of a rich man;[1] so that they too, along with the lesser citizens, were known under the denomination of The Inferiors.

It was to this class that Kinadon belonged. He was a young man of remarkable strength and courage, who had discharged with honour his duties in the Lykurgean discipline,[2] and had imbibed from it that sense of personal equality, and that contempt of privilege, which its theory as well as its practice suggested. Notwithstanding all exactness of duty performed, he found that the constitution, as practically worked, excluded him from the honours and distinctions of the state; reserving them for the select citizens known under the name of Peers. And this exclusion had become more marked and galling since the formation of the Spartan empire after the victory of Ægospotami; whereby the number of lucrative posts (harmosties and others) all monopolised by the Peers, had been so much multiplied. Debarred from the great political prizes, Kinadon was still employed by the Ephors, in consequence of his high spirit and military sufficiency, in that standing force which they kept for maintaining order at home.[3] He had been the agent ordered on several of those arbitrary seizures which they never scrupled to employ towards persons whom they regarded as dangerous. But this was no satisfaction to his mind; nay, probably, by bringing him into close contact with the men in authority, it contributed to lessen his respect for them. He desired

---

[1] See Ch. vi. of this History.
[2] Xen. Hellen. iii. 3, 5. Οὗτος (Κινάδων) δ' ἦν νεανίσκος καὶ τὸ εἶδος καὶ τὴν ψυχὴν εὔρωστος, οὐ μέντοι τῶν ὁμοίων.

The meaning of the term Οἱ ὅμοιοι fluctuates in Xenophon; it sometimes, as here, is used to signify the privileged Peers—again De Repub. Laced. viii. 1; and Anab. iv. 6, 14. Sometimes again it is used agreeably to the Lykurgean theory; whereby every citizen, who rigorously discharged his duty in the public drill, belonged to the number (De Rep. Lac. x. 7).

There was a variance between the theory and the practice.
[3] Xen. Hellen. iii. 3, 9. Τεταραγμένοι δὲ καὶ ἀλλ' ἤδη ὁ Κινάδων τοῖς Ἐφόροις τοιαῦτα. iii. 3, 7. Οἱ συντεταγμένοι ἡμῶν (Kinadon says) αὐτοὶ ἐκλέκτῳ κεκτήμεθα.

"to be inferior to no man in Sparta"[1]—and his conspiracy was undertaken to realise this object by breaking up the constitution.

<small>Police of the Ephors —information laid before them.</small> It has already been mentioned that amidst the general insecurity which pervaded the political society of Laconia, the Ephors maintained a secret police and system of espionage which reached its height of unscrupulous efficiency under the title of the Krypteia. Such precautions were now more than ever requisite; for the changes in the practical working of Spartan politics tended to multiply the number of malcontents, and to throw the Inferiors as well as the Periœki and the Neodamodes (manumitted Helots), into one common antipathy with the Helots, against the exclusive partnership of the Peers. Informers were thus sure of encouragement and reward, and the man who now came to the Ephors either was really an intimate friend of Kinadon, or had professed himself such in order to elicit the secret. "Kinadon (said he to the Ephors) brought me to the extremity of the market-place, and bade me count how many Spartans there were therein. I reckoned up about forty, besides the king, the Ephors, and the Senators. Upon my asking him why he desired me to count them, he replied—Because these are the men, and the only men, whom you have to look upon as enemies;[2] all others in the market-place, more than 4000 in number, are friends and comrades. Kinadon also pointed out to me the one or two Spartans whom we met in the roads, or who were lords in the country districts, as our only enemies; every one else around them being friendly to our purpose." "How many did he tell you were the accomplices actually privy to the scheme?"—asked the Ephors. "Only a few (was the reply); but those thoroughly trustworthy: these confidants themselves, however, said that all around them were accomplices—Inferiors, Periœki, Neodamodes, and Helots, all alike; for whenever any one among these classes talked about a Spartan, he could not disguise his

---

[1] Xen. Hellen. iii. 3, 11. μηδενὸς ἥττων εἶναι τῶν ἐν Λακεδαίμονι—was the declaration of Kinadon when seized and questioned by the Ephors concerning his purposes. Substantially it coincides with Aristotle (Polit. v. 6, 2)—ἢ ὅταν ἀνθρώδης τις ὢν μὴ μετέχῃ τῶν τιμῶν, οἷον Κινάδων ὁ τὴν ἐν Λακεδαίμονι συστήσας ἐπίθεσιν ἐπὶ τοὺς Σπαρτιάτας.

[2] Xen. Hellen. iii. 3, 5.

CHAP. LXXIII.    CONSPIRACY DISCLOSED.    73

intense antipathy—he talked as if he could eat the Spartans raw."[1]

"But how (continued the Ephors) did Kinadon reckon upon getting arms?" "His language was (replied the witness)—We of the standing force have our own arms all ready; and here are plenty of knives, swords, spits, hatchets, axes, and scythes—on sale in this market-place, to suit an insurgent multitude: besides, every man who tills the earth, or cuts wood and stone, has tools by him which will serve as weapons in case of need; especially in a struggle with enemies themselves unarmed." On being asked what was the moment fixed for execution—the witness could not tell; he had been instructed only to remain on the spot, and be ready.[2] *Widespread disaffection reckoned upon by the conspirators.*

It does not appear that this man knew the name of any person concerned, except Kinadon himself. So deeply were the Ephors alarmed, that they refrained from any formal convocation even of what was called the Lesser Assembly—including the Senate, of which the kings were members *ex officio*, and perhaps a few other principal persons besides. But the members of this assembly were privately brought together to deliberate on the emergency; Agesilaus probably among them. To arrest Kinadon at once in Sparta appeared imprudent; since his accomplices, of number as yet unknown, would be thus admonished either to break out in insurrection, or at least to make their escape. But an elaborate stratagem was laid for arresting him out of Sparta, without the knowledge of his accomplices. The Ephors, calling him before them, professed to confide to him (as they had done occasionally before) a mission to go to Aulon (a Laconian town on the frontier towards Arcadia and Triphylia) and there to seize *Alarm of the Ephors —their manœuvres for apprehending Kinadon privately.*

---

[1] Xen. Hellen. III. 3, 6. Αὑτοὶ μέντοι κάσιν ἔφασαν συνειδέναι καὶ εἴκοσιν καὶ νεοδαμώδεσι, καὶ τοῖς ὑπομείοσι, καὶ τοῖς περιοίκοις· ὅπου γάρ ἐν τούτοις τις λόγος γένοιτο περὶ Σπαρτιατῶν, οὐδένα δύνασθαι κρύπτειν τὸ μὴ οὐχ ἡδέως ἂν καὶ ὠμῶν ἐσθίειν αὐτῶν.

The expression of Homeric—ὠμὸν βεβρώτοις Πρίαμον, &c. (Iliad. iv. 35). The Greeks did not think themselves obliged to restrain the full expression of vindictive feeling. The poet Theognis wishes, "that he may one day come to drink the blood of those who had ill-used him" (v. 349 Gaisf.).

[2] Xen. Hellen. III. 3, 7. ὅτι ἐπιτάξειν οἱ κεκηρυγμένον εἴη.

some parties designated by name in a formal Skytalê or
warrant; including some of the Aulonite Periœki—some
Helots—and one other person by name, a woman of peculiar beauty resident at the place, whose influence was
understood to spread disaffection among all the Lacedæmonians who came thither, old as well as young.¹ When
Kinadon inquired what force he was to take with him on
the mission, the Ephors, to obviate all suspicion that they
were picking out companions with views hostile to him,
desired him to go to the Hippagretês (or commander of
the 300 youthful guards called Horsemen, though they
were not really mounted) and ask for the first six or seven
men of the guard² who might happen to be in the way.
But they (the Ephors) had already held secret communication with the Hippagretês, and had informed him both
whom they wished to be sent, and what the persons sent
were to do. They then dispatched Kinadon on his pretended mission, telling him that they should place at his
disposal three carts, in order that he might more easily
bring home the prisoners.

*Kinadon is seized, interrogated, and executed—his accomplices are arrested, and the conspiracy broken up.*

Kinadon began his journey to Aulon, without the
smallest suspicion of the plot laid for him by
the Ephors; who, to make their purpose sure,
sent an additional body of the guards after him,
to quell any resistance which might possibly
arise. But their stratagem succeeded as completely as they could desire. He was seized on
the road, by those who accompanied him ostensibly for his pretended mission. These men
interrogated him, put him to the torture,³ and heard from

¹ Xen. Hellen. III. 8, 6. Ἀγαγεῖν
δὲ ἐκέλευον καὶ τὴν γυναῖκα, ἣ καλ-
λίστη μὲν ἐλέγετο αὐτόθι εἶναι, λυ-
μαίνεσθαι δὲ ἐφόκει τοὺς ἀφικνουμί-
νους Λακεδαιμονίων καὶ πρεσβυτέρους
καὶ νεωτέρους.

² Xen. Hellen. III. 3, 9, 10.
The persons called Hippeis at
Sparta were not mounted; they
were a select body of 300 youthful
citizens, employed either on home
police or on foreign service.
See Herodot. vill. 124; Strabo, x.
p. 481; K. O. Müller, History of
the Dorians, B. III. cb. 12. s. 5, 6.

³ Xen. Hellen. III. 8, 9.
Ἔμελλον δὲ οἱ συλλαβόντες αὐτὸν
μὲν κατέχειν, τοὺς δὲ ξυνειδότας,
εὐθύμενοι αὐτοῦ, γράφαντες
ἀποπέμπειν τὴν ταχίστην τοῖς
ἐφόροις. Οὕτω δ' εἶχον οἱ ἔφοροι
πρὸς τὸ πρᾶγμα, ὥστε καὶ μορὰν
Ἱππέων ἔπεμψαν τοῖς ἀπ' Αὐλῶνος.
Ἐπεὶ δ' εἰλημμένου τοῦ ἀνδρὸς ἧκεν
Ἱππεύς, φέρων τὰ ὀνόματα ὧν
Κινάδων ἀπέγραψε, παραχρῆμα
τόν τε μάντιν Τισάμενον καὶ τοὺς
ἐπικαιριωτάτους ξυνελάμβανον. Ὡς
δ' ἀνήχθη ὁ Κινάδων, καὶ ἠλέγχετο,
καὶ ὡμολόγει πάντα, καὶ τοὺς ξυν-

his lips the names of his accomplices; the list of whom they wrote down, and forwarded by one of the guards to Sparta.

εἰδότας ἔλεγε, τέλος αὐτὸν ἤρωτα, τί καὶ βουλόμενος ταῦτα πράττοι; Polyænus (ii. 14, 1) in his account of this transaction, expressly mentions that the Hippeis or guards who accompanied Kinadon, put him to the torture (στρεβλοῦσαντες) when they seized him, in order to extort the names of his accomplices. Even without express testimony, we might pretty confidently have assumed this. From a man of spirit like Kinadon, the chief of a conspiracy, they were not likely to obtain such betrayal without torture.

I had affirmed that in the description of this transaction given by Xenophon, it did not appear whether Kinadon was able to write or not. My assertion was controverted by Colonel Mure (in his Reply to my Appendix), who cited the words φέρων τὰ ὀνόματα ὧν Κινάδων ἀνέγραψε, as containing an affirmation from Xenophon that Kinadon could write.

In my judgement, these words, taken in conjunction with what precedes, and with the probabilities of the fact, described, do not contain such an affirmation.

The guards were instructed to seize Kinadon, and *after having heard from Kinadon who his accomplices were, to write the names down and send them to the Ephors*. It is to be presumed that they executed these instructions as given; the more so, as what they were commanded to do was at once the safest and the most natural proceeding. For Kinadon was a man distinguished for personal stature and courage (τὸ εἶδος καὶ τὴν ψυχὴν εὔρωστος, iii. 3, 5), so that those who seized him would find it an indispensable precaution to pinion his arms. Assuming even that Kinadon could write—yet if he were to write, he must have his right arm free. And why should the guards take this risk, when all which the Ephors required was, that Kinadon should *pronounce* the names, to be written down by others? With a man of the qualities of Kinadon, it probably required the most intense pressure to force him to betray his comrades, even by word of mouth; it would probably be more difficult still, to force him to betray them by the more deliberate act of writing.

I conceive that ἥκων ἐπειδὴ, φέρων τὰ ὀνόματα ὧν ὁ Κινάδων ἀνέγραψε is to be construed with reference to the preceding sentence, and announces the carrying into effect of the instructions than reported as given by the Ephors. "A guard came, bearing the names of those whom Kinadon had given in." It is not necessary to suppose that Kinadon had written down these names with his own hand.

In the beginning of the Oration of Andokides (De Mysteriis), Pythonikus gives information of a mock celebration of the mysteries, committed by Alkibiades and others; citing as his witness the slave Andromachus; who is accordingly produced, and states to the assembly vivâ voce what he had seen and who were the persons present — Πρῶτος μὲν οὗτος (Andromachus) ταῦτα ἐμήνυσε, καὶ ἀπέγραψε τούτους (s. 13). It is not here meant to affirm that the slave Andromachus wrote down the names of these persons, which he had the moment before publicly

The Ephors, on receiving it, immediately arrested the parties principally concerned, especially the prophet Tisamenus; and examined them along with Kinadon, as soon as he was brought prisoner. They asked the latter, among other questions, what was his purpose in setting on foot the conspiracy; to which he replied—"I wanted to be inferior to no man at Sparta." His punishment was not long deferred. Having been manacled with a clog round his neck to which his hands were made fast—he was in this condition conducted round the city, with men scourging and pricking him during the progress. His accomplices were treated in like manner, and at length all of them were put to death.¹

**Dangerous discontent indicated at Sparta.** Such is the curious narrative, given by Xenophon, of this unsuccessful conspiracy. He probably derived his information from Agesilaus himself; since we cannot easily explain how he could have otherwise learnt so much about the most secret manœuvres of the Ephors, in a government proverbial for constant secrecy, like that of Sparta. The narrative opens to us a glimpse, though sadly transient and imperfect, of the internal dangers of the Spartan go-

announced to the assembly. It is by the words ἀπογράψαι τούτους that the orator describes the public oral announcement made by Andromachus, which was formally noted down by a secretary, and which led to legal consequences against the persons whose names were given in.

So again, in the old law quoted by Demosthenes (adv. Makart. p. 1068), 'Ἀπογραφάτω δὲ τὸν μὴ ποιοῦντα ταῦτα ὁ βουλόμενος πρὸς τὸν ἄρχοντα; and in Demosthenes adv. Nikostrat. p. 1247. Ἀ ἐκ τῶν νόμων τῷ ἰδιώτῃ τῷ ἀπογράψαντι γίγνεται, τῇ πόλει ἀφίημι: compare also Lysias, De Bonis Aristophanis, Or. xix. a. 53; it is not meant to affirm that ὁ ἀπογράφων was required to perform his process in writing, or was necessarily able to write. A citizen who could not write might do this,

as well as one who could. He *informed against* a certain person as delinquent; he *informed of* certain articles of property, as belonging to the state of one whose property had been confiscated to the city. The information, as well as the name of the informer, was taken down by the official person—whether the informer could himself write or not.

It appears to me that Kinadon, having been interrogated, *told* to the guards who first seized him, the names of his accomplices—just as he *told* these names afterwards to the Ephors (καὶ τοὺς ξυνειδότας ἔλεγε); and this, whether he was, or was not, able to write; a point, which the passage of Xenophon noway determines.

¹ Xenoph. Hellen. iii. 3, 11.

vernment. We were aware, from earlier evidences, of great discontent prevailing among the Helots, and to a certain extent among the Periœki. But the incident here described presents to us the first manifestation of a body of malcontents among the Spartans themselves; malcontents formidable both from energy and position, like Kinadon and the prophet Tisamenus. Of the state of disaffected feeling in the provincial townships of Laconia, an impressive proof is afforded by the case of that beautiful woman who was alleged to be so active in political proselytism at Aulon; not less than by the passionate expressions of hatred revealed in the deposition of the informer himself. Though little is known about the details, yet it seems that the tendency of affairs at Sparta was to concentrate both power and property in the hands of an oligarchy ever narrowing among the citizens; thus aggravating the dangers at home, even at the time when the power of the state was greatest abroad, and preparing the way for that irreparable humiliation which began with the defeat of Leuktra.

It can hardly be doubted that much more wide-spread discontent came to the knowledge of the Ephors than that which is specially indicated in Xenophon. And such discovery may probably have been one of the motives (as had happened in 424 B.C. on occasion of the expedition of Brasidas into Thrace) which helped to bring about the Asiatic expedition of Agesilaus, as an outlet for brave malcontents on distant and lucrative military service.

B.C. 397.

Derkyllidas had now been carrying on war in Asia Minor for near three years, against Tissaphernês and Pharnabazus, with so much efficiency and success, as both to protect the Asiatic Greeks on the coast, and to intercept all the revenues which those satraps either transmitted to court or enjoyed themselves. Pharnabazus had already gone up to Susa (during his truce with Derkyllidas in 397 B.C.), and besides obtaining a reinforcement which acted under himself and Tissaphernês in 396 B.C. against Derkyllidas in Lydia, had laid schemes for renewing the maritime war against Sparta.[1]

Proceedings of Derkyllidas and Pharnabazus in Asia.

---

[1] Diodor. xiv. 39; Xen. Hellen. iii. 8, 13.

It is now that we hear again mentioned the name of Konon, who having saved himself with nine triremes from the defeat of Ægospotami, had remained for the last seven years under the protection of Evagoras, prince of Salamis in Cyprus. Konon, having married at Salamis, and having a son[1] born to him there, indulged but faint hopes of ever returning to his native city, when, fortunately for him as well as for Athens, the Persians again became eager for an efficient admiral and fleet on the coast of Asia Minor. Through representations from Pharnabazus, as well as from Evagoras in Cyprus—and through correspondence of the latter with the Greek physician Ktêsias, who wished to become personally employed in the negotiation, and who seems to have had considerable influence with Queen Parysatis[2]—orders were obtained, and funds provided, to equip in Phœnicia and Kilikia a numerous fleet, under the command of Konon. While that officer began to show himself, and to act with such triremes as he found in readiness (about forty in number) along the southern coast of Asia Minor from Kilikia to Kaunus[3]—further preparations were vigorously prosecuted in the Phœnician ports, in order to make up the fleet to 300 sail.[4]

It was by a sort of accident that news of such equipment reached Sparta—in an age of the world when diplomatic residents were as yet unknown. A Syracusan merchant named Herodas, having visited the Phœnician ports for trading purposes, brought back to Sparta intelligence of the preparations which he had seen, sufficient to excite much uneasiness. The Spartans were taking counsel among

---

[1] Lysias, Orat. xix. (De Bonis Aristophanis) s. 39.

[2] See Ktesias, Fragmenta Persica, c. 63, ed. Bähr; Plutarch, Artax. c. 21.

We cannot make out these circumstances with any distinctness; but the general fact is plainly testified, and is besides very probable. Another Grecian surgeon (besides Ktesias) is mentioned as concerned—Polykritus of Mendê; and a Kretan dancer named Zeno—both established at the Persian court.

There is no part of the narrative of Ktesias, the loss of which is so much to be regretted as this; relating transactions, in which he was himself concerned, and seemingly giving original letters.

[3] Diodor. xiv. 39-79.

[4] Xen. Hellen. iii. 4, 1.

themselves, and communicating with their neighbouring allies, when Agesilaus, at the instance of Lysander, stood forward as a volunteer to solicit the command of a land-force for the purpose of attacking the Persians in Asia. He proposed to take with him only thirty full Spartan citizens or Peers, as a sort of Board or Council of Officers; 2000 Neodamodes or enfranchised Helots, whom the Ephors were probably glad to send away, and who would be selected from the bravest and most formidable; and 6000 hoplites from the land-allies, to whom the prospect of a rich service against Asiatic enemies would be tempting. Of these thirty Spartans Lysander intended to be leader, and thus reckoning on his pre-established influence over Agesilaus, to exercise the real command himself without the name. He had no serious fear of the Persian arms, either by land or sea. He looked upon the announcement of the Phœnician fleet to be an empty threat, as it had so often proved in the mouth of Tissaphernês during the late war; while the Cyreian expedition had inspired him further with ardent hopes of another successful Anabasis, or conquering invasion of Persia from the sea-coast inwards. But he had still more at heart to employ his newly-acquired ascendency in re-establishing everywhere the Dekarchies, which had excited such intolerable hatred and exercised so much oppression, that even the Ephors had refused to lend positive aid in upholding them, so that they had been in several places broken up or modified.[1] If the ambition of Agesilaus was comparatively less stained by personal and factious antipathies, and more Pan-hellenic in its aim, than that of Lysander—it was at the same time yet more unmeasured in respect to victory over the Great King, whom he dreamt of dethroning, or at least of expelling from Asia Minor and the coast.[2] So powerful was the influence exercised by the Cyreian expedition over the schemes and imagination of energetic Greeks; so sudden was the outburst of ambition in the mind of Agesilaus, for which no one before had given him credit.

[1] Xen. Hellen. III. 4, 2.
[2] Xen. Hellen. III. 5, 1. ἐλπίδας ἔχοντα μεγάλας αἱρήσειν βασιλέα, &c. Compare iv. 2, 3.

Xen. Agesilaus, I. 36. ἐπινοῶν καὶ ἐλπίζων καταλύσειν τὴν ἐπὶ τὴν Ἑλλάδα στρατεύσασαν πρότερον ἀρχήν, &c.

Though this plan was laid by two of the ablest men
in Greece, it turned out to be rash and improvident, so far as the stability of the Lacedæmonian empire was concerned. That empire ought
to have been made sure by sea, where its real
danger lay, before attempts were made to extend it by new inland acquisitions. And except for purposes of conquest, there was no need of further reinforcements in Asia Minor; since Derkyllidas was already there
with a force competent to make head against the satraps.
Nevertheless the Lacedæmonians embraced the plan eagerly;
the more so, as envoys were sent from many of the subject
cities, by the partisans of Lysander and in concert with
him, to entreat that Agesilaus might be placed at the head
of the expedition, with as large a force as he required.[1]

*Large plans of Agesilaus, for conquest in the interior of Asia.*

No difficulty probably was found in levying the proposed number of men from the allies, since there
was great promise of plunder for the soldiers in
Asia. But the altered position of Sparta with
respect to her most powerful allies was betrayed
by the refusal of Thebes, Corinth, and Athens,
to take any part in the expedition. The refusal
of Corinth, indeed, was excused professedly on
the ground of a recent inauspicious conflagration
of one of the temples in the city; and that of
Athens, on the plea of weakness and exhaustion not yet
repaired. But the latter, at least, had already begun to
conceive some hope from the projects of Konon.[2]

*General willingness of the Spartan allies to serve in the expedition, but refusal from Thebes, Corinth, and Athens.*

The mere fact that a king of Sparta was about to
take the command and pass into Asia, lent peculiar importance to the enterprise. The Spartan
kings, in their function of leaders of Greece,
conceived themselves to have inherited the
sceptre of Agamemnon and Orestês;[3] and Agesilaus, especially, assimilated his expedition to
a new Trojan war—an effort of united Greece,
for the purpose of taking vengeance on the
common Asiatic enemy of the Hellenic name.
The sacrifices having been found favourable,
Agesilaus took measures for the transit of the troops from

*Agesilaus compares himself with Aga-memnon—goes to sacrifice at Aulis—is contemp-tuously hindered by the Thebans.*

[1] Plutarch, Agesil. c. 6.     [2] Herodot. I. 68; vii. 159; Pausan.
[3] Xen. Hellen. iii. 5, 5; Pausan. iii. 16, 6.
iii. 9, 1.

various ports to Ephesus. But he himself, with one division, touched in his way at Geræstus, the southern point of Eubœa; wishing to cross from thence and sacrifice at Aulis, the port of Bœotia where Agamemnon had offered his memorable sacrifice immediately previous to departure for Troy. It appears that he both went to the spot, and began the sacrifice, without asking permission from the Thebans; moreover he was accompanied by his own prophet, who conducted the solemnities in a manner not consistent with the habitual practice of the temple or chapel of Artemis at Aulis. On both these grounds, the Thebans, resenting the proceeding as an insult, sent a body of armed men, and compelled him to desist from the sacrifice.[1] Not taking part themselves in the expedition, they probably considered that the Spartan king was presumptuous in assuming to himself the Pan-hellenic character of a second Agamemnon; and they thus inflicted a humiliation which Agesilaus never forgave.

Agesilaus seems to have reached Asia about the time when Derkyllidas had recently concluded his last armistice with Tissaphernês and Pharnabazus; an armistice intended to allow time for mutual communication both with Sparta and the Persian court. On being asked by the satrap what was his purpose in coming, Agesilaus merely renewed the demand which had before been made by Derkyllidas—of autonomy for the Asiatic Greeks. Tissaphernês replied by proposing a continuation of the same armistice, until he could communicate with the Persian court—adding that he hoped to be empowered to grant the demand. A fresh armistice was accordingly sworn to on both sides, for three months; Derkyllidas (who with his army came now under the command of Agesilaus) and Herippidas being sent to the satrap to receive his oath, and take oaths to him in return.[2]

B.C. 396. Arrival of Agesilaus at Ephesus —he concludes a fresh armistice with Tissaphernês.

While the army was thus condemned to temporary inaction at Ephesus, the conduct and position of Lysander began to excite intolerable jealousy in the superior officers;

[1] Xen. Hellen. III. 4, 3, 4; III. 5, 5; Plutarch, Agesilaus, c. 6; Pausan. III. 9, 2.
[2] Xen. Hellen. III. 4, 5, 6; Xen. Agesilaus, i. 10.

The term of three months is specified only in the latter passage. The former armistice of Derkyllidas was probably not expired when Agesilaus first arrived.

and most of all, in Agesilaus. So great and established was
the reputation of Lysander—whose statue had been
erected at Ephesus itself in the temple of Ar-
temis¹ as well as in many other cities—that all
the Asiatic Greeks looked upon him as the real
chief of the expedition. That *he* should be
real chief, under the nominal command of another,
was nothing more than what had happened before, in the year wherein he gained the great
victory of Ægospotami—the Lacedæmonians
having then also sent him out in the ostensible capacity of secretary to the admiral Arakus, in order to save
the inviolability of their own rule that the same man should
not serve twice as admiral.² It was through the instigation
of Lysander, and with a view to his presence, that the decemvirs and other partisans in the subject cities had sent
to Sparta to petition for Agesilaus; a prince as yet untried
and unknown. So that Lysander—taking credit, with
truth, for having ensured to Agesilaus first the crown, next
this important appointment—intended for himself, and was
expected by others, to exercise a fresh turn of command,
and to renovate in every town the discomfited or enfeebled
Dekarchies. Numbers of his partisans came to Ephesus to
greet his arrival, and a crowd of petitioners were seen
following his steps everywhere; while Agesilaus himself
appeared comparatively neglected. Moreover Lysander
resumed all that insolence of manner which he had contracted during his former commands, and which on this
occasion gave the greater offence, since the manner of
Agesilaus was both courteous and simple in a peculiar
degree.³

*Arrogant behaviour and overweening ascendency of Lysander—offensive to the army and to Agesilaus.*

The thirty Spartan counsellors, over whom Lysander
had been named to preside, finding themselves
neither consulted by him, nor solicited by others,
were deeply dissatisfied. Their complaints
helped to encourage Agesilaus, who was still
more keenly wounded in his own personal
dignity, to put forth a resolute and imperious

*Agesilaus humbles and degrades Lysander, who asks to be sent away.*

---

¹ Pausan. vi. 3, 8.
² Xen. Hellen. ii. 1, 7. This rôle does not seem to have been adhered to afterwards. Lysander was sent out again as commander in 403 B.C. It is possible indeed, that he may have been again sent out as nominal secretary to some other person named as commander.
³ Plutarch, Agesilaus, c. 7.

strength of will, such as he had not before been known to possess. He successively rejected every petition preferred to him by or through Lysander; a systematic purpose, which, though never formally announced,[1] was presently discerned by the petitioners, by the Thirty, and by Lysander himself. The latter thus found himself not merely disappointed in all his calculations, but humiliated to excess, though without any tangible ground of complaint. He was forced to warn his partisans, that his intervention was an injury and not a benefit to them; that they must desist from obsequious attention to him, and must address themselves directly to Agesilaus. With that prince he also remonstrated on his own account—"Truly, Agesilaus, you know how to degrade your friends."—"Ay, to be sure (was the reply), those among them who want to appear greater than I am; but such as seek to uphold me, I should be ashamed if I did not know how to repay with due honour."—Lysander was constrained to admit the force of this reply and to request, as the only means of escape from present and palpable humiliation, that he might be sent on some mission apart; engaging to serve faithfully in whatever duty he might be employed.[2]

This proposition, doubtless even more agreeable to Agesilaus than to himself, being readily assented to, he was dispatched on a mission to the Hellespont. Faithful to his engagement of forgetting past offences and serving with zeal, he found means to gain over a Persian grandee named Spithridatês, who had received some offence from Pharnabazus. Spithridatês revolted openly, carrying a regiment of 200 horse to join Agesilaus; who was thus enabled to inform himself fully about the satrapy of Pharnabazus, comprising the territory called Phrygia in the neighbourhood of the Propontis and the Hellespont.[3]

*Lysander is sent to command at the Hellespont—his valuable service there.*

---

[1] The sarcastic remarks which Plutarch ascribes to Agesilaus, calling Lysander "my meat-distributor" (κρεοδαίτην), are not warranted by Xenophon, and seem not to be probable under the circumstances (Plutarch, Lysand. c. 23; Plutarch, Agesil. c. 8).

[2] Xen. Hellen. III. 4, 7-10; Plutarch, Agesilaus, c. 7, 8; Plutarch,

Lysand. c. 23.

It is remarkable that in the Opusculum of Xenophon, a special Panegyric called *Agesilaus*, not a word is said about this highly characteristic proceeding between Agesilaus and Lysander at Ephesus; nor indeed is the name of Lysander once mentioned.

[3] Xen. Hellen. III. 4, 10.

The army under Tissaphernês had been already powerful at the moment when his timidity induced him to conclude the first armistice with Derkyllidas. But additional reinforcements, received since the conclusion of the second and more recent armistice, had raised him to such an excess of confidence, that even before the stipulated three months had expired, he sent to insist on the immediate departure of Agesilaus from Asia, and to proclaim war forthwith, if such departure were delayed. While this message, accompanied by formidable reports of the satrap's force, filled the army at Ephesus with mingled alarm and indignation, Agesilaus accepted the challenge with cheerful readiness; sending word back that he thanked the satrap for perjuring himself in so flagrant a manner, as to set the gods against him and ensure their favour to the Greek side.[1] Orders were forthwith given, and contingents summoned from the Asiatic Greeks, for a forward movement southward, to cross the Mœander, and attack Tissaphernês in Karia, where he usually resided. The cities on the route were required to provide magazines, so that Tissaphernês, fully anticipating attack in this direction, caused his infantry to cross into Karia, for the purpose of acting on the defensive; while he kept his numerous cavalry in the plain of the Mæander, with a view to overwhelm Agesilaus, who had no cavalry, in his march over that level territory towards the Karian hills and rugged ground.

But the Lacedæmonian king, having put the enemy on this false scent, suddenly turned his march northward towards Phrygia and the satrapy of Pharnabazus. Tissaphernês took no pains to aid his brother satrap, who on his side had made few preparations for defence. Accordingly Agesilaus, finding little or no resistance, took many towns and villages, and collected abundance of provisions, plunder, and slaves. Profiting by the guidance of the revolted Spithridatês, and marching as little as possible over the plains, he carried on lucrative and unopposed incursions as far as the neighbourhood of Daskylium, the residence of the satrap himself near the Propontis. Near the satrapic residence, however, his small body of cavalry,

[1] Xen. Hellen. III. 4, 11, 12; Xen. Agesil. i. 12-14; Plutarch, Agesil. c. 9.

ascending an eminence, came suddenly upon an equal detachment of Persian cavalry, under Rhathinês and Bagæus; who attacked them vigorously, and drove them back with some loss, until they were protected by Agesilaus himself coming up with the hoplites. The effect of such a check (and there were probably others of the same kind, though Xenophon does not specify them) on the spirits of the army was discouraging. On the next morning, the sacrifices being found unfavourable for farther advance, Agesilaus gave orders for retreating towards the sea. He reached Ephesus about the close of autumn; resolved to employ the winter in organizing a more powerful cavalry, which experience proved to be indispensable.[1]

This autumnal march through Phrygia was more lucrative than glorious. Yet it enables Xenophon to bring to view different merits of his hero Agesilaus; in doing which he exhibits to us ancient warfare and Asiatic habits on a very painful side. In common both with Kallikratidas and Lysander, though not with the ordinary Spartan commanders, Agesilaus was indifferent to the acquisition of money for himself. But he was not the less anxious to enrich his friends, and would sometimes connive at unwarrantable modes of acquisition for their benefit. Deserters often came in to give information of rich prizes or valuable prisoners; which advantages, if he had chosen, he might have appropriated to himself. But he made it a practice to throw both the booty and the honour in the way of some favourite officer; just as we have seen (in a former chapter), that Xenophon himself was allowed by the army to capture Asidatês and enjoy a large portion of his ransom.[2] Again when the army in the course of its march was at a considerable distance from the sea, and appeared to be advancing farther inland, the authorized auctioneers, whose province it was to sell the booty, found the buyers extremely slack. It was difficult to keep or carry what was

*Agesilaus indifferent to money for himself, but eager in enriching his friends.*

[1] Xen. Hellen. III. 4, 12-15; Xen. Agesil. l. 23. Ἐπεὶ μέντοι οὐδὲ ἐν τῇ Φρυγίᾳ ἀνὰ τὰ πεδία ἐδύνατο στρατεύεσθαι, διὰ τὴν Φαρναβάζου ἱππείαν, &c. Plutarch, Agesil. c. 9. These military operations of Agesilaus are loosely adverted to in the early part of c. 79 of the fourteenth Book of Diodorus.

[2] Xen. Agesil. l. 19; Xen. Anabas. vii. 8, 20-23; Plutarch, Reipub. Gerend. Præcept. p. 809 B. See above, Chapter lxxii. of this History.

bought, and opportunity for resale did not seem at hand. Agesilaus, while he instructed the auctioneers to sell upon credit, without insisting on ready money—at the same time gave private hints to a few friends that he was very shortly about to return to the sea. The friends thus warned, bidding for the plunder on credit and purchasing at low prices, were speedily enabled to dispose of it again at a seaport, with large profits.[1]

*His humanity towards captives and deserted children.* We are not surprised to hear that such lucrative graces procured for Agesilaus many warm admirers; though the eulogies of Xenophon ought to have been confined to another point in his conduct, now to be mentioned. Agesilaus, while securing for his army the plunder of the country over which he carried his victorious arms, took great pains to prevent both cruelty and destruction of property. When any town surrendered to him on terms, his exactions were neither ruinous nor grossly humiliating.[2] Amidst all the plunder realised, too, the most valuable portion was, the adult natives of both sexes, hunted down and brought in by the predatory light troops of the army, to be sold as slaves. Agesilaus was vigilant in protecting these poor victims from ill-usage; inculcating upon his soldiers the duty, "not of punishing them like wrong-doers, but simply of keeping them under guard as men."[3] It was the practice of the poorer part of the native population often to sell their little children for exportation to travelling slave-merchants, from inability to maintain them. The children thus purchased, if they promised to be handsome, were often mutilated, and fetched large prices as eunuchs, to supply the large demand for the harems and religious worship of many Asiatic towns. But in their haste to get out of the way of a plundering army, these slave-merchants were forced often to leave by the way-side the little children whom they had purchased, exposed to the wolves, the dogs, or starvation. In this wretched condition, they were found by Agesilaus on his march. His humane disposition

---

[1] Xen. Agesil. i. 18. πάντες συμπλήθη χρήματα ἔλαβον.

[2] Xen. Agesil. i. 20-22.

[3] Xen. Hellen. III. 4, 19; Xen. Agesil. i. 28. τοὺς ὑπὸ τῶν λῃστῶν ἁλισκομένους βαρβάρους.

So the word λῃστής, used in reference to the fleet, means the commander of a predatory vessel or privateer (Xen. Hellen. II. 1, 30).

prompted him to see them carried to a place of safety, where he gave them in charge of those old natives whom age and feebleness had caused to be left behind as not worth carrying off. By such active kindness, rare indeed in a Grecian general, towards the conquered, he earned the gratitude of the captives, and the sympathies of every one around.[1]

This interesting anecdote, imparting a glimpse of the ancient world in reference to details which Grecian historians rarely condescend to unveil, demonstrates the compassionate disposition of Agesilaus. We find in conjunction with it another anecdote, illustrating the Spartan side of his character. The prisoners who had been captured during the expedition were brought to Ephesus, and sold during the winter as slaves

*Spartan side of his character—exposure of naked prisoners—different practice of Asiatics and Greeks.*

[1] Xen. Agesil. L. 21. Καὶ πολλάκις μὲν προηγόρευε τοῖς στρατιώταις τοὺς ἁλισκομένους μὴ ὡς ἀδίκους τιμωρεῖσθαι, ἀλλ' ὡς ἀνθρώπους ὄντας φυλάσσειν. Πολλάκις δὲ, ὅποτε μεταστρατοπεδεύοιτο, εἰ αἴσθοιτο καταλελειμμένα παιδάρια μικρὰ ἐμπόρων, (ἃ πωλεῖν ἐκώλουν, διὰ τὸ νομίζειν μὴ δύνασθαι ἂν φέρειν αὐτὰ καὶ τρέφειν) ἐκμέλετο καὶ τούτων, ὅπως συγκομίζοιτό και· τοῖς δ' εὖ διὰ γῆρας καταλελειμμένοις αἰχμαλώτοις προσέταττεν ἐκμελεῖσθαι αὐτῶν, ὡς μήτε ὑπὸ κυνῶν, μήθ' ὑπὸ λύκων, διαφθείροιντο. Ὥστε οὐ μόνον οἱ πυνθανόμενοι ταῦτα, ἀλλὰ καὶ αὐτοὶ οἱ ἁλισκόμενοι, εὐμενεῖς αὐτῷ ἐγίγνοντο.

Herodotus affirms that the Thracians also sold their children for exportation—πωλεῦσι τὰ τέκνα ἐπ' ἐξαγωγῇ (Herod. v. 6): compare Philostratus, Vit. Apollon. viii. 7-12, p. 346; and Ch. xvi. of this History.

Herodotus mentions the Chian merchant Panionius (like the *Mitylenæus mango* in Martial—"Sed Mitylenæi roseus mangonis ephebus" Martial, vii. 79) as having conducted on a large scale the trade

of purchasing boys, looking out for such as were handsome, to supply the great demand in the East for eunuchs, who were supposed to make better and more attached servants. Herodot. viii. 104. ὅπως γὰρ κτήσαιτο (Panionius) παῖδας εἴδεος ἐπαμμένους, ἐκτέμνων, ἀγινέων ἐπώλεε ἐς Σάρδις τε καὶ Ἔφεσον χρημάτων μεγάλων· παρὰ γὰρ τοῖσι βαρβάροισι τιμιώτεροί εἰσι οἱ εὐνοῦχοι, πίστιος εἵνεκα τῆς πάσης, τῶν ἐνορχέων. Boys were necessary, as the operation was performed in childhood or youth—παῖδες ἐκτομίαι (Herodot. vi. 8-82: compare iii. 48). The Babylonians, in addition to their large pecuniary tribute, had to furnish to the Persian court annually 500 παῖδες ἐκτομίας (Herodot. iii. 92). For some farther remarks on the preference of the Persians both for the persons and the services of εὐνοῦχοι, see Dio Chrysostom. Orat. xxl. p. 270; Xenoph. Cyropæd. vii. 5, 61-65. Hellanikus (Fr. 169, ed. Didot) affirmed that the Persians had derived both the persons so employed, and the habit of employing them, from the Babylonians.

When Mr. Hanway was travelling

for the profit of the army. Agesilaus—being then busily employed in training his troops to military efficiency, especially for the cavalry service during the ensuing campaign—thought it advisable to impress them with contempt for the bodily capacity and prowess of the natives. He therefore directed the heralds who conducted the auction, to put the prisoners up to sale in a state of perfect nudity. To have the body thus exposed, was a thing never done, and even held disgraceful, by the native Asiatics; while among the Greeks, the practice was universal for purposes of exercise—or at least had become universal during the last two or three centuries—for we are told that originally the Asiatic feeling on this point had prevailed throughout Greece. It was one of the obvious differences between Grecian and Asiatic customs[1]—that in the former, both the exercises of the palæstra, as well as the matches in the solemn games, required competitors of every rank to contend naked. Agesilaus himself stripped thus habitually; Alexander prince of Macedon had done so, when he ran at the Olympic stadium[2]—also the combatants out of the great family of the Diagorids of Rhodes, when they gained their victories in the Olympic pankratium—and all those other noble pugilists, wrestlers, and runners, descended from gods and heroes, upon whom Pindar pours forth his complimentary odes.

On this occasion at Ephesus, Agesilaus gave special orders to put up the Asiatic prisoners to auction naked; not at all by way of insult, but in order to exhibit to the eye of the Greek soldier who contemplated them, how much he gained by his own bodily training and frequent exposure—and how inferior was the condition of men whose bodies never felt the sun or wind. They displayed a white skin, plump and soft limbs, weak and undeveloped muscles, like men accustomed to be borne in carriages instead of walking or running; from whence we indirectly learn that many of them were men in wealthy circumstances. And the purpose of Agesilaus was completely

near the Caspian, among the Kalmucks, little children of two or three years of age, were often tendered to him for sale, at two rubles per head (Hanway's Travels, ch. xvi. p. 65, 68).

[1] Herodot. i. 10. περὶ γὰρ τοῖσι Λυδοῖσι, σχεδὸν δὲ καὶ παρὰ τοῖσι ἄλλοισι βαρβάροισι, καὶ ἄνδρα ὀφθῆναι γυμνὸν, ἐς αἰσχύνην μεγάλην φέρει. Compare Thucyd. l. 6; Plato, Republic, v. 5, p. 452 D.

[2] Herodot. v. 22.

answered; since his soldiers, when they witnessed such evidences of bodily incompetence, thought that "the enemies against whom they had to contend were not more formidable than women."[1] Such a method of illustrating the difference between good and bad physical training would hardly have occurred to any one except a Spartan, brought up under the Lykurgean rules.

While Agesilaus thus brought home to the vision of his soldiers the inefficiency of untrained bodies, he kept them throughout the winter under hard work and drill, as well as in the palæstra as in arms. A force of cavalry was still wanting. To procure it, he enrolled all the richest Greeks in the various Asiatic towns, as conscripts to serve on horseback; giving each of them leave to exempt himself, however, by providing a competent substitute and equipment—man, horse, and arms.[2] Before the commencement of spring, an adequate force of cavalry was thus assembled at Ephesus, and put into tolerable exercise. Throughout the whole winter, that city became a place of arms, consecrated to drilling and gymnastic exercises. On parade as well as in the palæstra, Agesilaus himself was foremost in setting the example of obedience and hard work. Prizes were given to the diligent and improving, among hoplites, horsemen, and light troops; while the armourers, braziers, leather-cutters, &c., all the various artisans whose trade lay in muniments of war, were in the fullest employment. "It was a sight full of encouragement (says Xenophon, who was doubtless present and took part in it), to see Agesilaus

*Efforts of Agesilaus to train his army, and to procure cavalry.*

[1] Xen. Hellen. iii. 4, 19. Ἡγούμενος δὲ, καὶ τὸ καταφρονεῖν τῶν πολεμίων ῥώμην τινὰ ἐμβάλλειν πρὸς τὸ μάχεσθαι, προεῖπε τοῖς κήρυξι, τοὺς ὑπὸ τῶν λῃστῶν ἁλισκομένους βαρβάρους γυμνοὺς πωλεῖν. Ὁρῶντες οὖν οἱ στρατιῶται λευκοὺς μὲν, διὰ τὸ μηδέποτε ἐκδύεσθαι, μαλακοὺς δὲ καὶ ἀπόνους, διὰ τὸ ἀεὶ ἐπ᾽ ὀχημάτων εἶναι, ἐνόμισαν, οὐδὲν διοίσειν τὸν πόλεμον ἢ εἰ γυναιξὶ δέοι μάχεσθαι.

Xen. Agesil. i. 28—where he has it—αἰσχρὸν δὲ καὶ ἀπόνους, διὰ τὸ ἀεὶ ἐπ᾽ ὀχημάτων εἶναι (Polyænus, ii. 1, 6; Plutarch, Agesil. c. 9).

Frontinus (i. 18) recounts a proceeding somewhat similar on the part of Gelon, after his great victory over the Carthaginians at Himera in Sicily:—"Gelo Syracusarum tyrannus, bello adversus Pœnos suscepto, cum multos cepisset, infirmissimum quemque præcipue ex auxiliaribus, qui nigerrimi erant, nudatum in conspectu suorum prodxuit, ut persuaderet contemnendos."

[2] Xen. Hellen. iii. 4, 15; Xen. Agesil. 1. 23. Compare what is related about Scipio Africanus—Livy, xxix. 1.

and the soldiers leaving the gymnasium, all with wreaths on their heads; and marching to the temple of Artemis to dedicate their wreaths to the goddess."[1]

*B.C. 395.*

*Agesilaus renews the war against Tissaphernês, and gains a victory near Sardis.*

Before Agesilaus was in condition to begin his military operations for the spring, the first year of his command had passed over. Thirty fresh counsellors reached Ephesus from Sparta, superseding the first thirty under Lysander, who all went home forthwith. The army was now not only more numerous, but better trained, and more systematically arranged, than in the preceding campaign. Agesilaus distributed the various divisions under the command of different members of the new Thirty; the cavalry being assigned to Xenoklês, the Neodamode hoplites to Skythês, the Cyreians to Herippidas, the Asiatic contingents to Migdon. He then gave out that he should march straight against Sardis. Nevertheless Tissaphernês, who was in that place, construing this proclamation as a feint, and believing that the real march would be directed against Karia, disposed his cavalry in the plain of the Mæander as he had done in the preceding campaign; while his infantry were sent still farther southward within the Karian frontier. On this occasion, however, Agesilaus marched as he had announced, in the direction of Sardis. For three days he plundered the country without seeing an enemy; nor was it until the fourth day that the cavalry of Tissaphernês could be summoned back to oppose him; the infantry being even yet at a distance. On reaching the banks of the river Paktôlus, the Persian cavalry found the Greek light troops dispersed for the purpose of plunder, attacked them by surprise, and drove them in with considerable loss. Presently however Agesilaus himself came up, and ordered his cavalry to charge, anxious to bring on a battle before the Persian infantry could arrive in the field. In efficiency, it appears, the Persian cavalry was a full match for his cavalry, and in number apparently superior. But when he brought up his infantry, and caused his peltasts and younger hoplites to join the cavalry in a vigorous attack—victory soon declared on his side. The Persians were put to flight and many of them drowned in the Paktôlus. Their camp too was taken, with a valuable booty; including several camels,

[1] Xen. Hellen. iii. 4, 17, 18; Xen. Agesil. L 26, 27.

which Agesilaus afterwards took with him into Greece. This success ensured to him the unopposed mastery of all the territory round Sardis. He carried his ravages to the very gates of that city, plundering the gardens and ornamented ground, proclaiming liberty to those within, and defying Tissaphernês to come out and fight.[1]

The career of that timid and treacherous satrap now approached its close. The Persians in or near Sardis loudly complained of him as leaving them undefended, from cowardice and anxiety for his own residence in Karia; while the court of Susa was now aware that the powerful reinforcement which had been sent to him last year, intended to drive Agesilaus out of Asia, had been made to achieve absolutely nothing. To these grounds of just dissatisfaction was added a court-intrigue; to which, and to the agency of a person yet more worthless and cruel than himself, Tissaphernês fell a victim. The Queen Mother Parysatis had never forgiven him for having been one of the principal agents in the defeat and death of her son Cyrus. Her influence being now re-established over the mind of Artaxerxês, she took advantage of the existing discredit of the satrap to get an order sent down for his deposition and death. Tithraustês, the bearer of this order, seized him by stratagem at Kolossæ in Phrygia, while he was in the bath, and caused him to be beheaded.[2]

*Artaxerxês causes Tissaphernês to be put to death, and superseded by Tithraustês.*

The mission of Tithraustês to Asia Minor was accompanied by increased efforts on the part of Persia for prosecuting the war against Sparta with vigour, by sea as well as by land; and also for fomenting the anti-Spartan movement which burst out into hostilities this year in Greece. At first, however, immediately after the death of Tissaphernês, Tithraustês endeavoured to

B.C. 396

---

[1] Xen. Hellen. III. 4, 21-26; Xen. Agesil. i. 32, 33; Plutarch, Agesil. c. 10.

Diodorus (xiv. 80) professes to describe this battle; but his description is hardly to be reconciled with that of Xenophon, which is better authority. Among other points of difference, Diodorus affirms that the Persians had 50,000 infantry; and Pausanias also states (III. 9, 8) that the number of Persian infantry in this battle was greater than had ever been got together since the times of Darius and Xerxes. Whereas Xenophon expressly states that the Persian infantry had not come up, and took no part in the battle.

[2] Plutarch, Artaxerx. c. 23; Diodor. xiv. 80; Xen. Hellen. III. 4, 25.

open negotiations with Agesilaus; who was in military possession of the country round Sardis, while that city itself appears to have been occupied by Ariæus—probably the same Persian who had formerly been general under Cyrus, and who had now again revolted from Artaxerxês.¹ Tithraustês took credit to the justice of the King for having punished the late satrap; out of whose perfidy (he affirmed) the war had arisen. He then summoned Agesilaus, in the King's name, to evacuate Asia, leaving the Asiatic Greeks to pay their original tribute to Persia, but to enjoy complete autonomy, subject to that one condition. Had this proposition been accepted and executed, it would have secured these Greeks against Persian occupation or governors; a much milder fate for them than that to which the Lacedæmonians had consented in their conventions with Tissaphernês sixteen years before,² and analogous to the position in which the Chalkidians of Thrace had been placed with regard to Athens, under the peace of Nikias;³ subject to a fixed tribute, yet autonomous—with no other obligation or interference. Agesilaus replied that he had no power to entertain such a proposition without the authorities at home, whom he accordingly sent to consult. But in the interim he was prevailed upon by Tithraustês to conclude an armistice for six months, and to move out of his satrapy into that of Pharnabazus; receiving a contribution of thirty talents towards the temporary maintenance of the army.⁴ These satraps generally acted more like independent or even hostile princes, than cooperating colleagues; one of the many causes of the weakness of the Persian empire.

When Agesilaus had reached the neighbourhood of Kymê, on his march northward to the Hellespontine Phrygia, he received a despatch from home, placing the Spartan naval force in the Asiatic seas under his command, as well as the land-force, and empowering him to name whomsoever he chose as acting admiral.⁵ For the first time since the battle of Ægospotami, the maritime empire of Sparta was beginning to be threatened, and in-

*Margin note: Negotiations between the new satrap and Agesilaus—the satraps in Asia Minor hostile to each other.*

¹ Xen. Hellen. III. 35, 25; iv. 1, 27.
² Thucyd. viii. 36, 37, 58.
³ Thucyd. v. 18, 6.
⁴ Xen. Hellen. III. 4, 26; Diodor. xiv. 80. ἑξαμηνιαίους ἀνοχάς.
⁵ Xen. Hellen. III. 4, 27.

CHAP. LXXIII.   REVOLT OF RHODES.   93

creased efforts on her part were becoming requisite. Pharnabazus, going up in person to the court of Artaxerxês, had by pressing representations obtained a large subsidy for fitting out a fleet in Cyprus and Phœnicia, to act under the Athenian admiral Konon against the Lacedæmonians.[1] That officer—with a fleet of forty triremes, before the equipment of the remainder was yet complete—had advanced along the southern coast of Asia Minor to Kaunus, at the south-western corner of the peninsula, on the frontier of Karia and Lykia. In this port he was besieged by the Lacedæmonian fleet of 120 triremes under Pharax. But a Persian reinforcement strengthened the fleet of Konon to eighty sail, and put the place out of danger; so that Pharax, desisting from the siege, retired to Rhodes.

*B.C. 395. Commencement of action at sea against Sparta— the Athenian Konon, assisted by Persian ships and money, commands a fleet of eighty sail on the coast of Karia.*

The neighbourhood of Konon, however, who was now with his fleet of eighty sail near the Chersonesus of Knidus, emboldened the Rhodians to revolt from Sparta. It was at Rhodes that the general detestation of the Lacedæmonian empire, disgraced in so many different cities by the local Dekarchies and by the Spartan harmosts, first manifested itself. And such was the ardour of the Rhodian population, that their revolt took place while the fleet of Pharax was (in part at least) actually in the harbour, and they drove him out of it.[2] Konon, whose secret encouragements had helped to excite this insurrection, presently sailed to Rhodes with his fleet, and made the island his main station. It threw into his hands an unexpected advantage; for a numerous fleet of vessels arrived there shortly afterwards, sent by Nephereus the native king of Egypt (which was in revolt against the Persians) with marine stores and grain to the aid of the Lacedæmonians. Not having been apprised of the recent revolt, these vessels entered the harbour of Rhodes as if it

*Rhodes revolts from the Spartan empire— Konon captures an Egyptian corn-fleet at Rhodes.*

---

[1] Diodor. xiv. 89; Justin. vi. 1.
[2] Diodor. xiv. 79. 'Ῥόδιοι δὲ ἐκβαλόντες τὸν τῶν Πελοποννησίων στόλον, ἀπέστησαν ἀπὸ Λακεδαιμονίων, καὶ τὸν Κόνωνα προσεδέξαντο

μετὰ τοῦ στόλου παντὸς εἰς τὴν πόλιν.

Compare Androtion apud Pausaniam, vi. 7, 2.

were still a Lacedæmonian island; and their cargoes were thus appropriated by Konon and the Rhodians.[1]

*Anxiety of the Lacedæmonians— Agesilaus is appointed to command at sea as well as on land.*

In recounting the various revolts of the dependencies of Athens which took place during the Peloponnesian war, I had occasion to point out more than once that all of them took place not merely in the absence of any Athenian force, but even at the instigation (in most cases) of a present hostile force—by the contrivance of a local party—and without privity or previous consent of the bulk of the citizens. The present revolt of Rhodes, forming a remarkable contrast on all these points, occasioned the utmost surprise and indignation among the Lacedæmonians. They saw themselves about to enter upon a renewed maritime war, without that aid which they had reckoned on receiving from Egypt, and with aggravated uncertainty in respect to their dependencies and tribute. It was under this prospective anxiety that they took the step of nominating Agesilaus to the command of the fleet as well as of the army, in order to ensure unity of operations;[2] though a distinction of function, which they had hitherto set great value upon maintaining, was thus broken down—and though the two commands had never been united in any king before Agesilaus.[3] Pharax, the previous admiral, was recalled.[4]

*Severity of the Lacedæmonians towards the Rhodian Dorians— contrast of the former treatment of the same men by Athens.*

But the violent displeasure of the Lacedæmonians against the revolted Rhodians was still better attested by another proceeding. Among all the great families at Rhodes, none were more distinguished than the Diagoridæ. Its members were not only generals and high political functionaries in their native island, but had attained even Pan-hellenic celebrity by an unparalleled series of victories at the Olympic and other great solemnities. Dorieus, a member of this

---

[1] Diodor. xiv. 79; Justin. (vi. 2) calls this native Egyptian king *Hercynion.*

It seems to have been the uniform practice, for the corn-ships coming from Egypt to Greece to halt at Rhodes (Demosthen. cont. Dionysodor. p. 1285: compare Herodot. ii. 182).

[2] Xen. Hellen. ii. 4, 27.

[3] Plutarch, Agesil. c. 10; Aristotel. Politic. ii. 6, 22.

[4] The Lacedæmonian named Pharax, mentioned by Theopompus (Fragm. 218. ed. Didot: compare Athenæus, xii. p. 536) as a profligate and extravagant person, is more probably an officer who ser-

family, had gained the victory in the pankration at Olympia on three successive solemnities. He had obtained seven prizes in the Nemean, and eight in the Isthmian games. He had carried off the prize at one Pythian solemnity without a contest—no one daring to stand up against him in the fearful struggle of the pankration. As a Rhodian, while Rhodes was a subject-ally of Athens during the Peloponnesian war, he had been so pronounced in his attachment to Sparta as to draw on himself a sentence of banishment; upon which he had retired to Thurii, and had been active in hostility to Athens after the Syracusan catastrophe. Serving against her in ships fitted out at his own cost, he had been captured in 407 B.C. by the Athenians and brought in as prisoner to Athens. By the received practice of war in that day, his life was forfeited; and over and above such practice, the name of Dorieus was peculiarly odious to the Athenians. But when they saw before the public assembly a captive enemy, of heroic lineage as well as of unrivalled athletic majesty and renown, their previous hatred was so overpowered by sympathy and admiration, that they liberated him by public vote, and dismissed him unconditionally.[1]

This interesting anecdote, which has already been related in my sixty-fourth chapter, is here again noticed as a contrast to the treatment which the same Dorieus now underwent from the Lacedæmonians. What he had been doing since, we do not know; but at the time when Rhodes now revolted from Sparta, he was not only absent from the island, but actually in or near Peloponnesus. Such however was the wrath of the Lacedæmonians against Rhodians generally, that Dorieus was seized by their order, brought to Sparta, and there condemned and executed.[2] It seems hardly possible that he can have had any personal concern in the revolt. Had such been the fact, he would have been in the island—or would at least have taken care not to be within the reach of the Lacedæmonians when the revolt happened. Perhaps however

ved under Dionysius in Sicily and Italy, about forty years after the revolt of Rhodes. The difference of time appears so great, that we must probably suppose two different men bearing the same name.
[1] Xen. Hellen. l. 6, 19.

Compare a similar instance of merciful dealing, on the part of the Syracusan assembly, towards the Sikel prince Duketius (Diodor. xi. 92).
[2] Pausanias, vi. 7, 2.

other members of the Diagoridæ, his family, once so much attached to Sparta, may have taken part in it; for we know, by the example of the Thirty at Athens, that the Lysandrian Dekarchies and Spartan harmosts made themselves quite as formidable to oligarchical as to democratical politicians, and it is very conceivable that the Diagoridæ may have become less philo-Laconian in their politics.

*Sentiment of a multitude compared with that of individuals.*
This extreme difference in the treatment of the same man by Athens and by Sparta raises instructive reflections. It exhibits the difference both between Athenian and Spartan sentiment, and between the sentiment of a multitude and that of a few. The grand and sacred personality of the Hieronikê Dorieus, when exhibited to the senses of the Athenian multitude—the spectacle of a man in chains before them, who had been proclaimed victor and crowned on so many solemn occasions before the largest assemblages of Greeks ever brought together—produced an overwhelming effect upon their emotions; sufficient not only to efface a strong pre-established antipathy founded on active past hostility, but to countervail a just cause of revenge, speaking in the language of that day. But the same appearance produced no effect at all on the Spartan Ephors and Senate; not sufficient even to hinder them from putting Dorieus to death, though he had given them no cause for antipathy or revenge, simply as a sort of retribution for the revolt of the island. Now this difference depended partly upon the difference between the sentiment of Athenians and Spartans, but partly also upon the difference between the sentiment of a multitude and that of a few. Had Dorieus been brought before a select judicial tribunal at Athens, instead of before the Athenian public assembly—or had the case been discussed before the assembly in his absence —he would have been probably condemned, conformably to usage, under the circumstances; but the vehement emotion worked by his presence upon the multitudinous spectators of the assembly, rendered such a course intolerable to them. It has been common with historians of Athens to dwell upon the passions of the public assembly as if it were susceptible of excitement only in an angry or vindictive direction; whereas the truth is, and the example before us illustrates, that they were open-minded in one

direction as well as in another, and that the present emotion, whatever it might be, merciful or sympathetic as well as resentful, was intensified by the mere fact of multitude. And thus, where the established rule of procedure happened to be cruel, there was some chance of moving an Athenian assembly to mitigate it in a particular case, though the Spartan Ephors or Senate would be inexorable in carrying it out—if indeed they did not, as seems probable in the case of Dorieus, actually go beyond it in rigour.

While Konon and the Rhodians were thus raising hostilities against Sparta by sea, Agesilaus, on receiving at Kymê the news of his nomination to the double command, immediately despatched orders to the dependent maritime cities and islands, requiring the construction and equipment of new triremes. Such was the influence of Sparta, and so much did the local governments rest upon its continuance, that these requisitions were zealously obeyed. Many leading men incurred considerable expense, from desire to acquire his favour; so that a fleet of 120 new triremes was ready by the ensuing year. Agesilaus, naming his brother-in-law Peisander to act as admiral, sent him to superintend the preparations; a brave young man, but destitute both of skill and experience.[1]

<small>B.C. 396. Efforts of Agesilaus to augment the fleet—he names Peisander admiral.</small>

Meanwhile he himself pursued his march (about the beginning of autumn) towards the satrapy of Pharnabazus—Phrygia south and south-east of the Propontis. Under the active guidance of his new auxiliary Spithridatês, he plundered the country, capturing some towns, and reducing others to capitulate; with considerable advantage to his soldiers. Pharnabazus, having no sufficient army to hazard a battle in defence of his satrapy, concentrated all his force near his own residence at Daskylium, offering no opposition to the march of Agesilaus; who was induced by Spithridatês to traverse Phrygia and enter Paphlagonia, in hopes of concluding an alliance with the Paphlagonian prince Otys. That prince, in nominal dependence on Persia, could muster the best cavalry in the Persian empire. But he had recently refused to obey an invitation from the court at

<small>Operations of Agesilaus against Pharnabazus.</small>

[1] Xen. Hellen. III. 4, 28, 29; Plutarch, Agesil. c. 10.

Susa, and he now not only welcomed the appearance of Agesilaus, but concluded an alliance with him, strengthening him with an auxiliary body of cavalry and peltasts. Anxious to requite Spithridatês for his services, and vehemently attached to his son, the beautiful youth Megabatês—Agesilaus persuaded Otys to marry the daughter of Spithridatês. He even caused her to be conveyed by sea in a Lacedæmonian trireme—probably from Abydos, to Sinopê.[1]

Reinforced by the Paphlagonian auxiliaries, Agesilaus prosecuted the war with augmented vigour against the satrapy of Pharnabazus. He now approached the neighbourhood of Daskylium, the residence of the satrap himself, inherited from his father Pharnakês, who had been satrap before him. This was a well-supplied country, full of rich villages, embellished with parks and gardens for the satrap's hunting and gratification: the sporting tastes of Xenophon lead him also to remark that there were plenty of birds for the fowler, with rivers full of fish.[2] In this agreeable region Agesilaus passed the winter. His soldiers, abundantly supplied with provisions, became so careless, and straggled with so much contempt of their enemy, that Pharnabazus, with a body of 400 cavalry and two scythed chariots, found an opportunity of attacking 700 of them by surprise; driving them back with considerable loss, until Agesilaus came up to protect them with the hoplites.

*He lays waste the residence of the satrap, and surprises his camp— offence given to Spithridatês.*

This partial misfortune, however, was speedily avenged. Fearful of being surrounded and captured, Pharnabazus

---

[1] Xen. Hellen. iv. 1, 1-15.
The negotiation of this marriage by Agesilaus is detailed in a curious and interesting manner by Xenophon. His conversation with Otys took place in the presence of the thirty Spartan counsellors, and probably in the presence of Xenophon himself.
The attachment of Agesilaus to the youth Megabazus or Megabates, is marked in the Hellenica (iv. 1, 6-28)—but is more strongly brought out in the Agesilaus of

Xenophon (v. 6), and in Plutarch, Agesil. c. 11.
In the retreat of the Ten Thousand Greeks (five years before) along the southern coast of the Euxine, a Paphlagonian prince named Korylas is mentioned (Xen. Anab. v. 5, 22; v. 6, 8). Whether there was more than one Paphlagonian prince—or whether Otys was successor of Korylas—we cannot tell.

[2] Xen. Hellen. iv. 1, 16-33.

refrained from occupying any fixed position. He hovered about the country, carrying his valuable property along with him, and keeping his place of encampment as secret as he could. The watchful Spithridatês, nevertheless, having obtained information that he was encamped for the night in the village of Kanê, about 16 miles distant, Herippidas (one of the thirty Spartans) undertook a night-march with a detachment to surprise him. Two thousand Grecian hoplites, the like number of light-armed peltasts, and Spithridatês with the Paphlagonian horse, were appointed to accompany him. Though many of these soldiers took advantage of the darkness to evade attendance, the enterprise proved completely successful. The camp of Pharnabazus was surprised at break of day; his Mysian advanced guards were put to the sword, and he himself, with all his troops, was compelled to take flight with scarcely any resistance. All his stores, plate, and personal furniture, together with a large baggage-train and abundance of prisoners, fell into the hands of the victors. As the Paphlagonians under Spithridatês formed the cavalry of the victorious detachment, they naturally took more spoil and more prisoners than the infantry. They were proceeding to carry off their acquisitions, when Herippidas interfered and took everything away from them; placing the entire spoil of every description under the charge of Grecian officers, to be sold by formal auction in a Grecian city; after which the proceeds were to be distributed or applied by public authority. The orders of Herippidas were conformable to the regular and systematic proceeding of Grecian officers; but Spithridatês and the Paphlagonians were probably justified by Asiatic practice in appropriating that which they had themselves captured. Moreover, the order, disagreeable in itself, was enforced against them with Lacedæmonian harshness of manner,[1] unaccompanied by any guarantee that they would be allowed, even at last, a fair share of the proceeds. Resenting the conduct of Herippidas as combining injury with insult, they deserted in the night, and fled to Sardis, where the PersianАриæus was in actual revolt against the court of Susa. This was a serious loss, and still more serious chagrin, to Agesilaus. He was not only deprived of valuable auxiliary cavalry,

---

[1] Plutarch, Agesil. c. 11. πικρὸς ὧν ἐξεταστὴς τῶν πλανώντων, &c.

and of an enterprising Asiatic informant; but the report would be spread that he defrauded his Asiatic allies of their legitimate plunder, and others would thus be deterred from joining him. His personal sorrow too was aggravated by the departure of the youth Megabazus, who accompanied his father Spithridatês to Sardis.[1]

Personal conference between Agesilaus and Pharnabazus.

It was towards the close of this winter that a personal conference took place between Agesilaus and Pharnabazus, managed by the intervention of a Greek of Kyzikus named Apollophanês; who was connected by ties of hospitality with both, and served to each as guarantee for the good faith of the other. We have from Xenophon, himself probably present, an interesting detail of this interview. Agesilaus accompanied by his thirty Spartan counsellors, being the first to arrive at the place of appointment, all of them sat down upon the grass to wait. Presently came Pharnabazus, with splendid clothing and retinue. His attendants were beginning to spread fine carpets for him, when the satrap, observing how the Spartans were seated, felt ashamed of such a luxury for himself, and sat down on the grass by the side of Agesilaus. Having exchanged salutes, they next shook hands; after which Pharnabazus, who as the older of the two had been the first to tender his right-hand, was also the first to open the conversation. Whether he spoke Greek well enough to dispense with the necessity of an interpreter, we are not informed. "Agesilaus (said he), I was the friend and ally of you Lacedæmonians while you were at war with Athens: I furnished you with money to strengthen your fleet, and fought with you myself ashore on horseback, chasing your enemies into the sea. You cannot charge me with ever having played you false, like Tissaphernês, either by word or deed. Yet after this behaviour, I am now reduced by you to such a condition, that I have not a dinner in my own territory, except by picking up your leavings, like the beasts of the field. I see the fine residences, parks, and hunting-grounds,

---

[1] Xen. Hellen. iv. 1, 27; Plutarch, Agesil. c. 11.
Since the flight of Spithridatês took place secretly by night, the scene which Plutarch asserts to have taken place between Agesilaus and Megabazus cannot have occurred on the departure of the latter, but must belong to some other occasion; as indeed it seems to be represented by Xenophon (Agesil. v. 4).

bequeathed to me by my father, which formed the charm of my life, cut up or burnt down by you. Is this the conduct of men mindful of favours received, and eager to requite them? Pray answer me this question; for perhaps I have yet to learn what is holy and just."

The thirty Spartan counsellors were covered with shame by this emphatic appeal. They all held their peace; while Agesilaus, after a long pause, at length replied—"You are aware, Pharnabazus, that in Grecian cities, individuals become private friends and guests of each other. Such guests, if the cities to which they belong go to war, fight with each other, and sometimes by accident even kill each other, each in behalf of his respective city. So then it is that we, being at war with your king, are compelled to hold all his dominions as enemy's land. But in regard to you, we would pay any price to become your friends. I do not invite you to accept us as masters, in place of your present master; I ask you to become our ally, and to enjoy your own property as a freeman—bowing before no man and acknowledging no master. Now freedom is in itself a possession of the highest value. But this is not all. We do not call upon you to be a freeman, and yet poor. We offer you our alliance, to acquire fresh territory, not for the king, but for yourself; by reducing those who are now your fellow-slaves to become your subjects. Now tell me—if you thus continue a freeman and become rich, what can you want further to make you a thoroughly prosperous man?"

"I will speak frankly to you in reply (said Pharnabazus). If the king shall send any other general, and put me under him, I shall willingly become your friend and ally. But if he imposes the duty of command on me, so strong is the point of honour, that I shall continue to make war upon you to the best of my power. Expect nothing else."[1]

Agesilaus, struck with this answer, took his hand and said—"Would that with such high-minded sentiments you *could* become our friend! At any rate, let me assure you of this—that I will immediately quit your territory; and

[1] Xen. Hellen. iv. 1, 38. Ἐὰν μέντοι μοι τὴν ἀρχὴν προστάττῃ, τοιοῦτόν τι, ὡς ἔοικε, φιλοτιμία ἐστί, οὐ χρὴ εἰδέναι, ὅτι πολεμήσω ὑμῖν ὡς ἂν δύνωμαι ἄριστα. Compare about φιλοτιμία, Herodot. III. 53.

for the future, even should the war continue, I will respect both you and all your property, as long as I can turn my arms against any other Persians."

Here the conversation closed; Pharnabazus mounted his horse, and rode away. His son by Parapita, however—at that time still a handsome youth—lingered behind, ran up to Agesilaus, and exclaimed—"Agesilaus, I make you my guest." "I accept it with all my heart"—was the answer. "Remember me by this"—rejoined the young Persian—putting into the hands of Agesilaus the fine javelin which he carried. The latter immediately took off the ornamental trappings from the horse of his secretary Idæus, and gave them as a return present, upon which the young man rode away with them, and rejoined his father.[1]

<small>Friendship established between Agesilaus and the son of Pharnabazus—character of Agesilaus.</small> There is a touching interest and emphasis in this interview as described by Xenophon, who here breathes into his tame Hellenic chronicle something of the romantic spirit of the Cyropædia. The pledges exchanged between Agesilaus and the son of Pharnabazus were not forgotten by either. The latter—being in after-days impoverished and driven into exile by his brother, during the absence of Pharnabazus in Egypt—was compelled to take refuge in Greece; where Agesilaus provided him with protection and a home, and even went so far as to employ influence in favour of an Athenian youth, to whom the son of Pharnabazus was attached. This Athenian youth had outgrown the age and size of the boy-runners in the Olympic stadium; nevertheless Agesilaus, by strenuous personal interference, overruled the reluctance of the Eleian judges, and prevailed upon them to admit him as a competitor with the other boys.[2] The stress laid by Xenophon upon this favour illustrates the tone of Grecian sentiment, and shows us the variety of objects which personal ascendency was used to compass. Disinterested in regard to himself, Agesilaus was unscrupulous both in promoting the encroachments, and screening the injustices, of his friends.[3] The unfair privilege which he procured for this youth, though a small thing in itself, could hardly fail to offend a crowd of spectators familiar with the estab-

---

[1] Xen. Hellen. iv. 1, 29-41; Plutarch, Agesil. c. 13, 14; Xen. Agesil. iii. 5.
[2] Xen. Hellen. iv. 1, 40. πάντ' ἐποίησεν, ὅπως ἂν δι' ἐκεῖνον ἐγκριθείη εἰς τὸ στάδιον ἐν Ὀλυμπίᾳ, μέγιστος ὢν παίδων.
[3] Plutarch, Agesil. c. 5-13.

lished conditions of the stadium, and to expose the judges to severe censure.

Quitting the satrapy of Pharnabazus—which was now pretty well exhausted, while the armistice concluded with Tithraustês must have expired—Agesilaus took up his camp near the temple of Artemis, at Astyra in the plain of Thêbê (in the region commonly known as Æolis), near the Gulf of Elæus. He here employed himself in bringing together an increased number of troops with a view to penetrate farther into the interior of Asia Minor during the summer. Recent events had greatly increased the belief entertained by the Asiatics in his superior strength; so that he received propositions from various districts in the interior, inviting his presence, and expressing anxiety to throw off the Persian yoke. He sought also to compose the dissensions and misrule which had arisen out of the Lysandrian Dekarchies in the Greco-Asiatic cities, avoiding as much as possible sharp inflictions of death or exile. How much he achieved in this direction, we cannot tell — nor can it have been possible, indeed, to achieve much, without dismissing the Spartan harmosts and lessening the political power of his own partisans; neither of which he did.

His plans were now all laid for penetrating farther than ever into the interior, and for permanent conquest, if possible, of the western portion of Persian Asia. What he would have permanently accomplished towards this scheme, cannot be determined; for his aggressive march was suspended by a summons home, the reason of which will appear in the next chapter.

Meanwhile Pharnabazus had been called from his satrapy to go and take the command of the Persian fleet in Kilikia and the south of Asia Minor, in conjunction with Konon. Since the revolt of Rhodes from the Lacedæmonians (in the summer of the preceding year 395 B.C.), that active Athenian had achieved nothing. The burst of activity, produced by the first visit of Pharnabazus at the Persian court, had been paralysed by the jealousies of the Persian commanders, reluctant to serve under a Greek—by

B.C. 394.
Promising position and large preparations for Asiatic land-warfare, of Agesilaus—he is recalled with his army to Peloponnesus.

B.C. 394.
Efforts and proceedings of Konon in command of the Persian fleet—his personal visit to the Persian court.

¹ Xen. Hellen. iv. 1, 41; Xen. c. 14, 15; Isokratês, Or. v. (Philipp.) Agesil. i. 28-33; Plutarch, Agesil. s. 100.

peculation of officers who embezzled the pay destined for
the troops—by mutiny in the fleet from absence of pay—
and by the many delays arising while the satraps, unwilling
to spend their own revenues in the war, waited for orders
and remittances from court.[1] Hence Konon had been
unable to make any efficient use of his fleet, during those
months when the Lacedæmonian fleet was increased to
nearly double its former number. At length he resolved
—seemingly at the instigation of his countrymen at home[2]
as well as of Euagoras prince of Salamis in Cyprus, and
through the encouragement of Ktesias, one of the Grecian
physicians resident at the Persian court—on going himself
into the interior to communicate personally with Artaxerxês. Landing on the Kilikian coast, he crossed by land
to Thapsacus on the Euphratês (as the Cyreian army had
marched), from whence he sailed down the river in a boat
to Babylon. It appears that he did not see Artaxerxês,
from repugnance to that ceremony of prostration which
was required from all who approached the royal person.
But his messages, transmitted through Ktesias and others
—with his confident engagement to put down the maritime
empire of Sparta and counteract the projects of Agesilaus,
if the Persian forces and money were put into efficient
action—produced a powerful effect on the mind of the
monarch; who doubtless was not merely alarmed at the
formidable position of Agesilaus in Asia Minor, but also
hated the Lacedæmonians as main agents in the aggressive
enterprise of Cyrus. Artaxerxês not only approved his
views, but made to him a large grant of money, and transmitted peremptory orders to the coast that his officers
should be active in prosecuting the maritime war.

[1] Compare Diodor. xv. 41 ad fin.; and Thucyd. viii. 45.

[2] Isokratês (Or. viii. de Pace, s. 82) alludes to "many embassies" as having been sent by Athens to the king of Persia, to protest against the Lacedæmonian dominion. But this mission of Konon is the only one which we can verify, prior to the battle of Knidus.

Probably Damus the son of Pyri- lampês, an eminent citizen and trierarch of Athens, must have been one of the companions of Konon in this mission. He is mentioned in an oration of Lysias as having received from the Great King a present of a golden drinking-bowl or φιάλη; and I do not know on what other occasion he can have received it, except in this embassy (Lysias, Or. xix. De Bonis Aristoph. s. 27)

What was of still greater moment, Konon was permitted to name any Persian whom he chose, as admiral jointly with himself. It was by his choice that Pharnabazus was called from his satrapy, and ordered to act jointly as commander of the fleet. This satrap, the bravest and most straightforward among all the Persian grandees, and just now smarting with resentment at the devastation of his satrapy[1] by Agesilaus, cooperated heartily with Konon. A powerful fleet, partly Phœnician, partly Athenian or Grecian, was soon equipped, superior in number even to the newly-organized Lacedæmonian fleet under Peisander.[2] Euagoras, prince of Salamis in Cyprus,[3] not only provided many triremes, but served himself personally on board.

*Pharnabazus is named admiral jointly with Konon.*

It was about the month of July, 394 B.C., that Pharnabazus and Konon brought their united fleet to the south-western corner of Asia Minor; first probably to the friendly island of Rhodes, next off Loryma[4] and the mountain called

---

[1] Xen. Hellen. iv. 8, 6.

[2] The measures of Konon and the transactions preceding the battle of Knidus, are very imperfectly known to us; but we may gather them generally from Diodorus, xiv. 81; Justin, vi. 8, 4; Cornelius Nepos, Vit. Conon. c. 2, 8; Ktesias Fragment. c. 63, 64, ed. Bähr.

Isokratês (Orat. iv. (Panegyr.) s. 165: compare Orat. ix. (Euagor.) s. 77) speaks loosely as to the duration of time that the Persian fleet remained blocked up by the Lacedæmonians before Konon obtained his final and vigorous orders from Artaxerxes, unless we are to understand his *three years* as referring to the first news of outfit of ships of war in Phœnicia, brought to Sparta by Hêrodas, as Schneider understands them; and even then the statement that the Persian fleet remained πολιορκούμενον for all this time would be much exaggerated. Allowing for exaggeration, however, Isokratês coincides generally with the authorities above noticed.

It would appear that Ktesias the physician obtained about this time permission to quit the court of Persia, and come back to Greece. Perhaps he may have been induced (like Demokêdês of Kroton 120 years before) to promote the views of Konon in order to get for himself this permission.

In the meagre abstract of Ktesias given by Photius (c. 63) mention is made of some Lacedæmonian envoys who were now going up to the Persian court, and were watched or detained on the way. This mission can hardly have taken place before the battle of Knidus; for then Agesilaus was in the full tide of success, and contemplating the largest plans of aggression against Persia. It must have taken place, I presume, after the battle.

[3] Isokratês, Or. ix. (Euagoras) s. 67. Εὐαγόρου δὲ αὐτόν τε παρασχόντος, καὶ τῆς δυνάμεως τὴν πλείστην παρασκευάσαντος. Compare s. 63 of the same oration. Compare Pausanias, i. 3, 1.

[4] Diodor. xiv. 83. διέτριβον περὶ Δώρυμα τῆς Χερσονήσου.

Dorion on the peninsula of Knidus.¹ Peisander, with the
fleet of Sparta and her allies, sailed out from
Knidus to meet them, and both parties prepared
for a battle. The numbers of the Lacedæmonians are reported by Diodorus eighty-five
triremes; those of Konon and Pharnabazus at
above ninety. But Xenophon, without par-
ticularising the number on either side, seems
to intimate the disparity as far greater; stating
that the entire fleet of Peisander was considerably inferior even to the Grecian division under Konon,
without reckoning the Phœnician ships under Pharna-
bazus.² In spite of such inferiority, Peisander did not
shrink from the encounter. Though a young man without
military skill, he possessed a full measure of Spartan
courage and pride; moreover—since the Spartan maritime
empire was only maintained by the assumed superiority of
his fleet—had he confessed himself too weak to fight, his
enemies would have gone unopposed round the islands to
excite revolt. Accordingly he sailed forth from the harbour
of Knidus. But when the two fleets were ranged to opposite to each other, and the battle was about to commence
—so manifest and alarming was the superiority of the
Athenians and Persians, that his Asiatic allies on the left
division, noway hearty in the cause, fled almost without
striking a blow. Under such discouraging circumstances,
he nevertheless led his fleet into action with the greatest
valour. But his trireme was overwhelmed by numbers,
broken in various places by the beaks of the enemy's ships,
and forced back upon the land, together with a large portion of his fleet. Many of the crews jumped out and got
to land, abandoning their triremes to the conquerors.
Peisander too might have escaped in the same way; but
disdaining either to survive his defeat or to quit his ship,

---

*Marginal note:* B.C. 394. Battle of Knidus—complete defeat of the Lacedæmonian fleet—death of Peisander the admiral.

---

¹ It is hardly necessary to remark, that the word *Chersonesus* here (and in xiv. 89) does not mean the peninsula of Thrace commonly known by that name, forming the European side of the Hellespont —but the peninsula on which Knidus is situated.

¹ Pausan. vi. 3, 4. περὶ Κνίδον καὶ ὅσα τὸ Δώριον ὀνομαζόμενον.

² Xen. Hellen. iv. 8, 12. Φαρνάβαζον, ναύαρχον ὄντα, ἐν ταῖς Φοινίσσαις εἶναι. Κόνωνα δὲ, τὸ Ἑλληνικὸν ἔχοντα, τετάχθαι ἔμπροσθεν αὐτοῦ. Ἀντιπαραταξαμένου δὲ τοῦ Πεισάνδρου, καὶ πολὺ ἐλαττόνων αὐτῷ τῶν νεῶν φανεισῶν τῶν αὐτοῦ τοῦ μετὰ Κόνωνος Ἑλληνικοῦ, &c.

fell gallantly fighting aboard. The victory of Konon and Pharnabazus was complete. More than half of the Spartan ships was either captured or destroyed, though the neighbourhood of the land enabled a large proportion of the crews to escape to Knidus, so that no great number of prisoners were taken.[1] Among the allies of Sparta, the chief loss of course fell upon those who were most attached to her cause; the disaffected or lukewarm were those who escaped by flight at the beginning.

Such was the memorable triumph of Konon at Knidus; the reversal of that of Lysander at Ægospotami eleven years before. Its important effects will be recounted in the coming chapter.

B.C. 394. August 1-8.

[1] Xen. Hellen. iv. 3, 10-14; Diodor. xiv. 83; Cornelius Nepos, Conon, c. 4; Justin, vi. 3.

## CHAPTER LXXIV.

### FROM THE BATTLE OF KNIDUS TO THE REBUILDING OF THE LONG WALLS OF ATHENS.

*War In Central Greece against Sparta— called the Corinthian War.*

HAVING in my last chapter carried the series of Asiatic events down to the battle of Knidus, in the beginning of August, B.C. 394, at which period war was already raging on the other side of the Ægean, in Greece Proper—I now take up the thread of events from a period somewhat earlier, to show how this last-mentioned war, commonly called the Corinthian War, began.

*Relations of Sparta with the neighbouring states and with her allies after the accession of Agesilaus. Discontent among the allies.*

At the accession of Agesilaus to the throne, in 398 B.C., the power of Sparta throughout all Greece from Laconia to Thessaly, was greater than it had ever been, and greater than any Grecian state had ever enjoyed before. The burden of the long war against Athens she had borne in far less proportion than her allies; its fruits she had reaped exclusively for herself. There prevailed consequently among her allies a general discontent, which Thebes as well as Corinth manifested by refusing to take part in the recent expeditions; either of Pausanias against Thrasybulus and the Athenian exiles in Peiræus—or of Agis against the Eleians—or of Agesilaus against the Persians in Asia Minor. The Eleians were completely humbled by the invasions of Agis. All the other cities in Peloponnesus, from apprehension, from ancient habit, and from being governed by oligarchies who leaned on Sparta for support, were obedient to her authority—with the single exception of Argos, which remained, as before, neutral and quiet, though in sentiment unfriendly. Athens was a simple unit in the catalogue of Spartan allies, furnishing her contingent, like the rest, to be commanded by the xenâgus— or officer sent from Sparta for the special purpose of commanding such foreign contingents.

In the northern regions of Greece, the advance of

Spartan power is yet more remarkable. Looking back to the year 419 B.C. (about two years after the peace of Nikias), Sparta had been so unable to protect her colony of Herakleia, in Trachis on the Maliac Gulf, near the strait of Thermopylæ, that the Bœotians were obliged to send a garrison thither, in order to prevent it from falling into the hands of Athens. They even went so far as to dismiss the Lacedæmonian harmost.[1] In the winter of 409-408 B.C., another disaster had happened at Herakleia, in which the Lacedæmonian harmost was slain.[2] But about 399 B.C., we find Sparta exercising an energetic ascendency at Herakleia, and even making that place a central post for keeping down the people in the neighbourhood of Mount Œta and a portion of Thessaly. Herippidas the Lacedæmonian was sent thither to repress some factious movements, with a force sufficient to enable him to overawe the public assembly, to seize the obnoxious party in the place, and to put them to death, 500 in number, outside of the gates.[3] Carrying his arms farther against the Œtæans and Trachinians in the neighbourhood, who had been long at variance with the Laconian colonists at Herakleia, he expelled them from their abodes, and forced them to migrate with their wives and children into Thessaly.[4] Hence the Lacedæmonians were enabled to extent their influence into parts of Thessaly, and to place a harmost with a garrison in Pharsalus, resting upon Herakleia as a basis—which thus became a position of extraordinary importance for their dominion over the northern regions.

With the real power of Sparta thus greatly augmented on land, in addition to her vast empire at sea, bringing its ample influx of tribute—and among cities who had not merely long recognised her as leader, but had never recognised any one else—it required an unusual stimulus to raise any formidable hostile combination against her, notwithstanding a large spread of disaffection and antipathy. The stimulus came from Persia, from whose treasures the means had been before

[1] Thucyd. v. 52.
[2] Xen. Hellen. l. 2, 18.
[3] Diodor. xiv. 88; Polyæn. ii. 21.
[4] Diodorus, ul sup.: compare xiv. 81. τοὺς Τραχινίους φεύγοντας ἐκ τῶν πατρίδων ὑπὸ Λακεδαιμονίων, &c.

furnished to Sparta herself for subduing Athens. The news that a formidable navy was fitting out in Phœnicia, which had prompted the expedition of Agesilaus in the spring of 396 B.C., was doubtless circulated and heard with satisfaction among the Grecian cities unfriendly to Sparta; and the refusal of Thebes, Corinth, and Athens to take service under that prince—aggravated in the case of the Thebans by a positive offence given to him on the occasion of his sacrifice at Aulis—was enough to warn Sparta of the dangerous sentiments and tendencies by which she was surrounded near home.

It was upon these tendencies that the positive instigations and promises of Persia were brought to bear, in the course of the following year; and not merely promises, but pecuniary supplies, with news of revived naval warfare threatening the insular dominion of Sparta. Tithraustês, the new satrap who had put to death and succeeded Tissaphernês, had no sooner concluded the armistice mentioned above, and prevailed upon Agesilaus to remove his army into the satrapy of Pharnabazus, than he employed active measures for kindling war against Sparta in Greece, in order to create a necessity for the recall of Agesilaus out of Asia. He sent a Rhodian named Timokratês into Greece, as envoy to the cities most unfriendly to the Lacedæmonians, with a sum of fifty talents;[1] directing him to employ this money in gaining over the leading men in these cities, and to exchange solemn oaths of alliance and aid with Persia, for common hostility against Sparta. The island of Rhodes, having just revolted from the Spartan dominion, had admitted Konon with the Persian fleet

B.C. 395.
The satrap Tithraustês sends an envoy with money into Greece, to light up war against Sparta—his success at Thebes, Corinth, and Argos.

---

[1] Xen. Hellen. III. 5, 1. Πέμπει Τιμοκράτην 'Ρόδιον ἐς τὴν 'Ελλάδα δοὺς χρυσίον ἐς πεντήκοντα τάλαντα ἀργυρίου, καὶ κελεύει πειράσθαι, πιστὰ τὰ μέγιστα λαμβάνοντα, διδόναι τοῖς προεστηκόσιν ἐν ταῖς πόλεσιν, ἐφ' ᾧ τι πόλεμον ἐξοίσειν πρὸς Λακεδαιμονίους.

Timokratês is ordered to give the money; yet not absolutely, but only on a certain condition, in case he should find that such condition could be realised: that is, if by giving it he could procure from various leading Greeks sufficient assurances and guarantees that they would raise war against Sparta. As this was a matter more or less doubtful, Timokratês is ordered to try to give the money for this purpose. Though the construction of πειράσθαι couples it with διδόναι, the sense of the word more properly belongs to ἐξοίσειν—which designates the purpose to be accomplished.

(as I have mentioned in the last chapter), so that probably the Rhodian envoy was on a mission to Tithraustês on behalf of his countrymen. He was an appropriate envoy on this occasion, as having an animated interest in raising up new enemies to Sparta, and as being hearty in stirring up among the Thebans and Corinthians the same spirit which had led to the revolt of Rhodes. The effect which that revolt produced in alarming and exasperating the Spartans, has been already noticed; and we may fairly presume that its effect on the other side, in encouraging their Grecian enemies, was considerable. Timokratês visited Thebes, Corinth, and Argos, distributing his funds. He concluded engagements, on behalf of the satrap, with various leading men in each, putting them into communication with each other; Ismenias, Androkleidas, and others in Thebes—Timolaus and Polyanthês at Corinth—Kylon and others at Argos. It appears that he did not visit Athens; at least Xenophon expressly says that none of his money went there. The working of this mission—coupled, we must recollect, with the renewed naval warfare on the coast of Asia, and the promise of a Persian fleet against that of Sparta—was soon felt in the more pronounced manifestation of anti-Laconian sentiments in these various cities, and in the commencement of attempts to establish alliance between them.[1]

With that Laconian bias which pervades his Hellenica, Xenophon represents the coming war against Sparta as if it had been brought about mainly by these bribes from Persia to the leading men in these various cities. I have stated on more than one occasion, that the average public morality of Grecian individual politicians, in Sparta, Athens, and other cities, was not such as to exclude personal corruption; that it required a morality higher than the average, when such temptation was resisted—and a morality considerably higher than the average, if it were systematically resisted, and for a long life, as by Periklês and Nikias. There would be nothing therefore surprising, if Ismenias and the rest had received bribes under the circumstances here mentioned. But it appears highly improbable that the money given by Timokratês could have

The Persian money did not create hostility against Sparta, but merely brought out that which was pre-existing. Philo-Laconian sentiment of Xenophon.

[1] Xen. Hellen. iii. 5, 2; Pausan. iii. 9, 4; Plutarch, Artaxerxês, c. 20.

been a bribe; that is, given privately and for the separate use of these leaders. It was furnished for the promotion of a certain public object, which could not be accomplished without heavy disbursements; it was analogous to that sum of thirty talents which (as Xenophon himself tells us) Tithraustês had just given to Agesilaus, as an inducement to carry away his army into the satrapy of Pharnabazus (not as a present for the private purse of the Spartan king, but as a contribution to the wants of the army¹), or to that which the satrap Tiribazus gave to Antalkidas afterwards,² also for public objects. Xenophon affirms, that Ismenias and the rest, having received these presents from Timokratês, accused the Lacedæmonians, and rendered them odious—each in his respective city.³ But it is certain, from his own showing, that the hatred towards them existed in these cities, before the arrival of Timokratês. In Argos, such hatred was of old standing; in Corinth and Thebes, though kindled only since the close of the war, it was not the less pronounced. Moreover Xenophon himself informs us, that the Athenians, though they received none of the money,⁴ were quiteas ready for war as the other cities. If we therefore admit his statement as a matter of fact, that Timokratês gave private presents to various leading politicians, which is by no means improbable—we must dissent from the explanatory use which he makes of this fact, by setting it out prominently as the cause of the war. What these leading men would find it difficult to raise, was, not hatred of Sparta, but confidence and courage to brave the power of Sparta. And for this purpose the mission of Timokratês would be a valuable aid, by conveying assurances of Persian cooperation and support against Sparta. He must have been produced publicly either before the people, the Senate, or at least the great body of the anti-Laconian party in each city. And the money which he brought with him, though a portion of it may

¹ Xen. Hellen. lii. 4, 26.
² Xen. Hellen. iv. 8, 16.
³ Xen. Hellen. III. 5. 1. Οἱ μὲν δὴ δεξάμενοι τὰ χρήματα ἐς τὰς οἰκείας πόλεις διέβαλλον τοὺς Λακεδαιμονίους· ἐπεὶ δὲ ταύτας ἐς μῖσος αὐτῶν προήγαγον, συνίστασαν καὶ τὰς μεγίστας πόλεις πρὸς ἀλλήλας.

⁴ Xenophon, ut sup.
Pausanias (III. 9, 4) names some Athenians as having received part of the money. So Plutarch also, in general terms (Agesil. c. 15).
Diodorus mentions nothing respecting either the mission or the presents of Timokratês.

have gone in private presents, would serve to this party as the best warrant for the sincerity of the satrap. Whatever negotiations may have been in progress between the cities visited by Timokratês, no union had been brought about between them when the war, kindled by an accident, broke out as a "Bœotian War,"[1] between Thebes and Sparta separately. Between the Opuntian Lokrians and the Phokians, north of Bœotia, there was a strip of disputed borderland; respecting which the Phokians, imputing wrongful encroachment to the Lokrians, invaded their territory. The Lokrians, allied with Thebes, entreated her protection; upon which a body of Bœotians invaded Phokis; while the Phokians on their side threw themselves upon Lacedæmon, invoking her aid against Thebes.[2] "The Lacedæmonians (says Xenophon) were delighted to get a pretence for making war against the Thebans—having been long angry with them on several different grounds. They thought that the present was an excellent time for marching against them, and putting down their insolence; since Agesilaus was in full success in Asia, and there was no other war to embarrass them in Greece."[3] The various

*marginal note:* War between Sparta and Thebes— the Bœotian War.

---

[1] Πόλεμος Βοιωτικός (Diodor. xiv. 81).

[2] Xenophon (Hellen. lll. 5, 3) says—and Pausanias (iii. 9, 4) follows him—that the Theban leaders, wishing to bring about a war with Sparta, and knowing that Sparta would not begin it, purposely incited the Lokrians to encroach upon this disputed border, in order that the Phokians might resent it, and that thus a war might be lighted up. I have little hesitation in rejecting this version, which I conceive to have arisen from Xenophon's philo-Laconian and miso-Theban tendency, and in believing that the fight between the Lokrians and Phokians, as well as that between the Phokians and Thebans, arose without any design on the part of the latter to provoke Sparta. So Diodorus recounts it, in reference to the war between the Phokians and the Thebans; for about the Lokrians he says nothing (xiv. 81).

The subsequent events, as recounted by Xenophon himself, show that the Spartans were not only ready in point of force, but eager in regard to will, to go to war with the Thebans; while the latter were not at all ready to go to war with Sparta. They had not a single ally; for their application to Athens, in itself doubtful, was not made until after Sparta had declared war against them.

[3] Xen. Hellen. iii. 5, 5. Οἱ μέντοι Λακεδαιμόνιοι ἄσμενοι ἔλαβον πρόφασιν στρατεύειν ἐπὶ τοὺς Θηβαίους, πάλαι ὀργιζόμενοι αὐτοῖς, τῆς τε ἀντιλήψεως τῆς τοῦ Ἀπόλλωνος δεκάτης ἐν Δεκελείᾳ, καὶ τοῦ ἐπὶ τὸν Πειραιᾶ μὴ ἐθελῆσαι ἀκολουθῆσαι· ᾐτιῶντο δ' αὐτοὺς, καὶ Κορινθίους πεῖσαι μὴ συστρατεύειν.

grounds on which the Lacedæmonians rested their displeasure against Thebes, begin from a time immediately succeeding the close of the war against Athens, and the sentiment was now both established and vehement. It was they who now began the Bœotian war; not the Thebans, nor the bribes brought by Timokratês.

**Active operations of Sparta against Bœotia— Lysander is sent to act from Herakleia on the northward— Pausanias conducts an army from Peloponnesus.**

The energetic and ambitious Lysander, who had before instigated the expedition of Agesilaus across the Ægean, and who had long hated the Thebans—was among the foremost advisers of the expedition now decreed by the Ephors against Thebes,[1] as well as the chief commander appointed to carry it into execution. He was dispatched with a small force to act on the north of Bœotia. He was directed to start from Herakleia, the centre of Lacedæmonian influence in those regions—to muster the Herakleots, together with the various dependent populations in the neighbourhood of Œta, Œtæans, Malians, Ænianes, &c.—to march towards Bœotia, taking up the Phokians in his way—and to attack Haliartus. Under the walls of this town King Pausanias engaged to meet him on a given day, with the native Lacedæmonian force and the Peloponnesian allies. For this purpose, having obtained favourable border sacrifices, he marched forth to Tegea, and there employed himself in collecting the allied contingents from Peloponnesus.[2] But the allies generally were tardy and reluctant in the cause; while the Corinthians withheld all concurrence and support,[3]— though neither did they make any manifestation in favour of Thebes.

Ἀναμιμνήσκοντο δὲ καὶ, ὡς θύοντ' ἐν Αὐλίδι τὸν Ἀγησίλαον οὐκ εἴων, καὶ τὰ τεθυμένα ἱερὰ ὡς ἔρριψεν ἀπὸ τοῦ βωμοῦ· καὶ ὅτι οὐδ' εἰς τὴν Ἀσίαν συνεστράτευον Ἀγησιλάῳ. Ἐλογίζοντο δὲ καὶ καλὸν εἶναι τοῦ ἐξέγειν στρατιὰν ἐπ' αὐτούς, καὶ παῦσαι τῆς ἐς αὐτοὺς ὕβρεως· τά τε γὰρ ἐν τῇ Ἀσίᾳ καλῶς σφίσιν ἔχειν, κρατοῦντος Ἀγησιλάου, καὶ ἐν τῇ Ἑλλάδι οὐδένα ἄλλον πόλεμον ἐμποδὼν σφίσιν εἶναι. Compare vii. 1, 34.

The description here given by Xenophon himself—of the past dealing and established sentiment between Sparta and Thebes—refutes his allegation, that it was the bribes brought by Timokratês to the leading Thebans which first blew up the hatred against Sparta; and shows farther, that Sparta did not need any circuitous manœuvres of the Thebans, to furnish her with a pretext for going to war.

[1] Plutarch, Lysand. c. 28.
[2] Xen. Hellen. iii. 5, 6, 7.
[3] Xen. Hellen. iii. 5, 23.

The conduct of the Corinthians

Finding themselves thus exposed to a formidable attack on two sides, from Sparta at the height of her power, and from a Spartan officer of known ability—being moreover at the same time without a single ally—the Thebans resolved to entreat succour from Athens. A Theban embassy to Athens for any purpose, and especially for this purpose, was itself among the strongest marks of the revolution which had taken place in Grecian politics. *The Thebans apply to Athens for aid—remarkable proof of the altered sentiment in Greece.* The antipathy between the two cities had been so long and virulent, that the Thebans, at the close of the war, had endeavoured to induce Sparta to root out the Athenian population. Their conduct subsequently had been favourable and sympathising towards Thrasybulus in his struggle against the Thirty, and that leader had testified his gratitude by dedicating statues in the Theban Herakleion.[1] But it was by no means clear that Athens would feel herself called upon, either by policy or by sentiment, to assist them in the present emergency; at a moment when she had no Long Walls, no fortifications at Peiræus, no ships, nor any protection against the Spartan maritime power.

It was not until Pausanias and Lysander were both actually engaged in mustering their forces, that the Thebans sent to address the Athenian assembly. The speech of the Theban envoy sets forth strikingly the case against Sparta as it then stood. *Speech of the Theban envoy at Athens.* Disclaiming all concurrence with that former Theban deputy, who, without any instructions, had taken on himself to propose, in the Spartan assembly of allies, extreme severity towards the conquered Athenians —he reminded the Athenians that Thebes had by unanimous voice declined obeying the summons of the Spartans, to aid in the march against Thrasybulus and the Peiræus; and that this was the first cause of the anger of the Spartans against her. On that ground then, he appealed to the gratitude of democratical Athens against the Lacedæmonians. But he likewise invoked against them, with yet greater confidence, the aid of oligarchical Athens—or of those who at that time had stood opposed to Thrasybulus and the Peiræus; for it was Sparta who, after having first

here contributes again to refute the assertion of Xenophon about the effect of the bribes of Timokrates. [1] Pausanias, ix. 11, 4.

set up the oligarchy at Athens, had afterwards refused to
sustain it, and left its partisans to the generosity of their
democratical opponents, by whom alone they were saved
harmless.[1] Of course Athens was eager, if possible (so he
presumed), to regain her lost empire; and in this enterprise
he tendered the cordial aid of Thebes as an ally. He
pointed out that it was by no means an impracticable
enterprise; looking to the universal hatred which Sparta
had now drawn upon herself, not less on the part of ancient
allies than of prior enemies. The Athenians knew by experience that Thebes could be formidable as a foe: she
would now show that she could be yet more effective as a
friend, if the Athenians would interfere to rescue her.
Moreover, she was now about to fight, not for Syracusans
or Asiatics, but for her own preservation and dignity.
"We hesitate not to affirm, men of Athens (concluded the
Theban speaker), that what we are now invoking at your
hands is a greater benefit to you than it is to ourselves."[2]

Political feeling at Athens— good effects of the amnesty after the expulsion of the Thirty.
Eight years had now elapsed since the archonship of
Eukleides and the renovation of the democracy
after the crushing visitation of the Thirty. Yet
we may see, from the important and well-turned
allusion of the Theban speaker to the oligarchical portion of the assembly, that the two parties
still stood in a certain measure distinguished.
Enfeebled as Athens had been left by the war,
she had never since been called upon to take
any decisive and emphatic vote on a question of foreign
policy; and much now turned upon the temper of the oligarchical minority, which might well be conceived likely to
play a party-game and speculate upon Spartan countenance.
But the comprehensive amnesty decreed on the reestablishment of the democratical constitution—and the wise and
generous forbearance with which it had been carried out,
in spite of the most torturing recollections—were now
found to have produced their fruits. Majority and minority—democrats and oligarchs—were seen confounded in

[1] Xen. Hellen. iii. 5, 2.
Πολὺ δ᾽ ἔτι μᾶλλον ἀξιοῦμεν, ὅσοι
τῶν ἐν ἄστει ἐγένεσθε, προθύμως ἐπὶ
τοὺς Λακεδαιμονίους ἰέναι. Ἐκεῖνοι
γάρ, καταστήσαντες ὑμᾶς ἐς ὀλιγαρ-
χίαν καὶ ἐς ἔχθραν τῷ δήμῳ, ἀφικό-
μενοι πολλῇ δυνάμει, ὡς ὑμῖν σύμμαχοι, παρέδοσαν ὑμᾶς τῷ πλήθει·
ὥστε τὸ μὲν ἐπ᾽ ἐκείνοις εἶναι, ἀπο-
λώλατε, ὁ δὲ δῆμος οὑτοσὶ ὑμᾶς
ἔσωσε.

[2] Xen. Hellen. iii. 5, 9, 16.

one unanimous and hearty vote to lend assistance to Thebes, in spite of all risk from hostility with Sparta. We cannot indeed doubt that this vote was considerably influenced also by the revolt of Rhodes, by the re-appearance of Konon with a fleet in the Asiatic seas, and by private communications from that commander intimating his hope of acting triumphantly against the maritime empire of Sparta, through enlarged aid from Persia. The vote had thus a double meaning. It proclaimed not merely the restored harmony between democrats and oligarchs at Athens, but also their common resolution to break the chain by which they were held as mere satellites and units in the regiment of Spartan allies, and to work out anew the old traditions of Athens as a self-acting and primary power, at least—if not once again an imperial power. The vote proclaimed a renovated life in Athens. Its boldness, under the existing weakness of the city, is extolled two generations afterwards by Demosthenês.[1]

After having heard the Theban orator (we are told even by the philo-Laconian Xenophon[2]), "very many Athenian citizens rose and spoke in support of his prayer, and the whole assembly with one accord voted to grant it." Thrasybulus proposed the resolution, and communicated it to the Theban envoys. He told them that Athens knew well the risk which she was incurring while Peiræus was undefended; but that nevertheless she was prepared to show her gratitude by giving more in requital than she had received; for she was prepared to give the Thebans positive aid, in case they were attacked—while the Thebans had done nothing more for *her* than to refuse to join in an aggressive march against her.[3] *Unanimous vote of the Athenians to assist Thebes against Sparta.*

Without such assurance of succour from Athens, it is highly probable that the Thebans might have been afraid to face, single-handed, Lysander and the full force of Sparta.

[1] Demosthen. de Coronâ, c. 78. p. 258; also Philipp. l. c. 7. p. 44. Compare also Lysias, Orat. xvi. (pro Mantitheo, s. 15).
[2] Xen. Hellen. III. 5, 16. Τῶν δ' Ἀθηναίων ἀμπολλοὶ μὲν ξυνηγόρευον, πάντες δ' ἐψηφίσαντο βοηθεῖν αὐτοῖς.
[3] Xen. Hellen. ut sup. Pausanias (III. 9, 6) says that the Athenians sent envoys to the Spartans to entreat them not to act aggressively against Thebes, but to submit their complaint to equitable adjustment. This seems to me improbable. Diodorus (xiv. 81) briefly states the general fact in conformity with Xenophon.

But they now prepared for a strenuous defence. The first approach of Lysander with his army of Herakleots, Phokians, and others, from the north, was truly menacing; the more so, as Orchomenus, the second city next to Thebes in the Bœotian confederacy, broke off its allegiance and joined him. The supremacy of Thebes over the cities composing the Bœotian confederacy appears to have been often harsh and oppressive, though probably not equally oppressive towards all, and certainly not equally odious to all. To Platæa, on the extreme south of Bœotia, it had been long intolerable, and the unhappy fate of that little town has saddened many pages of my preceding volumes. To Orchomenus, on the extreme north, it was also unpalatable—partly because that town stood next in power and importance to Thebes— partly because it had an imposing legendary antiquity, and claimed to have been once the ascendent city receiving tribute from Thebes. The Orchomenians now joined Lysander, threw open to him the way into Bœotia, and conducted him with his army, after first ravaging the fields of Lebadeia, into the district belonging to Haliartus.[1]

Before Lysander quitted Sparta, the plan of operations concerted between him and Pausanias, was that they should meet on a given day in the territory of Haliartus. And in execution of this plan Pausanias had already advanced with his Peloponnesian army as far as Platæa in Bœotia. Whether the day fixed between them had yet arrived, when Lysander reached Haliartus, we cannot determine with certainty. In the imperfection of the Grecian calendar, a mistake on this point would be very conceivable—as had happened between the Athenian generals Hippokratês and Demosthenês in those measures which preceded the battle of Delium in 424 B.C.[2] But the engagement must have been taken by both parties, subject to obstructions in the way—since each would have to march through a hostile country to reach the place of meeting. The words of Xenophon, however, rather indicate that the day fixed had not yet arrived; nevertheless Lysander resolved at once to act against Haliartus, without waiting for Pausanias. There were as yet only a few

[1] Xen. Hellen. III. 5, 17; Plutarch, Lysand. c. 28.
[2] Thucyd. iv. 89. τεκμήνας διαμαρτίας τῶν ἡμερῶν, &c.

Thebans in the town, and he probably had good reason for judging that he would succeed better by rapid measures, before any more Thebans could arrive, than by delaying until the other Spartan army should join him; not to mention anxiety that the conquest should belong to himself exclusively, and confidence arising from his previous success at Orchomenus. Accordingly he addressed an invitation to the Haliartians to follow the example of the Orchomenians, to revolt from Thebes, and to stand upon their autonomy under Lacedæmonian protection. Perhaps there may have been a party in the town disposed to comply. But the majority, encouraged too by the Thebans within, refused the proposition; upon which Lysander marched up to the walls and assaulted the town. He was here engaged, close by the gates, in examining where he could best effect an entrance, when a fresh division of Thebans, apprised of his proceedings, was seen approaching from Thebes, at their fastest pace—cavalry as well as hoplites. They were probably seen from the watch-towers in the city earlier than they became visible to the assailants without; so that the Haliartians, encouraged by the sight, threw open their gates, and made a sudden sally. Lysander, seemingly taken by surprise, was himself slain among the first, with his prophet by his side, by a Haliartian hoplite named Neochôrus. His troops stood some time, against both the Haliartians from the town, and the fresh Thebans who now came up. But they were at length driven back with considerable loss, and compelled to retreat to rugged and difficult ground at some distance in their rear. Here however they made good their position, repelling their assailants with the loss of more than 200 hoplites.[1]

The success here gained, though highly valuable as an encouragement to the Thebans, would have been counterbalanced by the speedy arrival of Pausanias, had not Lysander himself been among the slain. But the death of so eminent a man was an irreparable loss to Sparta. His army, composed of heterogeneous masses, both collected and held together by his personal ascendency, lost confidence and dispersed in the ensuing night.[2] When Pausanias arrived soon afterwards, *Pausanias arrives in Bœotia after the death of Lysander—Thrasybulus and an Athenian army come to the aid of the Thebans.*

[1] Xen. Hellen. lll. 5, 18, 19, 20; Plutarch, Lysand. c. 28, 29; Paus. lll. 5, 4. The two last differ in various matters from Xenophon, whose account however, though brief, seems to me deserve the preference.

[2] Xen. Hellen. lll. 5, 21. ἀσύν-

he found no second army to join with him. Yet his own force was more than sufficient to impress terror on the Thebans, had not Thrasybulus, faithful to the recent promise, arrived with an imposing body of Athenian hoplites, together with cavalry under Orthobulus[1]—and imparted fresh courage as well as adequate strength to the Theban cause.

*Pausanias evacuates Bœotia, on receiving the dead bodies of Lysander and the rest for burial.*

Pausanias had first to consider what steps he would take to recover the bodies of the slain—that of Lysander among them; whether he would fight a battle and thus take his chance of becoming master of the field—or send the usual petition for burial-truce, which always implied confession of inferiority. On submitting the point to a council of officers and Spartan elders, their decision as well as his own was against fighting; not however without an indignant protest from some of the Spartan elders. He considered that the whole original plan of operations was broken up, since not only the great name and genius of Lysander had perished, but his whole army had spontaneously disbanded; that the Peloponnesian allies were generally lukewarm and reluctant, not to be counted upon for energetic behaviour in case of pressing danger; that he had little or no cavalry,[2] while the Theban cavalry was numerous and excellent; lastly, that the dead body of Lysander himself lay so close to the walls of Haliartus, that even if the Lacedæmonians were victorious, they could not carry it off without serious loss from the armed defenders in their towers.[3] Such were the reasons which determined Pausanias and the major part of the council to send and solicit a truce. But the Thebans refused to grant it except on condition that they should immediately evacuate Bœotia. Though such a requisition was contrary to the received practice of Greece,[4] which imposed on the victor

---

λαθόντες ἐν νυκτὶ τούς τε Φωκέας καὶ τοὺς ἄλλους ἅπαντας οἴκαδε ἀπέδοτους, &c.

[1] Lysias, Or. xvi. (pro Mantitheo) s. 13, 14.

[2] Accordingly we learn from an oration of Lysias, that the service of the Athenian horsemen in this expedition, who were commanded by Orthobulus, was judged to be extremely safe and easy; while that of the hoplites was dangerous (Lysias, Orat. xvi. pro Mantith. s. 15).

[3] Xen. Hellen. iii. 5, 23. Κορίνθιοι μὲν πεντέπωσιν οὐκ ἠκολούθουν αὐτοῖς, οἱ δὲ παρόντες οὐ προθύμως στρατεύοιντο, &c.

[4] See the conduct of the Thebans on this very point (of giving up

the duty of granting the burial-truce unconditionally, whenever it was asked, and inferiority thus publicly confessed—nevertheless such was the reluctant temper of the army, that they heard not merely with acquiescence, but with joy,[1] the proposition of departing. The bodies were duly buried—that of Lysander in the territory of Panopê, immediately across the Phokian border, but not far from Haliartus. And no sooner were these solemnities completed, than the Lacedæmonian army was led back to Peloponnesus; their dejection forming a mournful contrast to the triumphant insolence of the Thebans, who watched their march and restrained them, not without occasional blows, from straggling out of the road into the cultivated fields.[2]

The death of Lysander produced the most profound sorrow and resentment at Sparta. On returning thither Pausanias found himself the subject of such virulent accusation, that he thought it prudent to make his escape, and take sanctuary in the temple of Athênê Alea, at Tegea. He was impeached and put on trial, during his absence, on two counts; first, for having been behind the time covenanted, in meeting Lysander at Haliartus; next, for having submitted to ask a truce from the Thebans, instead of fighting battle, for the purpose of obtaining the bodies of the slain.

*Anger against Pausanias at Sparta; he escapes into voluntary exile; he is condemned in his absence.*

As far as there is evidence to form a judgement, it does not appear that Pausanias was guilty upon either of the two counts. The first is a question of fact; and it seems quite as likely that Lysander was before his time, as that Pausanias was behind his time, in arriving at Haliartus. Besides, Lysander, arriving there first, would have been quite safe, had he not resolved to attack without delay; in which the chances of war turned out against him, though the resolution in itself may have been well conceived. Next, as to truce solicited for burying the dead bodies—it does not appear that Pausanias could with any prudence have braved the chances of a battle. The facts of the case—even as summed up by Xenophon, who always exaggerates everything in favour of the Spartans—leed us to this conclusion. A few of the Spartan elders would doubtless prefer perishing on the field of battle, to the

*Condemnation of Pausanias not deserved.*

the slain at the solicitation of the conquered Athenians for burial) after the battle of Delium, and the discussion thereupon—in this History, Ch. IIII.
[1] Xen. Hellen. III. 5, 24. Οἱ δὲ ἄσμενοι τε ταῦτα ἤκουσαν, &c.
[2] Xen. Hellen. III. 5, 24.

humiliation of sending the herald to ask for a truce. But the mischief of fighting a battle under the influence of such a point of honour, to the exclusion of a rational estimate of consequences, will be seen when we come to the battle of Leuktra, where Kleombrotus son of Pausanias was thus piqued into an imprudence (at least this is alleged as one of the motives) to which his own life and the dominion of Sparta became forfeit.[1] Moreover the army of Pausanias, comprising very few Spartans, consisted chiefly of allies who had no heart in the cause, and who were glad to be required by the Thebans to depart. If he had fought a battle and lost it, the detriment to Sparta would have been most serious in every way; whereas, if he had gained a victory, no result would have followed except the acquisition of the bodies for burial; since the execution of the original plan had become impracticable through the dispersion of the army of Lysander.

Though a careful examination of the facts leads us (and seems also to have led Xenophon[2]) to the conclusion that Pausanias was innocent, he was nevertheless found guilty in his absence. He was in great part borne down by the grief felt at Sparta for the loss of Lysander, with whom he had been before in political rivalry, and for whose death he was made responsible. Moreover the old accusation was now revived against him[3]—for which he had been tried, and barely acquitted, eight years before—of having tolerated the re-establishment of the Athenian democracy at a time when he might have put it down. Without doubt this argument told prodigiously against him at the present juncture, when the Athenians had just now, for the first time since the surrender of their city, renounced their subjection to Sparta and sent an army to assist the Thebans in their defence. So violent was the sentiment against Pausanias that he was condemned to death in his

---

[1] Xen. Hellen. vi. 4, 5.

[2] The traveller Pausanias justifies the prudence of his regal namesake in avoiding a battle, by saying that the Athenians were in his rear, and the Thebans in his front; and that he was afraid of being assailed on both sides at once, like Leonidas at Thermopylæ, and like the troops enclosed in Sphakteria (Paus. iii. 5, 6).

But the matter of fact, on which this justification rests, is contradicted by Xenophon, who says that the Athenians had actually joined the Thebans, and were in the same ranks — ἐλθόντες ξυμπαρετάξαντο (Hellen. iii. 5, 22).

[3] Xen. Hellen. iii. 5, 25. Καὶ ὅτι τὸν δῆμον τῶν Ἀθηναίων λαβὼν ἐν τῷ Πειραιεῖ ἀνῆκε, &c. Compare Pausanias, iii. 5, 4.

absence, and passed the remainder of his life as an exile in sanctuary at Tegea. His son Agesipolis was invested with the sceptre in his place.

A brief remark will not be here misplaced. On no topic have Grecian historians been more profuse in their reproaches, than upon the violence and injustice of democracy, at Athens and elsewhere, in condemning unsuccessful, but innocent generals. Out of the many cases in which this reproach is advanced, there are very few wherein it has been made good. But even if we grant it to be valid against Athens and her democracy, the fate of Pausanias will show us that the Ephors and Senate of anti-democratical Sparta were capable of the like unjust misjudgement. Hardly a single instance of Athenian condemnation occurs, which we can so clearly prove to be undeserved, as this of a Spartan king.

*Sparta not less unjust in condemning unsuccessful generals than Athens.*

Turning from the banished king to Lysander—the Spartans had indeed valid reasons for deploring the fall of the latter. He had procured for them their greatest and most decisive victories, and the time was coming when they needed his services to procure them more; for he left behind him no man of equal warlike resource, cunning, and power of command. But if he possessed those abilities which powerfully helped Sparta to triumph over her enemies, he at the same time did more than any man to bring her empire into dishonour and to render its tenure precarious. His decemviral governments or Dekarchies, diffused through the subject cities, and each sustained by a Lacedæmonian harmost and garrison, were aggravations of local tyranny such as the Grecian world had never before undergone. And though the Spartan authorities presently saw that he was abusing the imperial name of the city for unmeasured personal aggrandisement of his own, and partially withdrew their countenance from his Dekarchies—yet the general character of their empire still continued to retain the impress of partisanship and subjugation which he had originally stamped upon it. Instead of that autonomy which Sparta had so repeatedly promised, it became subjection every way embittered. Such an empire was pretty sure to be short-lived; but the loss to Sparta herself, when her empire fell away, is not the only

*Character of Lysander —his mischievous influence, as well for Sparta, as for Greece generally.*

fault which the historian of Greece has to impute to Lysander. His far deeper sin consists in his having thrown away an opportunity—such as never occurred either before or afterwards—for organizing some permanent, honourable, self-maintaining, Pan-hellenic combination under the headship of Sparta. This is (as I have before remarked) what a man like Kallikratidas would have attempted, if not with far-sighted wisdom, at least with generous sincerity, and by an appeal to the best veins of political sentiment in the chief city as well as in the subordinates. It is possible that with the best intentions even he might have failed; so strong was the centrifugal instinct in the Grecian political mind. But what we have to reproach in Lysander is, that he never tried; that he abused the critical moment of cure for the purpose of infusing new poison into the system; that he not only sacrificed the interests of Greece to the narrow gains of Sparta, but even the interests of Sparta to the still narrower monopoly of dominion in his own hands. That his measures worked mischievously not merely for Greece, but for Sparta herself, aggravating all her bad tendencies—has been already remarked in the preceding pages.

That Lysander, with unbounded opportunities of gain, both lived and died poor, exhibits the honourable side of his character. Yet his personal indifference to money seems only to have left the greater space in his bosom for that thirst of power which made him unscrupulous in satiating the rapacity, as well as in upholding the oppressions, of coadjutors like the Thirty at Athens and the Decemvirs in other cities. In spite of his great success and ability in closing the Peloponnesian war, we shall agree with Pausanias[1] that he was more mischievous than profitable even to Sparta,—even if we take no thought of Greece generally. What would have been the effect produced by his projects in regard to the regal succession, had he been able to bring them to bear, we have no means of measuring. We are told that the discourse composed and addressed to him by the Halikarnassian rhetor Kleon, was found after his death among his papers by Agesilaus; who first learnt from it, with astonishment and alarm, the point to which the ambition of Lysander had tended, and was desirous of exposing his real character by making the discourse public

*His plans to make himself king at Sparta—discourse of the sophist Kleon.*

[1] Pausanias, ix. 52, l.

—but was deterred by the dissuasive counsel of the Ephor Lakratidas. But this story (attested by Ephorus[1]) looks more like an anecdote of the rhetorical schools than like a reality. Agesilaus was not the man to set much value on sophists or their compositions, nor is it easy to believe that he remained so long ignorant of those projects which Lysander had once entertained but subsequently dropped. Moreover the probability is, that Kleon himself would make the discourse public as a sample of his own talents, even in the lifetime of Lysander; not only without shame, but as representing the feelings of a considerable section of readers throughout the Grecian world.

Most important were the consequences which ensued from the death of Lysander and the retreat of Pausanias out of Bœotia. Fresh hope and spirits were infused into all the enemies of Sparta. An alliance was immediately concluded against her by Thebes, Athens, Corinth, and Argos. Deputies from these four cities were appointed to meet at Corinth, and to take active measures for inviting the cooperation of fresh allies; so that the war which had begun as a Bœotian war, now acquired the larger denomination of a Corinthian war, under which it lasted until the peace of Antalkidas. The alliance was immediately strengthened by the junction of the Eubœans—the Akarnanians—the Ozolian Lokrians—Ambrakia and Leukas (both particularly attached to Corinth),—and the Chalkidians of Thrace.[2]

*B.C. 395-394. Encouragement to the enemies of Sparta, from the death of Lysander—alliance against her between Thebes, Athens, Corinth, and Argos—the Eubœans and others join the alliance.*

We now enter upon the period when, for the first time, Thebes begins to step out of the rank of secondary powers, and gradually raises herself into a primary and ascendent city in Grecian politics. Throughout the Peloponnesian War, the Thebans had shown themselves excellent soldiers both on horseback and on foot, as auxiliaries to Sparta. But now the city begins to have a policy of its own, and individual citizens of ability become conspicuous. While waiting for Pelopidas and Epaminondas, with whom we shall presently become acquainted, we have at the present moment Ismenias; a wealthy The-

*Increased importance of Thebes —she now rises to the rank of a primary power—the Theban leader Ismenias.*

[1] Ephorus, Fr. 127, ed. Didot; Plutarch, Lysander, c. 30.   [2] Diodor. xiv. 81, 82; Xen. Hellen. iv. 2, 17.

ban, a sympathiser with Thrasybulus and the Athenian
exiles eight years before, and one of the great organizers
of the present anti-Spartan movement; a man, too, honoured
by his political enemies,[1] when they put him to death
fourteen years afterwards, with the title of "a great wicked
man,"—the same combination of epithets which Clarendon
applies to Oliver Cromwell.

*Successful operations of Ismenias to the north of Bœotia—capture of Herakleia from Sparta.*

It was Ismenias, who, at the head of a body of Bœotians
and Argeians, undertook an expedition to put
down the Spartan influence in the regions north
of Bœotia. At Pharsalus in Thessaly, the Lacedæmonians
had an harmost and garrison; at
Pheræ, Lykophron the despot was their ally:
while Larissa, with Medius the despot, was their
principal enemy. By the aid of the Bœotians,
Medius was now enabled to capture Pharsalus; Larissa,
with Krannon and Skotussa, was received into the Theban
alliance,[2] and Ismenias obtained also the more important
advantage of expelling the Lacedæmonians from Herakleia.
Some malcontents, left after the violent interference of the
Spartan Herippidas two years before, opened the gates of
Herakleia by night to the Bœotians and Argeians. The
Lacedæmonians in the town were put to the sword, but
the other Peloponnesian colonists were permitted to retire
in safety; while the old Trachinian inhabitants, whom the
Lacedæmonians had expelled to make room for their new
settlers—together with the Œtæans, whom they had driven
out of the districts in the neighbourhood—were now called
back to repossess their original homes.[3] The loss of
Herakleia was a serious blow to the Spartans in those
regions—protecting Eubœa in its recent revolt from them,
and enabling Ismenias to draw into his alliance the neighbouring
Malians, Ænianês, and Athamanês—tribes stretching
along the valley of the Spercheius westward to the
vicinity of Pindus. Assembling additional troops from
these districts (which, only a few months before, had
supplied an army to Lysander[4]), Ismenias marched against

---

[1] Xen. Hellen. v. 2, 36. 'Ὁ δ'
(Ἰσμηνίας) ἀπελογεῖτο μὲν πρὸς πάντα
ταῦτα, οὐ μέντοι ἐπειθέ γε τὸ μὴ οὐ
μεγαλοπράγμων τε καὶ κακοπράγμων
εἶναι.

It is difficult to make out anything
from the two allusions in Plato,
except that Ismenias was a wealthy
and powerful man (Plato, Menon,
p. 90 B.; Republ. l. p. 336 A.).

[2] Diodor. xiv. 82; Xen. Hellen.
iv. 3, 8; Xen. Agesil. ii. 2.

[3] Diodor. xiv. 38-82.

[4] Xenoph. Hellen. iii. 5, 4.

## RECALL OF AGESILAUS.

the Phokians, among whom the Spartan Lakisthenês had been left as harmost in command. After a severe battle, this officer with his Phokians were defeated near the Lokrian town of Naryx; and Ismenias came back victorious to the synod at Corinth.[1]

By such important advantages, accomplished during the winter of 395-394 B.C., the prospects of Grecian affairs as they stood in the ensuing spring became materially altered. The allies assembled at Corinth full of hope, and resolved to levy a large combined force to act against Sparta; who on her side seemed to be threatened with the loss of all her extra-Peloponnesian land-empire. Accordingly the Ephors determined to recall without delay Agesilaus with his army from Asia, and sent Epikydidas with orders to that effect. But even before this reinforcement could arrive, they thought it expedient to muster their full Peloponnesian force and to act with vigour against the allies at Corinth, who were now assembling in considerable numbers. Aristodemus—guardian of the youthful King Agesipolis son of Pausanias, and himself of the Eurystheneid race—marched at the head of a body of 6000 Lacedæmonian hoplites:[2] the Spartan xenâgi (or officers sent on purpose to conduct the contingents from the outlying allies), successively brought in 3000 hoplites from Elis, Triphylia, Akroreia, and Lasion —1500 from Sikyon—3000 from Epidaurus, Trœzen,

*B.C. 394. Synod of anti-Spartan allies at Corinth—their confident hopes—the Lacedæmonians send to recall Agesilaus from Asia.*

---

[1] Diodor. xiv. 82.
[2] Xen. Hellen. iv. 2, 16. Xenophon gives this total of 6000 as if it were of Lacedæmonians alone. But if we follow his narrative, we shall see that there were unquestionably in the army troops of Tegea, Mantineia, and the Achæan towns (probably also some of other Arcadian towns), present in the battle (iv. 2, 13, 18, 20). Can we suppose that Xenophon meant to include these allies in the total of 6000, along with the Lacedæmonians— which is doubtless a large total for Lacedæmonians alone? Unless this supposition be admitted, there is no resource except to assume an omission, either of Xenophon himself, or of the copyists; which omission in fact Gail and others do suppose. On the whole, I think they are right; for the number of hoplites on both sides would otherwise be prodigiously unequal; while Xenophon says nothing to imply that the Lacedæmonian victory was gained in spite of great inferiority of number, and something which even implies that it must have been nearly equal (iv. 2, 13)—though he is always disposed to compliment Sparta wherever he can.

Hermionê, and Halieis. None were sent from Phlius, on the plea (true or false¹) that in that city the moment was one of solemnity and holy truce. There were also hoplites from Tegea, Mantineia, and the Achæan towns, but their number is not given; so that we do not know the full muster-roll on the Lacedæmonian side. The cavalry, 600 in number, were all Lacedæmonian; there were moreover 300 Kretan bowmen—and 400 slingers from different rural districts of Triphylia.²

<small>Large muster near Corinth of Spartans and Peloponnesians on one side, of anti-Spartan allies on the other.</small>

The allied force of the enemy was already mustered near Corinth: 6000 Athenian hoplites—7000 Argeian—5000 Bœotian, those from Orchomenus being absent—3000 Corinthian—3000 from the different towns of Eubœa; making 24,000 in all. The total of cavalry was 1550: composed of 800 Bœotian, 600 Athenian, 100 from Chalkis in Eubœa, and 50 from the Lokrians. The light troops also were numerous —partly Corinthian, drawn probably from the serf-population which tilled the fields³—partly Lokrians, Malians, and Akarnanians.

<small>Boldness of the language against Sparta— speech of the Corinthian Timolaus.</small>

The allied leaders, holding a council of war to arrange their plans, came to a resolution that the hoplites should not be drawn up in deeper files than sixteen men,⁴ in order that there might be no chance of their being surrounded; and that the right wing, carrying with it command for the time, should be alternated from day to day between the different cities. The confidence which the events of the last few months had infused into these

---

¹ From a passage which occurs somewhat later (iv. 4, 15), we may suspect that this was an excuse, and that the Phliasians were not very well affected to Sparta. Compare a similar case of excuse ascribed to the Mantineians (v. 2, 2).

² Diodorus (xiv. 83) gives a total of 23,000 foot and 500 horse on the Lacedæmonian side, but without enumerating items. On the side of the confederacy he states a total of more than 15,000 foot and 500 horse (c. 82).

³ Xen. Hellen. iv. 2, 17. Καὶ φιλὸν δὲ, ξὺν τοῖς τῶν Κορινθίων, πλέον ἦν, &c. Compare Hesychius, v. Κυνόφαλοι; Welcker, Præfat. ad Theognidem, p.xxxv; K. O. Müller, History of the Dorians, iii. 4, 8.

⁴ Xen. Hellen. iv. 2, 13; compare iv. 2, 18—where he says of the Thebans — ἀμελήσαντες τοῦ ἐς ἀκριβείαν, βαθεῖαν παντελῶς ἐποιήσαντο τὴν φάλαγγα, &c., which implies and alludes to the resolution previously taken.

## ADVANCE OF THE SPARTANS.

leaders, now for the first time acting against their old leader Sparta, is surprising. "There is nothing like marching to Sparta (said the Corinthian Timolaus) and fighting the Lacedæmonians at or near their own home. We must burn out the wasps in their nest, without letting them come forth to sting us. The Lacedæmonian force is like that of a river; small at its source, and becoming formidable only by the affluents which it receives, in proportion to the length of its course."[1] The wisdom of this advice was remarkable: but its boldness was yet more remarkable, when viewed in conjunction with the established feeling of awe towards Sparta. It was adopted by the general council of the allies; but unfortunately the time for executing it had already passed; for the Lacedæmonians were already in march and had crossed their own border. They took the line of road by Tegea and Mantineia (whose troops joined the march), and advanced as far as Sikyon, where probably all the Arcadian and Achæan contingents were ordered to rendezvous.

The troops of the confederacy had advanced as far as Nemea when they learnt that the Lacedæmonian army was at Sikyon; but they then altered their plan, and confined themselves to the defensive. The Lacedæmonians on their side crossed over the mountainous post called Epieikia, under considerable annoyance from the enemy's light troops, who poured missiles upon them from the high ground. But when they had reached the level country, on the other side, along the shore of the Saronic Gulf, where they probably received the contingents from Epidaurus, Trœzen, Herminonê, and Halieis—the whole army thus reinforced marched forward without resistance, burning and ravaging the cultivated lands. The confederates retreated before them, and at length took up a position close to Corinth, amidst some rough ground with a ravine in their front.[2] The Lace-

*The allied Spartan allies take up a defensive position near Corinth—advance of the Lacedæmonians to attack them.*

---

[1] Xen. Hellen. iv. 2, 11, 12.
[2] Xen. Hellen. iv. 2, 14, 15.
In the passage—καὶ οἱ ἕτεροι μέντοι ἐλθόντες κατεστρατοπεδεύσαντο, ἔμπροσθεν χαράδραν τὴν χαράδραν—I apprehend that ἐκλιθέντες (which is sanctioned by four MSS., and preferred by Launclavius) is the proper reading, in place of ἐλθόντες. For it seems certain that the march of the confederates was one of retreat, and that the battle was fought very near to the walls of Corinth; since the defeated troops sought shelter within the town, and the Lacedæmonian pur-

dæmonians advanced forward until they were little more
than a mile distant from this position, and there encamped.

After an interval seemingly of a few days, the Bœotians, on the day when their turn came to occupy
the right wing and to take the lead, gave the
signal for battle.¹ The Lacedæmonians, prevented by the wooded ground from seeing
clearly, were only made aware of the coming
attack by hearing the hostile pæan. Taking
order of battle immediately, they advanced
forward to meet the assailants, when within a
furlong of their line. In each army, the right

*Battle of
Corinth—
victory of
the Lace-
dæmonians
in their
part of the
battle;
their allies
in the other
parts being
worsted.*

sners were so close upon them,
that the Corinthians within were
afraid to keep open the gates.
Hence we must reject the statement of Diodorus—that the battle
was fought on the banks of the
river Nemea (xiv. 83) as erroneous.

There are some difficulties and
obscurities in the description which
Xenophon gives of the Lacedæmonian march. His words run—ἐν
τούτῳ οἱ Λακεδαιμόνιοι, καὶ δὴ Τε-
γεάτας παρειληφότες καὶ Μαντινέας,
ἐξῄεσαν τὴν ἀμφίαλον. These
last three words are not satis-
factorily explained. Weiske and
Schneider construe τὴν ἀμφίαλον
(very justly) as indicating the
region lying immediately on the
Peloponnesian side of the isthmus
of Corinth, and having the Saronic
Gulf on one side, and the Corinthian Gulf on the other; in which
was included Sikyon. But then it
would not be correct to say, that
"the Lacedæmonians had gone out
by the bimarine way." On the
contrary, the truth is, that "they
had gone out into the bimarine
road or region"—which meaning
however would require a proposition—ἐξῄεσαν εἰς τὴν ἀμφίαλον.
Sturz in his Lexicon (v. ἐξιέναι)
renders τὴν ἀμφίαλον—viam ad mare
—which seems an extraordinary
sense of the word, unless instances
were produced to support it; and

even if instances were produced,
we do not see why the way from
Sparta to Sikyon should be called
by that name; which would more
properly belong to the road from
Sparta down the Eurotas to Helos.

Again, we do not know distinctly
the situation of the point or district
called τὴν Ἐπιεικίαν (mentioned
again, iv. 4, 19). But it is certain
from the map that when the confederates were at Nemea, and the
Lacedæmonians at Sikyon—the
former must have been exactly
placed so as to intercept the junction of the contingents from Epidaurus, Trœzen, and Hermionê,
with the Lacedæmonian army. To
secure this junction, the Lacedæmonians were obliged to force their
way across that mountainous region
which lies near Kleônæ and Nemea,
and to march in a line pointing
from Sikyon down to the Saronic
Gulf. Having reached the other
side of these mountains near the
sea, they would be in communication with Epidaurus and the other
towns of the Argolic peninsula.

The line of march which the
Lacedæmonians would naturally
take from Sparta to Sikyon and
Lechæum, by Tegea, Mantineia,
Orchomenus, &c., is described two
years afterwards in the case of
Agesilaus (iv. 5, 19).

¹ Xen. Hellen. iv. 2, 18. The

division took the lead—slanting to the right, or keeping the left shoulder forward, according to the tendency habitual with Grecian hoplites, through anxiety to keep the right or unshielded side from being exposed to the enemy, and at the same time to be protected by the shield of a right-hand neighbour.[1] The Lacedæmonians in the one army, and the Thebans in the other, each inclined themselves, and caused their respective armies to incline also, in a direction slanting to the right, so that the Lacedæmonians on their side considerably outflanked the Athenians on the opposite left. Out of the ten tribes of Athenian hoplites, it was only the six on the extreme left who came into conflict with the Lacedæmonians; while the remaining four contended with the Tegeans who stood next to the Lacedæmonians on their own line. But the six extreme Athenian tribes were completely beaten, and severely handled, being taken in flank as well as in front by the Lacedæmonians. On the other hand, the remaining four Athenian tribes vanquished and drove before them the Tegeans; and generally, along all the rest of the line, the Thebans, Argeians, and Corinthians were victorious— except where the troops of the Achæan Pellênê stood opposed to those of the Bœotian Thespiæ, where the battle was equal and the loss severe on both sides. The victorious confederates however were so ardent and incautious in pursuit, as to advance a considerable distance and return with disordered ranks; while the Lacedæmonians, who

---

[1] colouring which Xenophon puts upon this step is hardly fair to the Thebans, as is so constantly the case throughout his history. He says that "they were in no hurry to fight" (οὐδέν τι κατήπειγον τὴν μάχην {ωδατων} so long as they were on the left, opposed to the Lacedæmonians on the opposite right; but that as soon as they were on the right (opposed to the Achæans on the opposite left), they forthwith gave the word. Now it does not appear that the Thebans had any greater privilege on the day when they were on the right, than the Argeians or Athenians had when each were on the right respectively. The command had been determined to reside in the right division, wich post alternated from one to the other: why the Athenians or Argeians did not make use of this post to order the attack, we cannot explain.

So again, Xenophon says, that in spite of the resolution taken by the Council of War to have files sixteen deep, and no more—the Thebans made their files much deeper. Yet it is plain, from his own account, that no mischievous consequences turned upon this greater depth.

[2] See the instructive description of the battle of Mantineia—in Thucyd. v. 71.

were habitually self-restraining in this particular, kept their order perfectly, attacking the Thebans, Argeians, and Corinthians to great advantage when returning to their camp. Several of the Athenian fugitives obtained shelter within the walls of Corinth: in spite of the opposition of the philo-Laconian Corinthians, who insisted upon shutting the gates against them, and opening negotiations with Sparta. The Lacedæmonians however came so near, that it was at last thought impossible to keep the gates open longer. Many of the remaining confederates were therefore obliged to be satisfied with the protection of their ancient camp;[1] which seems however to have been situated in such defensible ground,[2] that the Lacedæmonians did not molest them in it.

*Lacedæmonian ascendency within Peloponnesus is secured, but no farther result gained.*
So far as the Lacedæmonians separately were concerned, the battle of Corinth was an important victory, gained (as they affirmed) with the loss of only eight men, and inflicting heavy loss upon the Athenians in the battle, as well as upon the remaining confederates in their return from pursuit. Though the Athenian hoplites suffered thus severely, yet Thrasybulus their commander,[3] who kept the field until the last, with strenuous efforts to rally them, was not satisfied with their behaviour. But on the other hand, all the allies of Sparta were worsted, and a considerable number of them slain. According to Diodorus, the total loss on the Lacedæmonian side was 1100; on the side of the confederates, 2600.[4] On the whole, the victory of the Lacedæmonians was not sufficiently decisive to lead to important results, though it completely secured their ascendency within Peloponnesus. We observe

---

[1] Xen. Hellen. iv. 2, 20-23. The allusion to this incident in Demosthenes (adv. Leptinem, a. 13. p. 472) is interesting, though indistinct.

[2] Xen. Hellen. iv. 2, 19. καὶ γάρ ἦν λάσιον τὸ χωρίον—which illustrates the expression in Lysias, Orat. xvi. (pro Mantitheo) s. 20. ἐν Κορίνθῳ χωρίων ἰσχυρῶν κατειλημμένων.

[3] Lysias, Orat. xvi. (pro Mantitheo) s. 19.

Plato in his panegyrical discourse (Menexenus, c. 17. p. 245 E.) ascribes the defeat and loss of the Athenians to "bad ground"—χρησαμένων δυσχωρίᾳ.

[4] Diodor. xiv. 83. The statement in Xenophon (Agesil. vii. 5) that near 10,000 men were slain on the side of the confederates, is a manifest exaggeration; if indeed the reading be correct.

here, as we shall have occasion to observe elsewhere, that the Peloponnesian allies do not fight heartily in the cause of Sparta. They seem bound to her more by fear than by affection.

The battle of Corinth took place about July 394 B.C., seemingly about the same time as the naval battle near Knidus (or perhaps a little earlier), and while Agesilaus was on his homeward march after being recalled from Asia. Had the Lacedæmonians been able to defer the battle until Agesilaus had come up so as to threaten Bœotia on the northern side, their campaign would probably have been much more successful. As it is, their defeated allies doubtless went home in disgust from the field of Corinth, so that the confederates were now enabled to turn their whole attention to Agesilaus.

B.C. 394.

That prince had received in Asia his summons of recall from the Ephors with profound vexation and disappointment, yet at the same time with patriotic submission. He had augmented his army, and was contemplating more extensive schemes of operations against the Persian satrapies in Asia Minor. He had established such a reputation for military force and skill, that numerous messages reached him from different inland districts, expressing their anxiety to be emancipated from Persian dominion, and inviting him to come to their aid. His ascendency was also established over the Grecian cities on the coast, whom he still kept under the government of partisan oligarchies and Spartan harmosts—yet seemingly with greater practical moderation, and less licence of oppression, than had marked the conduct of these men when they could count upon so unprincipled a chief as Lysander. He was thus just now not only at a high pitch of actual glory and ascendency, but nourishing yet brighter hopes of farther conquests for the future. And what filled up the measure of his aspirations—all these conquests were to be made at the expense, not of Greeks, but of the Persian. He was treading in the footsteps of Agamemnon, as Pan-hellenic leader against a Pan-hellenic enemy.

Agesilaus—his vexation on being recalled from Asia—his large plans of Asiatic conquest.

All these glorious dreams were dissipated by Epikydidas, with his sad message, and peremptory summons, from the Ephors. In the chagrin and disappointment of Agesilaus we can sincerely sympathise; but the panegyric

which Xenophon and others pronounce upon him for his
ready obedience is altogether unreasonable.[1]
There was no merit in renouncing his projects
of conquest at the bidding of the Ephors; because,
if any serious misfortune had befallen
Sparta at home, none of those projects could have
been executed. Nor is it out of place to remark,
that even if Agesilaus had not been recalled,
the extinction of the Lacedæmonian naval superiority by
the defeat of Knidus would have rendered all large plans
of inland conquest impracticable. On receiving his orders
of recall, he convened an assembly both of his allies and
of his army, to make known the painful necessity of his
departure; which was heard with open and sincere manifestations
of sorrow. He assured them that as soon as he
had dissipated the clouds which hung over Sparta at home,
he should come back to Asia without delay, and resume
his efforts against the Persian satraps; in the interim he
left Euxenus, with a force of 4000 men, for their protection.
Such was the sympathy excited by his communication,
combined with esteem for his character, that the cities
passed a general vote to furnish him with contingents of
troops for his march to Sparta. But this first burst of
zeal abated, when they came to reflect, that it was a service
against Greeks; not merely unpopular in itself, but presenting
a certainty of hard fighting with little plunder.
Agesilaus tried every means to keep up their spirits, by
proclaiming prizes both to the civic soldiers and to the
mercenaries, to be distributed at Sestos in the Chersonesus,
as soon as they should have crossed into Europe:
prizes for the best equipment, and best-disciplined soldiers
in every different arm.[2] By these means he prevailed
upon the bravest and most effective soldiers in his army to
undertake the march along with him; among them many
of the Cyreians, with Xenophon himself at their head.

*Regret of the Asiatic allies when he quits Asia—he leaves Euxenus in Asia with 4000 men.*

[1] Xen. Agesil. i. 37; Plutarch, Agesil. c. 15. Cornelius Nepos (Agesilaus, c. 4) almost translates the Agesilaus of Xenophon; but we can better feel the force of his panegyric, when we recollect that he had had personal cognisance of the disobedience of Julius Cæsar in his province to the orders of the Senate, and that the omnipotence of Sylla and Pompey in their provinces was then matter of recent history. "Cujus exemplum (says Cornelius Nepos about Agesilaus) utinam imperatores nostri sequi voluissent!"

[2] Xen. Hellen. iv. 2, 1-5; Xen. Agesil. i. 38; Plutarch, Agesil. c. 15.

Though Agesilaus, in leaving Greece, had prided himself on hoisting the flag of Agamemnon, he was now destined against his will to tread in the footsteps of the Persian Xerxes in his march from the Thracian Chersonese through Thrace, Macedonia, and Thessaly, to Thermopylæ and Bœotia. Never since the time of Xerxes had any army undertaken this march; which now bore an Oriental impress, from the fact that Agesilaus brought with him some camels, taken in the battle of Sardis.[1] Overawing or defeating the various Thracian tribes, he reached Amphipolis on the Strymon, where he was met by Derkyllidas, who had come fresh from the battle of Corinth and informed him of the victory. Full as his heart was of Panhellenic projects against Persia, he burst into exclamations of regret on hearing of the deaths of so many Greeks in battle, who could have sufficed, if united, to emancipate Asia Minor.[2] Sending Derkyllidas forward to Asia to make known the victory to the Grecian cities in his alliance, he pursued his march through Macedonia and Thessaly. In the latter country, Larissa, Krannon, and other cities in alliance with Thebes, raised opposition to bar his passage. But in the disunited condition of this country, no systematic resistance could be organized against him. Nothing more appeared than detached bodies of cavalry, whom he beat and dispersed, with the death of Polycharmus their leader. As the Thessalian cavalry however was the best in Greece, Agesilaus took great pride in having defeated them with cavalry disciplined by himself in Asia; backed however, it must be observed, by skillful and effective support from his hoplites.[3] After having passed the Achæan mountains or the line of Mount Othrys, he marched the rest of the way without opposition, through the strait of Thermopylæ to the frontier of Phokis and Bœotia.

In this latter part of his march, Agesilaus was met by the Ephor Diphridas in person, who urged him to hasten his march as much as possible and attack the Bœotians. He was further joined by two Lacedæmonian regiments[4]

B.C. 394.
Agesilaus crosses the Hellespont and marches homeward through Thrace, Macedonia, and Thessaly.

[1] Xen. Hellen. III. 4, 24.
[2] Xen. Agesil. vii. 5; Plutarch, Agesil. c. 16.
[3] Xen. Hellen. iv. 2, 4-8; Diodor. xiv. 83.
[4] Plutarch (Agesil. c. 17; compare also Plutarch, Apopth. p. 786, as corrected by Morus ad Xen.

from Corinth, and by fifty young Spartan volunteers as a body-guard, who crossed by sea from Sikyon. He was reinforced also by the Phokians and the Orchomenians—in addition to the Peloponnesian troops who had accompanied him to Asia, the Asiatic hoplites, the Cyreians, the peltasts, and the cavalry, whom he had brought with him from the Hellespont, and some fresh troops collected in the march. His army was thus in imposing force when he reached the neighbourhood of Chæroneia on the Bœotian border. It was here that they were alarmed by an eclipse of the sun, on the 14th of August, 394 B.C.; a fatal presage, the meaning of which was soon interpreted for them by the arrival of a messenger bearing news of the naval defeat of Knidus, with the death of Peisander, brother-in-law of Agesilaus. Deeply was the latter affected with this irreparable blow. He foresaw that, when known, it would spread dismay and dejection among his soldiers, most of whom would remain attached to him only so long as they believed the cause of Sparta to be ascendent and profitable.¹ Accordingly, he resolved, being now within a day's march of his enemies, to hasten on a battle without making known the bad news. Proclaiming that intelligence had been received of a seafight having taken place, in which the Lacedæmonians had been victorious, though Peisander himself was slain—he offered a sacrifice of thanksgiving and sent round presents of congratulation; which produced an encouraging effect, and made the skirmishers especially both forward and victorious.

To his enemies, now assembled in force on the plain of Koroneia, the real issue of the battle of Knidus was doubtless made known, spreading hope and cheerfulness through their ranks; though we are not informed what interpretation they

Hellen. iv. 3, 15) states two more or regiments as having joined Agesilaus from Corinth: Xenophon alludes only to one, besides that more which was in garrison at Orchomenus (Hellen. iv. 3, 15; Agesil. ii. 6).

¹ Xen. Hellen. iv. 3, 13.
Ὁ μὲν οὖν Ἀγησίλαος εὐθόμενος ταῦτα, τὸ μὲν πρῶτον χαλεπῶς ἔφερεν· ἐπεὶ μέντοι ἀνεθυμήθη, ὅτι τοῦ στρατεύματος τὸ πλεῖστον εἴη αὐτῷ, οἷον ἀγαθῶν μὲν γιγνομένων ἡδέως μετέχειν, εἰ δέ τι χαλεπὸν ὁρῷεν, οὐκ ἀνάγκη εἶναι κοινωνεῖν αὐτοῖς, &c. These indirect intimations of the real temper even of the philo-Spartan allies towards Sparta are

put upon the solar eclipse. The army was composed of nearly the same contingents as those who had recently fought at Corinth, except that we hear of the Æniânês in place of the Malians; but probably each contingent was less numerous, since there was still a necessity for occupying and defending the camp near Corinth. Among the Athenian hoplites, who had just been so roughly handled in the preceding battle, and who were now drafted off by lot to march into Bœotia, against both a general and an army of high reputation—there prevailed much apprehension and some reluctance; as we learn from one of them, Mantitheus, who stood forward to volunteer his services, and who afterwards makes just boast of it before an Athenian dikastery.[1] The Thebans and Bœotians were probably in full force, and more numerous than at Corinth, since it was their own country which was to be defended. The camp was established in the territory of Korôneia, not far from the great temple of Itonian Athênê, where the Pambœotia, or general Bœotian assemblies, were held, and where there also stood the trophy erected for the great victory over Tolmidês and the Athenians, about fifty years before.[2] Between the two armies there was no great difference of numbers, except as to the peltasts, who were more numerous in the army of Agesilaus, though they do not seem to have taken much part in the battle.

Having marched from Chæroneia, Agesilaus approached the plain of Koroneia from the river Kephissus, while the Thebans met him from the direction of Mount Helikon. He occupied the right wing of his army, the Orchomenians being on the left, and the Cyreians with the Asiatic allies in the centre. In the opposite line, the Thebans were on the right, and the Argeians on the left. Both armies approached slowly and in silence until they were separated only by an interval of a furlong, at which moment the Thebans on the right began the war-shout, and accelerated their

Battle of Koroneia— Agesilaus with most of his army is victorious; while the Thebans on their side are also victorious.

very valuable when coming from Xenophon, as they contradict all his partialities, and are dropped here almost reluctantly, from the necessity of justifying the conduct of Agesilaus in publishing a false proclamation to his army.

[1] Lysias, Orat. xvi. (pro Mantitheo) s. 20. φοβουμένων ἀπάντων αὐτοὺς, &c.

[2] Plutarch, Agesil. c. 19.

march to a run; the rest of the line following their example. When they got within half a furlong of the Lacedæmonians, the centre division of the latter under the command of Herippidas (comprising the Cyreians, with Xenophon himself, and the Asiatic allies) started forward on their side, and advanced at a run to meet them; seemingly getting beyond their own line,[1] and coming first to cross spears with the enemy's centre. After a sharp struggle, the division of Herippidas was here victorious, and drove back its opponents. Agesilaus on his right was yet more victorious, for the Argeians opposed to him fled without even crossing spears. These fugitives found safety on the high ground of Mount Helikon. But on the other hand, the Thebans on their own right, completely beat back the Orchomenians, and pursued them so far as to get to the baggage in the rear of the army. Agesilaus, while his friends around were congratulating him as conqueror, immediately wheeled round to complete his victory by attacking the Thebans; who on their side also faced about, and prepared to fight their way, in close and deep order, to rejoin their comrades on Helikon. Though Agesilaus might have let them pass, and assailed them in the rear with greater safety and equal effect, he preferred the more honourable victory of a conflict face to face. Such is the colouring which his panegyrist Xenophon[2] puts upon his manœuvre. Yet we may remark that if he had let the Thebans pass, he could not have pursued them far, seeing that their own comrades were at hand to sustain them —and also that having never yet fought against the Thebans, he had probably no adequate appreciation of their prowess.

*Terrible combat between the Thebans and Spartans: on the whole, the result is favourable to the Thebans.*
The crash which now took place was something terrific beyond all Grecian military experience,[3] leaving an indelible impression upon Xenophon who was personally engaged in it. The hoplites on both sides came to the fiercest and closest bodily struggle, pushing shields against each other, with all the weight of the incumbent mass behind impelling forward the foremost ranks— especially in the deep order of the Thebans.

---

[1] Xen. Hellen. iv. 8, 17. ἀντεξέδραμον ἀπὸ τῆς Ἀγησιλάου φάλαγγος, &c.

[2] Xen. Hellen. iv. 3, 19; Xen. Agesil. II. 12.

[3] Xen. Hellen. iv. 3, 16; Xen. Agesil. II. 9. Διηγήσομαι δὲ καὶ τὴν μάχην καὶ

The shields of the foremost combatants were thus stove in, their spears broken, and each man was engaged in such close embrace with his enemy, that the dagger was the only weapon which he could use. There was no systematic shout, such as usually marked the charge of a Grecian army ; the silence was only broken by a medley of furious exclamations and murmurs.[1] Agesilaus himself, who was among the front ranks, and whose size and strength were by no means on a level with his personal courage, had his body covered with wounds from different weapons[2]—was trodden down—and only escaped by the devoted courage of those fifty Spartan volunteers who formed his body-guard. Partly from his wounds, partly from the irresistible courage and stronger pressure of the Thebans, the Spartans were at length compelled to give way, so far as to afford a free passage to the former, who were thus enabled to march onward and rejoin their comrades; not without sustaining some loss by attacks on their rear.[3]

Agesilaus thus remained master of the field of battle, having gained a victory over his opponents taken collectively. But so far as concerns the Thebans separately, he had not only gained no victory, but had failed in his purpose of stopping their progress, and had had the worst of the combat. His wounds having been dressed, he was brought back on men's shoulders to give his final orders, and was then informed that a detachment of 80 Theban hoplites, left behind by the rest, had taken refuge in the temple of Itonian Athênê as suppliants. From generosity mingled with respect to the sanctity of the spot, he commanded that they should be dismissed unhurt, and then proceeded to give directions for the nightwatch, as it was already late. The field of battle presented a terrible spectacle: Spartan and Theban dead lying intermingled, some yet grasping their naked daggers, others pierced with the daggers of their enemies;

*Victory of Agesilaus, not without severe wounds — yet not very decisive — his conduct after the battle.*

γὰρ ἐγένετο οἵα οὐκ ἄλλη τῶν γ' ἐφ' ἡμῶν.

[1] Xen. Hellen. iv. 3, 19; Xen. Agesil. ii. 12.

Καὶ συμβαλόντες τὰς ἀσπίδας ἐωθοῦντο, ἐμάχοντο, ἀπέκτεινον, ἀπέθνησκον. Καὶ κραυγὴ μὲν οὐδεμία παρῆν, οὐ μὴν οὐδὲ σιγή· φωνὴ δὲ τις ἦν τοιαύτη, οἵαν ὀργή τε καὶ μάχη παράσχοιτ᾽ ἄν.

[2] Xen. Agesil. ii. 13. Ὁ δὲ, καίπερ πολλὰ τραύματα ἔχων πάντοσε καὶ παντοίοις ὅπλοις, &c.

Plutarch, Agesil. c. 18.

[3] Xen. Hellen. iv. 3, 19; Xen. Agesil. ii. 12.

around, on the blood-stained ground, were seen broken spears, smashed shields, swords and daggers scattered apart from their owners.[1] He directed the Spartan and Theban dead to be collected in separate heaps, and placed in safe custody for the night, in the interior of his phalanx: the troops then took their supper, and rested for the night. On the next morning, Gylis the Polemarch was ordered to draw up the army in battle-array, to erect a trophy, and to offer sacrifices of cheerfulness and thanksgiving, with the pipers solemnly playing, according to Spartan fashion. Agesilaus was anxious to make these demonstrations of victory as ostentatious as possible, because he really doubted whether he had gained a victory. It was very possible that the Thebans might feel confidence enough to renew the attack, and try to recover the field of battle, with their own dead upon it; which Agesilaus had, for that reason, caused to be collected in a separate heap and placed within the Lacedæmonian lines.[2] He was however soon relieved from doubt by a herald coming from the Thebans to solicit the customary truce for the burial of their dead; the understood confession of defeat. The request was immediately granted; each party paid the last solemnities to its own dead, and the Spartan force was then withdrawn from Bœotia. Xenophon does not state the loss on either side, but Diodorus gives it at 600 on the side of the confederates, 350 on that of the Lacedæmonians.[3]

Disqualified as he was by his wounds for immediate action, Agesilaus caused himself to be carried to Delphi, where the Pythian games were at that moment going on. He here offered to Apollo the tithe of the booty acquired during his two years' campaigns in Asia; a tithe equal

[1] Xen. Agesil. ii. 14. Ἐπεὶ γε μὴν ἐλήξεν ἡ μάχη, παρῆν δὴ θεάσασθαι ἔνθα συνέπεσον ἀλλήλοις, τὴν μὲν γῆν αἵματι πεφυρμένην, νεκροὺς δὲ πολεμίους φιλίους καὶ πολεμίους μετ' ἀλλήλων, ἀσπίδας δὲ διατεθρυμμένας, δόρατα συντεθραυσμένα, ἐγχειρίδια γυμνὰ κουλεῶν τὰ μὲν χαμαὶ, τὰ δ' ἐν μετὰ χειρός.
[2] Xen. Agesil. ii. 15. Τότε μὲν οὖν (καὶ γὰρ ἦν ἤδη ὀψὲ) συνελκύσαντες τοὺς τῶν πολεμίων νε-
ρους εἴσω φάλαγγος, ἐδειπνοποιήσαντο καὶ ἐκοιμήθησαν.
Schneider in his note on this passage, as well as ad Xen. Hellen. iv. 3, 21—condemns the expression τῶν πολεμίων as spurious and unintelligible. But in my judgement, these words bear a plain and appropriate meaning, which I have endeavoured to give in the text. Compare Plutarch, Agesil. c. 19.
[3] Diodor. xiv. 84.

to 100 talents.[1] Meanwhile the polemarch Gylis conducted the army first into Phokis, next on a predatory excursion into the Lokrian territory, where the nimble attack of the Lokrian light troops, amidst hilly ground, inflicted upon his troops a severe check, and cost him his life. After this the contingents in the army were dismissed to their respective homes, and Agesilaus himself, when tolerably recovered, sailed with the Peloponnesians homeward from Delphi across the Corinthian Gulf.[2] He was received at Sparta with every demonstration of esteem and gratitude, which was still farther strengthened by his exemplary simplicity and exact observance of the public discipline; an exactness not diminished either by long absence or enjoyment of uncontrolled ascendency. From this time forward he was the effective leader of Spartan policy, enjoying an influence greater than had ever fallen to the lot of any king before. His colleague Agesipolis, both young and of feeble character, was won over by his judicious and conciliatory behaviour, into the most respectful deference.[3]

*Army of Agesilaus withdraws from Bœotia—he goes to the Pythian games—sails homeward across the Corinthian Gulf—his honourable reception at Sparta.*

Three great battles had thus been fought in the space of little more than a month (July and August)—those of Corinth, Knidus, and Korôneia; the first and third on land, the second at sea, as described in my last chapter. In each of the two land-battles the Lacedæmonians had gained a victory: they remained masters of the field, and were solicited by the enemy to grant the burial-truce. But if we enquire what results these victories had produced, the answer must be that both were totally barren. The position of Sparta in Greece as against their enemies had undergone no improvement. In the battle of Corinth, her soldiers had indeed manifested signal superiority, and acquired much honour. But at the field of Korôneia, the honour of the day was rather on the side of the Thebans, who broke

B.C. 594.

*Results of the battles of Corinth and Korôneia. Sparta had gained nothing by the former, and had rather lost by the latter.*

---

[1] Xen. Hellen. iv. 3, 21; Plutarch, Agesil. c. 19. The latter says—εἰς Δελφοὺς ἀνασωθεὶς Πυθίων ἀγομένων, &c. Manso, Dr. Arnold, and others, contest the accuracy of Plutarch in this assertion respecting the time of year at which the Pythian games were celebrated, upon grounds which seem to me very insufficient.

[2] Xen. Hellen. iv. 3, 22, 23; iv. 4, 1.

[3] Plutarch, Agesil. c. 19, 20; Xen. Hellen. v. 3, 20.

through the most strenuous opposition, and carried their
point of joining their allies. And the purpose of Agesilaus
(ordered by the Ephor Diphridas) to invade Bœotia, completely failed.¹ Instead of advancing, he withdrew back
from Koroneia, and returned to Peloponnesus across the
Gulf from Delphi; which he might have done just as well
without fighting this murderous and hardly contested battle.
Even the narrative of Xenophon, deeply coloured as it is
both by his sympathies and his antipathies, indicates to us
that the predominant impression carried off by every one
from the field of Koroneia was that of the tremendous force
and obstinacy of the Theban hoplites—a foretaste of what
was to come at Leuktra!

If the two land victories of Sparta were barren of
results, the case was far otherwise with her naval
defeat at Knidus. That defeat was pregnant
with consequences following in rapid succession,
and of the most disastrous character. As with
Athens at Ægospotami—the loss of her fleet,
serious as that was, served only as the signal for
countless following losses. Pharnabazus and
Konon, with their victorious fleet, sailed from
island to island, and from one continental seaport
to another, in the Ægean, to expel the Lacedæmonian harmosts, and terminate the empire
of Sparta. So universal was the odium which it had inspired, that the task was found easy beyond expectation.
Conscious of their unpopularity, the harmosts in almost
all the towns, on both sides of the Hellespont, deserted
their posts and fled, on the mere news of the battle of
Knidus.² Everywhere Pharnabazus and Konon found
themselves received as liberators, and welcomed with
presents of hospitality. They pledged themselves not to
introduce any foreign force or governor, nor to fortify any
separate citadel, but to guarantee to each city its own
genuine autonomy. This policy was adopted by Pharnabazus at the urgent representation of Konon, who warned
him that if he manifested any design of reducing the cities
to subjection, he would find them all his enemies; that each

---

¹ Plutarch, Agesil. c. 17. Cornelius Nepos, Agesil. c. 4. "Ob-
sistere ei conati sunt Athenienses
et Bœoti," &c. But they did more
than endeavour: they succeeded in
barring his way, and compelling
him to retreat.

² Xenoph. Hellen. iv. 8, 1-5.

of them severally would cost him a long siege; and that a combination would ultimately be formed against him. Such liberal and judicious ideas, when seen to be sincerely acted upon, produced a strong feeling of friendship and even of gratitude, so that the Lacedæmonian maritime empire was dissolved without a blow, by the almost spontaneous movements of the cities themselves. Though the victorious fleet presented itself in many different places, it was nowhere called upon to put down resistance, or to undertake a single siege. Kos, Nisyra, Teos, Chios, Erythræ, Ephesus, Mitylênê, Samos, all declared themselves independent, under the protection of the new conquerors.[1] Pharnabazus presently disembarked at Ephesus and marched by land northward to his own satrapy; leaving a fleet of forty triremes under the command of Konon.

To this general burst of anti-Spartan feeling, Abydos, on the Asiatic side of the Hellespont, formed the solitary exception. That town, steady in hostility to Athens,[2] had been the great military station of Sparta for her northern Asiatic warfare, during the last twenty years. It was in the satrapy of Pharnabazus, and had been made the chief place of arms by Derkyllidas and Agesilaus, for their warfare against that satrap as well as for the command of the strait. Accordingly, while it was a main object with Pharnabazus to acquire possession of Abydos—there was nothing which the Abydenês dreaded so much as to become subject to him. In this view they were decidedly disposed to cling to Lacedæmonian protection; and it happened by a fortunate accident for Sparta that the able and experienced Derkyllidas was harmost in the town at the moment of the battle of Knidus. Having fought in the battle of Corinth, he had been sent to announce the news to Agesilaus, whom he had met on his march at Amphipolis, and who had sent him forward into Asia to communicate the victory to the allied cities;[3] neither of them at that moment anticipating

*Abydos holds faithfully to Sparta, under Derkyllidas.*

---

[1] Xen. Hellen. iv. 8, 1-3; Diodor. xiv. 84. About Samos, xiv. 97.

Compare also the speech of Derkyllidas to the Abydenês (Xen. Hellen. iv. 8, 4)—"Ὅσῳ δὴ μᾶλλον αἱ ἄλλαι πόλεις ξὺν τῇ τύχῃ ἀπεστράφησαν ἡμῶν, τοσούτῳ ὄντως ἡ ὑμετέρα πιστότης μείζων φανείη ἄν,

&c.

[2] Ἐκ γὰρ Ἀβύδου, τῆς τὸν ἅπαντα χρόνον ὑμῖν ἐχθρᾶς—says Demosthenes in the Athenian assembly (cont. Aristokrat. c. 89. p. 672; compare c. 82. p. 688).

[3] Xen. Hellen. iv. 8, 2.

the great maritime defeat then impending. The presence in Abydos of such an officer—who had already acquired a high military reputation in that region, and was at marked enmity with Pharnabazus—combined with the standing apprehensions of the Abydenês—was now the means of saving a remnant at least of maritime ascendency to Sparta. During the general alarm which succeeded the battle of Knidus, when the harmosts were everywhere taking flight, and when anti-Spartan manifestations, often combined with internal revolutions to overthrow the Dekarchs or their substitutes, were spreading from city to city—Derkyllidas assembled the Abydenês, heartened them up against the reigning contagion, and exhorted them to earn the gratitude of Sparta by remaining faithful to her while others were falling off; assuring them that she would still be found capable of giving them protection. His exhortations were listened to with favour. Abydos remained attached to Sparta, was put in a good state of defence, and became the only harbour of safety for the fugitive harmosts out of the other cities, Asiatic and European.

*Derkyllidas holds both Abydos and the Chersonesus opposite, in spite of Pharnabazus— anger of the latter.*

Having secured his hold upon Abydos, Derkyllidas crossed the strait to make sure also of the strong place of Sestos, on the European side, in the Thracian Chersonese.[1] In that fertile peninsula there had been many new settlers, who had come in and acquired land under the Lacedæmonian supremacy, especially since the building of the cross-wall by Derkyllidas to defend the isthmus against Thracian invasion. By means of these settlers, dependent on Sparta for the security of their tenures—and of the refugees from various cities all concentrated under his protection—Derkyllidas maintained his position effectively both at Abydos and at Sestos; defying the requisition of Pharnabazus that he should forthwith evacuate them. The satrap threatened war, and actually ravaged the lands round Abydos; but without any result. His wrath against the Lacedæmonians, already

[1] Lysander, after the victory of Ægospotami and the expulsion of the Athenians from Sestos, had assigned the town and district as a settlement for the pilots and Kelusta aboard his fleet. But the Ephors are said to have reversed the assignment, and restored the town to the Sestians (Plutarch, Lysand. c. 14). Probably however the new settlers would remain in part upon the lands vacated by the expelled Athenians.

considerable, was so aggravated by disappointment when he found that he could not yet expel them from his satrapy, that he resolved to act against them with increased energy, and even to strike a blow at them near their own home. For this purpose he transmitted orders to Konon to prepare a commanding naval force for the ensuing spring, and in the mean time to keep both Abydos and Sestos under blockade.[1]

As soon as spring arrived, Pharnabazus embarked on board a powerful fleet equipped by Konon; directing his course to Melos, to various islands among the Cycladês, and lastly to the coast of Peloponnesus. They here spent some time on the coast of Laconia and Messenia, disembarking at several points to ravage the country. They next landed on the island of Kythêra, which they captured, granting safe retirement to the Lacedæmonian garrison, and leaving in the island a garrison under the Athenian Nikophêmus. Quitting then the harbourless, dangerous, and ill-provided coast of Laconia, they sailed up the Saronic Gulf to the Isthmus of Corinth. Here they found the confederates—Corinthian, Bœotian, Athenian, &c.—carrying on war, with Corinth as their central post, against the Lacedæmonians at Sikyon. The line across the isthmus from Lechæum to Kenchreæ (the two ports of Corinth) was now made good by a defensive system of operations, so as to confine the Lacedæmonians within Peloponnesus; just as Athens, prior to her great losses in 446 B.C., while possessing both Megara and Pegæ, had been able to maintain the inland road midway between them, where it crosses the high and difficult crest of Mount Geraneia, thus occupying the only three roads by which a Lacedæmonian army could march from the Isthmus of Corinth into Attica or Bœotia.[2] Pharnabazus communicated in the most friendly manner with the allies, assured them of his strenuous support against Sparta, and left with them a considerable sum of money.[3]

---

[1] Xen. Hellen. iv. 8, 4—6.
[2] See Sir William Gell's Itinerary of Greece, p. 4. Ernst Curtius—Peloponnesos—p. 25, 20, and Thucyd. i. 106.
[3] Xen. Hellen. iv. 8, 7, 8; Diodor. xiv. 84.

*Assistance and encouragement given by Pharnabazus to the allies at Corinth—remarkable fact of a Persian satrap and fleet at Corinth.*

The appearance of a Persian satrap with a Persian fleet, as master of the Peloponnesian sea and the Saronic Gulf, was a phænomenon astounding to Grecian eyes. And if it was not equally offensive to Grecian sentiment, this was in itself a melancholy proof of the degree to which Panhellenic patriotism had been stifled by the Peloponnesian War and the Spartan empire. No Persian tiara had been seen near the Saronic Gulf since the battle of Salamis; nor could anything short of the intense personal wrath of Pharnabazus against the Lacedæmonians, and his desire to revenge upon them the damage inflicted by Derkyllidas and Agesilaus, have brought him now as far away from his own satrapy. It was this wrathful feeling of which Konon took advantage to procure from him a still more important boon.

*B.C. 395. Pharnabazus leaves the fleet with Konon in the Saronic Gulf, and aids him with money to rebuild the Long Walls of Athens.*

Since 404 B.C., a space of eleven years, Athens had continued without any walls round her seaport town Peiræus, and without any Long Walls to connect her city with Peiræus. To this state she had been condemned by the sentence of her enemies, in the full knowledge that she could have little trade—few ships either armed or mercantile—poor defence even against pirates, and no defence at all against aggression from the mistress of the sea. Konon now entreated Pharnabazus, who was about to go home, to leave the fleet under his command, and to permit him to use it in rebuilding the fortifications of Peiræus as well as the Long Walls of Athens. While he engaged to maintain the fleet by contributions from the islands, he assured the satrap that no blow could be inflicted upon Sparta so destructive or so mortifying, as the renovation of Athens and Peiræus with their complete and connected fortifications. Sparta would thus be deprived of the most important harvest which she had reaped from the long struggle of the Peloponnesian War. Indignant as he now was against the Lacedæmonians, Pharnabazus sympathised cordially with these plans, and on departing not only left the fleet under the command of Konon, but also furnished him with a considerable sum of money towards the expense of the fortifications.[1]

[1] Xen. Hellen. iv. 8, 9, 10.

Konon betook himself to the work energetically and without delay. He had quitted Athens in 407 B.C., as one of the joint admirals nominated after the disgrace of Alkibiadês. He had parted with his countrymen finally at the catastrophe of Ægospotami in 405 B.C., preserving the miserable fraction of eight or nine ships out of that noble fleet which otherwise would have passed entire into the hands of Lysander. He now returned, in 393 B.C., as a second Themistoklês, the deliverer of his country, and the restorer of her lost strength and independence. All hands were set to work; carpenters and masons being hired with the funds furnished by Pharnabazus, to complete the fortifications as quickly as possible. The Bœotians and other neighbours lent their aid zealously as volunteers¹—the same who eleven years before had danced to the sound of joyful music when the former walls were demolished; so completely had the feelings of Greece altered since that period. By such hearty cooperation, the work was finished during the course of the present summer and autumn without any opposition; and Athens enjoyed again her fortified Peiræus and harbour, with a pair of Long Walls, straight and parallel, joining it securely to the city. The third or Phalêric Wall (a single wall stretching from Athens to Phalêrum), which had existed down to the capture of the city by Lysander, was not restored; nor was it indeed by any means necessary to the security either of the city or of the port. Having thus given renewed life and security to Peiræus, Konon commemorated his great naval victory by a golden wreath in the acropolis, as well as by the erection of a temple in Peiræus to the honour of the Knidian Aphroditê, who was worshipped at Knidus with peculiar devotion by the local population.² He farther celebrated the completion of the walls by a splendid sacrifice and festival banquet. And the Athenian people not only inscribed on a pillar a public vote gratefully

Konon rebuilds the Long Walls —hearty cooperation of the allies.

¹ Xen. Hellen. iv. 8, 10; Diodor. xiv. 85.
Cornelius Nepos (Conon, c. 4) mentions fifty talents as a sum received by Konon from Pharnabazus as a present, and devoted by him to this public work. This is not improbable; but the total sum contributed by the satrap towards the fortifications must probably have been much greater.
² Demosthen. cont. Androtion. p. 616. c. 21. Pausanias (i. 1, 8) still saw this temple in Peiræus—very near to the sea; 550 years afterwards.

recording the exploits of Konon, but also erected a statue to his honour.¹

**Great importance of this restoration— how much it depended upon accident.**
The importance of this event in reference to the future history of Athens was unspeakable. Though it did not restore to her either her former navy, or her former empire, it reconstituted her as a city not only self-determining but even partially ascendent. It re-animated her, if not into the Athens of Periklês, at least into that of Isokratês and Demosthenês: it imparted to her a second fill of strength, dignity, and commercial importance, during the half century destined to elapse before she was finally overwhelmed by the superior military force of Macedon. Those who recollect the extraordinary stratagem whereby Themistoklês had contrived (eighty-five years before) to accomplish the fortification of Athens, in spite of the base but formidable jealousy of Sparta and her Peloponnesian allies, will be aware how much the consummation of the Themistoklean project had depended upon accident. Now, also, Konon in his restoration was favoured by unusual combinations such as no one could have predicted. That Pharnabazus should conceive the idea of coming over himself to Peloponnesus with a fleet of the largest force, was a most unexpected contingency. He was influenced neither by attachment to Athens, nor seemingly by considerations of policy, though the proceeding was one really conducive to the interests of Persian power—but simply by his own violent personal wrath against the Lacedæmonians. And this wrath would probably have been satisfied, if, after the battle of Knidus, he could have cleared his own satrapy of them completely. It was his vehement impatience, when he found himself unable to expel his old enemy Derkyllidas from the important position of Abydos, which chiefly spurred him on to take revenge on Sparta in her own waters. Nothing less than the satrap's personal presence would have placed at the disposal of Konon either a sufficient naval force, or sufficient funds, for the erection of the new walls, and the defiance of all impediment from Sparta. So strangely did events thus run, that the energy, by which Derkyllidas preserved Abydos, brought upon Sparta, indirectly, the greater mischief of

¹ Demosthen. cont. Leptin. c. 10. p. 477, 478; Athenæus, L 3; Cornelius Nepos, Conon, c. 4.

the new Kononian walls. It would have been better for Sparta that Pharnabazus should at once have recovered Abydos as well as the rest of his satrapy; in which case he would have had no wrongs remaining unavenged to incense him, and would have kept on his own side of the Ægean; feeding Konon with a modest squadron sufficient to keep the Lacedæmonian navy from again becoming formidable on the Asiatic side, but leaving the walls of Peiræus (if we may borrow an expression of Plato) "to continue asleep in the bosom of the earth."[1]

But the presence of Konon with his powerful fleet was not the only condition indispensable to the accomplishment of this work. It was requisite further that the interposition of Sparta should be kept off not merely by sea, but by land—and that too during all the number of months that the walls were in progress. Now the barrier against her on land was constituted by the fact, that the confederate force held the cross line within the isthmus from Lechæum to Kenchreæ, with Corinth as a centre.[2] But they were unable to maintain this line even through the ensuing year—during which Sparta, aided by dissensions at Corinth, broke through it, as will appear in the next chapter. Had she been able to break through it while the fortifications of Athens were yet incomplete, she would have deemed no effort too great to effect an entrance into Attica and interrupt the work, in which she might very probably have succeeded. Here then was the second condition, which was realised during the summer and autumn of 393 B.C., but which did not continue to be realised longer. So fortunate was it for Athens, that the two conditions were fulfilled both together during this particular year!

*Maintenance of the lines of Corinth against Sparta, was one essential condition to the power of rebuilding the Long Walls. The lines were not maintained longer than the ensuing year.*

[1] Plato, Legg. vi. p. 778. καθάπερ ἐάν ἐν τῇ γῇ κατακείμενα τὰ τείχη, &c.

[2] The importance of maintaining these lines, as a protection to Athens against invasion from Sparta, is illustrated in Xenoph. Hellen. v. 4, 19, and Andokides, Or. iii. De Pace, s. 30.

## CHAPTER LXXV.

### FROM THE REBUILDING OF THE LONG WALLS OF ATHENS TO THE PEACE OF ANTALKIDAS.

THE presence of Pharnabazus and Konon with their commanding force in the Saronic Gulf, and the liberality with which the former furnished pecuniary aid to the latter for rebuilding the full fortifications of Athens, as well as to the Corinthians for the prosecution of the war—seem to have given preponderance to the confederates over Sparta for that year. The plans of Konon[1] were extensive. He was the first to organise, for the defence of Corinth, a mercenary force which was afterwards improved and conducted with greater efficiency by Iphikratês; and after he had finished the fortifications of Peiræus with the Long Walls, he employed himself in showing his force among the islands, for the purpose of laying the foundations of renewed maritime power for Athens. We even hear that he caused an Athenian envoy to be despatched to Dionysius at Syracuse, with the view of despatching that despot from Sparta, and bringing him into connexion with Athens. Evagoras, despot of Salamis in Cyprus, the steady friend of Konon, was a party to this proposition, which he sought to strengthen by offering to Dionysius his sister in marriage.[2] There was a basis of sympathy between them arising from the fact that Evagoras was at variance with the Phenicians both in Phenicia and Cyprus, while Dionysius was in active hostilities with the Carthaginians (their kinsmen and colonists) in Sicily. Nevertheless the proposition met with little or no success. We find Dionysius afterwards still continuing to act as an ally of Sparta.

*Marginal notes:* B.C. 393. Large plans of Konon—organisation of a mercenary force at Corinth.

[1] Harpokration, v. ξενικὸν ἐν Κορίνθῳ. Philochorus, Fragm. 150, ed. Didot.
[2] Lysias, Orat. xix. (De Bonis Aristophanis) s. 21.

Profiting by the aid received from Pharnabazus, the Corinthians strengthened their fleet at Lechæum (their harbour in the Corinthian Gulf) so considerably, as to become masters of the Gulf, and to occupy Rhium, one of the two opposite capes which bound its narrow entrance. To oppose them, the Lacedæmonians on their side were driven to greater maritime effort. More than one naval action seems to have taken place, in those waters where the prowess and skill of the Athenian admiral Phormion had been so signally displayed at the beginning of the Peloponnesian War. At length the Lacedæmonian admiral Herippidas, who succeeded to the command of the fleet after his predecessor Polemarchus had been slain in battle, compelled the Corinthians to abandon Rhium, and gradually recovered his ascendency in the Corinthian Gulf; which his successor Teleutias, brother of Agésilaus, still farther completed.[1]

*Naval conflicts of the Corinthians and Lacedæmonians, in the Corinthian Gulf.*

While these transactions were going on (seemingly during the last half of 393 B.C. and the full year of 392 B.C.), so as to put an end to the temporary naval preponderance of the Corinthians—the latter were at the same time bearing the brunt of a desultory, but continued, land-warfare against the garrison of Lacedæmonians and Peloponnesians established at Sikyon. Both Corinth and Lechæum were partly defended by the presence of confederate troops, Bœotians, Argeians, Athenians, or mercenaries paid by Athens. But this did not protect the Corinthians against suffering great damage, in their lands and outlying properties, from the incursions of the enemy.

*B.C. 392. Land-warfare—the Lacedæmonians established at Sikyon—the anti-Spartan allies occupying the lines of Corinth from sea to sea.*

The plain between Corinth and Sikyon—fertile and extensive (speaking by comparison with Peloponnesus generally), and constituting a large part of the landed property of both cities, was rendered uncultivable during 393 and 392 B.C.; so that the Corinthian proprietors were obliged to withdraw their servants and cattle to Peiræum[2] (a portion of the Corinthian territory without the Isthmus properly so called, north-east of the Akrokorinthus, in a line between that eminence and the Megarian harbour of Pegæ). Here

*Sufferings of the Corinthians from the war being carried on in their territory. Many Corinthian proprietors become averse to the war.*

[1] Xen. Hellen. iv. 8, 11.    [2] Xen. Hellen. iv. 4, 1; iv. 5, 1.

the Sikyonian assailants could not reach them, because of
the Long Walls of Corinth, which connected that city by
a continuous fortification of 12 stadia (somewhat less than
a mile and a half) with its harbour of Lechæum. Nevertheless the loss to the proprietors of the deserted plain
was still so great, that two successive seasons of it were
quite enough to inspire them with a strong aversion to the
war;[1] the more so, as the damage fell exclusively upon

[1] I dissent from Mr. Fynes Clinton
as well as from M. Behdants (Vitæ
Iphicratis, &c. c. 4, who in the main
agrees with Dodwell's Annales
Xenophontei) in their chronological arrangement of these events.

They place the battle fought by
Praxitas within the Long Walls of
Corinth in 893 B.C., and the destruction of the Lacedæmonian mora or
division by Iphikratas (the monthly
date of which is marked by its
having immediately succeeded the
Isthmian games), in 392 B.C. I place
the former event in 392 B.C.; the
latter in 390 B.C., immediately after
the Isthmian games of 390 B.C.

If we study the narrative of Xenophon, we shall find, that after
describing (iv. 3) the battle of
Koroneia (August 394 B.C.) with
its immediate consequences, and
the return of Agesilaus home—he
goes on in the next chapter to
narrate the land-war about or near
Corinth, which he carries down
without interruption (through
Chapters 3, 4, 5, 6, 7, of Book Iv.)
to 389 B.C.

But in Chapter 8 of Book Iv., he
leaves the land-war, and takes up
the naval operations, from and
after the battle of Knidus (Aug.
394 B.C.). He recounts how Pharnabazus and Konon came across the
Ægean with a powerful fleet in the
spring of 393 B.C., and how after
various proceedings, they brought
the fleet to the Saronic Gulf and
the Isthmus of Corinth, where they
must have arrived at or near Mid-

summer 393 B.C.

Now it appears to me certain,
that these proceedings of Pharnabazus with the fleet, recounted in
the eighth chapter, come, in point
of date, before the seditious movements and the coup d'état at Corinth,
which are recounted in the fourth
chapter. At the time when Pharnabazus was at Corinth in Midsummer
393 B.C., the narrative of Xenophon
(iv. 8, 8-10) leads us to believe that
the Corinthians were prosecuting
the war zealously, and without
discontent: the money and encouragement which Pharnabazus
gave them were calculated to
strengthen such ardour. It was
by aid of this money that the Corinthians fitted out their fleet under
Agathinus, and acquired for a time
the maritime command of the Gulf.

The discontents against the war
(recounted in chap. 4 seq.) could
not have commenced until a considerable time after the departure
of Pharnabazus. They arose out
of causes which only took effect
after a long continuance—the hardships of the land-war, the losses of
property and slaves, the jealousy
towards Attica and Bœotia as being
undisturbed, &c. The Lacedæmonian and Peloponnesian aggressive
force at Sikyon cannot possibly
have been established before the
autumn of 394 B.C., and was most
probably placed there early in the
spring of 393 B.C. Its effects were
brought about, not by one great
blow, but by repetition of ravages

them—their allies in Bœotia, Athens, and Argos, having as yet suffered nothing. Constant military service for defence, with the conversion of the city into a sort of besieged post, aggravated their discomfort. There was another circumstance also, doubtless not without influence. The consequences of the battle of Knidus had been, first, to put down the maritime empire of Sparta, and thus to diminish the fear which she inspired to the Corinthians; next, to rebuild the fortifications, and renovate the shipping, commercial as well as warlike, of Athens;—a revival well calculated to bring back a portion of that anti-Athenian jealousy and apprehension which the Corinthians had felt so strongly a few years before. Perhaps some of the trade of Corinth may have been actually driven away by the disturbance of the war, to the renewed fortifications and greater security of Peiræus.

Fostered by this pressure of circumstances, the discontented philo-Laconian or peace-party which had always existed at Corinth, presently acquired sufficient strength, and manifested itself with sufficient publicity, to give much alarm to the government. The Corinthian government had always been, and still was, oligarchical. In what manner the administrators or the council were renewed, or how long individuals continued in office, indeed, we do not know. But of democracy, with its legal popular assemblies, open discussions, and authoritative resolves, there was

<small>B.C. 392. Growth and manifestation of a philo-Laconian party in Corinth. Oligarchical form of the government left open nothing but an appeal to force.</small>

<small>and destructive annoyance; and all the effects which it produced previous to Midsummer 693 B.C. would be more than compensated by the presence, the gifts, and the encouragement of Pharnabazus with his powerful fleet. Moreover, after his departure, too, the Corinthians were at first successful at sea and acquired the command of the Gulf, which however they did not retain for more than a year, if so much. Hence it is not likely that any strong discontent against the war began before the early part of 393 B.C.

Considering all these circumstances, I think it reasonable to believe that the *coup d'état* and massacre at Corinth took place (not in 393 B.C., as Mr. Clinton and M. Rebdantz place it, but) in 392 B.O.; and the battle within the Long Walls rather later in the same year.

Next, the opinion of the same two authors as well as of Dodwell —that the destruction of the Lacedæmonian more by Iphikratés took place in the spring of 343 B.C.—is also, in my view, erroneous. If this were true, it would be necessary to pack all the events mentioned in Xenophon, iv. 4, into</small>

nothing.[1] Now the oligarchical persons actually in power were vehemently anti-Laconian, consisting of men who had partaken of the Persian funds and contracted alliance with Persia, besides compromising themselves irrevocably (like Timolaus) by the most bitter manifestations of hostile sentiment towards Sparta. These men found themselves menaced by a powerful opposition-party, which had no constitutional means for making its sentiments predominant, and for accomplishing peaceably either a change of administrators or a change of public policy. It was only by an appeal to arms and violence that such a consummation could be brought about; a fact notorious to both parties—so that the oligarchical administrators, informed of the meetings and conversations going on, knew well that they had to expect nothing less than the breaking out of a conspiracy. That such anticipations were well-founded, we gather even from the partial recital of Xenophon; who states that Pasimêlus, the philo-Laconian leader, was on his guard and in preparation[2]—and counts it to him as a virtue that shortly afterwards he opened the gates to the Lacedæmonians.

*The Corinthian government forestal the conspiracy by a coup d'état.*

Anticipating such conspiracy, the government resolved to prevent it by a *coup d'état*. They threw themselves upon the assistance of their allies, invited in a body of Argeians, and made their blow the more sure by striking it on the last day of the festival called Eukleia, when it was least expected. Their proceeding, though dictated by precaution, was executed with the extreme of

---

the year 393 B.C.; which I hold to be impossible. If the destruction of the mora did not occur in the spring of 392 B.C., we know that it could not have occurred until the spring of 390 B.C.; that is, the next ensuing Isthmian games, two years afterwards. And this last will be found to be its true date; thus leaving full time, but not too much time, for the antecedent occurrences.

[1] Plutarch. Dion. c. 53.

[2] Xen. Hellen. iv. 4, 2. Γνόντες δὲ οἱ Ἀργεῖοι καὶ Βοιωτοὶ καὶ Ἀθηναῖοι καὶ Κορίνθιοι οἵ τε τῶν παρὰ βασιλέως χρημάτων μετεσχηκότες, καὶ οἱ τοῦ πολέμου αἰτιώτατοι γεγενημένοι, ὡς, εἰ μὴ ἐκποδών ποιήσαιντο τοὺς ἐπὶ τὴν εἰρήνην τετραμμένους, κινδυνεύσει πάλιν ἡ πόλις Λακωνίσαι —οὕτω δὴ καὶ σφαγὰς ἐπεχείρουν ποιεῖσθαι.

Iv. 4, 4. Οἱ δὲ νεώτεροι, ὑποπτεύσαντες Πασιμήλου τὸ μέλλον ἔσεσθαι, ἡσυχίαν ἔσχον ἐν τῷ Κρανίῳ· ὡς δὲ τῆς κραυγῆς ἤκθοντο, καὶ φεύγοντές τινες ἐκ τοῦ πράγματος ἀφίκοντο πρὸς αὐτοὺς, ἐκ τούτου ἀναδραμόντες κατὰ τὸν Ἀκροκόρινθον, προσβαλόντας μὲν Ἀργείους καὶ τοὺς ἄλλους ἀπεκρούσαντο, &c.

brutal ferocity aggravated by sacrilege; in a manner very different from the deep-laid artifices recently practised by the Spartan Ephors when they were in like manner afraid of the conspiracy of Kinadon—and more like the oligarchical conspirators at Korkyra (in the third year of the Peloponnesian War) when they broke into the assembled Senate, and massacred Peithias with sixty others in the Senate-house.[1] While the choice performers at Corinth were contending for the prize in the theatre, with judges formally named to decide—and while the market-place around was crowded with festive spectators—a number of armed men were introduced, probably Argeians, with leaders designating the victims whom they were to strike. Some of these select victims were massacred in the market-place, others in the theatre, and one even while sitting as a judge in the theatre. Others again fled in terror, to embrace the altars or statues in the market-place—which sanctuary nevertheless did not save their lives. Nor was such sacrilege arrested—repugnant as it was to the feelings of the assembled spectators and to Grecian feelings generally—until 120 persons had perished.[2] But the persons slain were chiefly elderly men; for the younger portion of the philo-Laconian party, suspecting some mischief, had declined attending the festival, and kept themselves separately assembled under their leader Pasimêlus, in the gymnasium and cypress-grove called Kranium, just without the city-gates. We find too that they were not only assembled, but actually in arms. For the moment that they heard the clamour in the market-place and learnt from some fugitives what was going on, they rushed up at once to the Akrokorinthus (or eminence and acropolis overhanging the city) and got possession of the citadel; which they maintained with such force and courage, that the Argeians, and the Corinthians who took part with the government, were repulsed in the attempt to dislodge them. This circumstance, indirectly revealed in the one-sided narrative of Xenophon, lets us into the real state of the city, and affords good ground for believing that Pasimêlus and his friends were prepared beforehand for an armed outbreak, but waited to execute it, until the festival was over,—a scruple

[1] Thucyd. III. 70.
[2] Diodorus (xiv. 86) gives this number, which seems very credible.

Xenophon (iv. 4, 4) only says πολλοί.

which the government, in their eagerness to forestal the
plot, disregarded; employing the hands and weapons of
Argeians who were comparatively unimpressed by solemnities peculiar to Corinth.¹

---

¹ In recounting this alternation
of violence projected, violence perpetrated, recourse on the one side
to a foreign ally, treason on the
other by admitting an avowed
enemy—which formed the modus
operandi of opposing parties in
the oligarchical Corinth—I invite
the reader to contrast it with the
democratical Athens.

At Athens, in the beginning of
the Peloponnesian War, there were
precisely the same causes at work,
and precisely the same marked
antithesis of parties, as those which
here disturbed Corinth. There was
first, a considerable Athenian minority who opposed the war with
Sparta from the first; next, when
the war began, the proprietors of
Attica saw their lands ruined, and
were compelled either to carry
away, or to lose, their servants
and cattle, so that they obtained
no returns. The intense discontent,
the angry complaints, the bitter
conflict of parties, which these
circumstances raised among the
Athenian citizens—not to mention
the aggravation of all these symptoms by the terrible epidemic—are
marked out in Thucydides, and
have been recorded in a preceding
volume of this history. Not only
the positive loss and suffering, but
all other causes of exasperation,
stood at a higher pitch at Athens
in the early part of the Peloponnesian War, than at Corinth in
302 B.C.

Yet what were the effects which
they produced? Did the minority
resort to a conspiracy—or the
majority to a coup d'état—or either
of them to invitation of foreign
aid against the other? Nothing of
the kind. The minority had always
open to them the road of pacific
opposition, and the chance of obtaining a majority in the Senate
or in the public assembly, which
was practically identical with the
totality of the citizens. Their
opposition, though pacific as to
acts, was sufficiently animated and
violent in words and propositions,
to serve as a real discharge for
imprisoned angry passion. If they
could not carry the adoption of
their general policy, they had the
opportunity of gaining partial victories which took off the edge of
a fierce discontent; witness the fine
imposed upon Periklês (Thucyd.
II. 65) in the year before his death,
which both gratified and mollified
the antipathy against him, and
brought about shortly afterwards
a strong reaction in his favour.
The majority, on the other hand,
knew that the predominance of its
policy depended upon its maintaining its hold on a fluctuating
public assembly, against the utmost
freedom of debate and attack,
within certain forms and rules prescribed by the constitution; attachment to the latter being the cardinal principle of political morality in both parties. It was this
system which excluded on both
sides the thought of armed violence.
It produced among the democratical citizens of Athens that characteristic insisted upon by Kleon in
Thucydidês—"constant and fearless
security and absence of treacherous
hostility among one another" (διὰ
γὰρ τὸ καθ' ἡμέραν ἀδεὲς καὶ ἀνεπιβούλευτον πρὸς ἀλλήλους, καὶ ἐς τοὺς
ξυμμάχους τὸ αὐτὸ ἔχετε—Thuc. iii.
37), the entire absence of which

Though Pasimêlus and his friends were masters of the citadel and had repulsed the assault of their enemies, yet the recent *coup d'état* had been completely successful in overawing their party in the city, and depriving them of all means of communicating with the Lacedæmonians at Sikyon. Feeling unable to maintain themselves, they were besides frightened by menacing omens, when they came to offer sacrifice, in order that they might learn whether the gods encouraged them to fight or not. The victims were found so alarming, as to drive them to evacuate the post and prepare for voluntary exile. Many of them (according to Diodorus 500[1]) actually went into exile; while others, and among them Pasimêlus himself, were restrained by the entreaties of their friends and relatives, combined with solemn assurances of peace and security from the government; who now probably felt themselves victorious, and were anxious to mitigate the antipathies which their recent violence had inspired. These pacific assurances were faithfully kept, and no farther mischief was done to any citizen.

*Numerous persons of the philo-Laconian party are banished: nevertheless Pasi-mêlus the leader is spared and remains at Corinth.*

But the political condition of Corinth was materially altered, by an extreme intimacy of alliance and communion now formed with Argos; perhaps combined with reciprocal rights of intermarriage, and of purchase and sale. The boundary pillars or hedges which separated the two territories were pulled up, and the city was entitled *Argos* instead of *Corinth* (says Xenophon). Such was probably the invidious phrase in which the opposition party described the very close political union now formed between the two cities; upheld by a strong Argeian force in the city and acropolis, together with some Athenian mercenaries under Iphikratês, and some Bœotians as a garrison in the port

*Intimate political union and consolidation between Corinth and Argos.*

---

stands so prominently forward in these deplorable proceedings of the oligarchical Corinth. Pasimêlus and his Corinthian minority had no assemblies, dikasteries, annual Senate, or constant habit of free debate and accusation, to appeal to; their only available weapon was armed violence, or treacherous correspondence with a foreign enemy. On the part of the Corinthian government, superior or more skilfully used force, or superior alliance abroad, was the only weapon of defence, in like manner.

[1] Diodor. xiv. 86; Xen. Hellen. iv. 4, 6.

of Lechæum. Most probably the government remained
still Corinthian, and still oligarchical, as before. But it
now rested upon Argeian aid, and was therefore dependent
chiefly upon Argos, though partly also upon the other two
allies.

To Pasimêlus and his friends such a state of things
was intolerable. Though personally they had
no ill-usage to complain of, yet the complete
predominance of their political enemies was quite
sufficient to excite their most vehement antipathies. They entered into secret correspondence
with Praxitas, the Lacedæmonian commander
at Sikyon, engaging to betray to him one of the
gates in the western Long Wall between Corinth
and Lechæum. The scheme being concerted,
Pasimêlus and his partisans got themselves placed,[1] partly
by contrivance and partly by accident, on the night-watch
at this gate; an imprudence, which shows that the government not only did not maltreat them, but even admitted
them to trust. At the moment fixed, Praxitas—presenting himself with a Lacedæmonian *mora* or regiment, a Sikyonian force, and the Corinthian exiles, — found the
treacherous sentinels prepared to open the gates. Having
first sent in a trusty soldier to satisfy him that there was
no deceit,[2] he then conducted all his force within the gates,
into the mid-space between the two Long Walls. So broad
was this space, and so inadequate did his numbers appear
to maintain it, that he took the precaution of digging a cross-ditch with a palisade to defend himself on the side towards
the city; which he was enabled to do undisturbed, since
the enemy (we are not told why) did not attack him all the
next day. On the ensuing day, however, Argeians, Corinthians, and Athenian mercenaries under Iphikratês, all
came down from the city in full force; the latter stood on the
right of the line, along the eastern wall, opposed to the
Corinthian exiles on the Lacedæmonian left; while the

---

[1] Xen. Hellen. iv. 4, 8. καὶ κατὰ τύχην καὶ κατ' ἐπιμέλειαν, &c.

[2] Xen. Hellen. iv. 4, 8. Nothing can show more forcibly the Laconian bias of Xenophon, than the credit which he gives to Pasimêlus for his good faith towards the Lacedæmonians whom he was letting in; overlooking or approving his treacherous betrayal towards his own countrymen, in thus opening a gate which he had been trusted to watch. τῷ δ' εἰσηγητῇ, καὶ οὕτως καλῶς ἀπεδείξατο, ὥστε ὁ εἰσελθὼν ἐξήγγειλα, πάντα εἶναι ἀδόλως, οἷά περ ἐλεγέτην.

Lacedæmonians themselves were on their own right, opposed to the Corinthians from the city; and the Argeians, opposed to the Sikyonians, in the centre.

It was here that the battle began; the Argeians, bold from superior numbers, attacked and broke the Sikyonians, tearing up the palisade, and pursuing them down to the sea with much slaughter;[1] upon which Pasimachus the Lacedæmonian commander of cavalry coming to their aid, caused his small body of horsemen to dismount and tie their horses to trees, and then armed them with shields taken from the Sikyonians, inscribed on the outside with the letter Sigma (Σ). With these he approached on foot to attack the Argeians, who mistaking them for Sikyonians, rushed to the charge with alacrity; upon which Pasimachus exclaimed—"By the two Gods, Argeians, these Sigmas which you see here will deceive you:" he then closed with them resolutely, but his numbers were so inferior that he was soon overpowered and slain. Meanwhile the Corinthian exiles on the left had driven back Iphikratês with his mercenaries (doubtless chiefly light troops) and pursued them even to the city gates; while the Lacedæmonians, easily repelling the Corinthians opposed to them, came out of their palisade and planted themselves with their faces towards the eastern wall, but at a little distance from it, to intercept the Argeians on their return. The latter were forced to run back as they could, huddling close along the eastern wall, with their right or unshielded side exposed as they passed to the spears of the Lacedæmonians. Before they could get to the walls of Corinth, they were met and roughly handled by the victorious Corinthian exiles. And even when they came to the walls, those within, unwilling to throw open the gates for fear of admitting the enemy, contented themselves with handing down ladders, over which the defeated Argeians clambered with distress and difficulty. Altogether, their loss in this disastrous retreat

*The Lacedæmonians are victorious—severe loss of the Argeians.*

---

[1] Xen. Hellen. iv. 4, 10. Καὶ τοὺς μὲν Σικυωνίους ἐτρέψαντο καὶ διασπάσαντες τὸ σταύρωμα ἐδίωκον ἐπὶ θάλασσαν, καὶ ἐπὶ πολλοὺς αὐτῶν ἀπέκτειναν.

It would appear from hence that there must have been an open portion of Lechæum, or a space apart from (but adjoining to) the wall which encircled Lechæum, yet still within the Long Walls. Otherwise the fugitive Sikyonians could hardly have got down to the sea.

was frightful. Their dead (says Xenophon) lay piled up like heaps of stones or wood.[1]

*The Lacedæmonians pull down a portion of the Long Walls between Corinth and Lechæum, so as to open a free passage across.—They capture Krommyon and Sidus.*

This victory of Praxitas and the Lacedæmonians, though it did not yet make them masters of Lechæum,[2] was nevertheless of considerable importance. Shortly afterwards they received reinforcements which enabled them to turn it to still better account. The first measure of Praxitas was to pull down a considerable breadth of the two walls, leaving a breach which opened free passage for any Lacedæmonian army from Sikyon to reach and pass the isthmus. He then marched his troops through the breach, forward on the road to Megara, capturing the two Corinthian dependencies of Krommyon and Sidus on the Saronic Gulf, in which he placed garrisons. Returning back by the road south of Corinth, he occupied Epieikia on the frontier of Epidaurus, as a protection to the territory of the latter against incursions from Corinth—and then disbanded his army.

*B.C. 391. Effective warfare carried on by the light troops under Iphikratês at Corinth—military genius and improvements of Iphikratês.*

A desultory warfare was carried on during the ensuing winter and spring between the opposite garrisons in Corinth and Sikyon. It was now that the Athenian Iphikratês, in the former place, began to distinguish himself at the head of his mercenary peltasts, whom, after their first organization by Konon, he had trained to effective tactics under the strictest discipline, and whose movements he conducted with consummate skill. His genius introduced improvements both in their armour and in their clothing. He lengthened by one half both the light javelin and

---

[1] Xen. Hellen. iv. 4, 12. Ὅστις ἐν ὀλίγῳ πολλοὶ ἔπεσον, ὥστε σιτιομένοι ὁρᾶν οἱ Ἀθηναῖοι σωροὺς σίτου, ξύλων, λίθων, τότε εἴδοντο σωροὺς νεκρῶν.

A singular form of speech.

[2] Diodorus (xiv. 16) represents that the Lacedæmonians on this occasion surprised and held Lechæum, defeating the general body of the confederates who came out from Corinth to retake it. But his narrative of all these circumstances differs materially from that of Xenophon; whom I here follow in preference, making allowance for great partiality, and for much confusion and obscurity.

Xenophon gives us plainly to understand, that Lechæum was not captured by the Lacedæmonians until the following year, by Agesilaus and Teleutias.

It is to be recollected that Xe-

## CHAP. LXXV.   IMPROVEMENTS OF IPHIKRATES.   161

the short sword, which the Thracian peltasts habitually carried; he devised a species of leggings, known afterwards by the name of Iphikratides; and he thus combined, better than had ever been done before, rapid motion—power of acting in difficult ground and open order—effective attack either by missiles or hand to hand—and dexterous retreat in case of need.¹ As yet he was but a young officer, in

---

Xenophon had particular means of knowing what was done by Agesilaus, and therefore deserves credit on that head—always allowing for partiality. Diodorus does not mention Agesilaus in connexion with the proceedings at Lechæum.

¹ Diodor. xv. 44 ; Cornelius Nepos, Vit. Iphicrat. c. 2; Polyæn. iii. 9, 19. Compare Rehdantz, Vitæ Iphicratis, Chabriæ, et Timothei, c. 2, 7 (Berlin, 1845)—a very useful and instructive publication.

In describing the improvements made by Iphikrates in the armature of his peltasts, I have not exactly copied either Nepos or Diodorus, who both appear to me confused in their statements. You would imagine, in reading their account (and so it has been stated by Weber, Prolegg. ad Demosth. cont. Aristokr. p. xxxv.), that there were no peltasts in Greece prior to Iphikrates; that he was the first to transform heavy-armed hoplites into light-armed peltasts, and to introduce from Thrace the light shield or *pelta*, not only smaller in size than the round ἀσπίς carried by the hoplite, but also without the ἴτυς, or surrounding metallic rim of the ἀσπίς, seemingly connected by outside bars or spokes of metal with the exterior central knob or projection (umbo) which the hoplite pushed before him in close combat. The *pelta*, smaller and lighter than the ἀσπίς, was apparently square or oblong and not round: though it had no ἴτυς, it often had thin plates of brass,

as we may see by Xenophon, Anab. v. 2, 29, so that the explanation of it given in the Scholia ad Platon. Legg. vii. p. 813 must be taken with reserve.

But Grecian peltasts existed before the time of Iphikrates (Xen. Hellen. l. 2, 1 and elsewhere). He did not first introduce them; he found them already there, and improved their armature. But Diodorus and Nepos affirm that he lengthened the *spears* of the peltasts to a measure half as long again as those of the hoplites (or twice as long, if we believe Nepos), and the swords in proportion— "ηὔξησι μὲν τὰ δόρατα ἡμιόλιῳ μεγέθει—hasta modum duplicavit." Now this I apprehend to be not exact; nor is it true (as Nepos asserts) that the Grecian hoplites carried "short spears"—"brevibus hastis." The spear of the Grecian hoplite was long (though not so long as that of the heavy and compact Macedonian phalanx afterwards became), and it appears to me incredible that Iphikrates should have given to his light and active peltast a spear twice as long, or half as long again, as that of the hoplite. Both Diodorus and Nepos have mistaken by making their comparison with the arms *of the hoplite*, to which the changes of Iphikrates had no reference. The peltast both before and after Iphikrates did not carry a spear but a *javelin*, which he employed as a missile, to hurl, not to thrust ; he was essentially an ἀκοντιστής

the beginning of his military career.[1] We must therefore presume that these improvements were chiefly of later date, the suggestions of his personal experience; but even now, the successes of his light troops were remarkable. Attacking Phlius, he entrapped the Phliasians into an ambuscade, and inflicted on them a defeat so destructive, that they were obliged to invoke the aid of a Lacedæmonian garrison for the protection of their city. He gained a victory near Sikyon, and carried his incursions over all Arcadia, to the very gates of the cities; damaging the Arcadian hoplites so severely, that they became afraid to meet him in the field. His own peltasts however, though full of confidence against these Peloponnesian hoplites, still retained their awe and their reluctance to fight against Lacedæmonians;[2] who on their side despised them, but despised their own allies still more. "Our friends fear these peltasts, as children fear hobgoblins"—said the Lacedæmonians sarcastically, endeavouring to set the example of courage by ostentatious demonstrations of their own round the walls of Corinth.[3]

---

or javelin-shooter (see Xenoph. Hellen. iv. 5, 14; vi. 1, 9). Of course the javelin might, in case of need, serve to thrust, but this was not its appropriate employment: *e converso*, the spear might be hurled (under advantageous circumstances), from the higher ground against an enemy below—Xen. Hellen. II. 4, 15; v. 4, 57), but its proper employment was, to be held and thrust forward.

What Iphikrates really did, was, to lengthen both the two offensive weapons which the peltast carried, before his time—the javelin, and the sword. He made the javelin a longer and heavier weapon, requiring a more practised hand to throw—but also competent to inflict more serious wounds, and capable of being used with more deadly effect if the peltasts saw an opportunity of coming to close fight on advantageous terms. Possibly Iphikrates not only lengthened the weapon, but also improved its point and efficacy in other ways; making it more analogous to the formidable Roman *pilum*. Whether he made any alteration in the *pelta* itself, we do not know.

The name *Iphikratides*, given to these new-fashioned leggings or boots, proves to us that Wellington and Blücher are not the first eminent generals who have lent an honourable denomination to boots and shoes.

[1] Justin. vi. 5.
[2] Xen. Hellen. iv. 4, 10; Diodor. xiv. 91.

Τοὺς μέντοι Λακεδαιμονίους οὕτως αἱ οἱ πελτασταὶ ἐδέδισαν, ὡς ἔντος ἀκοντίσματος οὐ προσῇεσαν τοῖς ὁπλίταις, &c.

Compare the sentiment of the light troops in the attack of Sphakteria, when they were awe-struck and afraid at first to approach the Lacedæmonian hoplites—τῇ γνώμῃ δεδουλωμένοι ὡς ἐπὶ Λακεδαιμονίους, &c. (Thucyd. iv. 34).

[3] Xen. Hellen. iv. 4, 17. ὥστε οἱ

The breach made in the Long Walls of Corinth by Praxitas had laid open the road for a Peloponnesian army to march either into Attica or Bœotia.¹ Fortunately for the Athenians, they had already completed the rebuilding of their own Long Walls; but they were so much alarmed by the new danger, that they marched with their full force, and with masons and carpenters accompanying,² to Corinth. Here, with that celerity of work for which they were distinguished,³ they in a few days re-established completely the western wall; the more important of the two, since it formed the barrier against the incursions of the Lacedæmonians from Sikyon. They had then a secure position, and could finish the eastern wall at their leisure; which they accordingly did, and then retired, leaving it to the confederate troops in Corinth to defend.

*B.C. 591.*
The Athenians restore the Long Walls between Corinth and Lechæum —expedition of the Spartan king Agesilaus, who, in concert with Teleutias, retakes the Long Walls and captures Lechæum.

This advantage, however, a very material one, was again overthrown by the expedition of the Lacedæmonian king Agesilaus during the same summer. At the head of

μὲν Λακεδαιμόνιοι καὶ ἐπισπώμενοι ἐτόλμων, ὡς οἱ σύμμαχοι φοβοῖντο τοὺς πελταστάς, ὥσπερ μορμόνας παιδάρια, &c.
This is a camp-jest of the time, which we have to thank Xenophon for preserving.
¹ Xenoph. Agesil. ii. 17. ἀναπετάσας τῆς Πελοποννήσου τὰς πύλας, &c.
Respecting the Long Walls of Corinth, as part of a line of defence which barred ingress to, or egress from, Peloponnesus — Colonel Leake remarks—"The narrative of Xenophon shows the great importance of the Corinthian Long Walls in time of war. They completed a line of fortification from the summit of the Acro-Corinthus to the sea, and thus intercepted the most direct and easy communication from the Isthmus into Peloponnesus. For the rugged mountain, which borders the southern side of the Isthmian plain,

has only two passes—one, by the opening on the eastern side of the Acro-Corinthus, which obliged an enemy to pass under the eastern side of Corinth, and was moreover defended by a particular kind of fortification, as some remains of walls still testify—the other, along the shore at Cenchreiæ, which was also a fortified place in the hands of the Corinthians. Hence the importance of the pass of Cenchreiæ, in all operations between the Peloponnesians, and an enemy without the Isthmus" (Leake, Travels in Morea, vol. iii. ch. xxviii. p. 254). Compare Plutarch, Aratus, c. 16; and the operations of Epaminondas as described by Diodorus, xv. 68.
² Xen. Hellen. iv. 4, 18. ἐλθόντες πανδημεὶ μετὰ λιθολόγων καὶ τεκτόνων, &c. The word πανδημεὶ shows how much they were alarmed.
³ Thucyd. vi. 98.

a full Lacedæmonian and Peloponnesian force, he first marched into the territory of Argos, and there spent some time in ravaging all the cultivated plain. From hence he passed over the mountain-road by Tenea[1] into the plain of Corinth, to the foot of the newly-repaired Long Walls. Here his brother Teleutias, who had recently superseded Herippidas as admiral in the Corinthian Gulf, came to cooperate with him in a joint attack, by sea and land, on the new Walls and on Lechæum.[2] The presence of this naval force rendered the Long Walls difficult to maintain, since troops could be disembarked in the interval between them, where the Sikyonians in the previous battle had been beaten and pursued down to the sea. Agesilaus and Teleutias were strong enough to defeat the joint force of the four confederated armies, and to master not only the Long Walls, but also the port of Lechæum[3] with its docks

[1] The words stand in the text of Xenophon—αὐτὸς εὐθὺς ὑπερβαλὼν κατὰ Τεγέαν εἰς Κόρινθον. A straight march from the Argeian territory to Corinth could not possibly carry Agesilaus by *Tegea*; Koppen proposes Τενέαν, which I accept, as geographically suitable. I am not certain however that it is right; the *Agesilaus* of Xenophon has the words κατὰ τὰ στενά.

About the probable situation of Tenea, see Colonel Leake, Travels in Morea, vol. iii. p. 521; also his Peloponnesiaca, p. 400.

[2] Xen. Hellen. iv. 4, 19—iv. 8, 10, 11.

It was rather late in the autumn of 393 B.C. that the Lacedæmonian maritime operations in the Corinthian Gulf began, against the fleet recently equipped by the Corinthians out of the funds lent by Pharnabazus. First the Lacedæmonian Polemarchus was named admiral; he was slain,—and his secretary Pollis, who succeeded to his command, retired afterwards wounded. Next came Herippidas to the command, who was succeeded by Teleutias. Now if we allow to Herippidas a year of command (the ordinary duration of a Lacedæmonian admiral's appointment), and to the other two something less than a year, since their time was brought to an end by accidents—we shall find that the appointment of Teleutias will fall in the spring or early summer of 391 B.C., the year of this expedition of Agesilaus.

[3] Andokides de Pace, s. 18; Xen. Hellen. iv. 4, 19. Παρεγένετο δὲ αὐτῷ (Ἀγησιλάῳ) καὶ ὁ ἀδελφὸς Τελευτίας κατὰ θάλασσαν, ἔχων τριήρεις περὶ δώδεκα· ὥστε μακαρίζεσθαι αὐτῶν τὴν μητέρα, ὅτι τῇ αὐτῇ ἡμέρᾳ ὧν ἐτέκεν ὁ μὲν κατὰ γῆν τὰ τείχη τῶν πολεμίων, ὁ δὲ κατὰ θάλασσαν τὰς ναῦς καὶ τὰ νεώρια ᾕρηκε.

This last passage indicates decidedly that Lechæum was not taken until this joint attack by Agesilaus and Teleutias. And the authority of Xenophon on the point is superior, in my judgement, to that of Diodorus (xiv. 86), who represents Lechæum to have been taken in the year before, on the occasion when the Lacedæmonians were first ad-

## CAPTURE OF LECHÆUM.

and the ships within them; thus breaking up the naval power of Corinth in the Krissæan Gulf. Lechæum now became a permanent post of hostility against Corinth, occupied by a Lacedæmonian garrison and occasionally by the Corinthian exiles; while any second rebuilding of the Corinthian Long Walls by the Athenians became impossible. After this important success, Agesilaus returned to Sparta. Neither he nor his Lacedæmonian hoplites, especially the Amyklæans, were ever willingly absent from the festival of the Hyakinthia: nor did he now disdain to take his station in the chorus,[1] under the

---

mitted by treachery within the Long Walls.

The passage from Aristeidês the rhetor, referred to by Wesseling, Mr. Clinton, and others, only mentions the battle at Lechæum—not the capture of the port. Xenophon also mentions a battle as having taken place close to Lechæum, between the two Long Walls, on the occasion when Diodorus talks of the capture of Lechæum; so that Aristeidês is more in harmony with Xenophon than with Diodorus.

A few months prior to this joint attack of Agesilaus and Teleutias, the Athenians had come with an army, and with masons and carpenters, for the express purpose of rebuilding the Long Walls which Praxitas had in part broken down. This step would have been both impracticable and useless, if the Lacedæmonians had stood then in possession of Lechæum.

There is one passage of Xenophon, indeed, which looks as if the Lacedæmonians had been in possession of Lechæum before this expedition of the Athenians to reëstablish the Long Walls—Αὐτοί (the Lacedæmonians) δ' ἐκ τοῦ Λεχαίου ὁρμώμενοι σὺν μόρᾳ καὶ τοῖς τῶν Κορινθίων φυγάσι, κύκλῳ περὶ τὸ ἄστυ τῶν Κορινθίων ἐστρατεύοντο (iv. 4, 17). But who-

ever reads attentively the sections from 16 to 19 inclusive, will see (I think) that this affirmation may well refer to a period after, and not before, the capture of Lechæum by Agesilaus; for it has reference to the general contempt shown by the Lacedæmonians for the peltasts of Iphikratês, as contrasted with the terror displayed by the Mantineians and others, of these same peltasts. Even if this were otherwise, however, I should still say that the passages which I have produced above from Xenophon show plainly that he represents Lechæum to have been captured by Agesilaus and Teleutias; and that the other words, ἐκ τοῦ Λεχαίου ὁρμώμενοι, if they really implied anything inconsistent with this, must be regarded as an inaccuracy.

I will add that the chapter of Diodorus, xiv. 86, puts into one year events which cannot all be supposed to have taken place in that same year.

Had Lechæum been in possession and occupation by the Lacedæmonians, in the year preceding the joint attack by Agesilaus and Teleutias, Xenophon would surely have mentioned it in iv. 4, 16; for it was a more important post than Sikyon, for acting against Corinth.

[1] Xen. Agesilaus, II. 17.

orders of the choric conductor, for the pæan in honour of
Apollo.

It was thus that the Long Walls, though rebuilt by
the Athenians in the preceding year, were again
permanently overthrown, and the road for
Lacedæmonian armies to march beyond the
Isthmus once more laid open. So much were
the Athenians and the Bœotians alarmed at this
new success, that both appear to have become
desirous of peace, and to have sent envoys to
Sparta. The Thebans are said to have offered
to recognise Orchomenus (which was now occupied by a Lacedæmonian garrison) as autonomous and disconnected from the Bœotian
federation; while the Athenian envoys seem to
have been favourably received at Sparta, and to have found
the Lacedæmonians disposed to make peace on better terms
than those which had been proposed during the late discussions with Tiribazus (hereafter to be noticed); recognising the newly-built Athenian Walls, restoring Lemnos,
Imbros, and Skyros to Athens, and guaranteeing autonomy
to each separate city in the Grecian world. The Athenian
envoys at Sparta having provisionally accepted these
terms, forty days were allowed for reference to the people
of Athens; to which place Lacedæmonian envoys were sent
as formal bearers of the propositions. The Argeians and
Corinthians, however, strenuously opposed the thoughts of
peace, urging the Athenians to continue the war; besides
which, it appears that many Athenian citizens thought
that large restitution ought to have been made of Athenian property forfeited at the end of the late war,—and
that the Thracian Chersonese ought to have been given
back as well as the three islands. On these and other
grounds, the Athenian people refused to sanction the
recommendation of their envoys; though Andokidês, one
of those envoys, in a discourse still extant, earnestly
advised that they should accept the peace.[1]

[1] Our knowledge of the abortive negotiations adverted to in the text, is derived, partly from the third Oration of Andokidês called De Pace—partly from a statement contained in the Argument of that Oration, and purporting to be borrowed from Philochorus—Φιλό-χορος μὲν οὖν λέγει καὶ ἐλθεῖν τοὺς πρέσβεις ἐκ Λακεδαίμονος, καὶ ἀπράκτους ἀνελθεῖν, μὴ πείσαντος τοῦ Ἀνδοκίδου.

Whether Philochorus had any additional grounds to rest upon,

## CHAP. LXXV.  ALARM AT THEBES AND ATHENS.  167

The war being thus continued, Corinth, though defended by a considerable confederate force, including other than this very oration itself, may appear doubtful. But at any rate, this important fragment (which I do not see noticed among the fragments of Philochorus in M. Didot's collection) counts for some farther evidence as to the reality of the peace proposed and discussed, but not concluded.

Neither Xenophon nor Diodorus make any mention of such mission to Sparta, or discussion at Athens, as that which forms the subject of the Andokidean oration. But on the other hand, neither of them says anything which goes to contradict the reality of the event; nor can we in this case found any strong negative inference on the mere silence of Xenophon, in the case of a pacific proposition which ultimately came to nothing.

If indeed we could be certain that the oration of Andokidês was genuine, it would of itself be sufficient to establish the reality of the mission to which it relates. It would be sufficient evidence, not only without corroboration from Xenophon, but even against any contradictory statement proceeding from Xenophon. But unfortunately, the rhetor Dionysius pronounced this oration to be spurious; which introduces a doubt and throws us upon the investigation of collateral probabilities. I have myself a decided opinion (already stated more than once), that another out of the four orations ascribed to Andokidês (I mean the fourth oration, entitled against Alkibiades) is spurious; and I was inclined to the same suspicion with respect to this present oration De Pace; a suspicion, which I expressed in a former volume (Ch. xlv.). But on studying over again with attention this oration De Pace, I find reason to retract my suspicion, and to believe that the oration may be genuine. It has plenty of erroneous allegations as to matter of fact, especially in reference to times prior to the battle of Ægospotami; but not one, so far as I can detect, which conflicts with the situation to which the orator addresses himself—nor which requires us to pronounce it spurious.

Indeed in considering this situation (which is the most important point to be studied when we are examining the genuineness of an oration), we find a partial coincidence in Xenophon, which goes to strengthen our affirmative confidence. One point much insisted upon in the oration, is, that the Bœotians were anxious to make peace with Sparta, and were willing to relinquish Orchomenus (s. 13-20). Now Xenophon also mentions, three or four months afterwards, the Bœotians as being anxious for peace, and as sending envoys to Agesilaus to ask on what terms it would be granted to them (Xen. Hellen. iv. 5, 6). This coincidence is of some value in reference to the authenticity of the oration.

Assuming the oration to be genuine, its date is pretty clearly marked, and is rightly placed by Mr. Fynes Clinton in 391 B.C. It was in the autumn or winter of that year, four years after the commencement of the war in Bœotia which began in 395 B.C. (s. 20). It was after the capture of Lechæum, which took place in the summer of 391 B.C.—and before the destruction of the Lacedæmonian mora by Iphikratês, which took place in the spring of 390 B.C. For An-

Athenian hoplites under Kallias, and peltasts under Iphikratês, became much pressed by the hostile posts at Lechæum as well as at Krommyon and Sidus—and by its own exiles as the most active of all enemies. Still however there remained the peninsula and the fortification of Peiræum as an undisturbed shelter for the Corinthian servants and cattle, and a source of subsistence for the city. Peiræum was an inland post northeast of Corinth, in the centre of that peninsula which separates the two innermost recesses of the Krissæan Gulf—the Bay of Lechæum on its south-west, the Bay called Alkyonis, between Kreusis and Olmiæ (now Psatho Bay), on its north-east. Across this latter bay Corinth communicated easily, through Peiræum and the fortified port of Œnoê, with Kreusis the port of Thespiæ in Bœotia.[1] The Corinthian exiles now prevailed upon Agesilaus to repeat his invasion of the territory, partly in order that they might deprive the city of the benefits which it derived from Peiræum—partly in order that they might also appropriate to themselves the honour of celebrating the Isthmian games, which were just approaching. The Spartan King accordingly marched forth, at the head of a force composed of Lacedæmonians and of the Peloponnesian allies, first to Lechæum, and thence to the Isthmus, specially so called; that is, the sacred precinct of Poseidon near Schœnus on the Saronic Gulf, at the

*B.C. 390.*
*Advantages derived by the Corinthians from possession of Peiræum. At the instigation of the exiles, Agesilaus marches forth with an army to attack it.*

dokidês emphatically intimates, that at the moment when he spoke, not one military success had yet been obtained against the Lacedæmonians—καίτοι ωείας τινὸς ἂν ἐκαίμει παρ' ἡμῶν εἰρήνης ἔτυχεν, εἰ μίαν μόνον μάχην ἡττήθησαν; (c. 19). This could never have been said *after* the destruction of the Lacedæmonian *mora*, which made so profound a sensation throughout Greece, and so greatly altered the temper of the contending parties. And it seems to me one proof (among others) that Mr. Fynes Clinton has not placed correctly the events subsequent to the battle of Corinth, when I observe that he assigns the destruction of the *mora* to the year 399 B.C., a year *before* the date which he rightly allots to the Andokidean oration. I have placed (though upon other grounds) the destruction of the *mora* in the spring of 390 B.C., which receives additional confirmation from this passage of Andokidês.

Both Valckenaer and Blotter (Lect. Andocid. c. x) consider the oration of Andokidês de Pace as genuine; Taylor and other critics hold the contrary opinion.

[1] Xen. Agesil. ii. 18.

narrowest breadth of the Isthmus, where the biennial Isthmian festival was celebrated.

It was the month of April or beginning of May, and the festival had actually begun, under the presidency of the Corinthians from the city who were in alliance with Argos; a body of Argeians being present as guards.[1] But on the approach of Agesilaus, they immediately retired to the city by the road to Kenchreæ, leaving their sacrifices half-finished. Not thinking fit to disturb their retreat, Agesilaus proceeded first to offer sacrifice himself, and then took a position close at hand, in the sacred ground of Poseidon, while the Corinthian exiles went through the solemnities in due form, and distributed the parsley wreaths to the victors. After remaining three days, Agesilaus marched away to attack Peiræum. He had no sooner departed than the Corinthians from the city came forth, celebrated the festival, and distributed the wreaths, a second time.

B.C. 390. Isthmian festival— Agesilaus disturbs the celebration. The Corinthian exiles, under his protection, celebrate it; then, when he is gone, the Corinthians from the city, and perform the ceremony over again.

---

[1] Xen. Hellen. iv. 5, 1; Plutarch, Agesil. c. 21.

Xenophon, who writes his history in the style and language of a partisan, says that "the Argeians celebrated the festival, Corinth having now become Argos." But it seems plain that the truth was as I have stated in the text—and that the Argeians stood by (with others of the confederates probably also) to protect the Corinthians of the city in the exercise of their usual privilege; just as Agesilaus, immediately afterwards, stood by to protect the Corinthian exiles while they were doing the same thing.

The Isthmian games were *trieteric*, that is, celebrated in every alternate year; in one of the spring months, about April or perhaps the beginning of May (the Greek months being lunar, no one of them would coincide regularly with any one of our calendar months, year after year); and in the *second* and *fourth* Olympic years. From Thucydidês, viii. 9, 10, we know that this festival was celebrated in April 412 B.C.; that is, towards the end of the *fourth* year of Olympiad 91, about two or three months before the festival of Olympiad 92.

Dodwell (De Cyclis Diss. vi. 2, just cited), Corsini (Diss. Agonistic. iv. 5), and Schneider in his note to this passage of Xenophon —all state the Isthmian games to have been celebrated in the *first* and *third* Olympic years; which is, in my judgement, a mistake. Dodwell erroneously states the Isthmian games mentioned in Thucydidês, viii. 9, to have been celebrated at the beginning of Olympiad 92, instead of the fourth quarter of the fourth year of Olympiad 91: a mistake pointed out by Krüger (ad loc.) as well as by Poppo and Dr. Arnold; although the argumentation of the latter, founded upon the time of the

> Peiræum was occupied by so numerous a guard, comprising Iphikratês and his peltasts, that Agesilaus, instead of directly attacking it, resorted to the stratagem of making a sudden retrograde march directly towards Corinth. Probably many of the citizens were at that moment absent for the second celebration of the festival; so that those remaining within, on hearing of the approach of Agesilaus, apprehended a plot to betray the city to him, and sent in haste to Peiræum to summon back Iphikratês with his peltasts.

*Agesilaus attacks Peiræum, which he captures, together with the Heræum, many prisoners, and much booty. B.C. 390.*

Having learnt that these troops had passed by in the night, Agesilaus forthwith again turned his course, and marched back to Peiræum, which he himself approached by the ordinary road, coasting round along the Bay of Lechæum, near the Therma, or warm springs which are still discernible;[1] while he sent a mora or division of troops to get round the place by a mountain-road more in the interior, ascending some woody heights commanding the town, and crowned by a temple of Poseidon.[2] The movement was quite effectual. The garrison and inhabitants of Peiræum, seeing that the place had become indefensible, abandoned it on the next day with all their cattle and property, to take refuge in the Heræum, or sacred ground of Hêrê Akræa, near the western cape of the peninsula.

---

Lacedæmonian festival of the Hyakinthia, is extremely uncertain. It is a still more strange idea of Dodwell, that the Isthmian games were celebrated at the same time as the Olympic games (Annal. Xenoph. ad ann. 392).

[1] See Ulrichs, Reisen und Forschungen in Griechenland, chap. l. p. 2. The modern village and port of Lutráki derives its name from these warm springs, which are quite close to it and close to the sea, at the foot of the mountain of Perachora or Peiræum; on the side of the bay opposite to Lechæum, but near the point where the level ground constituting the Isthmus (properly so-called), ends—and where the rocky or mountainous region, forming the westernmost portion of Geraneia (or the peninsula of Peiræum), begins. The language of Xenophon therefore when he comes to describe the back-march of Agesilaus is perfectly accurate—ἤδη δ᾽ ὑπερπεσόντος αὐτοῦ τὰ θερμὰ ἐς τὸ κατὰ τοῦ Ἀιγαίου, &c.(iv. 5, 8).

[2] Xen. Hellen. iv. 5, 4.

Xenophon here recounts how Agesilaus sent up ten men with fire in pans, to enable those on the heights to make fires and warm themselves; the night being very cold and rainy, the situation very high, and the troops not having come out with blankets or warm covering to protect them. They kindled large fires, and the neighbouring temple of Poseidon was accidentally burnt.

While Agesilaus marched thither towards the coast in pursuit of them, the troops descending from the heights attacked and captured Œnoê[1]—the Corinthian town of that name situated near the Alkyonian bay over against Kreusis in Bœotia. A large booty here fell into their hands, which was still farther augmented by the speedy surrender of all in the Heræum to Agesilaus, without conditions. Called upon to determine the fate of the prisoners, among whom were included men, women, and children—freemen and slaves—with cattle and other property—Agesilaus ordered that all those who had taken part in the massacre at Corinth in the market-place should be handed over to the vengeance of the exiles; and that all the rest should be sold as slaves.[2] Though he did not here inflict any harder measure than was usual in Grecian warfare, the reader who reflects that this sentence, pronounced by one on the whole more generous than most contemporary commanders, condemned numbers of free Corinthian men and women to a life of degradation, if not of misery—will understand by contrast the encomiums with which in another volume I set forth the magnanimity of Kallikratidas after the capture of Methymna; when he refused, in spite of the importunity of his allies, to sell either the Methymnæan or the Athenian captives—and when he proclaimed the exalted principle, that no free Greek should be sold into slavery by any permission of his.[3]

As the Lacedæmonians had been before masters of Lechæum, Krommyon, and Sidus, this last success shut up Corinth on its other side, and cut off its communication with Bœotia. The city not being in condition to hold out much longer, the exiles already began to lay their plans for surprising it by aid of friends within.[4] So trium-

---

[1] Xen. Hellen. iv. 5, 5.
This Œnoê must not be confounded with the Athenian town of that name, which lay on the frontiers of Attica towards Bœotia.
So also the town of Peiræum here noticed must not be confounded with another Peiræum, which was also in the Corinthian territory, but on the Saronic Gulf, and on the frontiers of Epidaurus (Thucyd. viii. 10).

[2] Xen. Hellen. iv. 5, 5–8.
[3] Xen. Hellen. l. 5, 14. See Ch. lxiv. of this History.
The sale of prisoners here directed by Agesilaus belies the encomiums of his biographers (Xen. Agesil. vii. 6; Cornel. Nep. Agesil. c. 5).
[4] Xen. Agesil. vii. 6; Cornelius Nepos, Ages. c. 5.
The story of Polyænus (iii. 9, 45) may perhaps refer to this point of

phant was the position of Agesilaus, that his enemies were all in alarm, and the Thebans, as well as others, sent fresh envoys to him to solicit peace. His antipathy towards the Thebans was so vehement, that it was a great personal satisfaction to him to see them thus humiliated. He even treated their envoys with marked contempt, affecting not to notice them when they stood close by, though Pharax, the proxenus of Thebes at Sparta, was preparing to introduce them.

*Triumphant position of Agesilaus. Danger of Corinth. The Thebans send fresh envoys to solicit peace—contemptuously treated by Agesilaus.*

Absorbed in this overweening pride, and exultation over conquered enemies, Agesilaus was sitting in a round pavilion, on the banks of the lake adjoining the Heræum,[1]—with his eyes fixed on the long train of captives brought out under the guard of armed Lacedæmonian hoplites, themselves the object of admiration to a crowd of spectators?—when news arrived, as if under the special intervention of retributive Nemesis, which changed unexpectedly the prospect of affairs.[2] A horseman was seen galloping up, his horse foaming with sweat. To the many inquiries addressed, he returned no answer, nor did he stop until he sprang from his horse at the feet of Agesi-

*Sudden arrival of bad news, which spoils the triumph.*

time. But it is rare that we can verify his anecdotes or those of the other Tactic writers. M. Rehdantz strives in vain to find proper places for the sixty-three different stratagems which Polyænus ascribes to Iphikratês.

[2] This lake is now called Lake Vuliasmeni. Considerable ruins were noticed by M. Dutroyat, in the recent French survey, near its western extremity; on which side it adjoins the temple of Hêrê Akræa, or the Heræum. See M. Boblaye, Recherches Géographiques sur les Ruines de la Morée, p. 86; and Colonel Leake's Peloponnesiaca, p. 399.

[2] Xen. Hellen. iv. 5, 6.
Τῶν δὲ Λακεδαιμονίων ἀπὸ τῶν ὅπλων σὺν τοῖς δόρασι κορηπολούθουν φύλακες τῶν αἰχμαλώτων, μάλα ὑπὸ

τῶν παρόντων θεωρούμενοι· οἱ γὰρ εὐτυχοῦντές και κρατοῦντες ἀεί πως ἀξιοθέατοι δοκοῦσιν εἶναι. Ἔτι δὲ καθημένου τοῦ Ἀγησιλάου, καὶ δεινότατος ἀπελλομένῳ τοῖς πεπραγμένοις, ἱππεύς τις προσήλαυνε, καὶ μάλα ἰσχυρῶς ἱδροῦντι τῷ ἵππῳ· ὑπὸ πολλῶν δὲ ἐρωτώμενος, ὅ,τι ἀγγέλλοι, οὐδενὶ ἀπεκρίνατο, &c.

It is interesting to mark in Xenophon the mixture of philo-Laconian complacency—of philosophical reflection—and of that care in bringing out the contrast of good fortune, with sudden reverse instantly following upon it, which forms so constant a point of effect with Grecian poets and historians.

[2] Plutarch, Agesil. c. 22. ἐπαθε δὲ πρᾶγμα νεμεσητόν, &c.

laus; to whom, with sorrowful tone and features, he made his communication. Immediately Agesilaus started up, seized his spear, and desired the herald to summon his principal officers. On their coming near, he directed them, together with the guards around, to accompany him without a moment's delay; leaving orders with the general body of the troops to follow as soon as they should have snatched some rapid refreshment. He then immediately put himself in march; but he had not gone far when three fresh horsemen met and informed him, that the task which he was hastening to perform had already been accomplished. Upon this he ordered a halt, and returned to the Heræum; where on the ensuing day, to countervail the bad news, he sold all his captives by auction.[1]

This bad news—the arrival of which has been so graphically described by Xenophon, himself probably among the bystanders and companions of Agesilaus—was nothing less than the defeat and destruction of a Lacedæmonian *mora* or military division by the light troops under Iphikratês. As it was an understood privilege of the Amyklæan hoplites in the Lacedæmonian army always to go home, even when on actual service, to the festival of the Hyakinthia, Agesilaus had left all of them at Lechæum. The festival day being now at hand, they set off to return. But the road from Lechæum to Sikyon lay immediately under the walls of Corinth, so that their march was not safe without an escort. Accordingly the polemarch commanding at Lechæum, leaving that place for the time under watch by the Peloponnesian allies, put himself at the head of the Lacedæmonian *mora* which formed the habitual garrison, consisting of 600 hoplites, and of a *mora* of cavalry (number unknown)—to protect the Amyklæans until they were out of danger from the enemy at Corinth. Having passed by Corinth, and reached a point within about three miles of the friendly town of Sikyon, he thought the danger over, and turned back with his *mora* of hoplites to Lechæum; still however leaving the officer of cavalry with orders to accompany the Amyklæans as much farther as they might choose, and afterwards to follow him on the return march.[2]

*Destruction of a Lacedæmonian mora by the light troops under Iphikratês.*

[1] Xen. Hellen. iv. 5, 7—8.   [2] Xen. Hellen. iv. 5, 11, 12.

Though the Amyklæans (probably not very numerous) were presumed to be in danger of attack from Corinth in their march, and though the force in that town was known to be considerable, it never occurred to the Lacedæmonian polemarch that there was any similar danger for his own *mora* of 600 hoplites; so contemptuous was his estimate of the peltasts, and so strong was the apprehension which these peltasts were known to entertain of the Lacedæmonians. But Iphikratês, who had let the whole body march by undisturbed, when he now saw from the walls of Corinth the 600 hoplites returning separately, without either cavalry or light troops, conceived the idea—perhaps in the existing state of men's minds, no one else would have conceived it—of attacking them with his peltasts as they repassed near the town. Kallias, the general of the Athenian hoplites in Corinth, warmly seconding the project, marched out his troops, and arrayed them in battle order not far from the gates; while Iphikratês with his peltasts began his attack upon the Lacedæmonian *mora* in flanks and rear. Approaching within missile distance, he poured upon them a shower of darts and arrows, which killed or wounded several, especially on the unshielded side. Upon this the polemarch ordered a halt, directed the youngest soldiers to drive off the assailants, and confided the wounded to the care of attendants to be carried forward to Lechæum.[1] But even the youngest soldiers, encumbered

*Daring and well-planned manœuvres of Iphikratês.*

---

[1] Xen. Hellen. iv. 5, 14. Τούτους μὲν ἐκέλευον τοὺς ὑπασπιστὰς ἀραμένους ἀποφέρειν εἰς Λέχαιον· οὗτοι καὶ μόνοι τῆς μόρας τῇ ἀληθείᾳ ἐσώθησαν.

We have here a remarkable expression of Xenophon—"These were the only men in the mora who were *really and truly saved*." He means, I presume, that they were the only men who were saved without the smallest loss of honour; being carried off wounded from the field of battle, and not having fled or deserted their posts. The others who survived, preserved themselves by flight; and we know that the treatment of those Lacedæmonians who ran away from the field (οἱ τρέσαντες), on their return to Sparta, was insupportably humiliating. See Xenoph. Rep. Laced. ix. 4; Plutarch, Agesil. c. 30. We may gather from these words of Xenophon, that a distinction was really made at Sparta between the treatment of these wounded men here carried off, and that of the other survivors of the beaten mora.

The ὑπασπισταί, or shield-bearers, were probably a certain number of attendants, who habitually carried the shields of the officers (compare Xen. Hellen. iv. 8, 39; Anab. iv. 2, 20), persons of im-

by their heavy shields, could not reach their nimbler enemies, who were trained to recede before them. And when, after an unavailing pursuit, they sought to resume their places in the ranks, the attack was renewed, so that nine or ten of them were slain before they could get back. Again did the polemarch give orders to march forward; again the peltasts renewed their attack, forcing him to halt; again he ordered the younger soldiers (this time, all those between 18 and 30 years of age, whereas on the former occasion, it had been those between 18 and 29) to rush out and drive them off.¹ But the result was just the same: the pursuers accomplished nothing, and only suffered increased loss of their bravest and most forward soldiers, when they tried to rejoin the main body. Whenever the Lacedæmonians attempted to make progress, these circumstances were again repeated, to their great loss and discouragement; while the peltasts became every moment more confident and vigorous.

Some relief was now afforded to the distressed *mora* by the coming up of their cavalry, which had finished the escort of the Amyklæans. Had this cavalry been with them at the beginning, the result might have been different; but it was now insufficient to repress the animated assaults of the peltasts. Moreover the Lacedæmonian horsemen were at no time very good, nor did they on this occasion venture to push their pursuit to a greater range than the younger hoplites could keep up with them. At length, after much loss in killed and wounded, and great distress to all, the polemarch contrived to get his detachment as far as an eminence about a quarter of a mile from the sea and about two miles from Lechæum. Here, while Iphikratês still continued to harass them with his peltasts, Kallias also was marching up with his hoplites to charge them hand to hand,—when the Lacedæmonians, enfeebled in numbers, exhausted in strength, and too much dispirited for close fight with a new enemy, broke and fled in all directions. Some took the road to Lechæum, which place a few of them reached,

*Few of the mora escape to Lechæum.*

pertinence, and rich hoplites. It seems hardly to be presumed that every hoplite had an ὑπασπιστής, in spite of what we read about the attendant Helots at the battle of Platæa (Herod. ix. 10–20) and in other places.

¹ Xen. Hellen. iv. 5, 15, 16. τὰ δύο ἀφ' ἥβης—τὰ πεντεκαίδεκα ἀφ' ἥβης.

along with the cavalry; the rest ran towards the sea at the nearest point, and observing that some of their friends were rowing in boats from Lechæum along the shore to rescue them, threw themselves into the sea, to wade or swim towards this new succour. But the active peltasts, irresistible in the pursuit of broken hoplites, put the last hand to the destruction of the unfortunate *mora*. Out of its full muster of 600, a very small proportion survived to re-enter Lechæum.¹

The horseman who first communicated the disaster to Agesilaus, had started off express immediately from Lechæum, even before the bodies of the slain had been picked up for burial. The hurried movement of Agesilaus had been dictated by the desire of reaching the field in time to contend for the possession of the bodies, and to escape the shame of soliciting the burial-truce. But the three horsemen who met him afterwards, arrested his course by informing him that the bodies had already been buried, under truce asked and obtained; which authorised Iphikratês to erect his well-earned trophy on the spot where he had first made the attack.²

*The Lacedæmonians bury the bodies of the slain, under truce asked and obtained. Trophy erected by Iphikratês.*

Such a destruction of an entire division of Lacedæmonian hoplites, by light troops who stood in awe of them and whom they despised, was an incident, not indeed of great political importance, but striking in respect of military

---

¹ Xen. Hellen. iv. 5, 17.
Xenophon affirms the number of slain to have been about 250—ἐν πάσαις δὲ ταῖς μάχαις καὶ .τῇ φυγῇ ἐκἰθανον περὶ πεντήκοντα καὶ διακοσίους. But he had before distinctly stated that the whole mora marching back to Lechæum under the polemarch, was 600 in number—ὁ μὲν πολέμαρχος σὺν τοῖς ὁπλίταις, οὖσιν ὡς ἑξακοσίοις, ἀπῄει πάλιν ἐπὶ τὸ Λέχαιον (iv. 5, 12). And it is plain, from several different expressions, that all of them were slain, excepting a very few survivors.
I think it certain therefore that one or other of these two numbers is erroneous; either the original aggregate of 600 is above the truth —or the total of slain, 250, is below the truth. Now the latter supposition appears to me by far the more probable of the two. The Lacedæmonians, habitually secret and misleading in their returns of their own numbers (see Thucyd. v. 74), probably did not choose to admit publicly a greater total of slain than 250. Xenophon has inserted this in his history, forgetting that his own details of the battle refuted the numerical statement. The total of 600 is more probable, than any smaller number, for the entire mora; and it is impossible to assign any reasons why Xenophon should overstate it.

² Xen. Hellen. iv. 5, 8-10.

effect and impression upon the Grecian mind. Nothing at all like it had occurred since the memorable capture of Sphakteria, thirty-five years before; a disaster less considerable in one respect, that the number of hoplites beaten was inferior by one-third—but far more important in another respect, that half the division had surrendered as prisoners; whereas in the battle near Corinth, though the whole mora (except a few fugitives) perished, it does not seem that a single prisoner was taken. *Great effect produced upon the Grecian mind by this event. Peculiar feelings of Spartans. Pride of the relatives of the slain.* Upon the Corinthians, Bœotians, and other enemies of Sparta, the event operated as a joyous encouragement, reviving them out of all their previous despondency. Even by the allies of Sparta, jealous of her superiority and bound to her by fear more than by attachment, it was welcomed with ill-suppressed satisfaction. But upon the army of Agesilaus (and doubtless upon the Lacedæmonians at home) it fell like a sudden thunderbolt, causing the strongest manifestations of sorrow and sympathy. To these manifestations there was only one exception—the fathers, brothers, or sons, of the slain warriors; who not only showed no sorrow, but strutted about publicly with cheerful and triumphant countenances, like victorious Athletes.[1] We shall find the like phænomenon at Sparta a few years subsequently, after the far more terrible defeat at Leuktra: the relatives of the slain were joyous and elate—those of the survivors, downcast and mortified;[2] a fact strikingly characteristic of the intense mental effect of the Spartan training, and of the peculiar associations which it generated. We may understand how terrible was the contempt which awaited a Spartan who survived defeat, when we find fathers positively rejoicing that their sons had escaped such treatment by death.

Sorely was Agesilaus requited for his supercilious insult towards the Theban envoys. When he at last consented to see them, after the news of the battle, their tone was completely altered. They said not a word about peace,

[1] Xen. Hellen. iv. 8, 10. Ἄτε δὴ ἀήθους τοῖς Λακεδαιμονίοις γεγενημένης τῆς τοιαύτης συμφορᾶς, πολὺ πένθος ἦν κατὰ τὸ Λακωνικὸν στράτευμα, πλὴν ὅσων ἐτέθνασαν ἐν χώρᾳ ἢ υἱοὶ ἢ πατέρες ἢ ἀδελφοί· οὗτοι δὲ, ὥσπερ νικηφόροι, λαμπροὶ καὶ ἀγαλλόμενοι τῷ οἰκείῳ πάθει περιῇσαν.

If any reader objects to the words which I have used in the text, I request him to compare them with the Greek of Xenophon.

[2] Xen. Hellen. vi. 4, 16.

but merely asked permission to pass through and communicate with their countrymen in Corinth. "I understand your purpose (said Agesilaus, smiling)—you want to witness the triumph of your friends, and see what it is worth. Come along with me and I will teach you." Accordingly, on the next day, he caused them to accompany him while he marched his army up to the very gates of Corinth,—defying those within to come out and fight. The lands had been so ravaged, that there remained little to destroy. But wherever there were any fruit-trees yet standing, the Lacedæmonians now cut them down. Iphikratês was too prudent to compromise his recent advantage by hazarding a second battle; so that Agesilaus had only the satisfaction of showing that he was master of the field, and then retired to encamp at Lechæum; from whence he sent back the Theban envoys by sea to Kreusis. Having then left a fresh mora or division at Lechæum, in place of that which had been defeated, he marched back to Sparta. But the circumstances of the march betrayed his real feelings, thinly disguised by the recent bravado of marching up to the gates of Corinth. He feared to expose his Lacedæmonian troops even to the view of those allies through whose territory he was to pass; so well was he aware that the latter (especially the Mantineians) would manifest their satisfaction at the recent defeat. Accordingly he commenced his day's march before dawn, and did not halt for the night till after dark: at Mantineia, he not only did not halt at all, but passed by, outside of the walls, before day had broken.[1] There cannot be a more convincing proof of the real dispositions of the allies towards Sparta, and of the sentiment of compulsion which dictated their continued adherence; a fact which we shall see abundantly illustrated as we advance in the stream of the history.

The retirement of Agesilaus was the signal for renewed enterprise on the part of Iphikratês; who retook Sidus and Krommyon, which had been garrisoned by Praxitas—as well as Peiræum and Œnoê, which had been left under occupation by Agesilaus. Corinth

[1] Xen. Hellen. iv. 6, 10.

was thus cleared of enemies on its eastern and northeastern sides. And though the Lacedæmonians still carried on a desultory warfare from Lechæum, yet such was the terror impressed by the late destruction of their mora, that the Corinthian exiles at Sikyon did not venture to march by land from that place to Lechæum, under the walls of Corinth—but communicated with Lechæum only by sea.[1] In truth we hear of no farther serious military operations undertaken by Sparta against Corinth, before the peace of Antalkidas. And the place became so secure, that the Corinthian leaders and their Argeian allies were glad to dispense with the presence of Iphikratês. That officer had gained so much glory by his recent successes, which the Athenian orators[2] even in the next generation never ceased to extol, that his temper, naturally haughty, became domineering; and he tried to procure, either for Athens or for himself, the mastery of Corinth—putting to death some of the philo-Argeian leaders. We know these circumstances only by brief and meagre allusion; but they caused the Athenians to recall Iphikratês with a large portion of his peltasts, and to send Chabrias to Corinth in his place.[3]

It was either in the ensuing summer—or perhaps immediately afterwards during the same summer, 390 B.C.—that Agesilaus undertook an expedition into Akarnania; at the instance of the Achæans, who threatened, if this were not done, to forsake the Lacedæmonian alliance. They had acquired possession of the Ætolian district of Kalydon, had brought the neighbouring villagers into a city residence, and garrisoned it as a dependence of the Achæan confederacy. But the Akarnanians—allies of Athens as well as Thebes, and aided by an Athenian squadron at Œniadæ—attacked them there, probably at the invitation of a portion

[1] Xen. Hellen. iv. 8, 19.
[2] Demosthenês—περὶ Συντάξεως—c. 8, p. 172.
[3] Diodor. xiv. 92; Xen. Hellen. iv. 8, 34.
Aristeidês (Panathen. p. 168) boasts that the Athenians were masters of the Acro-Corinthus, and might have kept the city as their own, but that they generously refused to do so.

of the inhabitants, and pressed them so hard, that they employed the most urgent instances to obtain aid from Sparta. Agesilaus crossed the Gulf at Rhium with a considerable force of Spartans and allies, and the full muster of the Achæans. On his arrival, the Akarnanians all took refuge in their cities, sending their cattle up into the interior highlands, to the borders of a remote lake. Agesilaus, having sent to Stratus to require them not merely to forbear hostilities against the Achæans, but to relinquish their alliance with Athens and Thebes, and to become allies of Sparta—found his demands resisted, and began to lay waste the country. Two or three days of operations designedly slack, were employed to lull the Akarnanians into security; after which, by a rapid forced march, Agesilaus suddenly surprised the remote spot in which their cattle and slaves had been deposited for safety. He spent a day here to sell this booty; merchants probably accompanying his army. But he had considerable difficulty in his return march, from the narrow paths and high mountains through which he had to thread his way. By a series of brave and well-combined hill-movements,— which probably reminded Xenophon of his own operations against the Karduchians in the retreat of the Ten Thousand —he defeated and dispersed the Akarnanians, though not without suffering considerably from the excellence of their light troops. Yet he was not successful in his attack upon any one of their cities, nor would he consent to prolong the war until seed-time, notwithstanding earnest solicitation from the Achæans, whom he pacified by engaging to return the next spring. He was indeed in a difficult and dangerous country, had not his retreat been facilitated by the compliance of the Ætolians; who calculated (though vainly) on obtaining from him the recovery of Naupaktus, then held (as well as Kalydon) by the Achæans.[1] Partial as the success of this expedition had been, however, it inflicted sufficient damage on the Akarnanians to accomplish its purpose. On learning that it was about to be repeated in the ensuing spring, they sent envoys to Sparta to solicit peace; consenting to abstain from hostilities against the Achæans, and to enrol themselves as members of the Lacedæmonian confederacy.[2]

[1] Diodor. xv. 73.   [2] Xen. Hellen. iv. 6, 1-14; iv. 7, 1.

It was in this same year that the Spartan authorities resolved on an expedition against Argos, of which Agesipolis, the other king, took the command. Having found the border sacrifices favourable, and crossed the frontier, he sent forward his army to Phlius, where the Peloponnesian allies were ordered to assemble; but he himself first turned aside to Olympia, to consult the oracle of Zeus.

It had been the practice of the Argeians, seemingly on more than one previous occasion,[1] when an invading Lacedæmonian army was approaching their territory, to meet them by a solemn message, intimating that it was the time of some festival (the Karneian or other) held sacred by both parties, and warning them not to violate the frontier during the holy truce. This was in point of fact nothing better than a fraud; for the notice was sent, not at the moment when the Karneian festival (or other, as the case might be) ought to come on according to the due course of seasons, but at any time when it might serve the purpose of arresting a Lacedæmonian invasion. But though the duplicity of the Argeians was thus manifest, so strong were the pious scruples of the Spartan king, that he could hardly make up his mind to disregard the warning. Moreover in the existing confusion of the calendar, there was always room for some uncertainty as to the question, which was the true Karneian moon; no Dorian state having any right to fix it imperatively for the others, as the Eleians fixed the Olympic truce, and the Corinthians the Isthmian. It was with a view to satisfy his conscience on this subject that Agesipolis now went to Olympia, and put the question to the oracle of Zeus; whether he might with a safe religious conscience refuse to accept the holy truce, if the Argeians should now tender it. The oracle, habitually dexterous in meeting a specific question with a general reply, informed him, that he might with a safe conscience decline a truce demanded wrongfully and for underhand purposes.[2] This was accepted

---

[1] Xen. Hellen. iv. 7, 2. Οἱ δ᾽ Ἀργεῖοι, ἐπεὶ ἤισθοντο οὐ δυνησόμενοι κωλύειν, ἔπεμψαν, ὥσπερ εἰώθεσαν, ἐστεφανωμένους δύο κήρυκας, ὑποφέροντας σπονδάς.

[2] Xen. Hellen. iv. 7, 2. Ὁ δὲ Ἀγησίπολις—ἐλθὼν εἰς τὴν Ὀλυμπίαν καὶ χρηστηριασάμενος, ἐπηρώτα τὸν

by Agesipolis as a satisfactory affirmative. Nevertheless, to make assurance doubly sure, he went directly forward to Delphi, to put the same question to Apollo. As it would have been truly embarrassing, however, if the two holy replies had turned out such as to contradict each other, he availed himself of the *præjudicium* which he had already received at Olympia, and submitted the question to Apollo at Delphi in this form— "Is thine opinion, on the question

θεόν, εἰ ὁσίως ἂν ἔχοι αὐτῷ, μὴ δεχομένῳ τὰς σπονδὰς τῶν Ἀργείων ὅτι οὐχ, ὁπότε καθήκοι ὁ χρόνος, ἀλλ' ὁπότε ἐμβάλλειν μέλλοιεν Λακεδαιμόνιοι, τότε ὑπέφερον τοὺς μῆνας. Ὁ δὲ θεὸς ἀπεσήμαινεν αὐτῷ, ὅσιον εἶναι μὴ δεχομένῳ σπονδὰς ἀδίκως ὑπερερομένας. Ἐντεῦθεν δ' εὐθὺς πορευθεὶς εἰς Δελφοὺς, ἐπήρετο αὖ τὸν Ἀπόλλω, εἰ κἀκείνῳ δοκοίη περὶ τῶν σπονδῶν, καθάπερ τῷ πατρί. Ὁ δ' ἀνευρίνατο, καὶ μάλα κατὰ ταὐτά.

I have given in the text what I believe to be the meaning of the words ὑποφέρειν τοὺς μῆνας—upon which Schneider has a long and not very instructive note, adopting an untenable hypothesis of Dodwell, that the Argeians on this occasion appealed to the sanctity of the Isthmian truce; which is not countenanced by anything in Xenophon, and which it belonged to the Corinthians to announce, not to the Argeians. The plural τοὺς μῆνας indicates (as Weiske and Manso understand it) that the Argeians sometimes put forward the name of one festival, sometimes of another. We may be pretty sure that the Karpeian festival was one of them; but what the others were we cannot tell. It is very probable that there were several festivals of common obligation either among all the Dorians, or between Sparta and Argos—πατρῴους τινὰς σπονδὰς ἐκ παλαιοῦ καθεστώσας τοῖς Δωριεῦσι πρὸς ἀλλήλους —to use the language of Pausanias (ii. 5, 6). The language of Xeno-

phon implies that the demand made by the Argeians, for observance of the Holy Truce, was in itself rightful, or rather, that it would have been rightful at a different season; but that they put themselves in the wrong by making it at an improper season and for a fraudulent political purpose.

For some remarks on other frandulent manœuvres of the Argeians, respecting the season of the Karneian truce, see an earlier passage of this History, Ch. lvi. The compound verb ὑποφέρειν τοὺς μῆνας seems to imply the *underhand* purpose with which the Argeians preferred their demand of the truce. What were the previous occasions on which they had preferred a similar demand, we are not informed. Two years before, Agesilaus had invaded and laid waste Argos; perhaps they may have tried, but without success, to arrest his march by a similar pious fraud.

It is to this proceeding, perhaps, that Andokidês alludes (Or. iii. De Pace, s. 27), where he says that the Argeians, though strenuous in insisting that Athens should help them to carry on the war for the possession of Corinth against the Lacedæmonians, had nevertheless made a separate peace with the latter covering their own Argeian territory from invasion—αὐτοὶ δ' ἰδίᾳ εἰρήνην ποιησάμενοι τὴν χώραν οὐ παρέχουσιν ἐμπολεμεῖν. Of this obscure passage I can give no better explanation.

of the holy truce, the same as that of thy father (Zeus)?"
"Most decidedly the same," replied the god. Such double
warranty, though the appeal was so drawn up as scarcely
to leave to Apollo freedom of speech,[1] enabled Agesipolis
to return with full confidence to Phlius, where his army
was already mustered; and to march immediately into the
Argeian territory by the road of Nemea. Being met on
the frontier by two heralds with wreaths and in solemn
attire, who warned him that it was a season of holy truce,
he informed them that the gods authorized his disobedience
to their summons, and marched on into the Argeian plain.

It happened that on the first evening after he had crossed
the border, the supper and the consequent liba-
tion having been just concluded, an earthquake       Earthquake
occurred; or, to translate the Greek phrase,         in Argos
"the god (Poseidon) shook." To all Greeks,           after the
and to Lacedæmonians especially, this was a          invasion of
solemn event, and the personal companions of         Agesipolis
Agesipolis immediately began to sing the pæan in honour   —he disre-
of Poseidon; the general impression among the soldiers    garde it.
being, that he would give orders for quitting the territory
immediately, as Agis had acted in the invasion of Elis a
few years before. Perhaps Agesipolis would have done
the same here, construing the earthquake as a warning
that he had done wrong in neglecting the summons of the
heralds — had he not been fortified by the recent oracles.
He now replied, that if the earthquake had occurred before
he crossed the frontier, he should have considered it as a
prohibition; but as it came after his crossing, he looked
upon it as an encouragement to go forward.

So fully had the Argeians counted on the success of
their warning transmitted by the heralds, that        He marches
they had made little preparation for defence.         up near to
Their dismay and confusion were very great:           Argos—
their property was still outlying, not yet remo-      much
ved into secure places, so that Agesipolis found      plunder
much both to destroy and to appropriate. He           taken—he
carried his ravages even to the gates of the city, piquing   retires.

[1] Aristotel. Rhetoric. ii. 23. Ἡγή- of putting the question to Apollo
σιππος ἐν Δελφοῖς ἐπηρώτα τὸν θεόν, at Delphi, after it had already been
συγχρώμενος πρότερον Ὀλυμπίασιν, εἰ put to Zeus at Dodona, is told
αὐτῷ ταὐτὰ δοκεῖ, ὥσπερ τῷ πατρί, about Agesilaus on another oc-
ὡς αἰσχρὸν ὃν τἀναντία εἰπεῖν. casion (Plutarch, Apophth. Lacon.
A similar story, about the manner p. 208 F.).

himself on advancing a little farther than Agesilaus had gone in his invasion two years before. He was at last driven to retreat by the terror of a flash of lightning in his camp, which killed several persons. And a project which he had formed, of erecting a permanent fort on the Argeian frontier, was abandoned in consequence of unfavourable sacrifices.[1]

*Transactions in Asia— efforts of Sparta to detach the Great King from Athens.*

Besides these transactions in and near the Isthmus of Corinth, the war between Sparta and her enemies was prosecuted during the same years both in the islands and on the coast of Asia Minor; though our information is so imperfect that we can scarcely trace the thread of events. The defeat near Knidus (394 B.C.),—the triumphant maritime force of Pharnabazus and Konon at the Isthmus of Corinth in the ensuing year (393 B.C.),—the restoration of the Athenian Long Walls and fortified port,—and the activity of Konon with the fleet among the islands²—so alarmed the Spartans with the idea of a second Athenian maritime empire, that they made every effort to detach the Persian force from the side of their enemies.

*The Spartan Antalkidas is sent as envoy to Tiribazus. Konon and other envoys sent also, from Athens and the anti-Spartan allies.*

The Spartan Antalkidas, a dexterous, winning, and artful man,³ not unlike Lysander, was sent as envoy to Tiribazus (392 B.C.); whom we now find as satrap of Ionia in the room of Tithraustês, after having been satrap of Armenia during the retreat of the Ten Thousand. As Tiribazus was newly arrived in Asia Minor, he had not acquired that personal enmity against the Spartans, which the active hostilities of Derkyllidas and Agesilaus had inspired to Pharnabazus and

---

[1] Xen. Hellen. iv. 7, 7; Pausan. iii. 5, 6.

It rather seems, by the language of these two writers, that they look upon the menacing signs, by which Agesipolis was induced to depart, as marks of some displeasure of the gods against his expedition.

[2] Xen. Hellen. iv. 8, 12. Compare Isokratês, Or. vii. (Areopag.) s. 13. ἑκάστης γάρ τῆς Ἑλλάδος ὑπὸ τῇν πόλιν ὑμῶν ὑποστάσης καὶ μετὰ τὴν Κόνωνος ναυμαχίαν καὶ μετὰ τὴν Τιμοθέου στρατηγίαν, &c. This oration however was composed a long

while after the events (about B.C. 853—see Mr. Clinton's Fast. H. in that year); and Isokratês exaggerates; mistaking the break-up of the Lacedæmonian empire for a resumption of the Athenian. Demosthenês also (cont. Lept. c. 16, p. 477) confounds the same two ideas; and even the Athenian vote of thanks to Konon, perpetuated on a commemorative column, countenanced the same impression— ἐπειδὴ Κόνων ἠλευθέρωσε τοὺς Ἀθηναίων συμμάχους, &c.

[3] Plutarch, Artaxerx. c. 22.

other Persians. Moreover jealousy between neighbouring satraps was an ordinary feeling, which Antalkidas now hoped to turn to the advantage of Sparta. To counteract his projects, envoys were also sent to Tiribazus, by the confederate enemies of Sparta—Athens, Thebes, Corinth, and Argos: and Konon, as the envoy of Athens, was incautiously dispatched among the number. On the part of Sparta, Antalkidas offered, first, to abandon to the King of Persia all the Greeks on the continent of Asia; next, as to all the other Greeks, insular as well as continental, he required nothing more than absolute autonomy for each separate city, great and small.[1] The Persian King (he said) could neither desire anything more for himself, nor have any motive for continuing the war against Sparta, when he should once be placed in possession of all the towns on the Asiatic coast, and when he should find both Sparta and Athens rendered incapable of annoying him, through the autonomy and disunion of the Hellenic world. But to neither of the two propositions of Antalkidas would Athens, Thebes, or Argos, accede. As to the first, they repudiated the disgrace of thus formally abandoning the Asiatic Greeks;[2] as to the second pro-

[1] Xen. Hellen. iv. 8, 12-14.
[2] Diodor. xiv. 110. He affirms that these cities strongly objected to this concession, five years afterwards, when the peace of Antalkidas was actually concluded; but that they were forced to give up their scruples and accept the peace including the concession, because they had not force enough to resist Persia and Sparta acting in hearty alliance.

Hence we may infer with certainty, that they also objected to it during the earlier discussions, when it was first broached by Antalkidas; and that their objections to it were in part the cause why the discussions reported in the text broke off without result.

It is true that Athens, during her desperate struggles in the last years of the Peloponnesian War, had consented to this concession, and even to greater, without doing herself any good (Thucyd. viii. 56). But she was not now placed in circumstances so imperious as to force her to be equally yielding.

Plato, in the Menexenus (c. 17. p. 245), asserts that all the allies of Athens—Bœotians, Corinthians, Argeians, &c., were willing to surrender the Asiatic Greeks at the requisition of Artaxerxes; but that the Athenians alone resolutely stood out, and were in consequence left without any allies. The latter part of this assertion, as to the isolation of Athens from her allies, is certainly not true; nor do I believe that the allies took essentially different views from Athens on the point. The Menexenus, eloquent and complimentary to Athens, must be followed cautiously as to matters of fact. Plato goes the length of denying that

position, guaranteeing autonomy to every distinct city of Greece, they would admit it only under special reserves, which it did not suit the purpose of Antalkidas to grant. In truth the proposition went to break up (and was framed with that view) both the Bœotian confederacy under the presidency of Thebes, and the union between Argos and Corinth; while it also deprived Athens of the chance of recovering Lemnos, Imbros, and Skyros[1]—islands which had been possessed and recolonised by her since the first commencement of the confederacy of Delos; indeed the two former, even from the time of Miltiadês the conqueror of Marathon.

*Antalkidas offers to surrender the Asiatic Greeks, and demands universal autonomy throughout the Grecian world—the anti-Spartan allies refuse to accede to those terms.*

Here commences a new era in the policy of Sparta. That she should abnegate all pretension to maritime empire, is noway difficult to understand —seeing that it had already been irrevocably overthrown by the defeat of Knidus. Nor can we wonder that she should abandon the Greeks on the Asiatic continent to Persian sway; since this was nothing more than she had already consented to do in her conventions with Tissaphernês and Cyrus during the latter years of the Peloponnesian War[2]—and consented, let us add, not under any of that stringent necessity which at the same time pressed upon Athens, but simply with a view to the maximum of victory over an enemy already enfeebled. The events which followed the close of that war (recounted in a former chapter) had indeed induced her to alter her determination, and again to espouse their cause. But the real novelty now first exhibited in her policy, is, the full development of what had before existed in manifest tendency.—hostility against all the partial land-confederacies of Greece, disguised under the plausible demand of universal autonomy for every town, great or small. How this autonomy was construed and carried into act, we shall see

*Hostility of Sparta to all the partial confederacies of Greece, now first proclaimed under the name of universal autonomy.*

---

the Athenians subscribed the convention of Antalkidas. Aristeidês (Panathen. p. 172) says that they were forced to subscribe it, because all their allies abandoned them.

[1] Xen. Hellen. iv. 8, 15.
[2] See a striking passage in the Or. xii. (Panathen.) of Isokratês, s. 110.

hereafter; at present, we have only to note the first proclamation of it by Antalkidas in the name of Sparta.

On this occasion, indeed, his mission came to nothing, from the peremptory opposition of Athens and the others. But he was fortunate enough to gain the approbation and confidence of Tiribazus; who saw so clearly how much both propositions tended to promote the interests and power of Persia, that he resolved to go up in person to court, and prevail on Artaxerxes to act in concert with Sparta. Though not daring to support Antalkidas openly, Tiribazus secretly gave him money to reinforce the Spartan fleet. He at the same time rendered to Sparta the far more signal service of arresting and detaining Konon, pretending that the latter was acting contrary to the interests of the King.[1] This arrest was a gross act of perfidy, since Konon not only commanded respect in his character of envoy—but had been acting with the full confidence, and almost under the orders, of Pharnabazus. But the removal of an officer of so much ability,—the only man who possessed the confidence of Pharnabazus,—was the most fatal of all impediments to the naval renovation of Athens. It was fortunate that Konon had had time to rebuild the Long Walls, before his means of action were thus abruptly intercepted. Respecting his subsequent fate, there exist contradictory stories. According to one, he was put to death by the Persians in prison; according to another, he found means to escape and again took refuge with Evagoras in Cyprus, in which island he afterwards died of sickness.[2] The latter story appears undoubtedly to be the true one. But it is certain that he never afterwards had the means of performing any public service, and that his career was cut short by this treacherous detention, just at the moment when its promise was the most splendid for his country.

*Side note:* Antalkidas gains the favour of Tiribazus, who espouses privately the cause of Sparta, though the propositions for peace fail. Tiribazus seizes Konon—Konon's career is now closed, either by death or imprisonment.

[1] Xen. Hellen. iv. 8, 16; Diodor. xiv. 85.
[2] Lysias, Or. xix. (De Bon. Aristoph.) s. 41, 42, 44; Cornelius Nepos, Conon, c. 5; Isokratês, Or. iv. (Panegyr.) s. 180.

Tiribazus, on going up to the Persian court, seems to have been detained there for the purpose of concerting measures against Evagoras prince of Salamis in Cyprus, whose revolt from Persia was on the point of breaking out. But the Persian court could not yet be prevailed upon to show any countenance to the propositions of Sparta or of Antalkidas. On the contrary, Struthas, who was sent down to Ionia as temporary substitute for Tiribazus, full of anxiety to avenge the ravages of Agesilaus, acted with vigorous hostility against the Lacedæmonians, and manifested friendly dispositions towards Athena.

*Tiribazus cannot prevail with the Persian court, which still continues hostile to Sparta. Struthas is sent down to act against the Lacedæmonians in Ionia.*

Thimbron (of whom we have before heard as first taking the command of the Cyreian army in Asia Minor, after their return from Thrace) received orders again to act as head of the Lacedæmonian forces in Asia against Struthas. The new commander, with an army estimated by Diodorus at 8000 men,[1] marched from Ephesus into the interior, and began his devastation of the territory dependent on Persia. But his previous command, though he was personally amiable,[2] had been irregular and disorderly, and it was soon observed that the same defects were now yet more prominent, aggravated by too liberal indulgence in convivial pleasures. Aware of his rash, contemptuous, and improvident mode of attack, Struthas laid a snare for him by sending a detachment of cavalry to menace the camp, just when Thimbron had concluded his morning meal in company with the flute-player Thersander—the latter not merely an excellent musician, but possessed of a full measure of Spartan courage. Starting from his tent at the news, Thimbron with Thersander, waited only to collect the few troops immediately at hand, without even leaving any orders for the remainder, and hastened to repel the assailants; who gave way easily, and seduced him into a pursuit. Presently

*B.C. 391. Victory of Struthas over Thimbron and the Lacedæmonian army. Thimbron is slain.*

---

[1] Diodor. xiv. 99.
[2] Xen. Hellen. iv. 8, 22. Ἦν δὲ οὗτος ἀνὴρ (Diphridas) εὐχαρὶς τε οὐχ ἧττον τοῦ Θιμβρωνος, μᾶλλόν τε συντεταγμένος, καὶ ἐγ- χειρητικώτερος στρατηγός· οὐδὲ γὰρ ἐκράτουν αὐτοῦ αἱ τοῦ σώματος ἡδοναὶ, ἀλλ' ἀεὶ, πρὸς ᾧ εἴη ἔργῳ, τοῦτο ἔπραττεν.

Struthas himself, appearing with a numerous and well-arrayed body of cavalry, charged with vigour the disorderly detachment of Thimbron. Both that general and Thersander, bravely fighting, fell among the first; while the army, deprived of their commander, as well as ill-prepared for a battle, made but an ineffective resistance. They were broken, warmly pursued, and the greater number slain. A few who contrived to escape the active Persian cavalry, found shelter in the neighbouring cities.[1]

This victory of Struthas, gained by the Persian cavalry, displays a degree of vigour and ability which, fortunately for the Greeks, was rarely seen in Persian operations. Our scanty information does not enable us to trace its consequences. We find Diphridas sent out soon after by the Lacedæmonians, along with the admiral Ekdikus, as successor of Thimbron, to bring together the remnant of the defeated army, and to protect those cities which had contributed to form it. Diphridas—a man with all the popular qualities of his predecessor, but a better and more careful officer—is said to have succeeded to some extent in this difficult mission. Being fortunate enough to take captive the son-in-law of Struthas with his wife (as Xenophon had captured Asidatês), he obtained a sufficiently large ransom to enable him to pay his troops for some time.[2] But it is evident that his achievements were not considerable, and that the Ionian Greeks on the continent are now left to make good their position, as they can, against the satrap at Sardis.

B.C. 390. Diphridas is sent to succeed Thimbron.

The forces of Sparta were much required at Rhodes; which island (as has been mentioned already) had revolted from Sparta about five years before (a few months anterior to the battle of Knidus), dispossessed the Lysandrian oligarchy, and established a democratical government. But since that period, an opposition-party in the island had gradually risen up, acquired strength, and come into correspondence with the oligarchical exiles; who on their side warmly solicited aid from Sparta, representing that Rhodes would otherwise become thoroughly dependent on Athens. Accordingly the Lacedæmonians sent eight triremes across the Ægean under the command of Ekdikus;

B.C. 890. Lacedæmonian fleet at Rhodes—intestine disputes in the island.

[1] Xen. Hellen. iv. 8, 18, 19.   [2] Xen. Hellen. iv. 8, 21, 22.

the first of their ships of war which had crossed since the
defeat of Knidus.[1] Though the Perso-Athenian naval
force in the Ægean had been either dismissed or paralysed
since the seizure of Konon, yet the Rhodian government
possessed a fleet of about twenty triremes, besides considerable force of other kinds; so that Ekdikus could not even
land on the island, but was compelled to halt at Knidus.
Fortunately, Teleutias the Lacedæmonian was now in the
Corinthian Gulf with a fleet of twelve triremes, which
were no longer required there; since Agesilaus and he had
captured Lechæum a few months before, and destroyed the
maritime force of the Corinthians in those waters. He
was now directed to sail with his squadron out of the Corinthian Gulf across to Asia, to supersede Ekdikus, and
take the command of the whole fleet for operations off
Rhodes. On passing by Samos, he persuaded the inhabitants to embrace the cause of Sparta, and to furnish him
with a few ships; after which he went onward to Knidus,
where, superseding Ekdikus, he found himself at the head
of twenty-seven triremes.[2] In his way from Knidus to
Rhodes, he accidentally fell in with the Athenian admiral
Philokratês, conducting ten triremes to Cyprus to the aid
of Evagoras in his struggle against the Persians. He was
fortunate enough to carry them as prisoners into Knidus,
where he sold the whole booty, and then proceeded with
his fleet, thus augmented to thirty-seven sail, to Rhodes.
Here he established a fortified post, enabling the oligarchical party to carry on an active civil war. But he was
defeated in a battle—his enemies being decidedly the
stronger force in the island, and masters of all the
cities.[3]

---

[1] Xen. Hellen. iv. 8, 21.
[2] Xen. Hellen. iv. 8, 23.
Diodorus (xiv. 97) agrees in this
number of 27 triremes, and in the
fact of aid having been obtained
from Samos, which island was
persuaded to detach itself from
Athens. But he recounts the circumstances in a very different
manner. He represents the oligarchical party in Rhodes as having risen in insurrection, and become masters of the island: he
does not name Teleutias, but Eu-
dokimus (Ekdikus?), Diphilus
(Diphridas?), and Philodikus, as
commanders.
The statement of Xenophon deserves the greater credence, in
my judgement. His means of information, as well as his interest,
about Teleutias (the brother of
Agesilaus) were considerable.
[3] Xen. Hellen. iv. 8, 24—26.
Although the three ancient Rhodian cities (Lindus, Ialysus, and
Kameirus) had coalesced (see
Diodor. xiii. 75) a few years before

The alliance with Evagoras of Cyprus, in his contention against Artaxerxês, was at this moment an unfortunate and perplexing circumstance for Athens, since she was relying upon Persian aid against Sparta, and since Sparta was bidding against her for it. But the alliance was one which she could not lightly throw off. For Evagoras had not only harboured Konon with the remnant of the Athenian fleet after the disaster of Ægospotami, but had earned a grant of citizenship and the honour of a statue at Athens, as a strenuous auxiliary in procuring that Persian aid which gained the battle of Knidus, and as a personal combatant in that battle, before the commencement of his dissension with Artaxerxês.[1] It would have been every way advantageous to Athens at this moment to decline assisting Evagoras, since, (not to mention the probability of offending the Persian court) she had more than enough to employ all her maritime force nearer home and for purposes more essential to herself. Yet in spite of these very serious considerations of prudence, the paramount feelings of prior obligation and gratitude, enforced by influential citizens who had formed connexions in Cyprus, determined the Athenians to identify themselves with his gallant struggles[2] (of which I shall speak more fully presently). So little was fickleness, or instability, or the easy oblivion of past feelings, a part of their real nature—though historians have commonly denounced it as among their prominent qualities.

*The Athenians send aid to Evagoras at Cyprus. Fidelity with which they adhered to him, though his alliance had now become inconvenient.*

The capture of their squadron under Philokratês, how-

---

into the great city of Rhodes, afterwards so powerful and celebrated—yet they still continued to exist, and apparently as fortified places. For Xenophon speaks of the democrats in Rhodes as τάς τε πόλεις ἔχοντας, &c. Whether the Philokratês here named as *Philokratês son of Ephialtês*, is the same person as the Philokratês accused in the Thirtieth Oration of Lysias—cannot be certainly made out. It is possible enough that there might be two contemporary Athenians bearing this name, which would explain the circumstance that Xenophon here names the father Ephialtês—a practice occasional with him, but not common.

[1] Isokratês, Or. ix. (Evagoras) s. 67, 68, 62; Epistola Philippi ap. Demosthen. Orat. p. 161. c. 4.

[2] Lysias, Orat. xix. (De Bonis Aristoph.) s. 87—44.

B.C. 389.

Thrasybulus is sent with a fleet from Athens to the Asiatic coast—his acquisitions in the Hellespont and Bosphorus.

ever, and the consequent increase of the Lacedæmonian naval force at Rhodes, compelled the Athenians to postpone further aid to Evagoras, and to arm forty triremes under Thrasybulus for the Asiatic coast; no inconsiderable effort, when we recollect that four years before, there was scarcely a single trireme in Peiræus, and not even a wall of defence around the place. Though sent immediately for the assistance of Rhodes, Thrasybulus judged it expedient to go first to the Hellespont; probably from extreme want of money to pay his men. Derkyllidas was still in occupation of Abydos, yet there was no Lacedæmonian fleet in the strait; so that Thrasybulus was enabled to extend the alliances of Athens both on the European and the Asiatic side—the latter being under the friendly satrap Pharnabazus. Reconciling the two Thracian princes, Seuthês and Amadokus, whom he found at war, he brought both of them into amicable relations with Athens, and then moved forward to Byzantium. That city was already in alliance with Athens; but on the arrival of Thrasybulus, the alliance was still further cemented by the change of its government into a democracy. Having established friendship with the opposite city of Chalkedon, and being thus master of the Bosphorus, he sold the tithe of the commercial ships sailing out of the Euxine;[1] leaving doubtless an adequate force to exact it. This was a striking evidence of revived Athenian maritime power, which seems also to have been now extended more or less to Samothrace, Thasus, and the coast of Thrace.[2]

Victory of Thrasybulus in Lesbos—he levies contributions along the Asiatic coast—he is slain near Aspendus.

From Byzantium Thrasybulus sailed to Mitylênê, which was already in friendship with Athens; though Methymna and the other cities in the island were still maintained by a force under the Lacedæmonian harmost Therimachus. With the aid of the Mitylenæans, and of the exiles from other Lesbian cities, Thrasybulus marched to the borders of Methymna, where he was met by Therimachus; who had also brought together his utmost force, but was now completely de-

[1] Xen. Hellen. iv. 8, 25—27. Polybius (iv. 38—47) gives instructive remarks and information about the importance of Byzantium and its very peculiar position, in the ancient world—as well as about the dues charged on the merchant-vessels going in to, or coming out of, the Euxine—and the manner in which these dues pressed upon general trade.

[2] Xen. Hellen. v. 1, 7.

feated and slain. The Athenians thus became masters of Antissa and Eresus, where they were enabled to levy a valuable contribution, as well as to plunder the refractory territory of Methymna. Nevertheless Thrasybulus, in spite of farther help from Chios and Mitylênê, still thought himself not in a situation to go to Rhodes with advantage. Perhaps he was not sure of pay in advance, and the presence of unpaid troops in an exhausted island might be a doubtful benefit. Accordingly, he sailed from Lesbos along the western and southern coast of Asia Minor, levying contributions at Halikarnassus[1] and other places, until he came to Aspendus in Pamphylia; where he also obtained money and was about to depart with it, when some misdeeds committed by his soldiers so exasperated the inhabitants that they attacked him by night unprepared in his tent, and slew him.[2]

Thus perished the citizen to whom, more than to any one else, Athens owed not only her renovated democracy, but its wise, generous, and harmonious working, after renovation. Even the philo-Laconian and oligarchical Xenophon bestows upon him a marked and unaffected eulogy.[3] His devoted patriotism in commencing and prosecuting the struggle against the Thirty, at a time when they not only were at the height of their power, but had plausible ground for calculating on the full auxiliary strength of Sparta, deserves high admiration. But the feature which stands yet more eminent in his character—a feature infinitely rare in the Grecian character generally—is, that the energy of a successful leader was combined with complete absence both of vindictive antipathies for the past, and of overbearing ambition for himself. Content to live himself as a simple citizen under the restored democracy, he taught his countrymen to forgive an oligarchical party from whom they had suffered atrocious wrongs, and set the example himself of acquiescing in the loss of his own large property. The

Character of Thrasybulus.

---

[1] Lysias, Or. xxviii. cont. Erg. s. 1, 20.
[2] Xen. Hellen. iv. 8, 28—30; Diodor. xiv. 94.
The latter states that Thrasybulus lost twenty-three triremes by a storm near Lesbos—which Xenophon does not notice, and which seems improbable.
[3] Xen. Hellen. iv. 8. 81. Καὶ Θρασύβουλος μὲν δὴ, μάλα δοκῶν ἀνὴρ ἀγαθὸς εἶναι, οὕτως ἀπελεύτησεν.

generosity of such a proceeding ought not to count for less, because it was at the same time dictated by the highest political prudence. We find, in an oration of Lysias against Ergoklês (a citizen who served in the Athenian fleet on this last expedition), in which the latter is accused of gross peculation—insinuations against Thrasybulus, of having countenanced the delinquency, though coupled with praise of his general character. Even the words as they now stand are so vague as to carry little evidence; but when we reflect that the oration was spoken after the death of Thrasybulus, they are entitled to no weight at all.[1]

The Athenians sent Agyrrhius to succeed Thrasybulus.

Agyrrhius succeeds Thrasybulus— Rhodes still holds out against the Lacedæmonians.
After the death of the latter, we may conclude that the fleet went to Rhodes, its original destination—though Xenophon does not expressly say so; the rather as neither Teleutias nor any subsequent Lacedæmonian commander appears to have become master of the island, in spite of the considerable force which they had there assembled.[2] The Lacedæmonians however, on their side,

---

[1] Lysias, cont. Ergo. Or. xxviii. s. 9.

Ergoklês is charged in this oration with gross abuse of power, oppression towards allies and citizens of Athens, and peculation for his own profit, during the course of the expedition of Thrasybulus; who is indirectly accused of conniving at such misconduct. It appears that the Athenians, as soon as they were informed that Thrasybulus had established the toll in the Bosphorus, passed a decree that an account should be sent home of all moneys exacted from the various cities, and that the colleagues of Thrasybulus should come home to go through the audit (s. 5); implying (so far as we can understand what is thus briefly noticed) that Thrasybulus himself should not be obliged to come home, but might stay on his Hellespontine or Asiatic command.

Ergoklês, however, probably one of these colleagues, resented this decree as an insult, and advised Thrasybulus to seize Byzantium, to retain the fleet, and to marry the daughter of the Thracian prince Seuthês. It is also affirmed in the oration that the fleet had come home in very bad condition (s. 2-4), and that the money, levied with so much criminal abuse, had been either squandered or fraudulently appropriated.

We learn from another oration that Ergoklês was condemned to death. His property was confiscated, and was said to amount to 80 talents, though he had been poor before the expedition; but nothing like that amount was discovered after the sentence of confiscation (Lysias, Or. xxx. cont. Philokrat. s. 3).

[2] Xen. Hellen. iv. 8, 31.

being also much in want of money, Teleutias was obliged (in the same manner as the Athenians) to move from island to island, levying contributions as he could.¹

When the news of the successful proceedings of Thrasybulus at Byzantium and the Hellespont, again establishing a toll for the profit of Athens, reached Sparta, it excited so much anxiety, that Anaxibius, having great influence with the Ephors of the time, prevailed on them to send him out as harmost to Abydos, in the room of Derkyllidas, who had now been in that post for several years. Having been the officer originally employed to procure the revolt of the place from Athens (in 411 B.C.),² Derkyllidas had since rendered service not less essential in preserving it to Sparta, during the extensive desertion which followed the battle of Knidus. But it was supposed, that he ought to have checked the aggressive plans of Thrasybulus; moreover Anaxibius promised, if a small force were entrusted to him, to put down effectually the newly-revived Athenian influence. He was presumed to know well those regions, in which he had once already been admiral, at the moment when Xenophon and the Cyreian army first returned; the harshness, treachery, and corruption, which he displayed in his dealing with that gallant body of men, have been already recounted in a former chapter.³ With three triremes, and funds for the pay of 1000 mercenary troops, Anaxibius accordingly went to Abydos. He began his operations with considerable vigour, both against Athens and against Pharnabazus. While he armed a land-force, which he employed in making incursions on the neighbouring cities in the territory of that satrap, —he at the same time reinforced his little squadron by three triremes out of the harbour of Abydos, so that he became strong enough to seize the merchant-vessels passing along the Hellespont to Athens or to her allies.⁴ The force which Thrasybulus had left at Byzantium to secure the strait-revenues, was thus inadequate to its object without farther addition.

*Anaxibius is sent to command at the Hellespont in place of Derkyllidas—his vigorous proceedings—he deprives Athens of the tolls of the strait.*

¹ Xen. Hellen. v. 1, 2.
² Thucyd. viii. 61; compare Xenoph. Anab. v. 6, 24.
³ See above, Chapter lxxi.
⁴ Xen. Hellen. iv. 8, 32, 33.

Fortunately, Iphikratês was at this moment disengaged
at Athens, having recently returned from
Corinth with his body of peltasts, for whom
doubtless employment was wanted. He was
accordingly sent with 1200 peltasts and eight
triremes, to combat Anaxibius in the Hellespont: which now became again the scene of
conflict, as it had been in the latter years of
the Peloponnesian War; the Athenians from
the European side, the Lacedæmonians from the Asiatic.
At first the warfare consisted of desultory, privateering,
and money-levying excursions on both sides.[1] But at
length, the watchful genius of Iphikratês discovered opportunity for a successful stratagem. Anaxibius, having
just drawn the town of Antandrus into his alliance, had
marched thither for the purpose of leaving a garrison in
it, with his Lacedæmonian and mercenary forces, as well
as 200 hoplites from Abydos itself. His way lay across
the mountainous region of Ida, southward to the coast of
the Gulf of Adramyttium. Accordingly Iphikratês, fore-
seeing that he would speedily return, crossed over in the
night from the Chersonese, and planted himself in ambush
on the line of return march, at a point where it traversed
the desert and mountainous extremities of the Abydene
territory, near the gold mines of Kremastê. The triremes
which carried him across were ordered to sail up the strait
on the next day, in order that Anaxibius might be apprised
of it, and might suppose Iphikratês to be employed on his
ordinary money-levying excursion.

The stratagem was completely successful. Anaxibius
returned on the next day, without the least suspicion of any enemy at hand, marching in careless order and with longstretched files, as well
from the narrowness of the mountain path as from the
circumstance that he was in the friendly territory of
Abydos. Not expecting to fight, he had unfortunately
either omitted the morning sacrifice, or taken no pains to
ascertain that the victims were favourable; so Xenophon
informs us,[2] with that constant regard to the divine jud-

---

[1] Xen. Hellen. iv. 8, 35, 36. τὸ
μὲν πρῶτον λῃσταὶ διακίμενοντες ἐπο-
λέμουν ἀλλήλοις..... Ὅπως δοκοίη,
ὥσπερ εἰώθει, ἐπ' ἀργυρολογίαν ἀν-
εστρατευμέναι.

[2] Xen. Hellen. iv. 8, 36. Ὁ Ἀντ-
ξίβιος ἀπεπορεύετο, ὡς μὲν ἐλέγετο,
οὐδὲ τῶν ἱερῶν γεγενημένων

gements and divine warnings which pervades both the Hellenica and the Anabasis. Iphikratês having suffered the Abydenes who were in the van to pass, suddenly sprang from his ambush, to assault Anaxibius with the Lacedæmonians and the mercenaries, as they descended the mountain pass into the plain of Kremastê. His appearance struck terror and confusion into the whole army; unprepared in its disorderly array for stedfast resistance—even if the minds of the soldiers had been ever so well strung—against well-trained peltasts, who were sure to prevail over hoplites not in steady rank. To Anaxibius himself, the truth stood plain at once. Defeat was inevitable, and there remained no other resource for him except to die like a brave man. Accordingly, desiring his shield-bearer to hand to him his shield, he said to those around him—"Friends, my honour commands me to die here; but do you hasten away and save yourselves before the enemy close with us." Such order was hardly required to determine his panic-stricken troops, who fled with one accord towards Abydos; while Anaxibius himself awaited firmly the approach of the enemy, and fell gallantly fighting on the spot. No less than twelve Spartan harmosts, those who had been expelled from their various governments by the defeat of Knidus, and who had remained ever since under Derkyllidas at Abydos, stood with the like courage and shared his fate. Such disdain of life hardly surprises us in conspicuous Spartan citizens, to whom preservation by flight was "no true preservation" (in the language of Xenophon[1]), but simply prolongation of life under intolerable disgrace at home. But what deserves greater remark is, that the youth to whom Anaxibius was tenderly attached and who was his constant companion, could not endure to leave him, stayed fighting by his side, and perished by the same honourable death.[2] So strong was the mutual devotion which this relation between persons

αὐτῷ ἐκείνῃ τῇ ἡμέρᾳ, ἀλλὰ κατεφρονήσας, ὅτι διὰ φιλίας τε ἐπορεύετο καὶ ἐς πόλιν φιλίαν, καὶ ὅτι ἥπους τῶν ἐπαντωντων, τὸν Ἰφικράτην ἀνακαλευκέναι τὴν ἐπὶ Προικοννήσου, ἀμελέστερον ἐπορεύετο.

[1] See the remarks a few pages back, upon the defeat and destruction of the Lacedæmonian mora

by Iphikratês, near Lechæum, page 174.

[2] Xen. Hellen. iv. 8, 39. Καὶ τὰ παιδικὰ μέντοι αὐτῷ παρίστατο, καὶ τῶν Λακεδαιμονίων δὲ τῶν συνειληλυθότων ἐκ τῶν πόλεων ἁρμοστήρων ὡς δώδεκα μαχόμενοι συναπέθανον· οἱ δ᾽ ἄλλοι φεύγοντες ἐκιπτον.

of the male sex inspired in the ancient Greek mind.
With these exceptions, no one else made any attempt
to stand. All fled, and were pursued by Iphikratês as
far as the gates of Abydos, with the slaughter of 50
out of the 200 Abydene hoplites, and 200 of the remaining troops.

This well-planned and successful exploit, while it added to the reputation of Iphikratês, rendered the Athenians again masters of the Bosphorus and the Hellespont, ensuring both the levy of the dues and the transit of their trading-vessels. But while the Athenians were thus carrying on naval war at Rhodes and the Hellespont, they began to experience annoyance nearer home, from Ægina.

*The Athenians are again masters of the Hellespont and the strait dues.*

That island (within sight as the eyesore of Peiræus, as Periklês was wont to call it) had been occupied fifty years before by a population eminently hostile to Athens, afterwards conquered and expelled by her—at last again captured in the new abode which they had obtained in Laconia—and put to death by her order. During the Peloponnesian War, Ægina had been tenanted by Athenian citizens as outsettlers or kleruchs; all of whom had been driven in, after the battle of Ægospotami. The island was then restored by Lysander to the remnant of the former population—as many of them at least as he could find.

*The island of Ægina— its past history.*

These new Æginetans, though doubtless animated by associations highly unfavourable to Athens, had nevertheless remained not only at peace, but also in reciprocal commerce, with her, until a considerable time after the battle of Knidus and the rebuilding of her Long Walls. And so they would have continued, of their own accord—since they could gain but little, and were likely to lose all the security of their traffic, by her hostility—had they not been forced to commence the war by Eteonikus, the Lacedæmonian harmost in the island;[1] one amidst many examples of the manner in which the smaller Grecian states were dragged into war, without any motive of their own, by the ambition of the

*The Æginetans are constrained by Sparta into war with Athens. The Lacedæmonian admiral Teleutias at Ægina. He is superseded by Hierax. His remarkable popularity among the seamen.*

[1] Xen. Hellen. v. 1, 1. ὧν δὲ ἐδλιν ὁ Ἐτεόνικος ἐν τῇ Αἰγίνῃ.

greater—by Sparta as well as by Athens.[1] With concurrence of the Ephors, Eteonikus authorised and encouraged all Æginetans to fit out privateers for depredation on Attica; which aggression the Athenians resented, after suffering considerable inconvenience, by sending a force of ten triremes to block up Ægina from the sea, with a body of hoplites under Pamphilus to construct and occupy a permanent fort in the island. This squadron, however, was soon driven off (though Pamphilus still continued to occupy the fort) by Teleutias, who came to Ægina on hearing of the blockade; having been engaged, with the fleet which he commanded at Rhodes, in an expedition among the Cyclades for the purpose of levying contributions. He seems to have been now at the term of his year of command, and while he was at Ægina, his successor Hierax arrived from Sparta on his way to Rhodes to supersede him. The fleet was accordingly handed over to Hierax at Ægina, while Teleutias went directly home to Sparta. So remarkable was his popularity among the seamen, that numbers of them accompanied him down to the water-edge, testifying their regret and attachment by crowning him with wreaths or pressing his hand. Some, who came down too late, when he was already under weigh, cast their wreaths on the sea, uttering prayers for his health and happiness.[2]

καὶ ἐπιμιξίᾳ χρωμένων τὸν πρόσθεν χρόνον τῶν Αἰγινητῶν πρὸς τοὺς Ἀθηναίους, ἐπεὶ φανερῶς κατὰ θάλατταν ἐπολεμεῖτο ὁ πόλεμος, ξυνδόξαν καὶ τοῖς ἐφόροις, ἐφίησι λῄζεσθαι τὸν βουλόμενον ἐκ τῆς Ἀττικῆς.

The meaning of the word πάλιν here is not easy to determine, since (as Schneider remarks) not a word had been said before about the presence of Eteonikus at Ægina. Perhaps we may explain it by supposing that Eteonikus found the Æginetans reluctant to engage in the war, and that he did not like to involve them in it without first going to Sparta to consult the Ephors. It was on coming back to Ægina (πάλιν) from Sparta, after having obtained the consent of the Ephors (ξυνδόξαν καὶ τοῖς ἐφόροις), that he issued the letters of marque.

Schneider's note explains τὸν πρόσθεν χρόνον incorrectly, in my judgement.

[1] Compare Xen. Hellen. vi. 3, 8; Thucyd. iii. 13. The old Æginetan antipathy against Athens, when thus again instigated, continued for a considerable time. A year or two afterwards, when the philosopher Plato was taken to Ægina to be sold as a slave, it was death to any Athenian to land in the island (Aristidês, Or. xlvi. p. 384; p. 306 Dindorf; Diogenês Laert. iii. 19; Plutarch, Dion. c. 5).

[2] Xen. Hellen. v. 1, 3. Ὁ δὲ Τελευτίας, μακαριώτατα δὴ ἀπέπλευσεν οἴκαδε, &c.

This description of the scene at

Hierax, while carrying back to Rhodes the remaining fleet which Teleutias had brought from that island, left his subordinate Gorgôpas as harmost at Ægina with twelve triremes; a force which protected the island completely, and caused the fortified post occupied by the Athenians under Pamphilus to be itself blocked up, insomuch that after an interval of four months, a special decree was passed at Athens to send a numerous squadron and fetch away the garrison. As the Æginetan privateers, aided by the squadron of Gorgôpas, now recommenced their annoyances against Attica, thirteen Athenian triremes were put in equipment under Eunomus as a guard-squadron against Ægina. But Gorgôpas and his squadron were now for the time withdrawn, to escort Antalkidas, the new Lacedæmonian admiral sent to Asia chiefly for the purpose of again negotiating with Tiribazus. On returning back, after landing Antalkidas at Ephesus, Gorgôpas fell in with Eunomus, whose pursuit however he escaped, landing at Ægina just before sunset. The Athenian admiral, after watching for a short time until he saw the Lacedæmonian seamen out of their vessels and ashore, departed as it grew dark to Attica, carrying a light to prevent his ships from parting company. But Gorgôpas, causing his men to take a hasty meal, immediately reembarked and pursued; keeping on the track by means of the light, and taking care not to betray himself either by the noise of oars or by the chant of the Keleustês. Eunomus had no suspicion of the accompanying enemy. Just after

the departure of Teleutias (for whom, as well as for his brother Agesilaus, Xenophon always manifests a marked sympathy) is extremely interesting. The reflection too, with which Xenophon follows it up, deserves notice—"I know well that in these incidents I am not recounting any outlay of money, or danger incurred, or memorable stratagem. But by Zeus, it does seem to me worth a man's while to reflect, by what sort of conduct Teleutias created such dispositions in his soldiers. This is a true man's achievement, more precious than any outlay or any danger."

What Xenophon here glances at in the case of Teleutias, is the scheme worked out in detail in the romance of the Cyropædia (τὸ ἐθέλοντων ἄρχειν—the exercising command in such manner as to have willing and obedient subjects)—and touched upon indirectly in various of his other compositions—the Hiero, the Œconomicus, and portions of the Memorabilia. The ideal of government, as it presented itself to Xenophon, was the paternal despotism, or something like it.

he had touched land near Cape Zôstêr in Attica, when his men were in the act of disembarking, Gorgôpas gave signal by trumpet to attack. After a short action by moonlight, four of the Athenian squadron were captured, and carried off to Ægina; with the remainder, Eunomus escaped to Peiræus.[1]

This victory, rendering both Gorgôpas and the Æginetans confident, laid them open to a stratagem skilfully planned by the Athenian Chabrias. That officer, who seems to have been dismissed from Corinth as Iphikratês had been before him, was now about to conduct a force of ten triremes and 800 peltasts to the aid of Evagoras; to whom the Athenians were thus paying their debt of gratitude, though they could ill spare any of their forces from home. Chabrias, passing over from Peiræus at night, landed without being perceived in a desert place of the coast of Ægina, and planted himself in ambush with his peltasts at some little distance inland of the Herakleion or temple of Heraklês, amidst hollow ground suitable for concealment. He had before made arrangement with another squadron and a body of hoplites under Demænetus; who arrived at day-break and landed in Ægina at a point called Tripyrgia, about two miles distant from the Herakleion, but farther removed from the city. As soon as their arrival became known, Gorgôpas hastened out of the city to repel them, with all the troops he could collect, Æginetans as well as marines out of the ships of war—and eight Spartans who happened to be his companions in the island. In their march from the city to attack the new comers, they had to pass near the Herakleion, and therefore near the troops in ambush; who, as soon as Gorgôpas and those about him had gone by, rose up suddenly and attacked them in the rear. The stratagem succeeded not less completely than that of Iphikratês at Abydos against Anaxibius. Gorgôpas and the Spartans near him were slain, the rest were defeated, and compelled to flee with considerable loss back to the city.[2]

*Gorgôpas is surprised in Ægina, defeated, and slain, by the Athenian Chabrias; who goes to assist Evagoras in Cyprus.*

After this brilliant success, Chabrias pursued his voyage to Cyprus, and matters appeared so secure on the side of Ægina, that Demænetus also was sent to the Hellespont

[1] Xen. Hellen. v. 1, 6-10.    [2] Xen. Hellen. v. 1, 12, 13.

to reinforce Iphikratês. For some time indeed, the Lacedæmonian ships at Ægina did nothing. Eteonikus, who was sent as successor to Gorgôpas,[1] could neither persuade nor constrain the seamen to go aboard, since he had no funds, while their pay was in arrears; so that Athens with her coast and her trading-vessels remained altogether unmolested. At length the Lacedæmonians were obliged to send again to Ægina Teleutias, the most popular and best-beloved of all their commanders, whom the seamen welcomed with the utmost delight. Addressing them under the influence of this first impression, immediately after he had offered sacrifice, he told them plainly that he had brought with him no money, but that he had come to put them in the way of procuring it; that he should himself touch nothing until they were amply provided, and should require of them to bear no more hardship or fatigue than he went through himself; that the power and prosperity of Sparta had all been purchased by willingly braving danger as well as toil, in the cause of duty; that it became valiant men to seek their pay, not by cringing to any one, but by their own swords at the cost of enemies. And he engaged to find them the means of doing this, provided they would now again manifest the excellent qualities which he knew them by experience to possess.[2]

This address completely won over the seamen, who received it with shouts of applause; desiring Teleutias to give his orders forthwith, and promising ready obedience. "Well (said he), now go and get your suppers, as you were intending to do; and then come immediately on ship-board, bringing with you provisions for one day. Advance me thus much out of your own means, that we may, by the will of the gods, make an opportune voyage."[3]

---

[1] So we may conclude from Xen. Hellen. v. 1, 13; Demosnetus is found at the Hellespont, v. 1, 26.
[2] Xen. Hellen. v. 1, 14-17.
[3] Xen. Hellen. v. 1, 16. Ἄγετε, ὦ ἄνδρες, δειπνήσατε μέν, ὥσπερ καὶ ὡς ἐμέλλετε· προσπορίσχετε δέ μοι μιᾶς ἡμέρας σῖτον ἕκαστα δὲ ἡμῖν ἐπὶ τὰς ναῦς αὐτίκα μάλα, ὅπως πλεύσωμεν, ἔνθα θεὸς θέλει, ἐν καιρῷ ἀφιξόμενοι.

Schneider doubts whether the words προσπορίσχετε δέ μοι are correct. But they seem to me to bear a very pertinent meaning. Teleutias had no money; yet it was necessary for his purpose that the seamen should come furnished with one day's provision beforehand. Accordingly he is obliged to ask

In spite of the eminent popularity of Teleutias, the men would probably have refused to go on board, had he told them beforehand his intention of sailing with his twelve triremes straight into the harbour of Peiræus. At first sight, the enterprise seemed insane, for there were triremes in it more than sufficient to overwhelm him. But he calculated on finding them all unprepared, with seamen as well as officers in their lodgings ashore, so that he could not only strike terror and do damage, but even realize half an hour's plunder before preparations could be made to resist him. Such was the security which now reigned there, especially since the death of Gorgôpas, that no one dreamt of an attack. The harbour was open, as it had been forty years before, when Brasidas (in the third year of the Peloponnesian War) attempted the like enterprise from the port of Megara.[1] Even then, at the maximum of the Athenian naval power, it was an enterprise possible, simply because every one considered it to be impossible; and it only failed because the assailants became terrified and flinched in the execution. *Sudden and successful attack of Teleutias upon the Peiræus.*

A little after dark, Teleutias quitted the harbour of Ægina, without telling any one whither he was going. Rowing leisurely, and allowing his men alternate repose on their oars, he found himself before morning within half a mile of Peiræus, where he waited until day was just dawning, and then led his squadron straight into the harbour. Everything turned out as he expected; there was not the least idea of being attacked, nor the least preparation for defence. Not a single trireme was manned or in fighting condition, but several were moored without their crews, together with merchant-vessels, loaded as well as empty. Teleutias directed the captains of his squadron to drive against the triremes, and disable them; but by no means to damage the beaks of their own ships by trying to disable the merchant-ships. Even at that early hour, many Athenians were abroad, and the arrival of the unexpected assailants struck every one with surprise and consternation. Loud and vague cries *Unprepared and unguarded condition of Peiræus —Teleutias gains rich plunder, and sails away in safety.*

them to get provision for themselves, or to lend it, as it were, to him; though they were already so dissatisfied from not having received their pay.
[1] Thucyd. ii. 94.

transmitted the news through all Peiræus, and from Peiræus up to Athens, where it was believed that their harbour was actually taken. Every man having run home for his arms, the whole force of the city rushed impetuously down thither, with one accord—hoplites as well as horsemen. But before such succours could arrive, Teleutias had full time to do considerable mischief. His seamen boarded the larger merchant-ships, seizing both the men and the portable goods which they found aboard. Some even jumped ashore on the quay (called the Deigma), laid hands on the tradesmen, ship-masters, and pilots, whom they saw near, and carried them away captive. Various smaller vessels with their entire cargoes were also towed away; and even three or four triremes. With all these Teleutias sailed safely out of Peiræus, sending some of his squadron to escort the prizes to Ægina, while he himself with the remainder sailed southward along the coast. As he was seen to come out of Peiræus, his triremes were mistaken for Athenian, and excited no alarm; so that he thus captured several fishing-boats, and passage-boats coming with passengers from the islands to Athens—together with some merchantmen carrying corn and other goods, at Sunium. All were carried safely into Ægina.[1]

He is enabled to pay his seamen—activity of the fleet—great loss inflicted upon Athenian commerce.

The enterprise of Teleutias, thus admirably concerted and executed without the loss of a man, procured for him a plentiful booty, of which probably not the least valuable portion consisted in the men seized as captives. When sold at Ægina, it yielded so large a return that he was enabled to pay down at once a month's pay to his seamen; who became more attached to him than ever, and kept the triremes in animated and active service under his orders.[2] Admonished by painful experience, indeed, the Athenians were now doubtless careful both in guarding and in closing Peiræus; as they had become forty years before after the unsuccessful attack of Brasidas. But in spite of the utmost vigilance, they suffered an extent of damage from the indefatigable Teleutias, and from the Æginetan privateers, quite sufficient to make them weary of the war.[3]

[1] Xen. Hellen. v. 1, 15-22.
[2] Xen. Hellen. v. 1, 24.
[3] Xen. Hellen. v. 1, 29.
Even ten years after this, how-

We cannot doubt indeed that the prosecution of the war must have been a heavy financial burthen upon the Athenians, from 395 B.C. downward to 397 B.C. How they made good the cost, without any contributory allies, or any foreign support, except what Konon obtained during one year from Pharnabazus—we are not informed. On the revival of the democracy in 403 B.C., the poverty of the city, both public and private, had been very great, owing to the long previous war, ending with the loss of all Athenian property abroad. At a period about three years afterwards, it seems that the Athenians were in arrears, not merely for the tribute-money which they then owed to Sparta as her subject allies, but also for debts due to the Bœotians on account of damage done; that they were too poor to perform in full the religious sacrifices prescribed for the year, and were obliged to omit some even of the more ancient; that the docks as well as tho walls were in sad want of repair.[1] Even the pay to those citizens who attended the public assemblies and sat as Dikasts in the dikasteries —pay essential to the working of the democracy—was restored only by degrees; beginning first at one obolus, and not restored to three oboli, at which it had stood before the capture, until after an interval of some years.[2] It was at this time too that the Theôric Board, or Paymasters for the general expenses of public worship and sacrifice, was first established; and when we read how much the Athenians were embarrassed for the means of celebrating the prescribed sacrifices, there was probably great necessity for the formation of some such office. The disbursements connected with this object had been administered, before 403 B.C., not by any special Board, but by the Hellenotamiæ, or treasurers of the tribute collected from the allies, who were not renewed after 403 B.C., as the Athenian empire had ceased to exist.[3] A portion of

ever, when the Lacedæmonian harmost Sphodrias marched from Thespiæ by night to surprise Peiræus, it was without gates on the landside — ἀπύλωτος — or at least without any such gates as would resist an assault (Xen. Hellen. v. 4, 20).

[1] Lysias. Orat. xxx. cont. Nikomachum, s. 21-30.

I trust this Oration so far as the matter of fact, that in the preceding year, some ancient sacrifices had been omitted from state-poverty; but the manner in which the speaker makes this fact tell against Nikomachus, may or may not be just.

[2] Aristophan. Ecclesias. 300-310.

[3] See the Inscription No. 147, in Boeckh's Corpus Inscriptt. Græcor.

the money disbursed by the Theôric Board for the religious festivals, was employed in the distribution of two oboli per head, called the diobely, to all present citizens, and actually received by all—not merely by the poor, but by persons in easy circumstances also.[1] This distribution was made at several festivals, having originally begun at the Dionysia, for the purpose of enabling the citizens to obtain places at the theatrical representations in honour of Dionysus; but we do not know either the number of festivals, or the amount of the total sum. It was, in principle, a natural corollary of the religious idea connected with the festival; not simply because the comfort and recreation of each citizen, individually taken, was promoted by his being enabled to attend the festival—but because the collective effect of the ceremony, in honouring and propitiating the god, was believed to depend in part upon a multitudinous attendance and lively manifestations.[2] Gradually, however, this distribution of Theôric or festival money came to be pushed to an abusive and mischievous excess, which is brought before our notice forty years afterwards, during the political career of Demosthenês. Until that time, we have no materials for speaking of it; and what I here notice is simply the first creation of the Theôric Board.

The means of Athens for prosecuting the war, and for paying her troops sent as well to Bœotia as to Corinth, must have been derived mainly from direct assessments on property, called eisphoræ. And some such assessments we find alluded to generally as having taken place during these years; though we know no details either as to frequency or amount.[3] But the restitution of the Long Walls and of

— Boeckh, Public Economy of Athens, b. 7. p. 179, 180, Engl. transl.,—and Schömann, Antiq. Jur. Publ. Græc. b. 77. p. 320.

[1] Demosthenês, Philippic. iv. p. 141. s. 43; Demosth. Orat. xliv. cont. Leocharem, p. 1091. s. 46.

[2] It is common to represent the festivals at Athens as if it were so many stratagems for feeding poor citizens at the public expense. But the primitive idea and sentiment of the Grecian religious festival— the satisfaction to the god de-

pendent upon multitudinous spectators sympathising, and enjoying themselves together (ὄμμιγα πάντας) —is much anterior to the development of democracy at Athens. See the old oracles in Demosthen. cont. Meidiam, p. 531. s. 56; Homer, Hymn. Apollin. 147; K. F. Herrmann, Gottesdienstlich. Alterthümer der Griechen, s. 8.

[3] See such direct assessments on property alluded to in various speeches of Lysias, Orat. xix. De Bonis Aristophan. s. 81, 45, 63;

Orat. xxvii. cont. Epikratem, s. 11; Orat. xxix. cont. Philokrat. s. 14. Boeckh (in his Public Econ. of Athens, iv. 4. p. 493, Engl. transl., which passage stands unaltered in the second edition of the German original, p. 542) affirms that a proposition for the assessment of a direct property-tax of one-fortieth, or 2½ per cent., was made about this time by a citizen named Euripides, who announced it as intended to produce 500 talents; that the proposition was at first enthusiastically welcomed by the Athenians, and procured for its author unbounded popularity; but that he was presently cried down and disgraced, because on farther examination the measure proved unsatisfactory and empty talk. Sievers also (Geschichte von Griech. bis zur Schlacht von Mantineia, pp. 100, 101) adopts the same view as Boeckh, that this was a real proposition of a property-tax of 2½ per cent. made by Euripides. After having alleged that the Athenians in these times supplied their treasury by the most unscrupulous injustice in confiscating the property of rich citizens — referring as proof to passages in the orators, none of which establishes his conclusion — Sievers goes on to say — "But that these violences did not suffice, is shown by the fact that the people caught with greedy impatience at other measures. Thus a new scheme of finance, which however was presently discovered to be insufficient or inapplicable, excited at first the most extravagant joy." He adds in a note: "The scheme proceeded from Euripides; it was a property-tax of 2½ per cent. See Aristophan. Ekklesias. 823; Boeckh, Staats-

hansh. ii. p. 27."

In my judgement, the assertion here made by Boeckh and Sievers rests upon no sufficient ground. The passage of Aristophanês does not warrant us in concluding anything at all about a proposition for a property-tax. It is as follows:—

Τὸ δ'ἔναγχος οὐχ ἅπαντες ἡμεῖς
ὤμνυμεν
Τάλαντ' ἔσεσθαι κεντακόσια τῇ πόλει
Τῆς τεσσαρακοστῆς, ἣν ἐπόρισ'
Εὐριπίδης;
Κεὐθὺς κατεχρύσου πᾶς ἀνὴρ Εὐριπίδην·
Ὅτε δὴ δ' ἀνασκοπουμένοις ἐφαίνετο
Ὁ Διὸς Κόρινθος, καὶ τὸ πρᾶγμ'
οὐκ ἤρκεσεν,
Πάλιν κατεπίττου πᾶς ἀνὴρ Εὐριπίδην.

What this "new financial scheme" (so Sievers properly calls it) was, which the poet here alludes to — we have no means of determining. But I venture to express my decided conviction that it cannot have been a property-tax. The terms in which it is described forbid that supposition. It was a scheme which seemed at first sight exceedingly promising and gainful to the city, and procured for its author very great popularity; but which on farther examination, proved to be mere empty boasting (ὁ Διὸς Κόρινθος). How can this be said about any motion for a property-tax? That any financier should ever have gained extraordinary popularity by proposing a property-tax, is altogether inconceivable. And a proposition to raise the immense sum of 500 talents (which Schömann estimates as the probable aggregate charge of the whole peace-establishment of Athens, Antiq. Jur. Public. Græc.

political power. That excellent harbour, commodious as a mercantile centre, and now again safe for the residence

s. 78. p. 815) at one blow by an assessment upon property! It would be as much as any financier could do to bear up against the tremendous *unpopularity* of such a proposition; and to induce the assembly even to listen to him, were the necessity ever so pressing. How odious are propositions for direct taxation, we may know without recurring to the specific evidence respecting Athens; but if any man requires such specific evidence, he may find it abundantly in the Philippics and Olynthiacs of Demosthenês. On one occasion (De Symmoriis, Or. xiv. s. 33. p. 185) that orator alludes to a proposition for raising 500 talents by direct property-tax as something extravagant, which the Athenians would not endure to hear mentioned.

Moreover—unpopularity apart—the motion for a property-tax could scarcely procure credit for a financier, because it is of all ideas the most simple and obvious. Any man can suggest such a scheme. But to pass for an acceptable financier, you must propose some measure which promises gain to the state without such undisguised pressure upon individuals.

Lastly, there is nothing *delusive* in a property-tax—nothing which looks gainful at first sight, and then turns out on farther examination (ἀνασκοπουμένοις) to be false or uncertain. It may indeed be more or less evaded; but this can only be known after it has been assessed, and when payment is actually called for.

· Upon these grounds, I maintain that the τεσσαρακοστή proposed by Euripidês was not a property-tax. What it was, I do not pretend to say; but τεσσαρακοστή may have

many other meanings; it might mean a duty of 2½ per cent. upon imports or exports, or upon the produce of the mines of Laurion; or it might mean a cheap coinage or base money, something in the nature of the Chian τεσσαρακοστά (Thucyd. viii. 100). All that the passage really teaches us, is, that some financial proposition was made by Euripidês which at first seemed likely to be lucrative, but would not stand an attentive examination. It is not even certain that Euripidês promised a receipt of 500 talents; this sum is only given to us as a comic exaggeration of that which foolish men at first fancied. Boeckh in more than one place reasons (erroneously, in my judgement) as if this 500 talents was a real and trustworthy estimate, and equal to 2½ per cent. upon the taxable property of the Athenians. He says (iv. 8. p. 520, Engl. transl.) that "Euripidês assumed as the basis of his proposal for levying a property-tax, a taxable capital of 20,000 talents"—and that "his proposition of ¹⁄₄₀ was *calculated* to produce 500 talents. No such conclusion can be fairly drawn from Aristophanês.

Again, Boeckh infers from another passage in the same play of the same author, that a small direct property-tax of one five-hundredth part had been recently imposed. After a speech from one of the old women, calling upon a young man to follow her, the young man replies (v. 1006)—

'Ἀλλ' οὐκ ἀνάγκη μοῦστιν, εἰ μὴ τῶν ἐμῶν
Τὴν πεντακοσιοστὴν κατέθηκε τῇ πόλει.

Boeckh himself admits (iv. 8. p. 520)

of metics and the importations of merchants, became speedily a scene of animated commerce, as we have seen it when surprised by Teleutias. The number of metics, or free resident non-citizens, became also again large, as it had been before the time of her reverses, and including a number of miscellaneous non-Hellenic persons, from Lydia, Phrygia, and Syria.[1] Both the port-duties, and the value of fixed property at Athens, was thus augmented so as in part to countervail the costs of war. Nevertheless these costs, continued from year to year, and combined with the damage done by Æginetan privateers, were seriously felt, and contributed to dispose the Athenians to peace.

In the Hellespont also, their prospects were not only on the decline, but had become seriously menacing. After going from Ægina to Ephesus in the preceding year, and sending back Gorgôpas with the Æginetan squadron, An-

that this passage is very obscure, and so I think every one will find it. Tyrwhitt was so perplexed by it that he altered ἡμῶν into ἐτῶν. Without presuming to assign the meaning of the passage, I merely contend that it cannot be held to justify the affirmation, as a matter of historical fact, that a property-tax of 1/100 had recently been levied at Athens, shortly before the representation of the Ekklesiazusæ.

I cannot refrain here from noticing another inference drawn by Sievers from a third passage in this same play—the Ekklesiazusæ (Geschichte Griechenlands vom Ende des Pelop. Kriegs bis zur Schlacht von Mantineia, p. 101). He says—"How melancholy is the picture of Athenian popular life, which is presented to us by the Ekklesiazusæ and the second Plutus, ten or twelve years after the restoration of the democracy! What an *impressive seriousness* (welch ein erschütternder Ernst) is expressed in the speech of Praxagora!" (v. 174 seqq.).

I confess that I find neither seriousness, nor genuine and trustworthy colouring, in this speech of Praxagora. It is a comic case made out for the purpose of showing that the women were more fit to govern Athens than the men, and setting forth the alleged follies of the men in terms of broad and general disparagement. The whole play is, throughout, thorough farce and full of Aristophanic humour. And it is surely preposterous to treat what is put into the mouth of Praxagora, the leading feminine character, as if it were historical evidence as to the actual condition or management of Athens. Let any one follow the speech of Praxagora into the proposition of reform which she is made to submit, and he will then see the absurdity of citing her discourse as if it were an harangue in Thucydides. History is indeed strangely transformed by thus turning comic wit into serious matter of evidence; and no history has suffered so much from the proceeding as that of Athens.

[1] Xenoph. Hellen. iv. 1, 19-24: compare vii. 1, 3, 4; Xenoph. De Vectigalibus, chapters i. ii. iii., &c.; Xenoph. De Repub. Athen. i. 17.

talkidas had placed the remainder of his fleet under his secretary Nikolochus, with orders to proceed to the Hellespont for the relief of Abydos. He himself landed, and repaired to Tiribazus, by whom he was conducted up to the court of Susa. Here he renewed the propositions for the pacification of Greece—on principles of universal autonomy, abandoning all the Asiatic Greeks as subject absolutely to the Persian king—which he had tried in vain to carry through two years before. Though the Spartans generally were odious to Artaxerxês, Antalkidas behaved with so much dexterity[1] as to gain the royal favour personally, while all the influence of Tiribazus was employed to second his political views. At length they succeeded in prevailing upon the King formally to adopt the peace, and to proclaim war against any Greeks who should refuse to accede to it, empowering the Spartans to enforce it everywhere as his allies and under his sanction. In order to remove one who would have proved a great impediment to this measure, the King was farther induced to invite the satrap Pharnabazus up to court, and to honour him with his daughter in marriage; leaving the satrapy of Daskylium under the temporary administration of Ariobarzanes, a personal friend and guest of Antalkidas.[2] Thus armed against all contingencies, Antalkidas and Tiribazus returned from Susa to the coast of Asia Minor in the spring of 387 B.C., not only bearing the formal diploma ratified by the King's seal but commanding ample means to carry it into effect; since, in addition to the full forces of Persia, twenty additional triremes were on their way from Syracuse and the Greco-Italian towns, sent by the despot Dionysius to the aid of the Lacedæmonians.[3]

On reaching the coast, Antalkidas found Nikolochus with his fleet of twenty-five sail blocked up in Abydos by the Athenians under Iphikratês; who, with thirty-two sail, were occupying the European side of the Hellespont. He immediately repaired to Abydos by land, and took an early opportunity of stealing out by night with

---

[1] Plutarch, Artaxerx. c. 22.   [2] Xen. Hellen. v. 1, 28.
[3] Xen. Hellen. v. 1, 25—27.

his fleet up the strait towards the Propontis; spreading the rumour that he was about to attack Chalkêdon, in concert with a party in the town. But he stopped at Perkotê, and lay hid in that harbour until he saw the Athenian fleet (which had gone in pursuit of him upon the false scent laid out) pass by towards Prokonnêsus. The strait being now clear, Antalkidas sailed down it again to meet the Syracusan and Italian ships, which he safely joined. Such junction, with a view to which his recent manœuvre had been devised, rendered him more than a match for his enemies. He had further the good fortune to capture a detached Athenian squadron of eight triremes, which Thrasybulus (a second Athenian citizen of that name) was conducting from Thrace to join the main Athenian fleet in the Hellespont. Lastly, additional reinforcements also reached Antalkidas from the zealous aid of Tiribazus and Ariobarzanes, insomuch that he found himself at the head of no less than eighty triremes, besides a still greater number which were under preparation in the various ports of Ionia.[1]

*Antalkidas in command of the Lacedæmonian and Syracusan fleets in the Hellespont, with Persian aid. His successes against the Athenians.*

Such a fleet, the greatest which had been seen in the Hellespont since the battle of Ægospotami, was so much superior to anything that could be brought to meet it, and indicated so strongly the full force of Persia operating in the interests of Sparta—that the Athenians began to fear a repetition of the same calamitous suffering which they had already undergone from Lysander. A portion of such hardship they at once began to taste. Not a single merchant-ship reached them from the Euxine, all being seized and detained by Antalkidas; so that their main supply of imported corn was thus cut off. Moreover, in the present encouraging state of affairs, the Æginetan privateers became doubly active in harassing the coasting trade of Attica; and this combination, of actual hardship with prospective alarm, created a paramount anxiety at Athens to terminate the war. Without Athens, the other allies would have no chance of success through their own forces; while the Argeians also, hitherto

*Distress and discouragement of Athens—anxiety of the anti-Spartan allies for peace.*

[1] Diodor. xiv. 2. These triremes were employed in the ensuing year for the prosecution of the war against Evagoras.

the most obstinate, had become on their own account desirous of peace, being afraid of repeated Lacedæmonian invasions of their territory. That Sparta should press for a peace, when the terms of it were suggested by herself, is not wonderful. Even to her, triumphant as her position now seemed, the war was a heavy burden.[1]

Such was the general state of feeling in the Grecian world, when Tiribazus summoned the contending parties into his presence, probably at Sardis, to hear the terms of the convention which had just come down from Susa. He produced the original edict, and having first publicly exhibited the regal seal, read aloud as follows:—

"King Artaxerxês thinks it just that the cities in Asia, and the islands of Klazomenæ and Cyprus, shall belong to him. He thinks it just also, to leave all the other Hellenic cities autonomous, both small and great—except Lemnos, Imbros, and Skyros, which are to belong to Athens, as they did originally. Should any parties refuse to accept this peace, I will make war upon them, along with those who are of the same mind, by land as well as by sea, with ships and with money."[2]

Instructions were given to all the deputies to report the terms of the edict to their respective cities, and to meet again at Sparta for acceptance or rejection. When the time of meeting arrived,[3] all the cities in spite of their repugnance to the abandonment of the Asiatic Greeks and partly also to the second condition, nevertheless felt themselves overruled by superior force and gave a reluctant consent. On taking the oaths, however, the Thebans tried indirectly to make good an exception in their own case, by claiming to take the oath not only on behalf of themselves, but on behalf of the Bœotian cities generally; a demand which Agesilaus in the name of Sparta repudiated, as virtually cancelling that item in the pacification whereby the small

---

[1] Xen. Hellen. v. 1, 28, 29.
[2] Xen. Hellen. v. 1, 31.
In this document there is the same introduction of the first person immediately following the third, as in the correspondence between Pausanias and Xerxes (Thucyd. I. 128, 129).
[3] Diodor. xiv. 110.

cities were pronounced to be autonomous as well as the great. When the Theban deputy replied that he could not relinquish his claim without fresh instructions from home, Agesilaus desired him to go at once and consult his countrymen. "You may tell them (said he) that if they do not comply, they will be shut out from the treaty."

It was with much delight that Agesilaus pronounced this peremptory sentence, which placed Thebes in so humiliating a dilemma. Antipathy towards the Thebans was one of his strongest sentiments, and he exulted in the hope that they would persist in their refusal; so that he would thus be enabled to bring an overwhelming force to crush their isolated city. So eagerly did he thirst for the expected triumph, that immediately on the departure of the Theban deputies, and before their answer could possibly have been obtained, he procured the consent of the ephors, offered the border sacrifice, and led the Spartan force out as far as Tegea. From that city he not only despatched messengers in all directions to hasten the arrival of the Periœki, but also sent forth the officers called xenâgi to the cities of the Peloponnesian allies, to muster and bring together the respective contingents. But in spite of all injunctions to despatch, his wishes were disappointed. Before he started from Tegea, the Theban deputies returned with the intimation that they were prepared to take the oath for Thebes alone, recognising the other Bœotian cities as autonomous. Agesilaus and the Spartans were thus obliged to be satisfied with the minor triumph, in itself very serious and considerable, of having degraded Thebes from her federal headship, and isolated her from the Bœotian cities.[1]

*Agesilaus refuses to allow the Thebans reserve, and requires unconditional acceptance. His eagerness, from hatred of Thebes, to get into a war with them single-handed. The Thebans are obliged to accept unconditionally.*

The unmeasured and impatient miso-Theban bitterness of Agesilaus, attested here by his friend and panegyrist, deserves especial notice; for it will be found to explain much of the misconduct of Sparta and her officers during the ensuing years.

There yet remained one compliance for Agesilaus to exact. The Argeian auxiliaries were not yet withdrawn

[1] Xen. Hellen. v. 1, 32, 33.

*Agesilaus forces the Corinthians to send away their Argeian auxiliaries. The philo-Argeian Corinthians go into exile: the philo-Lacedaemonian Corinthians are restored.*

from Corinth; and the Corinthian government might probably think that the terms of the peace, leaving their city autonomous, permitted them to retain or dismiss these auxiliaries at their own discretion. But it was not so that Agesilaus construed the peace; and his construction, right or wrong, was backed by the power of enforcement. He sent to inform both Argeians and Corinthians, that if the auxiliaries were not withdrawn, he would march his army forthwith into both territories. No resistance could be offered to his peremptory mandate. The Argeians retired from Corinth; and the vehement philo-Argeian Corinthians—especially those who had been concerned in the massacre at the festival of the Eukleia—retired at the same time into voluntary exile, thinking themselves no longer safe in the town. They found a home partly at Argos, partly at Athens,[1] where they were most hospitably received. Those Corinthians who had before been in exile, and who, in concert with the Lacedæmonian garrison at Lechæum and Sikyon, had been engaged in bitter hostility against their countrymen in Corinth—were immediately readmitted into the city. According to Xenophon, their readmission was pronounced by the spontaneous voice of the Corinthian citizens.[2] But we shall be more correct in affirming, that it was procured by the same intimidating summons from Agesilaus which had extorted the dismissal of the Argeians.[3] The restoration of the exiles from Lechæum on the present occasion was no more voluntary than that of the Athenian exiles had been eighteen years before, at the close of the Peloponnesian War—or than that of the Phliasian exiles was, two or three years afterwards.[4]

---

[1] Xen. Hellen. v. 1, 84; Demosthen. adv. Leptin. c. 13. p. 473.

[2] Xen. Hellen. v. 1, 34. Οἱ δ᾽ ἄλλοι πολῖται ἑκόντες κατεδέχοντο τοὺς πρόσθεν φεύγοντας.

[3] Such is in fact the version of the story in Xenophon's Encomium upon Agesilaus (ii. 21), where it is made a matter of honour to the latter, that he would not consent to peace, except with a compulsory clause (ἠνάγκασε) that the Corinthian and Theban exiles should be restored. The Corinthian exiles had been actively co-operating with Agesilaus against Corinth. Of Theban exiles we have heard nothing; but it is very probable that there were several serving with Agesilaus—and also pretty certain that he would insist upon their restoration.

[4] Xen. Hellen. v. 3, 8.

## CHAPTER LXXVI.

### FROM THE PEACE OF ANTALKIDAS DOWN TO THE SUBJUGATION OF OLYNTHUS BY SPARTA.

THE peace or convention[1] which bears the name of Antalkidas, was an incident of serious and mournful import in Grecian history. Its true character cannot be better described than in a brief remark and reply which we find cited in Plutarch. "Alas for Hellas (observed some one to Agesilaus) when we see our Lacŏnians *medising!*"—"Nay (replied the Spartan king), say rather the Medes (Persians) *laconising.*"[2]

These two propositions do not exclude each other. Both were perfectly true. The convention emanated from a separate partnership between Spartan and Persian interests. It was solicited by the Spartan Antalkidas, and propounded by him to Tiribazus on the express ground, that it was exactly calculated to meet the Persian king's purposes and wishes—as we learn even from the philo-Laconian Xenophon.[3] While Sparta and Persia were both great gainers, no other Grecian state gained anything, as the convention was originally framed. But after the first rejection, Antalkidas saw the necessity of conciliating Athens by the addition of a special article providing that Lemnos, Imbros, and Skyros should be restored to her.[4] This addition seems to have been first made in the abortive negotiations which form the subject of the discourse already mentioned, pronounced by Ando-

*Peace or convention of Antalkidas. Its import and character. Separate partnership between Sparta and Persia.*

---

[1] It goes by both names; Xenophon more commonly speaks of ἡ εἰρήνη—Isokratēs, of αἱ συνθῆκαι.
Though we say the peace of Antalkidas, the Greek authors say ἡ ἐπ' Ἀνταλκίδου εἰρήνη: I do not observe that they ever phrase it with the genitive case Ἀνταλκίδου simply, without a preposition.

[2] Plutarch, Artaxerxēs; c. 22 (compare Plutarch, Agesil. c. 23; and his Apophtheg. Lacon. p. 213 B). Ὁ μὲν γὰρ Ἀγησίλαος, πρὸς τὸν εἰπόντα—Φεῦ τῆς Ἑλλάδος, ὅπου μηδίζουσιν ἡμῖν οἱ Λάκωνες! ... Μᾶλλον, εἶπεν, οἱ Μῆδοι λακωνίζουσι.
[3] Xen. Hellen. iv. 8, 14.
[4] The restoration of these three

kidês. It was continued afterwards and inserted in the final decree which Antalkidas and Tiribazus brought down in the King's name from Susa; and it doubtless somewhat contributed to facilitate the adherence of Athens, though the united forces of Sparta and Persia had become so overwhelming, that she could hardly have had the means of standing out, even if the supplementary article had been omitted. Nevertheless, this condition undoubtedly did secure to Athens a certain share in the gain, conjointly with the far larger shares both of Sparta and Persia. It is however not less true, that Athens, as well as Thebes,[1] assented to the peace only under fear and compulsion. As to the other states of Greece, they were interested merely in the melancholy capacity of partners in the general loss and degradation.

That degradation stood evidently marked in the form,

*Degradation in the form of the convention —a fiat drawn up, issued, and enforced by Persia upon Greece.* origin, and transmission of the convention, even apart from its substance. It was a fiat issued from the court of Susa; as such it was ostentatiously proclaimed and "sent down" from thence to Greece. Its authority was derived from the King's seal, and its sanction from his concluding threat, that he would make war against all recusants. It was brought down by the satrap Tiribazus (along with Antalkidas), read by him aloud, and heard with submission by the assembled Grecian envoys, after he had called their special attention to the regal seal.[2]

---

Islands forms the basis of historical truth in the assertion of Isokrates, that the Lacedæmonians were so subdued by the defeat of Knidus, as to come and tender maritime empire to Athens—(αἰθαίν τὴν ἀρχὴν δώσοντας) Orat. vii. (Areopagit.) s. 74; Or. ix. (Evager.) s. 83. But the assertion is true respecting a later time; for the Lacedæmonians really did make this proposition to Athens after they had been enfeebled and humiliated by the battle of Leuktra; but not before (Xenoph. Hellen. vii. 1, 1).

[1] Diodor. xiv. 111.

[2] Xen. Hellen. v. 1, 3, 31. Ὅστ' ἐπεὶ παρήγγειλεν ὁ Τιριβάζος παρεῖναι τοὺς βουλομένους ὑπακοῦσαι, ἣν βασιλεὺς εἰρήνην κατέπεμ- ψοι, ταχέως πάντες παρεγίνοντο. Ἐπεὶ δὲ ἐυνῆλθον, ἐπιδείξας ὁ Τιριβάζος τὰ βασιλέως σημεῖα, ἀνεγίνωσκε τὰ γεγραμμένα, εἶχε δὲ ὦδε·

Ἀρταξέρξης βασιλεὺς νομίζει δί- καιον, τὰς μὲν ἐν τῇ Ἀσίᾳ πόλεις ἑαυτοῦ εἶναι, καὶ τῶν νήσων Κλαζο- μενὰς καὶ Κύπρον· τὰς δὲ ἄλλας Ἑλληνίδας πόλεις καὶ μικρὰς καὶ μεγάλας, αὐτονόμους εἶναι, πλὴν Λήμνου, καὶ Ἴμβρου καὶ Σκύρου,

## PEACE OF ANTALKIDAS.

Such was the convention which Sparta, the ancient president of the Grecian world, had been the first to solicit at the hands of the Persian king, and which she now not only set the example of sanctioning by her own spontaneous obedience, but even avouched as guarantee and champion against all opponents; preparing to enforce it at the point of the sword against any recusant state, whether party to it or not. Such was the convention which was now inscribed on stone, and placed as a permanent record in the temples of the Grecian cities;[1] nay even in the common sanctuaries—the Olympic, Pythian, and others—the great *foci* and rallying points of Pan-hellenic sentiment. Though called by the name of a convention, it was on the very face of it a peremptory mandate proceeding from the ancient enemy of Greece, an acceptance of which was nothing less than an act of obedience. While to him it was a glorious trophy, to all Pan-hellenic patriots it was the deepest disgrace and insult.[2] Effacing altogether the idea of an independent Hellenic world, bound together and regulated by the self-acting forces and common sympathies of its own members

ταύτας δὲ, ὥσπερ τὸ ἀρχαῖον, εἶναι Ἀθηναίων. Ὁπότεροι δὲ ταύτην τὴν εἰρήνην μὴ δέχονται, τούτοις ἐγὼ πολεμήσω, μετὰ τῶν ταῦτα βουλομένων, καὶ πέζῃ καὶ κατὰ θάλασσαν, καὶ ναυσὶ καὶ χρήμασι.

[1] Isokratês, Or. iv. (Panegyr.) s. 211. Καὶ ταύτας ἡμᾶς ἠνάγκασεν (the Persian king) ἐν στήλαις λιθίναις ἀναγράψαντας ἐν τοῖς κοινοῖς τῶν ἱερῶν ἀναθεῖναι, πολὺ κάλλιον τροπαίον τῶν ἐν ταῖς μάχαις γιγνομένων.

The Oratio Panegyrica of Isokratês (published about 380 B.C., seven years afterwards) from which I here copy, is the best evidence of the feelings with which an intelligent and patriotic Greek looked upon this treaty at the time; when it was yet recent, but when there had been full time to see how the Lacedæmonians carried it out. His other orations, though valuable and instructive, were published later, and represent the feelings of after-time.

Another contemporary, Plato in his Menexenus (c. 17. p. 245 D), stigmatises severely "the base and unholy act (αἴσχρὸν καὶ ἀνόσιον ἔργον) of surrendering Greeks to the foreigner," and asserts that the Athenians resolutely refused to sanction it. This is a sufficient mark of his opinion respecting the peace of Antalkidas.

[2] Isokrat. Or. iv. (Panegyr.) s. 207. Ἃ χρῆν ἀναιρεῖν, καὶ μηδεμίαν ἐᾶν ἡμέραν, νομίζοντας προστάγματα καὶ οὐ συνθήκας εἶναι, &c. (s. 213). Αἰσχρὸν ἡμᾶς ὅλης τῆς Ἑλλάδος ὑβριζομένης, μηδεμίαν ποιήσασθαι κοινὴν τιμωρίαν, &c.

The word προστάγματα exactly corresponds with an expression of Xenophon (put in the mouth of Autoklês the Athenian envoy at Sparta), respecting the dictation of the peace of Antalkidas by Artaxerxês—Καὶ ὅτι μὲν βασιλεὺς προσέταττεν αὐτονόμους τὰς πόλεις εἶναι, &c. (Xen. Hellen. vi, 3, 8).

—even the words of the convention proclaimed it as an act of intrusive foreign power, and erected the Barbarian King into a dictatorial settler of Grecian differences; a guardian[1] who cared for the peace of Greece more than the Greeks themselves. And thus, looking to the form alone, it was tantamount to that symbol of submission—the cession of earth and water—which had been demanded a century before by the ancestor of Artaxerxes from the ancestors of the Spartans and Athenians; a demand, which both Sparta and Athens then not only repudiated, but resented so cruelly, as to put to death the heralds by whom it was brought—stigmatising the Æginetans and others as traitors to Hellas for complying with it.[2] Yet nothing more would have been implied in such cession than what stood embodied in the inscription on that "colonna infame," which placed the peace of Antalkidas side by side with the Pan-hellenic glories and ornaments at Olympia.[3]

---

[1] Isokrat. Or. iv. (Panegyr.) s. 208. Καίτοι πῶς οὐ χρὴ διαλύειν ταύτας τὰς ὁμολογίας, ἐξ ὧν τοιαύτη δόξα γίγονεν, ὥστε ὁ μὲν Βάρβαρος κήδεται τῆς Ἑλλάδος καὶ φύλαξ τῆς εἰρήνης ἐστίν, ἡμῶν δὲ τινές εἰσιν οἱ λυμαινόμενοι καὶ κακῶς ποιοῦντες αὐτήν;

The word employed by Photius in his abstract of Theopompus (whether it be the expression of Theopompus himself, we cannot be certain—see Fragm. 111, ed. Didot), to designate the position taken by Artaxerxes in reference to this peace, is—τὴν εἰρήνην ἣν τοῖς Ἕλλησιν ἐβράβευσεν—which implies the peremptory decision of an official judge, analogous to another passage (139) of the Panegyr. Orat. of Isokrates—Νῦν δ' ἁπλῶς (Ἀρταξέρξης) ἐστίν, ὁ διοικῶν τὰ τῶν Ἑλλήνων καὶ μόνον οὐκ ἐπιστάθμους ἐν ταῖς πόλεσι καθίστας. Πλὴν γὰρ τούτου τί τῶν ἄλλων ὑπόλοιπόν ἐστιν; Οὐ περὶ τοῦ πολέμου κύριος ἐγένετο, καὶ τὴν εἰρήνην ἐπρυτάνευσε, καὶ τῶν παρόντων πραγμάτων ἐπιστάτης καθέστηκεν;

[2] Herodot. vi. 49. κατηγόρεον Αἰ-γινητάων τὰ πεποιήκοιεν, προδόντες τὴν Ἑλλάδα.

[3] Isokrates, Orat. xii. (Panathen.) s. 112—116.

Plutarch (Agesil. c. 23; Artaxerxes, c. 21, 22) expresses himself in terms of bitter and well-merited indignation of this peace—"if indeed (says he) we are to call this ignominy and betrayal of Greece by the name of peace, which brought with it as much infamy as the most disastrous war." Sparta (he says) lost her headship by her defeat at Leuktra, but her honour had been lost before, by the convention of Antalkidas.

It is in vain however that Plutarch tries to exonerate Agesilaus from any share in the peace. From the narrative (in Xenophon's Hellenics, v. 1. 33) of his conduct at the taking of the oaths, we see that he espoused it most warmly. Xenophon (in the Encomium of Agesilaus, vii. 7) takes credit to Agesilaus for being μισοπέρσης, which was true, from the year B.C. 396 to B.C. 394. But in B.C. 387, at the time of the peace of

## CONDUCT OF SPARTA.

Great must have been the change wrought by the intermediate events, when Sparta, the ostensible president of Greece—in her own estimation even more than in that of others!—had so lost all Pan-hellenic conscience and dignity, as to descend into an obsequious minister, procuring and enforcing a Persian mandate for political objects of her own. How insane would such an anticipation have appeared to Æschylus, or the audience who heard the Persæ! to Herodotus or Thucydidês! to Periklês and Archidamus! nay, even to Kallikratidas or Lysander! It was the last consummation of a series of previous political sins, invoking more and more the intervention of Persia to aid her against her Grecian enemies.

*Gradual loss of Pan-hellenic dignity, and increased submission towards Persia as a means of purchasing Persian help—on the part of Sparta.*

Her first application to the Great King for this purpose dates from the commencement of the Peloponnesian war, and is prefaced by an apology, little less than humiliating, from King Archidamus; who, not unconscious of the sort of treason which he was meditating, pleads that Sparta, when the Athenians are conspiring against her, ought not to be blamed for asking from foreigners as well as from Greeks aid for her own preservation.[2] From the earliest commencement to the seventh year of the war, many separate and successive envoys were dispatched by the Spartans to Susa; two of whom were

*Her first application before the Peloponnesian war; subsequent applications.*

---

Antalkidas, he had become μισο-
θηβαίος; his hatred of Persia had
given place to hatred of Thebes.
See also a vigorous passage of
Justin (viii. 4), denouncing the
disgraceful position of the Greek
cities at a later time in calling in
Philip of Macedon as arbiter; a
passage not less applicable to the
peace of Antalkidas; and perhaps
borrowed from Theopompus.

¹ Compare the language in which
the Ionians, on their revolt from
Darius king of Persia about 500
B.C., had implored the aid of Sparta
(Herodot. v. 49). Τὰ κατήκοντα γάρ
δοτι ταῦτα· Ἰώνων παῖδας δούλους
εἶναι ἀντ' ἐλευθέρων—ὀνειδός καὶ
ἄλγος μέγιστον μὲν αὐτοῖσι ἡμῖν,

ἔτι δὲ τῶν λοιπῶν ὑμῖν, ὅσῳ
προεστᾶτε τῆς Ἑλλάδος.
How striking is the contrast
between these words and the peace
of Antalkidas! and what would
have been the feelings of Herodotus himself if he could have heard
of the latter event!

² Thucyd. L. 82. Κἂν τούτῳ καὶ
τὰ ἡμέτερα αὐτῶν ἐξαρτυσόμεθα ξυμμάχων τε προσαγωγῇ καὶ Ἑλλήνων
καὶ βαρβάρων, εἴ ποθέν τινα ἢ
ναυτικοῦ ἢ χρημάτων δύναμιν
προσληψόμεθα, (ἀνεπίφθονον δὲ,
ὅσοι ὥσπερ καὶ ἡμεῖς ὑπ' Ἀθηναίων
ἐπιβουλευόμεθα, μὴ Ἕλληνας μόνον
ἀλλὰ καὶ βαρβάρους προσλαβόν-
τας διασωθῆναι), &c. Compare also
Plato, Menexenus, c. 14, p. 243 B.

seized in Thrace, brought to Athens, and there put to death. The rest reached their destination, but talked in so confused a way, and contradicted each other so much, that the Persian court, unable to understand what they meant,[1] sent Artaphernês with letters to Sparta (in the seventh year of the war) complaining of such stupidity, and asking for clearer information. Artaphernês fell into the hands of an Athenian squadron at Eion on the Strymon, and was conveyed to Athens; where he was treated with great politeness, and sent back (after the letters which he carried had been examined) to Ephesus. What is more important to note is, that Athenian envoys were sent along with him, with a view of bringing Athens into friendly communication with the Great King; which was only prevented by the fact that Artaxerxês Longimanus just then died. Here we see the fatal practice, generated by intestine war, of invoking Persian aid; begun by Sparta as an importunate solicitor—and partially imitated by Athens, though we do not know what her envoys were instructed to say, had they been able to reach Susa.

Nothing more is heard about Persian intervention until the year of the great Athenian disasters before Syracuse. Elate with the hopes arising out of that event, the Persians required no solicitation, but were quite as eager to tender interference for their own purposes, as Sparta was to invite them for hers. How ready Sparta was to purchase their aid by the surrender of the Asiatic Greeks, and that too without any stipulations in their favour, has been recounted in a preceding chapter.[2] She had not now the excuse—for it stands only as an excuse and not as a justification—of self-defence against aggression from Athens, which Archidamus had produced at the beginning of the war. Even then it was only a colourable excuse, not borne out by the reality of the case; but now, the avowed as well as the real object was something quite different—not to repel, but to crush,

B.C. 413.
Active partnership between Sparta and Persia against Athens, after the Athenian catastrophe at Syracuse. Athens is ready to follow her example.

---

[1] Thucyd. II. 7, 67; iv. 50.
[2] See Ch. LXXV. Compare the expressions of Demosthenes (cont. Aristokrat. c. 22. p. 646) attesting the prevalent indignation among the Athenians of his time, about this surrender of the Asiatic Greeks by Sparta—and his oration De Rhodior. Libertate, c. 13. p. 199, where he tells the peace

## SPARTA AT THE PEACE.

Athens. Yet to accomplish that object, not even of pretended safety, but of pure ambition, Sparta sacrificed unconditionally the liberty of her Asiatic kinsmen; a price which Archidamus at the beginning of the war would certainly never have endured the thoughts of paying, notwithstanding the then formidable power of Athens. Here, too, we find Athens following the example; and consenting, in hopes of procuring Persian aid, to the like sacrifice, though the bargain was never consummated. It is true that she was then contending for her existence. Nevertheless the facts afford melancholy proof how much the sentiment of Pan-hellenic independence became enfeebled in both the leaders, amidst the fierce intestine conflict terminated by the battle of Ægospotami.[1]

After that battle, the bargain between Sparta and Persia would doubtless have been fulfilled, and the Asiatic Greeks would have passed at once under the dominion of the latter—had not an entirely new train of circumstances arisen out of the very peculiar position and designs of Cyrus. That young prince did all in his power to gain the affections of the Greeks, as auxiliaries for his ambitious speculations; in which speculations both Sparta and the Asiatic Greeks took part, compromising themselves irrevocably against Artaxerxes, and still more against Tissaphernês. Sparta thus became unintentionally the enemy of Persia, and found herself compelled to protect the Asiatic Greeks against her hostility with which they were threatened; a protection easy for her to confer, not merely

*How Sparta became hostile to Persia after the battle of Ægospotami. The Persian force aids Athens against her, and breaks up her maritime empire.*

of Kallias, made by Athens with Persia in 449 B.C., in contrast with the peace of Antalkidas, contracted under the auspices of Sparta.

[1] This is strikingly set forth by Isokratês, Or. xii. (Panathen.) s. 157—173. In this passage, however, he distributes his blame too equally between Sparta and Athens, whereas the blame belongs of right to the former, in far greater proportion. Sparta not only began the practice of invoking the Great King, and purchasing his aid by disgraceful concessions—but she also carried it, at the peace of Antalkidas, to a more extreme point of selfishness and subserviences. Athens is guilty of following the bad example of her rival, but to a less extent, and under greater excuse on the plea of necessity.

Isokratês says in another place of this discourse, respecting the various acts of wrong-doing towards the general interests of Hellas—ἐπιδιιατίον τοὺς μὲν ἡμετέρους ὁψιμαθεῖς αὐτῶν γεγενημένους, Λακεδαιμονίους δὲ τὰ μὲν

from the unbounded empire which she then enjoyed over the Grecian world, but from the presence of the renowned Cyreian Ten Thousand, and the contempt for Persian military strength which they brought home from their retreat. She thus finds herself in the exercise of a Pan-hellenic protectorate or presidency, first through the ministry of Derkyllidas, next of Agesilaus, who even sacrifices at Aulis, takes up the sceptre of Agamemnon, and contemplates large schemes of aggression against the Great King. Here however the Persians play against her the same game which she had invoked them to assist in playing against Athens. Their fleet, which fifteen years before she had invited for her own purposes, is now brought in against herself, and with far more effect, since her empire was more odious as well as more oppressive than the Athenian. It is now Athens and her allies who call in Persian aid; without any direct engagement, indeed, to surrender the Asiatic Greeks, for we are told that after the battle of Knidus, Konon incurred the displeasure of the Persians by his supposed plans for re-uniting them with Athens,[1] and Athenian aid was still continued to Evagoras—yet nevertheless indirectly paving the way for that consummation. If Athens and her allies here render themselves culpable of an abnegation of Pan-hellenic sentiment, we may remark, as before, that they act under the pressure of stronger necessities than could ever be pleaded by Sparta; and that they might employ on their own behalf, with much greater truth, the excuse of self-preservation preferred by King Archidamus.

**No excuse for the subservience of Sparta to the Persians—she was probably afraid of a revived Athenian empire.**

But never on any occasion did that excuse find less real place than in regard to the mission of Antalkidas. Sparta was at that time so powerful, even after the loss of her maritime empire, that the allies at the Isthmus of Corinth, jealous of each other and held together only by common terror, could hardly stand on the defensive against her, and would probably have been disunited by reasonable offers on her part; nor would she have needed even to recall Agesilaus from Asia. Nevertheless the mission was probably dictated in great

πρώτους, τὰ δὲ μόνους ἐξαμαρ- τόντας (Panath. s. 103). Which is much nearer the truth than the passage before referred to.
[1] Cornelius Nepos, Conon. c. 5.

measure by a groundless panic, arising from the sight of the revived Long Walls and re-fortified Peiræus, and springing at once to the fancy, that a new Athenian empire, such as had existed forty years before, was about to start into life; a fancy little likely to be realised, since the very peculiar circumstances which had created the first Athenian empire were now totally reversed. Debarred from maritime empire herself, the first object with Sparta was, to shut out Athens from the like; the next, to put down all partial federations or political combinations, and to enforce universal autonomy, or the maximum of political isolation; in order that there might nowhere exist a power capable of resisting herself, the strongest of all individual states. As a means to this end, which was no less in the interest of Persia than in hers, she outbid all prior subserviences to the Great King—betrayed to him not only one entire division of her Hellenic kinsmen, but also the general honour of the Hellenic name in the most flagrant manner—and volunteered to *medise* in order that the Persians might repay her by *laconising*.[1] To ensure fully the obedience of all the satraps, who had more than once manifested dissentient views of their own, Antalkidas procured and brought down a formal order signed and sealed at Susa; and Sparta undertook, without shame or scruple, to enforce the same order—"the convention sent down by the King"—upon all her countrymen; thus converting them into the subjects, and herself into a sort of viceroy or satrap, of Artaxerxês. Such an act of treason to the Pan-hellenic cause was far more flagrant and destructive than that alleged confederacy with the Persian king, for which the Theban Ismenias was afterwards put to death, and that too by the Spartans themselves.[2] Unhappily it formed a precedent for the future, and was closely copied afterwards by Thebes;[3] foreboding but too clearly the short career which Grecian political independence had to run.

That large patriotic sentiment, which dictated the magnanimous answer sent by the Athenians[4] to the offers

---

[1] Isokrat. Or. iv. (Panegyr.) s. 145. Καὶ τῷ βαρβάρῳ τῷ τῆς Ἀσίας κρατοῦντι συμπράττουσι (the Lacedæmonians) ἕως ὡς μάλιστα ἀρχὴν ἔχωσιν.

[2] Xen. Hellen. v. 2, 35.
[3] Xen. Hellen. vii. 1, 33—39.
[4] Herodot. viii. 143.
The explanation which the Athenians give to the Spartan envoys,

of Mardonius in 479 B.C., refusing, in the midst of ruin present and prospective, all temptation to betray the sanctity of Pan-hellenic fellowship—that sentiment which had been during the two following generations the predominant inspiration of Athens, and had also been powerful, though always less powerful, at Sparta—was now, in the former, overlaid by more pressing apprehensions, and in the latter completely extinguished. Now it was to the leading states that Greece had to look, for holding up the great banner of Pan-hellenic independence; from the smaller states nothing more could be required than that they should adhere to and defend it, when upheld.[1] But so soon as Sparta was seen to solicit and enforce, and Athens to accept (even under constraint), the proclamation under the King's hand and seal brought down by Antalkidas—that banner was no longer a part of the public emblems of Grecian political life. The grand idea represented by it—of collective self-determining Hellenism—was left to dwell in the bosoms of individual patriots.

*Hellenism betrayed to the enemy, first by Sparta, next by the other leading states. Evidence that Hellenic independence was not destined to last much longer.*

If we look at the convention of Antalkidas apart from its form and warranty, and with reference to its substance, we shall find that though its first article was unequivocally disgraceful, its last was at least popular as a promise to the ear. Universal autonomy, to each city, small or great, was dear to Grecian political instinct.

*Promise of universal autonomy —popular to the Grecian ear—how carried out.*

of the reasons and feelings which dictated their answer of refusal to Alexander (viii. 144), are not less impressive than the answer itself.

But whoever would duly feel and appreciate the treason of the Spartans in soliciting the convention of Antalkidas, should read in contrast with it that speech which their envoys address to the Athenians, in order to induce the latter to stand out against the temptations of Mardonius (viii. 142).

[1] The sixth oration (called Archidamus) of Isokratês sets forth emphatically the magnanimous sentiments, and comprehensive principles, on which it becomes Sparta to model her public conduct—as altogether different from the simple considerations of prudence and security which are suitable to humbler states like Corinth, Epidaurus, or Phlius (Archidamus, s. 105, 106, 110).

Contrast these lofty pretensions with the dishonourable realities of the convention of Antalkidas—not thrust upon Sparta by superior force, but both originally sued out, and finally enforced, by her for her own political ends.

## PROMISE OF AUTONOMY.

I have already remarked more than once that the exaggerated force of this desire was the chief cause of the short duration of Grecian freedom. Absorbing all the powers of life to the separate parts, it left no vital force or integrity to the whole; especially, it robbed both each and all of the power of self-defence against foreign assailants. Though indispensable up to a certain point and under certain modifications, yet beyond these modifications, which Grecian political instinct was far from recognising, it produced a great preponderance of mischief. Although therefore this item of the convention was in its promise acceptable and popular—and although we shall find it hereafter invoked as a protection in various individual cases of injustice—we must inquire how it was carried into execution, before we can pronounce whether it was good or evil, the present of a friend or of an enemy.

The succeeding pages will furnish an answer to this inquiry. The Lacedæmonians, as "presidents (guarantees or executors) of the peace, sent down by the King,"[1] undertook the duty of execution; and we shall see that from the beginning they meant nothing sincerely. They did not even attempt any sincere and steady compliance with the honest, though undistinguishing, political instinct of the Greek mind; much less did they seek to grant as much as was really good, and to withhold the remainder. They defined autonomy in such manner, and meted it out in such portions, as suited their own political interests and purposes. The promise made by the convention, except in so far as it enabled them to increase their own power by dismemberment or party intervention, proved altogether false and hollow. For if we look back to the beginning of the Peloponnesian war, when they sent to Athens to require general autonomy throughout Greece, we shall find that the word had then a distinct

*The Spartans never intended to grant, nor ever really granted, general autonomy. They used the promise as a means of increased power to themselves.*

---

Compare also Isokratês, Or. xii. (Panathen.) s. 169—173, about the dimension of the leading Grecian states, and its baneful effects.

¹ Xen. Hellen. v. 1, 36.

'Εν δὲ τῷ πολέμῳ μᾶλλον ἀντιρρόπως τοῖς ἐναντίοις πράττοντες οἱ

Λακεδαιμόνιοι, πολλῷ ἐπιπυθέστεροι ἐγένοντο ἐκ τῆς ἐπ' Ἀνταλκίδου εἰρήνης καλουμένης· προστάται γὰρ γενόμενοι τῆς ὑπὸ βασιλέως καταπεμφθείσης εἰρήνης, καὶ τὴν αὐτονομίαν ταῖς πόλεσι πράττοντες, &c.

and serious import; demanding that the cities held in dependence by Athens should be left free, which freedom Sparta might have ensured for them herself at the close of the war, had she not preferred to convert it into a far harsher empire. But in 387 (the date of the peace of Antalkidas) there were no large bodies of subjects to be emancipated, except the allies of Sparta herself, to whom it was by no means intended to apply. So that in fact, what was promised, as well as what was realised, even by the most specious item of this disgraceful convention, was—"that cities should enjoy autonomy, not for their own comfort and in their own way, but for Lacedæmonian convenience;" a significant phrase (employed by Periklês,[1] in the debates preceding the Peloponnesian war) which forms a sort of running text for Grecian history during the sixteen years between the peace of Antalkidas and the battle of Leuktra.

I have already mentioned that the two first applications of the newly-proclaimed autonomy, made by the Lacedæmonians, were to extort from the Corinthian government the dismissal of its Argeian auxiliaries, and to compel Thebes to renounce her ancient presidency of the Bœotian federation. The latter especially was an object which they had long had at heart;[2] and by both, their ascendency in Greece was much increased. Athens too—terrified by the new development of Persian force as well as partially bribed by the restoration of her three islands, into an acceptance of the peace—was thus robbed of her Theban and Corinthian allies, and disabled from opposing the Spartan projects. But before we enter upon these projects, it will be convenient to turn for a short time to the proceedings of the Persians.

*Immediate point made against Corinth and Thebes— isolation of Athens.*

Even before the death of Darius Nothus (father of Artaxerxês and Cyrus) Egypt had revolted from the Persians, under a native prince named Amyrtæus. To the

---

[1] Thucyd. l. 144. Νῦν δὲ τούτοις (to the Lacedæmonian envoys) ἀνοσπινάμενοι ἀποαίρψομεν .... τὰς δὲ πόλεις ὅτι αὐτονόμους ἀφήσομεν, αἱ καὶ αὐτονόμους ἔχοντες ἐσπεισάμεθα, καὶ ὅταν κἀκεῖνοι τοῖς αὑτῶν ἀποδῶσι πόλεσι μὴ σφίσι τοῖς Λακεδαιμονίοις ἐπιτηδείως αὐτονομεῖσθαι, ἀλλὰ αὑτοῖς ἑκάστοις, ὡς βούλονται.

[2] Xen. Hellen. v. 1, 81. οὕπερ πάλαι ἐπεθύμουν.

Grecian leaders who accompanied Cyrus in his expedition against his brother, this revolt was well known to have much incensed the Persians; so that Klearchus, in the conversation which took place after the death of Cyrus about accommodation with Artaxerxês, intimated that the Ten Thousand could lend him effectual aid in reconquering Egypt.[1] It was not merely these Greeks who were exposed to danger by the death of Cyrus, but also the various Persians and other subjects who had lent assistance to him; all of whom made submission and tried to conciliate Artaxerxês, except Tamos, who had commanded the fleet of Cyrus on the coasts both of Ionia and of Kilikia. Such was the alarm of Tamos when Tissaphernês came down in full power to the coast, that he fled with his fleet and treasures to Egypt, to seek protection from King Psammetichus, to whom he had rendered valuable service. This traitor, however, having so valuable a deposit brought to him, forgot everything else in his avidity to make it sure, and put to death Tamos with all his children.[2] About 395 B.C., we find Nephereus king of Egypt lending aid to the Lacedæmonian fleet against Artaxerxês.[3] Two years afterwards (392-390 B.C.), during the years immediately succeeding the victory of Knidus, and the voyage of Pharnabazus across the Ægean to Peloponnesus—we hear of that satrap as employed with Abrokomas and Tithroustês in strenuous but unavailing efforts to reconquer Egypt.[4] Having thus repulsed the Persians, the Egyptian king

*Persian affairs—unavailing efforts of the Great King to reconquer Egypt.*

[1] Xen. Anab. ii. 5, 13.
It would appear that the revolt of Egypt from Persia must date between 414—411 B.C.; but this point is obscure. See Bœckh, Manetho und die Hundstern-Periode, pp. 358, 363, Berlin 1845; and Ley, Fata et Conditio Ægypti sub Imperio Persarum, p. 56.
M. Rehdantz, Vitæ Iphicratis, Timothei, et Chabriæ, p. 310, places the revolt rather earlier, about 414 B.C.; and Mr. Fynes Clinton (Fasti Hellen. Appendix, ch. 18, p. 317) countenances the same date.
[2] Diodor. xiv. 35.

This Psammetichus is presumed by Ley (in his Dissertation above cited, p. 20) to be the same person as Amyrtæus the Saite in the list of Manetho, under a different name. It is also possible, however, that he may have been king over part of Egypt, contemporaneous with Amyrtæus.
[3] Diodor. xiv. 79.
[4] This is the chronology laid down by M. Rehdantz (Vitæ Iphicratis, Chabriæ, et Timothei, Epimetr. ii. pp. 241, 242) on very probable grounds, principally from Isokratês, Orat. iv. (Panegyr.) s. 161, 162.

Akoris is found between 390-380 B.C.,[1] sending aid to Evagoras in Cyprus against the same enemy. And in spite of farther efforts made afterwards by Artaxerxês to reconquer Egypt, the native kings in that country maintained their independence for about sixty years in all, until the reign of his successor Ochus.

*Evagoras, despot of Salamis in Cyprus.*

But it was a Grecian enemy—of means inferior, yet of qualities much superior, to any of these Egyptians—who occupied the chief attention of the Persians immediately after the peace of Antalkidas: Evagoras despot of Salamis in Cyprus. Respecting that prince we possess a discourse of the most glowing and superabundant eulogy, composed after his death for the satisfaction (and probably paid for with the money) of his son and successor Nikoklês, by the contemporary Isokratês. Allowing as we must do for exaggeration and partiality, even the trustworthy features of the picture are sufficiently interesting.

*Descent of Evagoras—condition of the island of Cyprus.*

Evagoras belonged to a Salaminian stock or Gens called the Teukridæ, which numbered among its ancestors the splendid legendary names of Teukrus, Telamon, and Æakus; taking its departure, through them, from the divine name of Zeus. It was believed that the archer Teukrus, after returning from the siege of Troy to (the Athenian) Salamis, had emigrated under a harsh order from his father Telamon, and given commencement to the city of that name on the eastern coast of Cyprus.[2] As in Sicily, so in Cyprus, the Greek and Phœnician elements were found in near contact, though in very different proportions. Of the nine or ten separate city communities, which divided among them the whole sea-coast, the inferior towns being all dependent upon one or other of them—seven pass for Hellenic, the two most considerable being Salamis and Soli; three for Phœnician—Paphos, Amathus, and Kitium.

---

[1] Diodor. xv. 2, 8.
[2] Isokratês, Or. III. (Nikokl.) s. 50; Or. ix. (Evagoras) s. 21; Pausanias, ii. 29, 4; Diodor. xiv. 98.

The historian Theopompus, when entering upon the history of Evagoras, seems to have related many legendary tales respecting the Greek Gentes in Cyprus, and to have represented Agamemnon himself as ultimately migrating to it (Theopompus, Frag. 111, ed. Wichers; and ed. Didot. ap. Photium).

The tomb of the archer Teukrus was shown at Salamis in Cyprus. See the Epigram of Aristotle, Antholog. L B, 112.

Probably, however, there was in each a mixture of Greek and Phœnician population, in different proportions.[1] Each was ruled by its own separate prince or despot, Greek or Phœnician. The Greek immigrations, (though their exact date cannot be assigned) appear to have been later in date than the Phœnician. At the time of the Ionic revolt (B.C. 496), the preponderance was on the side of Hellenism; yet with considerable intermixture of Oriental custom. Hellenism was however greatly crushed by the Persian reconquest of the revolters, accomplished through the aid of the Phœnicians[2] on the opposite continent. And though doubtless the victories of Kimon and the Athenians (470-450 B.C.) partially revived it, yet Periklês, in his pacification with the Persians, had prudently relinquished Cyprus as well as Egypt;[3] so that the Grecian element in the former, receiving little extraneous encouragement, became more and more subordinate to the Phœnician.

It was somewhere about this time that the reigning princes of Salamis, who at the time of the Ionic revolt had been Greeks of the Teukrid Gens,[4] were supplanted and

[1] Movers, in his very learned investigations respecting the Phœnicians (vol. iii. ch. 6. p. 203-221 seq.), attempts to establish the existence of an ancient population in Cyprus, called Kitians; once extended over the island, and of which the town called Kitium was the remnant. He supposes them to have been a portion of the Canaanitish population, anterior to the Jewish occupation of Palestine. The Phœnician colonies in Cyprus he reckons as of later date, superadded to, and depressing these natives. He supposes the Kilikian population to have been in early times Canaanitish also. Engel (Kypros, vol. i. p. 168) inclines to admit the same hypothesis as highly probable.

The sixth century B.C. (from 600 downwards) appears to have been very unfavourable to the Phœnicians, bringing upon Tyre severe pressure from the Chaldæans, as it brought captivity upon the Jews. During the same period, the Grecian commerce with Egypt was greatly extended, especially by the reign of the Phil-Hellenic Amasis, who acquired possession of Cyprus. Much of the Grecian immigration into Cyprus probably took place at this time; we know of one body of settlers invited by Philokyprus to Soli, under the assistance of the Athenian Solon (Movers, p. 244 seq.).

[2] Herodot. v. 108.

Compare the description given by Herodotus of the costume and arms of the Cypriots in the armament of Xerxes—half Oriental (vii. 90). The Salaminians used chariots of war in battle (v. 113); as the Carthaginians did, before they learnt the art of training elephants (Diodor. xvi. 80; Plutarch, Timoleon, c. 27).

[3] See Chap. XLV. of this History.

[4] One of these princes however is mentioned as bearing the Phœnician name of Siromus (Herod. v. 104).

dethroned by a Phœnician exile who gained their confidence and made himself despot in their place.[1] To ensure his own sceptre, this usurper did everything in his power to multiply and strengthen the Phœnician population, as well as to discourage and degrade the Hellenic. The same policy was not only continued by his successor at Salamis, but seems also to have been imitated in several of the other towns; insomuch that during most part of the Peloponnesian war, Cyprus became sensibly dis-hellenised. The Greeks in the island were harshly oppressed; new Greek visitors and merchants were kept off by the most repulsive treatment, as well as by threats of those cruel mutilations of the body which were habitually employed as penalties by the Orientals; while Grecian arts, education, music, poetry, and intelligence, were rapidly on the decline.[2]

*Greek princes of Salamis are dispossessed by a Phœnician dynasty.*

Notwithstanding such untoward circumstances, in which the youth of the Teukrid Evagoras at Salamis was passed, he manifested at an early age so much energy both of mind and body, and so much power of winning popularity, that he became at once a marked man both among Greeks and Phœnicians. It was about this time that the Phœnician despot was slain, through a conspiracy

*Evagoras dethrones the Phœnician, and becomes despot of Salamis. B.C. 411-410.*

---

[1] We may gather this by putting together Herodot. iv. 162; v. 101-114; with Isokrates, Or. iv. (Evagoras) s. 22.

[2] Isokrates, Or. ix. (Evag.) s. 23, 35, 58.

Παραλαβών γάρ (Evagoras) τήν πόλιν ἐκβεβαρβαρωμένην, καὶ διὰ τὴν τῶν Φοινίκων ἀρχὴν οὔτε τοὺς Ἕλληνας προσδεχομένην, οὔτε τέχνας ἐπισταμένην, οὔτ᾽ ἐμπορίῳ χρωμένην, οὔτε λιμένα κεκτημένην, &c.

Πρὶν μὲν γὰρ λαβεῖν Εὐαγόραν τὴν ἀρχήν, οὕτως ἀπροσοίστως καὶ χαλεπῶς εἶχον, ὥστε καὶ τῶν ἀρχόντων τούτους ἐνόμιζον εἶναι βελτίστους οἵ τινες ὠμότατα πρὸς τοὺς Ἕλληνας διακείμενοι τυγχάνειεν, &c.

This last passage receives remarkable illustration from the oration of Lysias against Andokides, in which he alludes to the visit of the latter to Cyprus—μετὰ δὲ ταῦτα Κιλαύσων ὡς τὸν Κιτιέων βασιλέα, καὶ προδιδοὺς ληφθεὶς ὑπ᾽ αὐτοῦ ἐδέθη, καὶ οὐ μόνον τὸν θάνατον ἐφοβεῖτο ἀλλὰ τὰ καθ᾽ ἡμέραν αἰκίσματα, οἱόμενος τὰ ἀκρωτήρια ζῶντος ἀποτμηθήσεσθαι (s. 28).

Engel (Kypros, vol. i. p. 286) impugns the general correctness of this narrative of Isokrates. He produces no adequate reasons, nor do I myself see any, for this contradiction.

Not only Konon, but also his friend Nikophemus, had a wife and family at Cyprus, besides another family in Athens (Lysias, De Bonis Aristophanis, Or. xix. s. 37).

formed by a Kitian or Tyrian named Abdêmon, who got possession of his sceptre.[1] The usurper, mistrustful of his position and anxious to lay hands upon all conspicuous persons who might be capable of doing him mischief, tried to seize Evagoras; but the latter escaped and passed over to Soli in Kilikia. Though thus to all appearance a helpless exile, he found means to strike a decisive blow, while the new usurpation, stained by its first violences and rapacity, was surrounded by enemies, doubters, or neutrals, without having yet established any firm footing. He crossed over from Soli in Kilikia, with a small but determined band of about fifty followers—obtained secret admission by a postern gate of Salamis—and assaulted Abdêmon by night in his palace. In spite of a vastly superior number of guards, this enterprise was conducted with such extraordinary daring and judgement, that Abdêmon perished, and Evagoras became despot in his place.[2]

The splendour of this exploit was quite sufficient to seat Evagoras unopposed on the throne, amidst a population always accustomed to princely government; while among the Salaminian Greeks he was still farther endeared by his Teukrid descent.[3] His conduct fully justified the expectations entertained. Not merely did he refrain from bloodshed, or spoliation, or violence for the gratification of personal appetite; abstinences remarkable enough in any Grecian despot to stamp his reign with letters of gold, and the more remarkable in Evagoras, since he had the susceptible temperament of a Greek, though his great mental force always kept it under due control.[4] But he

*Able and beneficent government of Evagoras.*

---

[1] Theopompus (Fr. 111) calls Abdêmon a Kitian; Diodorus (xiv. 98) calls him a Tyrian. Movers (p. 306) thinks that both are correct, and that he was a Kitian living at Tyre, who had migrated from Salamis during the Athenian preponderance there. There were Kitians, not natives of the town of Kitium, but belonging to the ancient population of the island, living in the various towns of Cyprus; and there were also Kitians mentioned as resident at Sidon (Diogen. Laert. Vit. Zenon. s. 6).

[2] Isokratês, Or. ix. (Evagoras) s. 29-35; also Or. iii. (Nikokl.) s. 83; Theopomp. Fragm. 111, ed. Wichers and ed. Didot; Diodor. xiv. 98.

The two latter mention the name, Audymon or Abdêmon, which Isokratês does not specify.

[3] Isokratês, Or. iii. (Nikoklês, s. 33.

[4] Isokrat. Or. ix. s. 53. ἡγούμενος τῶν ἡδονῶν, ἀλλ' οὐκ ἀγόμενος ὑπ' αὐτῶν, &c.

was also careful in inquiring into, and strict in punishing crime, yet without those demonstrations of cruel infliction by which an Oriental prince displayed his energy.¹ His government was at the same time highly popular and conciliating, as well towards the multitude as towards individuals. Indefatigable in his own personal supervision, he examined everything for himself, shaped out his own line of policy, and kept watch over its execution.² He was foremost in all effort and in all danger. Maintaining undisturbed security, he gradually doubled the wealth, commerce, industry, and military force of the city, while his own popularity and renown went on increasing.

Above all, it was his first wish to renovate, both in Salamis and in Cyprus, that Hellenism which the Phœnician despots of the last fifty years had done so much to extinguish or corrupt. For aid in this scheme, he seems to have turned his thoughts to Athens, with which city he was connected as a Teukrid, by gentile and legendary sympathies—and which was then only just ceasing to be the great naval power of the Ægean. For though we cannot exactly make out the date at which Evagoras began to reign, we may conclude it to have been about 411 or 410 B.C. It seems to have been shortly after that period that he was visited by Andokidês the Athenian;³ moreover he must have been a prince not merely established, but powerful, when he ventured to harbour Konon in 405 B.C., after the battle of Ægospotami. He invited to Salamis fresh immigrants from Attica and

*His anxiety to revive Hellenism in Cyprus— he looks to the aid of Athens.*

¹ Isokr. Or. ix. 51. οὐδένα μὲν ἀδικῶν, τοὺς δὲ χρηστοὺς τιμῶν, καὶ σφόδρα μὲν ἀπάντων ἄρχων, νομίμως δὲ τοὺς ἐξαμαρτάνοντας κολάζων (s. 58)—ὃς οὐ μόνον τὴν ἑαυτοῦ πόλιν πλείονος ἀξίαν ἐποίησεν, ἀλλὰ καὶ τὸν τόπον ὅλον, τὸν περιέχοντα τὴν νῆσον, ἐπὶ πραότητα καὶ μετριότητα προήγαγεν, &c.: compare s. 81.

These epithets, *lawful punishment, mild dealing,* &c., cannot be fully understood except in contrast with the mutilations alluded to by Lysias, in the passage cited in a note of my preceding page; also

with exactly similar mutilations, mentioned by Xenophon as systematically inflicted upon offenders by Cyrus the younger (Xenoph. Anabas. i. 9, 13). Οὐδείς γάρ ἡμῶν (says Isokratês about the Persians) οὕτως αἰκίζεται τοὺς οἰκέτας, ὡς ἐκεῖνοι τοὺς ἐλευθέρους κολάζουσιν— Or. iv. (Paneg.) 142.

² Isokratês, Or. ix. (Evag.) s. 50-56.

The language of the encomiast, though exaggerated, must doubtless be founded in truth, as the result shows.

³ Lysias cont. Andokid. s. 28.

other parts of Greece, as the prince Philokyprus of Soli had done under the auspices of Solon,[1] a century and a half before. He took especial pains to revive and improve Grecian letters, arts, teaching, music, and intellectual tendencies. His encouragement was so successfully administered, that in a few years, without constraint or violence, the face of Salamis was changed. The gentleness and sociability, the fashions and pursuits, of Hellenism, became again predominant; with great influence of example over all the other towns of the island.

Had the rise of Evagoras taken place a few years earlier, Athens might perhaps have availed herself of the opening to turn her ambition eastward, in preference to that disastrous impulse which led her westward to Sicily. But coming as he did only at that later moment when she was hard pressed to keep up even a defensive war, he profited rather by her weakness than by her strength. During those closing years of the war, when the Athenian empire was partially broken up, and when the Ægean, instead of the tranquillity which it had enjoyed for fifty years under Athens, became a scene of contest between two rival money-levying fleets—many outsettlers from Athens, who had acquired property in the islands, the Chersonesus, or elsewhere, under her guarantee, found themselves insecure in every way, and were tempted to change their abodes. Finally, by the defeat of Ægospotami (B.C. 405), all such out-settlers as then remained were expelled, and forced to seek shelter either at Athens (at that moment the least attractive place in Greece), or in some other locality. To such persons, not less than to the Athenian admiral Konon with his small remnant of Athenian triremes saved out of the great defeat, the proclaimed invitations of Evagoras would present a harbour of refuge nowhere else to be found. Accordingly we learn that numerous settlers of the best character, from different parts of Greece, crowded to Salamis.[2] Many Athenian women, during the years of destitution and suffering which preceded as well as followed the battle of Ægospotami, were well pleased to emigrate and find husbands in that

*Relations of Evagoras with Athens during the closing years of the Peloponnesian war.*

[1] Plutarch, Solon, c. 26.
[2] Isokrates, Or. ix. (Evag.) s. 89. Cf: compare Lysias, Or. xix. (De

Aristoph. Ran.) s. 38-46; and Diodor. xiv. 98.

city;[1] while throughout the wide range of the Lacedæmonian empire, the numerous victims exiled by the Harmosts and Dekarchies had no other retreat on the whole so safe and tempting. The extensive plain of Salamis afforded lands for many colonists. On what conditions, indeed, they were admitted, we do not know; but the conduct of Evagoras as a ruler gave universal satisfaction.

During the first years of his reign, Evagoras doubtless paid his tribute regularly, and took no steps calculated to offend the Persian king. But as his power increased, his ambition increased also. We find him towards the year 390 B.C., engaged in a struggle not merely with the Persian king, but with Amathus and Kitium in his own island. By what steps, or at what precise period, this war began, we cannot determine. At the time of the battle of Knidus (394 B.C.) Evagoras not only paid his tribute, but was mainly instrumental in getting the Persian fleet placed under Konon to act against the Lacedæmonians, himself serving aboard.[*] It was in fact (if we may believe Isokratês) to the extraordinary energy, ability, and power, displayed by him on

*Evagoras at war with the Persians—he receives aid both from Athens and from Egypt—he is at first very successful, so as even to capture Tyre.*

---

[1] Isokratês, l. c. καιδοκοιεῖσθαι δὲ τοὺς πλείστους αὐτῶν γυναῖκας λαμβάνοντες παρ' ἡμῶν, &c.

For the extreme distress of Athenian women during these trying times, consult the statement in Xenophon, Memorab. II. 7, 2-4.

The Athenian Andokidês is accused of having carried out a young woman of citizen family—his own cousin, and daughter of an Athenian named Aristeidês—to Cyprus, and there to have sold her to the despot of Kitium for a cargo of wheat. But being threatened with prosecution for this act before the Athenian Dikastery, he stole her away again and brought her back to Athens; in which act however he was detected by the prince, and punished with imprisonment from which he had the good fortune to escape. (Plutarch, Vit. X. Orat. p. 834; Photius, Cod. 261; Tzetzes, Chil. Iad. vi. 367.)

How much there may be of truth in this accusation, we have no means of determining. But it illustrates the way in which Athenian maidens, who had no dowry at home, were provided for by their relatives elsewhere. Probably Andokidês took this young woman out, under the engagement to find a Grecian husband for her in Cyprus. Instead of doing this, he sold her for his own profit to the harem of the prince; or at least is accused of having so sold her.

[*] Thus much appears even from the meagre abstract of Ktesias, given by Photius (Ktesiæ Persica, c. 63. p. 80, ed. Bähr.)

Both Ktesias and Theopompus (Fr. III. ed. Wichers, and ed. Didot) recounted the causes which brought about the war between the Persian king and Evagoras.

that occasion in the service of Artaxerxês himself, that the jealousy and alarm of the latter against him are to be ascribed. Without any provocation, and at the very moment when he was profiting by the zealous services of Evagoras, the Great King treacherously began to manœuvre against him and forced him into the war in self-defence.[1] Evagoras accepted the challenge, in spite of the disparity of strength, with such courage and efficiency, that he at first gained marked successes. Seconded by his son Pnytagoras, he not only worsted and humbled Amathus, Kitium, and Soli—which cities, under the prince Agyris, adhered to Artaxerxês—but also equipped a large fleet, attacked the Phœnicians on the mainland with so much vigour as even to take the great city of Tyre; prevailing moreover upon some of the Kilikian towns to declare against the Persians.[2] He received powerful aid from Akoris, the native and independent king in Egypt, as well as from Chabrias and the force sent out by the Athenians.[3] Beginning apparently about 390 B.C., the war against Evagoras lasted something more than ten years, costing the Persians great efforts and an immense expenditure of money. Twice did Athens send a squadron to his assistance, from gratitude for his long protection to Konon and his energetic efforts before in the battle of Knidus—though she thereby ran every risk of making the Persians her enemies.

The satrap Tiribazus saw that so long as he had on his hands a war in Greece, it was impossible for him to concentrate his force against the prince of Salamis and the Egyptians. Hence, in part, the extraordinary effort made by the Persians to dictate, in conjunction with Sparta, the peace of Antalkidas, and to get together such a fleet in Ionia as should overawe Athens and Thebes into submission. It was one of the conditions

*Struggle of Evagoras against the whole force of the Persian empire after the peace of Antalkidas.*

---

[1] Isokratês, Or. ix. (Evag.) s. 71, 73, 74. πρὸς δὲ τούτον (Evagoras) οὕτως ἐκ πολλοῦ περιδεῶς ἔσχε (Ἀρταξερξῆς), ὥστε μεταξὺ ῥᾳθυμῶν εὖ, πολεμεῖν πρὸς αὐτὸν ἐπεχείρησαν, δίκαια μὲν οὐ ποιῶν, &c.— ἐπειδὴ ἠναγκάσθη πολεμεῖν (i.e. Evagoras).

[2] Isokr. Or. ix. (Evag.) s. 75, 76; Diodor. xiv. 98; Ephorus, Frag. 134, ed. Didot.

[3] Cornelius Nepos, Chabrias, c. 2; Demosthenês adv. Leptinem, p. 479, s. 84.

of that peace that Evagoras should be abandoned;[1] the whole island of Cyprus being acknowledged as belonging to the Persian king. Though thus cut off from Athens, and reduced to no other Grecian aid than such mercenaries as he could pay, Evagoras was still assisted by Akoris of Egypt, and even by Hekatomnus prince of Karia with a secret present of money.[2] But the peace of Antalkidas being now executed in Asia, the Persian satraps were completely masters of the Grecian cities on the Asiatic seaboard, and were enabled to convey round to Kilikia and Cyprus not only their own fleet from Ionia, but also additional contingents from these very Grecian cities. A large portion of the Persian force acting against Cyprus was thus Greek, yet seemingly acting by constraint, neither well paid nor well used,[3] and therefore not very efficient.

The satraps Tiribazus and Orontês commanded the land force, a large portion of which was transported across to Cyprus: the admiral Gaos was at the head of the fleet, which held its station at Kitium in the south of the island. It was here that Evagoras, having previously gained a battle on land, attacked them. By extraordinary efforts he had got together a fleet of 200 triremes, nearly equal in number to theirs; but after a hard-fought contest, in which he at first seemed likely to be victorious, he underwent a complete naval defeat, which disqualified him from keeping the sea, and enabled the Persians to block up Salamis as well by sea as by land.[4] Though thus reduced to his own single city, however, Evagoras defended

*Evagoras, after a ten years' war, is reduced, but obtains an honourable peace, mainly owing to the dispute between the two satraps jointly commanding.*

---

[1] Isokrat. Or. iv. (Panegyr.) s. 161. Εὐαγόραν—ὃς ἐν ταῖς συνθήκαις ἐκδοτὸς ἐστιν, &c.

We must observe, however, that Cyprus had been secured to the king of Persia, even under the former peace, so glorious to Athens, concluded by Periklês about 449 b.c., and called the peace of Kallias. It was therefore neither a new demand on the part of Artaxerxês, nor a new concession on the part of the Greeks, at the peace of Antalkidas.

[2] Diodor. xv. 2.

It appears that Artaxerxês had counted much upon the aid of Hekatomnus for conquering Evagoras (Diodor. xiv. 98).

About 360 b.c., Isokratês reckons Hekatomnus as being merely dependant in name on Persia; and ready to revolt openly on the first opportunity (Isokratês, Or. iv. (Paneg.) s. 189).

[3] Isokratês. Or. iv. (Panegyr.) s. 163, 164, 179.

[4] Diodor. xv. 4.

himself with unshaken resolution, still sustained by aid
from Akoris in Egypt; while Tyre and several towns in
Kilikia also continued in revolt against Artaxerxês; so
that the efforts of the Persians were distracted, and the
war was not concluded until ten years after its commencement.[1] It cost them on the whole (if we may believe
Isokratês[2]) 15,000 talents in money, and such severe losses
in men, that Tiribazus acceded to the propositions of Evagoras for peace, consenting to leave him in full possession
of Salamis, under payment of a stipulated tribute, "like a
slave to his master." These last words were required by
the satrap to be literally inserted in the convention; but
Evagoras peremptorily refused his consent, demanding
that the tribute should be recognized as paid by "one king
to another." Rather than concede this point of honour, he
even broke off the negotiation, and resolved again to defend
himself to the uttermost. He was rescued, after the siege
had been yet farther prolonged, by a dispute which broke out
between the two commanders of the Persian army. Orontês,
accusing Tiribazus of projected treason and rebellion
against the King, in conjunction with Sparta, caused him

[1] Compare Isokratês, Or. iv.
(Panegyr.) s. 187, 188—with Isokratês, Or. ix. (Evag.) s. 77.
The war was not concluded—and
Tyre as well as much of Kilikia
was still in revolt—when Isokratês
published the Panegyrical Oration.
At that time, Evagoras had maintained the contest six years, counting either from the peace of Antalkidas (387 B.C.) or from his naval
defeat about a year or two afterwards; for Isokratês does not make
it quite clear from what point of
commencement he reckons the six
years.
We know that the war between
the king of Persia and Evagoras had
begun as early as 390 B.C., in which
year an Athenian fleet was sent to
assist the latter (Xenoph. Hellen.
iv. 8, 24). Both Isokratês and Diodorus state that it lasted ten years;
and I therefore place the conclusion
of it in 380 or 379 B.C., soon after
the date of the Panegyrical Oration
of Isokratês. I dissent on this
point from Mr. Clinton (see Fasti
Hellenici, ad annos 387-376 B.C.,
and his Appendix, No. 19—where
the point is discussed). He supposes the war to have begun after
the peace of Antalkidas, and to
have ended in 376 B.C. I agree with
him in making light of Diodorus,
but he appears to me on this occasion to contradict the authority
of Xenophon—or at least only to
evade the necessity of contradicting
him by resorting to an inconvenient
hypothesis, and by representing
the two Athenian expeditions sent
to assist Evagoras in Cyprus, first
in 390 B.C., next in 388 B.C., as
relating to "*hostile measures before
the war began*" (p. 380). To me it
appears more natural and reasonable to include these as a part of
the war.

[2] Isokratês, Or. ix. s. 72-74.

to be sent for as prisoner to Susa, and thus became sole commander. But as the besieging army was already wearied out by the obstinate resistance of Salamis, he consented to grant the capitulation, stipulating only for the tribute, and exchanging the offensive phrase enforced by Tiribazus, for the amendment of the other side.[1]

It was thus that Evagoras was relieved from his besieging enemies, and continued for the remainder of his life as tributary prince of Salamis under the Persians.

About B.C. 380—379. Assassination of Evagoras, as well as of his son Puytagoras, by an eunuch slave of Nikokreon.

He was no farther engaged in war, nor was his general popularity among the Salaminians diminished by the hardships which they had gone through along with him.[2] His prudence calmed the rankling antipathy of the Great King, who would gladly have found a pretext for breaking the treaty. His children were numerous, and lived in harmony as well with him as with each other. Isokratês specially notices this fact, standing as it did in marked contrast with the family-relations of most of the Grecian despots, usually stained with jealousies, antipathies, and conflict, often with actual bloodshed.[3] But he omits to notice the incident whereby Evagoras perished; an incident not in keeping with that superhuman good fortune and favour from the Gods, of which the Panegyrical Oration boasts as having been vouchsafed to the hero throughout his life.[4] It was seemingly not very long after the peace, that a Salaminian named Nikokreon formed a conspiracy against his life and dominion, but was detected, by a singular accident, before the moment of execution, and forced to seek safety in flight. He left behind him a youthful daughter in his harem, under the care of an eunuch (a Greek, born in Elis) named

[1] Diodor. xv. 8, 9.
This remarkable anecdote, of susceptible Grecian honour on the part of Evagoras, is noway improbable, and seems safe to admit on the authority of Diodorus. Nevertheless, it forms so choice a morsel for a panegyrical discourse such as that of Isokratês, that one cannot but think he would have inserted it had it come to his knowledge. His silence causes great surprise—not without some suspicion as to the truth of the story.

[2] Isokratês, Or. iii. (Nikoklês) s. 40—a passage which must be more true of Evagoras than of Nikoklês.

[3] Isokrat. Or. ix. s. 88. Compare his Orat. viii. (De Pace) s. 138.

[4] Isokratês, ib. s. 85. εὐτυχέστερον καὶ θεοφιλέστερον, &c.

## ASSASSINATION OF EVAGORAS.

Thrasydæus; who, full of vindictive sympathy in his master's cause, made known the beauty of the young lady both to Evagoras himself and to Pnytagoras, the most distinguished of his sons, partner in the gallant defence of Salamis against the Persians. Both of them were tempted, each unknown to the other, to make a secret assignation for being conducted to her chamber by the eunuch: both of them were there assassinated by his hand.[1]

Thus perished a Greek of pre-eminent vigour and intelligence, remarkably free from the vices usual in Grecian despots, and forming a strong contrast in this respect with his contemporary Dionysius, whose military energy is so deeply stained by crime and violence. Nikoklês, the son of Evagoras, reigned at Salamis after him, and showed much regard, accompanied by munificent presents, to the

*Nikoklês, son of Evagoras, becomes despot of Salamis.*

---

[1] I give this incident, in the main, as it is recounted in the fragment of Theopompus, preserved as a portion of the abstract of that author by Photius (Theopom. Fr. 111, ed. Wichers and ed. Didot).

Both Aristotle (Polit. v. 8, 10) and Diodorus (xv. 47) allude to the assassination of Evagoras by the eunuch; but both these authors conceive the story differently from Theopompus. Thus Diodorus says —Nikoklês the eunuch assassinated Evagoras and became "despot of Salamis." This appears to be a confusion of Nikoklês with Nikokreon. Nikoklês was the son of Evagoras, and the manner in which Isokratês addresses him affords the surest proof that he had no hand in the death of his father.

The words of Aristotle are—ἡ (ἐπίθεσις) τοῦ εὐνούχου Εὐαγόρᾳ τῷ Κυπρίῳ· διὰ γὰρ τὸ τὴν γυναῖκα παραλίσθαι τὸν υἱὸν αὐτοῦ ἀπέκτεινεν ὡς ὑβρισμένος. So perplexing is the passage in its literal sense, that M. Barthélemy St. Hilaire, in the note to his translation, conceives ὁ εὐνοῦχος to be a surname

or sobriquet given to the conspirator, whose real name was Nikoklês. But this supposition is, in my judgement, contradicted by the fact, that Theopompus marks the same fact, of the assassin being an eunuch, by another word—Θρασυδαίου τοῦ ἡμιάρρενος, &c. ἦν Ἠλεῖος τὸ γένος, &c.

It is evident that Aristotle had heard the story differently from Theopompus, and we have to choose between the two. I prefer the version of the latter; which is more marked as well as more intelligible, and which furnishes the explanation why Pnytagoras—who seems to have been the most advanced of the sons, being left in command of the besieged Salamis when Evagoras quitted it to solicit aid in Egypt—did not succeed his father, but left the succession to Nikoklês, who was evidently (from the representation even of an eulogist like Isokratês) not a man of much energy. The position of this eunuch in the family of Nikokreon seems to mark the partial prevalence of Oriental habits.

Athenian Isokratês; who compliments him as a pacific and well-disposed prince, attached to Greek pursuits and arts, conversant by personal study with Greek philosophy, and above all, copying his father in that just dealing and absence of wrong towards person or property, which had so much promoted the comfort as well as the prosperity of the city.[1]

*B.C. 387-385. Condition of the Asiatic Greeks after being transferred to Persia— much changed for the worse. Exposure of the Ionian islands also.*

We now revert from the episode respecting Evagoras —interesting not less from the eminent qualities of that prince than from the glimpse of Hellenism struggling with the Phœnician element in Cyprus—to the general consequences of the peace of Antalkidas in Central Greece. For the first time since the battle of Mykalê in 479 B.C., the Persians were now really masters of all the Greeks on the Asiatic coast. The satraps lost no time in confirming their dominion. In all the cities which they suspected, they built citadels and planted permanent garrisons. In some cases, their mistrust or displeasure was carried so far as to raze the town altogether.[2] And thus these cities, having already once changed their position greatly for the worse, by passing from easy subjection under Athens to the harsh rule of Lacedæmonian harmosts and native decemvirs—were now transferred to masters yet more oppressive and more completely without the pale of Hellenic sympathy. Both in public extortion, and in wrong-doing towards individuals, the commandant and his mercenaries whom the satrap maintained, were probably more rapacious, and certainly more unrestrained, than even the harmosts of Sparta. Moreover the Persian grandees required beautiful boys as eunuchs for their service, and beautiful women as inmates of their harems.[3] What was taken for their convenience admitted neither of recovery nor redress; and Grecian women, if not more beautiful than many of the native Asiatics, were at least more intelligent, lively, and seductive—as we may read in the history of that Phokæan lady, the companion of Cyrus, who was

---

[1] Isokratês, Or. iii. (Nikoklês) s. 37-48: Or. ix. (Evagoras) s. 100; Or. xv. (Permut.) s. 43. Diodorus (xv. 47) places the assassination of Evagoras in 374 B.C.

[2] Isokratês, Or. iv. (Paneg.) s. 142.

186, 190. Τὰς τε πόλεις τὰς Ἑλληνίδες οὕτω τρυφῶς κορυλήψει, ὥστε τὰς μὲν κατασκάπτειν, ἐν δὲ ταῖς ἀπροσδόκητι ἐντειχίζειν.

[3] See Herodot. vi. 9; ix. 76.

taken captive at Kunaxa. Moreover, these Asiatic Greeks, when passing into the hands of Oriental masters, came under the maxims and sentiment of Orientals, respecting the infliction of pain or torture—maxims not only more cruel than those of the Greeks, but also making little distinction between freemen and slaves.[1] The difference between the Greeks and Phœnicians in Cyprus, on this point, has been just noticed; and doubtless the difference between Greeks and Persians was still more marked. While the Asiatic Greeks were thus made over by Sparta and the Perso-Spartan convention of Antalkidas, to a condition in every respect worse, they were at the same time transferred, as reluctant auxiliaries, to strengthen the hands of the Great King against other Greeks—against Evagoras in Cyprus—and above all, against the islands adjoining the coast of Asia—Chios, Samos, Rhodes, &c.[2] These islands were now exposed to the same hazard, from their overwhelming Persian neighbours, as that from which they had been rescued nearly a century before by the Confederacy of Delos, and by the Athenian empire into which that Confederacy was transformed. All the tutelary combination that the genius, the energy, and the Panhellenic ardour, of Athens, had first organized, and so long kept up—was now broken up; while Sparta, to whom its extinction was owing, in surrendering the Asiatic Greeks, had destroyed the security even of the islanders.

It soon appeared, however, how much Sparta herself had gained by this surrender in respect to dominion nearer home. The government of Corinth—wrested from the party friendly to Argos, deprived of Argeian auxiliaries,

[1] Isokrat. Or. iv. (Paneg.) s. 142. Οἱς (to the Asiatic Greeks after the peace of Antalkidas) οὐκ ἐξαρκεῖ δεσμολογεῖσθαι καὶ τὰς ἀπορθήσεις ὁρᾶν ἀπὸ τῶν ἐχθρῶν κατηγομένας, ἀλλὰ πρὸς ταῖς κοιναῖς συμφοραῖς δεινότερα πάσχουσι τῶν παρ' ἡμῖν ἀργυρωνήτων· οὐδεὶς γὰρ ἡμῶν οὕτως αἰκίζεται τοὺς οἰκέτας, ὡς ἐκεῖνοι τοὺς ἐλευθέρους κολάζουσιν.

[2] Isokrat. Or. iv. (Paneg.) s. 143, 154, 189, 190. How immediately the inland kings, who had acquired possession of the continental Grecian cities, aimed at acquiring the islands also—is seen in Herodot. i. 27. Chios and Samos, indeed, surrendered without resisting, to the first Cyrus, when he was master of the continental towns, though he had no naval force (Herod. i. 143-169). Even after the victory of Mykalê, the Spartans deemed it impossible to protect these islanders against the Persian masters of the continent (Herod. ix. 106). Nothing except the energy and organisation of the Athenians proved that it was possible to do so.

and now in the hands of the restored Corinthian exiles who were the most devoted partisans of Sparta—looked to her for support, and made her mistress of the Isthmus, either for offence or for defence. She thus gained the means of free action against Thebes, the enemy upon whom her attention was first directed. Thebes was now the object of Spartan antipathy, not less than Athens had formerly been; especially on the part of King Agesilaus, who had to avenge the insult offered to himself at the sacrifice near Aulis, as well as the strenuous resistance on the field of Koroneia. He was at the zenith of his political influence; so that his intense miso-Theban sentiment made Sparta, now becoming aggressive on all sides, doubly aggressive against Thebes. More prudent Spartans, like Antalkidas, warned him[1] that his persevering hostility would ultimately kindle in the Thebans a fatal energy of military resistance and organization. But the warning was despised until it was too fully realised in the development of the great military genius of Epaminondas, and in the defeat of Leuktra.

*Great power gained by Sparta through the peace of Antalkidas. She becomes practically mistress of Corinth, and the Corinthian Isthmus. Miso-Theban tendencies of Sparta—especially of Agesilaus.*

I have already mentioned that in the solemnity of exchanging oaths to the peace of Antalkidas, the Thebans had hesitated at first to recognise the autonomy of the other Bœotian cities; upon which Agesilaus had manifested a fierce impatience to exclude them from the treaty, and to attack them single-handed.[2] Their timely submission balked him in his impulse; but it enabled him to enter upon a series of measures highly humiliating to the dignity as well as to the power of Thebes.

*Sparta organised anti-Theban oligarchies in the Bœotian cities with a Spartan harmost in several. Most of these cities seem to have been favourable to Thebes, though Orchomenus and Thespiæ were adverse.*

All the Bœotian cities were now proclaimed autonomous under the convention. As solicitor, guarantee, and interpreter, of that convention, Sparta either had, or professed to have, the right of guarding their autonomy against dangers, actual or contingent, from their previous Vorort or presiding city. For this purpose she availed herself of this moment of change to organize in each of

[1] Plutarch, Agesil. c. 18; Plutarch, Lykurg. c. 13.
[2] Xen. Hellen. v. 1, 33.

them a local oligarchy, composed of partisans adverse to Thebes as well as devoted to herself, and upheld in case of need by a Spartan harmost and garrison.¹ Such an internal revolution grew almost naturally out of the situation; since the previous leaders, and the predominant sentiment in most of the towns, seem to have been favourable to Bœotian unity, and to the continued presidency of Thebes. These leaders would therefore find themselves hampered, intimidated, and disqualified, under the new system, while those who had before been an opposition minority would come forward with a bold and decided policy, like Kritias and Theramenês at Athens after the surrender of the city to Lysander. The new leaders doubtless would rather invite than repel the establishment of a Spartan harmost in their town, as a security to themselves against resistance from their own citizens as well as against attacks from Thebes, and as a means of placing them under the assured conditions of a Lysandrian Dekarchy. Though most of

¹ Xen. Hellen. v. 4, 46. Ἐν τόσῳ γὰρ τοῖς πόλεσι δυναστεῖαι καθιστήκεσαν, ὥσπερ ἐν Θήβαις. Respecting the Bœotian city of Tanagra, he says—ὅτι γὰρ τότε καὶ τὴν Ταναγραν οἱ περὶ Ὑπατόδωρον, φίλοι ὄντες τῶν Λακεδαιμονίων, εἶχον (v. 4, 49).
Schneider in his note on the former of these two passages, explains the word δυναστεῖαι as follows—"Sunt factiones optimatium qui Lacedæmoniis favebant, cum præsidio et harmostâ Laconico." This is perfectly just; but the words ὥσπερ ἐν Θήβαις seem also to require an explanation. These words allude to the "factio optimatinm" at Thebes, of whom Leontiadês was the chief; who betrayed the Kadmeia (the citadel of Thebes) to the Lacedæmonian troops under Phœbidas in 382 B.C.; and who remained masters of Thebes, subservient to Sparta and upheld by a standing Lacedæmonian garrison in the Kadmeia, until they were overthrown by the memorable conspiracy of Pelopidas and Mellon in 379 B.C. It is to this oligarchy under Leontiadês at Thebes, devoted to Spartan interests and resting on Spartan support—that Xenophon compares the governments planted by Sparta, after the peace of Antalkidas, in each of the Bœotian cities. What he says, of the government of Leontiadês and his colleagues at Thebes, is—"that they deliberately introduced the Lacedæmonians into the acropolis, and enslaved Thebes to them, in order that they might themselves exercise a despotism"—τοὺς τε τῶν πολιτῶν εἰσηγητέντας εἰς τὴν ἀκρόπολιν αὐτούς, καὶ βουληθέντας Λακεδαιμονίοις τὴν πόλιν δουλεύειν, ὥστε αὐτοὶ τυραννεῖν (v. 4, 1: compare v. 2, 36). This character—conveying a strong censure in the mouth of the philo-Laconian Xenophon—belongs to all the governments planted by Sparta in the Bœotian cities after the peace of Antalkidas, and indeed to the Dekarchies generally which she established throughout her empire.

R 2

the Bœotian cities were thus, on the whole, favourable to
Thebes—and though Sparta thrust upon them the boon,
which she called autonomy, from motives of her own, and
not from their solicitation—yet Orchomenus and Thespiæ,
over whom the presidency of Thebes appears to have been
harshly exercised, were adverse to her, and favourable to
the Spartan alliance.¹ These two cities were strongly
garrisoned by Sparta, and formed her main stations in
Bœotia.²

The presence of such garrisons, one on each side of
Thebes— the discontinuance of the Bœotarchs, with the
breaking up of all symbols and proceedings of the Bœotian
federation—and the establishment of oligarchies devoted
to Sparta in the other cities—was doubtless a deep wound
to the pride of the Thebans. But there was another wound
still deeper, and this the Lacedæmonians forthwith proceeded to inflict—the restoration of Platæa.

A melancholy interest attaches both to the locality of
this town, as one of the brightest scenes of
Grecian glory,—and to its brave and faithful
population, victims of an exposed position
combined with numerical feebleness. Especially,
we follow with a sort of repugnance the
capricious turns of policy which dictated the
Spartan behaviour towards them. One hundred
and twenty years before, the Platæans had thrown themselves upon Sparta to entreat her protection against
Thebes. The Spartan king Kleomenês had then declined
the obligation as too distant, and had recommended them
to ally themselves with Athens.³ This recommendation,
though dictated chiefly by a wish to raise contention
between Athens and Thebes, was complied with; and the
alliance, severing Platæa altogether from the Bœotian
confederacy, turned out both advantageous and honourable
to her until the beginning of the Peloponnesian war. At
that time, it suited the policy of the Spartans to uphold
and strengthen in every way the supremacy of Thebes
over the Bœotian cities. It was altogether by Spartan
intervention, indeed, that the power of Thebes was re-
established, after the great prostration as well as disgrace

*The Spartans restore Platæa. Former conduct of Sparta towards Platæa.*

¹ Xenoph. Memorab. III. 5, 2; Thucyd. iv. 133; Diodor. xv. 78.
² Xen. Hellen. v. 4, 15—20; Dio- dor. xv. 32—37; Isokratês, Or. xiv. (Plataic.) s. 14, 15.
³ Herodot. vi. 108.

which she had undergone, as traitor to Hellas and zealous in the service of Mardonius.[1] Athens, on the other hand, was at that time doing her best to break up the Bœotian federation, and to enrol its various cities as her allies: in which project, though doubtless suggested by and conducive to her own ambition, she was at that time (460-445 B.C.) perfectly justifiable on Pan-hellenic grounds; seeing that Thebes as their former chief had so recently enlisted them all in the service of Xerxes, and might be expected to do the same again if a second Persian invasion should be attempted. Though for a time successful, Athens was expelled from Bœotia by the defeat of Koroneia; and at the beginning of the Peloponnesian war, the whole Bœotian federation (except Platæa) was united under Thebes, in bitter hostility against her. The first blow of the war, even prior to any declaration, was struck by Thebes in her abortive nocturnal attempt to surprise Platæa. In the third year of the war, King Archidamus, at the head of the full Lacedæmonian force, laid siege to the latter town; which, after an heroic defence and a long blockade, at length surrendered under the extreme pressure of famine; yet not before one half of its brave defenders had forced their way out over the blockading wall, and escaped to Athens, where all the Platæan old men, women, and children, had been safely lodged before the siege. By a cruel act which stands among the capital iniquities of Grecian warfare, the Lacedæmonians had put to death all the Platæan captives, two hundred in number, who fell into their hands; the town of Platæa had been razed, and its whole territory, joined to Thebes, had remained ever since cultivated on Theban account.[2] The surviving Platæans had been dealt with kindly and hospitably by the Athenians. A qualified right of citizenship was conceded to them at Athens, and when Skionê was recaptured in 420 B.C., that town (vacant by the slaughter of its captive citizens) was handed over to the Platæans as a residence.[3] Compelled to evacuate Skionê, they were obliged, at the close of the Peloponnesian war,[4] to return to Athens, where the remainder of them were residing at the time of the peace of Antalkidas; little dreaming that

[1] See Ch. xlv. of this History. (Panegyr.) s. 126; Or. xii. (Panathen.)
[2] Thucyd. iii. 68. s. 101.
[3] Thucyd. v. 32; Isokrates, Or. iv. [4] Plutarch, Lysand. c. 14.

those who had destroyed their town and their fathers forty years before, would now turn round and restore it.[1]

Such restoration, whatever might be the ostensible grounds on which the Spartans pretended to rest it, was not really undertaken either to carry out the convention of Antalkidas, which guaranteed only the autonomy of *existing* towns—or to repair previous injustice, since prior destruction had been the deliberate act of themselves, and of King Archidamus the father of Agesilaus—but simply as a step conducive to the present political views of Sparta. And towards this object it was skilfully devised. It weakened the Thebans, not only by wresting from them what had been, for about forty years, a part of their territory and property; but also by establishing upon it a permanent stronghold in the occupation of their bitter enemies, assisted by a Spartan garrison. It furnished an additional station for such a garrison in Bœotia, with the full consent of the newly-established inhabitants. And more than all, it introduced a subject of contention between Athens and Thebes, calculated to prevent the two from hearty cooperation afterwards against Sparta. As the sympathy of the Platæans with Athens was no less ancient and cordial than their antipathy against Thebes, we may probably conclude that the restoration of the town was an act acceptable to the Athenians; at least at first, until they saw the use made of it, and the position which Sparta came to occupy in reference to Greece generally. Many of the Platæans, during their residence at Athens, had intermarried with Athenian women,[2] who now probably accompanied their husbands to the restored little town on the north of Kithæron, near the southern bank of the river Asôpus.

*Motives of Sparta in restoring Platæa. A politic step, as likely to sever Thebes from Athens.*

Had the Platæans been restored to a real and honourable autonomy, such as they enjoyed in alliance with Athens before the Peloponnesian war, we should have cordially sympathised with the event. But the sequel will prove—and their own subsequent statement emphatically sets forth—that they were a mere dependency of Sparta, and an outpost for Spartan operations against Thebes.[3] They were a part of the great

*Platæa becomes a dependency and outpost of Sparta. Main object of Sparta to prevent the reconstitution of the Bœotian federation.*

[1] Pausanias, ix. 1, 8.    s. 54.
[2] Isokratês, Or. xiv. (Plataic.)    [3] See the Orat. xiv. (called Pla-

revolution which the Spartans now brought about in Bœotia; whereby Thebes was degraded from the president of a federation into an isolated autonomous city, while the other Bœotian cities, who had been before members of the federation, were elevated each for itself into the like autonomy; or rather (to substitute the real truth¹ in place of Spartan professions) they became enrolled and sworn in as dependent allies of Sparta, under oligarchical factions devoted to her purposes and resting upon her for support. That the Thebans should submit to such a revolution, and above all, to the sight of Platæa as an independent neighbour with a territory abstracted from themselves—proves how much they felt their own weakness, and how irresistible at this moment was the ascendency of their great enemy, in perverting to her own ambition the popular lure of universal autonomy held out by the peace of Antalkidas. Though compelled to acquiesce, the Thebans waited in hopes of some turn of fortune which would enable them to reorganize the Bœotian federation; while their hostile sentiment towards Sparta was not the less bitter for being suppressed. Sparta on her part kept constant watch to prevent the reunion of Bœotia;² an object in which she was for a time completely successful, and was even enabled, beyond her hopes, to become possessed of Thebes itself,³ through a party of traitors within—as will presently appear.

---

taisons) of Isokrates; which is a pleading probably delivered in the Athenian assembly by the Platæans (after the second destruction of their city) and doubtless founded upon their own statements. The painful dependence and compulsion under which they were held by Sparta, is proclaimed in the most unequivocal terms (s. 15, 23, 46); together with the presence of a Spartan harmost and garrison in their town (s. 14).

¹ Xenophon says, truly enough, that Sparta made the Bœotian cities αὐτονόμους ἀπὸ τῶν Θηβαίων (v. 1. 36), which she had long desired to do. Autonomy, in the sense of disconnection from Thebes, was ensured to them—but in no

other sense.

² To illustrate the relations of Thebes, the other Bœotian cities, and Sparta, between the peace of Antalkidas and the seizure of the Kadmeia by Sparta (387-383 B.C.)—compare the speech of the Akanthian envoys, and that of the Theban Leontiades, at Sparta (Xenoph. Hellen. v. 2, 16-34). Τρεῖς (the Spartans) τῆς μὲν Βοιωτίας ἐπιμεληθῆναι, ὅπως μὴ καθ᾽ ἕνα ἦν, &c. Καὶ ὑμεῖς γε τότε μὲν ἀεὶ προσείχετε τὸν νοῦν, μῶν ἀκούσησθε βιαζομένους αὐτοὺς (the Thebans) τὴν Βοιωτίαν ὑφ᾽ αὐτοῖς εἶναι· νῦν δὲ, ἐπεὶ τάδε κέπρακται, οὐδὲν ὑμᾶς δεῖ Θηβαίους φοβεῖσθαι, &c. Compare Diodor. xv. 20.

³ In the Orat. (14) Platäic. of

In these measures regarding Bœotia, we recognise the vigorous hand, and the miso-Theban spirit, of Agesilaus. He was at this time the great director of Spartan foreign policy, though opposed by his more just and moderate colleague King Agesipolis,[1] as well as by a section of the leading Spartans; who reproached Agesilaus with his project of ruling Greece by means of subservient local despots or oligarchies in the various cities,[2] and who contended that the autonomy promised by the peace of Antalkidas ought to be left to develope itself freely, without any coercive intervention on the part of Sparta.[3]

Spartan policy at this time directed by the partisan spirit of Agesilaus, opposed by his colleague Agesipolis.

---

[1] Isokratês, s. 80—we find it stated among the accusations against the Thebans, that during this period (i. e. between the peace of Antalkidas and the seizure of the Kadmeia) they became sworn in as members of the Spartan alliance and as ready to act with Sparta conjointly against Athens. If we could admit this as true, we might also admit the story of Epaminondas and Pelopidas serving in the Spartan army at Mantineia (Plutarch, Pelop. c. 3). But I do not see how it can be even partially true. If it had been true, I think Xenophon could not have failed to mention it: all that he does say, tends to contradict it.

[2] Diodor. xv. 29.

[3] How currently this reproach was advanced against Agesilaus, may be seen in more than one passage of the Hellenica of Xenophon; whose narrative is both so partial, and so ill-constructed, that the most instructive information is dropped only in the way of unintentional side wind, where we should not naturally look for it. Xen. Hellen. v. 3, 16. καλλιον δὲ λεγοντων Λακεδαιμονιων ως ολιγων ἑνεκεν ἀνθρωπων πολει (Phlios) ἐκεχθανοιτο (Agesilaus) πλειον πεντακισχιλιων ἀνδρων. Again, v. 4, 13.

(Αγησιλαος) εὖ εἰδως, ὅτι, εἰ στρατηγοιη, λεξειαν οἱ πολιται, ὡς Αγησιλαος, ὅπως βοηθησειε τοις τυραννοις, πραγματα τῇ πολει παρεχει, &c. Compare Plutarch, Agesil. c. 34-36.

² Diodorus indeed affirms, that this was really done, for a short time; that the cities which had before been dependent allies of Sparta were now emancipated and left to themselves; that a reaction immediately ensued against those Dekarchies or oligarchies which had hitherto managed the cities in the interests of Sparta; that this reaction was so furious, as everywhere to kill, banish, or impoverish, the principal partisans of Spartan supremacy; and that the accumulated complaints and sufferings of these exiles drove the Spartans, after having "endured the peace like a heavy burthen" (ὥσπερ βαρυ φορτιον—xv. 5) for a few months, to shake it off, and to re-establish by force their own supremacy as well as the government of their friends in all the various cities. In this statement there is nothing intrinsically improbable. After what we have heard of the Dekarchies under Sparta, no extent of violence in the reaction against them is incredible, nor can we doubt that such reaction would

Far from any wish thus to realise the terms of peace which they had themselves imposed, the Lacedæmonians took advantage of an early moment after becoming free from their enemies in Bœotia and Corinth, to strain their authority over their allies beyond its previous limits. Passing in review [1] the conduct of each during the late war, they resolved to make an example of the city of Mantineia. Some acts, not of positive hostility, but of equivocal fidelity, were imputed to the Mantineians. They were accused of having been slack in performance of their military obligations, sometimes even to the length of withholding their contingent altogether, under pretence of a season of religious truce; of furnishing corn in time of war to the hostile Argeians; and of plainly manifesting their disaffected feeling towards Sparta—chagrin at every success which she obtained—satisfaction, when she chanced to experience a reverse.[2] The Spartan Ephors now sent an envoy to Mantineia, denouncing all such past behaviour, and peremptorily requiring that the walls of the city should be demolished, as the only security for future penitence and amendment. As compliance was refused, they despatched an army, summoning the allied contingents generally for the purpose of enforcing the sentence. They entrusted the command to

*B.C. 385-383. Oppressive behaviour of the Spartans towards Mantineia. They require the walls of the city to be demolished.*

---

carry with it some new injustice, along with much well-merited retribution. Hardly any but Athenian citizens were capable of the forbearance displayed by Athens both after the Four Hundred and after the Thirty. Nevertheless I believe that Diodorus is here mistaken, and that he has assigned to the period immediately succeeding the peace of Antalkidas, those reactionary violences which took place in many cities about sixteen years subsequently, *after the battle of Leuktra.* For Xenophon, in recounting what happened after the peace of Antalkidas, mentions nothing about any real autonomy granted by Sparta to her various subject allies, and sub-

sequently revoked; which he would never have omitted to tell us, had the fact been so, because it would have supplied a plausible apology for the high-handed injustice of the Spartans, and would have thus lent aid to the current of partiality which manifests itself in his history.

[1] Xen. Hellen. v. 2, 1-8. Αἰσθόμενοι τοὺς Λακεδαιμονίους ἐπικαλοῦντας τοὺς συμμάχους, ὁποῖοί τινες ἕκαστοι ἐν τῷ πολέμῳ αὐτοῖς ἐγίγνοντο, &c.

[2] Xen. Hellen. v. 2, 2. He had before stated, that the Mantineians had really shown themselves pleased, when the Lacedæmonian Mora was destroyed near Corinth by Iphikratês (iv. 5, 18).

King Agesipolis, since Agesilaus excused himself from the
duty, on the ground that the Mantineians had rendered
material service to his father Archidamus in the dangerous
Messenian war which had beset Sparta during the early
part of his reign.[1]

*Agesipolis blockades the city, and forces it to surrender, by damming up the river Ophis. The Mantineians are forced to break up their city into villages.* Having first attempted to intimidate the Mantineians by ravaging their lands, Agesipolis commenced the work of blockade by digging a ditch round the town; half of his soldiers being kept on guard, while the rest worked with the spade. The ditch being completed, he prepared to erect a wall of circumvallation. But being apprised that the preceding harvest had been so good, as to leave a large stock of provision in the town, and to render the process of starving it out tedious both for Sparta and for her allies, —he tried a more rapid method of accomplishing his object. As the river Ophis, of considerable breadth for a Grecian stream, passed through the middle of the town, he dammed up its efflux on the lower side;[2] thus causing it to inundate the interior of the city

---

[1] Xen. Hellen. v. 2, 3.

[2] In 1627, during the Thirty Years' War, the German town of Wolfenbüttel was constrained to surrender in the same manner, by damming up the river Ocker which flowed through it: a contrivance of General Count Pappenheim, the Austrian besieging commander. See Colonel Mitchell's Life of Wallenstein, p. 107.

The description given by Xenophon of Mantineia as it stood in 385 B.C., with the river Ophis, a considerable stream, passing through the middle of it, is perfectly clear. When the city, after having been now broken up, was rebuilt in 370 B.C., the site was so far changed that the river no longer ran through it. But the present course of the river Ophis, as given by excellent modern topographical examiners, Colonel Leake and Kiepert, is at a very considerable distance from the Mantineia rebuilt in 370 B.C.; the situation of which is accurately known, since the circuit of its walls still remains distinctly marked. The Mantineia of 870 B.C., therefore, as compared with the Mantineia in 385 B.C., must have been removed to a considerable distance—or else the river Ophis must have altered its course. Colonel Leake supposes that the Ophis had been artificially diverted from its course, in order that it might be brought through the town of Mantineia; a supposition, which he founds on the words of Xenophon—σοφωτέρων γενομένων ταύτῃ γε τῶν ἀνθρώπων, τὸ μὴ διὰ τοιγῶν ποταμὸν ποιεῖσθαι (Hellen. v. 2, 7). But it is very difficult to agree with him on this point, when we look at his own map (annexed to the Peloponnesiaca) of the Mantinice and Tegeatis, and ob-

and threaten the stability of the walls; which seem to have been of no great height, and built of sun-burnt bricks. Disappointed in their application to Athens for aid,¹ and unable to provide extraneous support for their tottering towers, the Mantineians were compelled to solicit a capitulation. But Agesipolis now refused to grant the request, except on condition that not only the fortifications of their city, but the city itself, should be in great part demolished; and that the inhabitants should be re-distributed into those five villages, which had been brought together, many years before, to form the aggregate city of Mantineia. To this also the Mantineians were obliged to submit, and the capitulation was ratified.

Though nothing was said in the terms of it about the chiefs of the Mantineian democratical government, yet these latter, conscious that they were detested both by their own oligarchical opposition and by the Lacedæmonians, accounted themselves certain of being put to death. And such would assuredly have been their fate, had not Pausanias (the late king of Sparta, now in exile at Tegea), whose good opinion they had always enjoyed, obtained as a personal favour from his son Agesipolis the lives of the most obnoxious, sixty in number, on condition that they should depart into exile. Agesipolis had much difficulty in accomplishing the wishes of his father. His Lacedæmonian soldiers were ranged in arms on both sides of the gate by which the obnoxious men went out; and Xenophon notices it as a signal mark of Lacedæmonian discipline, that they could keep their spears unemployed when disarmed enemies were thus within their reach; especially as the oligarchical Mantineians manifested the most murderous propensities, and were exceedingly difficult to control.² As at Peiræus before, so here at

*Democratical leaders of Mantineia—owed their lives to the mediation of the exiled King Pausanias.*

---

serve the great distance between the river Ophis and Mantineia; nor do the words of Xenophon seem necessarily to imply any artificial diversion of the river. It appears easier to believe that the river has changed its course. See Leake, Travels in Morea, vol. iii. ch. xxiv. p. 71; and Peloponnesiaca, p. 880; and Ernst Curtius,

Peloponnesos, p. 239—who still however leaves the point obscure.
¹ Diodor. xv. 5.
² Xen. Hellen. v. 2, 6. Ὀλιγίσκων δὲ ἀπολιγίσθαι τῶν ἀρχολιζόντων, καὶ τῶν τοῦ δήμου προστατῶν, διακρίζετο ὁ ἀνήρ (see before, v. 8, 3) παρὰ τοῦ Ἀγησιπόλιδος, ἀσφαλείαν αὐτοῖς ἔσεσθαι, ἀπαλλαττομένοις ἐκ τῆς πόλεως, ἐξήκοντα οὖσι. Καὶ

Mantineia again—the liberal, but unfortunate, King Pausanias is found interfering in the character of mediator to soften the ferocity of political antipathies.

**Mantineia is pulled down and distributed into five villages.**
The city of Mantineia was now broken up, and the inhabitants were distributed again into the five constituent villages. Out of four-fifths of the population, each man pulled down his house in the city, and rebuilt it in the village near to which his property lay. The remaining fifth continued to occupy Mantineia as a village. Each village was placed under oligarchical government and left unfortified. Though at first (says Xenophon) the change proved troublesome and odious, yet presently, when men found themselves resident upon their landed properties—and still more, when they felt themselves delivered from the vexatious demagogues—the new situation became more popular than the old. The Lacedæmonians were still better satisfied. Instead of one city of Mantineia, five distinct Arcadian villages now stood enrolled in their catalogue of allies. They assigned to each a separate xenâgus (Spartan officer destined to the command of each allied contingent), and the military service of all was henceforward performed with the utmost regularity.[1]

**High-handed despotism of Sparta towards Mantineia—signal partiality of Xenophon.**
Such was the dissection or cutting into parts of the ancient city Mantineia; one of the most odious acts of high-handed Spartan despotism. Its true character is veiled by the partiality of the historian, who recounts it with a confident assurance, that after the trouble of moving was over, the population felt themselves decidedly bettered by the change. Such an assurance is only to be credited, on the ground that, being cap-

ἀμφοτέρωθεν μὲν τῆς ὁδοῦ, ἀρξάμενοι ἀπὸ τῶν κυκλῶν, ἔχοντες τὰ δόρατα οἱ Λακεδαιμόνιοι ἔστησαν, θεώμενοι τοὺς ἐξιόντας· καὶ μισοῦντες μὲν οὐ τοὺς ὅμως ἀπείχοντο αὐτῶν ῥᾷον, ἢ οἱ βέλτιστοι τῶν Μαντινέων· καὶ τοῦτο μὲν εἰρήσθω μέγα τεκμήριον πολιαρχίας.

I have remarked more than once, and the reader will here observe a new example, how completely the word βέλτιστοι—which is applied to the wealthy or aristocratical party in politics, as its equivalent is in other languages, by writers who sympathise with them—is divested of all genuine ethical import as to character.

[1] Xen. Hellen. v. 2, 7.

He says of this breaking up of the city of Mantineia, διῳκίσθη ἡ Μαντίνεια τετραχῇ, καθάπερ τὸ ἀρχαῖον ᾤκουν. Ephorus (Fr. 138, ed. Didot) states that it was distributed

tives under the Grecian laws of war, they may have been thankful to escape the more terrible liabilities of death or personal slavery, at the price of forfeiting their civic community. That their feelings towards the change were those of genuine aversion, is shown by their subsequent conduct after the battle of Leuktra. As soon as the fear of Sparta was removed, they flocked together with unanimous impulse, to re-constitute and re-fortify their dismantled city.¹ It would have been strange indeed had the fact been otherwise; for attachment to a civic community was the strongest political instinct of the Greek mind. The citizen of a town was averse—often most unhappily averse—to compromise the separate and autonomous working of his community by joining in any larger political combination, however equitably framed, and however it might promise on the whole an increase of Hellenic dignity. But still more vehemently did he shrink from the idea of breaking up his town into separate villages, and exchanging the character of a citizen for that of a villager, which

into the five original villages; and Strabo affirms that there were five original constituent villages (viii. p. 337). Hence it is probable that Mantineia the city was still left, after this διοίκισις, to subsist as one of the five unfortified villages; so that Ephorus, Strabo and Xenophon may be thus made to agree, in substance.

¹ This is mentioned by Xenophon himself (Hellen. vi. 5, 8). The Lacedæmonians, though they remonstrated against it, were at that time too much humiliated to interfere by force and prevent it. The reason why they did not interfere by force (according to Xenophon) was that a general peace had just then been sworn, guaranteeing autonomy to every distinct town, so that the Mantineians under this peace had a right to do what they did—στρατεύειν γε μέντοι ἐπ' αὐτοὺς οὐ δυνατὸν ἔδοξε εἶναι, ἐπ' αὐτονομίᾳ τῆς εἰρήνης γεγενημένης (vi. 5, 5). Of this second peace, Athens was the originator and the voucher;

but the autonomy which it guaranteed was only the same as had been professedly guaranteed by the peace of Antalkidas, of which Sparta had been the voucher.

General autonomy, as interpreted by Athens, was a different thing from general autonomy as it had been when interpreted by Sparta. The Spartans, when they had in their own hands both the power of interpretation and the power of enforcement, did not scruple to falsify autonomy so completely as to lay siege to Mantineia and break up the city by force; while, when interpretation and enforcement had passed to Athens, they at once recognised that the treaty precluded them from a much less violent measure of interference.

We may see by this, how thoroughly partial and Philo-Laconian is the account given by Xenophon of the διοίκισις of Mantineia; how completely he keeps out of view the odious side of that proceeding.

was nothing less than great social degradation, in the eyes of Greeks generally, Spartans not excepted.¹

*Mischievous influence of Sparta during this period of her ascendency, in decomposing the Grecian world into the smallest fragments.*

In truth the sentence executed by the Spartans against Mantineia was, in point of dishonour as well as of privation, one of the severest which could be inflicted on free Greeks. All the distinctive glory and superiority of Hellenism—all the intellectual and artistic manifestations—all that there was of literature and philosophy, or of refined and rational sociality—depended upon the city-life of the people. And the influence of Sparta, during the period of her empire, was peculiarly mischievous and retrograde, as tending not only to decompose the federations such as Bœotia into isolated towns, but even to decompose suspected towns such as Mantineia into villages; all for the purpose of rendering each of them exclusively dependent upon herself. Athens during her period of empire had exercised no such disuniting influence; still less Thebes, whom we shall hereafter find coming forward actively to found the new and great cities of Megalopolis and Messênê. The imperial tendencies of Sparta are worse than those of either Athens or Thebes; including less of improving or Pan-hellenic sympathies, and leaning the most systematically upon subservient factions in each subordinate city. In the very treatment of Mantineia just recounted, it is clear that the attack of Sparta was welcomed at least, if not originally invited, by the oligarchical party of the place, who sought to grasp the power into their own hands and to massacre their political opponents. In the first object they completely succeeded, and their government probably was more assured in the five villages than it would have been in the entire town. In the second, nothing prevented them from succeeding except the accidental intervention of the exile Pausanias; an accident, which alone rescued the Spartan name from the additional disgrace of a political massacre, over and above the lasting odium incurred by the act itself—by breaking up all

¹ See the remarkable sentence of the Spartans, in which they reject the claim of the Pisatans to preside over and administer the Olympic festival (which had been their ancient privilege) because they were χωρῖται and not fit for the task (Xen. Hellen. iii. 2, 31): compare χωριτικὸς (Xen. Cyrop. iv. 5, 54).

ancient autonomous city, which had shown no act of overt enmity, and which was so moderate in its democratical manifestations as to receive the favourable criticism of judges rather disinclined towards democracy generally.[1] Thirty years before, when Mantineia had conquered certain neighbouring Arcadian districts, and had been at actual war with Sparta to preserve them, the victorious Spartans exacted nothing more than the reduction of the city to its original district;[2] now, they are satisfied with nothing less than the partition of the city into unfortified villages, though there had been no actual war preceding. So much had Spartan power, as well as Spartan despotic propensity, progressed during this interval.

The general language of Isokratês, Xenophon, and Diodorus[3] indicates that this severity towards Mantineia was only the most stringent among a series of severities, extended by the Lacedæmonians through their whole confederacy, and operating upon all such of its members as gave them ground for dissatisfaction or mistrust. During the ten years after the surrender of Athens, they had been lords of the Grecian world both by land and sea, with a power never before possessed by any Grecian state; until the battle of Knidus, and the combination of Athens, Thebes, Argos, and Corinth, seconded by Persia, had broken up their empire at sea, and much endangered it on land. At length the peace of Antalkidas, enlisting Persia on their side (at the price of the liberty of the Asiatic Greeks), had enabled them to dissolve the hostile combination against them. The general autonomy, of which they were the authorised interpreters, meant nothing more than a separation of the Bœotian cities from Thebes,[4] and of Corinth from Argos—being noway intended to apply to the relation between Sparta and her allies. Having thus their hands free, the Lacedæmonians applied themselves to raise their ascendancy on land to the point where it had stood before the battle of Knidus, and even to regain as much as possible of their empire at sea. To bring back a

*The treatment of Mantineia was only one among a series of other acts of oppressive intervention, committed by Sparta towards her various allies.*

---

[1] Aristot. Polit. vi. 2, 2.
[2] Thucyd. v. 81.
[3] Isokratês, Or. iv. (Panegyr.) s. 133, 134, 146, 206; Or. viii. (De Pace) s. 123; Xen. Hellen. v. 2, 1-8; Diodor. xv. 5, 9-19.
[4] Xen. Hellen. v. 1, 35.

dominion such as that of the Lysandrian Harmosts and Dekarchies, and to reconstitute a local oligarchy of their most devoted partisans, in each of those cities where the government had been somewhat liberalised during the recent period of war—was their systematic policy.

*Return of the philo-Laconian exiles in the various cities, as partisans for the purposes of Sparta— case of Phlius.*

Those exiles who had incurred the condemnation of their fellow-citizens for subserviency to Sparta, now found the season convenient for soliciting Spartan intervention to procure their return. It was in this manner that a body of exiled political leaders from Phlius—whose great merit it was that the city when under their government had been zealous in service to Sparta, but had now become lukewarm or even disaffected in the hands of their opponents—obtained from the Ephors a message, polite in form but authoritative in substance, addressed to the Phliasians, requiring that the exiles should be restored, as friends of Sparta banished without just cause.[1]

*Competition of Athens with Sparta for ascendency at sea. Athens gains ground, and gets together some rudiments of a maritime confederacy.*

While the Spartan power, for the few years succeeding the peace of Antalkidas, was thus decidedly in ascending movement on land, efforts were also made to re-establish it at sea. Several of the Cyclades and other smaller islands were again rendered tributary. In this latter sphere however Athens became her competitor. Since the peace, and the restoration of Lemnos, Imbros, and Skyros, combined with the refortified Peiræus and its Long Walls—Athenian commerce and naval power had been reviving, though by slow and humble steps. Like the naval force of England compared with France, the warlike marine of Athens rested upon a considerable commercial marine, which latter hardly existed at all in Laconia. Sparta had no seamen except constrained Helots or paid foreigners;[2] while the commerce of Peiræus both required and maintained a numerous population of this character. The harbour of Peiræus was convenient in respect of accommodation, and well-stocked with artisans—while Laconia had few artisans, and was notoriously destitute of

---

[1] Xen. Hellen. v. 2, 8-10. The consequences of this forced return are not difficult to foresee; they will appear in a subsequent page.

[2] Xen. Hellen. vii. 1, 8-12.

harbours.[1] Accordingly in this maritime competition, Athens, though but the shadow of her former self, started at an advantage as compared with Sparta, and, in spite of the superiority of the latter on land, was enabled to compete with her in acquiring tributary dependencies among the smaller islands of the Ægean. To these latter, who had no marine of their own, and who (like Athens herself) required habitual supplies of imported corn, it was important to obtain both access to Peiræus and protection from the Athenian triremes against that swarm of pirates, who showed themselves after the peace of Antalkidas when there was no predominant maritime state: besides which, the market of Peiræus was often supplied with foreign corn from the Crimea, through the preference shown by the princes of Bosphorus to Athens, at a time when vessels from other places could obtain no cargo.[2] A moderate tribute paid to Athens would secure to the tributary island greater advantages than if paid to Sparta—with at least equal protection. Probably the influence of Athens over these islanders was farther aided by the fact, that she administered the festivals, and lent out the funds, of the holy temple at Delos. We know by inscriptions remaining, that large sums were borrowed at interest from the temple treasure, not merely by individual islanders, but also by the island-cities collectively—Naxos, Andros, Tenos, Siphnos, Seriphos. The Amphiktyonic council who dispensed these loans (or at least the presiding members) were Athenians, named annually at Athens.[3] Moreover these islanders rendered religious homage and attendance at the Delian festivals, and were thus brought within the range of a central Athenian influence, capable, under favourable circumstances, of being strengthened and rendered even politically important.

By such helps, Athens was slowly acquiring to herself a second maritime confederacy, which we shall pre-

[1] Xen. Hellen. iv. 8, 7.
[2] Isokratês, Orat. xvii. (Trapezit.) s. 71.
[3] See the valuable inscription called the Marmor Sandvicense, which contains the accounts rendered by the annual Amphiktyons at Delos, from 377—373 B.C.
Boeckh, Staatshaushaltung der

Athener, vol. ii. p. 214, ed. 1; vol. ii. p. 78 seq., ed. 2nd.
The list of cities and individuals who borrowed money from the temple is given in these accounts, together with the amount of interest either paid by them, or remaining in arrear.

sently find to be of considerable moment, though never approaching the grandeur of her former empire: so that in the year 380 B.C., when Isokratês published his Panegyrical Discourse (seven years after the peace of Antalkidas), though her general power was still slender compared with the overruling might of Sparta,[1] yet her navy had already made such progress, that he claims for her the right of taking the command by sea, in that crusade which he strenuously enforces, of Athens and Sparta in harmonious unity at the head of all Greece, against the Asiatic barbarians.[2]

*Ideas entertained by some of the Spartan leaders, of acting against the Persians for the rescue of the Asiatic Greeks.— Panegyrical Discourse of Isokratês.*

It would seem that a few years after the peace of Antalkidas, Sparta became somewhat ashamed of having surrendered the Asiatic Greeks to Persia; and that King Agesipolis and other leading Spartans encouraged the scheme of a fresh Grecian expedition against Asia, in compliance with propositions from some disaffected subjects of Artaxerxês.[3] Upon some such project, currently discussed though never realised, Isokratês probably built his Panegyrical Oration, composed in a lofty strain of patriotic eloquence (380 B.C.), to stimulate both Sparta and Athens in the cause, and calling on both, as joint chiefs

---

[1] This is the description which Isokratês himself gives (Orat. xv. (Permutat.) s. 61) of the state of the Grecian world when he published his Panegyrical Discourse—ὅτι Λακεδαιμόνιοι μὲν ἦρχον τῶν Ἑλλήνων, ἡμεῖς δὲ ταπεινῶς ἐπράττομεν, &c.

[2] The Panegyrical Discourse of Isokratês, the date of it being pretty exactly known, is of great value for enabling us to understand the period immediately succeeding the peace of Antalkidas.

He particularly notices the multiplication of pirates, and the competition between Athens and Sparta about tribute from the islands in the Ægean (s. 133). Τίς γὰρ ἂν τοιαύτης κατασταίη ἐπιθυμήσειεν, ἐν ᾗ κατακοντιστὰι μὲν τὴν θάλασσαν κατέχουσι, πελτασταὶ

δὲ τὰς πόλεις καταλαμβάνουσι, &c.

.... Καίτοι χρὴ τοὺς φύσει καὶ μὴ διὰ τύχην μέγα φρονοῦντας τοιούτοις ἔργοις ἐπιχειρεῖν, πολὺ μᾶλλον ἢ τοὺς νησιώτας δασμολογεῖν, οὓς ἐξὸν ἐστιν ἐλέειν, ὁρῶντας τούτους μὲν διὰ σπανιότητα τῆς γῆς ὄρη γεωργεῖν ἀναγκαζομένους, τοὺς δ' ἠπειρώτας δι' ἀφθονίαν τῆς χώρας τὴν μὲν πλείστην αὐτῆς ἀργὸν περιορῶντας, &c., (s. 151).

.... Ὃ, ἡμεῖς (Athenians and Spartans) οὐδεμίαν ποιούμεθα πρόνοιαν, ἀλλὰ περὶ μὲν τῶν Κυκλάδων νήσων ἀμφισβητοῦμεν, τοσαύτας δὲ τὸ πλῆθος καὶ τηλικαύτας τὸ μέγεθος δυνάμεις οὕτως εἰκῇ τῷ βαρβάρῳ παραδεδώκαμεν.

Compare Xenoph. Hellen. vi. 1, 12—μὴ εἰς νησύδρια ἀποβλέποντας, &c.

[3] Diodor. xv. 9, 19.

of Greece, to suspend dissension at home for a great Panhellenic manifestation against the common enemy abroad. But whatever ideas of this kind the Spartan leaders may have entertained, their attention was taken off, about 382 B.C., by movements in a more remote region of the Grecian world, which led to important consequences.

Since the year 414 B.C. (when the Athenians were engaged in the siege of Syracuse), we have heard nothing either of the kings of Macedonia, or of the Chalkidic Grecian cities in the peninsula of Thrace adjoining Macedonia. Down to that year, Athens still retained a portion of her maritime empire in those regions. The Platæans were still in possession of Skiônê (on the isthmus of Pallênê) which she had assigned to them; while the Athenian admiral Euetion, seconded by many hired Thracians, and even by Perdikkas king of Macedonia, undertook a fruitless siege to reconquer Amphipolis on the Strymon.[1] But the fatal disaster at Syracuse having disabled Athens from maintaining such distant interests, they were lost to her along with her remaining empire—perhaps earlier; though we do not know how. At the same time during the last years of the Peloponnesian war, the kingdom of Macedonia greatly increased in power; partly, we may conceive, from the helpless condition of Athens—but still more from the abilities and energy of Archelaus, son and successor of Perdikkas.

*State of Macedonia and Chalkidikê —growth of Macedonian power during the last years of the Peloponnesian war.*

The course of succession among the Macedonian princes seems not to have been settled, so that disputes and bloodshed took place at the death of several of them. Moreover there were distinct tribes of Macedonians, who, though forming part, really or nominally, of the dominion of the Temenid princes, nevertheless were immediately subject to separate but subordinate princes of their own. The reign of Perdikkas had been much troubled in this manner. In the first instance, he had stripped his own brother Alketas of the crown,[2] who appears, (so far as we can

*Perdikkas and Archelaus—energy and ability of the latter.*

---

[1] Thucyd. vii. 9.
[2] This is attested by Plato, Gorgias, c. 26. p. 471 A.

.... Ὅς γε (Archelaus son of Perdikkas) πρῶτον μὲν τοῦτον αὐτὸν τὸν δεσπότην καὶ θεῖον (Alketas) μετακεμψάμενος, ὡς ἀποδώσων.

make out) to have had the better right to it; next he had also expelled his younger brother Philippus from his subordinate principality. To restore Amyntas the son of Philippus, was one of the purposes of the Thrakian prince Sitalkês, in the expedition undertaken conjointly with Athens, during the second year of the Peloponnesian war.¹ On the death of Perdikkas (about 413 B.C.), his eldest or only legitimate son was a child of seven years old; but his natural son² Archelaus was of mature age and unscrupulous ambition. The dethroned Alketas was yet alive, and had now considerable chance of re-establishing himself on the throne: Archelaus, inviting him and his son under pretence that he would himself bring about their re-establishment, slew them both amidst the intoxication of a banquet. He next dispatched the boy, his legitimate brother, by suffocating him in a well; and through these crimes made himself king. His government however was so energetic and able, that Macedonia reached a degree of military power such as none of his predecessors had ever possessed. His troops, military equipments, and fortified places, were much increased in numbers; while he also cut straight roads of communication between the various portions of his territory—a novelty seemingly everywhere, at that time.³ Besides such improved organization (which unfortunately we are not permitted to know in detail), Archelaus founded

τὴν ἀρχὴν ἣν Περδίκκας αὐτὸν ἀφείλετο, &c.

This statement of Plato, that Perdikkas expelled his brother Alketas from the throne, appears not to be adverted to by the commentators. Perhaps it may help to explain the chronological embarrassments connected with the reign of Perdikkas, the years of which are assigned by different authors, at 23, 28, 35, 40, 41. See Mr. Clinton, Fasti Hellen. ch. iv. p. 222—where he discusses the chronology of the Macedonian kings: also Krebs, Lection. Diodorex, p. 159.

There are no means of determining when the reign of Perdikkas began—nor exactly, when it ended. We know from Thucydidês that he was king in 432, and in 414 B.C. But the fact of his acquiring the crown by the expulsion of an older brother, renders it less wonderful that the beginning of his reign should be differently stated by different authors; though these authors seem mostly to conceive Perdikkas as the immediate successor of Alexander, without any notice of Alketas.

¹ Thucyd. L 57; II. 97-100.

² The mother of Archelaus was a female slave belonging to Alketas; it is for this reason that Plato calls Alketas δεσπότην καὶ ὅσιον of Archelaus (Plato, Gorgias, c. 26. p. 471 A.).

³ Thucyd. II. 100. ὁδοὺς εὐθείας ἔτεμε, &c.

a splendid periodical Olympic festival, in honour of the Olympian Zeus and the Muses,[1] and maintained correspondence with the poets and philosophers of Athens. He prevailed upon the tragic poets Euripidês and Agathon, as well as the epic poet Chœrilus, to visit him in Macedonia, where Euripidês especially was treated with distinguished favour and munificence,[2] remaining there until his death in 406 or 405 B.C. Archelaus also invited Sokratês, who declined the invitation—and appears to have shown some favour to Plato.[3] He perished in the same year as Sokrates (399 B.C.), by a violent death; two Thessalian youths, Krateuas and Hellanokratês, together with a Macedonian named Dekamnichus, being his assassins during a hunting party. The two first were youths to whom he was strongly attached, but whose dignity he had wounded by insulting treatment and non-performance of promises: the third was a Macedonian, who, for having made an offensive remark upon the bad breath of Euripidês, had been given up by the order of Archelaus to the poet, in order that he might be flogged for it. Euripidês actually caused the sentence to be inflicted: but it was not till six years after his death that Dekamnichus, who had neither forgotten nor forgiven the affront, found the opportunity of taking revenge by instigating and aiding the assassins of Archelaus.[4]

These incidents, recounted on the authority of Aristotle, and relating as well to the Macedonian king Archelaus as to the Athenian citizen and poet Euripidês, illustrate the political contrast between Macedonia and Athens. The govern-

*Contrast of Macedonia and Athens.*

[1] Arrian, I. 11; Diodor. xvii. 16.
[2] Plutarch, De Vitioso Pudore, c. 7, p. 531 E.
[3] Aristotel. Rhetoric. II. 24; Seneca, de Beneficiis, v. 6; Ælian, V. H. xiv. 17.
[4] See the statements, unfortunately very brief, of Aristotle (Politic. v. 8, 10-13). Plato (Alkibiad. II. c. 5, p. 141 D), while mentioning the assassination of Archelaus by his παιδικά, represents the motive of the latter differently from Aristotle, as having been an ambitious desire to possess himself of the throne. Diodorus (xiv. 37) represents Krateuas as having killed Archelaus unintentionally in a hunting party.

Καὶ τῆς Ἀρχελάου δ' ἐπιθέσεως Δεκάμνιχος ἡγεμὼν ἐγένετο, παροξύνων τοὺς ἐπιθεμένους πρῶτος· αἴτιον δὲ τῆς ὀργῆς, ὅτι αὐτὸν ἐξέδωκε μαστιγῶσαι Εὐριπίδῃ τῷ ποιητῇ· ὁ δὲ Εὐριπίδης ἐχαλέπαινεν εἰπόντος τι αὐτοῦ εἰς δυσωδίαν τοῦ στόματος (Arist. Pol. l. c.).

Dekamnichus is cited by Aristotle as one among the examples of persons actually scourged; which

ment of the former is one wholly personal—dependent on
the passions, tastes, appetites, and capacities, of the king.
The ambition of Archelaus leads both to his crimes for
acquiring the throne, and to his improved organization of
the military force of the state afterwards; his admiration
for the poets and philosophers of Athens makes him sympathise warmly with Euripidês, and ensure to the latter
personal satisfaction for an offensive remark; his appetites,
mingling licence with insult, end by drawing upon him
personal enemies of a formidable character. *L'État, c'est
moi*—stands marked in the whole series of proceedings;
the personality of the monarch is the determining element.
Now at Athens, no such element exists. There is, on the
one hand, no easy way of bringing to bear the ascendency
of an energetic chief to improve the military organization
—as Athens found to her cost, when she was afterwards
assailed by Philip, the successor after some interval, and
in many respects the parallel, of Archelaus. But on the
other hand, neither the personal tastes nor the appetites,
of any individual Athenian, count as active causes in the
march of public affairs, which is determined by the
established law and by the pronounced sentiments of the
body of citizens. However gross an insult might have
been offered to Euripidês at Athens, the Dikasts would
never have sentenced that the offender should be handed
over to him to be flogged. They would have inflicted
such measure of punishment as the nature of the wrong,
and the pre-existing law, appeared to them to require.
Political measures, or judicial sentences, at Athens, might
be well- or ill-judged; but at any rate, they were always
dictated by regard to a known law and to the public con-
ceptions entertained of state-interests, state-dignity, and
state-obligations, without the avowed intrusion of any
man's personality. To Euripidês—who had throughout
his whole life been the butt of Aristophanês and other
comic writers, and who had been compelled to hear, in the
crowded theatre, taunts far more galling than what is
ascribed to Dekamnichus—the contrast must have been
indeed striking, to have the offender made over to him,
and the whip placed at his disposal, by order of his new
patron. And it is little to his honour, that he should have

proves that Euripidês availed himself of the privilege accorded by
Archelaus.

availed himself of the privilege, by causing the punishment to be really administered;—a punishment which he could never have seen inflicted, during the fifty years of his past life, upon any free Athenian citizen.

Krateuas did not survive the deed more than three or four days, after which Orestês son of Archelaus, a child, was placed on the throne, under the guardianship of Aeropus. The latter however, after about four years, made away with his ward, and reigned in his stead for two years. He then died of sickness, and was succeeded by his son Pausanias; who, after a reign of only one year, was assassinated and succeeded by Amyntas.[1] This Amyntas (chiefly celebrated as the father of Philip and the grandfather of Alexander the Great), though akin to the royal family, had been nothing more than an attendant of Aeropus,[2] until he made himself king by putting to death Pausanias.[3] He reigned, though with interruptions, twenty-four years (393—369 B.C.); years, for the most part, of trouble and humiliation for Macedonia, and of occasional exile for himself. The vigorous military organization introduced by Archelaus appears to have declined; while the frequent dethronements and assassinations of kings, beginning even with Perdikkas the father of Archelaus, and continued down to Amyntas, unhinged the central authority and disunited the various portions of the Macedonian name; which naturally tended to separation, and could only be held together by a firm hand.

*Succeeding Macedonian kings—Orestês, Aeropus, Pausanias, Amyntas. Assassination frequent.*

The interior regions of Macedonia were bordered, to the north, north-east, and north-west, by warlike barbarian tribes, Thracian and Illyrian, whose invasions were not unfrequent and often formidable. Tempted probably by the unsettled position of the government, the Illyrians poured in upon Amyntas during the first year of his reign: perhaps they may have been invited by other princes of the interior,[4] and at all events their coming would operate as a signal for

*Amyntas is expelled from Macedonia by the Illyrians—he makes over much of the sea-coast to the Olynthian confederacy.*

[1] Diodor. xiv. 84—89.
[2] Ælian, V. H. xii. 43; Dexippus ap. Syncell. p. 263; Justin, vii. 4.
[3] Diodor. xiv. 89. Ἐτελεύτησε δὲ καὶ Παυσανίας ὁ τῶν Μακεδόνων βα- σιλεύς, ἐπιτρεθεὶς ὑπὸ Ἀμύντου βδ- λῳ, ὅς τε ἐνιαυτὸν τὴν δὲ βασιλείαν κατέσχεν Ἀμύντας, &c.
[4] See in Thucyd. iv. 112—the relations of Arrhibæus, prince of the

malcontents to declare themselves. Amyntas—having only acquired the sceptre a few months before by assassinating his predecessor, and having little hold on the people—was not only unable to repel them, but found himself obliged to evacuate Pella, and even to retire from Macedonia altogether. Despairing of his position, he made over to the Olynthians a large portion of the neighbouring territory—Lower Macedonia or the coast and cities round the Thermaic Gulf.[1] As this cession is represented to have been made at the moment of his distress and expatriation, we may fairly suspect that it was made for some reciprocal benefit or valuable equivalent; of which Amyntas might well stand in need, at a moment of so much exigency.

<small>B.C. 392.
Chalkidians of Olynthus—they take into their protection the Macedonian cities on the coast, when Amyntas runs away before the Illyrians. Commencement of the Olynthian confederacy.</small>

It is upon this occasion that we begin to hear again of the Chalkidians of Olynthus, and the confederacy which they gradually aggregated round their city as a centre. The confederacy seems to have taken its start from this cession of Amyntas—or rather, to speak more properly, from his abdication; for the cession of what he could not keep was of comparatively little moment, and we shall see that he tried to resume it as soon as he acquired strength. The effect of his flight was, to break up the government of Lower or maritime Macedonia, and to leave the cities therein situated defenceless against the Illyrians, or other invaders from the interior. To these cities, the only chance of security, was to throw themselves upon the Greek cities on the coast, and to organise in conjunction with the latter a confederacy for mutual support. Among all the Greeks on that coast, the most strenuous and persevering (so they had proved themselves in their former contentions against Athens when at the summit of her power) as well

---

<small>Macedonians called Lynkestæ in the interior country, with the Illyrian invaders—B.C. 423.

Archelaus had been engaged at a more recent period in war with a prince of the interior named Arrhibæus—perhaps the same person (Aristot. Polit. v. 8, 11).

[1] Diodor. xiv. 92; xv. 19. Άπο-

τομὲ δὲ τὴν ἀρχήν, Ὀλυνθίοις μὲν τὴν συνεγγὺς χώραν ἐδωρήσατο, &c. Τῷ δήμῳ τῶν Ὀλυνθίων δωρησαμένου πολλὴν τῆς ὁμόρου χώρας, διὰ τὴν ἀπόγνωσιν τῆς ἑαυτοῦ δυναστείας, &c.

The flight of Amyntas, after a year's reign, is confirmed by Dexippus ap. Syncell. p. 263.</small>

as the nearest, were the Chalkidians of Olynthus. These Olynthians now put themselves forward—look into their alliance and under their protection the smaller towns of maritime Macedonia immediately near them—and soon extended their confederacy so as to comprehend all the larger towns in this region—including even Pella, the most considerable city of the country.[1] As they began this enterprise at a time when the Illyrians were masters of the country so as to drive Amyntas to despair and flight, we may be sure that it must have cost them serious efforts, not without great danger if they failed. We may also be sure that the cities themselves must have been willing, not to say eager, coadjutors; just as the islanders and Asiatic Greeks clung to Athens at the first formation of the confederacy of Delos. The Olynthians could have had no means of conquering even the less considerable Macedonian cities, much less Pella, by force and against the will of the inhabitants.

How the Illyrians were compelled to retire, and by what steps the confederacy was got together, we are not permitted to know. Our information (unhappily very brief) comes from the Akanthian envoy Kleigenês, speaking at Sparta about ten years afterwards (B.C. 383), and describing in a few words the confederacy as it then stood. But there is one circumstance which this witness—himself hostile to Olynthus and coming to solicit Spartan aid against her—attests emphatically; the equal, generous, and brotherly principles, upon which the Olynthians framed their scheme from the beginning. They did not

*Equal and liberal principles on which the confederacy was framed from the beginning. Accepted willingly by the Macedonian and Greco-Macedonian cities.*

[1] Xenoph. Hellen. v. 2, 12—"Ὅτι μὲν γὰρ τῶν ἐπὶ Θρᾴκης μεγίστη πόλις Ὄλυνθος, σχεδὸν πάντες ἐπίστασθε. Οὗτοι τῶν πόλεων προσηγάγοντο ἐστὶν ἃς, ἐφ' ᾧτε τοῖς αὐτοῖς χρῆσθαι νόμοις καὶ συμπολιτεύειν· ἔπειτα δὲ καὶ τῶν μειζόνων προσέλαβόν τινας. Ἐκ δὲ τούτου ἐπεχείρησαν καὶ τὰς τῆς Μακεδονίας πόλεις ἐλευθεροῦν ἀπὸ Ἀμύντου, τοῦ βασιλέως Μακεδόνων. Ἐπεὶ δὲ εἰσήκουσαν αἱ ἐγγύτατα αὐτῶν, ταχὺ καὶ ἐπὶ τὰς πόρρω καὶ μείζους ἐπορεύοντο· καὶ ἀπηλίκομεν ἡμεῖς ἔχοντες ἤδη ἄλλας τε πολλὰς, καὶ Πέλλαν, ἥπερ μεγίστη τῶν ἐν Μακεδονίᾳ πόλεων. Καὶ Ἀμύνταν δὲ αἰσθανόμεθα ἀποχωροῦντά τε ἐκ τῶν πόλεων, καὶ ὅσον οὐκ ἐκπεπτωκότα ἤδη ἐκ πάσης Μακεδονίας.

We know from Diodorus that Amyntas fled the country in despair, and ceded a large proportion at least of Lower Macedonia to the Olynthians. Accordingly the struggle, between the latter and Amyntas (here alluded to), must have taken place when he came back and tried to resume his dominion.

present themselves as an imperial city enrolling a body of dependent allies, but invited each separate city to adopt common laws and reciprocal citizenship with Olynthus, with full liberty of intermarriage, commercial dealing, and landed proprietorship. That the Macedonian cities near the sea should welcome so liberal a proposition as this, coming from the most powerful of their Grecian neighbours, cannot at all surprise us; especially at a time when they were exposed to the Illyrian invaders, and when Amyntas had fled the country. They had hitherto always been subjects:[1] their cities had not (like the Greek cities) enjoyed each its own separate autonomy within its own walls: the offer, now made to them by the Olynthians, was one of freedom in exchange for their past subjection under the Macedonian kings, combined with a force adequate to protect them against Illyrian and other invaders. Perhaps also these various cities—Anthemus, Therma, Chalastra, Pella, Alôrus, Pydna, &c.—may have contained, among the indigenous population, a certain proportion of domiciliated Grecian inhabitants, to whom the proposition of the Olynthians would be especially acceptable.

*The Olynthians extend their confederacy among the Grecian cities in Chalkidic Thrace—their liberal procedure—several cities join—others cling to their own autonomy, but are afraid of open resistance.*

We may thus understand why the offer of Olynthus was gladly welcomed by the Macedonian maritime cities. They were the first who fraternised as voluntary partners in the confederacy; which the Olynthians, having established this basis, proceeded to enlarge farther, by making the like liberal propositions to the Greek cities in their neighbourhood. Several of these latter joined voluntarily; others were afraid to refuse; insomuch that the confederacy came to include a considerable number of Greeks—especially Potidæa, situated on the isthmus of Pallênê, and commanding the road of communication between the cities within Pallênê and the continent. The Olynthians carried out with scrupulous sincerity their professed principles of equal and intimate partnership, avoiding all encroachment or offensive pre-eminence in favour of their own city. But in spite of this liberal procedure, they

---

[1] Xen. Hellen. v. 2, 12—τὰς τῆς Μακεδονίας πόλεις ἐλευθέρουν ἀπὸ Ἀμύντου, &c.: compare v. 2, 38.

found among their Grecian neighbours obstructions which they had not experienced from the Macedonian. Each of the Grecian cities had been accustomed to its own town-autonomy and separate citizenship, with its peculiar laws and customs. All of them were attached to this kind of distinct political life, by one of the most tenacious and universal instincts of the Greek mind; all of them would renounce it with reluctance, even on consenting to enter the Olynthian confederacy, with its generous promise, its enlarged security, and its manifest advantages; and there were even some who, disdaining every prospective consideration, refused to change their condition at all except at the point of the sword.

Among these last were Akanthus and Apollonia, the largest cities (next to Olynthus) in the Chalkidic peninsula, and therefore the least unable to stand alone. To these the Olynthians did not make application, until they had already attracted within their confederacy a considerable number of other Grecian as well as Macedonian cities. They then invited Akanthus and Apollonia to come in, upon the same terms of equal union and fellow-citizenship. The proposition being declined, they sent a second message intimating that, unless it were accepted within a certain time, they would enforce it by compulsory measures. So powerful already was the military force of the Olynthian confederacy, that Akanthus and Apollonia, incompetent to resist without foreign aid, dispatched envoys to Sparta to set forth the position of affairs in the Chalkidic peninsula, and to solicit intervention against Olynthus. *Akanthus and Apollonia resist the proposition. Olynthos menaces. They then solicit Spartan intervention against her.*

Their embassy reached Sparta about B.C. 383, when the Spartans, having broken up the city of Mantineia into villages and coerced Phlius, were in the full swing of power over Peloponnesus— and when they had also dissolved the Bœotian federation, placing harmosts in Platæa and Thespiæ as checks upon any movement of Thebes. The Akanthian Kleigenês, addressing himself to the assembly of Spartans and their allies, drew an alarming picture of the recent growth and prospective tendencies of Olynthus, invoking the interference of Sparta against that city. The Olynthian confederacy (he said) already comprised many cities, small *Speech of Kleigenês the Akanthian envoy at Sparta.*

and great, Greek as well as Macedonian—Amyntas having lost his kingdom. Its military power, even at present great, was growing every day.[1] The territory, comprising a large breadth of fertile corn-land, could sustain a numerous population. Wood for ship-building[2] was close at hand, while the numerous harbours of the confederate cities ensured a thriving trade as well as a steady revenue from custom-duties. The neighbouring Thracian tribes would be easily kept in willing dependence, and would thus augment the military force of Olynthus; even the gold mines of Mount Pangæus would speedily come within her assured reach. "All that I now tell you (such was the substance of his speech) is matter of public talk among the Olynthian people, who are full of hope and confidence. How can you Spartans, who are taking anxious pains to prevent the union of the Bœotian cities,[3] permit the aggregation of so much more formidable a power, both by land and by sea, as this of Olynthus? Envoys have already been sent thither from Athens and Thebes—and the Olynthians have decreed to send an embassy in return, for contracting alliance with those cities; hence your enemies will derive a large additional force. We of Akanthus and Apollonia, having declined the proposition to join the confederacy voluntarily, have received notice that, if we persist, they will constrain us. Now we are anxious to retain our paternal laws and customs, continuing as a city

---

[1] Xen. Hellen. v. 2, 14. The number of Olynthian troops is given in Xenophon as 800 hoplites—a far greater number of peltasts—and 1000 horsemen, assuming that Akanthus and Apollonia joined the confederacy. It has been remarked by Mr. Mitford and others, that these numbers, as they here stand, must be decidedly smaller than the reality. But we have no means of correction open to us. Mr. Mitford's suggestion of 8000 hoplites in place of 800 rests upon no authority. Demosthenes states that Olynthus by herself, and before she had brought all the Chalkidians into confederacy (οὔπω Χαλκιδέων πάντων εἰς ἓν συνηρισμένω.—De Fals.

Leg. c. 75. p. 425) possessed 400 horsemen, and a citizen population of 5000; no more than this (he says) at the time when the Lacedæmonians attacked them. The historical statements of the great orator, for a time which nearly coincides with his own birth, are to be received with caution.

[2] Compare Boeckh, Public Economy of Athens, p. 54. s. 100, Eng. Tr.

[3] Xen. Hellen. v. 2, 16. Ἐννοήσατε δὲ καὶ τόδε, πῶς εἰκός, ὑμᾶς τῆς μὲν Βοιωτίας ἐπιμεληθῆναι, ὅπως μὴ καθ' ἓν εἴη, πολὺ δὲ μείζονος ἀθροιζομένης δυνάμεως ἀμελῆσαι, &c.

I translate here the substance of the speech, not the exact words.

by ourselves.[1] But if we cannot obtain aid from you, we shall be under the necessity of joining them—as several other cities have already done, from not daring to refuse; cities, who would have sent envoys along with us, had they not been afraid of offending the Olynthians. These cities, if you interfere forthwith, and with a powerful force, will now revolt from the new confederacy. But if you postpone your interference, and allow time for the confederacy to work, their sentiments will soon alter. They will come to be knit together in attached unity, by the co-burgership, the intermarriage, and the reciprocity of landed possessions, which have already been enacted prospectively. All of them will become convinced that they have a common interest both in belonging to, and in strengthening the confederacy—just as the Arcadians, when they follow you, Spartans, as allies, are not only enabled to preserve their own property, but also to plunder others. If, by your delay, the attractive tendencies of the confederacy should come into real operation, you will presently find it not so much within your power to dissolve."[2]

This speech of the Akanthian envoy is remarkable in more than one respect. Coming from the lips of an enemy, it is the best of all testimonies to the liberal and comprehensive spirit in which the Olynthians were acting. They are accused —not of injustice, nor of selfish ambition, nor of degrading those around them—but literally, of organizing a new partnership on principles too generous and too seductive; of gently superseding, instead of violently breaking down, the barriers, between the various cities, by reciprocal ties of property and family among the citizens of each; of uniting them all into a new political aggregate,

*Envoys from Amyntas at Sparta.*

---

[1] Xenoph. Hellen. v. 2, 14. Ἡμεῖς δέ, ὦ ἄνδρες Λακεδαιμόνιοι, βουλόμεθα μὲν τοῖς πατρίοις νόμοις χρῆσθαι, καὶ αὐτονομεῖσθαι εἶναι· εἰ μέντοι μὴ βοηθήσει τις, ἀνάγκη καὶ ἡμῖν μετ' ἐκείνων γίγνεσθαι.

[2] Xen. Hellen. v. 2, 18. Δεῖ γε μὴν ὑμᾶς καὶ τόδε εἰδέναι, ὡς, ἣν εἰρήκαμεν δύναμιν μεγάλην οὖσαν, οὕτω δυσκάθεκτός τις ἐστίν· αἱ γὰρ ἔχουσαι τῶν πόλεων τῆς πολιτείας κοινωνοῦσαι, αὗται, ἂν τι ἴδωσιν ἀντίπαλον, ταχὺ ἀποστήσονται· εἰ μέντοι συγκλεισθήσονται ταῖς τε ἐπιγαμίαις καὶ ἐγκτήσεσι παρ' ἀλλήλαις, ἃς ἐψηφισμένοι εἰσί—καὶ γνώσονται, ὅτι μετὰ τῶν κρατούντων ἕπεσθαι κερδαλέον ἐστίν, ὥσπερ Ἀρκάδες, ὅταν μεθ' ὑμῶν ἴωσι, τά τε αὑτῶν σώζουσι, καὶ τὰ ἀλλότρια ἁρπάζουσιν —ἴσως οὐκέθ' ὁμοίως εὔλυτα ἔσται.

in which not only all would enjoy equal rights, but all without exception would be gainers. The advantage, both in security and in power, accruing prospectively to all, is not only admitted by the orator, but stands in the front of his argument. "Make haste and break up the confederacy (he impresses upon Sparta) before its fruit is ripe, so that the confederates may never taste it nor find out how good it is; for if they do, you will not prevail on them to forego it." By implication, he also admits—and he says nothing tending even to raise a doubt—that the cities which he represents, Akanthus and Apollonia, would share along with the rest in this same benefit. But the Grecian political instinct was nevertheless predominant—"We wish to preserve our paternal laws, and to be a city by ourselves." Thus nakedly is the objection stated; when the question was, not whether Akanthus should lose its freedom and become subject to an imperial city like Athens—but whether it should become a free and equal member of a larger political aggregate, cemented by every tie which could make union secure, profitable, and dignified. It is curious to observe how perfectly the orator is conscious that this repugnance, though at the moment preponderant, was nevertheless essentially transitory, and would give place to attachment when the union became to be felt as a reality; and how eagerly he appeals to Sparta to lose no time in clenching the repugnance, while it lasted. He appeals to her, not for any beneficial or Pan-hellenic objects, but in the interests of her own dominion, which required that the Grecian world should be as it were, pulverised into minute, self-acting, atoms, without cohesion—so that each city, or each village, while protected against subjection to any other, should farther be prevented from equal political union or fusion with any other; being thus more completely helpless and dependent in reference to Sparta.

It was not merely from Akanthus and Apollonia, but also from the dispossessed Macedonian king Amyntas, that envoys reached Sparta to ask for aid against Olynthus. It seems that Amyntas, after having abandoned the kingdom and made his cession to the Olynthians, had obtained some aid from Thessaly and tried to reinstate himself by force. In this scheme he had failed, being defeated by the Olynthians. Indeed we find another person named Argæus, mentioned as competitor for the Macedonian sceptre, and possessing it for two years.[1]

After hearing these petitioners, the Lacedæmonians first declared their own readiness to comply with the prayer, and to put down Olynthus; next, they submitted the same point to the vote of the assembled allies.[2] Among these latter, there was no genuine antipathy against the Olynthians, such as that which had prevailed against Athens before the Peloponnesian war, in the synod then held at Sparta. But the power of Sparta over her allies was now far greater than it had been then. Most of their cities were under oligarchies, dependent upon her support for authority over their fellow-citizens; moreover the recent events in Bœotia and at Mantineia had operated as a serious intimidation. Anxiety to keep the favour of Sparta was accordingly paramount, so that most of the speakers, as well as most of the votes, declared for the war,[3] and a combined army of ten thousand men was voted to be raised.

To make up such a total, a proportional contingent was assessed upon each confederate; combined with the proviso, now added for the first time, that each might furnish money instead of men, at the rate of three Æginæan oboli (half an Æginæan drachma) for each hoplite. A cavalry-soldier, to those cities which furnished such, was reckoned as equivalent to four hoplites; a hoplite, as equivalent to two peltasts; or pecuniary contribution on the same scale. All cities in default were made liable to a forfeit of one stater (four drachmæ) per day, for every soldier not sent; the forfeit to be enforced by Sparta.[4]

---

[1] Diodor. xiv. 92; xv. 19. Demosthenês speaks of Amyntas as having been expelled from his kingdom by the Thessalians (cont. Aristokrat. c. 29. p. 657). If this be historically correct, it must be referred to some subsequent war in which he was engaged with the Thessalians; perhaps to the time when Jason of Pheræ acquired dominion over Macedonia (Xenoph. Hellen. vi. 1, 11).

[2] See above in this History, Ch. xlviii.

[3] Xen. Hellen. v. 2, 20. Ἐκ τούτου μέντοι, πολλοὶ μὲν ξυνηγόρευον στρατιάν ποιεῖν, μάλιστα δὲ οἱ βουλόμενοι Λακεδαιμονίοις χαρίζεσθαι, &c.

[4] Xen. Hellen. v. 2, 21, 22.

Diodorus (xv. 31) mentions the fact that an hoplite was reckoned equivalent to two peltasts, in reference to a Lacedæmonian musterroll of a few years afterwards; but it must have been equally necessary to fix the proportion on the present occasion.

Such licensed substitution of pecuniary payment for personal service, is the same as I have already described to have taken place nearly a century before in the confederacy of Delos under the presidency of Athens.¹ It was a system not likely to be extensively acted upon among the Spartan allies, who were at once poorer and more warlike than those of Athens. But in both cases it was favourable to the ambition of the leading state; and the tendency becomes here manifest, to sanction, by the formality of a public resolution, that increased Lacedæmonian ascendency which had already grown up in practice.

*Anxiety of the Akanthians for instant intervention. The Spartan Eudamidas is sent against Olynthus at once, with such force as could be got ready. He checks the career of the Olynthians.*

The Akanthian envoys, while expressing their satisfaction with the vote just passed, intimated that the muster of these numerous contingents would occupy some time, and again insisted on the necessity of instant intervention, even with a small force; before the Olynthians could find time to get their plans actually in work or appreciated by the surrounding cities. A moderate Lacedæmonian force (they said), if dispatched forthwith, would not only keep those who had refused to join Olynthus, steady to their refusal, but also induce others, who had joined reluctantly, to revolt. Accordingly the Ephors appointed Eudamidas at once, assigning to him 2000 hoplites—Neodamodês (or enfranchised Helots), Periœki, and Skiritæ or Arcadian borderers. Such was the anxiety of the Akanthians for haste, that they would not let him delay even to get together the whole of this moderate force. He was put in march immediately, with such as were ready; while his brother Phœbidas was left behind to collect the remainder and follow him. And it seems that the Akanthians judged correctly. For Eudamidas, arriving in Thrace after a rapid march, though he was unable to contend against the Olynthians in the field, yet induced Potidæa to revolt from them, and was able to defend those cities, such as Akanthus and Apollonia, which resolutely stood aloof.² Amyntas brought a force to co-operate with him.

¹ See Ch. xlv. of this History.
² Xen. Hellen. v. 2, 24; Diodor. xv. 21.

The delay in the march of Phœbidas was productive of consequences no less momentous than unexpected. The direct line from Peloponnesus to Olynthus lay through the Theban territory; a passage which the Thebans, whatever might have been their wishes, were not powerful enough to refuse, though they had contracted an alliance with Olynthus,[1] and though proclamation was made that no Theban citizens should join the Lacedæmonian force. Eudamidas, having departed at a moment's notice, passed through Bœotia without a halt in his way to Thrace. But it was known that his brother Phœbidas was presently to follow; and upon this fact the philo-Laconian party in Thebes organised a conspiracy.

*Phœbidas, brother of Eudamidas, remains behind to collect fresh force, and march to join his brother in Thrace. He passes through the Theban territory and near Thebes.*

They obtained from the Ephors, and from the miso-Theban feelings of Agesilaus, secret orders to Phœbidas, that he should cooperate with them in any party movement which they might find opportunity of executing;[2] and when he halted with his detachment near the gymnasium a little way without the walls, they concerted matters as well with him as among themselves. Leontiadês, Hypatês, and Archias, were the chiefs of the party in Thebes favourable to Sparta; a party decidedly in minority, yet still powerful, and at this moment so strengthened by the unbounded ascendency of the Spartan name, that Leontiadês himself was one of the polemarchs of the city. Of the anti-Spartan, or predominant sentiment in Thebes,—which included most of the wealthy and active citizens, those who came successively into office as hipparchs or generals of the cavalry[3]—the leaders

*Conspiracy of Leontiadês and the philo-Laconian party in Thebes, to betray the town and citadel to Phœbidas.*

---

[1] Xen. Hellen. v. 2, 27-34.

[2] This is the statement of Diodorus (xv. 20), and substantially that of Plutarch (Agesil. c. 24), who intimates that it was the general belief of the time. And it appears to me more probable than the representation of Xenophon—that the first idea arose when Phœbidas was under the walls of Thebes, and that the Spartan leader was persuaded by Leontiadês to act on his own responsibility. The behaviour of Agesilaus and of the Ephors after the fact, is like that of persons who had previously contemplated the possibility of it. But the original suggestion must have come from the Theban faction themselves.

[3] Plutarch (De Genio Socratis, c. 5, p. 578 B.) states that most of these generals of cavalry (τῶν ἱππαρχικῶν νομίμως) were afterwards in exile with Pelopidas at Athens.

were Ismenias and Androkleidês. The former especially, the foremost as well as ablest conductor of the late war against Sparta, was now in office as Polemarch, conjointly with his rival Leontiadês.

*The opposing leaders —Leontiadês and Ismenias— were both Polemarchs. Leontiadês contrives the plot and introduces Phœbidas into the Kadmeia.*

While Ismenias, detesting the Spartans, kept aloof from Phœbidas, Leontiadês assiduously courted him and gained his confidence. On the day of the Thesmophoria,[1] a religious festival celebrated by the women apart from the men, during which the acropolis or Kadmeia was consecrated to their exclusive use—Phœbidas, affecting to have concluded his halt, put himself in march to proceed as if towards Thrace; seemingly rounding the walls of Thebes, but not going into it. The Senate was actually assembled in the portico of the agora, and the heat of a summer's noon had driven every one out of the streets, when Leontiadês, stealing away from the Senate, hastened on horseback to overtake Phœbidas, caused him to face about, and conducted the Lacedæmonians straight up to the Kadmeia; the gates of which as well as those of the town, were opened to his order as Polemarch.

We have little or no information respecting the government of Thebes. It would seem to have been at this moment a liberalised oligarchy. There was a senate, and two Polemarchs (perhaps the Polemarchs may have been more than two in all, though the words of Xenophon rather lead us to suppose only two)—and there seems also to have been a civil magistrate, chosen by lot (ὁ πρεσβύτατος ἄρχων) and renewed annually, whose office was marked by his constantly having in his possession the sacred spear of state (τὸ ἱερὸν δόρυ) and the city-seal (Plutarch, De Gen. Socr. c. 31. p. 597-B.-C.).

At this moment, it must be recollected, there were no such officers as Bœotarchs; since the Lacedæmonians, enforcing the peace of Antalkidas, had put an end to the Bœotian federation.

[1] The rhetor Aristeidês (Or. xiii. Eleusin. p. 452 Cant.; p. 418 Dind.) states that the Kadmeia was seized during the Pythian festival. This festival would take place, July or August 382 B.C.; near the beginning of the third year of the (99th) Olympiad. See above in this History, Ch. liv. Respecting the year and month in which the Pythian festival was held, there is a difference of opinion among commentators. I agree with those who assign it to the first quarter of the third Olympic year. And the date of the march of Phœbidas would perfectly harmonise with this supposition.

Xenophon mentions nothing about the Pythian festival as being in course of celebration when Phœbidas was encamped near Thebes; for it had no particular reference to Thebes.

There were not only no citizens in the streets, but none even in the Kadmeia; no male person being permitted to be present at the feminine Thesmophoria; so that Phœbidas and his army became possessed of the Kadmeia without the smallest opposition. At the same time they became possessed of an acquisition of hardly less importance—the persons of all the assembled Theban women; who served as hostages for the quiet submission, however reluctant, of the citizens in the town below. Leontiadês handed to Phœbidas the key of the gates, and then descended into the town, giving orders that no man should go up without his order.[1]

The assembled senate heard with consternation the occupation of the acropolis by Phœbidas. Before any deliberation could be taken among the senators, Leontiadês came down to resume his seat. The lochages and armed citizens of his party, to whom he had previously given orders, stood close at hand. "Senators (said he), be not intimidated by the news that the Spartans are in the Kadmeia; for they assure us that they have no hostile purpose against any one who does not court war against them. But I, as Polemarch, am empowered by law to seize any one whose behaviour is manifestly and capitally criminal. Accordingly I seize this man Ismenias, as the great inflamer of war. Come forward, capitains and soldiers, lay hold of him, and carry him off where your orders direct." Ismenias was accordingly seized and hurried off as a prisoner to the Kadmeia; while the senators, thunderstruck and overawed, offered no resistance. Such of them as were partisans of the arrested polemarch, and many even of the more neutral members, left the Senate and went home, thankful to escape with their lives. Three hundred of them, including Androkleidas, Pelopidas, Mellon, and others, sought safety by voluntary exile to Athens: after which the remainder of the Senate, now composed of few or none except philo-Spartan partisans, passed a vote formally dismissing Ismenias, and appointing a new polemarch in his place.[2]

*Leontiadês overawes the Senate, and arrests Ismenias: Pelopidas and the leading friends of Ismenias go into exile.*

This blow of high-handed violence against Ismenias forms a worthy counterpart to the seizure of Theramenês

[1] Xen. Hellen. v. 2, 28, 29.   [2] Xen. Hellen. v. 2, 30, 31.

by Kritias,[1] twenty-two years before, in the Senate of
Athens under the Thirty. Terror-striking in itself, it was probably accompanied by similar deeds
of force against others of the same party. The
sudden explosion and complete success of the
conspiracy, plotted by the Executive Chief

*Phœbidas in the Kadmeia—terror and submission at Thebes.*

himself, the most irresistible of all conspirators—the presence of Phœbidas in the Kadmeia, and of a compliant Senate in the town—the seizure or flight of Ismenias and all his leading partisans—were more than sufficient to crush all spirit of resistance on the part of the citizens; whose first anxiety probably was, to extricate their wives and daughters from the custody of the Lacedæmonians in the Kadmeia. Having such a price to offer, Leontiadês would extort submission the more easily, and would probably procure a vote of the people ratifying the new *régime*, the Spartan alliance, and the continued occupation of the acropolis. Having accomplished the first settlement of his authority, he proceeded without delay to Sparta, to make known the fact that "order reigned" at Thebes.

The news of the seizure of the Kadmeia and of the
revolution at Thebes had been received at
Sparta with the greatest surprise, as well as
with a mixed feeling of shame and satisfaction.
Everywhere throughout Greece, probably, it
excited a greater sensation than any event since
the battle of Ægospotami. Tried by the recognised public law of Greece, it was a flagitious

*Mixed feelings at Sparta—great importance of the acquisition to Spartan interests.*

iniquity, for which Sparta had not the shadow of a pretence. It was even worse than the surprise of Platæa by the Thebans before the Peloponnesian war, which admitted of the partial excuse that war was at any rate impending; whereas in this case, the Thebans had neither done nor threatened anything to violate the peace of Antalkidas. It stood condemned by the indignant sentiment of all Greece, unwillingly testified even by the philo-Laconian Xenophon[2] himself. But it was at the same time an immense accession to Spartan power. It had been achieved with pre-eminent skill and success; and Phœbidas might well claim to have struck for Sparta the most important blow since Ægospotami, relieving her from one of her two really formidable enemies.[3]

[1] Xen. Hellen. ii. 3. See above in this History, Ch. lxv.
[2] Xen. Hellen. v. 4, 1.
[3] It is curious that Xenophon,

## CHAP. LXXVI.   EFFECT OF THE NEWS AT SPARTA.

Nevertheless, far from receiving thanks at Sparta, he became the object of wrath and condemnation, both with the Ephors and the citizens generally. Every one was glad to throw upon him the odium of the proceeding, and to denounce him as having acted without orders. Even the Ephors, who had secretly authorized him beforehand to cooperate generally with the faction at Thebes, having doubtless never given any specific instructions, now indignantly disavowed him. Agesilaus alone stood forward in his defence, contending that the only question was, whether his proceeding at Thebes had been injurious or beneficial to Sparta. If the former, he merited punishment; if the latter, it was always lawful to render service, even *impromptu* and without previous orders.

*Displeasure at Sparta more pretended than real, against Phœbidas: Agesilaus defends him.*

Tried by this standard, the verdict was not doubtful. For every man at Sparta felt how advantageous the act was in itself; and felt it still more, when Leontiadês reached the city, humble in solicitation as well as profuse in promise. In his speech addressed to the assembled Ephors and Senate, he first reminded them how hostile Thebes had hitherto been to them, under Ismenias and the party just put down—and how constantly they had been in jealous alarm, lest Thebes should reconstitute by force the Bœotian federation. "Now (added he) your fears may be at an end: only take as good care to uphold our government, as we shall take to obey your orders. For the future, you will have nothing to do but to send us a short dispatch, to get every service which you require."[1]

*Leontiadês at Sparta— his humble protestations and assurances —the Ephors decide that they will retain the Kadmeia, but at the same time fine Phœbidas.*

---

treating Phœbidas as a man more warm-hearted than wise, speaks of him as if he had rendered no real service to Sparta by the capture of the Kadmeia (v. 2, 28). The explanation of this is, that Xenophon wrote his history at a later period, after the defeat at Leuktra and the downfall of Sparta: which downfall was brought about by the reaction against her overweening and oppressive dominion, especially after the capture of the

Kadmeia—or (in the pious creed of Xenophon) by the displeasure of the gods, which such iniquity drew down upon her (v. 4, 1). In this way, therefore, it is made out that Phœbidas had not acted with true wisdom, and that he had done his country more harm than good; a criticism which we may be sure that no man advanced, at the time of the capture itself, or during the three years after it.

[1] Xen. Hellen. v. 2, 34.

It was resolved by the Lacedæmonians, at the instance of Agesilaus, to retain their garrison now in the Kadmeia, to uphold Leontiadês with his colleagues in the government of Thebes, and to put Ismenias upon his trial. Yet they at the same time, as a sort of atonement to the opinion of Greece, passed a vote of censure on Phœbidas, dismissed him from his command, and even condemned him to a fine. The fine, however, most probably was never exacted; for we shall see by the conduct of Sphodrias afterwards that the displeasure against Phœbidas, if at first genuine, was certainly of no long continuance.

*The Lacedæmonians cause Ismenias to be tried and put to death. Iniquity of this proceeding.*

That the Lacedæmonians should at the same time condemn Phœbidas and retain the Kadmeia— has been noted as a gross contradiction. Nevertheless we ought not to forget, that had they evacuated the Kadmeia, the party of Leontiadês at Thebes, which had compromised itself for Sparta as well as for its own aggrandizement, would have been irretrievably sacrificed. The like excuse, if excuse it be, cannot be urged in respect to their treatment of Ismenias; whom they put upon his trial at Thebes, before a court consisting of three Lacedæmonian commissioners, and one from each allied city. He was accused, probably by Leontiadês and his other enemies, of having entered into friendship and conspiracy with the Persian king to the detriment of Greece[1] —of having partaken in the Persian funds brought into Greece by Timokratês the Rhodian—and of being the real author of that war which had disturbed Greece from 395 B.C. down to the peace of Antalkidas. After an unavailing defence, he was condemned and executed. Had this doom been inflicted upon him by his political antagonists

Καὶ ὑμεῖς τε (says Leontiadês to the Lacedæmonian Ephors) τότε μὲν ἀεὶ προσείχετε τὸν νοῦν, πότε ἐκοῦσαι σθε διαζομένους αὐτοὺς τὴν Βοιωτίαν ὑφ' αὑτοῖς εἶναι· νῦν δ', ἐὰν τάδε πέπρακται, οὐδὲν ὑμᾶς δεῖ Θηβαίους φοβεῖσθαι· ἀλλ' ἀρκέσει ὑμῖν μικρά σκυτάλη, ὥστε ἐκείθε, πάντα πράττεσθαι, ὅσων ἂν δέησθε— ἐὰν, ὥσπερ ἡμεῖς ὑμῶν, οὕτω καὶ ὑμεῖς ἡμῶν, ἐπιμέλησθε.

Xenophon mentions the displeasure of the Ephors and the Spartans generally against Phœbidas (χαλεπῶς ἔχοντες τῷ Φοιβίδᾳ), but not the fine, which is certified by Diodorus (xv. 20), by Plutarch (Pelopidas, c. 6, and De Genio Socratis, p. 576 A), and Cornelius Nepos (Pelopid. c. 1).

[1] Xen. Hellen. v. 2, 85; Plutarch, De Genio Socratis, p. 576 A. Plutarch in another place (Pelopid. c. 5) represents Ismenias as having been conveyed to Sparta and tried there.

as a consequence of their intestine victory, it would have been too much in the analogy of Grecian party-warfare to call for any special remark. But there is something peculiarly revolting in the prostitution of judicial solemnity and Pan-hellenic pretence, which the Lacedæmonians here committed. They could have no possible right to try Ismenias as a criminal at all; still less to try him as a criminal on the charge of confederacy with the Persian king —when they had themselves, only five years before, acted not merely as allies, but even as instruments, of that monarch, in enforcing the peace of Antalkidas. If Ismenias had received money from one Persian satrap, the Spartan Antalkidas had profited in like manner by another—and for the like purpose too of carrying on Grecian war. The real motive of the Spartans was doubtless to revenge themselves upon this distinguished Theban for having raised against them the war which began in 395 B.C. But the mockery of justice by which that revenge was masked, and the impudence of punishing in him as treason that same foreign alliance with which they had ostentatiously identified themselves, lends a deeper enormity to the whole proceeding.

Leontiadês and his partisans were thus established as rulers in Thebes, with a Lacedæmonian garrison in the Kadmeia to sustain them and execute their orders. The once-haughty Thebes was enrolled as a member of the Lacedæmonian confederacy. Sparta was now enabled to prosecute her Olynthian expedition with redoubled vigour. Eudamidas and Amyntas, though they repressed the growth of the Olynthian confederacy, had not been strong enough to put it down; so that a larger force was necessary, and the aggregate of ten thousand men, which had been previously decreed, was put into instant requisition, to be commanded by Teleutias, brother of Agesilaus. *Vigorous action of the Spartans against Olynthus—Teleutias is sent there with a large force, including a considerable Theban contingent. Derdas co-operates with him.*
The new general, a man of very popular manners, was soon on his march at the head of this large army, which comprised many Theban hoplites as well as horsemen furnished by the new rulers in their unqualified devotion to Sparta. He sent forward envoys to Amyntas in Macedonia, urging upon him the most strenuous efforts for the purpose of recovering the Macedonian cities which had joined the

Olynthians—and also to Derdas, prince of the district of Upper Macedonia, called Elimeia, inviting his cooperation against that insolent city, which would speedily extend her dominion (he contended) from the maritime region to the interior, unless she were put down.[1]

*Strenuous resistance of the Olynthians—excellence of their cavalry.*
B.C. 382.

Though the Lacedæmonians were masters everywhere and had their hands free—though Teleutias was a competent officer with powerful forces—and though Derdas joined with 400 excellent Macedonian horse—yet the conquest of Olynthus was found no easy enterprise.[2] The Olynthian cavalry, in particular, was numerous and efficient. Unable as they were to make head against Teleutias in the field or repress his advance, nevertheless, in a desultory engagement which took place near the city gates they defeated the Lacedæmonian and Theban cavalry, threw even the infantry into confusion, and were on the point of gaining a complete victory, had not Derdas with his cavalry on the other wing made a diversion which forced them to come back for the protection of the city. Teleutias, remaining master of the field, continued to ravage the Olynthian territory during the summer, for which however the Olynthians retaliated by frequent marauding expeditions against the cities in alliance with him.[3]

*Teleutias being at first successful and having become overconfident, sustains a terrible defeat from the Olynthians under the walls of their city.*
B.C. 381.

In the ensuing spring, the Olynthians sustained various partial defeats, especially one near Apollonia from Derdas. They were more and more confined to their walls; insomuch that Teleutias became confident and began to despise them. Under these dispositions on his part, a body of Olynthian cavalry showed themselves one morning, passed the river near their city, and advanced in calm array towards the Lacedæmonian camp. Indignant at such an appearance of daring, Teleutias directed Tlemonidas with the peltasts to disperse them; upon which the Olynthians slowly retreated, while the peltasts

---

[1] Xen. Hellen. v. 2, 38.
[2] Demosthenês (De Fals. Leg. c. 76, p. 425) speaks with proper commendation of the brave resistance made by the Olynthians against the great force of Sparta. But his expressions are altogether misleading as to the tenor and result of the war. If we had no other information than his, we should be led to imagine that the Olynthians had been victorious, and the Lacedæmonians baffled.
[3] Xenoph. Hellen. v. 2, 40—43.

rushed impatiently to pursue them, even when they recrossed the river. No sooner did the Olynthians see that half the peltasts had crossed it than they suddenly turned, charged them vigorously, and put them to flight with the loss of their commander Tlemonidas and a hundred others. All this passed in sight of Teleutias, who completely lost his temper. Seizing his arms, he hurried forward to cover the fugitives with the hoplites around him, sending orders to all his troops, hoplites, peltasts, and horsemen, to advance also. But the Olynthians, again retreating, drew him on towards the city, with such inconsiderate forwardness, that many of his soldiers, ascending the eminence on which the city was situated, rushed close up to the walls.[1] Here however they were received by a shower of missiles which forced them to recede in disorder; upon which the Olynthians again sallied forth, probably from more than one gate at once, and charged them first with cavalry and peltasts, next with hoplites. The Lacedæmonians and their allies, disturbed and distressed by the first, were unable to stand against the compact charge of the last; Teleutias himself, fighting in the foremost ranks, was slain, and his death was a signal for the flight of all around. The whole besieging force dispersed and fled in different directions—to Akanthus, to Spartôlus, to Potidæa, to Apollonia. So vigorous and effective was the pursuit by the Olynthians, that the loss of the fugitives was immense. The whole army was in fact ruined;[2] for probably many of the allies who escaped became discouraged and went home.

At another time, probably, a victory so decisive, might have deterred the Lacedæmonians from farther proceedings, and saved Olynthus. But now, they were so completely masters everywhere else, that they thought only of repairing the dishonour by a still more imposing demonstration. Their king Agesipolis was placed at the head of an expedition on the largest scale; and his name called forth eager cooperation, both in men and money, from the allies. He marched with thirty

B.C. 380.
Agesipolis is sent to Olynthus from Sparta with a reinforcement. He dies of a fever.

---

[1] Thucyd. i. 63—with the Scholiast.

[2] Xen. Hellen. v. 8, 4—5. συμπλήθεις ἀπέκτειναν ἀνθρώπους καὶ

ὅτι περ ὄφελος ἦν τούτου τοῦ στρατεύματος.

Diodorus (xv. 21) states the loss at 1200 men.

Spartan counsellors, as Agesilaus had gone to Asia; besides a select body of energetic youth as volunteers, from the Periœki, from the illegitimate sons of Spartans, and from strangers or citizens who had lost their franchise through poverty, introduced as friends of richer Spartan citizens to go through the arduous Lykurgean training.[1] Amyntas and Derdas also were instigated to greater exertions than before, so that Agesipolis was enabled, after receiving their reinforcements in his march through Macedonia, to present himself before Olynthus with an overwhelming force, and to confine the citizens within their walls. He then completed the ravage of their territory, which had been begun by Teleutias; and even took Torônê by storm. But the extreme heat of the summer weather presently brought upon him a fever, which proved fatal in a week's time; although he had caused himself to be carried for repose to the shady grove, and clear waters, near the temple of Dionysus at Aphytis. His body was immersed in honey and transported to Sparta, where it was buried with the customary solemnities.[2]

Polybiadês, who succeeded Agesipolis in the command, prosecuted the war with undiminished vigour; and the Olynthians, debarred from their home produce as well as from importation, were speedily reduced to such straits as to be compelled to solicit peace. They were obliged to break up their own federation, and to enrol themselves as sworn members of the Lacedæmonian confederacy,

---

[1] Xen. Hellen. v. 3, 9. Πολλοὶ δὲ αὐτῷ καὶ τῶν περιοίκων ἐθελονταὶ καλοὶ κἀγαθοὶ ἠκολούθουν, καὶ ξένοι τῶν τροφίμων καλουμένων, καὶ νόθοι τῶν Σπαρτιατῶν, μάλα εὐειδεῖς τε καὶ τῶν ἐν τῇ πόλει καλῶν οὐκ ἄπειροι.

The phrase—ξένοι τῶν τροφίμων—is illustrated by a passage from Phylarchus in Athenæus, vi. p. 271 (referred to by Schneider in his note here). I have already stated that the political franchise of a Spartan citizen depended upon his being able to furnish constantly his quota to the public mess-table. Many of the poor families became unable to do this, and thus lost their qualification and their training; but rich citizens sometimes paid their quota for them, and enabled them by such aid to continue their training as ξύντροφοι, τρόφιμοι, μόθακες, &c., as companions of their own sons. The two sons of Xenophon were educated at Sparta (Diog. Laërt. ii. 54), and would thus be ξένοι τῶν τροφίμων καλουμένων. If either of them was now old enough, he might probably have been one among the volunteers to accompany Agesipolis.

[2] Xen. Hellen. v. 3, 18; Pausan. iii. 5, 9.

with its obligations of service to Sparta.¹ The Olynthian union being dissolved, the component Grecian cities were enrolled severally as allies of Sparta, while the maritime cities of Macedonia were deprived of their neighbouring Grecian protector, and passed again under the dominion of Amyntas.

Both the dissolution of this growing confederacy, and the reconstitution of maritime Macedonia, were signal misfortunes to the Grecian world. Never were the arms of Sparta more mischievously or more unwarrantably employed. That a powerful Grecian confederacy should be formed in the Chalkidic peninsula, in the border region where Hellas joined the non-Hellenic tribes—was an incident of signal benefit to the Hellenic world generally. It would have served as a bulwark to Greece against the neighbouring Macedonians and Thracians, at whose expense its conquests, if it made any, would have been achieved. That Olynthus did not oppress her Grecian neighbours—that the principles of her confederacy were of the most equal, generous, and seducing character—that she employed no greater compulsion than was requisite to surmount an unreflecting instinct of town-autonomy—and that the very towns who obeyed this instinct would have become sensible themselves, in a very short time, of the benefits conferred by the confederacy on each and every one—these are facts certified by the urgency of the reluctant Akanthians, when they entreat Sparta to leave no interval for the confederacy to make its working felt. Nothing but the intervention of Sparta could have crushed this liberal and beneficent promise; nothing but the accident, that during the three years from 382 to 379 B.C., she was at the maximum of her power and had her hands quite free, with Thebes and its Kadmeia under her garrison. Such prosperity did not long continue unabated. Only a few months after the submission of Olynthus, the Kadmeia was retaken by the Theban exiles, who raised so vigorous a war against Sparta, that she would have been disabled from meddling with Olynthus—as we shall find illustrated

¹ Xen. Hellen. v. 3, 26; Diodor. xv. 22, 23.

by the fact (hereafter to be recounted) that she declined interfering in Thessaly to protect the Thessalian cities against Jason of Pheræ. Had the Olynthian confederacy been left to its natural working, it might well have united all the Hellenic cities around it in harmonious action, so as to keep the sea-coast in possession of a confederacy of free and self-determining communities, confining the Macedonian princes to the interior. But Sparta threw in her extraneous force, alike irresistible and inauspicious, to defeat these tendencies; and to frustrate that salutary change—from fractional autonomy and isolated action into integral and equal autonomy with collective action—which Olynthus was labouring to bring about. She gave the victory to Amyntas, and prepared the indispensable basis upon which his son Philip afterwards rose, to reduce not only Olynthus, but Akanthus, Apollonia, and the major part of the Grecian world, to one common level of subjection. Many of those Akanthians, who spurned the boon of equal partnership and free communion with Greeks and neighbours, lived to discover how impotent were their own separate walls as a bulwark against Macedonian neighbours; and to see themselves confounded in that common servitude which the imprudence of their fathers had entailed upon them. By the peace of Antalkidas, Sparta had surrendered the Asiatic Greeks to Persia; by crushing the Olynthian confederacy, she virtually surrendered the Thracian Greeks to the Macedonian princes. Never again did the opportunity occur of placing Hellenism on a firm, consolidated, and self-supporting basis, round the coast of the Thermaic Gulf.

*B.C. 380. Intervention of Sparta with the government of Phlius. The Phliasian government favoured by Agesipolis, persecuted by Agesilaus.*

While the Olynthian expedition was going on, the Lacedæmonians were carrying on, under Agesilaus, another intervention within Peloponnesus, against the city of Phlius. It has already been mentioned that certain exiles of this city had recently been recalled, at the express command of Sparta. The ruling party in Phlius had at the same time passed a vote to restore the confiscated property of these exiles; reimbursing out of the public treasury, to those who had purchased it, the price which they had paid— and reserving all disputed points for judicial decision.[1] The returned exiles now again came to Sparta, to profer complaint that they could obtain no just restitution of their property; that the tribunals of the city were in the hands of their opponents, many of them directly interested as purchasers, who refused them the right of appealing to any extraneous and impartial authority; and that there were even in the city itself many who thought them wronged. Such allegations were probably more or less founded in truth. At the same time, the appeal to Sparta, abrogating the independence of Phlius, so incensed the ruling Phliasians that they passed a sentence of fine against all the appellants. The latter insisted on this sentence as a fresh count for strengthening their complaints at Sparta; and as a farther proof of anti-Spartan feeling, as well as of high-handed injustice, in the Phliasian rulers.[2] Their cause was warmly espoused by Agesilaus, who had personal relations of hospitality with some of the exiles; while it appears that his colleague king Agesipolis was on good terms with the ruling party at Phlius—had received from them zealous aid, both in men and money, for his Olynthian expedition —and had publicly thanked them for their devotion to Sparta.[3] The Phliasian government, emboldened by the proclaimed testimonial of Agesipolis, certifying their fidelity, had fancied that they stood upon firm ground, and that no Spartan coercion would be enforced against them. But the marked favour of Agesipolis, now absent in Thrace, told rather against them in the mind of Agesilaus; pursuant to that jealousy which usually prevailed between the two Spartan kings. In spite of much remonstrance at Sparta, from many who deprecated hostilities against a city of 5000 citizens, for the profit of a handful of exiles—he not only seconded the proclamation of war against Phlius by the Ephors, but also took the command of the army.[4]

The army being mustered, and the border sacrifices favourable, Agesilaus marched with his usual rapidity towards Phlius; dismissing those Phliasian envoys, who

[1] Xen. Hellen. v. 2, 10.
[2] Xen. Hellen. v. 3, 10, 11.
[3] Xen. Hellen. v. 5, 10. ἡ Φλιασίων πόλις, ἐπαινεθεῖσα μὲν ὑπὸ τοῦ Ἀγησιπόλιδος, ὅ τι πολλὰ καὶ ταχέως αὐτῷ χρήματα ἐς τὴν στρατιὰν ἔδοσαν, &c.
[4] Xen. Hellen. v. 3, 12, 13; Plutarch, Agesil. c. 21; Diodor. xv. 20.

met him on the road and bribed or entreated him to desist, with the harsh reply that the government had already deceived Sparta once, and that he would be satisfied with nothing less than the surrender of the acropolis. This being refused, he marched to the city, and blocked it up by a wall of circumvallation. The besieged defended themselves with resolute bravery and endurance, under a citizen named Delphion; who, with a select troop of 300, maintained constant guard at every point, and even annoyed the besiegers by frequent sallies. By public decree, every citizen was put upon half-allowance of bread, so that the siege was prolonged to double the time which Agesilaus, from the information of the exiles as to the existing stock of provisions, had supposed to be possible. Gradually, however, famine made itself felt; desertions from within increased, among those who were favourable, or not decidedly averse, to the exiles; desertions, which Agesilaus took care to encourage by an ample supply of food, and by enrolment as Phliasian emigrants on the Spartan side. At length, after about a year's blockade,[1] the provisions within were exhausted, so that the besieged were forced to entreat permission from Agesilaus to despatch envoys to Sparta and beg for terms. Agesilaus granted their request. But being at the same time indignant that they submitted to Sparta rather than to him, he sent to ask the Ephors that the terms might be referred to his dictation. Meanwhile he redoubled his watch over the city; in spite of which, Delphion, with one of his most active subordinates, contrived to escape at this last hour. Phlius was now compelled to surrender at discretion to Agesilaus, who named a Council of One Hundred (half from the exiles, half from those within the city) vested with absolute powers of life and death over all the citizens, and authorized to frame a constitution for the future government of the city. Until

*marginal notes:* Agesilaus marches an army against Phlius—reduces the town by blockade, after a long resistance. The Lacedæmonians occupy the acropolis, naming a Council of One Hundred as governors.

[1] Xen. Hellen. v. 3, 25.
Καὶ τὰ μὲν περὶ Φλιοῦντα οὕτως οὐ περιείλκετο ἐν ὅλῳ μηνὶ καὶ ἐνιαυτῷ.

This general expression "the matters relative to Phlius," comprises not merely the blockade, but the preliminary treatment and complaints of the Phliasian exiles. One year therefore will be as much as we can allow for the blockade —perhaps more than we ought to allow.

this should be done, he left a garrison in the acropolis, with assured pay for six months.¹

Had Agesipolis been alive, perhaps the Phliasians might have obtained better terms. How the omnipotent Hekatontarchy named by the partisan feelings of Agesilaus,² conducted themselves, we do not know. But the presumptions are all unfavourable, seeing that their situation as well as their power was analogous to that of the Thirty at Athens and the Lysandrian Dekarchies elsewhere.

The surrender of Olynthus to Polybiadês, and of Phlius to Agesilaus, seem to have taken place B.C. 379. nearly at the same time.

¹ Xen. Hellen. v. 3, 17—16.
² The panegyrist of Agesilaus finds little to commend in these Phliasian proceedings, except the φιλεταιρεία or partisan-attachment of his hero (Xenoph. Agesil. ii. 21).

## CHAPTER LXXVII.

### FROM THE SUBJUGATION OF OLYNTHUS BY THE LACEDÆMONIANS DOWN TO THE CONGRESS AT SPARTA, AND PARTIAL PEACE, IN 371 B.C.

AT the beginning of 379 B.C., the empire of the Lacedæmonians on land had reached a pitch never before paralleled. On the sea, their fleet was but moderately powerful, and they seem to have held divided empire with Athens over the smaller islands; while the larger islands (so far as we can make out) were independent of both. But the whole of inland Greece, both within and without Peloponnesus—except Argos, Attica, and perhaps the more powerful Thessalian cities—was now enrolled in the confederacy dependent on Sparta. Her occupation of Thebes, by a Spartan garrison and an oligarchy of local partisans, appeared to place her empire beyond all chance of successful attack; while the victorious close of the war against Olynthus carried everywhere an intimidating sense of her far-reaching power. Her allies too—governed as they were in many cases by Spartan harmosts, and by oligarchies whose power rested on Sparta—were much more dependent upon her than they had been during the time of the Peloponnesian war.

Such a position of affairs rendered Sparta an object of the same mingled fear and hatred (the first preponderant) as had been felt towards imperial Athens fifty years before, when she was designated as the "despot city."[1] And this sentiment was farther aggravated by the recent peace of Antalkidas, in every sense the work of Sparta; which she had first procured, and afterwards carried into execution. That peace was disgraceful enough as being dictated by the king of Persia, enforced in his name, and surrendering

---
[1] Thucyd. L. 121. πόλιν τύραννον.

to him all the Asiatic Greeks. But it became yet more disgraceful when the universal autonomy which it promised was seen to be so executed, as to mean nothing better than subjection to Sparta. Of all the acts yet committed by Sparta, not only in perversion of the autonomy promised to every city, but in violation of all the acknowledged canons of right dealing between city and city—the most flagrant was, her recent seizure and occupation of the Kadmeia at Thebes. Her subversion (in alliance with, and partly for the benefit of, Amyntas king of Macedonia) of the free Olynthian confederacy was hardly less offensive to every Greek of large or Pan-hellenic patriotism. She appeared as the confederate of the Persian king on one side, of Amyntas the Macedonian on another, of the Syracusan despot Dionysius on a third—as betraying the independence of Greece to the foreigner, and seeking to put down everywhere within it, that free spirit which stood in the way of her own harmosts and partisan oligarchies.

Unpopular as Sparta was, however, she stood out incontestably as the head of Greece. No man dared to call in question her headship, or to provoke resistance against it. The tone of patriotic and free-spoken Greeks at this moment is manifested in two eminent residents at Athens —Lysias and Isokratês. Of these two rhetors, the former composed an oration which he publicly read at Olympia during the celebration of the 99th Olympiad, B.C. 384, three years after the peace of Antalkidas. In this oration (of which unhappily only a fragment remains, preserved by Dionysius of Halikarnassus), Lysias raises the cry of danger to Greece, partly from the Persian king, partly from the despot Dionysius of Syracuse.[1] He calls

*Strong complaint of the rhetor Lysias, expressed at the Olympic festival of 384 B.C.*

[1] Lysias, Frag. Orat. xxxiii. (Olymp.) ed. Bekker ap. Dionys. Hal. Judic. de Lysiâ, p. 520-525, Reisk.

...... Ὁρῶν οὕτως αἰσχρῶς διακειμένην τὴν Ἑλλάδα, καὶ πολλὰ μὲν αὐτῆς ὄντα ὑπὸ τῷ βαρβάρῳ, πολλὰς δὲ πόλεις ὑπὸ τυράννων ἀναστάτους γεγενημένας.

...... Ὁρῶμεν γὰρ τοὺς κινδύνους καὶ μεγάλους καὶ πανταχόθεν περιεστηκότας. Ἐπίστασθε δὲ, ὅτι

ἡ μὲν ἀρχὴ τῶν κρατούντων τῆς θαλάσσης, τῶν δὲ χρημάτων βασιλεὺς ταμίας· τὰ δὲ τῶν Ἑλλήνων σώματα, τῶν δύνασθαι δαπανᾶσθαι μένων· ναῦς δὲ πολλὰς αὐτὸς κέκτηται, πολλὰς δ' ὁ τύραννος τῆς Σικελίας.....

...... Ὥστε ἄξιον—τοὺς προγόνους μιμεῖσθαι, οἱ τοὺς μὲν βαρβάρους ἐποίησαν, τῆς ἀλλοτρίας ἐπιθυμοῦντας, τῆς σφετέρας αὐτῶν ἀστερῆσθαι· τοὺς δὲ τυράννους ἐξελάσαντες, κοινὴν

upon all Greeks to lay aside hostility and jealousies one with the other, and to unite in making head against these two really formidable enemies, as their ancestors had previously done, with equal zeal for putting down despots and for repelling the foreigner. He notes the number of Greeks (in Asia) handed over to the Persian king, whose great wealth would enable him to hire an indefinite number of Grecian soldiers, and whose naval force was superior to anything which the Greeks could muster; while the strongest naval force in Greece was that of the Syracusan Dionysius. Recognising the Lacedæmonians as chiefs of Greece, Lysias expresses his astonishment that they should quietly permit the fire to extend itself from one city to another. They ought to look upon the misfortunes of those cities which had been destroyed, both by the Persians and by Dionysius, as coming home to themselves; not to wait patiently, until the two hostile powers had united their forces to attack the centre of Greece, which yet remained independent.

Of the two common enemies—Artaxerxês and Dionysius—whom Lysias thus denounces, the latter had sent to this very Olympic festival a splendid Theôry, or legation to offer solemn sacrifice in his name; together with several chariots to contend in the race, and some excellent rhapsodes to recite poems composed by himself.

*Demonstration against the Syracusan despot Dionysius, at that festival.*

---

πᾶσι τὴν ἐλευθερίαν κατέστησεν. Θαυμάζω δὲ Λακεδαιμονίους πάντων μάλιστα, τίνι ποτὲ γνώμῃ χρώμενοι, καιομένην τὴν Ἑλλάδα περιορῶσιν, ἡγεμόνες ὄντες τῶν Ἑλλήνων, &c.

. . . . . . Οὐ τοίνυν ὁ ἐπιὼν καιρὸς τοῦ παρόντος βελτίων· οὐ γάρ ἀλλοτρίας δεῖ τὰς τῶν ἀπολωλότων συμφορὰς νομίζειν, ἀλλ' οἰκείας· οὐδ' ἀναμεῖναι, ἕως ἂν ἐπ' αὐτοὺς ἡμᾶς αἱ δυνάμεις ἀμφοτέρων (of Artaxerxês and Dionysius) ἔλθωσιν, ἀλλ' ἕως ἔτι ἔξεστι, τὴν τούτων ὕβριν κωλῦσαι.

Ephorus appears to have affirmed that there was a plan concerted between the Persian king and Dionysius, for attacking Greece in concert and dividing it between them (see Ephori Fragm. 141, ed. Didot). The assertion is made by the rhetor Aristeidês, and the allusion to Ephorus is here preserved by the Scholiast on Aristeidês (who however is mistaken, in referring it to Dionysius the younger). Aristeidês ascribes the frustration of this attack to the valour of two Athenian generals, Iphikratês and Timotheus; the former of whom captured the fleet of Dionysius, while the latter defeated the Lacedæmonian fleet at Leukas. But these events happened in 375-372 B.C., when the power of Dionysius was not so formidable or aggressive as it had been between 387-383 B.C.; moreover

The Syracusan legation, headed by Thearidês, brother of Dionysius, were clothed with rich vestments and lodged in a tent of extraordinary magnificence, decorated with gold and purple; such probably as had not been seen since the ostentatious display made by Alkibiadês[1] in the ninetieth Olympiad (B.C. 420). While instigating the spectators present to exert themselves as Greeks for the liberation of their fellow-Greeks enslaved by Dionysius, Lysias exhorted them to begin forthwith their hostile demonstration against the latter, by plundering the splendid tent before them, which insulted the sacred plain of Olympia with the spectacle of wealth extorted from Grecian sufferers. It appears that this exhortation was partially, but only partially, acted upon.[2] Some persons assailed the tents, but were probably restrained by the Eleian superintendents without difficulty.

the ships of Dionysius taken by Iphikratês were only ten in number, a small squadron. Aristeidês appears to me to have misconceived the date to which the assertion of Ephorus really referred.

[1] See Pseudo-Andokidês cont. Alkibiad. s. 30; and Ch. iv. of this History.

[2] Dionys. Hal. Judic. de Lysiâ, p. 519; Diodor. xiv. 109. ὥστε τινάς τολμῆσαι διαρπάζειν τὰς σκηνάς. Dionysius does not specify the date of this oration of Lysias; but Diodorus places it at Olympiad 99 —B.C. 388—the year before the peace of Antalkidas. On this point I venture to depart from him, and assign it to Olympiad 98, or 384 B.C., three years after the peace; the rather as his Olympic chronology appears not clear, as may be seen by comparing xv. 7 with xiv. 109.

1. The year 388 B.C. was a year of war, in which Sparta with her allies on one side—and Thebes, Athens, Corinth, and Argos, on the other—were carrying on strenuous hostilities. The war would hinder the four last-mentioned states from sending any public legation to sacrifice at the Olympic festival.

Lysias, as an Athenian metic, could hardly have gone there at all; but he certainly could not have gone there to make a public and bold oratorical demonstration.

2. The language of Lysias implies that the speech was delivered *after* the cession of the Asiatic Greeks to Persia—ὁρῶν πολλὰ μὲν αὐτῆς (Ἑλλάδος) ὄντα ὑπὸ τῷ βαρβάρῳ, &c. This is quite pertinent after the peace of Antalkidas; but not at all admissible before that peace. The same may be said about the phrase—οὐ γὰρ ἀλλοτρίας δεῖ τὰς τῶν ἀκολουθότων συμφορὰς νομίζειν, ἀλλ' οἰκείας; which must be referred to the recent subjection of the Asiatic Greeks by Persia, and of the Italian and Sicilian Greeks by Dionysius.

3. In 388 B.C.—when Athens and so large a portion of the greater cities of Greece were at war with Sparta and therefore contesting her headship—Lysias would hardly have publicly talked of the Spartans as ἡγεμόνες τῶν Ἑλλήνων, οὐκ ἀδίκως, καὶ διὰ τὴν ἔμφυτον ἀρετὴν καὶ διὰ τὴν πρὸς τὸν πόλεμον ἐπιστήμην. This remark is made also by Sievers (Geschich. Griech. his sur Schlacht von Mantineia, p. 138).

Yet the incident, taken in conjunction with the speech of Lysias, helps us to understand the apprehensions and sympathies which agitated the Olympic crowd in B.C. 384. This was the first Olympic festival after the peace of Antalkidas; a festival memorable, not only because it again brought thither Athenians, Bœotians, Corinthians, and Argeians, who must have been prevented by the preceding war from coming either in B.C. 388 or in B.C. 392—but also as it exhibited the visitors and Theôries from the Asiatic Greeks, for the first time since they had been handed over by Sparta to the Persians—and the like also from those numerous Italians and Sicilian Greeks whom Dionysius had enslaved. All these sufferers, especially the Asiatics, would doubtless be full of complaints respecting the hardship of their new lot, and against Sparta as having betrayed them; complaints, which would call forth genuine sympathy in the Athenians, Thebans, and all others who had submitted reluctantly to the peace of Antalkidas. There was thus a large body of sentiment prepared to respond to the declamations of Lysias. And many a Grecian patriot, who would be ashamed to lay hands on the Syracusan tents or envoys, would yet yield a mournful assent to the orator's remark, that the free Grecian world was on fire[1] at both sides; that Asiatics, Italians, and Sicilians, had already passed into the hands of Artaxerxês and Dionysius; and that, if these two formidable enemies should coalesce, the liberties even of central Greece would be in great danger.

It is easy to see how much such feeling of grief and shame would tend to raise antipathy against Sparta. Lysias, in that portion of his speech which we possess, disguises his censure against her under the forms of surprise. But Isokratês, who composed an analogous discourse four years afterwards (which may perhaps have been read at the next Olympic festival of B.C. 380), speaks out more plainly. He denounces the Lacedæmonians as traitors to the general security and

*Panegyrical oration of Isokratês.*

Nor would he have declaimed so ardently against the Persian king, at a time when Athens was still not despairing of Persian aid against Sparta.

On these grounds (as well as on others which I shall state when I recount the history of Dionysius), it appears to me that this oration of Lysias is unsuitable to B.C. 388 —but perfectly suitable to 384 B.C.

[1] Lysias, Orat. Olymp. Frag. ἀσιομένην τὴν Ἑλλάδα περιορῶσιν, &c.

freedom of Greece, and as seconding foreign kings as well as Grecian despots to aggrandize themselves at the cost of autonomous Grecian cities—all in the interest of their own selfish ambition. No wonder (he says) that the free and self-acting Hellenic world was every day becoming contracted into a narrower space, when the presiding city Sparta assisted Artaxerxês, Amyntas, and Dionysius to absorb it—and herself undertook unjust aggressions against Thebes, Olynthus, Phlius, and Mantineia.[1]

The preceding citations, from Lysias and Isokratês, would be sufficient to show the measure which intelligent contemporaries took, both of the state of Greece and of the conduct of Sparta, during the eight years succeeding the peace of Antalkidas (387—379 B.C.). But the philo-Laconian Xenophon is still more emphatic in his condemnation of Sparta. Having described her triumphant and seemingly unassailable position after the subjugation of Olynthus and Phlius, he proceeds to say [2]—"I could produce numerous other incidents, both in and out of Greece, to prove that the gods take careful note of impious men and of evil-doers; but the events which I am now about to relate are quite sufficient. The Lacedæmonians, who had sworn to leave each city autonomous, having violated their

*Censure upon Sparta, pronounced by the philo-Laconian Xenophon.*

oaths by seizing the citadel of Thebes, were punished by
the very men whom they had wronged—though no
one on earth had ever before triumphed over them. And
the Theban faction who had introduced them into the
citadel, with the deliberate purpose that their city should
be enslaved to Sparta in order that they might rule des-
potically themselves—were put down by no more than
seven assailants, among the exiles whom they had
banished."

*His manner of marking the point of transition in his history —from Spartan glory to Spartan disgrace.*

What must have been the hatred, and sense of abused
ascendency, entertained towards Sparta by
neutral or unfriendly Greeks, when Xenophon,
alike conspicuous for his partiality to her and
for his dislike of Thebes, could employ these
decisive words in ushering in the coming phase
of Spartan humiliation, representing it as a
well-merited judgement from the gods? The
sentence which I have just translated marks, in
the commonplace manner of the Xenophontic Hellenica,
the same moment of pointed contrast and transition—past
glory suddenly and unexpectedly darkened by supervening
misfortune—which is foreshadowed in the narrative of
Thucydidês by the dialogue between the Athenian envoys
and the Melian[1] council; or in the Œdipus and Antigonê
of Sophoklês,[2] by the warnings of the prophet Teiresias.

*B.C. 379. Thebes under Leontiadês and the philo-Spartan oligarchy, with the Spartan garrison in the Kadmeia—oppressive and tyrannical government.*

The government of Thebes had now been for three
years (since the blow struck by Phœbidas) in
the hands of Leontiadês and his oligarchical
partisans, upheld by the Spartan garrison in
the Kadmeia. Respecting the details of its
proceedings we have scarce any information.
We can only (as above remarked) judge of it
by analogy of the Thirty tyrants at Athens,
and of the Lysandrian Dekarchies, to which it
was exactly similar in origin, position, and
interests. That the general spirit of it must
have been cruel, oppressive, and rapacious—we
cannot doubt; though in what degree we have
no means of knowing. The appetites of uncontrolled rulers, as well as those of a large foreign garrison,
would ensure such a result: besides which, those rulers

---

[1] See above in this History—the close of Chapter lvi.
[2] Soph. Œdip. Tyr. 450; Antigon. 1056.

## CHAP. LXXVII. THEBES UNDER THE OLIGARCHY. 295

must have been in constant fear of risings or conspiracies amidst a body of high-spirited citizens who saw their city degraded, from being the chief of the Bœotian federation, into nothing better than a captive dependency of Sparta. Such fear was aggravated by the vicinity of a numerous body of Theban exiles, belonging to the opposite or anti-Spartan party; three or four hundred of whom had fled to Athens at the first seizure of their leader Ismenias, and had been doubtless joined subsequently by others. So strongly did the Theban rulers apprehend mischief from these exiles, that they hired assassins to take them off by private murder at Athens; and actually succeeded in thus killing Androkleidas, chief of the band and chief successor of the deceased Ismenias—though they missed their blows at the rest.[1] And we may be sure that they made the prison in Thebes subservient to multiplied enormities and executions, when we read not only that 150 prisoners were found in it when the government was put down,[2] but also that in the fervour of that revolutionary movement, the slain gaoler was an object of such fierce antipathy, that his corpse was trodden and spit upon by a crowd of Theban women.[3] In Thebes, as in other Grecian cities, the women not only took no part in political disputes, but rarely even showed themselves in public;[4] so that this furious demonstration of vindictive sentiment must have been generated by the loss or maltreatment of sons, husbands, and brothers.

The Theban exiles found at Athens not only secure shelter, but genuine sympathy with their complaints against Lacedæmonian injustice. The generous countenance which had been shown by the Thebans, twenty-four years before, to Thrasybulus and the other Athenian refugees, during the omnipotence of the Thirty—was

*Discontent at Thebes, though under compression. Theban exiles at Athens.*

---

[1] Plutarch, Pelopidas, c. 6: compare Plutarch, De Gen. Socr. c. 29. p. 596 B.
[2] Xenoph. Hellen. v. 4, 14.
[3] Plutarch, De Gen. Socr. c. 33. p. 598 B. C. ᾧ καὶ μεθ' ἡμέραν ἐπενέθησαν καὶ προσέπτυσαν οὐκ ὀλίγαι γυναῖκες.
Among the prisoners was a distinguished Theban of the democratic party, named Amphitheus. He was about to be shortly executed, and the conspirators, personally attached to him, seem to have accelerated the hour of their plot partly to preserve his life (Plutarch, De Gen. Socrat. p. 577 D. p. 586 F.).
[4] The language of Plutarch (De Gen. Socrat. c. 33. p. 598 C.) is

now gratefully requited under this reversal of fortune to both cities;[1] and requited too in defiance of the menaces of Sparta, who demanded that the exiles should be expelled —as she had in the earlier occasion demanded that the Athenian refugees should be dismissed from Thebes. To protect these Theban exiles, however, was all that Athens could do. Their restoration was a task beyond her power —and seemingly yet more beyond their own. For the existing government of Thebes was firmly seated, and had the citizens completely under control. Administered by a small faction, Archias, Philippus, Hypatês, and Leontiadês (among whom the two first were at this moment polemarchs, though the last was the most energetic and resolute)—it was at the same time sustained by the large garrison of 1500 Lacedæmonians and allies,[2] under Lysanoridas and two other harmosts, in the Kadmeia—as well as by the Lacedæmonian posts in the other Bœotian cities around— Orchomenus, Thespiæ, Platæa, Tanagra, &c. Though the general body of Theban sentiment in the city was decidedly adverse to the government, and though the young men while exercising in the palæstra (gymnastic exercises being more strenuously prosecuted at Thebes than anywhere else except at Sparta) kept up by private communication the ardour of an earnest, but compressed, patriotism—yet

Illustrated by the description given in the harangue of Lykurgus cont. Leokrat. (c. xl. s. 40)—of the universal alarm prevalent in Athens after the battle of Chæroneia, such that even the women could not stay in their houses—ἀναξίως αὐτῶν καὶ τῆς πόλεως ὁρωμέναις, &c. Compare also the words of Makaria, in the Herakleidæ of Euripidês, 475; and Diodor. xlii. 55—in his description of the capture of Selinus in Sicily.

[1] Plutarch, Pelopidas, c. 6. See this sentiment of gratitude on the part of Athenian democrats, towards those Thebans who had sheltered them at Thebes during the exile along with Thrasybulus —strikingly brought out in an oration of Lysias, of which unfortunately only a fragment remains (Lysias, Frag. 46, 47, Bekk.; Dionys. Hal. Judic. de Isæo, p. 604). The speaker of this oration had been received at Thebes by Kephisodotus the father of Phereníkus; the latter was now in exile at Athens; and the speaker had not only welcomed him (Phereníkus) to his house with brotherly affection, but also delivered this oration on his behalf before the Dikastery; Phereníkus having rightful claims on the property left behind by the assassinated Androkleidas.

[2] Diodor. xv. 26; Plutarch, Pelopidas, c. 12; Plutarch, De Gen. Socr. c. 17. p. 586 E.

In another passage of the treatise (the last sentence but one) he sets down the numbers in the Kadmeia at 6000; but the smaller number is most likely to be true.

all manifestation or assemblage was forcibly kept down, and the commanding posts of the lower town, as well as the citadel, were held in vigilant occupation by the ruling minority.[1]

For a certain time, the Theban exiles at Athens waited in hopes of some rising at home, or some positive aid from the Athenians. At length, in the third winter after their flight, they began to despair of encouragement from either quarter, and resolved to take the initiative upon themselves. Among them were numbered several men of the richest and highest families at Thebes, proprietors of chariots, of jockeys, and of training establishments for contending at the various festivals: Pelopidas, Mellon, Damokleidas, Theopompus, Pherenikus, and others.[2] *The Theban exiles at Athens, after waiting some time in hopes of a rising at Thebes, resolve to begin a movement themselves.*

Of these the most forward in originating aggressive measures, though almost the youngest, was Pelopidas; whose daring and self-devotion, in an enterprise which seemed utterly desperate, soon communicated itself to a handful of his comrades. The exiles, keeping up constant private correspondence with their friends in Thebes, felt assured of the sympathy of the citizens generally, if they could once strike a blow. Yet nothing less would be sufficient than the destruction of the four rulers, Leontiades and his colleagues—nor would any one within the city devote himself to so hopeless a danger. It was this conspiracy which Pelopidas, Mellon, and five or ten other exiles (the entire band is differently numbered, by some as seven, by others, twelve[3]) undertook to execute. Many of their friends in Thebes came in as auxiliaries to them, who would not have *Pelopidas takes the lead—he, with Mellon and five other exiles, undertakes the task of destroying the rulers of Thebes. Co-operation of Phyllidas the secretary, and Charon at Thebes.*

---

[1] Plutarch, De Gen. Socr. c. 4. p. 577 B; c. 17. p. 587 B; c. 25. p. 594 C; c. 27. p. 595 A.

[2] Plutarch, Pelopidas, c. 7, 8. Plutarch, De Gen. Socrat. c. 17. p. 587 D. Τῶν Μελλωνος ἁρμηλατῶν 'ἐπιστάτης ...... Ἀρ' οὐ Κλίδωνα λέγεις, τὸν κέλητι τὰ Ἡραῖα νικῶντα ἐρούσιν;

[3] Xenophon says seven (Hellen. v. 4, 1, 2); Plutarch and Cornelius Nepos say twelve (Plutarch, De Gen. Socr. c. 1. p. 576 C.; Plutarch, Pelopidas, c. 8—13; Cornel. Nepos, Pelopidas, c. 2).

It is remarkable that Xenophon never mentions the name of Pelopidas in this conspiracy; nor indeed (with one exception) throughout his Hellenica.

embarked in the design as primary actors. Of all auxiliaries, the most effective and indispensable was Phyllidas, the secretary of the polemarchs; next to him, Charon, an eminent and earnest patriot. Phyllidas, having been dispatched to Athens on official business, entered into secret conference with the conspirators, concerted with them the day for their coming to Thebes, and even engaged to provide for them access to the persons of the polemarchs. Charon not only promised them concealment in his house, from their first coming within the gates, until the moment of striking their blow should have arrived—but also entered his name to share in the armed attack. Nevertheless, in spite of such partial encouragements, the plan still appeared desperate to many who wished heartily for its success. Epaminondas, for example—who now for the first time comes before us—resident at Thebes, and not merely sympathising with the political views of Pelopidas, but also bound to him by intimate friendship—dissuaded others from the attempt, and declined participating in it. He announced distinctly that he would not become an accomplice in civil bloodshed. It appears that there were men among the exiles whose violence made him fear that they would not, like Pelopidas, draw the sword exclusively against Leontiadês and his colleagues, but would avail themselves of success to perpetrate unmeasured violence against other political enemies.[1]

*B.C. 379.*
*Plans of Phyllidas for admitting the conspirators into Thebes and the government-house—he invites the polemarchs to a banquet.*

The day for the enterprise was determined by Phyllidas the secretary, who had prepared an evening banquet for Archias and Philippus, in celebration of the period when they were going out of office as polemarchs—and who had promised on that occasion to bring into their company some women remarkable for beauty, as well as of the best families in Thebes.[2] In concert with the general body of Theban exiles at Athens, who held themselves ready on the borders of Attica, together with some Athenian sympathisers, to march to Thebes the instant that they should receive intimation—and in concert also with two out of

---

[1] Plutarch, De Gen. Socr. c. 3. p. 576 E.; p. 577 A.
[2] Xen. Hellen. v. 4, 4. τὰς σεμνοτάτας καὶ καλλίστας τῶν ἐν Θήβαις. Plutarch, De Gen. Socr. c. 4. p. 577 C.; Plutarch, Pelopid. c. 9.
The Theban women were distinguished for majestic figure and beauty (Dikæarchus, Vit. Græc. p. 144, ed. Fuhr.).

the ten Stratêgi of Athens, who took on themselves privately to countenance the enterprise, without any public vote—Pelopidas and Mellon, and their five companions,[1] crossed Kithæron from Athens to Thebes. It was wet weather, about December B.C. 379; they were disguised as rustics or hunters, with no other arms than a concealed dagger; and they got within the gates of Thebes one by one at nightfall, just when the latest farming-men were coming home from their fields. All of them arrived safe at the house of Charon, the appointed rendezvous.

It was, however, by mere accident that they had not been turned back, and the whole scheme frustrated. For a Theban named Hipposthenidas, friendly to the conspiracy, but faint-hearted, who had been let into the secret against the will of Phyllidas—became so frightened as the moment of execution approached, that he took upon himself, without the knowledge of the rest, to dispatch Chlidon, a faithful slave of Mellon, ordering him to go forth on horseback from Thebes, to meet his master on the road, and to desire that he and his comrades would go back to Attica, since circumstances had happened to render the project for the moment impracticable. Chlidon, going home to fetch his bridle, but not finding it in its usual place, asked his wife where it was. The woman, at first pretending to look for it, at last confessed that she had lent it to a neighbour. Chlidon became so irritated with this delay, that he got into loud altercation with his wife, who on her part wished him ill-luck with his journey. He at last beat her, until neighbours ran in to interpose. His departure was thus accidentally frustrated, so that the intended message of countermand never reached the conspirators on their way.[2]

*The scheme very nearly frustrated—accident which prevented Chlidon from delivering his message.*

In the house of Charon they remained concealed all the ensuing day, on the evening of which the banquet of Archias and Philippus was to take place. Phyllidas had laid his plan for introducing them at that banquet, at the moment

---

[1] Plutarch (Pelopid. c. 25; De Gen. Socr. c. 24. p. 594 D.) mentions Menekleidas, Damokleidas, and Theopompus among them. Compare Cornel. Nepos, Pelopid. c. 2.

[2] Plutarch, Pelopidas, c. 8; Plutarch, De Gen. Socrat. 17. p. 586 B.; c. 18. p. 597 D.-E.

when the two polemarchs had become full of wine, in female attire, as being the women whose visit was expected. The hour had nearly arrived, and they were preparing to play their parts, when an unexpected messenger knocked at the door, summoning Charon instantly into the presence of the polemarchs. All within were thunderstruck with the summons, which seemed to imply that the plot had been divulged, perhaps by the timid Hipposthenidas. It was agreed among them that Charon must obey at once. Nevertheless he himself, even in the perilous uncertainty which beset him, was most of all apprehensive lest the friends whom he had sheltered should suspect him of treachery towards themselves and their cause. Before departing, therefore, he sent for his only son, a youth of fifteen and of conspicuous promise in every way. This youth he placed in the hands of Pelopidas, as a hostage for his own fidelity. But Pelopidas and the rest, vehemently disclaiming all suspicion, entreated Charon to put his son away, out of the reach of that danger in which all were now involved. Charon, however, could not be prevailed on to comply, and left his son among them to share the fate of the rest. He went into the presence of Archias and Philippus; whom he found already half-intoxicated, but informed, by intelligence from Athens, that some plot, they knew not by whom, was afloat. They had sent for him to question him, as a known friend of the exiles; but he had little difficulty, aided by the collusion of Phyllidas, in blinding the vague suspicions of drunken men, anxious only to resume their conviviality.[1] He was allowed to retire and rejoin his friends. Nevertheless soon after his departure—so many were the favourable chances which befel these improvident

*Pelopidas and Mellon get secretly into Thebes, and conceal themselves in the house of Charon. Sudden summons sent by the polemarchs to Charon. Charon places his son in the hands of Pelopidas as a hostage— warning to the polemarchs from Athens— they leave it abroad.*

[1] Xenophon does not mention this separate summons and visit of Charon to the polemarchs—nor anything about the scene with his son. He only notices Charon as having harboured the conspirators in his house, and seems even to speak of him as a person of little consequence— κατά Χαρωνί τινι, &c. (v. 4, 3).

The anecdote is mentioned in both the compositions of Plutarch (De Gen. Socr. c. 28. p. 595; and Pelopidas, c. 9), and is too interesting to be omitted, being perfectly consistent with what we read in Xenophon; though it has perhaps somewhat of a theatrical air.

CHAP. LXXVII.   THE POLEMARCHS SLAIN.   301

men—a fresh message was delivered to Archias the polemarch, from his namesake Archias the Athenian Hierophant, giving an exact account of the names and scheme of the conspirators, which had become known to the philo-Laconian party at Athens. The messenger who bore this dispatch delivered it to Archias with an intimation, that it related to very serious matters. "Serious matters for to-morrow," said the polemarch, as he put the dispatch, unopened and unread, under the pillow of the couch on which he was reclining.[1]

Returning to their carousal, Archias and Philippus impatiently called upon Phyllidas to introduce the women according to his promise. Upon this the secretary retired, and brought the conspirators, clothed in female attire, into an adjoining chamber; then going back to the polemarchs, he informed them that the women would not come in unless all the domestics were first dismissed. An order was forthwith given that these latter should depart, while Phyllidas took care that they should be well provided with wine at the lodging of one among their number. The polemarchs were thus left only with one or two friends at table, half-intoxicated as well as themselves; among them Kabeirichus, the archon of the year, who always throughout his term kept the consecrated spear of office in actual possession, and had it at that moment close to his person. Phyllidas now conducted the pretended women into the banqueting-room; three of them attired as ladies of distinction, the four others following as female attendants. Their long veils, and ample folds of clothing, were quite sufficient as disguise—even had the guests at table been sober—until they sat down by the side of the polemarchs; and the instant of lifting their veils was the signal for using their daggers. Archias and Philippus were slain at once and with little resistance; but Kabeirichus

*Phyllidas brings the conspirators, in female attire, into the room where the polemarchs are banqueting—Archias, Philippus, and Kabeirichus are assassinated.*

---

[1] Plutarch, Pelopidas, c. 10; Plutarch, De Gen. Socr. c. 30. p. 598 F. Εἰς αὔριον τὰ σπουδαῖα. This occurrence also finds no place in the narrative of Xenophon. Cornelius Nepos, Pelopidas, c. 3. Æneas (Poliorcetic. 31) makes a general reference to the omission of immediate opening of letters arrived, as having caused the capture of the Kadmeia; which was however only its remote consequence.

with his spear tried to defend himself, and thus perished with the others, though the conspirators had not originally intended to take his life.[1]

*Leontiadês and Hy- patês are slain in their houses.* Having been thus far successful, Phyllidas conducted three of the conspirators—Pelopidas, Kephisodôrus, and Damokleidas—to the house of Leontiadês, into which he obtained admittance by announcing himself as the bearer of an order from the polemarchs. Leontiadês was reclining after supper, with his wife sitting spinning wool by his side, when they entered his chamber. Being a brave and powerful man, he started up, seized his sword, and mortally wounded Kephisodôrus in the throat; a desperate struggle then ensued between him and Pelopidas in the narrow doorway, where there was no room for a third to approach. At length, however, Pelopidas overthrew and killed him,

---

[1] The description given by Xenophon, of this assassination of the polemarchs at Thebes, differs materially from that of Plutarch. I follow Xenophon in the main; introducing however several of the details found in Plutarch, which are interesting, and which have the air of being authentic. Xenophon himself intimates (Hellen. v. 4, 7), that besides the story given in the text, there was also another story told by some—that Mellon and his companions had got access to the polemarchs in the guise of drunken revellers. It is this latter story which Plutarch has adopted, and which carries him into many details quite inconsistent with the narrative of Xenophon. I think the story, of the conspirators having been introduced in female attire, the more probable of the two. It is borne out by the exact analogy of what Herodotus tells us respecting Alexander son of Amyntas, prince of Macedonia (Herod. v. 20).

Compare Plutarch, Pelopidas, c. 10, 11; Plutarch, De Gen. Socrat. c. 31. p. 597. Polyænus (II. 4, 3) gives a story with many different circumstances, yet agreeing in the fact that Pelopidas in female attire killed the Spartan general. The story alluded to by Aristotle (Polit. v. 5, 10), though he names both Thebes and Archias, can hardly refer to this event.

It is Plutarch however who mentions the presence of Kabeirichus the archon at the banquet, and the curious Theban custom that the archon during his year of office never left out of his hand the consecrated spear. As a Bœotian born, Plutarch was doubtless familiar with these old customs.

From what other authors Plutarch copied the abundant details of this revolution at Thebes, which he interweaves in the life of Pelopidas and in the treatise called De Genio Socratis—we do not know. Some critics suppose him to have borrowed from Dionysodôrus and Anaxis—Bœotian historians whose work comprised this period, but of whom not a single fragment is preserved (see Fragm. Histor. Græc. ed. Didot, vol. ii. p. 84).

after which they retired, enjoining the wife with threats to remain silent, and closing the door after them with peremptory commands that it should not be again opened. They then went to the house of Hypatês, whom they slew while he attempted to escape over the roof.[1]

The four great rulers of the philo-Laconian party in Thebes, having been now put to death, Phyllidas proceeded with the conspirators to the prison. Here the gaoler, a confidential agent in the oppressions of the deceased governors, hesitated to admit him; but was slain by a sudden thrust with his spear, so as to ensure free admission to all. To liberate the prisoners, probably for the most part men of kindred politics with the conspirators—to furnish them with arms taken from the battle-spoils hanging up in the neighbouring porticoes—and to range them in battle order near the temple of Amphion— were the next proceedings; after which they began to feel some assurance of safety and triumph.[2] Epaminondas and Gorgidas, apprised of what had occurred, were the first who appeared in arms with a few friends to sustain the cause; while proclamation was everywhere made aloud, through heralds, that the despots were slain—that Thebes was free—and that all Thebans who valued freedom should muster in arms in the market-place. There were at that moment in Thebes many trumpeters who had come to contend for the prize at the approaching festival of the Herakleia. Hipposthenidas engaged these men to blow their trumpets in different parts of the city, and thus everywhere to excite the citizens to arms.[3]

*Phyllidas opens the prison, and sets free the prisoners. Epaminondas and many other citizens appear in arms.*

---

[1] Xen. Hell. v. 4, 9; Plutarch, Pelop. c. 11, 12; and De Gen. Socr. p. 597 D–F. Here again Xenophon and Plutarch differ; the latter represents that Pelopidas got into the house of Leontiadês *without* Phyllidas—which appears to me altogether improbable. On the other hand, Xenophon mentions nothing about the defence of Leontiadês and his personal conflict with Pelopidas, which I copy from Plutarch. So brave a man as Leontiadês, awake and sober, would not let himself be slain without a defence dangerous to assailants. Plutarch, in another place, singles out the death of Leontiadês as the marking circumstance of the whole glorious enterprise, and the most impressive to Pelopidas (Plutarch —Non posse suaviter vivi secundum Epicurum—p. 1099 A-E.).

[2] Xenoph. Hellen. v. 4, 8; Plutarch, Pelop. c. 12; De Gen. Socr. p. 598 B.

[3] This is a curious piece of detail, which we learn from Plutarch (De Gen. Socr. c. 34. p. 598 D.). The Orchomenian Inscriptions

Although during the darkness surprise was the prevalent feeling, and no one knew what to do—yet so soon as day dawned, and the truth became known, there was but one feeling of joy and patriotic enthusiasm among the majority of the citizens.¹ Both horsemen and hoplites hastened in arms to the agora. Here for the first time since the seizure of the Kadmeia by Phœbidas, a formal assembly of the Theban people was convened, before which Pelopidas and his fellow-conspirators presented themselves. The priests of the city crowned them with wreaths, and thanked them in the name of the local gods; while the assembly hailed them with acclamations of delight and gratitude, nominating with one voice Pelopidas, Mellon, and Charon as the first renewed Bœotarchs.² The revival of this title, which had been dropt since the peace of Antalkidas, was in itself an event of no mean significance; implying not merely that Thebes had waked up again into freedom, but that the Bœotian confederacy also had been, or would be, restored.

*Universal joy among the citizens on the ensuing morning, when the event was known. General assembly in the market-place—Pelopidas, Mellon, and Charon are named the first Bœotarchs.*

Messengers had been forthwith dispatched by the conspirators to Attica to communicate their success; upon which all the remaining exiles, with the two Athenian generals privy to the plot and a body of Athenian volunteers, or *corps francs*, all of whom were ready on the borders awaiting the summons—flocked to Thebes to complete the work. The Spartan generals, on their side also, sent to Platæa and Thespiæ for aid. During the whole night, they had been distracted and alarmed by the disturbance in the city; lights showing themselves here and there with trumpets sounding and shouts for the recent success.³ Apprised speedily of the slaughter of the polemarchs, from

*Aid to the conspirators from private sympathisers in Attica. Alarm of the Spartans in the Kadmeia—they send for reinforcements.*

---

In Boeckh's Collection record the prizes given to these Σαλπιγκταί or trumpeters (see Boeckh, Corp. Inscr. No. 1584, 1585, &c.).

¹ The unanimous joy with which the consummation of the revolution was welcomed in Thebes—and the ardour with which the citizens turned out to support it by armed force—is attested by Xenophon, no very willing witness—Hellen. v. 4, 9. ἐπεὶ δ' ἡμέρα ἦν καὶ φανερὸν ἦν τὸ γεγενημένον, ταχὺ δὴ καὶ οἱ ὁπλῖται καὶ οἱ ἱππεῖς σὺν τοῖς ὅπλοις ἐξεβοήθουν.

² Plutarch, Pelop. c. 13.

³ Plutarch, De Gen. Socr. p. 598 E; Pelop. c. 12.

whom they had been accustomed to receive orders, they knew not whom to trust or to consult, while they were doubtless beset by affrighted fugitives of the now defeated party, who would hurry up to the Kadmeia for safety. They reckoned at first on a diversion in their favour from the forces at Plataea and Thespiae. But these forces were not permitted even to approach the city-gate; being vigorously charged, as soon as they came in sight, by the newly-mustered Theban cavalry, and forced to retreat with loss. The Lacedæmonians in the citadel were thus not only left without support, but saw their enemies in the city reinforced by the other exiles, and by the auxiliary volunteers.[1]

*Pelopidas and the Thebans prepare to storm the Kadmeia—the Lacedæmonian garrison capitulate and are dismissed—several of the oligarchical Thebans are put to death in trying to go away along with them. The barmost who surrendered the Kadmeia is put to death by the Spartans.*

Meanwhile Pelopidas and the other new Bœotarchs found themselves at the head of a body of armed citizens, full of devoted patriotism and unanimous in hailing the recent revolution. They availed themselves of this first burst of fervour to prepare for storming the Kadmeia without delay, knowing the importance of forestalling all aid from Sparta. And the citizens were already rushing up to the assault—proclamation being made of large rewards to those who should first force their way in—when the Lacedæmonian commander sent proposals for a capitulation.[2] Undisturbed egress from Thebes, with the honours of war, being readily guaranteed to him by oath, the Kadmeia was then surrendered. As the Spartans were marching out of the gates, many Thebans of the defeated party went forth also. But against these latter the exasperation of the victors was so ungovernable, that several of the most odious were seized as they passed, and put to death; in some

---

[1] Xenophon expressly mentions that the Athenians who were invited to come, and who actually did come, to Thebes, were the two generals and the volunteers; all of whom were before privy to the plot and were in readiness on the borders of Attica—τοὺς πρὸς τοῖς ὁρίοις Ἀθηναίων, καὶ τοὺς δύο τῶν στρατηγῶν—οἱ Ἀθηναῖοι ἀπὸ τῶν ὁρίων ἤδη ἐτρῆσαν (Hellen. v. 4, θ, 10).

[2] Xen. Hellen. v. 4, 10, 11. προσέβαλον πρὸς τὴν ἀκρόπολιν—τὴν προθυμίαν τῶν προσιόντων ἑκάντων δωρῶν, &c.

Diodorus. xv. 25. ἔπειτα τοὺς πολίτας ἐπὶ τὴν ἐλευθερίαν παρακαλέσαντες (the successful Theban conspirators, Pelopidas, &c.) εὐνέφρους ἔσχον ἅπαντας τοὺς Θηβαίους.

cases, even their children along with them. And more of them would have been thus dispatched, had not the Athenian auxiliaries, with generous anxiety, exerted every effort to get them out of sight and put them into safety.¹ We are not told—nor is it certain—that these Thebans were protected under the capitulation. Even had they been so, however, the wrathful impulse might still have prevailed against them.

Of the three harmosts who thus evacuated the Kadmeia without a blow, two were put to death, the third was heavily fined and banished by the authorities at Sparta.² We do not know what the fortifications of the Kadmeia were, nor how far it was provisioned. But we can hardly wonder that these officers were considered to have dishonoured the Lacedæmonian arms, by making no attempt to defend it; when we recollect that hardly more than four or five days would be required to procure adequate relief from home—and that forty-three years afterwards, the Macedonian garrison in the same place maintained itself against the Thebans in the city for more than fourteen days, until the return of Alexander from Illyria.³ The first messenger who brought news to Sparta of the conspiracy and revolution at Thebes, appears to have communicated at the same time that the garrison had evacuated the Kadmeia and was in full retreat, with a train of Theban exiles from the defeated party.⁴

¹ Xen. Hellen. v. 4, 12.
² Xen. Hellen. v. 4, 13; Diodor. xv. 27.
Plutarch (Pelopid. c. 13) augments the theatrical effect by saying that the Lacedæmonian garrison on its retreat, actually met at Megara the reinforcements under King Kleombrotus, which had advanced thus far, on their march to relieve the Kadmeia. But this is highly improbable. The account of Xenophon intimates clearly that the Kadmeia was surrendered on the next morning after the nocturnal movement. The commanders capitulated in the first moment of distraction and despair, without even standing an assault.
³ Arrian, i. 8.

⁴ In recounting this revolution at Thebes, and the proceedings of the Athenians in regard to it, I have followed Xenophon almost entirely.

Diodorus (xv. 25, 26) concurs with Xenophon in stating that the Theban exiles got back from Attica to Thebes by night, partly through the concurrence of the Athenians (συνεκβεβλημένων τῶν Ἀθηναίων)—slew the rulers—called the citizens to freedom next morning, finding all hearty in the cause—and then proceeded to besiege the 1500 Lacedæmonians and Peloponnesians in the Kadmeia.

But after thus much of agreement, Diodorus states what followed, in a manner quite inconsistent

This revolution at Thebes came like an electric shock upon the Grecian world. With a modern reader, the

with Xenophon; thus (he tells us)— The Lacedæmonian commander sent instant intelligence to Sparta of what had happened, with request for a reinforcement. The Thebans at once attempted to storm the Kadmeia, but were repulsed with great loss, both of killed and wounded. Fearing that they might not be able to take the fort before reinforcement should come from Sparta, they sent envoys to Athens to ask for aid, reminding the Athenians that they (the Thebans) had helped to emancipate Athens from the Thirty, and to restore the democracy (ὁκομιμνήσκοντες μέν ὅτι καὶ αὐτοὶ συγκαταγάγοιεν τὸν δῆμον τῶν Ἀθηναίων καθ' ὃν καιρὸν ὑπὸ τῶν τριάκοντα κατεδουλώθησαν). The Athenians, partly from desire to requite this favour, partly from a wish to secure the Thebans as allies against Sparta, passed a public vote to assist them forthwith. Demophon the general got together 5000 hoplites and 500 horsemen, with whom he hastened to Thebes on the next day; and all the remaining population were prepared to follow, if necessary (πανδημεί). All the other cities in Bœotia also sent aid to Thebes, too—so that there was assembled there a large force of 12,000 hoplites and 2000 horsemen. This united force, the Athenians being among them, assaulted the Kadmeia day and night, relieving each other; but were repelled with great loss of killed and wounded. At length the garrison found themselves without provisions; the Spartans were tardy in sending reinforcement; and sedition broke out among the Peloponnesian allies who formed the far larger part of the garrison. These Peloponnesians, refusing to fight longer, insisted upon capitulating; which the Lacedæmonian governor was obliged perforce to do, though both he and the Spartans along with him desired to hold out to the death. The Kadmeia was accordingly surrendered, and the garrison went back to Peloponnesus. The Lacedæmonian reinforcement from Sparta arrived only a little too late.

All these circumstances stated by Diodorus are not only completely different from Xenophon, but irreconcileable with his conception of the event. We must reject either the one or the other.

Now, Xenophon is not merely the better witness of the two, but is in this case sustained by all the collateral probabilities of the case.

1. Diodorus represents the Athenians as having despatched by public vote, assistance to Thebes, in order to requite the assistance which the Thebans had before sent to restore the Athenian democracy against the Thirty. Now this is incorrect in point of fact. The Thebans had *never sent any assistance*, positive or ostensible, to Thrasybulus and the Athenian democrats against the Thirty. They had assisted Thrasybulus underhand, and without any public government-act; and they had refused to serve along with the Spartans against him. But they never sent any force to help him against the Thirty. Consequently, the Athenians could not now have sent any public force to Thebes, *in requital* for a similar favour done before by the Thebans to them.

2. Had the Athenians passed a formal vote, sent a large public army, and taken vigorous part in

x 2

assassination of the four leaders, in their houses and at
the banquet, raises a sentiment of repugnance
which withdraws his attention from the other
features of this memorable deed. Now an
ancient Greek not only had no such repugnance,
but sympathised with the complete revenge for
the seizure of the Kadmeia and the death of

*Powerful sensation produced by this incident throughout the Grecian world.*

several bloody assaults on the
Lacedæmonian garrison in the
Kadmeia—this would have been
the most flagrant and unequivocal commencement of hostilities
against Sparta. No Spartan envoys
could, after that, have gone to
Athens, and stayed safely in the
house of the Proxenus—as we know
from Xenophon that they did. Besides—the story of Sphodrias (presently to be recounted) proves
distinctly that Athens was at peace
with Sparta, and had committed
no act of hostility against her, for
three or four months at least after
the revolution at Thebes. It therefore refutes the narrative of Diodorus about the public vote of the
Athenians, and the public Athenian force under Demophon, aiding
in the attack of the Kadmeia.
Strange to say—Diodorus himself,
three chapters afterwards (xv. 29)
relates this story about Sphodrias,
just in the same manner (with little
difference) as Xenophon; ushering
in the story with a declaration,
that *the Athenians were still at
peace with Sparta*, and forgetting
that he had himself recounted a
distinct rupture of that peace on
the part of the Athenians.

2. The news of the revolution at
Thebes must necessarily have taken
the Athenian public completely by
surprise (though some few Athenians were privy to the scheme),
because it was a scheme which had
no chance of succeeding except by
profound secrecy. Now, that the
Athenian public, hearing the news

for the first time—having no positive act to complain of on the part
of Sparta, and much reason to fear
her power—having had no previous
circumstances to work them up,
or prepare them for any dangerous
resolve—should identify themselves
at once with Thebes, and provoke
war with Sparta in the impetuous
manner stated by Diodorus—this
is, in my judgement, eminently
improbable, requiring good evidence to induce us to believe it.

4. Assume the statement of Diodorus to be true—what reasonable
explanation can be given of the
erroneous version which we read
in Xenophon? The facts as he
recounts them conflict most pointedly with his Philo-Laconian partialities; first, the overthrow of
the Lacedæmonian power at Thebes, by a handful of exiles; still
more, the whole story of Sphodrias
and his acquittal.

But assume the statement of
Xenophon to be true—and we can
give a very plausible explanation
how the erroneous version in Diodorus arose. A few months later,
after the acquittal of Sphodrias at
Sparta, the Athenians really did
enter heartily into the alliance of
Thebes, and sent a large public
force (indeed 5000 hoplites, the
same number as those of Demophon, according to Diodorus, c. 32)
to assist her in repelling Agesilaus
with the Spartan army. It is by
no means unnatural that their
public vote and expedition undertaken about July 378 B.C.—should

Ismenias; while he admired, besides, the extraordinary personal daring of Pelopidas and Mellon—the skilful forecast of the plot, and the sudden overthrow, by a force so contemptibly small, of a government which the day before seemed unassailable.[1] It deserves note that we here see the richest men in Thebes undertaking a risk, single-handed and with their own persons, which must have appeared on a reasonable estimate little less than desperate. From the Homeric Odysseus and Achilles down to the end of free Hellenism, the rich Greek strips in the palæstra,[2] and exposes his person in the ranks as a soldier like the poorest citizens; being generally superior to them in strength and bodily efficiency.

have been erroneously thrown back to December 379 B.C. The Athenian orators were fond of boasting that Athens had saved the Thebans from Sparta; and this might be said with some truth, in reference to the aid which she really rendered afterwards. Isokrates (Or. xiv. Plataic. s. 31) makes this boast in general terms; but Deinarchos (cont. Demosthen. s. 40) is more distinct, and gives in a few words a version the same as that which we find in Diodorus; so also does Aristeidês, in two very brief allusions (Panathen. p. 172, and Or. xxxviii. Socialis, p. 484—479). Possibly Aristeidês as well as Diodorus may have copied from Ephorus; but however this may be, it is easy to understand the mistake out of which their version grew.

5. Lastly, Plut. mentions nothing about the public vote of the Athenians, and the regular division of troops under Demophon which Diodorus asserts to have aided in the storming of the Kadmeia. See Plutarch (De Gen. Socrat. ad fin. Agesil. c. 23; Pelopid. 12, 13). He intimates only, as Xenophon does, that there were some Athenian volunteers who assisted the exiles.

M. Bohdanis (Vitæ Iphicratis, Chabriæ, &c. p. 88-43) discusses this discrepancy at considerable length, and often the opinion of various German authors in respect to it, with none of whom I altogether concur.

In my judgement, the proper solution is, to reject altogether (as belonging to a later time) the statement of Diodorus, respecting the public vote at Athens, and the army said to have been sent to Thebes under Demophon; and to accept the more credible narrative of Xenophon; which ascribes to Athens a reasonable prudence, and great fear of Sparta—qualities such as Athenian orators would not be disposed to boast of. According to that narrative, the question about sending Athenians to aid in storming the Kadmeia could hardly have been submitted for public discussion, since that citadel was surrendered at once by the intimidated garrison.

[1] The daring coup de main of Pelopidas and Mellon, against the government of Thebes, bears a remarkable analogy to that by which Evagoras got into Salamis and overthrew the previous despot (Isokratês, Or. ix. Evagor. s. 34).

[2] See, in illustration of Greek sentiment on this point, Xeno-

As the revolution in Thebes acted forcibly on the Grecian mind from the manner in which it was accomplished, so by its positive effects it altered forthwith the balance of power in Greece. The empire of Sparta, far from being undisputed and nearly universal over Greece, is from henceforward only maintained by more or less of effort, until at length it is completely overthrown.[1]

*It alters the balance of power, and the tenure of Spartan empire.*

The exiles from Thebes, arriving at Sparta, inflamed both the Ephors, and the miso-Theban Agesilaus, to the highest pitch. Though it was then the depth of winter,[2] an expedition was decreed forthwith against Thebes, and the allied contingents were summoned. Agesilaus declined to take the command of it, on the ground that he was above sixty years of age, and therefore no longer liable to compulsory foreign service. But this (says Xenophon[3]) was not his real reason. He was afraid that his enemies at Sparta would say—"Here is Agesilaus again putting us to expense, in order that he may uphold despots in other cities"—as he had just done, and had been reproached with doing, at Phlius; a second proof that the reproaches against Sparta (which I have cited a few pages above from Lysias and Isokratês) of allying

*Indignation in Sparta at the revolution of Thebes—a Spartan army sent forth at once, under King Kleombrotus. He retires from Bœotia without achieving anything.*

---

[1] phon, Hellen. III. 4, 19; and Xenophon, Enc. Ages. L 28.

[2] If indeed we could believe Isokratês, speaking through the mouth of a Platæan, it would seem that the Thebans, immediately after their revolution, sent an humble embassy to Sparta deprecating hostility, entreating to be admitted as allies, and promising service even against their benefactors the Athenians, just as devoted as the deposed government had rendered; an embassy which the Spartans haughtily answered by desiring them to receive back their exiles, and to cast out the assassins Pelopidas and his comrades. It is possible that the Thebans may have sent to try the possibility of escaping Spartan enmity; but it is highly improbable that they made any such promises as those here mentioned; and it is certain that they speedily began to prepare vigorously for that hostility which they saw to be approaching.

See Isokratês, Or. xiv. (Plataic.) s. 3L

This oration is put into the mouth of a Platæan, and seems to be an assemblage of nearly all the topics which could possibly be enforced, truly or falsely, against Thebes.

[3] Xen. Hellen. v. 4, 14. μάλα χειμῶνος ὄντος.

[4] Xen. Hellen. v. 4, 13. εὖ εἰδὼς ὅτι, εἰ στρατηγοίη, λέξειαν οἱ πολῖται, ὡς Ἀγησίλαος, ὅπως βοηθήσειε τοῖς τυράννοις, πράγματα τῇ πόλει παρέχοι. Plutarch, Agesil. c. 24.

herself with Greek despots as well as with foreigners to put down Grecian freedom, found an echo even in Sparta herself. Accordingly Kleombrotus the other king of Sparta took the command. He had recently succeeded his brother Agesipolis, and had never commanded before.

Kleombrotus conducted his army along the Isthmus of Corinth through Megara to Plataea, cutting to pieces an outpost of Thebans, composed chiefly of the prisoners set free by the recent revolution, who had been placed for the defence of the intervening mountain pass. From Plataea he went forward to Thespiae, and from thence to Kynoskephalae in the Theban territory, where he lay encamped for sixteen days; after which he retreated to Thespiae. It appears that he did nothing, and that his inaction was the subject of much wonder in his army, who are said to have even doubted whether he was really and earnestly hostile to Thebes. Perhaps the exiles, with customary exaggeration, may have led him to hope that they could provoke a rising in Thebes, if he would only come near. At any rate the bad weather must have been a serious impediment to action; since in his march back to Peloponnesus through Kreusis and Ægosthenæ the wind blew a hurricane, so that his soldiers could not proceed without leaving their shields and coming back afterwards to fetch them. Kleombrotus did not quit Bœotia, however, without leaving Sphodrias as harmost at Thespiae, with one-third of the entire army, and with a considerable sum of money to employ in hiring mercenaries and acting vigorously against the Thebans.[1]

B.C. 378. Kleombrotus passes by the Athenian frontier—alarm at Athens—condemnation of the two Athenian generals who had favoured the enterprise of Pelopidas.

The army of Kleombrotus, in its march from Megara to Plataea, had passed by the skirts of Attica; causing so much alarm to the Athenians, that they placed Chabrias with a body of peltasts, to guard their frontier and the neighbouring road through Eleutheræ into Bœotia. This was the first time that a Lacedæmonian army had touched Attica (now no longer guarded by the lines of Corinth, as in the war between 394 and 369 B.C.) since the retirement of King Pausanias in 404 B.C.; furnishing a proof of the exposure of the country, such as to revive in the Athenian mind all the terrible recollections of Dekeleia and the

[1] Xen. Hellen. v. 4, 15-18.

Peloponnesian war. It was during the first prevalence of this alarm—and seemingly while Kleombrotus was still with his army at Thespiæ or Kynoskephalæ, close on the Athenian frontier—that three Lacedæmonian envoys, Etymoklês and two others, arrived at Athens to demand satisfaction for the part taken by the two Athenian generals and the Athenian volunteers, in concerting and aiding the enterprise of Pelopidas and his comrades. So overpowering was the anxiety in the public mind to avoid giving offence to Sparta, that these two generals were both of them accused before the Dikastery. The first of them was condemned and executed; the second, profiting by this warning (since, pursuant to the psephism of Kannônus,[1] the two would be put on trial separately), escaped, and a sentence of banishment was passed against him.[2] These two generals had been unquestionably guilty of a grave abuse of their official functions. They had brought the state into public hazard, not merely without consulting the senate or assembly, but even without taking the sense of their own board of Ten. Nevertheless the severity of the sentence pronounced indicates the alarm, as well as the displeasure, of the general body of Athenians; while it served as a disclaimer in fact, if not in form, of all political connection with Thebes.[3]

[1] See above in this History, Ch. lxiv. about the psephism of Kannônus.

[2] Xen. Hellen. v. 4, 19; Plutarch, Pelopid. c. 14.

Xenophon mentions the Lacedæmonian envoys at Athens, but does not expressly say that they were sent to demand reparation for the conduct of these two generals or of the volunteers. I cannot doubt however that the fact was so; for in those times there were no resident envoys—none but envoys sent on special missions.

[3] The trial and condemnation of these two generals has served as the ground-work for harsh reproach against the Athenian democracy. Wachsmuth (Hellen. Alterth. i. p. 654) denounces it as "a judicial horror, or abomination—ein Graulgericht." Rehdantz (Vitæ Iphicratis, Chabriæ, &c. p. 44, 45) says —"Quid? quia invasionem Lacedæmoniorum viderant in Bœotiam factam esse, non puduit eos, damnare imperatores quorum facta suis decretis comprobaverant?".....
"Igitur hanc illius facinoris excusationem habebimus: Rebus quæ a Thebanis agebantur (i. e. by the propositions of the Thebans seeking peace from Sparta, and trying to get enrolled as her allies—alleged by Isokratês, which I have noticed above as being, in my judgement, very inaccurately recorded) cogniti, Athenienses, quo entxius suberneraut, eo majore pœnitentiâ perculsi sunt..... Sed tantum abfuit ut sibimet irascerentur, at, a more Athenicnsium, punirentur

## ALARM AT ATHENS.

Even before the Lacedæmonian envoys had quitted Athens, however, an incident, alike sudden and memorable,

*qui perfecerant id quod tum populus exoptaverat.*" The censures of Wachsmuth, Rehdantz, &c. assume as a matter of fact,—1. That the Athenians had passed a formal vote in the public assembly to send assistance to Thebes, under two generals, who accordingly went out in command of the army and performed their instructions. 2. That the Athenians, becoming afterwards repentant or terrified, tried and condemned these two generals for having executed the commission entrusted to them.

I have already shown grounds (in a previous note) for believing that the first of these affirmations is incorrect; the second, as dependent on it, will therefore be incorrect also.

These authors here appear to me to single out a portion of each of the two inconsistent narratives of Xenophon and Diodorus, and blend them together in a way which contradicts both.

Thus, they take from Diodorus the allegation, that the Athenians sent to Thebes by public vote a large army, which fought along with the Thebans against the Kadmeia—an allegation, which not only is not to be found in Xenophon, but which his narrative plainly, though indirectly, excludes.

Next, they take from Xenophon the allegation, that the Athenians tried and condemned the two generals who were accomplices in the conspiracy of Mellon against the Theban rulers—τὼ δύο στρατηγώ, οἳ συνηκιστάσθην τὴν τοῦ Μέλλωνος ἐπὶ τοὺς περὶ Λεοντιάδην ἐπανάστασιν (v. 4, 19). Now the mention of these two generals follows naturally and consistently in Xenophon.

He had before told us that there were two out of the Athenian generals, who both assisted underhand in organizing the plot, and afterwards went with the volunteers to Thebes. But it cannot be fitted on to the narrative of Diodorus, who never says a word about this condemnation by the Athenians —nor ever mentions any two Athenian generals, at all. He tells us that the Athenian army which went to Thebes was commanded by Demophon; he notices no colleague whatever. He says in general words, that the conspiracy was organized "with the assistance of the Athenians" (συνκτλοθομένων Ἀθηναίων); not saying a word about any two generals as especially active.

Wachsmuth and Rehdantz take it for granted, most gratuitously, that these two condemned generals (mentioned by Xenophon and not by Diodorus) are identical with Demophon and another colleague, commanders of an army which went out by public vote (mentioned by Diodorus and not by Xenophon).

The narratives of Xenophon and Diodorus (as I have before observed) are distinct and inconsistent with each other. We have to make our option between them. I adhere to that of Xenophon, for reasons previously given. But if any one prefers that of Diodorus, he ought then to reject altogether the story of the condemnation of the two Athenian generals (*who nowhere appear in Diodorus*), and to suppose that Xenophon was misinformed upon that point, as upon the other facts of the case.

That the two Athenian generals (assuming the Xenophontic narrative as true) should be tried and

completely altered the Athenian temper. The Lacedæmonian harmost Sphodrias (whom Kleombrotus had left at Thespiæ to prosecute the war
against Thebes), being informed that Peiræus
on its land-side was without gates or night-
watch—since there was no suspicion of attack—
conceived the idea of surprising it by a night-
march from Thespiæ, and thus of mastering at
one stroke the commerce, the wealth, and the
naval resources of Athens. Putting his troops under
march one evening after an early supper, he calculated on
reaching the Peiræus the next morning before day-light.
But his reckoning proved erroneous. Morning overtook
him when he had advanced no farther than the Thriasian
plain near Eleusis; from whence, as it was useless to proceed farther, he turned back and retreated to Thespiæ;
not, however, without committing various acts of plunder
against the neighbouring Athenian residents.

*B.C. 878. Attempt of Sphodrias from Thespiæ to surprise the Peiræus by a night-march. He fails.*

This plan against Peiræus appears to have been not
ill-conceived. Had Sphodrias been a man competent to organise and execute movements as
rapid as those of Brasidas, there is no reason
why it might not have succeeded; in which case
the whole face of the war would have been
changed, since the Lacedæmonians, if once
masters of Peiræus, both could and would have
maintained the place. But it was one of those injustices,

*Different constructions put upon this attempt and upon the character of Sphodrias.*

punished, when the consequences of their unauthorised proceeding were threatening to come with severity upon Athens—appears to me neither improbable nor un-reasonable. Those who are shocked by the severity of the sentence, will do well to read the remarks which the Lacedæmonian envoys make (Xen. Hellen. v. 4, 23) on the conduct of Sphodrias.

To turn from one severe sentence to another—whoever believes the narrative of Diodorus in preference to that of Xenophon, ought to re-gard the execution of those two Lacedæmonian commanders who surrendered the Kadmeia as exceedingly cruel. According to Diodorus, these officers had done everything which brave men could do; they had resisted a long time, repelled many attacks, and were only prevented from farther holding out by a mutiny among their garrison.

Here again, we see the superiority of the narrative of Xenophon over that of Diodorus. According to the former, these Lacedæmonian com-manders surrendered the Kadmeia without any resistance at all. Their condemnation, like that of the two Athenian generals, becomes a matter easy to understand and explain.

which no one ever commends until it has been successfully consummated—"consilium—quod non potest laudari nisi peractum."[1] As it failed, it has been considered, by critics as well as by contemporaries, not merely as a crime but as a fault, and its author Sphodrias as a brave man, but singularly weak and hot-headed.[2] Without admitting the full extent of this censure, we may see that his present aggression grew out of an untoward emulation of the glory which Phœbidas, in spite of the simulated or transient displeasure of his countrymen, had acquired by seizing the Kadmeia. That Sphodrias received private instructions from Kleombrotus (as Diodorus states) is not sufficiently proved; while the suspicion, intimated by Xenophon as being abroad, that he was wrought upon by secret emissaries and bribes from his enemies the Thebans, for the purpose of plunging Athens into war with Sparta, is altogether improbable;[3] and seems merely an hypothesis

[1] Tacit. Hister. i. 38. Compare (in Plutarch, Anton. c. 32) the remark of Sextus Pompey to his captain Menas, when the latter asked his permission to cut the cables of the ship, while Octavius and Antony were dining on board, and to seize their persons —"I cannot permit any such thing; but you ought to have done it without asking my permission." A reply familiar to the readers of Shakspeare's Antony and Cleopatra.

[2] Kallisthenes, Frag. 2, ed. Didot, apud Harpokration. v. Σφοδρίας; Diodor. xv. 29; Plutarch, Pelopidas, c. 14; Plutarch, Agesil. c. 24. The miscalculation of Sphodrias as to the time necessary for his march to Peiræus is not worse than other mistakes which Polybius (in a very instructive discourse, ix. 12, 20, seemingly extracted from his lost commentaries on Tactics) recounts as having been committed by various other able commanders.

[3] Παίθουσι τὸν ἐν ταῖς Θεσπιαῖς ἁρμοστὴν Σφοδρίαν, χρήματα δόντες, ὡς ὑκωπτεύετο—Xenoph. Hellen. v. 4, 20; Diodor. xv. 29; Plutarch, Pelopid. c. 14; Plutarch, Agesil. c. 24, 25. Diodorus affirms private orders from Kleombrotus to Sphodrias. In rejecting the suspicion mentioned by Xenophon—that it was the Theban leaders who instigated and bribed Sphodrias—we may remark—1. That the plan might very possibly have succeeded; and its success would have been ruinous to the Thebans. Had they been the instigators, they would not have failed to give notice of it at Athens at the same time; which they certainly did not do. 2. That if the Lacedæmonians had punished Sphodrias, no war would have ensued. Now every man would have predicted, that assuming the scheme to fail, they certainly would punish him. 3. The strong interest taken by Agesilaus afterwards in the fate of Sphodrias, and the high encomium which he passed on the general character of the latter—are quite consistent with a belief on his part that Sphodrias (like Phœbidas) may have done wrong towards a foreign city from over-ambition in the service of his

suggested by the consequences of the act—which were such, that if his enemies had bribed him, he could not have served them better.

*Alarm and wrath produced at Athens by the attempt of Sphodrias. The Lacedæmonian envoys at Athens seized, but dismissed.*

The presence of Sphodrias and his army in the Thriasian plain was communicated shortly after daybreak at Athens, where it excited no less terror than surprise. Every man instantly put himself under arms for defence; but news soon arrived that the invader had retired. When thus reassured, the Athenians passed from fear to indignation. The Lacedæmonian envoys, who were lodging at the house of Kallias the proxenus of Sparta, were immediately put under arrest and interrogated. But all three affirmed that they were not less astonished, and not less exasperated, by the march of Sphodrias than the Athenians themselves; adding, by way of confirmation, that had they been really privy to any design of seizing the Peiræus, they would have taken care not to let themselves be found in the city, and in their ordinary lodging at the house of the proxenus, where of course their persons would be at once seized. They concluded by assuring the Athenians, that Sphodrias would not only be indignantly disavowed, but punished capitally, at Sparta. And their reply was deemed so satisfactory, that they were allowed to depart; while an Athenian embassy was sent to Sparta to demand the punishment of the offending general.[1]

*Trial of Sphodrias at Sparta. He is acquitted, greatly through the private favour and sympathies of Agesilaus.*

The Ephors immediately summoned Sphodrias home to Sparta, to take his trial on a capital charge. So much did he himself despair of his case, that he durst not make his appearance; while the general impression was, both at Sparta and elsewhere, that he would certainly be condemned. Nevertheless, though thus absent and undefended, he was acquitted, purely through private favour and esteem for his general character. He was of the party of Kleombrotus,

country. But if Agesilaus (who detested the Thebans beyond measure) had believed that Sphodrias was acting under the influence of bribes from them, he would not merely have been disposed to let justice take its course, but would have approved and promoted the condemnation.

On a previous occasion (Hellen. III. 5, 3) Xenophon had imputed to the Thebans a similar refinement of stratagem; seemingly with just as little cause.

[1] Xen. Hellen. v. 4, 22; Plutarch, Agesil. c. 24.

so that all the friends of that prince espoused his cause as a matter of course. But as he was of the party opposed to Agesilaus, his friends dreaded that the latter would declare against him, and bring about his condemnation. Nothing saved Sphodrias except the peculiar intimacy between his son Kleonymus and Archidamus' son of Agesilaus. The mournful importunity of Archidamus induced Agesilaus, when this important cause was brought before the senate of Sparta, to put aside his judicial conviction and give his vote in the following manner—"To be sure, Sphodrias is guilty; upon that there cannot be two opinions. Nevertheless, we cannot put to death a man like him, who, as boy, youth, and man, has stood unblemished in all Spartan honour. Sparta cannot part with soldiers like Sphodrias."[1] The friends of Agesilaus, following this opinion and coinciding with those of Kleombrotus, ensured a favourable verdict. And it is remarkable, that Etymoklês himself, who as envoy at Athens had announced as a certainty that Sphodrias would be put to death—as senator and friend of Agesilaus voted for his acquittal.[2]

This remarkable incident (which comes to us from a witness not merely philo-Laconian, but also personally intimate with Agesilaus) shows how powerfully the course of justice at Sparta was overruled by private sympathy interests— especially those of the two kings. It especially illustrates what has been stated in a former chapter respecting the oppressions exercised by the Spartan harmosts and the dekadarchies, for which no redress was attainable at Sparta. Here was a case where not only the guilt of Sphodrias stood confessed, but in which also his acquittal was sure

Comparison of Sparta with Athenian procedure.

[1] Xen. Hellen. v. 4. 32. Ἐκεῖνος γε (Ἀγησίλαος) πρὸς πάντας ὅσοις διαλέγεται, ταὐτὰ λέγει· Μὴ ἀδικεῖν μὲν Σφοδρίαν ἀδύνατον εἶναι· ὅστις μέντοι, καὶς τε ὢν καὶ παιδίσκος καὶ ἡβῶν, πάντα τὰ καλὰ ποιῶν διετέλεσε, χαλεπὸν εἶναι τοιοῦτον ἄνδρα ἀποκτιννύναι· τὴν γὰρ Σπάρτην τοιούτων δεῖσθαι στρατιωτῶν.

Xenophon explains at some length (v. 4, 25-33) and in a very interesting manner, both the relations between Kleonymus and Archidamus, and the appeal of Archidamus to his father. The statement has all the air of being derived from personal knowledge, and nothing but the fear of prolixity hinders me from giving it in full.

Compare Plutarch, Agesilaus, c. 25; Diodor. xv. 29.

[2] Xen. Hellen. v. 4, 22-32.

to be followed by a war with Athens. If, under such circumstances, the Athenian demand for redress was overruled by the favour of the two kings, what chance was there of any justice to the complaint of a dependent city or an injured individual against the harmost? The contrast between Spartan and Athenian proceeding is also instructive. Only a few days before, the Athenians had condemned, at the instance of Sparta, their two generals who had without authority lent aid to the Theban exiles. In so doing, the Athenian dikastery enforced the law against clear official misconduct—and that, too, in a case where their sympathies went along with the act, though their fear of a war with Sparta was stronger. But the most important circumstance to note is, that at Athens there is neither private influence, nor kingly influence, capable of overruling the sincere judicial conscience of a numerous and independent dikastery.

The result of the acquittal of Sphodrias must have been well known beforehand to all parties at Sparta. Even by the general voice of Greece, the sentence was denounced as iniquitous.[1] But the Athenians, who had so recently given strenuous effect to the remonstrances of Sparta against their own generals, were stung by it to the quick; and only the more stung, in consequence of the extraordinary compliments to Sphodrias on which the acquittal was made to turn. They immediately contracted hearty alliance with Thebes, and made vigorous preparations for war against Sparta both by land and sea. After completing the fortifications of Peiræus, so as to place it beyond the reach of any future attempt, they applied themselves to the building of new ships of war and to the extension of their naval ascendency at the expense of Sparta.[2]

B.C. 378.
The Athenians declare war against Sparta and contract alliance with Thebes.

From this moment, a new combination began in Grecian politics. The Athenians thought the moment favourable to attempt the construction of a new confederacy, analogous to the Confederacy of Delos, formed a century before; the basis on which had been ultimately reared the formidable Athenian empire, lost at the close of the Peloponnesian war. Towards such construction there was so far a tendency, that Athens had already a

[1] Xen. Hellen. v. 4, 24.   [2] Xen. Hellen. v. 4. 34-63.

small body of maritime allies; while rhetors like Isokratês (in his Panegyrical Discourse, published two years before) had been familiarising the public mind with larger ideas. But the enterprise was now pressed with the determination and vehemence of men smarting under recent insult. The Athenians had good ground to build upon; since, while the discontent against the ascendency of Sparta was widely spread, the late revolution in Thebes had done much to lessen that sentiment of fear upon which such ascendency chiefly rested. To Thebes, the junction with Athens was pre-eminently welcome, and her leaders gladly enrolled their city as a constituent member of the new confederacy.[1] They cheerfully acknowledged the presidency of Athens—reserving however, tacitly or expressly, their own rights as presidents of the Bœotian federation, as soon as that could be reconstituted; which reconstitution was at this moment desirable even for Athens, seeing that the Bœotian towns were now dependent allies of Sparta under harmosts and oligarchies.

*Exertions of Athens to form a new maritime confederacy, like the Confederacy of Delos. Thebes enrolls herself as a member.*

The Athenians next sent envoys round to the principal islands and maritime cities in the Ægean, inviting all of them to an alliance on equal and honourable terms. The principles were in the main the same as those upon which the Confederacy of Delos had been formed against the Persians, almost a century before. It was proposed that a congress of deputies should meet at Athens, one from each city, small as well as great, each with one vote; that Athens should be president, yet each individual city autonomous; that a common fund should be raised, with a common naval force, through assessment imposed by this congress upon each, and applied as the same authority might prescribe; the general purpose being defined to be, maintenance of freedom and security from foreign aggression, to each confederate, by the common force of all. Care was taken to banish as much as possible those associations of tribute and subjection

*Athens sends round envoys to the islands in the Ægean. Liberal principles on which the new confederacy is formed. The Athenians formally renounce all pretensions to their lost properties out of Attica, and engage to abstain from future Kleruchies.*

[1] Xen. Hellen. v. 4, 34; Xen. De (Platæo.) s. 20, 23, 27; Diodor. xv. Vectigal. v. 7; Isokratês, Or. xiv. 29.

which rendered the recollection of the former Athenian empire unpopular.¹ And as there were many Athenian citizens, who, during those times of supremacy, had been planted out as kleruchs or outsettlers in various dependencies, but had been deprived of their properties at the close of the war—it was thought necessary to pass a formal decree,² renouncing and barring all revival of these

---

¹ The contribution was now called σύνταξις, not φόρος: see Isokratês, De Pace, s. 37-46; Plutarch, Phokion, c. 7; Harpokration v. Σύνταξις. Plutarch, De Fortuna Athen. p. 351. Ἰσόψηφον αὐτοῖς τὴν Ἑλλάδα κατέστησαν.
² Isokratês, Or. xiv. (Plataic.) s. 47. Καὶ τῶν μὲν κτημάτων τῶν ὑμετέρων αὐτῶν ἀπέστητε, βουλόμενοι τὴν συμμαχίαν ὡς μεγίστην ποιῆσαι, &c.
Diodor. xv. 2¹, 29. Ἐψηφίσαντο δὲ καὶ τὰς γενομένας κληρουχίας ἀποκαταστῆσαι τοῖς πρότερον κυρίοις γεγονόσι, καὶ νόμον ἔθεντο μηδένα τῶν Ἀθηναίων γεωργεῖν ἐκτὸς τῆς Ἀττικῆς. Διὰ δὲ ταύτης τῆς φιλανθρωπίας ἀνακτησάμενοι τὴν παρὰ τοῖς Ἕλλησιν εὔνοιαν, ἰσχυροτέραν ἐποιήσαντο τὴν ἰδίαν ἡγεμονίαν.

Isokratês and Diodorus speak loosely of this vote, in language which might make us imagine that it was one of distinct restitution, giving back property actually enjoyed. But the Athenians had never actually regained the outlying private property lost at the close of the war, though they had much desired it, and had cherished hopes that a favourable turn of circumstances might enable them to effect the recovery. As the recovery, if effected, would be at the cost of those whom they were now soliciting as allies, the public and formal renunciation of such rights was a measure of much policy, and contributed greatly to appease uneasiness in the islands; though in

point of fact nothing was given up except rights to property not really enjoyed.

An Inscription has recently been discovered at Athens, recording the original Athenian decree, of which the main provisions are mentioned in my txtL It bears date in the archonship of Nausinikus. It stands with the restorations of M. Boeckh (fortunately a portion of it has been found in tolerably good preservation), in the Appendix to the new edition of his work—"Ueber die Staatshaushaltung der Athener — Verbesserungen und Nachträge zu den drei Bänden der Staatshaushaltung der Athener," p. xx.

Ἀπὸ δὲ Ναυσινίκου ἄρχοντος μὴ ἐξεῖναι μήτε ἰδίᾳ μήτε δημοσίᾳ Ἀθηναίων μηδενὶ ἐγκτήσασθαι ἐν ταῖς τῶν συμμάχων χώραις μήτε οἰκίαν μήτε χωρίον, μήτε πριάμενῳ, μήτε ὑποθεμένῳ, μήτε ἄλλῳ τρόπῳ μηδενί. Ἐάν δέ τις ὠνῆται ἢ κτᾶται ἢ τίθηται τρόπῳ ὁτῳοῦν, ἐξεῖναι τῷ βουλομένῳ τῶν συμμάχων φῆναι πρὸς τοὺς συνέδρους τῶν συμμάχων. Οἱ δὲ σύνεδροι ἀπο- -μενοι ἀποδόντων (τὸ μὲν ἥμισυ τῷ φῄναντι, τὸ δὲ ἄλλο κοινὸν) ἔστω τῶν συμμάχων. Ἐάν δέ τις [ἢ] ἐπὶ πολέμῳ ἐπὶ τοὺς ποιησομένους τὴν συμμαχίαν, ἢ κατὰ γῆν ἢ κατὰ θάλασσαν, βοηθεῖν Ἀθηναίους καὶ τοὺς συμμάχους τούτοις καὶ κατὰ γῆν καὶ κατὰ θάλασσαν παντὶ σθένει κατὰ τὸ δυνατόν. Ἐὰν δέ τις εἴπῃ ἢ ἐπιψηφίσῃ, ἢ ἄρχων ἢ ἰδιώτης, παρὰ ταῦτα τὸ ψήφισμα, ὡς λύσει τι δεῖ τῶν ἐν τῷδε τῷ ψηφίσματι εἰρημένων, ὑπαρχέτω μὲν αὐτῷ ἀτίμῳ εἶναι, καὶ τὰ

suspended rights. It was farther decreed that henceforward no Athenian should on any pretence hold property, either in house or land, in the territory of any one of the confederates; neither by purchase, nor as security for money lent, nor by any other mode of acquisition. Any Athenian infringing this law was rendered liable to be informed against before the synod; who, on proof of the fact, were to deprive him of the property—half of it going to the informer, half to the general purposes of the confederacy.

Such were the liberal principles of confederacy now proposed by Athens—who, as a candidate for power, was straightforward and just, like the Herodotean Deiokês[1]—and formally ratified, as well by the Athenians as by the general voice of the confederate deputies assembled within their walls. The formal decree and compact of alliance was inscribed on a stone column and placed by the side of the statue of Zeus Eleutherius or the Liberator; a symbol, of enfranchisement from Sparta accomplished, as well as of freedom to be maintained against Persia and other enemies.[2] Periodical meetings of the confederate

*Envoys sent round by Athens —Chabrias, Timotheus, Kallistratos.*

χρήματα αὐτοῦ δημόσια ἔστω καὶ τῆς θεοῦ τὸ ἐπιδέκατον· καὶ κριτέσθω ἐν Ἀθηναίοις καὶ τοῖς συμμάχοις ὡς διαλύων τὴν συμμαχίαν. Ζημιούντων δὲ αὐτὸν θανάτῳ ἢ φυγῇ ὅπου Ἀθηναῖοι καὶ οἱ σύμμαχοι κρατοῦσι. Ἐὰν δὲ θανάτῳ τιμηθῇ, μὴ ταφήτω ἐν τῇ Ἀττικῇ μηδὲ ἐν τῇ τῶν συμμάχων.

Then follows a direction, that the Secretary of the Senate of Five Hundred shall inscribe the decree on a column of stone, and place it by the side of the statue of Zeus Eleutherius; with orders to the Treasurers of the Goddess to disburse sixty drachmas for the cost of so doing.

It appears that there is annexed to this Inscription a list of such cities as had already joined the confederacy, together with certain other names added afterwards, of cities which joined subsequently.

The Inscription itself directs such list to be recorded—εἰς δὲ τὴν στήλην ταύτην ἀναγράφειν τῶν τε οὐσῶν πόλεων συμμαχίδων τὰ ὀνόματα, καὶ ἥτις ἂν ἄλλη σύμμαχος γίγνηται.

Unfortunately M. Boeckh has not annexed this list, which moreover he states to have been preserved only in a very partial and fragmentary condition. He notices only, as contained in it, the towns of Poieessa and Koréus in the island of Keos—and Antissa and Eresus in Lesbos; all four as autonomous communities.

[1] Herodot. i. 96. Ὁ δὲ, οἷα δὴ μνώμενος ἀρχήν, ἰθύς τε καὶ δίκαιος ἦν.

[2] This is the sentiment connected with Ζεὺς Ἐλευθέριος—Pausanias, the victor of Plataea, offers to Zeus Eleutherius a solemn sacrifice and thanksgiving immediately after the battle, in the agora of the town

deputies were provided to be held (how often we do not know) at Athens, and the synod was recognised as competent judge of all persons, even Athenian citizens, charged with treason against the confederacy. To give fuller security to the confederates generally, it was provided in the original compact, that if any Athenian citizen should either speak, or put any question to the vote, in the Athenian assembly, contrary to the tenor of that document—he should be tried before the synod for treason; and that, if found guilty, he might be condemned by them to the severest punishment.

Three Athenian leaders stood prominent as commissioners in the first organisation of the confederacy, and in the dealings with those numerous cities whose junction was to be won by amicable inducement—Chabrias, Timotheus son of Konon, and Kallistratus.[1] The first of the three is already known to the reader. He and Iphikratês were the most distinguished warriors whom Athens numbered among her citizens. But not having been engaged in any war, since the peace of Antalkidas in 387 B.C., she had had no need of their services; hence both of them had been absent from the city during much of the last nine years, and Iphikratês seems still to have been absent. At the time when that peace was concluded, Iphikratês was serving in the Hellespont and Thrace, Chabrias with Evagoras in Cyprus; each having been sent thither by Athens at the head of a body of mercenary peltasts. Instead of dismissing their troops, and returning to Athens as peaceful citizens, it was not less agreeable to the military tastes of these generals than conducive to their importance and their profit, to keep together their bands, and to take foreign service. Accordingly Chabrias had continued in service first in Cyprus, next with the native Egyptian king Akoris. The Persians, against whom he served, found his hostility so inconvenient, that Pharnabazus demanded of the Athenians to recall him, on pain of the Great King's displeasure; and requested at the same time that Iphikratês might be sent to aid the Persian satraps in organizing a great expedition against Egypt. The Athenians, to whom the goodwill of Persia was now of peculiar importance,

(Thucyd. ii. 71). So the Syracusans immediately after the expulsion of the Gelonian dynasty (Diodor xi. 72) and Mæandrius at Samos (Herodot. iii. 142).
[1] Diodor. xv. 29.

complied on both points; recalled Chabrias, who thus became disposable for the Athenian service,[1] and dispatched Iphikratês to take command along with the Persians.

Iphikratês, since the peace of Antalkidas, had employed his peltasts in the service of the kings of Thrace: first of Seuthês, near the shores of the Propontis, whom he aided in the recovery of certain lost dominions—next of Kotys, whose favour he acquired, and whose daughter he presently married.[2] Not only did he enjoy great scope for warlike operations and plunder, among the "butter-eating Thracians"[3]—but he also acquired, as dowry, a large stock of such produce as Thracian princes had at their disposal, together with a boon even more important—a seaport village not far from the mouth of the Hebrus, called Drys, where he established a fortified post, and got together a Grecian colony dependent on himself.[4] Miltiadês, Alkibiadês, and other eminent Athenians had done the same thing before him; though Xenophon had refused a similar

*Service of Iphikratês in Thrace after the peace of Antalkidas. He marries the daughter of the Thracian prince Kotys, and acquires possession of a Thracian seaport, Drys.*

---

[1] Diodor. xv. 29.

[2] Cornel. Nepos, Iphicrates, c. 2; Chabrias, c. 2, 3.

[3] See an interesting Fragment (preserved by Athenæus, iv. p. 131) of the comedy called Protesilaus—by the Athenian poet Anaxandridês (Meineke, Comic. Græc. Frag. III. p. 182). It contains a curious description of the wedding of Iphikratês with the daughter of Kotys in Thrace; enlivened by an abundant banquet and copious draughts of wine given to crowds of Thracians in the market-place—

δαινύειν δ' ἄνδρας βουτυρο-
φάγας
αὐχμηροκόμους μυριοπληθεῖς, &c.

brazen vessels as large as wine vats, full of broth—Kotys himself girt round, and serving the broth in a golden basin, then going about to taste all the bowls of wine and water ready mixed, until he was himself the first man intoxicated. Iphikratês brought from Athens several of the best players on the harp and flute.

The distinction between the butter-eaten, or rubbed on the skin, by the Thracians, and the olive-oil habitually consumed in Greece, deserves notice. The word αὐχμηροκόμους seems to indicate the absence of those scented unguents which, at the banquet of Greeks, would have been applied to the hair of the guests, giving to it a shining gloss and moisture. It appears that the Lacedæmonian women, however, sometimes anointed themselves with butter, and not with oil: see Plutarch, adv. Koloten, p. 1109 B.

The number of warlike stratagems in Thrace, ascribed to Iphikratês by Polyænus and other Tactic writers, indicates that his exploits there were renowned as well as long-continued.

[4] Theopomp. Fragm. 175, ed. Didot; Demosth. cont. Aristokrat. p. 664.

proposition when made to him by the earlier Seuthês.[1] Iphikratês thus became a great man in Thrace, yet by no means abandoning his connection with Athens, but making his position in each subservient to his importance in the other. While he was in a situation to favour the projects of Athenian citizens for mercantile and territorial acquisitions in the Chersonese and other parts of Thrace—he could also lend the aid of Athenian naval and military art, not merely to princes in Thrace, but to others even beyond those limits—since we learn that Amyntas king of Macedonia became so attached or indebted to him as to adopt him for his son.[2] When sent by the Athenians to Persia, at the request of Pharnabazus (about 378 B.C. apparently), Iphikratês had fair ground for anticipating that a career yet more lucrative was opening before him.[3]

---

[1] Xenoph. Anab. vii. 2, 39; vii. 5, 8; vii. 6, 43. Xen. Hellen. i. 5, 17; Plutarch, Alkibiad. c. 36.

See also a striking passage (in Lysias, Orat. xxviii. cont. Ergokl. s. 6) about the advice given to Thrasybulus by a discontented fellow-citizen, to seize Byzantium, marry the daughter of Seuthês, and defy Athens.

[2] Æschinês, Fals. Leg. c. 13. p. 249.

As analogy for the adoption of Iphikratês, we find Ada queen of Karia adopting Alexander the Great as her son. He did not decline the adoption. Arrian, i. 23, 12. καλῶς οἱ τιθεμένη Ἀλέξανδρον. Καὶ Ἀλέξανδρος τὸ ὄνομα τοῦ παιδὸς οὐκ ἀπηξίωσε. At what time Amyntas took this step, we cannot distinctly make out: Amyntas died in 370 B.C., while from 378-371 B.C., Iphikratês seems to have been partly on service with the Persian satraps, partly in command of the Athenian fleet in the Ionian Sea (see Rehdantz, Vitæ Iphicratis, &c. ch. 4). Therefore the adoption took place at some time between 387-378 B.C.; perhaps after the restoration of Amyntas to his maritime dominions by the Lacedæmonian expedition against Olynthus — 382-380 B.C. Amyntas was so weak and insecure, from the Thessalians and other land-neighbours (see Demosth. cont. Aristokrat. p. 657. s. 112), that it was much to his advantage to cultivate the favour of a warlike Athenian established on the Thracian coast, like Iphikratês.

[3] From these absences of men like Iphikratês and Chabrias, a conclusion has been drawn severely condemning the Athenian people. They were so envious and ill-tempered (it has been said), that none of their generals could live with comfort at Athens; all lived abroad as much as they could. Cornelius Nepos (Chabrias, c. 5) makes the remark, borrowed originally from Theopompus (Fr. 117, ed. Didot), and transcribed by many modern commentators as if it were exact and literal truth—"Hoc Chabrias nuntio (i. e. on being recalled from Egypt, in consequence of the remonstrance of Pharnabazus) Athenas rediit neque ibi diutius est moratus quam fuit necesse. Non enim libenter erat ante oculos civium suorum, quod

Iphikratês being thus abroad, the Athenians joined with Chabrias, in the mission and measures for organizing

et vivebat laute, et indulgebat sibi liberalius, quam ut invidiam vulgi posset effugere. Est enim hoc commune vitium in magnis libertisque civitatibus, ut invidia gloriæ comes sit, et libenter de his detrahant, quos eminere videant altius; neque animo æquo pauperes alienam opulentiam intuentur fortunam. Itaque Chabrias, quoad ei licebat, plurimum aberat. Neque vero solus ille aberat Athenis Iphikratêr, sed omnes fere principes fecerunt idem, quod tantum se ab invidiâ putabant ab futuros, quantum a conspectu suorum recessissent. Itaque Conon plurimum Cypri vixit, Iphikratêr in Thraciâ, Timotheus Lesbi, Chares in Sigæo."

That the people of Athens, among other human frailties, had their fair share of envy and jealousy, is not to be denied; but that these attributes belonged to them in a marked or peculiar manner, cannot (in my judgement) be shown by the evidence here alluded to.

"Chabrias was fond of a life of enjoyment and luxurious indulgence." If instead of being an Athenian, he had been a Spartan, he would undoubtedly have been compelled to expatriate in order to gratify this taste; for it was the express drift and purpose of the Spartan discipline, not to equalise property, but to equalise the habits, enjoyments, and personal toils, of the rich and poor. This is a point which the admirers of Lykurgus— Xenophon and Plutarch—attest not less clearly than Thucydidês, Plato, Aristotle, and others. If then it were considered a proof of envy and ill-temper, to debar rich men from spending their money in procuring enjoyments, we might fairly consider the reproach as made out against Lykurgus and Sparta. Not so against Athens. There was no

city in Greece where the means of luxurious and comfortable living were more abundantly exhibited for sale, nor where a rich man was more perfectly at liberty to purchase them. Of this the proofs are everywhere to be found. Even the son of this very Chabrias—Ktêsippus—who inherited the appetite for enjoyment, without the greater qualities of his father—found the means of gratifying his appetite so unfortunately easy at Athens, that he wasted his whole substance in such expenses (Plutarch, Phokion, c. 7; Athenæus, iv. p. 165). And Charês was even better liked at Athens in consequence of his love of enjoyment and licence—if we are to believe another Fragment (238) of the same Theopompus.

The allegation of Theopompus and Nepos, therefore, is neither true as matter of fact, nor sufficient, if it had been true, to sustain the hypothesis of a malignant Athenian public, with which they connect it. Iphikratês and Chabrias did not stay away from Athens because they loved enjoyments or feared the envy of their countrymen; but because both of them were large gainers by doing so, in importance, in profit, and in tastes. Both of them were men πολεμικοί καὶ φιλοπόλεμοι ἀγάπωσι (to use an expression of Xenophon respecting the Lacedæmonian Klearchus—Anab. ii. 6, 1); both of them loved war and had great abilities for war—qualities quite compatible with a strong appetite for enjoyment; while neither of them had either taste or talent for the civil routine and debate of Athens when at peace. Besides, each of them was commander of a body of peltasts, through whose means he could obtain lucrative service as well as

their new confederacy, two other colleagues, of whom we now hear for the first time—Timotheus son of Konon, and Kallistratus the most celebrated orator of his time.¹ The abilities of Kallistratus were not military at all; while Timotheus and Chabrias were men of distinguished military merit. But in acquiring new allies and attracting deputies to her proposed congress, Athens stood in need of persuasive appeal, conciliatory dealing, and substantial fairness in all her

*B.C. 378. Timotheus and Kallistratus—their great success in winning the islanders into confederacy with Athens.*

foreign distinction; so that we can assign a sufficient reason why both of them preferred to be absent from Athens during most part of the nine years that the peace of Antalkidas continued. Afterwards, Iphikrates was abroad three or four years, in service with the Persian satraps, by order of the Athenians; Chabrias also went a long time afterwards, again on foreign service, to Egypt, at the same time when the Spartan king Agesilaus was there (yet without staying long away, since we find him going out on command from Athens to the Chersonese in 358-358 B.C.—Demosth. cont. Aristokr. p. 677, s. 204); but neither he, nor Agesilaus, went there to escape the mischief of envious countrymen. Demosthenes does not talk of Iphikrates as being uncomfortable in Athens, or anxious to get out of it: see Orat. cont. Meidiam. p. 535, s. 83.

Again, as to the case of Konon and his residence in Cyprus: It is truly surprising to see this fact cited as an illustration of Athenian jealousy or ill-temper. Konon went to Cyprus immediately after the disaster of Ægospotami, and remained there, or remained away from Athens, for eleven years (405-393 B.C.) until the year after his victory at Knidus. It will be recollected that he was one of the six Athenian generals who commanded the fleet at Ægospotami. That disaster, while it brought irretrievable ruin upon Athens, was at the same time such as to brand with well-merited infamy the generals commanding. Konon was so far less guilty than his colleagues, as he was in a condition to escape with eight ships when the rest were captured. But he could not expect, and plainly did not expect, to be able to show his face again in Athens, unless he could redeem the disgrace by some signal fresh service. He nobly paid this debt to his country, by the victory of Knidus in 394 B.C.; and then came back the year afterwards, to a grateful and honourable welcome at Athens. About a year or more after this, he went out again as envoy to Persia in the service of his country. He was there seized and imprisoned by the satrap Tiribazus, but contrived to make his escape, and died at Cyprus, as it would appear, about 390 B.C. Nothing therefore can be more unfounded than the allegation of Theopompus, "that Konon lived abroad at Cyprus, because he was afraid of undeserved ill-temper from the public at Athens." For what time Timotheus may have lived at Lesbos, we have no means of saying. But from the year 370 B.C. down to his death, we hear of him so frequently elsewhere, in the service of his country, that his residence cannot have been long.

¹ Æschines, Fals. Leg. c. 40, p. 283.

propositions, not less than of generalship. We are told that Timotheus, doubtless popular as son of the liberator Konon, from the recollections of the battle of Knidus—was especially successful in procuring new adhesions; and probably Kallistratus,[1] going round with him to the different islands, contributed by his eloquence not a little to the same result. On their invitation, many cities entered as confederates.[2] At this time (as in the earlier confederacy of Delos) all who joined must have been unconstrained members. And we may understand the motives of their junction, when we read the picture drawn by Isokratês (in 380 B.C.) of the tyranny of the Persians on the Asiatic mainland, threatening to absorb the neighbouring islands. Not only was there now a new basis of imposing force, presented by Athens and Thebes in union—but there was also a wide-spread hatred of imperial Sparta, aggravated since her perversion of the pretended boon of autonomy, promised by the peace of Antalkidas; and the conjunction of these sentiments caused the Athenian mission of invitation to be extremely successful. All the cities in Euboea (except Histiæa, at the north of the island)—as well as Chios, Mitylênê, Byzantium, and Rhodes—the three former of whom had continued favourably inclined to Athens ever since the peace of Antalkidas[3]—all entered into the confederacy. An Athenian fleet under Chabrias, sailing among the Cyclades and the other islands of the Ægean, aided in the expulsion of the Lacedæmonian harmosts,[4] together

---

[1] The employment of the new word συντέλεις, instead of the unpopular term φόρους, is expressly ascribed to Kallistratus—Harpokration in Voce.

[2] Isokratês gives the number 24 cities (Or. xv. Permut. s. 120). So also Deinarchus cont. Demosthen. s. 15; cont. Philokl. s. 17. The statement of Æschinês, that Timotheus brought 75 cities into the confederacy, appears large, and most probably includes all that that general either acquired or captured (Æsch. Fals. Leg. c. 21. p. 243). Though I think the number twenty-four probable enough, yet it is difficult to identify what towns they

were. For Isokratês, so far as he particularises, includes Samos, Sestos, and Krithôtê, which were not acquired until many years afterwards—in 346-365 B.C.

Neither of these orators distinguish between those cities which Timotheus brought or persuaded to come into the confederacy, when it was first formed (among which we may reckon Euboea, or most part of it—Plutarch, De Glor. Athen. p. 351 A.)—from those others which he afterwards took by siege, like Samos.

[3] Isokratês, Or. xiv. Plataic. s. 60.

[4] Isokratês, Or. xiv. (Plat) s. 20. Οἱ μὲν γὰρ ὑφ' ὑμῶν κατὰ κράτος

with their devoted local oligarchies, wherever they still subsisted; and all the cities thus liberated became equal members of the newly-constituted congress at Athens. After a certain interval there came to be not less than seventy cities, many of them separately powerful, which sent deputies to it;[1] an aggregate sufficient to intimidate Sparta, and even to flatter Athens with the hope of restoration to something like her former lustre.

*Synod of the new confederates assembled at Athens— votes for war on a large scale.*
The first votes both of Athens herself, and of the newly-assembled congress, threatened war upon the largest scale. A resolution was passed to equip 20,000 hoplites, 500 horsemen, and 200 triremes.[2] Probably the insular and Ionic deputies promised each a certain contribution of money, but nothing beyond. We do not, however, know how much—nor how far the engagements, large or small, were realized—nor whether Athens was authorised to enforce execution against defaulters—or was in circumstances to act upon such authority, if granted to her by the congress. It was in this way that Athens had first rendered herself unpopular in the confederacy of Delos—by enforcing the resolutions of the confederate synod against evasive or seceding members. It was in this way that what was at first a voluntary association had ultimately slid into an empire by constraint. Under the new circumstances of 378 B.C., we may presume that the confederates, though ardent and full of promises on first assembling at Athens, were even at the outset not exact, and became afterwards still less exact, in performance; yet that Athens was forced to be reserved in claiming, or in exercising, the right of enforcement. To obtain a vote of contribution by the majority of deputies present, was only the first step in the process; to obtain punctual payment, when the Athenian fleet was sent round for the purpose of collecting—yet without incurring dangerous

ἑλόντες εὐθὺς μὲν ἁρμοστοῦ καὶ δουλείας ἀπηλλάγησαν, τῶν δὲ τοῦ συνεδρίου καὶ τῆς ἐλευθερίας μετέχουσιν, &c.
The adverb of time here used indicates about 377 B.C., about a year before the battle of Leuktra.
[1] Diodor. xv. 30.
[2] Diodor. xv. 29.

Polybius (II. 62) states that the Athenians sent out (not merely, voted to send out) 10,000 hoplites, and manned 100 triremes.
Both these authors treat the resolution as if it were taken by the Athenians alone; but we must regard it in conjunction with the newly-assembled synod of allies.

unpopularity—was the second step, but by far the most doubtful and difficult.

It must, however, be borne in mind that at this moment, when the confederacy was first formed, both Athens and the other cities came together from a spontaneous impulse of hearty mutuality and co-operation. A few years afterwards, we shall find this changed; Athens selfish, and the confederates reluctant.[1]

Inflamed as well by their position of renovated headship, as by fresh animosity against Sparta, the Athenians made important efforts of their own, both financial and military. Equipping a fleet, which for the time was superior in the Ægean, they ravaged the hostile territory of Histiæa in Eubœa, and annexed to their confederacy the islands of Peparêthus and Skiathus. They imposed upon themselves also a direct property-tax; to what amount, however, we do not know.

It was on the occasion of this tax that they introduced a great change in the financial arrangements and constitution of the city; a change conferring note upon the archonship of Nausinikus (B.C. 378—377). The great body of substantial Athenian citizens as well as metics were now classified anew for purposes of taxation. It will be remembered that even from the time of Solon[1] the citizens of Athens had been distributed into four classes—Pentakosiomedimni, Hippeis, Zeugitæ, Thêtes—distinguished from each other by the amount of their respective properties. Of these Solonian classes, the fourth, or poorest, paid no direct taxes; while the three former were taxed according to assessments representing a certain proportion of their actual property. The taxable property of the richest (or Pentakosiomedimni, including all at or above the minimum

*marginal notes:* B.O. 378. Members of the confederacy were at first willing and harmonious —a fleet is equipped. New property-tax imposed at Athens. The Solonian census.

[1] Xen. De Vectigal. v. 5. οὗτοι καὶ τότ', ἐπεὶ τοῦ ἀδικεῖν ἀπεσχόμεθα, πάλιν ὑπὸ τῶν νησιωτῶν ἑκόντων προστάται τοῦ ναυτικοῦ ἐγενόμεθα;

In the early years of this confederacy, votive offerings of wreaths or crowns, in token of gratitude to Athens, were decreed by the Eubœans, as well as by the general body of allies. These crowns were still to be seen thirty years afterwards at Athens, with commemorative inscriptions (Demosthen. cont. Androtion. c. 21. p. 616; cont. Timokrat. c. 41. p. 756.)

[2] For the description of the Solonian census, see Ch. XI. of this History.

income of 500 medimni of corn per annum) was entered in
the tax-book at a sum equal to twelve times their income;
that of the Hippeis (comprising all who possessed between
300 and 500 medimni of annual income) at ten times their
income; that of the Zeugitæ (or possessors of an annual
income between 200 and 300 medimni) at five times their
income. A medimnus of corn was counted as equivalent
to a drachma; which permitted the application of this same
class-system to moveable property as well as to land. So
that, when an actual property-tax (or *eisphora*) was imposed, it operated as an equal or proportional tax, so far
as regarded all the members of the same class; but as a
graduated or progressive tax, upon all the members of
the richer class as compared with those of the poorer.

The three Solonian property-classes above named
appear to have lasted, though probably not
without modifications, down to the close of the
Peloponnesian war; and to have been in great
part preserved, after the renovation of the democracy in B.C. 403, during the archonship of
Eukleidês.[1] Though eligibility to the great
offices of state had before that time ceased to be
dependent on pecuniary qualification, it was
still necessary to possess some means of distinguishing the wealthier citizens, not merely in
case of direct taxation being imposed, but also because the
liability to serve in liturgies or burdensome offices was consequent on a man's enrolment as possessor of more than
a given minimum of property. It seems, therefore, that
the Solonian census, in its main principles of classification
and graduation, was retained. Each man's property being
valued, he was ranged in one of three or more classes
according to its amount. For each of the classes, a fixed
proportion of taxable capital to each man's property was
assumed, and each was entered in the schedule, not for his
whole property, but for the sum of taxable capital corresponding to his property, according to the proportion
assumed. In the first or richest class, the taxable capital
bore a greater ratio to the actual property than in the less
rich; in the second, a greater ratio than in the third. The

*The Solonian census retained in the main, though with modifications, at the restoration under the archonship of Eukleidês in 403 B.C.*

---

[1] This is M. Boeckh's opinion, seemingly correct, as far as can be made out on a subject very imperfectly known (Public Economy of Athens, B. iv. ch. 5).

sum of all these items of taxable capital, in all the different classes, set opposite to each man's name in the schedule, constituted the aggregate census of Attica; upon which all direct property-tax was imposed, in equal proportion upon every man.

Respecting the previous modifications in the register of taxable property, or the particulars of its distribution into classes, which had been introduced in 403 B.C. at the archonship of Eukleidês, we have no information. Nor can we make out how large or how numerous were the assessments of direct property-tax, imposed at Athens between that archonship and the archonship of Nausinikus in 378 B.C. But at this latter epoch the register was again considerably modified, at the moment when Athens was bracing herself up for increased exertions. A new valuation was made of the property of every man possessing property to the amount of 25 minæ (or 2500 drachmæ) and upwards. Proceeding upon this valuation, every one was entered in the schedule for a sum of taxable capital equal to a given fraction of what he possessed. But this fraction was different in each of the different classes. How many classes there were, we do not certainly know; nor can we tell, except in reference to the lowest class taxed, what sum was taken as the minimum for any one of them. There could hardly have been less, however, than three classes, and there may probably have been four. But respecting the first or richest class, we know that each man was entered in the schedule for a taxable capital equal to one-fifth of his estimated property; and that possessors of 15 talents were included in it. The father of Demosthenês died in this year, and the boy Demosthenês was returned by his guardians to the first class, as possessor of 15 talents; upon which his name was entered on the schedule with a taxable capital of three talents set against him; being one-fifth of his actual property. The taxable capital of the second class was entered at a fraction less than one-fifth of their actual property (probably enough, one-sixth, the same as all the registered metics); that of the third, at a fraction still smaller; of the fourth (if there was a fourth) even smaller than the third. This last class descended down to

*Archonship of Nausinikus in 378 B.C.—New census and schedule then introduced, of all citizens worth 25 minæ and upwards, distributed into classes and entered for a fraction of their total property; each class for a different fraction.*

the minimum of 25 minæ, or 2500 drachmæ; below which no account was taken.[1]

Besides the taxable capitals of the citizens, thus graduated, the schedule also included those of the metics or resident aliens; who were each enrolled (without any difference of greater or smaller property, above 25 minæ) at a taxable capital equal to one-sixth of his actual property;[2] being a proportion less than the richest class of citizens, and probably equal to the second class in order of wealth. All these items summed up, amounted to 5750 or 6000 talents,[3] forming the aggregate schedule of taxable property; that is, something near about 6000 talents. A property-tax was no part of the regular ways and means of the state. It was imposed only on special occasions; and whenever it was imposed, it was assessed upon this schedule—every man, rich or poor, being rated equally according to his taxable capital as there entered. A property-tax of 1 per cent. would thus produce 60 talents; 2 per cent., 120 talents, &c. It is highly probable that

*All metics, worth more than 25 minæ, were registered in the schedule; all in one class, each man for one-sixth of his property. Aggregate schedule.*

---

[1] Demosthen. cont. Aphob. i. p. 815, 816; cont. Aphob. ii. p. 836; cont. Aphob. de Perjur. p. 842. Compare Boeckh, Publ. Econ. Ath. iv. 7.

In the exposition which M. Boeckh gives of the new property-schedule introduced under the archonship of Nausinikus, he inclines to the hypothesis of four distinct Classes, thus distributed (p. 671 of the new edition of his Staatshaushaltung der Athener):—

1. The first class included all persons who possessed property to the value of 12 talents and upwards. They were entered on the schedule, each for one-fifth, or 20 per cent. of his property.

2. The second class comprised all who possessed property to the amount of 6 talents, but below 12 talents. Each was enrolled in the schedule, for the amount of 16 per cent. upon his property.

3. The third class included all whose possessions amounted to the value of 2 talents, but did not reach 6 talents. Each was entered in the schedule at the figure of 12 per cent. upon his property.

4. The fourth class comprised all from the minimum of 25 minæ, but below the maximum of 2 talents. Each was entered in the schedule for the amount of 8 per cent. upon his property.

This detail rests upon no positive proof; but it serves to illustrate the principle of distribution, and of graduation, then adopted.

[2] Demosthen. cont. Androtion. p. 612. c. 17. τὸ ἕκτον μέρος εἰσφέρειν μετὰ τῶν μετοίκων.

[3] Polybius states the former sum (ii. 62), Demosthenês the latter (De Symmoriis, p. 183. c. 4). Boeckh however has shown, that Polybius did not correctly conceive what the sum which he stated really meant.

CHAP. LXXVII.    METICS IN THE CENSUS.    333

the exertions of Athens during the archonship of Nausinikus, when this new schedule was first prepared, may have caused a property-tax to be then imposed, but we do not know to what amount.¹

Along with this new schedule of taxable capital, a new distribution of the citizens now took place into certain bodies called Symmories. As far as we can make out, on a very obscure subject, it seems that these Symmories were twenty in number, two to each tribe; that each contained sixty citizens, thus making 1200 in all; that these 1200 were the wealthiest citizens on the schedule —containing, perhaps, the two first out of the

*The Symmories— containing the 1200 wealthiest citizens— the 300 wealthiest, leaders of the Symmories.*

---

¹ I am obliged again upon this point to dissent from M. Boeckh, who sets it down as positive matter of fact that a property-tax of 5 per cent., amounting to 500 talents, was imposed and levied in the archonship of Nansinikus (Publ. Econ. Ath. iv. 7, 8. p. 517-521, Eng. Transl.). The evidence upon which this is asserted, is, a passage of Demosthenes cont. Androtion. (p. 606. c. 14). 'Τρίν παρά τάς εἰσφοράς τάς ἐπὶ Ναυσινίκου, ταρ' Ισως τάλαντα τριακόσια ἢ μικρῷ πλείω, ἔλλειμμα τίτταρα καὶ δέκα ἐστὶ τάλαντα' ὧν ἐκτὰ οὖτος (Androtion) εἰσέπραξεν. Now these words imply —not that a property-tax of about 500 talents had been levied or called for during the archonship of Nausinikus, but—that a total sum of 300 talents, or thereabouts, had been levied (or called for) by all the various property-taxes imposed from the archonship of Nausinikus down to the date of the speech. The oration was spoken about 355 B.C.; the archonship of Nausinikus was in 378 B.C. What the speaker affirms therefore, is, that a sum of 300 talents had been levied or called for by all the various property-taxes imposed between these two dates; and that the aggregate sum of arrears due upon all of them,

at the time when Androtion entered upon his office, was 14 talents. Taylor, indeed, in his note, thinking that the sum of 300 talents is very small, as the aggregate of all property-taxes imposed for 23 years, suggests that it might be proper to read ἐπὶ Ναυσινίκου instead of ἐκ Ναυσινίκου; and I presume that M. Boeckh adopts that reading. But it would be unsafe to found an historical assertion upon such a change of text, even if the existing text were more indefensible than it actually is. And surely the plural number τάς εἰσφοράς proves that the orator has in view, not the single property-tax imposed in the archonship of Nausinikus, but two or more property-taxes, imposed at different times. Besides, Androtion devoted himself to the collection of outstanding arrears generally, in whatever year they might have accrued. He would have no motive to single out those which had accrued in the year 378 B.C.; moreover those arrears would probably have become confounded with others, long before 355 B.C. Demosthenes selects the year of Nausinikus as his initial period, because it was then that the new schedule, and a new reckoning, began.

four classes enrolled. Among these 1200, however, the 300 wealthiest stood out as a separate body; thirty from each tribe. These 300 were the wealthiest men in the city, and were called "the leaders or chiefs of the Symmories." The 300, and the 1200, corresponded, speaking roughly, to the old Solonian classes of Pentakosiomedimni and Hippeis; of which latter class there had also been 1200, at the beginning of the Peloponnesian war.[1] The liturgies, or burdensome and costly offices, were discharged principally by the Three Hundred, but partly also by the Twelve Hundred. It would seem that the former was a body essentially fluctuating, and that after a man had been in it for some time, discharging the burdens belonging to it, the Stratêgi or Generals suffered him to be mingled with the Twelve Hundred, and promoted one of the latter body to take his place in the Three Hundred. As between man and man, too, the Attic law always admitted the process called Antidosis or Exchange of Property. Any citizen who believed himself to have been overcharged with costly liturgies, and that another citizen, as rich or richer than himself, had not borne his fair share—might, if saddled with a new liturgy, require the other to undertake it in his place; and in case of refusal, might tender to him an exchange of properties, under an engagement that he would undertake the new charge, if the property of the other were made over to him.

*Citizens not wealthy enough to be included in the Symmories, yet still entered in the schedule and liable to property-tax. Purpose of the Symmories—extension of the principle to the trierarchy.*

It is to be observed that besides the 1200 wealthiest citizens who composed the Symmories, there were a more considerable number of less wealthy citizens not included in them, yet still liable to the property-tax; persons who possessed property, from the minimum of 25 minæ, up to some maximum that we do not know, at which point the Symmories began—and who corresponded, speaking loosely, to the third class or Zeugitæ of the Solonian census. The two Symmories of each tribe (comprising its 120 richest members) superintended the property-register of each tribe, and collected the contributions due from its less wealthy registered members. Occasionally, when the state required immediate pay-

[1] Respecting the Symmories, compare Boeckh, Staatshaushaltung der Athener, Iv. 9, 10; Schömann, Antiq. Jur. Publ. Græcor. s. 78; Parreidt, De Symmoriis, p. 16 sqq.

ment, the thirty richest men in each tribe (making up altogether the 300) advanced the whole sum of tax chargeable upon the tribe, having their legal remedy of enforcement against the other members for the recovery of the sum chargeable upon each. The richest citizens were thus both armed with rights and charged with duties, such as had not belonged to them before the archonship of Nausinikus. By their intervention (it was supposed) the schedule would be kept nearer to the truth as respects the assessment on each individual, while the sums actually imposed would be more immediately forthcoming, than if the state directly interfered by officers of its own. Soon after, the system of Symmories was extended to the trierarchy; a change which had not at first been contemplated. Each Symmory had its chiefs, its curators, its assessors, acting under the general presidency of the Stratêgi. Twenty-five years afterwards, we also find Demosthenês (then about thirty years of age) recommending a still more comprehensive application of the same principle, so that men, money, ships, and all the means and forces of the state, might thus be parcelled into distinct fractions, and consigned to distinct Symmories, each with known duties of limited extent for the component persons to perform, and each exposed not merely to legal process, but also to loss of esteem, in the event of non-performance. It will rather appear, however, that, in practice, the system of Symmories came to be greatly abused, and to produce pernicious effects never anticipated.

At present, however, I only notice this new financial and political classification introduced in 378 B.C., as one evidence of the ardour with which Athens embarked in her projected war against Sparta. The feeling among her allies the Thebans was no less determined. The government of Leontiadês and the Spartan garrison had left behind it so strong an antipathy, that the large majority of citizens, embarking heartily in the revolution against them, lent themselves to all the orders of Pelopidas and his colleagues; who, on their part, had no other thought but to repel the common enemy. The Theban government now became probably democratical in form; and still more democratical in spirit, from the unanimous ardour pervading the whole mass. Its military force was put under the best training; the most fertile portion of the plain north of Thebes, from which the chief subsistence of

*Enthusiasm at Thebes in defence of the new government against Sparta. Military training—the Sacred Band.*

the city came, was surrounded by a ditch and a palisade,[1] to repel the expected Spartan invasion; and the memorable Sacred Band was now for the first time organized. This was a brigade of 300 hoplites, called the Lochus or regiment of the city, as being consecrated to the defence of the Kadmeia or acropolis.[2] It was put under constant arms and training at the public expense, like the Thousand at Argos, of whom mention was made in my fifty-fifth chapter. It consisted of youthful citizens from the best families, distinguished for their strength and courage amidst the severe trials of the palæstra in Thebes, and it was marshalled in such manner that each pair of neighbouring soldiers were at the same time intimate friends; so that the whole band were thus kept together by ties which no dangers could sever. At first its destination, under Gorgidas its commander (as we see by the select Three Hundred who fought in 424 B.C. at the battle of Delium[3]), was to serve as front rank men for the general body of hoplites to follow. But from a circumstance to be mentioned presently, it came to be employed by Pelopidas and Epaminondas as a regiment by itself, and in a charge was then found irresistible.[4]

Epaminondas. We must remark that the Thebans had always been good soldiers, both as hoplites and as cavalry. The existing enthusiasm therefore, with the more sustained training, only raised good soldiers into much better. But Thebes was now blest with another good fortune, such as had never yet befallen her. She found among her citizens a leader of the rarest excellence. It is now for the first time that Epaminondas the son of Polymnis begins to stand out in the public life of Greece. His family, poor rather than rich, was among the most ancient in Thebes, belonging to those Gentes called Sparti,

[1] Xen. Hellen. v. 4, 39.
[2] Plutarch, Pelopid. c. 18, 19.
[3] Diodor. xii. 70.
These pairs of neighbours who fought side by side at Delium, were called Heniochi and Parabatæ—Charioteers and Side-companions; a name borrowed from the analogy of chariot-fighting, as described in the Iliad and probably in many of the lost epic poems; the charioteer being himself an excellent warrior, though occupied for the moment with other duties—Diomêdês and Sthenelus, Pandarus and Æneas, Patroklus and Automedon, &c.
[4] Plutarch, Pelopidas, c. 18, 19. Ὁ συντεχθεὶς ὑπὸ Ἐπαμινώνδου ἱερὸς λόχος (Hieronymus apud Athenæum, xiii. p. 602 A.). There was a Carthaginian military division which bore the same title, composed of chosen and wealthy citizens, 2500 in number (Diodor. xvi. 80).

whose heroic progenitors were said to have sprung from the dragon's teeth sown by Kadmus.[1] He seems to have been now of middle age; Pelopidas was younger, and of a very rich family; yet the relations between the two were those of equal and intimate friendship, tested in a day of battle wherein the two were ranged side by side as hoplites, and where Epaminondas had saved the life of his wounded friend, at the cost of several wounds, and the greatest possible danger, to himself.[2]

Epaminondas had discharged, with punctuality, those military and gymnastic duties which were incumbent on every Theban citizen. But we are told that in the gymnasia he studied to acquire the maximum of activity rather than of strength; the nimble movements of a runner and wrestler —not the heavy muscularity, purchased in part by excessive nutriment, of the Bœotian pugilist.[3] He also learned music, vocal and instrumental, and dancing; by which in those days was meant, not simply the power of striking the lyre or blowing the flute, but all that belonged to the graceful, expressive, and emphatic, management

*His previous character and training—musical and intellectual as well as gymnastic. Conversation with philosophers, Eoratic as well as Pythagorean.*

[1] Pausan. viii. 11, 5. Dikæarchus, only one generation afterwards, complained that he could not find out the name of the mother of Epaminondas (Plutarch, Agesil. c. 19).

[2] Plutarch, Pelop. o. 4; Pausan. ix. 13, 1. According to Plutarch, Epaminondas had attained the age of forty years, before he became publicly known (De Occ. Vivendo, p. 1129 C.). Plutarch affirms that the battle (in which Pelopidas was desperately wounded and saved by Epaminondas) took place at Mantineia, when they were fighting on the side of the Lacedæmonians, under King Agesipolis, against the Arcadians; the Thebans being at that time friends of Sparta, and having sent a contingent to her aid. I do not understand what battle Plutarch can here mean. The Thebans were never so united with Sparta, as to send any contingent to her aid, after the capture of Athens (in 404 B.C.). Most critics think that the war referred to by Plutarch is, the expedition conducted by Agesipolis against Mantineia, whereby the city was broken up into villages—in 385 B.C.: see Mr. Clinton's Fasti Hellenici ad 385 B.C. But, in the first place, there cannot have been any Theban contingent then assisting Agesipolis; for Thebes was on terms unfriendly with Sparta—and certainly was not her ally. In the next place, there does not seem to have been any battle, according to Xenophon's account.

I therefore am disposed to question Plutarch's account, as to the alleged battle of Mantineia: though I think it probable that Epaminondas may have saved the life of Pelopidas at some earlier conflict, before the peace of Antalkidas.

[3] Cornel. Nepos, Epamin. c. 2;

either of the voice or of the body; rhythmical pronunciation, exercised by repetition of the poets—and disciplined movements, for taking part in a choric festival with becoming consonance amidst a crowd of citizen performers. Of such gymnastic and musical training, the combination of which constituted an accomplished Grecian citizen, the former predominated at Thebes, the latter at Athens. Moreover at Thebes, the musical training was based more upon the flute (for the construction of which, excellent reeds grew near the Lake Kopaïs); at Athens more upon the lyre, which admitted of vocal accompaniment by the player. The Athenian Alkibiadês [1] was heard to remark, when he threw away his flute in disgust, that flute-playing was a fit occupation for the Thebans, since they did not know how to speak; and in regard to the countrymen of Pindar [2] generally, the remark was hardly less true than contemptuous. On this capital point, Epaminondas formed a splendid exception. Not only had he learnt the lyre [3] as well as the flute from the best masters, but also, dissenting from his brother Kapheisias and his friend Pelopidas, he manifested from his earliest years an ardent intellectual impulse which would have been remarkable even in an Athenian. He sought with eagerness the conversation of the philosophers within his reach, among whom were the Theban Simmias and the Tarentine Spintharus, both of them once companions of Sokratês; so that the stirring influence of the Sokratic method would thus find its way, partially and at second-hand, to the bosom of Epaminondas. As the relations between Thebes and Athens, ever since the close of the Peloponnesian war, had become more and more friendly, growing at length into alliance and joint war against the Spartans—we may reasonably presume that he profited by teachers at the latter city as well as at the former. But the person to whom he particularly devoted himself, and whom he not

---

Plutarch, Apophth. Reg. p. 192 D.; Aristophan. Acharn. 872.
Compare the citations in Athenæus, x. p. 417. The perfection of form required in the runner was also different from that required in the wrestler (Xenoph. Memor. III. 5, 4; III. 10, 6).

[1] Plutarch, Alkib. c. 2.

[2] Pindar, Olymp. vi. 90. ἀρχαῖον ὄνειδος—Βοιώτιον ὖν, &c.

[3] Aristoxenus mentions the flute, Cicero and Cornelius Nepos the lyre (Aristoxen. Fr. 60 ed. Didot. ap. Athenæ. iv. p. 184; Cicero, Tusc. Disp. I. 2, 4; Cornel. Nepos, Epamin. c. 2).

only heard as a pupil, but tended almost as a son, during the close of an aged life—was, a Tarentine exile named Lysis; a member of the Pythagorean brotherhood, who, from causes which we cannot make out, had sought shelter at Thebes and dwelt there until his death.[1] With him, as well as with other philosophers, Epaminondas discussed all the subjects of study and inquiry then afloat. By perseverance in this course for some years, he not only acquired considerable positive instruction, but also became practised in new and enlarged intellectual combinations; and was, like Periklês,[2] emancipated from that timorous interpretation of nature which rendered so many Grecian commanders the slaves of signs and omens. His patience as a listener, and his indifference to showy talk on his own account, were so remarkable, that Spintharus (the father of Aristoxenus), after numerous conversations, with him, affirmed that he had never met with any one who understood more or talked less.[3]

[1] Aristoxenus, Frag. 11, ed. Didot; Plutarch, De Gen. Socr. p. 683; Cicero, De Offic. l. 44, 155; Pausan. In. 13, 1; Ælian, V. H. iii. 17.
The statement (said to have been given by Aristoxenus, and copied by Plutarch as well as by Jamblichus) that Lysis, who taught Epaminondas, had been one of the persons actually present in the synod of Pythagoreans at Kroton when Kylon burnt down the house, and that he with another had been the only persons who escaped—cannot be reconciled with chronology.
[2] Compare Diodor. xv. 39 with Plutarch, Periklês, c. 8, and Plutarch, Demosthenês, c. 20.
[3] Plutarch, De Gen. Socrat. p. 576 D. μετειλήφει παιδείας διαφόρου καὶ περιττῆς—(p. 585 D.) τὴν ἀρίστην τροφὴν ἐν φιλοσοφίᾳ—(p. 592 F.) Σπίνθαρος ὁ Ταραντῖνος οὐκ ὀλίγον αὐτῷ (Epaminondas) συνδιατρίψας ἐνταῦθα χρόνον, ἔτι δήπου λέγει, μηδενὶ τοῦ τῶν καθ' ἑαυτὸν ἀνθρώπων ἐντετυχέναι, μήτε πλείονα γιγνώσκοντι μήτε ἐλάττονα φθεγγομένῳ.

Compare Cornel. Nepos, Epamin. c. 3—and Plutarch, De Audiend. c. 3. p. 39 F.
We may fairly presume that this judgement of Spintharus was communicated by him to his son Aristoxenus, from whom Plutarch copied it; and we know that Aristoxenus in his writings mentioned other particulars respecting Epaminondas(Athenæus, iv. p. 184). We see thus that Plutarch had access to good sources of information respecting the latter. And as he had composed a life of Epaminondas (Plutarch, Agesil. c. 28), though unfortunately it has not reached us, we may be confident that he had taken some pains to collect materials for the purpose, which materials would naturally be employed in his dramatic dialogue, "De Genio Socratis." This strengthens our confidence in the interesting statements which that dialogue furnishes respecting the character of Epaminondas; as well as in the incidental allusions interspersed among Plutarch's other writings.

z 2

Nor did such reserve proceed from any want of ready powers of expression. On the contrary, the eloquence of Epaminondas, when he entered upon his public career, was shown to be not merely pre-eminent among Thebans, but effective even against the best Athenian opponents.[1] But his disposition was essentially modest and unambitious, combined with a strong intellectual curiosity and a great capacity; a rare combination amidst a race usually erring on the side of forwardness and self-esteem. Little moved by personal ambition, and never cultivating popularity by unworthy means, Epaminondas was still more indifferent on the score of money. He remained in contented poverty to the end of his life, not leaving enough to pay his funeral expenses, yet repudiating not merely the corrupting propositions of foreigners, but also the solicitous tenders of personal friends;[2] though we are told that, when once serving the costly office of choregus, he permitted his friend Pelopidas to bear a portion of the expense.[3] As he thus stood exempt from two of the besetting infirmities which most frequently misguided eminent Greek statesmen, so there was a third characteristic not less estimable in his moral character; the gentleness of his political antipathies—his repugnance to harsh treatment of conquered enemies—and his refusal to mingle in intestine bloodshed. If ever there were men whose conduct seemed to justify unmeasured retaliation, it was Leontiadês and his fellow-traitors. They had opened the doors of the Kadmeia to the Spartan Phœbidas, and had put to death the Theban leader Ismenias. Yet Epaminondas disapproved of the scheme of Pelopidas and the other exiles to assassinate them, and declined to take part in it; partly on prudential grounds, but partly also on conscientious scruples.[4]

*His eloquence—his unambitious disposition—gentleness of his political resentments.*

[1] Cornel. Nepos, Epaminond. c. 5; Plutarch, Præcept. Reip. Gerend. p. 819 C. Cicero notices him as the only man with any pretensions to oratorical talents, whom Thebes, Corinth, or Argos had ever produced (Brutus, c. 13, 50).

[2] Plutarch (De Gen. Socr. p. 583, 584; Pelopid. c. 3; Fab. Max. c. 27; Compar. Alcibiad. and Coriol. c. 4);

Cornel. Nepos, Epamin. c. 4.

[3] Plutarch, Aristeidês, c. 1; Justin, vi. 8.

[4] Plutarch, De Gen. Socr. p. 576 F. Ἐπαμεινώνδας δέ, μὴ πείθων ὡς οἴεται βέλτιον εἶναι ταῦτα μὴ πράσσειν αἰσχρῶς ἀντιτείνει πρὸς ἃ μὴ πέφυκε, μηδὲ δοκιμάζει, ἐκπαραλευόμενος.

........ Ἐπεὶ δὲ οὐ πείθει τοὺς

## POSITION OF THEBES.

None of his virtues was found so difficult to imitate by his subsequent admirers, as this mastery over the resentful and vindictive passions.[1] Before Epaminondas could have full credit for these virtues, however, it was necessary that he should give proof of the extraordinary capacities for action with which they were combined, and that he should achieve something to earn that exclamation of praise which we shall find his enemy Agesilaus afterwards pronouncing, on seeing him at the head of the invading Theban army near Sparta—"Oh! thou man of great deeds!"[2] In the year B.C. 379, when the Kadmeia was emancipated, he was as yet undistinguished in public life, and known only to Pelopidas with his other friends; among whom, too, his unambitious and inquisitive disposition was a subject of complaint as keeping him unduly in the background.[3] But the unparalleled phænomena of that year supplied a spur which overruled all backwardness, and smothered all rival inclinations. The Thebans, having just recovered their city by an incredible turn of fortune, found themselves exposed singlehanded to the full attack of Sparta and her extensive confederacy. Not even Athens had yet declared in their favour, nor had they a single other ally. Under such

*Conduct of Epaminondas at the Theban revolution of 379 B.C.—he acquires influence, through Pelopidas, in the military organisation of the city.*

πολλοὺς, ἀλλὰ ταύτην ὡρμήκαμεν τὴν ὁδὸν, ἐὰν αὑτὸν κελεύει φόνου καθαρὸν ὄντα καὶ ἀναίτιον ἐφεστάναι τοῖς καιροῖς, μετὰ τοῦ δικαίου τῷ συμφέροντι προσοισόμενον. Compare the same dialogue, p. 594 B.; and Cornelius Nepos, Pelopidas, c. 4.

Isokrates makes a remark upon Evagoras of Salamis, which may be well applied to Epaminondas; that the objectionable means, without which the former could not have got possession of the sceptre, were performed by others and not by him; while all the meritorious and admirable functions of command were reserved for Evagoras (Isokratês, Or. ix. (Evag.) s. 28).

[1] See the striking statements of Plutarch and Pausanias about

Philopœmen—καίπερ Ἐπαμινώνδου βουλόμενος εἶναι μάλιστα ζηλωτής, τὸ δραστήριον καὶ συνετὸν αὐτοῦ καὶ ὑπὸ χρημάτων ἀπαθὲς ἰσχυρῶς ἐμιμεῖτο, τῷ δὲ πράῳ καὶ βαθεῖ καὶ φιλανθρώπῳ παρὰ τὰς πολιτικὰς διαφορὰς ἐμμένειν οὐ δυνάμενος, δι' ὀργὴν καὶ φιλονεικίαν, μᾶλλον ἐδόκει στρατιωτικῆς ἢ πολιτικῆς ἀρετῆς οἰκεῖος εἶναι. To the like purpose Pausanias, viii. 49, 2; Plutarch, Pelopidas, c. 25; Cornel. Nepos, Eparmin. c. 3—"patiens admirandum in modum."

[2] Plutarch, Agesilaus, c. 32. Ὢ τοῦ μεγαλοπράγμονος ἀνθρώπου!

[3] Plutarch, De Gen. Socr. p. 576 E. Ἐπαμινώνδας δὲ, Βοιωτῶν ἀξιόντων τῷ πεπαιδεῦσθαι πρὸς ἀρετὴν ἀξιῶν διαφέρειν, ἀμβλὺς ἐστι καὶ ἀπρόθυμος.

circumstances, Thebes could only be saved by the energy of all her citizens—the unambitious and philosophical as well as the rest. As the necessities of the case required such simultaneous devotion, so the electric shock of the recent revolution was sufficient to awaken enthusiasm in minds much less patriotic than that of Epaminondas. He was among the first to join the victorious exiles in arms, after the contest had been transferred from the houses of Archias and Leontiadês to the open market-place; and he would probably have been among the first to mount the walls of the Kadmeia, had the Spartan harmost awaited an assault. Pelopidas being named Bœotarch, his friend Epaminondas was naturally placed among the earliest and most forward organizers of the necessary military resistance against the common enemy; in which employment his capacities speedily became manifest. Though at this moment almost an unknown man, he had acquired, in B.C. 371, seven years afterwards, so much reputation both as speaker and as general, that he was chosen as the expositor of Theban policy at Sparta, and trusted with the conduct of the battle of Leuktra, upon which the fate of Thebes hinged. Hence we may fairly conclude, that the well-planned and successful system of defence, together with the steady advance of Thebes against Sparta, during the intermediate years, was felt to have been in the main his work.[1]

The turn of politics at Athens which followed the acquittal of Sphodrias was an unspeakable benefit to the Thebans, in seconding as well as encouraging their defence. The Spartans, not unmoved at the new enemies raised up by their treatment of Sphodrias, thought it necessary to

---

[1] Bauch, in his instructive biography of Epaminondas (Epaminondas, und Thebens Kampf um die Hegemonie: Breslau, 1834, p. 26), seems to conceive that Epaminondas was never employed in any public official post by his countrymen, until the period immediately preceding the battle of Leuktra. I cannot concur in this opinion. It appears to me that he must have been previously employed in such posts as enabled him to show his military worth. For all the proceedings of 371 B.C. prove that in that year he actually possessed a great and established reputation, which must have been acquired by previous acts in a conspicuous position; and as he had no great family position to start from, his reputation was probably acquired only by slow degrees.

The silence of Xenophon proves nothing in contradiction of this supposition; for he does not mention Epaminondas even at Leuktra.

make some efforts on their side. They organized on a more systematic scale the military force of their confederacy, and even took some conciliatory steps with the view of effacing the odium of their past misrule.[1] The full force of their confederacy—including, as a striking mark of present Spartan power, even the distant Olynthians[2]—was placed in motion against Thebes in the course of the summer under Agesilaus; who contrived, by putting in sudden requisition a body of mercenaries acting in the service of the Arcadian town Kleitor against its neighbour the Arcadian Orchomenus, to make himself master of the passes of Kithæron, before the Thebans and Athenians could have notice of his passing the Lacedæmonian border.[3] Then crossing Kithæron into Bœotia, he established his head-quarters at Thespiæ, a post already under Spartan occupation. From thence he commenced his attacks upon the Theban territory, which he found defended partly by a considerable length of ditch and palisade—partly by the main force of Thebes, assisted by a division of mixed Athenians and mercenaries, sent from Athens under Chabrias. Keeping on their own side of the palisade, the Thebans suddenly sent out their cavalry, and attacked Agesilaus by surprise, occasioning some loss. Such sallies were frequently repeated, until, by a rapid march at break of day, he forced his way through an opening in the breastwork into the inner country, which he laid waste nearly to the city walls.[4] The Thebans and Athenians, though not offering him battle on equal terms, nevertheless kept the field against him, taking care to hold positions advantageous for defence. Agesilaus on his side did not feel confident enough to attack them against such odds. Yet on one occasion he had made up his mind to do so: and was marching up to the charge, when he was daunted by the firm attitude and excellent array of the troops of Chabrias. They had received orders to await his approach, on a high and advantageous ground, without moving until signal should be given; with their shields resting on the knee, and their spears protended. So im-

*B.C. 378. Agesilaus marches to attack Thebes with the full force of the Spartan confederacy—good system of defence adopted by Thebes—aid from Athens under Chabrias.*

[1] Diodor. xv. 31.
[2] Xen. Hellen. v. 4, 54; Diodor. xv. 31.
[3] Xen. Hellen. v. 4, 38-39.
[4] Xen. Hellen. v. 4, 41.

posing was their appearance that Agesilaus called off his troops without daring to complete the charge.¹ After a month or more of devastations on the lands of Thebes, and a string of desultory skirmishes in which he seems to have lost rather than gained, Agesilaus withdrew to Thespiæ; the fortifications of which he strengthened, leaving Phœbidas with a considerable force in occupation, and then leading back his army to Peloponnesus.

*Agesilaus retires, leaving Phœbidas in command at Thespiæ—desultory warfare of Phœbidas against Thebes—he is defeated and slain. Increase of the Theban strength in Bœotia, against the philo-Spartan oligarchies in the Bœotian cities.*

Phœbidas—the former captor of the Kadmeia—thus stationed at Thespiæ, carried on vigorous warfare against Thebes; partly with his own Spartan division, partly with the Thespian hoplites, who promised him unshrinking support. His incursions soon brought on reprisals from the Thebans; who invaded Thespiæ, but were repulsed by Phœbidas with the loss of all their plunder. In the pursuit, however, hurrying incautiously forward, he was slain by a sudden turn of the Theban cavalry;¹ upon which all his troops fled, chased by the Thebans to the very gates of Thespiæ. Though the Spartans, in consequence of this misfortune, despatched by sea another general and division to replace Phœbidas, the cause of the Thebans was greatly strengthened by their recent victory. They pushed their success not only against Thespiæ, but against the other Bœotian cities, still held by local oligarchies in dependence on Sparta. At the same time these oligarchies were threatened by the growing strength of their own popular or philo-Theban citizens, who crowded in considerable numbers as exiles to Thebes.²

---

¹ Diodor. xv. 33; Polyæn. II. 1, 2; Cornel. Nepos, Chabrias, c. 1.— "obolxo genu scuto"—Demosthen. cont. Leptinem, p. 479.

The Athenian public having afterwards voted a statue to the honour of Chabrias, he made choice of this attitude for the design (Diodor. xv. 33).

² Xen. Hellen. v. 4, 42-45; Diodor. xv. 33.

² Xen. Hellen. v. 4, 46. Ἐκ δὲ τούτου πάλιν αὖ τὰ τῶν Θηβαίων ἀνεζωπυρεῖτο, καὶ ἐστρατεύοντο εἰς Θεσπιὰς, καὶ εἰς τὰς ἄλλας τὰς περιοικίδας πόλεις. Ὁ μέντοι δῆμος ἐξ αὐτῶν εἰς τὰς Θήβας ἀπεχώρει· ἐν πάσαις γὰρ ταῖς πόλεσι δυναστεῖαι καθειστήκεσαν, ὥσπερ ἐν Θήβαις· ὥστε καὶ οἱ ἐν ταύταις ταῖς πόλεσι φίλοι τῶν Λακεδαιμονίων βοηθείας ἐδέοντο.

## AGESILAUS IN BŒOTIA.

A second expedition against Thebes, undertaken by Agesilaus in the ensuing summer with the main army of the confederacy, was neither more decisive nor more profitable than the preceding. Though he contrived, by a well-planned stratagem, to surprise the Theban palisade and lay waste the plain, he gained no serious victory; and even showed, more clearly than before, his reluctance to engage except upon perfectly equal terms.[1] It became evident that the Thebans were not only strengthening their position in Bœotia, but also acquiring practice in warfare and confidence against the Spartans; insomuch that Antalkidas and some other companions remonstrated with Agesilaus, against carrying on the war so as only to give improving lessons to his enemies in military practice—and called upon him to strike some decisive blow. He quitted Bœotia, however, after the summer's campaign, without any such step.[2] In his way he appeased an intestine conflict which was about to break out in Thespiæ. Afterwards, on passing to Megara, he experienced a strain or hurt, which grievously injured his sound leg (it has been mentioned already that he was lame of one leg), and induced his surgeon to open a vein in the limb for reducing the inflammation. When this was done, however, the blood could not be stopped until he swooned. Having been conveyed home to Sparta in great suffering, he was confined to his couch for several months; and he remained during a much longer time unfit for active command.[3]

The functions of general now devolved upon the other king Kleombrotus, who in the next spring conducted the army of the confederacy to invade Bœotia anew. But on this occasion, the Athenians and Thebans had occupied the passes of Kithæron, so that he was unable even to enter the country, and was obliged to dismiss his troops without achieving anything.[4]

*Marginal notes:* B.C. 377. Second expedition of Agesilaus into Bœotia —he gains no decisive advantage. The Thebans acquire greater and greater strength. Agesilaus retires—he is disabled by a hurt in the leg. B.C. 376. Kleombrotus conducts the Spartan force to invade Bœotia—he is stopped by Mount Kithæron, being unable to get over the passes—he retires without reaching Bœotia.

[1] Xen. Hellen. v. 4, 47, 51. The anecdotes in Polyænus (ii. 1, 18-20), mentioning faint-heartedness and alarm among the allies of Agesilaus, are likely to apply (certainly in part) to this campaign.
[2] Diodor. xv. 33, 34; Plutarch, Agesil. c. 26.
[3] Xen. Hellen. v. 4, 58.
[4] Xen. Hellen. v. 4, 59.

His inglorious retreat excited such murmurs among the allies when they met at Sparta, that they resolved to fit out a large naval force, sufficient both to intercept the supplies of imported corn to Athens, and to forward an invading army by sea against Thebes, to the Bœotian port of Kreusis in the Krissæan Gulf. The former object was attempted first. Towards midsummer, a fleet of sixty triremes, fitted out under the Spartan admiral Pollis, was cruising in the Ægean; especially round the coast of Attica, near Ægina, Keos, and Andros. The Athenians, who, since their recently renewed confederacy, had been undisturbed by any enemies at sea, found themselves thus threatened, not merely with loss of power, but also with loss of trade and even famine; since their cornships from the Euxine, though safely reaching Geræstus (the southern extremity of Eubœa), were prevented from doubling Cape Sunium. Feeling severely this interruption, they fitted out at Peiræus a fleet of 80 triremes,[1] with crews mainly composed of citizens; who, under the admiral Chabrias, in a sharply contested action near Naxos, completely defeated the fleet of Pollis, and regained for Athens the mastery of the sea. Forty-nine Lacedæmonian triremes were disabled or captured, eight with their entire crews.[2] Moreover, Chabrias might have destroyed all or most of the rest, had he not suspended his attack, having eighteen of his own

*Resolution of Sparta to equip a large fleet, under the admiral Pollis. The Athenians send out a fleet under Chabrias—victory of Chabrias at sea near Naxos. Recollection of the battle of Arginusæ.*

[1] Xen. Hellen. v. 4, 61. ἀνήγαγεν αὐτοὶ εἰς τὰς ναῦς, &c. Boeckh (followed by Dr. Thirlwall, Hist. Gr. ch. 38. vol. v. p. 58) connects with this maritime expedition an Inscription (Corp. Insc. No. 84. p. 124) recording a vote of gratitude, passed by the Athenian assembly in favour of Phanokritus, a native of Parium in the Propontis. But I think that the vote can hardly belong to the present expedition. The Athenians could not need to be informed by a native of Parium about the movements of a hostile fleet near Ægina and Keos. The information given by Phanokritus must have related more probably, I think, to some occasion of the transit of hostile ships along the Hellespont, which a native of Parium would be the likely person first to discover and communicate.

[2] Diodor. xv. 35; Demosthen. cont. Leptin. c. 17. p. 480.

I give the number of prize-ships taken in this action, as stated by Demosthenes; in preference to Diodorus, who mentions a smaller number. The orator, in enumerating the exploits of Chabrias in this oration, not only speaks from a written memorandum in his hand, which he afterwards causes to be read by the clerk—but also seems exact and special as to numbers,

## VICTORY AT NAXOS.

ships disabled, to pick up both the living men and the dead bodies on board, as well as all Athenians who were swimming for their lives. He did this (we are told[1]) from distinct recollection of the fierce displeasure of the people against the victorious generals after the battle of Arginusæ. And we may thus see, that though the proceedings on that memorable occasion were stained both by illegality and by violence, they produced a salutary effect upon the public conduct of subsequent commanders. Many a brave Athenian (the crews consisting principally of citizens) owed his life, after the battle of Naxos, to the terrible lesson administered by the people to their generals in 406 B.C., thirty years before.

This was the first great victory (in September, 376 B.C.[7]) which the Athenians had gained at sea since the Peloponnesian war; and while it thus filled them with joy and confidence, it led to a material enlargement of their maritime confederacy. The fleet of Chabrias—of which a squadron was detached under the orders of Phokion, a young Athenian now distinguishing himself for the first time and often hereafter to be mentioned—sailed victorious round the Ægean, made prize of

B.C. 376-375. Extension of the Athenian maritime confederacy, in consequence of the victory of Naxos.

so as to inspire greater confidence than usual.

[1] Diodor. xv. 35. Chabrias ἐπέσχετο παντελῶς τοῦ διωγμοῦ, ἀναμνησθεὶς τῆς ἐν Ἀργινούσαις ναυμαχίας, ἐν ᾗ τοὺς νικήσαντας στρατηγοὺς ὁ δῆμος ἀντὶ μεγάλης εὐεργεσίας θανάτῳ περιέβαλεν, αἰτιασάμενος ὅτι τοὺς τετελευτηκότας κατὰ τὴν ναυμαχίαν οὐκ ἔθαψαν· εὐλαβήθη οὖν (see Wesseling and Stephens's note) μή ποτε τῆς περιστάσεως ὁμοίας γενομένης κινδυνεύσῃ παθεῖν παραπλήσια. Διόπερ ἀποστὰς τοῦ διώκειν, ἀνελέγετο τῶν πολιτῶν τοὺς διανηχομένους, καὶ τοὺς μὲν ἔτι ζῶντας διδάωσι, τοὺς δὲ τετελευτηκότας ἔθαψεν. Εἰ δὲ μὴ περὶ ταύτην ἐγένετο τὴν ἐπιμέλειαν, ῥᾳδίως ἂν ἅπαντα τὸν πολεμίων στόλον διέφθειρε. This passage illustrates what I remarked in my preceding Ch. lxiv. respecting the battle of Arginusæ

and the proceedings at Athens afterwards. I noticed that Diodorus incorrectly represented the excitement at Athens against the generals as arising from their having neglected to pick up the bodies of the slain warriors for burial—and that he omitted the more important fact, that they left many living and wounded warriors to perish. It is curious, that in the first of the two sentences above cited, Diodorus repeats his erroneous affirmation about the battle of Arginusæ; while in the second sentence he corrects the error, telling us that Chabrias, profiting by the warning, took care to pick up the living men on the wrecks and in the water, as well as the dead bodies.

[7] Plutarch, Phokion, c. 6; Plutarch, Camillus, c. 19.

twenty other triremes in single ships, brought in 3000 prisoners with 110 talents in money, and annexed seventeen new cities to the confederacy, as sending deputies to the synod and furnishing contributions. The discreet and conciliatory behaviour of Phokion, especially, obtained much favour among the islanders and determined several new adhesions to Athens.[1] To the inhabitants of Abdêra in Thrace, Chabrias rendered an inestimable service, by aiding them to repulse a barbarous horde of Triballi, who quitting their abode from famine, had poured upon the sea-coast, defeating the Abderites and plundering their territory. The citizens, grateful for a force left to defend their town, willingly allied themselves with Athens, whose confederacy thus extended itself to the coast of Thrace.[2]

*B.C. 375.*
*Circumnavigation of Peloponnesus by Timotheus with an Athenian fleet—his victory over the Lacedæmonian fleet—his success in extending the Athenian confederacy—his just dealing.*

Having prosperously enlarged their confederacy to the east of Peloponnesus, the Athenians began to aim at the acquisition of new allies in the west. The fleet of 60 triremes, which had recently served under Chabrias, was sent, under the command of Timotheus, the son of Konon, to circumnavigate Peloponnesus and alarm the coast of Laconia; partly at the instance of the Thebans, who were eager to keep the naval force of Sparta occupied, so as to prevent her from conveying troops across the Krissæan Gulf from Corinth to the Bœotian port of Kreusis.[3] This Periplus of Peloponnesus—the first which the fleet of Athens had attempted since her humiliation at Ægospotami—coupled with the ensuing successes, was long remembered by the countrymen of Timotheus. His large force, just dealing, and conciliatory professions, won new and valuable allies. Not only Kephallenia, but the still more important island of Korkyra, voluntarily accepted his propositions; and as he took care to avoid all violence or interference with the political constitution, his popularity all around augmented every day. Alketas, prince of the Molossi—the Chaonians with other Epirotic tribes—and the Akarnanians on the coast—all embraced his alliance.[4] While near

---

[1] Demosthen. cont. Leptin. p. 490; Plutarch, Phokion, c. 7.
[2] Diodor. xv. 36. He states, by mistake, that Chabrias was afterwards assassinated at Abdêra.
[3] Xen. Hellen. v. 4, 62.
[4] Xen. Hellen. v. 4, 64; Diodor. xv. 56.

Alyzia and Leukas on this coast, he was assailed by the Peloponnesian ships under Nikolochus, rather inferior in number to his fleet. He defeated them, and being shortly afterwards reinforced by other triremes from Korkyra, he became so superior in those waters, that the hostile fleet did not dare to show itself. Having received only 13 talents on quitting Athens, we are told that he had great difficulty in paying his fleet; that he procured an advance of money, from each of the sixty trierarchs in his fleet, of seven minæ towards the pay of their respective ships; and that he also sent home requests for large remittances from the public treasury;[1] measures which go to bear out that honourable repugnance to the plunder of friends or neutrals, and care to avoid even the suspicion of plunder, which his panegyrist Isokratês ascribes to him.[2] This was a feature unhappily rare among the Grecian generals on both sides, and tending to become still rarer, from the increased employment of mercenary bands.

The demands of Timotheus on the treasury of Athens were not favourably received. Though her naval position was now more brilliant and commanding than it had been since the battle of Ægospotami —though no Lacedæmonian fleet showed itself to disturb her in the Ægean[3]—yet the cost of the war began to be seriously felt. Privateers from the neighbouring island of Ægina annoyed her commerce, requiring a perpetual coast-guard; while the contributions from the deputies to the confederate synod were not sufficient to dispense with the necessity of a heavy direct property-tax at home.[4]

B.C. 874.
Financial difficulties of Athens.

---

[1] Xen. Hellen. v. 4, 66; Isokratês, De Permutat. s. 116; Cornelius Nepos, Timotheus, c. 2.

The advance of seven minæ respectively, obtained by Timotheus from the sixty trierarchs under his command, is mentioned by Demosthenês cont. Timotheum (o. 3. p. 1187). I agree with M. Boeckh (Public Economy of Athens, ii. 24. p. 284) in referring this advance to his expedition to Korkyra and other places in the Ionian Sea in 375-374 B.C.; not to his subsequent expedition of 873 B.C., to which Rehdantz, Lachmann, Schlosser,

and others would refer it (Vitæ Iphicratis, &c. p. 89). In the second expedition, it does not appear that he ever had really sixty triremes, or sixty trierarchs, under him. Xenophon (Hellen. v. 4, 63) tells us that the fleet sent with Timotheus to Korkyra consisted of sixty ships; which is the exact number of trierarchs named by Demosthenês.

[2] Isokratês, Orat. De Permutat. s. 128, 131, 135.

[3] Isokratês, De Permutat. s. 117; Cornel. Nepos, Timoth. c. 2.

[4] Xen. Hellen. vi. 2, 1.

In this synod the Thebans, as members of the confederacy, were represented.[1] Application was made to them to contribute towards the cost of the naval war; the rather, as it was partly at their instance that the fleet had been sent round to the Ionian Sea. But the Thebans declined compliance,[2] nor were they probably in any condition to furnish pecuniary aid. Their refusal occasioned much displeasure at Athens, embittered by jealousy at the strides which they had been making during the last two years, partly through the indirect effect of the naval successes of Athens. At the end of the year 377 B.C., after the two successive invasions of Agesilaus, the ruin of two home-crops had so straitened the Thebans, that they were forced to import corn from Pagasæ in Thessaly; in which enterprise their ships and seamen were at first captured by the Lacedæmonian harmost at Oreus in Eubœa, Alketas. His negligence however soon led not only to an outbreak of their seamen who had been taken prisoners, but also to the revolt of the town from Sparta, so that the communication of Thebes with Pagasæ became quite unimpeded. For the two succeeding years, there had been no Spartan invasion of Bœotia; since in 376 B.C., Kleombrotus could not surmount the heights of Kithæron—while in 375 B.C., the attention of Sparta had been occupied by the naval operations of Timotheus in the Ionian Sea. During these two years, the Thebans had exerted themselves vigorously against the neighbouring cities of Bœotia, in most of which a strong party, if not the majority of the population, was favourable to them, though the government was in the hands of the philo-Spartan oligarchy, seconded by Spartan harmosts and garrisons.[3] We hear of one victory gained by the Theban cavalry near Platæa, under Charon; and of another near Tanagra, in which Panthoides, the Lacedæmonian harmost in that town, was slain.[4]

---

[1] See Isokratês, Or. xiv. (Plataic.) s. 21, 23, 37.

[2] Xen. Hellen. vi. 2, 1. Οἱ δ' Ἀθηναῖοι, ἀδοξαινομένους μὲν ὁρῶντες διὰ πρὸς τοὺς Θηβαίους, χρήματα δ' οὐ συμβαλλομένους εἰς τὸ ναυτικόν, ἀυτοὶ δ' ἀποναιδόμενοι καὶ χρημάτων διαφοραῖς καὶ ἱππασίαις ἐξ Αἰγίνης, καὶ φυλακαῖς τῆς χώρας, ἐπεθύμησαν παύσασθαι τοῦ πολέμου.

[3] Xen. Hellen. v. 4, 46-55.

[4] Plutarch, Pelopidas, c. 15-25.

But the most important of all their successes was that of Pelopidas near Tegyra. That commander, hearing that the Spartan harmost, with his two (moræ or) divisions in garrison at Orchomenus, had gone away on an excursion into the Lokrian territory, made a dash from Thebes with the Sacred Band and a few cavalry, to surprise the place. It was the season in which the waters of the Lake Kopais were at the fullest, so that he was obliged to take a wide circuit to the north-west, and to pass by Tegyra, on the road between Orchomenus and the Opuntian Lokris. On arriving near Orchomenus, he ascertained that there were still some Lacedæmonians in the town, and that no surprise could be effected; upon which he retraced his steps. But on reaching Tegyra, he fell in with the Lacedæmonian commanders, Gorgoleon and Theopompus, returning with their troops from the Lokrian excursion. As his numbers were inferior to theirs by half, they rejoiced in the encounter; while the troops of Pelopidas were at first dismayed, and required all his encouragement to work them up. But in the fight that ensued, closely and obstinately contested in a narrow pass, the strength, valour, and compact charge of the Sacred Band proved irresistible. The two Lacedæmonian commanders were both slain; their troops opened, to allow the Thebans an undisturbed retreat; but Pelopidas, disdaining this opportunity, persisted in the combat until all his enemies dispersed and fled. The neighbourhood of Orchomenus forbade any long pursuit, so that Pelopidas could only erect his trophy, and strip the dead, before returning to Thebes.[1]

*Victory of Pelopidas at Tegyra over the Lacedæmonians.*

This combat, in which the Lacedæmonians were for the first time beaten in fair field by numbers inferior to their own, produced a strong sensation in the minds of both the contending parties. The confidence of the Thebans, as well as their exertion, was redoubled; so that by the year 374 B.C., they had cleared Bœotia of the Lacedæmonians, as well as of the local oligarchies which sustained them; persuading or constraining the cities again to come into union with Thebes, and

*The Thebans expel the Lacedæmonians out of all Bœotia, except Orchomenus—they reorganise the Bœotian federation.*

---

[1] Plutarch, Pelopidas, c. 17; Diodor. xv. 37.
Xenophon does not mention the combat at Tegyra. Diodorus mentions, what is evidently this battle, near Orchomenus, but he does not

reviving the Bœotian confederacy. Haliartus, Korôneia, Lebadeia, Tanagra, Thespiæ, Platæa and the rest, thus became again Bœotian;[1] leaving out Orchomenus alone (with its dependency Chæroneia), which was on the borders of Phokis, and still continued under Lacedæmonian occupation. In most of these cities the party friendly to Thebes was numerous, and the change, on the whole, popular; though in some the prevailing sentiment was such, that adherence was only obtained by intimidation. The change here made by Thebes, was, not to absorb these cities into herself, but to bring them back to the old federative system of Bœotia; a policy, which she had publicly proclaimed on surprising Platæa in 431 b.c.[2] While resuming her own ancient rights and privileges as head of the Bœotian federation, she at the same time guaranteed to the other cities —by convention, probably express, but certainly implied— their ancient rights, their security, and their qualified autonomy, as members; the system which had existed down to the peace of Antalkidas.

The position of the Thebans was materially improved by this re-conquest or re-confederation of Bœotia. Becoming masters of Kreusis, the port of Thespiæ,[3] they fortified it, and built some triremes to repel any invasion from Peloponnesus by sea across the Krissæan Gulf. Feeling thus secure against invasion, they began to retaliate upon their neighbours and enemies the Phokians; allies of Sparta, and auxiliaries in the recent attacks on Thebes—yet also, from ancient times, on friendly terms with

name Tegyra.
Kallisthenês seems to have described the battle of Tegyra, and to have given various particulars respecting the religious legends connected with that spot (Kallisthenês, Fragm. 3, ed. Didot, ap. Stephan. Byz. v. Τεγύρα).

[1] That the Thebans thus became again presidents of all Bœotia, and revived the Bœotian confederacy— is clearly stated by Xenophon, Hellen. v. 4, 63; vi. 1, 1.

[2] Thucyd. ii. 2. Ἀνίκεν ὁ κῆρυξ (the Theban herald after the Theban troops had penetrated by night into the middle of Platæa) εἴ τις βούλεται

κατὰ τὰ πάτρια τῶν πάντων Βοιωτῶν ξυμμαχεῖν, τίθεσθαι παρ' αὐτοὺς τὰ ὅπλα, νομίζοντες σφίσι ῥᾳδίως τούτῳ τῷ τρόπῳ προσχωρήσειν τὴν πόλιν.

Compare the language of the Thebans about τὰ πάτρια τῶν Βοιωτῶν (III. 61, 65, 66). The description which the Thebans give of their own professions and views, when they attacked Platæa in 431 B.C., may be taken as fair analogy to judge of their professions and views towards the recovered Bœotian towns in 378-375 B.C.

[3] Xen. Hellen. vi. 4, 3; compare Diodor. xv. 53.

Athens.[1] So hard pressed were the Phokians—especially as Jason of Pheræ in Thessaly was at the same time their bitter enemy[2]—that unless assisted, they would have been compelled to submit to the Thebans, and along with them Orchomenus, including the Lacedæmonian garrison then occupying it; while the treasures of the Delphian temple would also have been laid open, in case the Thebans should think fit to seize them. Intimation being given by the Phokians to Sparta, King Kleombrotus was sent to their aid, by sea across the Gulf, with four Lacedæmonian divisions of troops, and an auxiliary body of allies.[3] This reinforcement, compelling the Thebans to retire, placed both Phokis and Orchomenus in safety. While Sparta thus sustained them, even Athens looked upon the Phokian cause with sympathy. When she saw that the Thebans had passed from the defensive to the offensive—partly by her help, yet nevertheless refusing to contribute to the cost of her navy—her ancient jealousy of them became again so powerful, that she sent envoys to Sparta to propose terms of peace. What these terms were, we are not told; nor does it appear that the Thebans even received notice of the proceeding. But the peace was accepted at

*B.C. 374. They invade Phokis—Kleombrotus is sent thither with an army for defence—Athens makes a separate peace with the Lacedæmonians.*

---

[1] Diodor. xv. 81; Xen. Hellen. vi. 8, 1; iii. 5, 21.
[2] Xen. Hellen. vi. 4, 21-27.
[3] Xen. Hellen. vi. 1, 2; vi. 21. This expedition of Kleombrotus to Phokis is placed by Mr. Fynes Clinton in 376 B.C. (Fast. Hel. ad 875 B.C.). To me it seems to belong rather to 374 B.C. It was not undertaken until the Thebans had reconquered all the Bœotian cities (Xen. Hell. vi. 1, 1); and this operation seems to have occupied them all the two years—876 and 875 B.C. See v. 4, 63, where the words οὔτ' —ἐν ᾧ Τιμόθεος περιέπλευσε must be understood to include, not simply the time which Timotheus took in *actually circumnavigating* Peloponnesus, but the year which he spent afterwards in the Ionian Sea, and the time which he occupied in performing his exploits near Korkyra, Leukas, and the neighbourhood generally. The 'Periplus', for which Timotheus was afterwards honoured at Athens (see Æschines cont. Ktesiphont. c. 90 p. 465) meant the exploits performed by him during the year and with the fleet of the 'Periplus'.
It is worth notice that the Pythian games were celebrated in this year 374 B.C.—ἐπὶ Σωκρατίδου ἄρχοντος; that is, in the first quarter of that archon, or the third Olympic year; about the beginning of August. Chabrias won a prize at these games with a chariot and four; in celebration of which, he afterwards gave a splendid banquet at the point of seashore called Κωλιάς, near Athens (Demosthen. cont. Neæram, c. 11. p. 1356).

Sparta, and two of the Athenian envoys were despatched at once from thence, without even going home, to Korkyra; for the purpose of notifying the peace to Timotheus, and ordering him forthwith to conduct his fleet back to Athens.[1]

*B.C. 374.*
*Demand made upon the Lacedæmonians from Thessaly, for aid to Pharsalus.*

*Polydamas of Pharsalus applies to Sparta for aid against Pheræ.*

This proposition of the Athenians, made seemingly in a moment of impetuous dissatisfaction, was much to the advantage of Sparta, and served somewhat to countervail a mortifying revelation which had reached the Spartans a little before from a different quarter.

Polydamas, an eminent citizen of Pharsalus in Thessaly, came to Sparta to ask for aid. He had long been on terms of hospitality with the Lacedæmonians; while Pharsalus had not merely been in alliance with them, but was for some time occupied by one of their garrisons.[2] In the usual state of Thessaly, the great cities Larissa, Pheræ, Pharsalus, and others, each holding some smaller cities in a state of dependent alliance, were in disagreement with each other, often even in actual war. It was rare that they could be brought to concur in a common vote for the election of a supreme chief or Tagus. At his own city of Pharsalus, Polydamas was now in the ascendent, enjoying the confidence of all the great family factions who usually contended for predominance; to such a degree, indeed, that he was entrusted with the custody of the citadel and the entire management of the revenues, receipts as well as disbursements. Being a wealthy man, "hospitable and ostentatious in the Thessalian fashion", he advanced money from his own purse to the treasury whenever it was low, and repaid himself when public funds came in.[3]

---

[1] Xen. Hellen. vi. 2, 1, 2.
Kallias seems to have been one of the Athenian envoys (Xen. Hellen. vi. 3, 4).

[2] Diodor. xiv. 82.

[3] Xen. Hellen. vi. 1, 6. Καὶ ὅπου μὲν ἐνδεὴς εἴη, παρ' ἑαυτοῦ προσετίθει· ὅπου δὲ περιγίνοιτο τῆς προσόδου, ἀπελάμβανεν· ἦν δὲ καὶ ἄλλως φιλόξενός τε καὶ μεγαλοπρεπὴς τὸν Θετταλικὸν τρόπον.

Such loose dealing of the Thessalians with their public revenues helps us to understand how Philip of Macedon afterwards got into his hands the management of their harbours and customs duties (Demosthen. Olynth. i. p. 16; ii. p. 20). It forms a striking contrast with the exactness of the Athenian people about their public receipts and disbursements, as testified in the inscriptions yet remaining.

But a greater man than Polydamas had now arisen in Thessaly—Jason, despot of Pheræ; whose formidable power, threatening the independence of Pharsalus, he now came to Sparta to denounce. Though the force of Jason can hardly have been very considerable when the Spartans passed through Thessaly, six years before, in their repeated expeditions against Olynthus, he was now not only despot of Pheræ, but master of nearly all the Thessalian cities (as Lykophron of Pheræ had partially succeeded in becoming thirty years before,[1]) as well as of a large area of tributary circumjacent territory. The great instrument of his dominion was, a standing and well-appointed force of 6000 mercenary troops, from all parts of Greece. He possessed all the personal qualities requisite for conducting soldiers with the greatest effect. His bodily strength was great; his activity indefatigable; his self-command, both as to hardship and as to temptation, alike conspicuous. Always personally sharing both in the drill and in the gymnastics of the soldiers, and encouraging military merits with the utmost munificence, he had not only disciplined them, but inspired them with extreme warlike ardour and devotion to his person. Several of the neighbouring tribes, together with Alketas prince of the Molossi in Epirus, had been reduced to the footing of his dependent allies. Moreover he had already defeated the Pharsalians, and stripped them of many of the towns which had once been connected with them, so that it only remained for him now to carry his arms against their city. But Jason was prudent as well as daring. Though certain of success, he wished to avoid the odium of employing force, and the danger of having malcontents for subjects. He therefore proposed to Polydamas in a private interview, that he (Polydamas) should bring Pharsalus under Jason's dominion, accepting for himself the second place in Thessaly, under Jason installed as Tagus or president. The whole force of Thessaly thus

*Jason of Pheræ—his energetic character and formidable power.*

[1] Xen. Hellen. II. 3, 4. The story (told in Plutarch, De Gen. Socrat. p. 683 F.) of Jason sending a large sum of money to Thebes, at some period anterior to the recapture of the Kadmeia, for the purpose of corrupting Epaminondas—appears not entitled to credit. Before that time, Epaminondas was too little known to be worth corrupting; moreover, Jason did not become *tagus* of Thessaly until long after the recapture of the Kadmeia (Xen. Hellen. vi. 1, 18, 19).

united, with its array of tributary nations around, would be decidedly the first power in Greece, superior on land either to Sparta or Thebes, and at sea to Athens. And as to the Persian king, with his multitudes of unwarlike slaves, Jason regarded him as an enemy yet easier to overthrow; considering what had been achieved first by the Cyreians, and afterwards by Agesilaus.

*His prudent dealing with Polydamas.*

Such were the propositions, and such the ambitious hopes, which the energetic despot of Pheræ had laid before Polydamas; who replied, that he himself had long been allied with Sparta, and that he could take no resolution hostile to her interests. "Go to Sparta, then (rejoined Jason), and give notice there, that I intend to attack Pharsalus, and that it is for them to afford you protection. If they cannot comply with the demand, you will be unfaithful to the interests of your city if you do not embrace my offers." It was on this mission that Polydamas was now come to Sparta, to announce that unless aid could be sent to him, he should be compelled unwillingly to sever himself from her. "Recollect (he concluded) that the enemy against whom you will have to contend is formidable in every way, both from personal qualities and from power; so that nothing short of a first-rate force and commander will suffice. Consider and tell me what you can do."

*The Lacedæmonians find themselves unable to spare any aid for Thessaly— they dismiss Polydamas with a refusal. He comes to terms with Jason, who becomes Tagus of Thessaly.*

The Spartans, having deliberated on the point, returned a reply in the negative. Already a large force had been sent under Kleombrotus as essential to the defence of Phokis; moreover the Athenians were now the stronger power at sea. Lastly, Jason had hitherto lent no active assistance to Thebes and Athens—which he would assuredly be provoked to do, if a Spartan army interfered against him in Thessaly. Accordingly the Ephors told Polydamas plainly, that they were unable to satisfy his demands, recommending him to make the best terms that he could both for Pharsalus and for himself. Returning to Thessaly, he resumed his negotiation with Jason, and promised substantial compliance with what was required. But he entreated to be spared the dishonour of admitting a foreign garrison into the citadel which had been confidentially entrusted to his care;

engaging at the same time to bring his fellow-citizens into voluntary union with Jason, and tendering his two sons as hostages for faithful performance. All this was actually brought to pass. The politics of the Pharsalians were gently brought round, so that Jason, by their votes as well as the rest, was unanimously elected Tagus of Thessaly.[1]

The dismissal of Polydamas implied a mortifying confession of weakness on the part of Sparta. It marks too an important stage in the real decline of her power. Eight years before, at the instance of the Akanthian envoys backed by the Macedonian Amyntas, she had sent three powerful armies in succession to crush the liberal and promising confederacy of Olynthus, and to re-transfer the Grecian cities on the sea-coast to the Macedonian crown. *Evidence of the decline of Spartan power during the last eight years.* The region to which her armies had been then sent, was the extreme verge of Hellas. The parties in whose favour she acted, had scarcely the shadow of a claim, as friends or allies; while those *against* whom she acted, had neither done nor threatened any wrong to her: moreover the main ground on which her interference was invoked, was to hinder the free and equal confederation of Grecian cities. Now, a claim, and a strong claim, is made upon her by Polydamas of Pharsalus, an old friend and ally. It comes from a region much less distant; lastly, her political interest would naturally bid her arrest the menacing increase of an aggressive power already so formidable as that of Jason. Yet so seriously has the position of Sparta altered in the last eight years (382-374 B.C.) that she is now compelled to decline a demand which justice, sympathy, and political policy alike prompted her to grant. So unfortunate was it for the Olynthian confederacy, that their honourable and well-combined aspirations fell exactly during those few years in which Sparta was at her maximum of power! So unfortunate was such coincidence of time not only for Olynthus, but for Greece generally:—since nothing but Spartan interference restored the Macedonian kings to the sea-coast, while the Olynthian confederacy, had it been allowed to expand, might probably have confined them to

---

[1] See the interesting account of this mission, and the speech of Polydamas, which I have been compelled greatly to abridge (in Xen. Hellen. vi. 1, 4-18).

the interior, and averted the death-blow which came upon
Grecian freedom in the next generation from their hands.
The Lacedæmonians found some compensation for
their reluctant abandonment of Polydamas, in
the pacific propositions from Athens which
liberated them from one of their chief enemies.
But the peace thus concluded was scarcely even
brought to execution. Timotheus being ordered
home from Korkyra, obeyed and set sail with
his fleet. He had serving along with him some
exiles from Zakynthus; and as he passed by
that island in his homeward voyage, he disembarked these exiles upon it, aiding them in
establishing a fortified post. Against this proceeding the Zakynthian government laid complaints at Sparta, where it was so deeply resented,
that redress having been in vain demanded at
Athens, the peace was at once broken off, and war again
declared. A Lacedæmonian squadron of 25 sail was despatched to assist the Zakynthians,[1] while plans were formed

B.C. 874.
Peace between
Athens and
Sparta—
broken off
almost immediately.
The Lacedæmonians
declare war
again, and
resume
their plans
upon
Zakynthus
and Korkyra.

[1] Xen. Hellen. vi. 2, 8; Diodor. xv. 45.

The statements of Diodorus are not clear in themselves; besides that on some points, though not in the main, they contradict Xenophon. Diodorus states that those exiles whom Timotheus brought back to Zakynthus, were the philo-Spartan leaders, who had been recently expelled for their misrule under the empire of Sparta. The statement must doubtless be incorrect. The exiles whom Timotheus restored must have belonged to the anti-Spartan party in the island.

But Diodorus appears to me to have got into confusion by representing that universal and turbulent revolution against the philo-Spartan oligarchies, which really did not take place until after the battle of Leuktra—as if it had taken place some three years earlier. The events recounted in Diodor. xv. 40, seem to me to belong to a period *after* the battle

of Leuktra.

Diodorus also seems to have made a mistake in saying that the Athenians sent *Ktesikles* as auxiliary commander to *Zakynthus* (xv. 46); whereas this very commander is announced by himself in the next chapter (as well as by Xenophon, who calls him *Stesikles*) as sent to *Korkyra* (Hellen. v. 2, 10).

I conceive Diodorus to have inadvertently mentioned this Athenian expedition under Stesikles or Ktesikles, twice over; once as sent to Zakynthus—then again, as sent to *Korkyra*. The latter is the truth. No Athenian expedition at all appears on this occasion to have gone to Zakynthus; for Xenophon enumerates the Zakynthians among those who helped to fit out the fleet of Mnasippus (v. 2, 3).

On the other hand, I see no reason for calling in question the reality of the two Lacedæmonian expeditions, in the last half of 374 B.C.—one under Aristokrates to

for the acquisition of the more important island of Korkyra. The fleet of Timotheus having now been removed home, a malcontent Korkyræan party formed a conspiracy to introduce the Lacedæmonians as friends, and betray the island to them. A Lacedæmonian fleet of 22 triremes accordingly sailed thither, under colour of a voyage to Sicily. But the Korkyræan government, having detected the plot, refused to receive them, took precautions for defence, and sent envoys to Athens to entreat assistance.

The Lacedæmonians now resolved to attack Korkyra openly, with the full naval force of their confederacy. By the joint efforts of Sparta, Corinth, Leukas, Ambrakia, Elis, Zakynthus, Achaia, Epidaurus, Trœzen, Hermionê, and Halieis— strengthened by pecuniary payments from other confederates, who preferred commuting their obligation to serve beyond sea—a fleet of sixty triremes and a body of 1500 mercenary hoplites, were assembled; besides some Lacedæmonians, probably Helots or Neodamodes.[1] At the same time, application was sent to Dionysius the Syracusan despot, for his cooperation against Korkyra, on the ground that the connection of that island with Athens had proved once, and might prove again, dangerous to his city.

B.C. 373. Lacedæmonian armament under Mnasippus, collected from all the confederates, invades Korkyra.

It was in the spring of 373 B.C. that this force proceeded against Korkyra, under the command of the Lacedæmonian Mnasippus; who, having driven in the Korkyræan fleet with the loss of four triremes, landed on the island, gained a victory, and confined the inhabitants within the walls of the city. He next carried his ravages round the adjacent lands, which were found in the highest state of cultivation and full of the richest produce; fields admirably tilled—vineyards in surpassing condition—with splendid farm-buildings, well-appointed wine-cellars, and abund-

Mnasippus besieges the city—high cultivation of the adjoining lands.

Zakynthos, the other under Alkidas to Korkyra—which Diodorus mentions (Diod. xv. 45, 46). It is true that Xenophon does not notice either of them; but they are noway inconsistent with the facts which he does state.

[1] Xen. Hellen. vi. 2, 3, 5, 10:

compare v. 2, 21—about the commutation of personal service for money.

Diodorus (xv. 47) agrees with Xenophon in the main about the expedition of Mnasippus, though differing on several other contemporary points.

ance of cattle as well as labouring-slaves. The invading soldiers, while enriching themselves by depredations on cattle and slaves, became so pampered with the plentiful stock around, that they refused to drink any wine that was not of the first quality.¹ Such is the picture given by Xenophon, an unfriendly witness, of the democratical Korkyra, in respect of its landed economy, at the time when it was invaded by Mnasippus; a picture not less memorable than that presented by Thucydides (in the speech of Archidamus), of the flourishing agriculture surrounding democratical Athens, at the moment when the hand of the Peloponnesian devastator was first felt there in 431 B.C.²

*The Korkyræans blocked up in the city —supplies intercepted —want begins—no hope of safety except in aid from Athens. Reinforcement arrives from Athens—large Athenian fleet preparing under Timotheus.*

With such plentiful quarters for his soldiers, Mnasippus encamped on a hill near the city walls, cutting off those within from supplies out of the country, while he at the same time blocked up the harbour with his fleet. The Korkyræans soon began to be in want. Yet they seemed to have no chance of safety except through aid from the Athenians; to whom they had sent envoys with pressing entreaties,³ and who had now reason to regret their hasty consent (in the preceding year) to summon home the fleet of Timotheus from the island. However, Timotheus was again appointed admiral of a new fleet to be sent thither; while a division of 600 peltasts, under Stesiklês, was directed to be despatched by the quickest route, to meet the immediate necessities of the Korkyræans, during

¹ Xen. Hellen. vi. 2, 6. Ἐπειδὴ δὲ ἀκίβη (when Mnasippus landed), ἐκράτει τε τῆς γῆς καὶ ἐδήου ἀξειργασμένην μὲν καγκαλῶς καὶ πεφυτευμένην τὴν χώραν, μεγαλοπρεπεῖς δὲ οἰκήσεις καὶ οἰνῶνας κατεσκευασμένους ἔχουσαν ἐπὶ τῶν ἀγρῶν· ὥστ᾽ ἔφασαν τοὺς στρατιώτας εἰς τοῦτο τρυφῆς ἐλθεῖν, ὥστ᾽ οὐκ ἐθέλειν πίνειν, εἰ μὴ ἀνθοσμίας εἴη. Καὶ ἀνδράποδα δὲ καὶ βοσκήματα πάμπολλα ἡλίσκετο ἐκ τῶν ἀγρῶν.
Οἶνον, implied in the antecedent word οἰνῶνας, is understood after πίνειν.

² Thucyd. i. 82. (Speech of Archidamus) μὴ γὰρ ἄλλο τι νομίσητε τὴν γῆν αὐτῶν (of the Athenians) ἢ ὅμηρον ἔχειν, καὶ οὐχ ἧσσον ὅσῳ ἄμεινον ἐξείργασται.
Compare the earlier portion of the same speech (c. 80), and the second speech of the same Archidamus (ii. 11).
To the same purpose Thucydides speaks, respecting the properties of the wealthy men established throughout the area of Attica—οἱ δὲ δυνατοὶ καλὰ κτήματα κατὰ τὴν χώραν οἰκοδομίαις τε καὶ πολυτελέσι κατασκευαῖς ἀπολωλεκότες (i. e. by the invasion)—Thucyd. ii. 65.

³ The envoys from Korkyra to Athens (mentioned by Xenophon,

the delays unavoidable in the preparation of the main fleet and its circumnavigation of Peloponnesus. The peltasts were conveyed by land across Thessaly and Epirus, to the coast opposite Korkyra; upon which island they were enabled to land through the intervention of Alketas solicited by the Athenians. They were fortunate enough to get into the town; where they not only brought the news that a large Athenian fleet might be speedily expected, but also contributed much to the defence. Without such encouragement and aid, the Korkyræans would hardly have held out; for the famine within the walls increased daily; and at length became so severe, that many of the citizens deserted, and numbers of slaves were thrust out. Mnasippus refused to receive them, making public proclamation that every one who deserted should be sold into slavery; and since deserters nevertheless continued to come, he caused them to be scourged back to the city-gates. As for the unfortunate slaves, being neither received by him nor readmitted within, many perished outside of the gates from sheer hunger.[1]

Such spectacles of misery portended so visibly the approaching hour of surrender, that the besieging army became careless, and the general insolent. Though his military chest was well-filled, through the numerous pecuniary payments which he had received from allies in commutation of personal service—yet he had 'dismissed several of his mercenaries without pay, and had kept all of them unpaid for the last two months. His present temper made him not only more harsh towards his own soldiers,[2] but also less vigilant in the conduct of the siege. Accordingly the besieged, detecting from their watch-towers the negligence of the guards, chose a favourable opportunity and made a vigorous sally. Mnasippus, on seeing his outposts driven in, armed

*Mnasippus becomes careless and insolent from over-confidence—he offends his mercenaries—the Korkyræans make a successful sally— Mnasippus is defeated and slain— the city supplied with provisions.*

v. 2, 9) would probably cross Epirus and Thessaly, through the aid of Alketas. This would be a much quicker way for them than the circumnavigation of Peloponnesus; and it would suggest the same way for the detachment of Stesiklês presently to be mentioned.

[1] Xen. Hellen. vi. 2, 15.
[2] Xen. Hellen. vi. 2, 16.
Ὁ δ' αὖ Μνάσιππος ὁρῶν ταῦτα, ἠνώμιζέ τε ὅσον οὐκ ἤδη ἔχειν τὴν πόλιν, καὶ περὶ τοὺς μισθοφόρους ἐκαινούργει, καὶ τοὺς μέν τινας αὐτῶν ἀπομισθοὺς ἐπεπίηκει, τοῖς δ' οὖσι καὶ δυοῖν ἤδη μηνοῖν ὠφείλε τὸν

himself and hastened forward with the Lacedæmonians around him to sustain them; giving orders to the officers of the mercenaries to bring their men forward also. But these officers replied, that they could not answer for the obedience of soldiers without pay; upon which Mnasippus was so incensed, that he struck them with his stick and with the shaft of his spear. Such an insult inflamed still farther the existing discontent. Both officers and soldiers came to the combat discouraged and heartless, while the Athenian peltasts and the Korkyræan hoplites, rushing out of several gates at once, pressed their attack with desperate energy. Mnasippus, after displaying great personal valour, was at length slain, and all his troops, being completely routed, fled back to the fortified camp in which their stores were preserved. Even this too might have been taken, and the whole armament destroyed, had the besieged attacked it at once. But they were astonished at their own success. Mistaking the numerous camp-followers for soldiers in reserve, they retired back to the city.

Their victory was however so complete, as to re-open easy communication with the country, to procure sufficient temporary supplies, and to afford a certainty of holding out until reinforcement from Athens should arrive. Such reinforcement, indeed, was already on its way, and had been announced as approaching to Hypermenés (second under the deceased Mnasippus), who had now succeeded to the command. Terrified at the news, he hastened to sail round from his station—which he had occupied with the fleet to block up the harbour—to the fortified camp. Here he first put the slaves, as well as the property, aboard of his transports, and sent them away; remaining himself to defend the camp with the soldiers and marines—but remaining only a short time, and then taking these latter also aboard the triremes. He thus completely evacuated the island, making off for Leukas. But such had been the hurry—and so great the terror lest the Athenian fleet should arrive—that much corn and wine, many slaves, and even many sick and wounded soldiers, were left behind. To the victorious Korkyræans, these acquisitions were not needed

*Approach of the Athenian reinforcement—Hypermenés, successor of Mnasippus, conveys away the armament, leaving his sick and much property behind.*

μισθὸν, οὐκ ἀπορῶν, ὡς ἐλέγετο, χρημάτων, &c.

to enhance the value of a triumph which rescued them from capture, slavery, or starvation.[1]

The Athenian fleet had not only been tardy in arriving, so as to incur much risk of finding the island already taken—but when it did come, it was commanded by Iphikratês, Chabrias, and the orator Kallistratus[2]—not by Timotheus, whom the original vote of the people had nominated. It appears that Timotheus—who (in April 373 B.C.), when the Athenians first learnt that the formidable Lacedæmonian fleet had begun to attack Korkyra, had been directed to proceed thither forthwith with a fleet of 60 triremes—found a difficulty in manning his ships at Athens, and therefore undertook a preliminary cruise to procure both seamen and contributory funds, from the maritime allies. His first act was to transport the 600 peltasts under Stesiklês to Thessaly, where he entered into relations with Jason of Pheræ. He persuaded the latter to become the ally of Athens, and to further the march of Stesiklês with his division by land across Thessaly, over the passes of Pindus, to Epirus; where Alketas, who was at once the ally of Athens, and the dependent of Jason, conveyed them by night across the strait from Epirus to Korkyra. Having thus opened important connection with the powerful Thessalian despot, and obtained from him a very seasonable service, together (perhaps) with some seamen from Pagasæ to man his fleet —Timotheus proceeded onward to the ports of Macedonia, where he also entered into relations with Amyntas, receiving from him signal marks of private favour—and then to Thrace as well as the neighbouring islands. His voyage procured for him valuable subsidies in money and supplies of seamen, besides some new adhesions and deputies to the Athenian confederacy.

*B.C. 373.* Tardy arrival of the Athenian fleet—it is commanded not by Timotheus, but by Iphikratês—causes of the delay—preliminary voyage of Timotheus, very long protracted.

This preliminary cruise of Timotheus, undertaken with the general purpose of collecting means for the expedition to Korkyra, began in the month of April or commencement of May 373 B.C.[3] On

*B.C. 373.*

---

[1] Xen. Hellen. vi. 2, 18-26; Diodor. xv. 47.
[2] Xen. Hellen. vi. 2, 39.
[3] The manner in which I have described the preliminary cruise of Timotheus, will be found (I think) the only way of uniting into one consistent narrative the scattered fragments of information which we possess respecting his proceed-

**Discontent at Athens, in consequence of the absence of Timotheus—distress of the armament assembled at Kalauria—Iphikrates and Kallistratus accuse Timotheus. Iphikrates named admiral in his place.**

departing, it appears, he had given orders to such of the allies as were intended to form part of the expedition, to assemble at Kalauria (an island off Trœzen, consecrated to Poseidon), where he would himself come and take them up to proceed onward. Pursuant to such order, several contingents mustered at this island; among them the Bœotians, who sent several triremes, though in the preceding year it had been alleged against them that they contributed nothing to sustain the naval exertions of Athens. But Timotheus stayed out a long time. Reliance was placed upon him, and upon the money which he was to bring home, for the pay of the fleet; and the unpaid triremes accordingly fell into distress and

inge in this year. The date of his setting out from Athens is exactly determined by Demosthenes, adv. Timoth. p. 1186—the month Munychion, in the archonship of Sokratides—April 373 B.C. Diodorus says that he proceeded to Thrace, and that he acquired several new members for the confederacy (xv. 47); Xenophon states that he sailed towards the islands (Hellen. vi. 2, 13); two statements not directly the same, yet not incompatible with each other. In his way to Thrace, he would naturally pass up the Eubœan strait and along the coast of Thessaly.

We know that Steslkles and his peltasts must have got to Korkyra, not by sea circumnavigating Peloponnesus, but by land across Thessaly and Epirus; a much quicker way. Xenophon tells us that the Athenians "asked Alketas to help them to cross over from the mainland of Epirus to the opposite island of Korkyra; and that they were in consequence carried across by night"—'Ἀλκέτου δὲ ἐδεήθησαν συνδιαβιβάσαι τούτους καὶ οὗτοι μὲν νυκτὸς διακομισθέντες εἰς τῆς χώρας, εἰσῆλθον εἰς τὴν πόλιν.

Now these troops could not have got to Epirus without crossing Thessaly; nor could they have crossed Thessaly without the permission and escort of Jason. Moreover, Alketas himself was the dependent of Jason, whose goodwill was therefore doubly necessary (Xen. Hellen. vi. 1, 7).

We farther know that in the year preceding (374 B.C.), Jason was not yet in alliance with Athens, nor even inclined to become so, though the Athenians were very anxious for it (Xen. Hellen. vi. 1, 10). But in November 373 B.C., Jason (as well as Alketas) appears as the established ally of Athens; not as then becoming her ally for the first time, but as so completely an established ally, that he comes to Athens for the express purpose of being present at the trial of Timotheus and of deposing in his favour—'Ἀφικομένου γὰρ Ἀλκέτου καὶ Ἰάσονος ὡς τούτου (Timotheus) ἐν τῷ Μαιμακτηριῶνι μηνὶ τῷ ἐπ' Ἀστείου ἄρχοντος, ἐπὶ τὸν ἀγῶνα τὸν τούτου, βοηθησάντων αὐτῷ καὶ κατηγορίαν εἰς τὴν οἰκίαν τὴν ἐν Πειραιεῖ, &c. (Demosthen. adv. Timoth. c. 5. p. 1190). Again—Αὐτὸν δὲ τοῦτον (Timotheus) ἐξαι-

disorganization at Kalauria, awaiting his return.[1] In the mean time, fresh news reached Athens that Korkyra was much pressed; so that great indignation was felt against the absent admiral, for employing in his present cruise a precious interval essential to enable him to reach the island in time. Iphikratês (who had recently come back from serving with Pharnabazus, in an unavailing attempt to reconquer Egypt for the Persian king) and the orator Kallistratus, were especially loud in their accusations against him. And as the very salvation of Korkyra required pressing haste, the Athenians cancelled the appointment of Timotheus even during his absence—naming Iphikratês, Kallistratus, and Chabrias, to equip a fleet and go round to Korkyra without delay.[2]

Before they could get ready, Timotheus returned; bringing several new adhesions to the confederacy, with a flourishing account of general success.[3] He went down

του μὲν ὧν μὲν τῶν ἐπιτηδείων καὶ οἰκείων αὐτῷ ἁπάντων, ὅτι δὲ καὶ Ἀλκέτου καὶ Ἰάσονος, συμμάχων ὄντων ὑμῖν, μόλις μὲν ἐπείσθητε δεῖναι (Demosthen. ib. c. 3. p. 1187). We see from hence therefore that the first alliance between Jason and Athens had been contracted in the early part of 373 B.C.; we see farther that it had been contracted by Timothens in his preliminary cruise, which is the only reasonable way of explaining the strong interest felt by Jason as well as by Alketas in the fate of Timotheus, inducing them to take the remarkable step of coming to Athens to promote his acquittal. It was Timotheus who had first made the alliance of Athens with Alketas (Diodor. xv. 36; Cornel. Nepos, Timoth. c. 2), a year or two before.

Combining all the circumstances here stated, I infer with confidence, that Timotheus, in his preliminary cruise, visited Jason, contracted alliance between him and Athens, and prevailed upon him to forward the division of Biesiklês across

Thessaly to Epirus and Korkyra. In this oration of Demosthenês, there are three or four exact dates mentioned, which are a great aid to the understanding of the historical events of the time. That oration is spoken by Apollodorus, claiming from Timotheus the repayment of money lent to him by Pasion the banker, father of Apollodorus; and the dates specified are copied from entries made by Pasion at the time in his commercial books (c. 1. p. 1186; c. 9. p. 1197).

[1] Demosthen. adv. Timoth. c. 8. p. 1188. ἀμισθον μὲν τὸ στρατευμα καταλελύσθαι ἐν Καλαυρίᾳ, &c.—ibid. c. 10. p. 1199. προσῆκε γάρ τῷ μὲν Βοιωτίῳ ἄρχοντι παρὰ τούτου (Τιμοθεους) τὴν τροφὴν τοῖς ἐν ταῖς ναυσὶ παραλαμβάνειν· ἐκ γὰρ τῶν κοινῶν συντάξεων ἡ μισθοφορία ἦν τῷ στρατεύματι· τὰ δὲ χρήματα οὐ (Τιμοθεους) ἔλαβες ἐξέλεξας ἐκ τῶν συμμάχων καὶ οἱ ἴδει αὐτῶν λόγον ἀποδοῦναι.

[2] Xenoph. Hellen. vi. 2, 12, 13, 39; Demosthen. adv. Timoth. c. 5. p. 1188.

[3] Diodor. xv. 47.

to Kalauria to supply the deficiencies of funds, and make up
for the embarrassments which his absence had occasioned.
But he could not pay the Bœotian trierarchs
without borrowing money for the purpose on his
own credit; for though the sum brought home
from his voyage was considerable, it would
appear that the demands upon him had been
greater still. At first an accusation, called for
in consequence of the pronounced displeasure
of the public, was entered against him by Iphikratês and Kallistratus. But as these two had
been named joint admirals for the expedition
to Korkyra, which admitted of no delay—his trial
was postponed until the autumn; a postponement advantageous to the accused, and doubtless seconded by his
friends.[1]

*Return of Timotheus—an accusation is entered against him, but trial is postponed until the return of Iphikratês from Korkyra.*

Meanwhile Iphikratês adopted the most strenuous
measures for accelerating the equipment of his
fleet. In the present temper of the public, and
in the known danger of Korkyra, he was allowed
(though perhaps Timotheus, a few weeks earlier,
would not have been allowed) not only to impress
seamen in the port, but even to coerce the
trierarchs with severity,[2] and to employ all the
triremes reserved for the coast-guard of Attica,
as well as the two sacred triremes called Paralus
and Salaminia. He thus completed a fleet of
seventy sail, promising to send back a large
portion of it directly, if matters took a favourable turn at Korkyra. Expecting to find on the
watch for him a Lacedæmonian fleet fully equal
to his own, he arranged his voyage so as to combine the
maximum of speed with training to his seamen, and with
preparation for naval combat. The larger sails of an
ancient trireme were habitually taken out of the ship

*Rapid and energetic movements of Iphikratês towards Korkyra—his excellent management of the voyage. On reaching Kephallenia, he learns the flight of the Lacedæmonians from Korkyra.*

---

[1] I collect what is here stated from Demosthen. adv. Timoth. c. 5. p. 1188; c. 10, p. 1199. It is there said that Timotheus was about to sail home from Kalauria to take his trial; yet it is certain that his trial did not take place until the month Mæmakterion or November. Accordingly the trial must have been postponed, in consequence of the necessity for Iphikratês and Kallistratus going away at once to preserve Korkyra.

[2] Xen. Hellen. vi. 2, 14. Ὁ δὲ (Ἰφικράτης) ἐπεὶ κατέστη στρατηγός, μάλα ὀξέως τάς ναῦς ἐκλήρουτο, καὶ τοὺς τριηράρχους ἠνάγκαζε.

previous to a battle, as being inconvenient aboard: Iphikratês left such sails at Athens,—employed even the smaller sails sparingly—and kept his seamen constantly at the oar; which greatly accelerated his progress, at the same time that it kept the men in excellent training. Every day he had to stop, for meals and rest, on an enemy's shore; and these halts were conducted with such extreme dexterity as well as precision, that the least possible time was consumed, not enough for any local hostile force to get together. On reaching Sphakteria, Iphikratês learnt for the first time the defeat and death of Mnasippus. Yet not fully trusting the correctness of his information, he still persevered both in his celerity and his precautions, until he reached Kephallenia, where he first fully satisfied himself that the danger of Korkyra was past. The excellent management of Iphikratês throughout this expedition is spoken of in terms of admiration by Xenophon.[1]

Having no longer any fear of the Lacedæmonian fleet, the Athenian commander probably now sent back the home-squadron of Attica which he had been allowed to take, but which could ill be spared from the defence of the coast.[2] After making himself master of some of the Kephallenian cities, he then proceeded onward to Korkyra; where the squadron of ten triremes from Syracuse was now on the point of arriving; sent by Dionysius to aid the Lacedæmonians, but as yet uninformed of their flight. Iphikratês, posting scouts on the hills to give notice of their approach, set apart twenty triremes to be ready for moving at the first signal. So excellent was his discipline (says Xenophon), that "the moment the signal was made, the ardour of all the crews was a fine thing to see; there was not a man who did not hasten at a run to take his place aboard."[3] The ten Syracusan triremes, after their voyage across from the Japygian cape, had halted to rest their men on one of the northern points of Korkyra; where they were found by Iphikratês and captured, with all their crews and the admiral Anippus; one alone escaping, through the strenuous efforts of her captain, the Rhodian Melanopus. Iphikratês returned in triumph, towing his nine prizes into the har-

*He goes on to Korkyra, and captures by surprise the ten Syracusan triremes sent by Dionysius to the aid of Sparta.*

[1] Xen. Hellen. vi. 2, 27, 32.  [2] Compare vi. 2, 14—with vi. 2, 39.
[3] Xen. Hellen. vi. 2, 34.

bour of Korkyra. The crews, being sold or ransomed, yielded to him a sum of 60 talents; the admiral Anippus was retained in expectation of a higher ransom, but slew himself shortly afterwards from mortification.¹

*Iphikratês in want of money— he sends home Kallistratus to Athens— he finds work for his seamen at Korkyra —he obtains funds by service in Akarnania.*

Though the sum thus realised enabled Iphikratês for the time to pay his men, yet the suicide of Anippus was a pecuniary disappointment to him, and he soon began to need money. This consideration induced him to consent to the return of his colleague Kallistratus; who— an orator by profession, and not on friendly terms with Iphikratês—had come out against his own consent. Iphikratês had himself singled out both Kallistratus and Chabrias as his colleagues. He was not indifferent to the value of their advice, nor did he fear the criticisms, even of rivals, on what they really saw in his proceedings. But he had accepted the command under hazardous circumstances; not only from the insulting displacement of Timotheus, and the provocation consequently given to a powerful party attached to the son of Konon— but also under great doubts whether he could succeed in relieving Korkyra, in spite of the rigorous coercion which he applied to man his fleet. Had the island been taken and had Iphikratês failed, he would have found himself exposed to severe crimination, and multiplied enemies, at Athens. Perhaps Kallistratus and Chabrias, if left at home, might in that case have been among his assailants— so that it was important to him to identify both of them with his good or ill success, and to profit by the military ability of the latter as well as by the oratorical talent of the former.² As the result of the expedition, however,

---

¹ Xen. Hellen. vi. 2, 35, 36; Diodor. xv. 47.

We find a story recounted by Diodorus (xvi. 57), that the Athenians under Iphikratês captured, off Korkyra, some triremes of Dionysius, carrying sacred ornaments to Delphi and Olympia. They detained and appropriated the valuable cargo, of which Dionysius afterwards loudly complained.

This story (if there be any truth in it) can hardly allude to any other triremes than those under Anippus. Yet Xenophon would probably have mentioned the story, if he had heard it; since it presents the enemies of Sparta as committing sacrilege. And whether the triremes were carrying sacred ornaments or not, it is certain that they were coming to take part in the war, and were therefore legitimate prizes.

² Xen. Hellen. vi. 2, 39. The meaning of Xenophon here is not

was altogether favourable, all such anxieties were removed. Iphikratês could well afford to part with both his colleagues; and Kallistratus engaged, that if permitted to go home, he would employ all his efforts to keep the fleet well-paid from the public treasury; or if this were impracticable, that he would labour to procure peace.[1] So terrible are the difficulties which the Grecian generals now experience in procuring money from Athens (or from other cities in whose service they are acting), for payment of their troops! Iphikratês suffered the same embarrassment which Timotheus had experienced the year before—and which will be found yet more painfully felt as we advance forward in the history. For the present he subsisted his seamen by finding work for them on the farms of the Korkyræans, where there must doubtless have been ample necessity for repairs after the devastations of Mnasippus; while he crossed over to Akarnania with his peltasts and hoplites, and there obtained service with the townships friendly to Athens against such others as were friendly to Sparta; especially against the warlike inhabitants of the strong town called Thyrieia.[2]

The happy result of the Korkyræan expedition, imparting universal satisfaction at Athens, was not less beneficial to Timotheus than to Iphikratês. It was in November 373 B.C., that the former, as well as his quæstor or military treasurer Antimachus, underwent each his trial. Kallistratus, having returned home, pleaded against the quæstor, perhaps against Timotheus also, as one of the

very clear, nor is even the text perfect.

Ἐγὼ μὲν δὴ ταύτην τὴν στρατηγίαν τῶν Ἰφικράτους οὐχ ἥκιστα ἐκείνων ἕνεκα καὶ τὸ προωκληκέναι καὶ εὖ ὅτι ἑαυτῷ (this shows that Iphikratês himself singled them out) Καλλίστρατόν τε τὸν δημήγορον, οὐ μάλα ἐπιτήδειον ὄντα, καὶ Χαβρίαν, μάλα στρατηγικὸν νομιζόμενον. Εἶτα γὰρ φρονίμους αὐτοὺς ἡγούμενος εἶναι, συμβούλους λαβεῖν ἐβούλετο, σώφρον μοι δοκεῖ διαπράξασθαι· εἴτε ἀντιπάλους νομίζων, οὕτω θρασέως (some words in the text seem to

be wanting) ..... μήτε καταρρᾳθυμῶν μήτε καταμελῶν φαίνεσθαι μηδὲν, μεγαλοφρονοῦντος ἐφ' ἑαυτῷ τοῦτό μοι δοκεῖ ἀνδρὸς εἶναι.

I follow Dr. Thirlwall's translation of οὐ μάλα ἐπιτήδειον, which appears to me decidedly preferable. The word ἥρει (vl. 5, 3) shows that Kallistratus was an unwilling colleague.

[1] Xen. Hellen. vi. 3, 3. ὑκοσχόμενος γὰρ Ἰφικράτει (Kallistratus) εἰ αὐτὸν ἀφίει, ἢ χρήματα εἰσπράξειν τῷ ναυτικῷ, ἢ εἰρήνην ποιήσειν, &c.

[2] Xen. Hellen. iv. 2, 37, 38.

accusers;[1] though probably in a spirit of greater gentleness
and moderation, in consequence of his recent joint success
and of the general good temper prevalent in the
city. And while the edge of the accusation
against Timotheus was thus blunted, the defence was strengthened not merely by numerous
citizen friends speaking in his favour with increased confidence, but also by the unusual
phænomenon of two powerful foreign supporters.
At the request of Timotheus, both Alketas of
Epirus, and Jason of Pheræ, came to Athens
a little before the trial, to appear as witnesses
in his favour. They were received and lodged
by him in his house in the Hippodamian Agora,
the principal square of the Peiræus. And as he
was then in some embarrassment for want of
money, he found it necessary to borrow various
articles of finery in order to do them honour
—clothes, bedding, and two silver drinking-bowls—
from Pasion, a wealthy banker near at hand. These two
important witnesses would depose to the zealous service
and estimable qualities of Timotheus; who had inspired
them with warm interest, and had been the means of
bringing them into alliance with Athens; an alliance,
which they had sealed at once by conveying Stesiklês and
his division across Thessaly and Epirus to Korkyra. The
minds of the Dikastery would be powerfully affected by
seeing before them such a man as Jason of Pheræ, at that
moment the most powerful individual in Greece; and we
are not surprised to learn that Timotheus was acquitted.
His treasurer Antimachus, not tried by the same Dikastery,
and doubtless not so powerfully befriended, was less fortunate. He was condemned to death, and his property
confiscated; the Dikastery doubtless believing, on what
evidence we do not know, that he had been guilty of fraud
in dealing with the public money, which had caused serious
injury at a most important crisis. Under the circumstances
of the case, he was held responsible as treasurer, for the
pecuniary department of the money-levying command confided to Timotheus by the people.

[1] Demosthen. cont. Timoth. c. 9. p. 1197, 1193.

CHAP. LXXVII.   CONDUCT OF TIMOTHEUS.   371

As to the military conduct, for which Timotheus himself would be personally accountable, we can only remark that having been invested with the command for the special purpose of relieving the besieged Korkyra, he appears to have devoted an unreasonable length of time to his own self-originated cruise elsewhere; though such cruise was in itself beneficial to Athens; insomuch that if Korkyra had really been taken, the people would have had good reason for imputing the misfortune to his delay.¹ And although he was now acquitted, his reputation suffered so much by the whole affair, that in the ensuing spring he was glad to accept an

*Timotheus had been guilty of delay, not justifiable under the circumstances— though acquitted, his reputation suffered— he accepts command under Persia.*

¹ The narrative here given of the events of 373 B.C., so far as they concern Timotheus and Iphikratês, appears to me the only way of satisfying the exigences of the case, and following the statements of Xenophon and Demosthenes.

Schneider in his note, indeed, implies, and Rehdantz (Vitæ Iphicratis, &c. p. 86) contends, that Iphikratês did not take the command of the fleet, nor depart from Athens, until *after* the trial of Timotheus. There are some expressions in the oration of Demosthenes, which might seem to countenance this supposition; but it will be found hardly admissible, if we attentively study the series of facts.

1. Mnasippus arrived with his armament at Korkyra, and began the siege, either before April, or at the first opening of April, 373 B.C. For his arrival there, and the good condition of his fleet, was known at Athens *before* Timotheus received his appointment as admiral of the fleet for the relief of the island (Xen. Hellen. vi. 2, 10, 11, 12).

2. Timotheus sailed from Peiræus on this appointed voyage, in April, 373 B.C.

3. Timotheus was tried at Athens in November 373 B.C.; Alketas and Jason being then present, as allies of Athens and witnesses in his favour.

Now, if the truth were, that Iphikratês did not depart from Athens with his fleet until after the trial of Timotheus in November, we must suppose that the siege of Korkyra by Mnasippus lasted seven months, and the cruise of Timotheus nearly five months. Both the one and the other are altogether improbable. The Athenians would never have permitted Korkyra to incur so terrible a chance of capture, simply in order to wait for the trial of Timotheus. Xenophon does not expressly say how long the siege of Korkyra lasted; but from his expressions about the mercenaries of Mnasippus (that already pay was owing to them for *as much as two months*—καὶ δυοῖν ἤδη μηνοῖν—vi. 2, 16), we should infer that it could hardly have lasted more than three months in all. Let us say, that it lasted four months; the siege would then be over in August; and we know that the fleet of Iphikratês arrived just after the siege was concluded.

Besides, is it credible, that Timotheus—named as admiral for the express purpose of relieving Korkyra, and knowing that Mnasippus

2 B 2

invitation of the Persian satraps, who offered him the command of the Grecian mercenaries in their service for the

was already besieging the place with a formidable fleet — would have spent so long a time as *five* months in his preliminary cruise? I presume Timotheus to have stayed out in this cruise about two months; and even this length of time would be quite sufficient to raise strong displeasure against him at Athens, when the danger and privations of Korkyra were made known as hourly increasing. At the time when Timotheus came back to Athens, he found all this displeasure actually afloat against him, excited in part by the strong censures of Iphikratês and Kallistratus (Dem. cont. Timoth. p. 1187. c. 3). The adverse orations in the public assembly, besides inflaming the wrath of the Athenians against him, caused a vote to be passed deposing him from his command to Korkyra, and nominating in his place Iphikratês, with Chabrias and Kallistratus. Probably those who proposed this vote would at the same time give notice that they intended to prefer a judicial accusation against Timotheus for breach or neglect of duty. But it would be the interest of all parties to postpone *actual trial* until the fate of Korkyra should be determined, for which purpose the saving of time would be precious. Already too much time had been lost, and Iphikratês was well aware that his whole chance of success depended upon celerity; while Timotheus and his friends would look upon postponement as an additional chance of softening the public displeasure, besides enabling them to obtain the attendance of Jason and Alketas. Still, though trial was postponed, Timotheus was from this moment under impeachment.

The oration composed by Demosthenês therefore (delivered by Apollodorus as plaintiff, several years afterwards) — though speaking loosely, and not distinguishing the angry speeches against Timotheus *in the public assembly* (in June 873 B.C., or thereabouts, whereby his deposition was obtained), from the accusing speeches against him at his actual trial in November 373 B.C., *before the dikastery* — is nevertheless not incorrect in saying —ἐπειδὴ δ' ἀπεχειροτονήθη μὲν ὑφ' ὑμῶν στρατηγὸς διὰ τὸ μὴ περιπλεῦσαι Πελοπόννησον, ἐπὶ κρίσει δὲ παρεδόθετο εἰς τὸν δῆμον, αἰτίας τῆς μεγίστης τυχών (c. 3. p. 1167)—and again respecting his coming from Kalauria to Athens—μέλλων τοίνυν καταπλεῖν ἐπὶ τὴν κρίσιν, ἐν Καλαυρίᾳ ὁρμιζόμενος, &c. (p. 1188-1189). That Timotheus had been handed over to the people for trial — that he was sailing back from Kalauria *for his trial*—might well be asserted respecting his position in the month of June, though his trial did not actually take place until November. I think it cannot be doubted that the triremes at Kalauria would form a part of that fleet which actually went to Korkyra under Iphikratês; not waiting to go thither until after the trial of Timotheus in November, but departing as soon as Iphikratês could get ready, probably about July 373 B.C.

Rehdantz argues that if Iphikratês departed with the fleet in July, he must have returned to Athens in November to the trial of Timotheus, which is contrary to Xenophon's affirmation that he remained in the Ionian sea until 371 B.C. But if we look attentively at the oration of Demosthenês, we shall see that

Egyptian war; the same command from which Iphikratês had retired a little time before.¹ That admiral, whose naval force had been reinforced by a large number of Korkyræan triremes, was committing without opposition incursions against Akarnania, and the western coast of Peloponnesus; insomuch that the expelled Messenians, in their distant exile at Hesperides in Libya, began to conceive hopes of being restored by Athens to Naupaktus, which they had occupied under her protection during the Peloponnesian war.² And while the Athenians

there is no certain ground for affirming Iphikratês to have been present in Athens in November, during the actual trial of Timotheus. The phrases in p. 1187—ἀριστήκαι δ' αὐτῷ Καλλίστρατος καὶ Ἰφικράτης..... οὗτω δὲ διέθεσαν ὑμᾶς κατηγοροῦντες τούτου αὐτοί τε καὶ οἱ συνηγορεύοντες αὐτοῖς, &c., may be well explained, so far as Iphikratês is concerned, by supposing them to allude to those pronounced censures in the public assembly whereby the vote of deposition against Timotheus was obtained, and whereby the general indignation against him was first excited. I therefore see no reason for affirming that Iphikratês was actually present at the trial of Timotheus in November. But Kallistratus was really present at the trial (see c. 9. p. 1197, 1199); which consists well enough with the statement of Xenophon, that this orator obtained permission from Iphikratês to leave him at Korkyra and come back to Athens (vi. 3, 3). Kallistratus directed his accusation mainly against Antimachus, the treasurer of Timotheus. And it appears to me that under the circumstances of the case, Iphikratês, having carried his point of superseding Timotheus in the command and gaining an important success at Korkyra—might be well-pleased to be dispensed from the obligation of formally accusing him before the Dikastery, in opposition to Jason and Alketas, as well as to a powerful body of Athenian friends. Diodorus (xv. 47) makes a statement quite different from Xenophon. He says that Timotheus was at first deposed from his command, but afterwards forgiven and reappointed by the people (jointly with Iphikratês) in consequence of the great accession of force which he had procured in his preliminary cruise. Accordingly the fleet, 130 triremes in number, was despatched to Korkyra under the joint command of Iphikratês and Timotheus. Diodorus makes no mention of the trial of Timotheus. This account is evidently quite distinct from that of Xenophon; which latter is on all grounds to be preferred, especially as its main points are in conformity with the Demosthenic oration.

¹ Demosth. cont. Timoth. s. 6. p. 1191; o. 8. p. 1194.

We see from another passage of the same oration that the creditors of Timotheus reckoned upon his making a large sum of money in the Persian service (s. 1. p. 1185). This farther illustrates what I have said in a previous note, about the motives of the distinguished Athenian officers to take service in foreign parts away from Athens.

² Xen. Hellen. vi. 3, 33; Pausanias, iv. 26, 3.

were thus masters at sea both east and west of Peloponnesus. Sparta and her confederates, discouraged by the ruinous failure of their expedition against Korkyra in the preceding year, appear to have remained inactive. With such mental predispositions, they were powerfully affected by religious alarm arising from certain frightful earthquakes and inundations with which Peloponnesus was visited during this year, and which were regarded as marks of the wrath of the god Poseidon. More of these formidable visitations occurred this year in Peloponnesus than had ever before been known; especially one, the worst of all, whereby the two towns of Helikê and Bura in Achaia were destroyed, together with a large portion of their population. Ten Lacedæmonian triremes, which happened to be moored on this shore on the night when the calamity occurred, were destroyed by the rush of the waters.[2]

Under these depressing circumstances, the Lacedæmonians had recourse to the same manœuvre which had so well served their purpose fifteen years before, in 368-367 B.C. They sent Antalkidas again as envoy to Persia, to entreat both pecuniary aid,[3] and a fresh Persian intervention enforcing anew the peace which bore his name; which peace had now been infringed (according to Lacedæmonian construction) by the reconstitution of the Bœotian confederacy under Thebes as president. And it appears that in the course of the autumn or winter, Persian envoys actually did come to Greece, requiring that the belligerents should all desist from war, and wind up their dissensions on the principles of the peace of Antalkidas.[4] The Persian satraps, at this

---

[1] See a curious testimony to this fact in Demosthen. cont. Nearav. c. 12. p. 1357.

[2] Diodor. xl. 48, 49; Pausan. vii. 25; Ælian. Hist. Animal. xi. 19. Kallisthenes seems to have described at large, with appropriate religious comments, numerous physical portents which occurred about this time (see Kallisthen. Fragm. 8, ed. Didot).

[3] This second mission of Antalkidas is sufficiently verified by an indirect allusion of Xenophon (vi. 3, 12). His known philo-Laconian sentiments sufficiently explain why he avoids directly mentioning it.

[4] Diodor. xv. 50.

CHAP. LXXVII.    MISSION OF ANTALKIDAS.    375

time renewing their efforts against Egypt, were anxious for the cessation of hostilities in Greece, as a means of enlarging their numbers of Grecian mercenaries; of which troops Timotheus had left Athens a few months before to take the command.

Apart, however, from this prospect of Persian intervention, which doubtless was not without effect —Athens herself was becoming more and more disposed towards peace. That common fear and hatred of the Lacedæmonians, which had brought her into alliance with Thebes in 378 B.C., was now no longer predominant. She was actually at the head of a considerable maritime confederacy; and this she could hardly hope to increase by continuing the war, since the Lacedæmonian naval power had already been humbled. Moreover she found the expense of warlike operations very burdensome, nowise defrayed either by the contributions of her allies or by the results of victory. The orator Kallistratus—who had promised either to procure remittances from Athens to Iphikratês, or to recommend the conclusion of peace— was obliged to confine himself to the latter alternative, and contributed much to promote the pacific dispositions of his countrymen.[1]

*Athens disposed towards peace.*

Moreover, the Athenians had become more and more alienated from Thebes. The ancient antipathy, between these two neighbours, had for a time been overlaid by common fear of Sparta. But as soon as Thebes had re-established her authority in Bœotia, the jealousies of Athens again began to arise. In 374 B.C., she had concluded a peace with the Spartans, without the concurrence of Thebes; which peace was broken almost as soon as made, by the

*Athens had ceased to be afraid of Sparta, and had become again jealous of Thebes.*

---

Diodorus had stated (a few chapters before, xv. 38) that Persian envoys had also come into Greece a little before the peace of 374 B.C., and had been the originators of that previous peace. But this appears to me one of the cases (not a few altogether in his history) in which he repeats himself, or gives the same event twice over under analogous circumstances. The intervention of the Persian envoys bears much more suitably on the period immediately preceding the peace of 371 B.C., than upon that which preceded the peace of 374 B.C.—when, in point of fact, no peace was ever fully executed.

Dionysius of Halikarnassus also (Judic. de Lysiâ, p. 479) represents the king of Persia as a party to the peace sworn by Athens and Sparta in 371 B.C.

[1] Xen. Hellen. vi. 3, 3.

Spartans themselves, in consequence of the proceedings of
Timotheus at Zakynthus. The Phokians—against whom,
as having been active allies of Sparta in her invasions of
Bœotia, Thebes was now making war—had also been ancient
friends of Athens, who sympathised with their sufferings.[1]
Moreover the Thebans on their side probably resented the
unpaid and destitute condition in which their seamen had
been left by Timotheus at Kalauria, during the expedition
for the relief of Korkyra, in the preceding year;[2] an expedition, of which Athens alone reaped both the glory and
the advantage. Though they remained members of the
confederacy, sending deputies to the congress at Athens,
the unfriendly spirit on both sides continued on the increase,
and was farther exasperated by their violent proceeding
against Platæa in the first half of 372 B.C.

During the last three or four years, Platæa, like the
other towns of Bœotia, had been again brought
into the confederacy under Thebes. Re-
established by Sparta after the peace of Antalkidas as a so-called autonomous town, it had
been garrisoned by her as a post against Thebes,
and was no longer able to maintain a real autonomy after the Spartans had been excluded from
Bœotia in 376 B.C. While other Bœotian cities
were glad to find themselves emancipated from
their philo-Laconian oligarchies and rejoined to
the federation under Thebes, Platæa—as well
as Thespiæ—submitted to the union only by
constraint; awaiting any favourable opportunity
for breaking off, either by means of Sparta or of Athens.
Aware probably of the growing coldness between the
Athenians and Thebans, the Platæans were secretly trying
to persuade Athens to accept and occupy their town,
annexing Platæa to Attica:[3] a project hazardous both to
Thebes and Athens, since it would place them at open war
with each other, while neither was yet at peace with
Sparta.

*Equivocal position of the restored Platæa, now that the Lacedæmonians had been expelled from Bœotia. The Platæans try to persuade Athens to incorporate them with Attica.*

[1] Xen. Hellen. vi. 3, 1.
[2] Demosth. cont. Timoth. p. 1189, s. 17.
[3] Diodor. xv. 46. I do not know from whom Diodorus copied this statement; but it seems extremely reasonable.

This intrigue, coming to the knowledge of the Thebans, determined them to strike a decisive blow. Their presidency, over more than one of the minor Bœotian cities, had always been ungentle, suitable to the roughness of their dispositions. Towards Platæa, especially, they not only bore an ancient antipathy, but regarded the re-established town as little better than a Lacedæmonian encroachment, abstracting from themselves a portion of territory which had become Theban, by prescriptive enjoyment lasting for forty years from the surrender of Platæa in 427 B.C. As it would have been to them a loss as well as embarrassment, if Athens should resolve to close with the tender of Platæa—they forestalled the contingency by seizing the town for themselves. Since the re-conquest of Bœotia by Thebes, the Platæans had come again, though reluctantly, under the ancient constitution of Bœotia: they were living at peace with Thebes, acknowledging her rights as president of the federation, and having their own rights as members guaranteed in return by her, probably under positive engagement—that is, their security, their territory, and their qualified autonomy, subject to the federal restrictions and obligations. But though thus at peace with Thebes,[1] the Platæans

*Marginal note:* The Thebans forestal this negotiation by seizing Platæa, and expelling the inhabitants, who again take refuge at Athens.

---

[1] This seems to me what is meant by the Platæan speaker in Isokrates, when he complains more than once that Platæa had been taken by the Thebans in time of peace—εἰρήνης οὔσης. The speaker, in protesting against the injustice of the Thebans, appeals to two guarantees which they have violated; for the purpose of his argument, however, the two are not clearly distinguished, but run together into one. The first guarantee was, the peace of Antalkidas, under which Platæa had been restored, and to which Thebes, Sparta, and Athens were all parties. The second guarantee was, that given by Thebes when she conquered the Bœotian cities in 377-376 B.C., and reconstituted the federation; whereby she ensured to the Platæans existence as a city, with so much of autonomy as was consistent with the obligations of a member of the Bœotian federation. When the Platæan speaker accuses the Thebans of having violated "the oaths and the agreement" (ὅρκους καὶ συνθήκας), he means the terms of the peace of Antalkidas, subject to the limits afterwards imposed by the submission of Platæa to the federal system of Bœotia. He calls for the tutelary interference of Athens, as a party to the peace of Antalkidas.

Dr. Thirlwall thinks (Hist. Gr. vol. v. ch. 38. p. 70-72) that the Thebans were parties to the peace of 374 B.C. between Sparta and Athens; that they accepted it, intending deliberately to break it; and that under that peace, the Lacedæmonian harmosts and garri-

knew well what was her real sentiment towards them, and their own towards her. If we are to believe, what seems very probable, that they were secretly negotiating with Athens to help them in breaking off from the federation— the consciousness of such an intrigue tended still farther to keep them in anxiety and suspicion. Accordingly being apprehensive of some aggression from Thebes, they kept themselves habitually on their guard. But their vigilance was somewhat relaxed, and most of them went out of the city to their farms in the country, on the days, well known beforehand, when the public assemblies in Thebes were held. Of this relaxation the Bœotarch Neoklês took advantage.[1] He conducted a Theban armed force, immediately from the assembly, by a circuitous route through Hysiæ to Plataea; which town he found deserted by most of its male adults and unable to make resistance. The Plataeans— dispersed in the fields, finding their walls, their wives, and their families, all in possession of the victor—were under the necessity of accepting the terms proposed to them. They were allowed to depart in safety and to carry away all their moveable property; but their town was destroyed and its territory again annexed to Thebes. The unhappy fugitives were constrained for the second time to seek refuge at Athens, where they were again kindly received, and restored to the same qualified right of citizenship as they had enjoyed prior to the peace of Antalkidas.[2]

sons were withdrawn from Thespiæ and other places in Bœotia. I am unable to acquiesce in this view; which appears to me negatived by Xenophon, and neither affirmed nor implied in the Plataic discourse of Isokratês. In my opinion, there were no Lacedæmonian harmosts in Buœtia (except at Orchomenus in the north) in 374 B.C. Xenophon tells us (Hellen. v. 4, 63; vi. 1, 1) that the Thebans "were recovering the Bœotian cities—had subdued the Bœotian cities"—in or before 375 B.C., so that they were able to march out of Bœotia and invade Phokis; which implies the expulsion or retirement of all the Lacedæmonian forces from the southern part of Bœotia.

The reasoning in the Plataic discourse of Isokratês is not very clear or discriminating; nor have we any right to expect that it should be, in the pleading of a suffering and passionate man. But the expression εἰρήνης οὔσης and εἰρήνη may always (in my judgement) be explained, without referring it, as Dr. Thirlwall does, to the peace of 874 B.C., or supposing Thebes to have been a party to that peace.

[1] Pausanias, ix. 1, 8.
[2] Diodor. xv. 47.

Pausanias (ix. 1, 8) places this capture of Plataea in the third year (counting the years from midsummer to midsummer) before the battle of Leuktra; or in the year

It was not merely with Plataea, but also with Thespiæ, that Thebes was now meddling. Mistrusting the dispositions of the Thespians, she constrained them to demolish the fortifications of their town;[1] as she had caused to be done fifty-two years before, after the victory of Delium,[2] on suspicion of leanings favourable to Athens. Such proceedings on the part of the Thebans in Bœotia excited strong emotion at Athens; where the Platæans not only appeared as suppliants, with the tokens of misery conspicuously displayed, but also laid their case pathetically before the assembly, and invoked aid to regain their town of which they had been just bereft. On a question at once so touching and so full of political consequences, many speeches were doubtless composed and delivered, one of which has fortunately reached us; composed by Isokratês, and perhaps actually delivered by a Platæan speaker before the public assembly. The hard fate of this inter-

*Strong feeling excited in Athens against the Thebans, on account of their dealings with Platæa and Thespiæ. The Plataic discourse of Isokratês.*

of the archon Asteius at Athens; which seems to me the true date, though Mr. Clinton supposes it (without ground, I think) to be contradicted by Xenophon. The year of the archon Asteius reaches from midsummer 373 to midsummer 372 B.C. It is in the latter half of the year of Asteius (between January and July 372 B.C.) that I suppose Platæa to have been taken.

[1] I infer this from Isokratês, Or. xiv. (Plataic.) s. 21-38: compare also sect. 10. The Platæan speaker accuses the Thebans of having destroyed the walls of some Bœotian cities (over and above what they had done to Platæa), and I venture to apply this to Thespiæ. Xenophon indeed states that the Thespians were at this very period treated exactly like the Platæans; that is, driven out of Bœotia, and their town destroyed; except that they had not the same claim on Athens (Hellen. vi. 3, 1—ἀπολιδας γενομένους: compare also vi. 3, 5). Diodorus also (xv. 46) speaks of

the Thebans as having destroyed Thespiæ. But against this, I gather, from the Plataic Oration of Isokratês, that the Thespians were not in the same plight with the Platæans when that oration was delivered; that is, they were not expelled collectively out of Bœotia. Moreover Pausanias also expressly says that the Thespians were present in Bœotia at the time of the battle of Leuktra, and that they were expelled shortly afterwards. Pausanias at the same time gives a distinct story, about the conduct of the Thespians, which it would not be reasonable to reject (ix. 13, 3; ix. 14, 1). I believe therefore that Xenophon has spoken inaccurately in saying that the Thespians were ἀπολιδες *before* the battle of Leuktra. It is quite possible that they might have sent supplications to Athens (ἱκετεύοντας—Xen. Hell. vi. 3, 1) in consequence of the severe mandate to demolish their walls.

[2] Thucyd. iv. 133.

esting little community is here impressively set forth; including the bitterest reproaches, stated with not a little of rhetorical exaggeration, against the multiplied wrongs done by Thebes, as well towards Athens as towards Platæa. Much of his invective is more vehement than conclusive. Thus when the orator repeatedly claims for Platæa her title to autonomous existence, under the guarantee of universal autonomy sworn at the peace of Antalkidas[1]—the Thebans would doubtless reply, that at the time of that peace, Platæa was no longer in existence; but had been extinct for forty years, and was only renovated afterwards by the Lacedæmonians for their own political purposes. And the orator intimates plainly, that the Thebans were noway ashamed of their proceeding, but came to Athens to justify it, openly and avowedly; moreover several of the most distinguished Athenian speakers espoused the same side.[2] That the Platæans had cooperated with Sparta in her recent operations in Bœotia against both Athens and Thebes, was an undeniable fact; which the orator himself can only extenuate by saying that they acted under constraint from a present Spartan force—but which was cited on the opposite side as a proof of their philo-Spartan dispositions, and of their readiness again to join the common enemy as soon as he presented himself.[3] The Thebans would accuse Platæa of subsequent treason to the confederacy; and they even seem to have contended, that they had rendered a positive service to the general Athenian confederacy of which they were members,[4] by expelling the inhabitants of Platæa and dismantling Thespiæ; both towns being not merely devoted to Sparta, but also adjoining Kithæron, the frontier line whereby a Spartan army would invade Bœotia. Both in the public assembly of Athens, and in the general congress of the confederates

---

[1] Isokratês, Or. xiv. (Plataic.) s. 11, 13, 15, 42, 46, 47, 60.
[2] Isokratês, Or. xiv. (Plat.) s. 3. Εἰ μὲν οὖν μὴ Θηβαίους ἑωρῶμεν ἐκ παντὸς τρόπου παρεσκευασμένους κωλύειν ὑμᾶς ὡς οὐδὲν εἰς ἡμᾶς ἐξημαρτήκασι, διὰ βραχέων ἂν ἐποιησάμεθα τοὺς λόγους· ἐπειδὴ δ' εἰς τοῦτ' ἀτυχίας ἤλθομεν, ὥστε μὴ μόνον ἡμῖν εἶναι τὸν ἀγῶνα πρὸς τούτους ἀλλὰ καὶ τῶν ῥητόρων τοὺς δυνατωτάτους,

οὓς ἀπὸ τῶν ἡμετέρων αὑτοῖς οὗτοι παρασκευάσαντο συνηγόρους, &c. Compare sect. 36.
[3] Isokr. Or. xiv. (Plat.) s. 12, 13, 14, 16, 28, 33, 40.
[4] Isokrat. Or. xiv. (Plat.) s. 23-27. λέγουσιν ὡς ὑπὲρ τοῦ κοινοῦ τῶν συμμάχων ταῦτ' ἐπράξαν—φασὶ τὸ Θηβαίους ἔχειν τὴν ἡμετέραν, τοῦτο σύμφερον εἶναι τοῖς συμμάχοις, &c.

at that city, animated discussions were raised upon the whole subject;[1] discussions, wherein, as it appears, Epaminondas, as the orator and representative of Thebes, was found a competent advocate against Kallistratus, the most distinguished speaker in Athens; sustaining the Theban cause with an ability which greatly enhanced his growing reputation.[2]

But though the Thebans and their Athenian supporters, having all the prudential arguments on their side, carried the point so that no step was taken to restore the Plataeans, nor any hostile declaration made against those to whom they owed their expulsion—yet the general result of the debates, animated by keen sympathy with the Plataean sufferers, tended decidedly to poison the good feeling, and loosen the ties, between Athens and Thebes. This change showed itself by an increased gravitation towards peace with Sparta; strongly advocated by the orator Kallistratus, and now promoted not merely by the announced Persian intervention, but by the heavy cost of war, and the absence of all prospective gain from its continuance. The resolution was at length taken—first by Athens, and next, probably, by the majority of the confederates assembled at Athens—to make propositions of peace to Sparta, where it was well known that similar dispositions prevailed towards peace. Notice of this intention was given to the Thebans, who were invited to send envoys thither also, if they chose to become parties. In the spring of 371 B.C., at the time

*B.C. 371. Increased tendency of the Athenians towards peace with Sparta—Athens and the Athenian confederacy give notice to Thebes. General congress for peace at Sparta.*

---

[1] Isokrat. Or. xiv. (Plat.) s. 18, 24.
[2] Diodorus (xv. 88) mentions the parliamentary conflict between Epaminondas and Kallistratus, assigning it to the period immediately antecedent to the abortive peace concluded between Athens and Sparta three years before. I agree with Wesseling (see his note ad loc.) in thinking that these debates more properly belong to the time immediately preceding the peace of 371 B.C. Diodorus has made great confusion between the two; sometimes repeating twice over the same antecedent phenomena—as if they belonged to both—sometimes assigning to one what properly belongs to the other.

The altercation between Epaminondas and *Kallistratus* (ἐν τῷ κοινῷ συνεδρίῳ) seems to me more properly appertaining to debates in the assembly of the confederacy at Athens—rather than to debates at Sparta, in the preliminary discussions for peace, where the altercations between Epaminondas and *Agesilaus* occurred.

when the members of the Lacedæmonian confederacy were assembled at Sparta, both the Athenian and Theban envoys, and those from the various members of the Athenian confederacy, arrived there. Among the Athenian envoys, two at least—Kallias (the hereditary Dadach or Torchbearer of the Eleusinian ceremonies) and Autoklês—were men of great family at Athens; and they were accompanied by Kallistratus the orator.¹ From the Thebans, the only man of note was Epaminondas, then one of the Bœotarchs.

Of the debates which took place at this important congress, we have very imperfect knowledge; and of the more private diplomatic conversations, not less important than the debates, we have no knowledge at all. Xenophon gives us a speech from each of the three Athenians, and from no one else. That of Kallias, who announces himself as hereditary proxenus of Sparta at Athens, is boastful and empty, but eminently philo-Laconian in spirit;² that of Autoklês is in the opposite tone, full of severe censure on the past conduct of Sparta; that of Kallistratus, delivered after the other two —while the enemies of Sparta were elate, her friends humiliated, and both parties silent, from the fresh effect of the reproaches of Autoklês³—is framed in a spirit of conciliation; admitting faults on both sides, but deprecating the continuance of war, as injurious to both, and showing how much the joint interests of both pointed towards peace.⁴

B.C. 371.
May-June.
Speeches of the Athenian envoys Kallias, Autoklês, Kalli-stratus.

Kallistratus and his policy.

This orator, representing the Athenian diplomacy of the time, recognises distinctly the peace of Antalkidas as the basis upon which Athens was prepared to treat—autonomy to each city, small as well as great; and in this way, coinciding with the views of the Persian king, he dismisses with indifference the menace that Antalkidas was on his way back from Persia with money to aid the Lacedæmonians in the war. It was not from fear of the Persian treasures (he urged)—as the

¹ Xen. Hellen. vl. 3, 3.
It seems doubtful from the language of Xenophon, whether Kallistratus was one of the envoys appointed, or only a companion.
² Xen. Hellen. vi. 3, 4-8.

³ Xen. Hellen. vi. 8, 7-10. Τοῦτ' εἰπών, εἰωθὴν μὲν παρὰ πάντων ἐπῄνεσεν (Autoklês), ἠδομένους δὲ τοὺς ἀχθομένους τοῖς Λακεδαιμονίοις ἐποίησε.
⁴ Xen. Hellen. vi. 8, 10-17.

enemies of peace asserted—that Athens sought peace.[1] Her affairs were now so prosperous both by sea and land, as to prove that she only did so on consideration of the general evils of prolonged war, and on a prudent abnegation of that rash confidence which was always ready to contend for extreme stakes[2]—like a gamester playing double or quits. The time had come for both Sparta and Athens now to desist from hostilities. The former had the strength on land, the latter was predominant at sea; so that each could guard the other; while the reconciliation of the two would produce peace throughout the Hellenic world, since in each separate city, one of the two opposing local parties rested on Athens, the other on Sparta.[3] But it was indispensably necessary that Sparta should renounce that system of aggression (already pointedly denounced by the Athenian Autoklês) on which she had acted since the peace of Antalkidas; a system, from which she had at last reaped bitter fruits, since her unjust seizure of the Kadmeia had ended by throwing into the arms of the Thebans all those Bœotian cities, whose separate autonomy she had bent her whole policy to ensure.[4]

Two points stand out in this remarkable speech, which takes a judicious measure of the actual position of affairs: first, autonomy to every city; and autonomy in the genuine sense, not construed and enforced by the separate interests of Sparta, as it had been at the peace of Antalkidas; next, the distribution of such pre-eminence or headship, as was consistent with this universal autonomy, between Sparta and Athens; the former on land, the latter at sea; as the means of ensuring tranquillity in Greece. That "autonomy perverted to Lacedæmonian purposes"—which Periklês had denounced before the Peloponnesian war as the condition of Peloponnesus, and which

*He proposes that Sparta and Athens shall divide between them the headship of Greece— Sparta on land, Athens at sea—recognising general autonomy.*

---

[1] Xen. Hellen. vi. 3, 12, 13.
[2] Xen. Hellen. vi. 3, 16.
[3] Xen. Hellen. vi. 5, 14. Καὶ γὰρ δὴ κατὰ γῆν μὲν τίς ἄν, ὑμῶν φίλων ὄντων, ἱκανὸς γένοιτο ἡμᾶς λυπῆσαι; κατὰ θάλατταν γε μή, τίς ἂν ὑμᾶς βλάψαι τι, ἡμῶν ὑμῖν ἐπιτηδείων ὄντων;
[4] Xen. Hellen. vi. 5, 11. Καὶ ὑμῖν δὲ ἔγωγε ὁρῶ διὰ τὰ ἀγνωμόνως πραχθέντα ἔστιν ὅτε καὶ πολλὰ ἀντίτυπα γιγνόμενα· ὧν ἦν καὶ ἡ καταληφθεῖσα ἐν Θήβαις Καδμεία· νῦν γοῦν, ὡς (?) ἐσπουδάσατε αὐτονόμους τὰς πόλεις γίγνεσθαι, πᾶσαι πάλιν, ἐπεὶ ἠδικήθησαν οἱ Θηβαῖοι, ἐπ' ἐκείνοις γεγένηται.

had been made the political canon of Greece by the peace of Antalkidas—was now at an end. On the other hand, Athens and Sparta were to become mutual partners and guarantees; dividing the headship of Greece by an ascertained line of demarcation, yet neither of them interfering with the principle of universal autonomy. Thebes, and her claim to the presidency of Bœotia, were thus to be set aside by mutual consent.

It was upon this basis that the peace was concluded.

*Peace is concluded. Autonomy of each city to be recognised: Sparta to withdraw her harmosts and garrisons.*

The armaments on both sides were to be disbanded; the harmosts and garrisons everywhere withdrawn, in order that each city might enjoy full autonomy. If any city should fail in observance of these conditions, and continue in a career of force against any other, all were at liberty to take arms for the support of the injured party; but no one who did not feel disposed, was bound so to take arms. This last stipulation exonerated the Lacedæmonian allies from one of their most vexatious chains.

*Oaths exchanged. Sparta takes the oath for herself and her allies. Athens takes it for herself: her allies take it after her, successively.*

To the conditions here mentioned, all parties agreed; and on the ensuing day, the oaths were exchanged. Sparta took the oath for herself and her allies; Athens took the oath for herself only; her allies afterwards took it severally, each city for itself. Why such difference was made, we are not told; for it would seem that the principle of severance applied to both confederacies alike.

*The oath proposed to the Thebans. Epaminondas, the Theban envoy, insists upon taking the oath in the name of the Bœotian federation.*

Next came the turn of the Thebans to swear; and here the fatal hitch was disclosed. Epaminondas, the Theban envoy, insisted on taking the oath, not for Thebes separately, but for Thebes as president of the Bœotian federation, including all the Bœotian cities. The Spartan authorities, on the other hand, and Agesilaus as the foremost of all, strenuously opposed him. They required that he should swear for Thebes alone, leaving the Bœotian cities to take the oath each for itself.

Already in the course of the preliminary debates, Epaminondas had spoken out boldly against the ascendency of Sparta. While most of the deputies stood overawed by her dignity, represented by the energetic Agesilaus as spokesman—he, like the Athenian Autoklês, and with strong sympathy from many of the deputies present, had proclaimed that nothing kept alive the war except her unjust pretensions, and that no peace could be durable unless such pretensions were put aside.[1] Accepting the conditions of peace as finally determined, he presented himself to swear to them in the name of the Bœotian federation. But Agesilaus, requiring that each of the Bœotian cities should take the oath for itself, appealed to those same principles of liberty which Epaminondas himself had just invoked, and asked him whether each of the Bœotian cities had not as good a title to autonomy as Thebes. Epaminondas might have replied by asking, why Sparta had just been permitted to take the oath for her allies as well as for herself. But he took a higher ground. He contended that the presidency of Bœotia was held by Thebes on as good a title as the sovereignty of Laconia by Sparta.[2] He would remind the assembly that when Bœotia was first conquered and settled by its present inhabitants, the other towns had all been planted out from Thebes as their chief and mother-city; that the federal union of all, administered by Bœotarchs chosen by and from all, with Thebes as president, was coeval with the first settlement of the country; that the separate autonomy of each was qualified by an established institution, devolving on the Bœotarchs and councils sitting at Thebes the management of the foreign relations of all jointly. All this had been already pleaded by the Theban orator fifty-six years earlier, before the five Spartan commissioners assembled to determine the fate of the captives after the surrender of Platæa; when he required the condemnation of the Platæans as guilty of treason to the ancestral institutions of Bœotia;[3] and the Spartan commissioners had recognised

---

[1] Plutarch, Agesil. c. 27.
[2] Plutarch, Agesil. c. 28.
[3] Thucyd. III. 61. ἡμῶν (the Thebans) κτισάντων Πλάταιαν ὕστερον τῆς ἄλλης Βοιωτίας καὶ ἄλλα χωρία μετ' αὐτῆς, ἃ ξυμμίκτους ἀνθρώπους ἐξελάσαντες ἔσχομεν, οὐκ ἠξίουν οὗτοι (the Platæans), ὥσπερ ἐτάχθη τὸ πρῶτον, ἡγεμονεύεσθαι ὑφ' ἡμῶν, ἔξω δὲ τῶν ἄλλων Βοιωτῶν

the legitimacy of these institutions by a sweeping sentence of death against the transgressors. Moreover, at a time when the ascendency of Thebes over the Bœotian cities had been greatly impaired by her anti-Hellenic cooperation with the invading Persians, the Spartans themselves had assisted her with all their power to re-establish it, as a countervailing force against Athens.[1] Epaminondas could show, that the presidency of Thebes over the Bœotian cities was the keystone of the federation; a right not only of immemorial antiquity, but pointedly recognised and strenuously vindicated by the Spartans themselves. He could show farther that it was as old, and as good, as their own right to govern the Laconian townships; which latter was acquired and held (as one of the best among their own warriors had boastfully proclaimed[2]) by nothing but Spartan valour and the sharpness of the Spartan sword.

**Indignation of the Spartans, and especially of Agesilaus—brief questions exchanged—Thebes is excluded from the treaty.**
An emphatic speech of this tenor, delivered amidst the deputies assembled at Sparta, and arraigning the Spartans not merely in their supremacy over Greece, but even in their dominion at home—was as it were the shadow cast before, by coming events. It opened a question such as no Greek had ever ventured to raise. It was a novelty startling to all—extravagant probably in the eyes of Kallistratus and the Athenians—but to the Spartans themselves, intolerably poignant and insulting.[3] They had already a

---

παραβαίνοντες τὰ πάτρια, ἐπειδὴ προσηναγκάζοντο, προσεχωρήσαν πρὸς Ἀθηναίους, &c.

Again (c. 55) he says respecting the oligarchical Platæans who admitted the Theban detachment when it came by night to surprise Platæa—εἰ δὲ ἄνδρες ὑμῶν οἱ πρῶτοι καὶ χρήμασι καὶ γένει βουλόμενοι τῆς μὲν ἔξω ξυμμαχίας ὑμᾶς παῦσαι, ἐς δὲ τὰ κοινὰ τῶν πάντων Βοιωτῶν πάτρια καταστῆσαι, ἐπεκαλέσαντο ἑκόντες, &c.

Again (c. 66), κατὰ τὰ πάντων Βοιωτῶν πάτρια, &c. Compare II. 2.
[1] Diodor. xi. 81.
[2] Thucyd. iv. 126. Brasidas, addressing his soldiers when serving in Macedonia, on the approach of the Illyrians:—

Ἀγαθοῖς γάρ εἶναι προσήκει ὑμῖν τὰ πολέμια, οὐ διὰ ξυμμάχων παρουσίαν ἑκάστοτε, ἀλλὰ δι' οἰκείαν ἀρετὴν, καὶ μηδὲν πλῆθος πεφοβῆσθαι ἑτέρων· οἵ γε μηδὲ ἀπὸ πολιτειῶν τοιούτων ἥκετε, ἐν αἷς οὐ πολλοὶ ὀλίγων ἄρχουσιν, ἀλλὰ πλείονων μᾶλλον ἐλάσσους· οὐκ ἄλλῳ τινὶ κτησάμενοι τὴν δυναστείαν ἢ τῷ μαχόμενοι κρατεῖν.

[3] One may judge of the revolting effect produced by such a proposition, before the battle of Leuktra—by reading the language which Isokratês puts into the mouth of the Spartan prince Archidamus,

long account of antipathy to clear off with Thebes; their own wrong-doing in seizing the Kadmeia—their subsequent humiliation in losing it and being unable to recover it—their recent short-comings and failures, in the last seven years of war against Athens and Thebes jointly. To aggravate this deep-seated train of hostile associations, their pride was now wounded in an unforeseen point, the tenderest of all. Agesilaus, full to overflowing of the national sentiment, which in the mind of a Spartan passed for the first of virtues, was stung to the quick. Had he been an Athenian orator like Kallistratus, his wrath would have found vent in an animated harangue. But a king of Sparta was anxious only to close these offensive discussions with scornful abruptness, thus leaving to the presumptuous Theban no middle ground between humble retractation and acknowledged hostility. Indignantly starting from his seat, he said to Epaminondas—"Speak plainly—will you, or will you not, leave to each of the Bœotian cities its separate autonomy?" To which the other replied—"Will *you* leave each of the Laconian towns autonomous?" Without saying another word, Agesilaus immediately caused the name of the Thebans to be struck out of the roll, and proclaimed them excluded from the treaty.[1]

---

five or six years after that battle, protesting that all Spartan patriots ought to perish rather than consent to the relinquishment of Messenia —περὶ μὲν ἄλλων τινῶν ἀμφισβητήσεις ἐγίγνοντο, περὶ δὲ Μεσσήνης, οὔτε βασιλεὺς, οὐδ' ἡ τῶν Ἀθηναίων πόλις, οὐδὲ αὐτοῦ ἡμῖν ἐνεκάλεσεν ὡς ἀδίκως κεκτημένοις αὐτήν (Isok. Arch. s. 32). In the spring of 371 B.C., what had once been Messenia was only a portion of Laconia, which no one thought of distinguishing from the other portions (see Thucyd. iv. 3, 11).

[1] Plutarch, Agesil. c. 28; Pausanias, ix. 13, 1: compare Diodor. xv. 51. Pausanias erroneously assigns the debate to the congress preceding the peace of Antalkidas in 387 B.C.; at which time Epaminondas was an unknown man.

Plutarch gives this interchange of brief questions, between Agesilaus and Epaminondas, which is in substance the same as that given by Pausanias, and has every appearance of being the truth. But he introduces it in a very bold and abrupt way, such as cannot be conformable to the reality. To raise a question about the right of Sparta to govern Laconia, was a most daring novelty. A courageous and patriotic Theban might venture upon it as a retort against those Spartans who questioned the right of Thebes to her presidency of Bœotia; but he would never do so without assigning his reasons to justify an assertion so startling to a large portion of his hearers. The reasons which I here ascribe to Epaminondas are such as we know to have formed the Theban creed, in reference to the Bœotian

B.C. 371.
General peace sworn, including Athens, Sparta, and the rest— Thebes alone is excluded.

Such was the close of this memorable congress at Sparta in June 371 B.C. Between the Spartans and Athenians, and their respective allies, peace was sworn. But the Thebans were excluded, and their deputies returned home (if we may believe Xenophon[1]) discouraged and mournful. Yet such a man as Epaminondas must have been well-aware that neither his claims nor his arguments would be admitted by Sparta. If therefore he was disappointed with the result, this must be because he had counted upon, but did not obtain, support from the Athenians or others.

Advantageous position of Athens— prudence in her to make peace now.

The leaning of the Athenian deputies had been adverse rather than favourable to Thebes throughout the congress. They were disinclined, from their sympathies with the Platæans, to advocate the presidential claims of Thebes, though on the whole it was the political interest of Athens that the Bœotian federation should be cities; such as were actually urged by the Theban orator in 427 B.C., when the fate of the Platæan captives was under discussion. After Epaminondas had once laid out the reasons in support of his assertion, he might then, if the same brief question were angrily put to him a second time, meet it with another equally brief counter-question or retort. It is this final interchange of thrusts which Plutarch has given, omitting the arguments previously stated by Epaminondas, and necessary to warrant the seeming paradox which he advances. We must recollect that Epaminondas does not contend that Thebes was entitled to as much power in Bœotia as Sparta in Laconia. He only contends that Bœotia, under the presidency of Thebes, was as much an integral political aggregate, as Laconia under Sparta—in reference to the Grecian world.

Xenophon differs from Plutarch in his account of the conduct of the Theban envoys. He does not mention Epaminondas at all, nor any envoy by name; but he says that "the Thebans, having entered their name among the cities which had taken the oaths, came on the next day and requested, that the entry might be altered, and that 'the Bœotians' might be substituted in place of 'the Thebans,' as having taken the oath. Agesilaus told them that he could make no change; but he would strike their names out if they chose, and he accordingly did strike them out" (vi. 3, 19). It seems to me that this account is far less probable than that of Plutarch, and bears every mark of being incorrect. Why should such a man as Epaminondas (who doubtless was the envoy) consent at first to waive the presidential pretensions of Thebes, and to swear for her alone? If he did consent, why should he retract the next day? Xenophon is anxious to make out Agesilaus to be as much in the right as may be; since the fatal consequences of his proceedings manifested themselves but too soon.

[1] Xenoph. Hellen. vi. 3, 20.

maintained, as a bulwark to herself against Sparta. Yet the relations of Athens with Thebes, after the congress as before it, were still those of friendship, nominal rather than sincere. It was only with Sparta, and her allies, that Thebes was at war, without a single ally attached to her. On the whole, Kallistratus and his colleagues had managed the interests of Athens in this congress with great prudence and success. They had disengaged her from the alliance with Thebes, which had been dictated seven years before by common fear and dislike of Sparta, but which had no longer any adequate motive to countervail the cost of continuing the war; at the same time, the disengagement had been accomplished without bad faith. The gains of Athens, during the last seven years of war, had been considerable. She had acquired a great naval power, and a body of maritime confederates; while her enemies the Spartans had lost their naval power in the like proportion. Athens was now the ascendent leader of maritime and insular Greece—while Sparta still continued to be the leading power on land, but only on land; and a tacit partnership was now established between the two, each recognising the other in their respective halves of the Hellenic hegemony.[1] Moreover, Athens had the prudence to draw her stake, and quit the game, when at the maximum of her acquisitions, without taking the risk of future contingences.

On both sides, the system of compulsory and indefeasible confederacies was renounced; a renunciation, which had already been once sworn to, sixteen years before, at the peace of Antalkidas, but treacherously perverted by Sparta in the execution. Under this new engagement, the allies of Sparta or Athens ceased to constitute an organized permanent body voting by its majority, passing resolutions permanently binding upon dissentients, arming the chief state with more or less power of enforcement against all, and forbidding voluntary secessions of individual members. They became a mere uncemented aggregate of individuals, each acting for himself; taking counsel together, as long as they chose, and cooperating so far as all were in harmony; but no one being bound by any decision of the others, nor

*Terms of the peace—compulsory and indefeasible confederacies are renounced—voluntary alliances alone maintained.*

[1] Diodor. xv. 38-82.

recognising any right in the others to compel him even to performance of what he had specially promised, if it became irksome. By such change, therefore, both Athens and Sparta were losers in power; yet the latter to a much greater extent than the former, inasmuch as her reach of power over her allies had been more comprehensive and stringent.

We here see the exact point upon which the requisition addressed by Sparta to Thebes, and the controversy between Epaminondas and Agesilaus, really turned. Agesilaus contended that the relation between Thebes and the other Bœotian cities, was the same as what subsisted between Sparta and her allies; that accordingly, when Sparta renounced the indefeasible and compulsory character of her confederacy, and agreed to deal with each of its members as a self-acting and independent unit, she was entitled to demand that Thebes should do the same in reference to the Bœotian towns. Epaminondas, on the contrary, denied the justice of this parallel. He maintained that the proper subject of comparison to be taken, was the relation of Sparta, not to her extra-Laconian allies, but to the Laconian townships; that the federal union of the Bœotian towns under Thebes was coeval with the Bœotian settlement, and among the most ancient phænomena of Greece; that in reference to other states, Bœotia, like Laconia or Attica, was the compound and organized whole, of which each separate city was only a fraction; that other Greeks had no more right to meddle with the internal constitution of these fractions, and convert each of them into an integer—than to insist on separate independence for each of the townships of Laconia. Epaminondas did not mean to contend that the power of Thebes over the Bœotian cities was as complete and absolute in degree, as that of Sparta over the Laconian townships; but merely that her presidential power, and the federal system of which it formed a part, were established, indefeasible, and beyond the interference of any Hellenic convention—quite as much as the internal government of Sparta in Laconia.

*Real point in debate between Agesilaus and Epaminondas.*

Once already this question had been disputed between Sparta and Thebes, at the peace of Antalkidas. Once already had it been decided by the superior power of the former, extorting submission from the latter. The last sixteen years had reversed the previous decision, and enabled the Thebans to reconquer those presidential rights of which the former peace had deprived them. Again therefore the question stood for decision, with keener antipathy on both sides—with diminished power in Sparta—but with increased force, increased confidence, and a new leader whose inestimable worth was even yet but half-known—in Thebes. The Athenians—friendly with both, yet allies of neither—suffered the dispute to be fought out without interfering. How it was settled will appear in the next chapter.

## CHAPTER LXXVIII.

### BATTLE OF LEUKTRA AND ITS CONSEQUENCES.

**B.C. 371. Measures for executing the stipulations made at the congress of Sparta.**

IMMEDIATELY after the congress at Sparta in June 371 B.C., both the Athenians and Lacedæmonians took steps to perform the covenants sworn respectively to each other as well as to the allies generally. The Athenians despatched orders to Iphikratês, who was still at Korkyra or in the Ionian Sea, engaged in incursions against the Lacedæmonian or Peloponnesian coasts—that he should forthwith conduct his fleet home, and that if he had made any captures subsequent to the exchange of oaths at Sparta they should all be restored;[1] so as to prevent the misunderstanding which had occurred fifty-two years before with Brasidas,[2] in the peninsula of Pallênê. The Lacedæmonians on their side sent to withdraw their harmosts and their garrisons from every city still under occupation. Since they had already made such promise once before at the peace of Antalkidas, but had never performed it—commissioners,[3] not Spartans, were now named from the general congress, to enforce the execution of the agreement.

**Violent impulse of the Spartans against Thebes.**

No great haste, however, was probably shown in executing this part of the conditions; for the whole soul and sentiment of the Spartans were absorbed by their quarrel with Thebes. The miso-Theban impulse now drove them on with a fury which overcame all other thoughts; and which, though doubtless Agesilaus and others considered it at the time as legitimate patriotic resentment for the recent insult, appeared to the philo-Laconian Xenophon, when he looked back upon it

---

[1] Xen. Hellen. vi. 4, 1.
[2] Thucyd. iv.
[3] Diodor. xv. 38. ἐξαγωγεῖς, Xen. Hellen. l. c.
Diodorus refers the statements in this chapter to the peace between Athens and Sparta in 374 B.C. I have already remarked that they belong properly to the peace of 371 B.C.; as Wesseling suspects in his note.

from the subsequent season of Spartan humiliation, to be a misguiding inspiration sent by the gods[1]—like that of the Homeric Atê. Now that Thebes stood isolated from Athens and all other allies out of Bœotia, Agesilaus had full confidence of being able to subdue her thoroughly. The same impression of the superiority of Spartan force was also entertained both by the Athenians and by other Greeks; to a great degree even by the Thebans themselves. It was anticipated that the Spartans would break up the city of Thebes into villages (as they had done at Mantineia) —or perhaps retaliate upon her the fate which she had inflicted upon Platæa—or even decimate her citizens and her property to the profit of the Delphian god, pursuant to the vow that had been taken more than a century before, in consequence of the assistance lent by the Thebans to Xerxês.[2] Few persons out of Bœotia doubted of the success of Sparta.

To attack Thebes, however, an army was wanted; and as Sparta, by the peace just sworn, had renounced everything like imperial ascendency over her allies, leaving each of them free to send or withhold assistance as they chose—to raise an army was no easy task; for the allies, generally speaking, being not at all inflamed with the Spartan antipathy against Thebes, desired only to be left to enjoy their newly-acquired liberty. But it so happened, that at the moment when peace was sworn, the Spartan king Kleombrotus was actually at the head of an army, of Lacedæmonians and allies, in Phokis, on the north-western frontier of Bœotia. Immediately on hearing of the peace, Kleombrotus sent home to ask for instructions as to his future proceedings. By the unanimous voice of the Spartan authorities and assembly, with Agesilaus as the most vehement of all,[3] he was directed to march against the Thebans, unless they should flinch at the last moment (as they had done at the peace of Antalkidas), and relinquish their presidency over the other Bœotian cities. One citizen alone, named Prothous, interrupted this unanimity. He protested against the order, first, as a violation of their oaths, which required them to disband the army and recon-

*King Kleombrotus is ordered to march into Bœotia, out of Phokis.*

[1] Xen. Hellen. vi. 4, 3. ἤδη γάρ, ὡς ἔοικε, τὸ δαιμόνιον ἦγεν, &c.
[2] Xen. Hellen. vi. 3, 20; Plutarch, Pelopid. c. 20; Diodor. xv. 51.
[3] Plutarch, Agesilaus, c. 28.

stitute it on the voluntary principle—next, as imprudent
in regard to the allies, who now looked upon such liberty
as their right, and would never serve with cordiality unless
it were granted to them. But Prothous was treated with
disdain as a silly alarmist,[1] and the peremptory order was
despatched to Kleombrotus; accompanied, probably, by a
reinforcement of Spartans and Lacedæmonians, the number
of whom, in the ensuing battle, seems to have been greater
than can reasonably be imagined to have been before
serving in Phokis.

Meanwhile no symptoms of concession were manifested
at Thebes.[2] Epaminondas, on his return, had
found cordial sympathy with the resolute tone
which he had adopted both in defence of the
Bœotian federation and against Sparta. Though
every one felt the magnitude of the danger, it
was still hoped that the enemy might be prevented from penetrating out of Phokis into Bœotia.
Epaminondas accordingly occupied with a strong force the
narrow pass near Koroneia, lying between a spur of Mount
Helikon on one side and the Lake Kopais on the other;
the same position as had been taken by the Bœotians, and
forced by the army returning from Asia under Agesilaus,
twenty-three years before. Orchomenus lay northward
(that is, on the Phokian side) of this position; and its
citizens, as well as its Lacedæmonian garrison, now doubtless formed part of the invading army of Kleombrotus.
That prince, with a degree of military skill rare in the
Spartan commanders, baffled all the Theban calculations.
Instead of marching by the regular road from Phokis into
Bœotia, he turned southward by a mountain road scarcely
deemed practicable, defeated the Theban division under
Chæreas which guarded it, and crossed the ridge of Helikon
to the Bœotian port of Kreusis on the Krissæan Gulf.
Coming upon this place by surprise, he stormed it, capturing twelve Theban triremes which lay in the harbour.
He then left a garrison to occupy the port, and marched

*His forces
the defences of
Bœotia,
and encamps at
Leuktra.*

---

[1] Xen. Hellen. vi. 4, 2, 3. ἐκεῖνον
μὲν φλυαρεῖν ἡγήσατο, &c.

[2] It is stated that either the Lacedæmonians from Sparta or Kleombrotus from Phokis, sent a new formal requisition to Thebes, that the Bœotian cities should be left autonomous; and the requisition was repudiated (Diodor. xv. 51; Aristeidês, Orat. (Leuktr.) ii. xxxiv. p. 544, ed. Dindorf). But such mission seems very doubtful.

without delay over the mountainous ground into the territory of Thespiæ on the eastern declivity of Helikon; where he encamped on the high ground, at a place of ever-memorable name, called Leuktra.[1]

Here was an important success, skilfully gained; not only placing Kleombrotus within an easy march of Thebes, but also opening a sure communication by sea with Sparta, through the port of Kreusis, and thus eluding the difficulties of Mount Kithæron. Both the king and the Lacedæmonians around him were full of joy and confidence; while the Thebans on their side were struck with dismay as well as surprise. It required all the ability of Epaminondas, and all the daring of Pelopidas, to uphold the resolution of their countrymen, and to explain away or neutralize the terrific signs and portents, which a dispirited Greek was sure to see in every accident of the road. At length, however, they succeeded in this, and the Thebans with their allied Bœotians were marched out from Thebes to Leuktra, where they were posted on a declivity opposite to the Spartan camp. They were commanded by the seven Bœotarchs, of whom Epaminondas was one. But such was the prevalent apprehension of joining battle with the Spartans on equal terms, that even when actually on the ground, three of these Bœotarchs refused to concur in the order for fighting, and proposed to shut themselves up in Thebes for a siege, sending their wives and families away to Athens. Epaminondas was vainly combating their determination, when the seventh Bœotarch, Branchylidês, arrived from the passes of Kithæron, where he had been on guard, and was prevailed upon to vote in favour of the bolder course.

Though a majority was thus secured for fighting, yet the feeling throughout the Theban camp was more that of brave despair than of cheering hope; a conviction that it was better to perish in the field, than to live in exile with the Lacedæmonians masters of the Kadmeia. Some encouraging omens, however, were transmitted to the camp, from the temples in Thebes as well as from that of Trophonius at Lebadeia:[2] and a Spartan exile named Leandrias, serving in the Theban ranks, ventured to assure them that they were now on the very spot foredoomed for the overthrow

*Epaminondas and the Thebans at Leuktra—Leukira—discouragement in the army.*

[1] Xen. Hellen. vi. 4, 3, 4; Diodor. xv. 53; Pausan. ix. 13, 2.
[2] Kallisthenês, ap. Cic. de Divinatione, i. 34. Fragm. 9. ed. Didot.

of the Lacedæmonian empire. Here stood the tomb of two females (daughters of a Leuktrian named Skedasus) who had been violated by two Lacedæmonians and had afterwards slain themselves. Skedasus, after having in vain attempted to obtain justice from the Spartans for this outrage, came back, imprecating curses on them, and slew himself also. The vengeance of these departed sufferers would now be sure to pour itself out on Sparta, when her army was in their own district and near their own tomb. And the Theban leaders, to whom the tale was full of opportune encouragement, crowned the tomb with wreaths, invoking the aid of its inmates against the common enemy now present.[1]

New order of battle adopted by Epaminondas.

While others were thus comforted by the hope of superhuman aid, Epaminondas, to whom the order of the coming battle had been confided, took care that no human precautions should be wanting. His task was arduous; for not only were his troops dispirited, while those of the enemy were confident—but their numbers were inferior, and some of the Bœotians present were hardly even trustworthy. What the exact numbers were on either side we are not permitted to know. Diodorus assigns about 6000 men to the Thebans; Plutarch states the numbers of Kleombrotus at 11,000.[2] Without placing faith in these figures, we see good reason

---

[1] Xen. Hellen. vi. 4, 7; Diodor. xv. 54; Pausan. ix. 13, 5; Plutarch, Pelopid. c. 20, 21; Polyænus, ii. 3, 8.

The latter relates that Pelopidas in a dream saw Skedasus, who directed him to offer on this tomb "an auburn virgin" to the deceased females. Pelopidas and his friends were greatly perplexed about the fulfilment of this command; many urged that it was necessary for some maiden to devote herself or to be devoted by her parents, as a victim for the safety of the country, like Menœkeus and Makaria in the ancient legends; others denounced the idea as cruel and inadmissible. In the midst of the debate, a mare, with a chestnut filly, galloped up, and stopped not far off; upon which the prophet Theokritus exclaimed—"Here comes the victim required, sent by the special providence of the gods." The chestnut filly was caught and offered as a sacrifice on the tomb; every one being in high spirits from a conviction that the mandate of the gods had been executed.

The prophet Theokritus figures in the treatise of Plutarch De Genio Socratis (c. 5. p. 578 D.) as one of the companions of Pelopidas in the conspiracy whereby the Theban oligarchy was put down and the Lacedæmonians expelled from the Kadmeia.

[2] Diodor. xv. 52-56; Plutarch, Pelop. c. 20.

for believing that the Theban total was decidedly inferior. For such inferiority Epaminondas strove to make up by skilful tactics, and by a combination at that time novel as well as ingenious. In all former Grecian battles, the opposite armies had been drawn up in line, and had fought along the whole line; or at least such had been the intention of the generals—and if it was not realized, the cause was to be sought in accidents of the ground, or backwardness or disorder on the part of some division of the soldiers. Departing from this habit, Epaminondas now arrayed his troops so as to bring his own left to bear with irresistible force upon the Spartan right, and to keep back the rest of his army comparatively out of action. Knowing that Kleombrotus, with the Spartans and all the official persons, would be on the right of their own line, he calculated that, if successful on this point against the best troops, he should find little resistance from the remainder. Accordingly he placed on his own left wing chosen Theban hoplites, to the prodigious depth of fifty shields, with Pelopidas and the Sacred Band in front. His order of advance was disposed obliquely or in echelon, so that the deep column on the left should join battle first, while the centre and right kept comparatively back and held themselves more in a defensive attitude.

In 371 B.C., such a combination was absolutely new, and betokened high military genius. It is therefore no disgrace to Kleombrotus that he was not prepared for it, and that he adhered to the ordinary Grecian tactics of joining battle at once along the whole line. But so unbounded was the confidence reigning among the Spartans, that there never was any occasion on which peculiar precautions were less thought of. When, from their entrenched camp on the Leuktrian eminence, they saw the Thebans encamped on an opposite eminence, separated from them by a small breadth of low ground and moderate declivities—their only impatience was to hurry on the decisive moment, so as to prevent the enemy from escaping. Both the partisans and the opponents of Kleombrotus united in provoking order for battle, each in their own language. The partisans urged him, since he had never yet done anything against the Thebans, to strike a decisive blow, and clear himself from the disparaging comparisons which rumour instituted

between him and Agesilaus; the opponents gave it to be
understood, that if Kleombrotus were now backward, their
suspicions would be confirmed that he leaned in his heart
towards the Thebans.[1] Probably the king was himself
sufficiently eager to fight, and so would any other Spartan
general have been, under the same circumstances, before
the battle of Leuktra. But even had he been otherwise,
the impatience, prevalent among the Lacedæmonian portion
of his army, left him no option. Accordingly, the decided
resolution to fight was taken. The last council was held,
and the final orders issued by Kleombrotus after his morning meal, where copious libations of wine both attested
and increased the confident temper of every man. The
army was marched out of the camp, and arrayed on the
lower portion of the declivity; Kleombrotus with the Spartans and most of the Lacedæmonians being on the right,
in an order of twelve deep. Some Lacedæmonians were
also on the left, but respecting the order of the other parts
of the line, we have no information. The cavalry was
chiefly posted along the front.

Battle of Leuktra. Meanwhile, Epaminondas also marched down his
declivity, in his own chosen order of battle; his
left wing being both forward, and strengthened
into very deep order, for desperate attack. His cavalry
too were posted in front of his line. But before he commenced his march, he sent away his baggage and attendants
home to Thebes; while at the same time he made proclamation that any of his Bœotian hoplites, who were not
hearty in the cause, might also retire if they chose. Of
such permission the Thespians immediately availed themselves;[2] so many were there, in the Theban camp, who
estimated the chances to be all in favour of Lacedæmonian
victory. But when these men, a large portion of them
unarmed, were seen retiring, a considerable detachment
from the army of Kleombrotus, either with or without
orders, ran after to prevent their escape, and forced them
to return for safety to the main Theban army. The most
zealous among the allies of Sparta present—the Phokians,
the Phliasians, and the Herakleots, together with a body
of mercenaries—executed this movement; which seems to
have weakened the Lacedæmonians in the main battle,
without doing any mischief to the Thebans.

[1] Xen. Hellen. vi. 4, 5.  [2] Polyæn. II. 2, 1; Pausan. ix. 13, 8; ix. 14, 1.

The cavalry first engaged, in front of both lines; and here the superiority of the Thebans soon became manifest. The Lacedæmonian cavalry—at no time very good, but at this moment unusually bad, composed of raw and feeble novices, mounted on horses provided by the rich—was soon broken and driven back upon the infantry, whose ranks were disturbed by the fugitives. To re-establish the battle, Kleombrotus gave the word for the infantry to advance, himself personally leading the right. The victorious cavalry probably hung upon the Lacedæmonian infantry of the centre and left, and prevented them from making much forward movement; while Epaminondas and Pelopidas with their left, advanced according to their intention to bear down Kleombrotus and his right wing. The shock here was terrible; on both sides victory was resolutely and desperately disputed, in a close hand-combat, with pushing of opposite shields and opposite masses. But such was the overwhelming force of the Theban charge—with the Sacred Band or chosen warriors in front, composed of men highly trained in the palæstra,[1] and the deep column of fifty shields propelling behind—that even the Spartans, with all their courage, obstinacy, and discipline, were unable to stand up against it. Kleombrotus; himself either in or near the front, was mortally wounded, apparently early in the battle; and it was only by heroic and unexampled efforts, on the part of his comrades around, that he was carried off yet alive, so as to preserve him from falling into the hands of the enemy. Around him also fell the most eminent members of the Spartan official staff; Deinon the Polemarch, Sphodrias with his son Kleonymus, and several others. After an obstinate resistance, and a fearful slaughter, the right wing of the Spartans was completely beaten, and driven back to their camp on the higher ground.

It was upon this Spartan right wing, where the Theban left was irresistibly strong, that all the stress of the battle fell—as Epaminondas had intended that it should. In no other part of the line does there appear to have been any serious fighting; partly through his deliberate scheme of not pushing forward either his centre or his right—partly through the preliminary victory of the Theban cavalry,

[1] Plutarch, Symposiac. ii. 5. p. 639 F.

which probably checked in part the forward march of the
enemy's line—and partly also, through the lukewarm
adherence, or even suppressed hostility, of the allies marshalled under the command of Kleombrotus.[1] The Phokians
and Herakleots—zealous in the cause from hatred of
Thebes—had quitted the line to strike a blow at the
retiring baggage and attendants; while the remaining allies,
after mere nominal fighting and little or no loss, retired
to the camp as soon as they saw the Spartan right defeated
and driven back to it. Moreover, even some Lacedæmonians
on the left wing, probably astounded by the lukewarmness
of those around them, and by the unexpected calamity
on their own right, fell back in the same manner. The
whole Lacedæmonian force, with the dying king, was thus
again assembled and formed behind the entrenchment on
the higher ground, where the victorious Thebans did not
attempt to molest them.[2]

But very different were their feelings as they now
stood arrayed in the camp, from that exulting
boastfulness with which they had quitted it an
hour or two before; and fearful was the loss
when it came to be verified. Of seven hundred
Spartans who had marched forth from the camp,
only three hundred returned to it.[3] One
thousand Lacedæmonians, besides, had been left
on the field, even by the admission of Xenophon;
probably the real number was even larger. Apart from
this, the death of Kleombrotus was of itself an event impressive to every one, the like of which had never occurred
since the fatal day of Thermopylæ. But this was not all.
The allies who stood along-side of them in arms were now
altered men. All were sick of their cause, and averse to

*Spartan camp after the defeat—confession of defeat by sending to solicit the burial-truce.*

---

[1] Pausanias (ix. 13, 4: compare viii. 6, 1) lays great stress upon this indifference or even treachery of the allies. Xenophon says quite enough to authenticate the reality of the fact (Hellen. vi. 4, 15-24): see also Cicero de Offic. ii. 7, 26.
Polyænus has more than one anecdote respecting the dexterity of Agesilaus in dealing with faint-hearted conduct or desertion on the part of the allies of Sparta (Polyæn. ii. 1 18-20).

[2] Xen. Hellen. vi. 4, 13, 14.
[3] Xen. Hellen. l. c. Plutarch (Agesil. c. 28) states 1000 Lacedæmonians to have been slain; Pausanias (ix. 13, 4) gives the number as more than 1000; Diodorus mentions 4000 (xv. 56), which is doubtless above the truth, though the number given by Xenophon may be fairly presumed as somewhat below it. Dionysius of Halikarnassus (Antiq. Roman. ii. 17) states that 1700 Spartans perished.

farther exertion; some scarcely concealed a positive satisfaction at the defeat. And when the surviving polemarchs, now commanders, took counsel with the principal officers as to the steps proper in the emergency, there were a few, but very few, Spartans who pressed for renewal of the battle, and for recovering by force their slain brethren in the field, or perishing in the attempt. All the rest felt like beaten men; so that the polemarchs, giving effect to the general sentiment, sent a herald to solicit the regular truce for burial of their dead. This the Thebans granted, after erecting their own trophy.[1] But Epaminondas, aware that the Spartans would practise every stratagem to conceal the magnitude of their losses, coupled the grant with a condition that the allies should bury their dead first. It was found that the allies had scarce any dead to pick up, and that nearly every slain warrior on the field was a Lacedæmonian.[2] And thus the Theban general, while he placed the loss beyond possibility of concealment, proclaimed at the same time such public evidence of Spartan courage, as to rescue the misfortune of Leuktra from all aggravation on the score of dishonour. What the Theban loss was, Xenophon does not tell us. Pausanias states it at forty-seven men,[3] Diodorus at three hundred. The former number is preposterously small, and even the latter is doubtless under the truth; for a victory in close fight, over soldiers like the Spartans, must have been dearly purchased. Though the bodies of the Spartans were given up to burial, their arms were retained; and the shields of the principal officers were seen by the traveller Pausanias at Thebes 500 years afterwards.[4]

Twenty days only had elapsed, from the time when Epaminondas quitted Sparta after Thebes had been excluded from the general peace, to the day when he stood victorious on the field of Leuktra.[5] The event came like a thunderclap upon every one in Greece, upon victors as well as vanquished— upon allies and neutrals, near and distant, alike. The general expectation had been that Thebes would be speedily overthrown and dismantled;

B.C. 371. Great surprise, and immense alteration of feeling, produced throughout Greece by the Theban victory.

[1] Xen. Hellen. vi. 4, 15.
[2] Pausan. ix. 13, 4; Plutarch, Apophtheg. Reg. p. 198 B.; Cicero, de Officiis, II. 7.
[3] Pausan. ix. 13, 4; Diodor. xv. 55.
[4] Pausan. ix. 16, 3.
[5] This is an important date preserved by Plutarch (Agesil. c. 28).

instead of which, not only she had escaped, but had inflicted a crushing blow on the military majesty of Sparta.

It is in vain that Xenophon—whose account of the battle is obscure, partial, and imprinted with that chagrin which the event occasioned to him[1]—ascribes the defeat to untoward accidents,[2] or to the rashness and convivial carelessness of Kleombrotus; upon whose generalship Agesilaus and his party at Sparta did not scruple to cast ungenerous reproach,[3] while others faintly exculpated him by saying that he had fought contrary to his better judgement, under fear of unpopularity. Such criticisms, coming from men wise after the fact, and consoling themselves for the public calamity by censuring the unfortunate commander, will not stand examination. Kleombrotus represented on this occasion the feeling universal among his countrymen. He was ordered to march against Thebes

---

The congress was broken up at Sparta on the fourteenth of the Attic month Skirrophorion (June), the last month of the year of the Athenian archon Alkisthenês; the battle was fought on the fifth of the Attic month of Hekatombæon, the first month of the next Attic year, of the archon Phrasikleidês; about the beginning of July.

[2] Diodorus differs from Xenophon on one important matter connected with the battle; affirming that Archidamus son of Agesilaus was present and fought, together with various other circumstances, which I shall discuss presently, in a future note. I follow Xenophon.

[3] Xen. Hellen. vi. 4, 8. Εἰς δ᾽ οὖν τὴν μάχην τοῖς μὲν Λακεδαιμονίοις πάντα τἀναντία ἐγίγνετο, τοῖς δὲ (to the Thebans) πάντα καὶ ὑπὸ τῆς τύχης κατωρθοῦτο.

[3] Isokratês, in the Oration vi. called Archidamus (composed about five years after the battle, as if to be spoken by Archidamus son of Agesilaus), puts this statement distinctly into the mouth of Archidamus—μέχρι μὲν τουτηοὶ τῆς ἡμέρας

ἐδυστυχήναμεν δοκοῦμεν ἐν τῇ μάχῃ τῇ πρὸς Θηβαίους, καὶ τοῖς μὲν σώμασι κρατηθῆναι διὰ τὸν οὐκ ὀρθῶς ἡγησάμενον, &c. (s. 9).

I take his statement as good evidence of the real opinion entertained both by Agesilaus and by Archidamus; an opinion the more natural, since the two contemporary kings of Sparta were almost always at variance, and at the head of opposing parties; especially true about Agesilaus and Kleombrotus, during the life of the latter.

Cicero (probably copying Kallisthenês or Ephorus) says, de Officiis, i. 24, 84—"Illa plaga (Lacedæmoniis) pestifera, quâ, quum Cleombrotus invidiam timens temere cum Epaminondâ conflixisset, Lacedæmoniorum opes corruerunt." Polybius remarks (ix. 23, we know not from whom he borrowed) that all the proceedings of Kleombrotus during the empire of Sparta, were marked with a generous regard for the interests and feelings of the allies; while the proceedings of Agesilaus were of the opposite character.

with the full belief, entertained by Agesilaus and all the Spartan leaders, that her unassisted force could not resist him. To fight the Thebans on open ground was exactly what he and every other Spartan desired. While his manner of forcing the entrance of Bœotia, and his capture of Kreusis, was a creditable manœuvre, he seems to have arranged his order of battle in the manner usual with Grecian generals at the time. There appears no reason to censure his generalship, except in so far as he was unable to divine—what no one else divined—the superior combinations of his adversary, then for the first time applied to practice.

To the discredit of Xenophon, Epaminondas is never named in his narrative of the battle, though he recognises in substance that the battle was decided by the irresistible Theban force brought to bear upon one point of the enemy's phalanx; a fact which both Plutarch and Diodorus[1] expressly refer to the genius of the general. All the calculations of Epaminondas turned out successful. The bravery of the Thebans, cavalry as well as infantry, seconded by the training which they had received during the last few years, was found sufficient to carry his plans into full execution. To this circumstance, principally, was owing the great revolution of opinion throughout Greece which followed the battle. Every one felt that a new military power had arisen, and that the Theban training, under the generalship of Epaminondas, had proved itself more than a match on a fair field, with shield and spear, and with numbers on the whole inferior—for the ancient Lykurgean discipline; which last had hitherto stood without a parallel as turning out artists and craftsmen in war, against mere citizens in the opposite ranks, armed, yet without the like training.[2] Essentially stationary and old-fashioned, the Lykurgean discipline was now overborne by the progressive military improvement of other states, handled by a pre-

---

[1] Diodor. xv. 55. Epaminondas, ἰδίᾳ τινὶ καὶ περιττῇ τάξει χρησάμενος, διὰ τῆς ἰδίας στρατηγίας περιεποιήσατο τὴν περιβόητον νίκην..... διὸ καὶ λοξὴν ποιήσας τὴν φάλαγγα, τῷ τοὺς ἐπιλέκτους ἔχοντι κέρατι ἔγνω κρῖναι τὴν μάχην, &c. Compare Plutarch, Pelop. c. 23.

[2] See Aristotel. Politic. viii. 8, 8, 5.
Compare Xenophon, De Repub. Laced. xiii. 5. τοὺς μὲν ἄλλους αὐτοσχεδιαστὰς εἶναι τῶν στρατιωτικῶν, Λακεδαιμονίους δὲ μόνους τῷ ὄντι τεχνίτας τῶν πολεμικῶν—and Xenophon, Memorab. ii. 8, 13, 14.

eminent tactician; a misfortune predicted by the Corinthians[1] at Sparta sixty years before, and now realized, to the conviction of all Greece, on the field of Leuktra.

**Effect of the news at Sparta— heroic self-command.** But if the Spartan system was thus invaded and overpassed in its privilege of training soldiers, there was another species of teaching wherein it neither was nor could be overpassed—the hard lesson of enduring pain and suppressing emotion.

Memorable indeed was the manner in which the news of this fatal catastrophe was received at Sparta. To prepare the reader by an appropriate contrast, we may turn to the manifestation at Athens twenty-seven years before, when the trireme called Paralus arrived from Ægospotami, bearing tidings of the capture of the entire Athenian fleet. "The moan of distress (says the historian[2]) reached all up the Long Walls from Peiræus to Athens, as each man communicated the news to his neighbour: on that night, not a man slept, from bewailing for his lost fellow-citizens and for his own impending ruin." Not such was the scene at Sparta, when the messenger arrived from the field of Leuktra, although there was everything calculated to render the shock violent. For not only was the defeat calamitous and humiliating beyond all former parallel, but it came at a moment when every man reckoned on victory. As soon as Kleombrotus, having forced his way into Bœotia, saw the unassisted Thebans on plain ground before him, no Spartan entertained any doubt of the result. Under this state of feeling, a messenger arrived with the astounding revelation, that the army was totally defeated, with the loss of the king, of 400 Spartans, and more than 1000 Lacedæmonians; and that defeat stood confessed, by having solicited the truce for interment of the slain. At the moment when he arrived, the festival called the Gymnopædia was actually being celebrated on its last day; and the chorus of grown men was going through its usual solemnity in the theatre. In spite of all the poignancy of the intelligence, the Ephors would not permit the solemnity to be either interrupted or abridged. "*Of necessity,*

---

[1] Thucyd. I. 71. ἀρχαιότροπα ὑμῶν (of you Spartans) τὰ ἐπιτηδεύματα πρὸς αὐτούς ἐστιν. Ἀνάγκη δ' ὥσπερ τέχνης ἀεὶ τὰ ἐπιγιγνόμενα κρατεῖν· καὶ ἡσυχαζούσῃ μὲν πόλει τὰ ἀκίνητα νόμιμα ἄριστα, πρὸς πολλὰ δὲ ἀναγκαζομένοις ἰέναι, πολλῆς καὶ τῆς ἐπιτεχνήσεως δεῖ, &c.

[2] Xen. Hellen. II. 2, 3.

*I suppose they were grieved,*—but they went through the whole as if nothing had happened, only communicating the names of the slain to their relations, and issuing a general order to the women, to make no noise or wailing, but to bear the misfortune in silence." That such an order should be issued, is sufficiently remarkable; that it should be issued and obeyed, is what could not be expected; that it should not only be issued and obeyed, but overpassed, is what no man could believe if it were not expressly attested by the contemporary historian. "On the morrow (says he) you might see those whose relations had been slain, walking about in public with bright and cheerful countenances; but of those whose relatives survived, scarce one showed himself; and the few who were abroad, looked mournful and humbled."[1]

In comparing this extraordinary self-constraint and obedience to orders, at Sparta, under the most trying circumstances—with the sensitive and demonstrative temper, and spontaneous outburst of feeling, at Athens, so much more nearly approaching to the Homeric type of Greeks—we must at the same time remark, that in reference to active and heroic efforts for the purpose of repairing past calamities and making head against preponderant odds, the Athenians were decidedly the better of the two. I have already recounted the prodigious and unexpected energy displayed by Athens, after the ruinous loss of her two armaments before Syracuse, when no one expected that she could have held out for six months: I am now about to

*Difference of Athens and Sparta—Athens, equal in active energy.*

---

[1] Xen. Hellen. vi. 4, 16. Γινομένων δὲ τούτων, ὁ μὲν εἰς τὴν Λακεδαίμονα ἀγγελῶν τὸ πάθος ἀφικνεῖται, Γυμνοπαιδιῶν τε οὐσῶν τῆς τελευταίας, καὶ τοῦ ἀνδρικοῦ χόρου ἔνδον ὄντος. Οἱ δὲ ἔφοροι, ἐπεὶ ἤκουσαν τὸ πάθος, ἐλυποῦντο μέν, ὥσπερ οἶμαι, ἀνάγκη· τὸν μέντοι χόρον οὐκ ἐξήγαγον, ἀλλὰ διαγωνίσασθαι εἴων. Καὶ τὰ μὲν ὀνόματα πρὸς τοὺς οἰκείους ἑκάστου τῶν τεθνηκότων ἀπέδοσαν· προεῖπον δὲ ταῖς γυναιξί, μὴ ποιεῖν κραυγήν, ἀλλὰ σιγῆ τὸ πάθος φέρειν. Τῇ δὲ ὑστεραίᾳ ἦν ὁρᾶν, ὧν μὲν ἐτέθνασαν οἱ προσήκοντες, λιπαροὺς καὶ φαιδροὺς ἐν τῷ φανερῷ ἀναστρεφομένους· ὧν δὲ ζῶντες ἠγγελμένοι ἦσαν, ὀλίγους ἂν εἶδες, τούτους δὲ σκυθρωποὺς καὶ ταπεινοὺς περιϊόντας—and Plutarch, Agesil. c. 29.

See a similar statement of Xenophon, after he has recounted the cutting in pieces of the Lacedæmonian mora near Lechæum, about the satisfaction and even triumph of those in the Lacedæmonians who had lost relations in the battle; while every one else was mournful (Xen. Hellen. iv. 5, 10). Compare also Justin, xxviii. 4—the behaviour after the defeat of Sellasia.

recount the proceedings of Sparta, after the calamity at
Leuktra—a calamity great and serious indeed, yet in positive
amount inferior to what had befallen the Athenians at Syracuse. The reader will find that, looking to the intensity
of active effort in both cases, the comparison is all to the
advantage of Athens; excusing at least, if not justifying,
the boast of Periklês[1] in his memorable funeral harangue
—that his countrymen, without the rigorous drill of Spartans, were yet found noway inferior to Spartans in daring
exertion, when the hour of actual trial arrived.

*Reinforce-
ments sent
from
Sparta.*
It was the first obligation of the Ephors to provide
for the safety of their defeated army in Bœotia;
for which purpose they put in march nearly the
whole remaining force of Sparta. Of the Lacedæmonian Moræ, or military divisions (seemingly
six in the aggregate), two or three had been sent with
Kleombrotus; all the remainder were now despatched, even
including elderly citizens up to near sixty years of age,
and all who had been left behind in consequence of other
public offices. Archidamus took the command (Agesilaus
still continuing to be disabled), and employed himself in
getting together the aid promised from Tegea—from the
villages representing the disintegrated Mantineia—from
Corinth, Sikyon, Phlius, and Achaia; all these places being
still under the same oligarchies which had held them under
Lacedæmonian patronage, and still adhering to Sparta.
Triremes were equipped at Corinth, as a means of trans-
porting the new army across to Kreusis, and thus joining
the defeated troops at Leuktra; the port of Kreusis, the
recent acquisition of Kleombrotus, being now found inestimable, as the only means of access into Bœotia.[2]

*Proceed-
ings in
Bœotia
after the
battle of
Leuktra.
The The-
ban victory
not well re-
ceived at
Athens.*
Meanwhile the defeated army still continued in its
entrenched camp at Leuktra, where the Thebans
were at first in no hurry to disturb it. Besides
that this was a very arduous enterprise, even
after the recent victory—we must recollect the
actual feeling of the Thebans themselves, upon
whom their own victory had come by surprise,
at a moment when they were animated more by
despair than by hope. They were doubtless absorbed in the intoxicating triumph and exultation of the
moment, with the embraces and felicitations of their

[1] Thucyd. ii. 39.    [2] Xen. Hellen. vi. 4, 17-19.

families in Thebes, rescued from impending destruction by their valour. Like the Syracusans after their last great victory[1] over the Athenian fleet in the Great Harbour, they probably required an interval to give loose to their feelings of ecstasy, before they would resume action. Epaminondas and the other leaders, aware how much the value of Theban alliance was now enhanced, endeavoured to obtain reinforcement from without, before they proceeded to follow up the blow. To Athens they sent a herald, crowned with wreaths of triumph, proclaiming their recent victory. They invited the Athenians to employ the present opportunity for taking full revenge on Sparta, by joining their hands with those of Thebes. But the sympathies of the Athenians, were now rather hostile than friendly to Thebes, besides that they had sworn peace with Sparta, not a month before. The Senate, who were assembled in the acropolis when the herald arrived, heard his news with evident chagrin, and dismissed him without even a word of courtesy; while the unfortunate Plataeans, who were doubtless waiting in the city in expectation of the victory of Kleombrotus, and of their own speedy re-establishment, found themselves again struck down and doomed to indefinite exile.

To Jason of Pherae in Thessaly, another Theban herald was sent for the same purpose, and very differently received. That despot sent back word that he would come forthwith by sea, and ordered triremes to be equipped for the purpose. But this was a mere deception; for at the same time, he collected the mercenaries and cavalry immediately near to him, and began his march by land. So rapid were his movements, that he forestalled all opposition—though he had to traverse the territory of the Herakleots and Phokians, who were his bitter enemies—and joined the Thebans safely in Bœotia.[2] But when the Theban leaders proposed that he should attack the Lacedæmonian camp in flank, from the high ground, while they would march straight up the hill and attack it in front—Jason strongly dissuaded the enterprise as too perilous; recommending that they should permit the

*Jason of Pherae arrives at Leuktra—the Spartan army retires from Bœotia under capitulation.*

[1] See Thucyd. vii. 73.
[2] Xen. Hellen. vi. 4, 20, 21.
However, since the Phokians formed part of the beaten army at Leuktra, it must be confessed that Jason had less to fear from them at this moment, than at any other.

enemy's departure under capitulation. "Be content (said he) with the great victory which you have already gained. Do not compromise it by attempting something yet more hazardous, against Lacedæmonians driven to despair in their camp. Recollect that a few days ago, *you* yourselves were in despair, and that your recent victory is the fruit of that very feeling. Remember that the gods take pleasure in bringing about these sudden changes of fortune."[1] Having by such representations convinced the Thebans, he addressed a friendly message to the Lacedæmonians, reminding them of their dangerous position, as well as of the little trust to be reposed in their allies—and offering himself as mediator to negotiate for their safe retreat. Their acquiescence was readily given; and at his instance, a truce was agreed to by both parties, assuring to the Lacedæmonians the liberty of quitting Bœotia. In spite of the agreement, however, the Lacedæmonian commander placed little faith either in the Thebans or in Jason, apprehending a fraud for the purpose of inducing him to quit the camp and of attacking him on the march. Accordingly, he issued public orders in the camp for every man to be ready for departure after the evening meal, and to march in the night to Kithæron, with a view of passing that mountain on the next morning. Having put the enemy on this false scent, he directed his real night-march by a different and not very easy way, first to Kreusis, next to Ægosthena in the Megarian territory.[2] The Thebans offered no opposition; nor is it at all probable that they intended any fraud, considering that Jason was here the

---

[1] Pausanias states that immediately after the battle, Epaminondas gave permission to the allies of Sparta to depart and go home, by which permission they profited, so that the Spartans now stood alone in the camp (Paus. ix. 14, 1). This however is inconsistent with the account of Xenophon (vi. 4, 26), and I think improbable.

Sievers (Geschichte, &c. p. 247) thinks that Jason preserved the Spartans by outwitting and deluding Epaminondas. But it appears to me that the storming of the Spartan camp was an arduous enterprise wherein more Thebans than Spartans would have been slain: moreover, the Spartans were masters of the port of Kreusis, so that there was little chance of starving out the camp before reinforcements arrived. The capitulation granted by Epaminondas seems to have been really the wisest proceeding.

[2] Xen. Hellen. vi. 5, 22-25.

The road from Kreusis to Leuktra, however, must have been that by which Kleombrotus arrived.

guarantee, and that he at least had no motive to break his word.

It was at Ægosthena that the retreating Lacedæmonians met Archidamus, who had advanced to that point with the Laconian forces, and was awaiting the junction of his Peloponnesian allies. The purpose of his march being now completed, he advanced no farther. The armament was disbanded, and Lacedæmonians as well as allies returned home.[1]

[1] This is the most convenient place for noticing the discrepancy, as to the battle of Leuktra, between Diodorus and Xenophon. I have followed Xenophon.

Diodorus (xv. 54) states both the arrival of Jason in Bœotia, and the outmarch of Archidamus from Sparta, to have taken place, not *after* the battle of Leuktra, but *before* it. Jason (he says) came with a considerable force to the aid of the Thebans. He prevailed upon Kleombrotus, who doubted the sufficiency of his own numbers, to agree to a truce and to evacuate Bœotia. But as Kleombrotus was marching homeward, he met Archidamus with a second Lacedæmonian army, on his way to Bœotia, by order of the Ephors, for the purpose of reinforcing him. Accordingly Kleombrotus, finding himself thus unexpectedly strengthened, openly broke the truce just concluded, and marched back with Archidamus to Leuktra. Here they fought the battle, Kleombrotus commanding the right wing, and Archidamus the left. They sustained a complete defeat, in which Kleombrotus was slain; the result being the same on both statements.

We must here make our election between the narrative of Xenophon and that of Diodorus. That the authority of the former is greater speaking generally, I need hardly remark; nevertheless his philo-Laconian partialities become so glaring and preponderant, during these latter books of the Hellenica (where he is discharging the mournful duty of recounting the humiliation of Sparta), as to afford some colour for the suspicions of Palmerius, Morus, and Schneider, who think that Xenophon has concealed the direct violation of truce on the part of the Spartans, and that the facts really occurred as Diodorus has described them. See Schneider ad Xen. Hellen. vi. 4, 5, 6.

It will be found, however, on examining the facts, that such suspicion ought not here to be admitted, and that there are grounds for preferring the narrative of Xenophon.

1. He explains to us how it happened that the remains of the Spartan army, after the defeat of Leuktra, escaped out of Bœotia. Jason arrives after the battle, and prevails upon the Thebans to allow them to retreat under a truce; Archidamus also arrives after the battle to take them up. If the defeat had taken place under the circumstances mentioned by Diodorus—Archidamus and the survivors would have found it scarcely possible to escape out of Bœotia.

2. If Diodorus relates correctly, there must have been a violation of truce on the part of Kleombrotus and the Lacedæmonians, as glaring as any that occurs in Grecian history. But such vio-

In all communities, the return of so many defeated soldiers, liberated under a capitulation by the enemy, would have been a scene of mourning. But in Sparta it was pregnant with grave and dangerous consequences. So terrible was the scorn and ignominy heaped upon the Spartan citizen who survived a defeat, that life became utterly intolerable to him. The mere fact sufficed for his condemnation, without any inquiry into justifying or extenuating circumstances. No citizen at home would speak to him or be seen consorting with him in tent, game, or chorus; no other family would intermarry with his; if he was seen walking about with an air of cheerfulness, he was struck and ill-used by the passers-by, until he assumed that visible humility which was supposed to become his degraded position. Such rigorous treatment (which we learn from the panegyrist Xenophon[1]) helps to explain the satisfaction of the Spartan father and mother, when they learnt that their son was among the slain and not among the survivors. Defeat of Spartan troops had hitherto been rare. But in the case of the prisoners at Sphakteria, when released from captivity and brought back to a degraded existence at Sparta, some uneasiness had been felt, and some precautions deemed necessary to prevent them from becoming dangerous malcontents.[2] Here was another case yet more formidable. The vanquished returning from Leuktra were numerous, while the severe loss sustained in the battle amply attested

*Treatment of the defeated citizens on reaching Sparta— suspension of the law.*

lation is never afterwards alluded to by any one, among the misdeeds of the Lacedæmonians.

3. A part, and an essential part, of the story of Diodorus, is, that Archidamus was present and fought at Leuktra. But we have independent evidence rendering it almost certain that he was not there. Whoever reads the Discourse of Isokratês called *Archidamus* (Or. vi. sect. 9, 10, 129), will see that such observations could not have been put into the mouth of Archidamus, if he had been present there, and (of course) in joint command with Kleombrotus.

4. If Diodorus be correct, Sparta must have levied a new army from her allies, just after having sworn the peace, which peace exonerated her allies from everything like obligation to follow her headship; and a new army, not for the purpose of extricating defeated comrades in Bœotia, but for pure aggression against Thebes. This, to say the least, is eminently improbable.

On these grounds, I adhere to Xenophon and depart from Diodorus.

[1] Xenoph. Rep. Lac. c. iz.; Plutarch, Agesil. c. 30.
[2] Thucyd. v. 34.

their bravery. Aware of the danger of enforcing against them the established custom, the Ephors referred the case to Agesilaus; who proposed that for that time and case the customary penalties should be allowed to sleep; but should be revived afterwards and come into force as before. Such was the step accordingly taken;[1] so that the survivors from this fatal battle-field were enabled to mingle with the remaining citizens without dishonour or degradation. The step was indeed doubly necessary, considering the small aggregate number of fully qualified citizens; which number always tended to decline—from the nature of the Spartan political franchise combined with the exigences of Spartan training[2]—and could not bear even so great a diminution as that of the four hundred slain at Leuktra. "Sparta (says Aristotle) could not stand up against a single defeat, but was ruined through the small number of her citizens."[3]

The cause here adverted to by Aristotle, as explaining the utter loss of ascendency abroad, and the capital diminution both of power and of inviolability at home, which will now be found to come thick upon Sparta, was undoubtedly real and important. But a fact still more important was, the alteration of opinion produced everywhere in Greece with regard to Sparta, by the sudden shock of the battle of Leuktra. All the prestige and old associations connected with her long-established power vanished; while the hostility and fears, inspired both by herself and by her partisans, but hitherto reluctantly held back in silence—now burst forth into open manifestation.

*Lowered estimation of Sparta in Greece—prestige of military superiority lost.*

The ascendency, exercised down to this time by Sparta north of the Corinthian Gulf, in Phokis and elsewhere, passed away from her, and became divided between the vic-

---

[1] Plutarch, Agesil. c. 30; Plutarch, Apophtheg. Lacon. p. 214 B.; Apophtheg. Reg. p. 191 C.; Polyænus, ii. 1, 13.

A similar suspension of penalties, for the special occasion, was enacted after the great defeat of Agis and the Lacedæmonians by Antipater, B.C. 330. Akrotatas, son of King Kleomenês, was the only person at Sparta who opposed the suspension (Diodor. xix. 70). He incurred the strongest unpopularity for such opposition. Compare also Justin, xxviii. 4—describing the public feeling at Sparta after the defeat at Sellasia.

[2] The explanation of Spartan citizenship will be found in an earlier part of this History, Ch. vi.

[3] Aristotel. Politic. ii. 8, 12. Μίαν γὰρ πληγὴν οὐχ ὑπήνεγκεν ἡ πόλις, ἀλλ' ἀπώλετο διὰ τὴν ὀλιγανθρωπίαν.

torious Thebans and Jason of Pheræ. The Thebans, and
the Bœotian confederates who were now in
cordial sympathy with them, excited to enthusiasm by their recent success, were eager for
fresh glories, and readily submitted to the full
exigences of military training; while under a
leader like Epaminondas, their ardour was turned
to such good account, that they became better
soldiers every month.[1] The Phokians, unable to defend
themselves single-handed, were glad to come under the
protection of the Thebans—as less bitterly hostile to them
than the Thessalian Jason—and concluded with them
obligations of mutual defence and alliance.[2] The cities
of Eubœa, together with the Lokrians (both Epiknemidian
and Opuntian), the Malians and the town of Herakleа,
followed the example. The latter town was now defenceless;
for Jason, in returning from Bœotia to Thessaly, had
assaulted it and destroyed its fortifications; since by its
important site near the pass of Thermopylæ, it might easily
be held as a position to bar his entrance into Southern
Greece.[3] The Bœotian town of Orchomenus, which had
held with the Lacedæmonians even until the late battle,
was now quite defenceless; and the Thebans, highly exasperated against its inhabitants, were disposed to destroy
the city, reducing the inhabitants to slavery. Severe as
this proposition was, it would not have exceeded the customary rigours of war: nor even what might have befallen
Thebes herself, had Kleombrotus been victorious at Leuktra.
But the strenuous remonstrance of Epaminondas prevented
it from being carried into execution. Alike distinguished
for mild temper and for long-sighted views, he reminded
his countrymen that in their present aspiring hopes towards ascendency in Greece, it was essential to establish a
character for moderation of dealing[4] not inferior to their
military courage, as attested by the recent victory. Accordingly, the Orchomenians were pardoned upon submission, and re-admitted as members of the Bœotian confed-

---

[1] Xen. Hellen. vi. 5, 24. Καὶ γὰρ
οἱ μὲν Βοιωτοὶ πάντες ἐγυμνάζοντο
περὶ τὰ ὅπλα, ἀγαλλόμενοι τῇ ἐν
Λεύκτροις νίκῃ, &c.
These are remarkable words from
the unwilling pen of Xenophon:
compare vii. 5, 12.

[2] Xen. Hellen. vi. 5, 23; vii. 5, 4;
Diodor. xv. 57.

[3] Xen. Hellen. vi. 4, 27; vi. 6, 23.

[4] Diodor. xv. 57.

cracy. To the Thespians, however, the same lenity was not extended. They were expelled from Bœotia, and their territory annexed to Thebes. It will be recollected that immediately before the battle of Leuktra, when Epaminondas caused proclamation to be made that such of the Bœotians as were disaffected to the Theban cause might march away, the Thespians had availed themselves of the permission and departed.[1] The fugitive Thespians found shelter, like the Platæans, at Athens.[2]

While Thebes was commemorating her recent victory by the erection of a treasury-chamber,[3] and the dedication of pious offerings at Delphi—while the military organization of Bœotia was receiving such marked improvement, and the cluster of dependent states attached to Thebes was thus becoming larger, under the able management of Epaminondas—Jason in Thessaly was also growing more powerful every day. He was tagus of all Thessaly; with its tributary neighbours under complete obedience—with Macedonia partially dependent on him—and with a mercenary force, well-paid and trained, greater than had ever been assembled in Greece. By dismantling Heraklea, in his return home from Bœotia, he had laid open the strait of Thermopylæ, so as to be sure of access into southern Greece whenever he chose. His personal ability and ambition, combined with his great power, inspired universal alarm; for no man knew whither he would direct his arms; whether to Asia, against the Persian king, as he was fond of boasting[4]—or northward against the cities in Chalkidikê—or southward against Greece.

*Power and ambition of Jason.*

The last-mentioned plan seemed the most probable, at the beginning of 370 B.C., half a year after the battle of Leuktra: for Jason proclaimed distinctly his intention of being present at the Pythian festival (the season for which was about August 1, 370 B.C., near Delphi), not only with splendid presents and sacrifices to Apollo, but also at the head of a numerous army. Orders had been given that his troops should hold themselves ready for military service[5]—about

*Plans of Jason— Pythian festival.*

[1] Pausan. ix. 13, 3; ix. 14, 1.
[2] Xen. Hellen. vi. 3, 1.
I have already given my reasons (in a note on the preceding chapter) for believing that the Thespians were not ἀνάστατοι before the battle of Leuktra.
[3] Pausanias, x. 11, 4.
[4] Isokratês, Or. v. (Philip.) s. 141.
[5] Xen. Hellen. vi. 4, 20. παρήγγειλε

the time when the festival was to be celebrated; and requisitions had been sent round, demanding from all his tributaries victims for the Pythian sacrifice, to a total of not less than 1000 bulls, and 10,000 sheep, goats, and swine; besides a prize-bull to take the lead in the procession, for which a wreath of gold was to be given. Never before had such honour been done to the god; for those who came to offer sacrifice were usually content with one or more beasts bred on the neighbouring plain of Kirrha.[1] We must recollect, however, that this Pythian festival of 370 B.C. occurred under peculiar circumstances; for the two previous festivals in 374 B.C. and 378 B.C. must have been comparatively unfrequented; in consequence of the war between Sparta and her allies on one side, and Athens and Thebes on the other—and also of the occupation of Phokis by Kleombrotus. Hence the festival of 370 B.C., following immediately after the peace, appeared to justify an extraordinary burst of pious magnificence, to make up for the niggardly tributes to the god during the two former; while the hostile dispositions of the Phokians would be alleged as an excuse for the military force intended to accompany Jason.

*Assassination of Jason at Pheræ.*

But there were other intentions, generally believed though not formally announced, which no Greek could imagine without uneasiness. It was affirmed that Jason was about to arrogate to himself the presidency and celebration of the festival, which belonged of right to the Amphiktyonic assembly. It was feared, moreover, that he would lay hands on the rich treasures of the Delphian temple; a scheme said to

δὲ καὶ ὡς στρατευσομένοις εἰς τὸν περὶ τὰ Πύθια χρόνον Θετταλοῖς ἐπρασιτυάζεσθαι.

I agree with Dr. Arnold's construction of this passage (see his Appendix ad Thucyd. v. 1, at the end of the second volume of his edition of Thucydides) as opposed to that of Mr. Fynes Clinton. At the same time, I do not think that the passage proves much either in favour of his view, or against the view of Mr. Clinton, about the month of the Pythian festival; which I incline to conceive as celebrated about August 1; a little later than Dr. Arnold, a little earlier than Mr. Clinton, supposes. Looking to the lunar months of the Greeks, we must recollect that the festival would not always coincide with the same month or week of our year.

I cannot concur with Dr. Arnold in setting aside the statement of Plutarch respecting the coincidence of the Pythian festival with the battle of Koroneia.

[1] Xen. Hellen. vi. 4, 29, 30. βοῦν ἡγεμόνα, &c.

have been conceived by the Syracusan despot Dionysius fifteen years before, in conjunction with the Epirot Alketas, who was now dependent upon Jason.[1] As there were no visible means of warding off this blow, the Delphians consulted the god to know what they were to do if Jason approached the treasury; upon which the god replied, that he would himself take care of it—and he kept his word. This enterprising despot, in the flower of his age and at the summit of his power, perished most unexpectedly before the day of the festival arrived.[2] He had been reviewing his cavalry near Pheræ, and was sitting to receive and answer petitioners, when seven young men approached, apparently in hot dispute with each other, and appealing to him for a settlement. As soon as they got near, they set upon him and slew him.[3] One was killed on the spot by the guards, and another also as he was mounting on horseback; but the remaining five contrived to reach horses ready prepared for them and to gallop away out of the reach of pursuit. In most of the Grecian cities which these fugitives visited, they were received with distinguished honour, as having relieved the Grecian world from one who inspired universal alarm,[4] now that Sparta was unable to resist him, while no other power had as yet taken her place.

Jason was succeeded in his dignity, but neither in his power, nor ability, by two brothers—Polyphron and Polydorus. Had he lived longer, he would have influenced most seriously the subsequent destinies of Greece. What else he would have done, we cannot say; but he would have interfered materially with the development of Theban power.

*Relief to Thebes by the death of Jason—satisfaction in Greece.*

---

[1] Diodor. xv. 13.
[2] Xen. Hellen. vi. 4, 30. ἀνεκρίνοντο τὸν θεόν, ὅτι αὐτῷ μελήσει. Ὁ δ᾽ οὖν ἀνὴρ, τηλικοῦτος ὤν, καὶ τοσαῦτα καὶ τοιαῦτα διανοούμενος, &c.

Xenophon evidently considers the sudden removal of Jason as a consequence of the previous intention expressed by the god to take care of his own treasure.
[3] Xen. Hellen. vi. 4, 31, 32. The cause which provoked these young men is differently stated: compare Diodor. xv. 60; Valer. Maxim. ix. 10, 2.
[4] Xen. Hellen. vi. 4. 82.

The death of Jason, in the spring or early summer of 370 B.C., refutes the compliment which Cornelius Nepos (Timoth. c. 4) pays to Timotheus; who can never have made war upon Jason after 373 B.C., when he received the latter at Athens in his house.

Thebes was a great gainer by his death, though perfectly innocent of it, and though in alliance with him to the last; insomuch that his widow went to reside there for security.[1] Epaminondas was relieved from a most formidable rival, while the body of Theban allies north of Bœotia became much more dependent than they would have remained, if there had been a competing power like that of Jason in Thessaly. The treasures of the god were preserved a few years longer, to be rifled by another hand.

<small>Proceedings in Peloponnesus after the defeat of Leuktra. Expulsion of the Spartan harmosts and dekarchies.</small> While these proceedings were going on in Northern Greece, during the months immediately succeeding the battle of Leuktra, events not less serious and stirring had occurred in Peloponnesus. The treaty sworn at Sparta twenty days before that battle, bound the Lacedæmonians to disband their forces, remove all their harmosts and garrisons, and leave every subordinate city to its own liberty of action. As they did not scruple to violate the treaty by the orders sent to Kleombrotus, so they probably were not zealous in executing the remaining conditions; though officers were named, for the express purpose of going round to see that the evacuation of the cities was really carried into effect.[2] But it probably was not accomplished in twenty days; nor would it perhaps have been ever more than nominally accomplished, if Kleombrotus had been successful in Bœotia. But after these twenty days came the portentous intelligence of the fate of that prince and his army. The invincible arm of Sparta was broken; she had not a man to spare for the maintenance of foreign ascendency. Her harmosts disappeared at once (as they had disappeared from the Asiatic and insular cities twenty-three years before, immediately after the battle of Knidus[3]) and returned home. Nor was this all. The Lacedæmonian ascendency had been maintained everywhere by local oligarchies or dekarchies, which had been for the most part violent and oppressive. Against these governments, now deprived of their foreign support, the long-accumulated flood of internal discontent burst with irresistible force, stimulated probably by returning exiles. Their past misgovernment was avenged by severe sentences and proscription, to the length

<small>[1] Xen. Hellen. vi. 4, 37.  [2] Diodor. xv. 38, ἐξαγωγεῖς.
[3] Xenoph. Hellen. iv. 8, 1-5.</small>

of great reactionary injustice; and the parties banished by this anti-Spartan revolution became so numerous, as to harass and alarm seriously the newly-established governments. Such were the commotions which, during the latter half of 371 B.C., disturbed many of the Peloponnesian towns—Phigaleia, Phlius, Corinth, Sikyon, Megara, &c., though with great local difference both of detail and of result.[1]

But the city where intestine commotion took place in its most violent form was Argos. We do not know how this fact was connected with the general state of Grecian politics at the time; for Argos had not been in any way subject to Sparta, nor a member of the Spartan confederacy, nor (so far as we know) concerned in the recent war, since the peace of Antalkidas in 387 B.C. The Argeian government was a

*Skytalism at Argos—violent intestine feud.*

---

[1] Diodor. xv. 38, 40.
Diodorus mentions these commotions as if they had taken place after the peace concluded in 374 B.C., and not after the peace of 371 B.C. But it is impossible that they can have taken place after the former, which, in point of fact, was broken off almost as soon as sworn—was never carried into effect—and comprised no one but Athens and Sparta. I have before remarked that Diodorus seems to have confounded, both in his mind and his history, these two treaties of peace together, and has predicated of the former what really belongs to the latter. The commotions which he mentions come in most naturally and properly, immediately after the battle of Leuktra.
He affirms the like reaction against Lacedæmonian supremacy and its local representatives in the various cities, to have taken place even after the peace of Antalkidas in 387 B.C. (xv. 5). But if such reaction began at that time, it must have been promptly repressed by Sparta, then in undiminished and even advancing power.

Another occurrence, alleged to have happened after the battle of Leuktra, may be properly noticed here. Polybius (ii. 39), and Strabo seemingly copying him (viii. p. 384), assert that both Sparta and Thebes agreed to leave their disputed questions of power to the arbitration of the Achæans, and to abide by their decision. Though I greatly respect the authority of Polybius, I am unable here to reconcile his assertion either with the facts which unquestionably occurred, or with general probability. If any such arbitration was ever consented to, it must have come to nothing; for the war went on without interruption. But I cannot bring myself to believe that it was even consented to, either by Thebes or by Sparta. The exuberant confidence of the former, the sense of dignity on the part of the latter, must have indisposed both to such a proceeding; especially to the acknowledgment of umpires like the Achæan cities, who enjoyed little estimation in 370 B.C., though they acquired a good deal a century and a half afterwards.

democracy, and the popular leaders were vehement in their
denunciations against the oligarchical opposition party—
who were men of wealth and great family position. These
last, thus denounced, formed a conspiracy for the forcible
overthrow of the government. But the conspiracy was
discovered prior to execution, and some of the suspected
conspirators were interrogated under the torture to make
them reveal their accomplices; under which interrogation,
one of them deposed against thirty conspicuous citizens.
The people, after a hasty trial, put these thirty men to
death, and confiscated their property, while others slew
themselves to escape the same fate. So furious did the
fear and wrath of the people become, exasperated by the
popular leaders, that they continued their executions until
they had put to death 1200 (or as some say, 1500) of the
principal citizens. At length the popular leaders became
themselves tired and afraid of what they had done; upon
which the people were animated to fury against them, and
put them to death also.[1]

This gloomy series of events was termed the Skytalism,
or Cudgelling, from the instrument (as we are told) by
which these multiplied executions were consummated;
though the name seems more to indicate an impetuous
popular insurrection than deliberate executions. We know
the facts too imperfectly to be able to infer anything more
than the brutal working of angry political passion amidst
a population like that of Argos or Korkyra, where there
was not (as at Athens) either a taste for speech, or the
habit of being guided by speech, and of hearing both sides
of every question fully discussed. Cicero remarks that he
had never heard of any Argeian orator. The acrimony of
Demosthenês and Æschinês was discharged by mutual
eloquence of vituperation, while the assembly or the
dikastery afterwards decided between them. We are told
that the assembled Athenian people, when they heard the
news of the Skytalism at Argos, were so shocked at it,
that they caused the solemnity of purification to be performed round the assembly.[2]

---

[1] Diodor. xv. 57, 58.
[2] Plutarch, Reipubl. Gerend. Præcept. p. 814 B.; Isokratês, Or. v.
(Philip.) s. 52: compare Dionys.
Halic. Antiq. Rom. vii. 66.

CHAP. LXXVIII. POSITION OF SPARTA. 419

Though Sparta thus saw her confidential partisans deposed, expelled, or maltreated, throughout so many of the Peloponnesian cities—and though as yet there was no Theban interference within the isthmus, either actual or prospective—yet she was profoundly discouraged, and incapable of any effort either to afford protection or to uphold ascendency. One single defeat had driven her to the necessity of contending for home and family;[1] probably too the dispositions of her own Periœki and Helots in Laconia, were such as to require all her force as well as all her watchfulness. At any rate, her empire and her influence over the sentiments of Greeks out of Laconia, became suddenly extinct, to a degree which astonishes us, when we recollect that it had become a sort of tradition in the Greek mind, and that, only nine years before, it had reached as far as Olynthus. How completely her ascendency had passed away, is shown in a remarkable step taken by Athens, seemingly towards the close of 371 B.C., about four months after the battle of Leuktra. Many of the Peloponnesian cities, though they had lost both their fear and their reverence for Sparta, were still anxious to continue members of a voluntary alliance under the presidency of some considerable city. Of this feeling the Athenians took advantage, to send envoys and invite them to enter into a common league at Athens, on the basis of the peace of Antalkidas, and of the peace recently sworn at Sparta.[2] Many of them, obeying the summons, entered into an engagement to the following effect: "I will adhere to the peace sent

*Discouragement of Sparta and helplessness of Sparta.*

*Athens places herself at the head of a new Peloponnesian land confederacy.*

[1] Xen. Hellen. vii. 1, 10.
The discouragement of the Spartans is revealed by the unwilling, though indirect, intimations of Xenophon—not less than by their actual conduct—Hellen. vi. 5, 21; vii. 1, 30-32: compare Plutarch, Agesil. c. 30.

[2] Xen. Hellen. vi. 6, 1-3.
Ἐνθυμηθέντες οἱ Ἀθηναῖοι ὅτι οἱ Πελοποννήσιοι ἔτι οἴονται, χρῆναι ἀκολουθεῖν, καὶ οὔπω διαξιοῦντο οἱ Λακεδαιμόνιοι, ὥσπερ τοὺς Ἀθηναίους διέθεσαν—μεταπέμπονται τὰς πόλεις, ὅσαι βούλονται τῆς εἰρήνης μετέχειν,

ἣν βασιλεὺς κατέπεμψεν.
In this passage, Morus and some other critics maintain that we ought to read οὔπω (which seems not to be supported by any MSS.), in place of οὕτω. Zeune and Schneider have admitted the new reading into the text; yet they doubt the propriety of the change, and I confess that I share their doubts. The word οὕτω will construe, and gives a clear sense; a very different sense from οὔπω, indeed—yet one more likely to have been intended by Xenophon.

2 E 2

down by the Persian king, and to the resolutions of the Athenians and the allies generally. If any of the cities who have sworn this oath shall be attacked, I will assist her with all my might." What cities, or how many, swore to this engagement, we are not told; we make out indirectly that Corinth was one;[1] but the Eleians refused it, on the ground that their right of sovereignty over the Marganeis, the Triphylians, and the Skilluntians, was not recognised. The formation of the league itself, however, with Athens as president, is a striking fact, as evidence of the sudden dethronement of Sparta, and as a warning that she would henceforward have to move in her own separate orbit, like Athens after the Peloponnesian war. Athens stepped into the place of Sparta as president of the Peloponnesian confederacy, and guarantee of the sworn peace; though the cities which entered into this new compact were not for that reason understood to break with their ancient president.[2]

*Accusation preferred in the Amphiktyonic assembly, by Thebes against Sparta.*

Another incident too, apparently occurring about the present time, though we cannot mark its exact date—serves to mark the altered position of Sparta. The Thebans preferred in the assembly of Amphiktyons an accusation against her, for the unlawful capture of their citadel the Kadmeia by Phœbidas, while under a sworn peace; and for the sanction conferred by the Spartan authorities on this act, in detaining and occupying the place. The Amphiktyonic assembly found the Spartans guilty, and condemned them to a fine of 500 talents. As the fine was not paid, the assembly, after a certain interval, doubled it; but the second sentence remained unexecuted as well as the first, since there were no means of enforcement.[3] Probably neither those who preferred the charge, nor those who passed the vote, expected that the Lacedæmonians would really submit to pay the fine. The

---

[1] Xen. Hellen. vi. 5, 37.

[2] Thus the Corinthians still continued allies of Sparta (Xen. Hellen. vii. 4, 8).

[3] Diodor. xvi. 23-29; Justin. viii. 1. We may fairly suppose that both of them borrow from Theopompus, who treated at large of the memorable Sacred War against the Phokians, which began in 355 B.C., and in which the conduct of Sparta was partly determined by this previous sentence of the Amphiktyons. See Theopompi Fragm. 182-184, ed. Didot.

utmost which could be done, by way of punishment for such contumacy, would be to exclude them from the Pythian games, which were celebrated under the presidency of the Amphiktyons; and we may perhaps presume that they really were thus excluded.

The incident however deserves peculiar notice, in more than one point of view. First, as indicating the lessened dignity of Sparta. Since the victory of Leuktra and the death of Jason, Thebes had become preponderant, especially in Northern Greece, where the majority of the nations or races voting in the Amphiktyonic assembly were situated. It is plainly through the ascendency of Thebes, that this condemnatory vote was passed. Next, as indicating the incipient tendency, which we shall hereafter observe still farther developed, to extend the functions of the Amphiktyonic assembly beyond its special sphere of religious solemnities, and to make it the instrument of political coercion or revenge in the hands of the predominant state. In the previous course of this history, an entire century has passed without giving occasion to mention the Amphiktyonic assembly as taking part in political affairs. Neither Thucydidês nor Xenophon, though their united histories cover seventy years, chiefly of Hellenic conflict, ever speak of that assembly. The latter, indeed, does not even notice this fine imposed upon the Lacedæmonians, although it falls within the period of his history. We know the fact only from Diodorus and Justin; and unfortunately, merely as a naked fact, without any collateral or preliminary details. During the sixty or seventy years preceding the battle of Leuktra, Sparta had always had her regular political confederacy and synod of allies convened by herself: her political ascendency was exercised over them *eo nomine*, by a method more direct and easy than that of perverting the religious authority of the Amphiktyonic assembly, even if such a proceeding were open to her.[1] But when Thebes, after the battle of Leuktra, became the more powerful state individually, she had no such established confederacy and synod of allies to sanction her propositions and to share or abet her antipathies. The Amphiktyonic assembly, meeting alternately

[1] See Tittmann, Ueber den Bund der Amphiktyonen, pp. 192-107 (Berlin, 1812).

at Delphi and at Thermopylæ, and composed of twelve
ancient races, principally belonging to Northern Greece,
as well as most of them inconsiderable in power—presented itself as a convenient instrument for her purposes.
There was a certain show of reason for considering the
seizure of the Kadmeia by Phœbidas as a religious offence;
since it was not only executed during the Pythian festival,
but was in itself a glaring violation of the public law and
interpolitical obligations recognised between Grecian
cities; which, like other obligations, were believed to be
under the sanction of the gods; though probably, if the
Athenians and Platæans had preferred a similar complaint
to the Amphiktyons against Thebes for her equally unjust
attempt to surprise Platæa under full peace in the spring
of 431 B.C.—both Spartans and Thebans would have
resisted it. In the present case, however, the Thebans
had a case against Sparta sufficiently plausible, when
combined with their overruling ascendency, to carry a
majority in the Amphiktyonic assembly, and to procure
the imposition of this enormous fine. In itself the sentence
produced no direct effect—which will explain the silence
of Xenophon. But it is the first of a series of proceedings,
connected with the Amphiktyons, which will be found
hereafter pregnant with serious results for Grecian stability
and independence.

Proceedings in Arcadia. Among all the inhabitants of Peloponnesus, none
were more powerfully affected, by the recent
Spartan overthrow at Leuktra, than the Arcadians. Tegea, their most important city, situated
on the border of Laconia, was governed by an oligarchy
wholly in the interest of Sparta; Orchomenus was of like
sentiment; and Mantineia had been broken up into separate
villages (about fifteen years before) by the Lacedæmonians
themselves—an act of high-handed injustice committed at
the zenith of their power after the peace of Antalkidas. The
remaining Arcadian population were in great proportion
villagers; rude men, but excellent soldiers, and always ready
to follow the Lacedæmonian banners, as well from old habit
and military deference, as from the love of plunder.[1]

The defeat of Leuktra effaced this ancient sentiment.
The Arcadians not only ceased to count upon victory and
plunder in the service of Sparta, but began to fancy that

[1] Xen. Hellen. v. 2, 15.

their own military prowess was not inferior to that of the Spartans; while the disappearance of the harmosts left them free to follow their own inclinations. It was by the Mantineians that the movement was first commenced. Divested of Grecian city-life, and condemned to live in separate villages, each under its own philo-Spartan oligarchy, they had nourished a profound animosity, which manifested itself on the first opportunity of deposing these oligarchies and coming again together. The resolution was unanimously adopted to re-establish Mantineia with its walls, and resume their political consolidation; while the leaders banished by the Spartans at their former intervention, now doubtless returned to become foremost in the work.[1] As the breaking up of Mantineia had been one of the most obnoxious acts of Spartan omnipotence, so there was now a strong sympathy in favour of its re-establishment. Many Arcadians from other quarters came to lend auxiliary labour. Moreover the Eleians sent three talents as a contribution towards the cost. Deeply mortified by this proceeding, yet too weak to prevent it by force, the Spartans sent Agesilaus with a friendly remonstrance. Having been connected with the city by paternal ties of hospitality, he had declined the command of the army of coercion previously employed against it; nevertheless, on this occasion, the Mantineian leaders refused to convene their public assembly to hear his communication, desiring that he would make known his purpose to them. Accordingly, he intimated that he had come with no view of hindering the re-establishment of the city, but simply to request that they would defer it until the consent of Sparta could be formally given; which (he promised) should soon be forthcoming, together with a handsome subscription to lighten the cost. But the Mantineian leaders answered, that compliance was impossible, since a public resolution had already been taken to prosecute the work forthwith. Enraged at such a rebuff, yet without power to resent it, Agesilaus was compelled to return home.[2] The Mantineians persevered and completed

B.C. 371.
Re-establishment of the city of Mantineia by its own citizens.

[1] Xen. Hellen. v. 2, 6; vi. 5, 3.
[2] Xen. Hellen. vi. 5, 4, 5.
Pausanias (viii. 8, 6; ix. 14, 2) states that the Thebans re-established the city of Mantineia. The act emanated from the spontaneous impulse of the Mantineians and other Arcadians, before the Thebans

the rebuilding of their city, on a level site, and in an elliptical form, surrounded with elaborate walls and towers.

The affront here offered, probably studiously offered, by Mantineian leaders who had either been exiles themselves, or sympathised with the exiles—was only the prelude to a series of others (presently to be recounted) yet more galling and intolerable. But it was doubtless felt to the quick both by the Ephors and by Agesilaus, as a public symptom of that prostration into which they had so suddenly fallen. To appreciate fully such painful sentiment, we must recollect that an exaggerated pride and sense of dignity, individual as well as collective, founded upon military excellence and earned by incredible

*Humiliating refusal experienced by Agesilaus from the Mantineians— keenly painful to a Spartan.*

had yet begun to interfere actively in Peloponnesus, which we shall presently find them doing. But it was doubtless done in reliance upon Theban support, and was in all probability made known to, and encouraged by, Epaminondas. It formed the first step to that series of anti-Spartan measures in Arcadia, which I shall presently relate.

Either the city of Mantineia now built was not exactly in the same situation as the one dismantled in 385 B.C., since the river Ophis did not run through it, as it had run through the former—or else the course of the Ophis has altered. If the former, there would be three successive sites, the oldest of them being on the hill called Ptolis, somewhat north of Gurzuli. Ptolis was perhaps the larger of the primary constituent villages. Ernst Curtius (Peloponnesos, p. 242) makes the hill Gurzuli to be the same as the hill called Ptolis; Colonel Leake distinguishes the two, and places Ptolis on his map northward of Gurzuli (Peloponnesiaca, p. 378-381). The summit of Gurzuli is about one mile distant from the centre of Mantineia (Leake, Peloponnès. p. 383).

The walls of Mantineia, as rebuilt in 370 B.C., form an ellipse of about eighteen stadia, or a little more than two miles in circumference. The greater axis of the ellipse points north and south. It was surrounded with a wet ditch, whose waters join into one course at the west of the town, and form a brook which Sir William Gell calls the Ophis (Itinerary of the Morea, p. 142). The face of the wall is composed of regularly cut square stones; it is about ten feet thick in all—four feet for an outer wall, two feet for an inner wall, and an intermediate space of four feet filled up with rubbish. There were eight principal double gates, each with a narrow winding approach, defended by a round tower on each side. There were quadrangular towers, eighty feet apart, all round the circumference of the walls (Ernst Curtius, Peloponnesos, p. 236, 237).

These are instructive remains, indicating the ideas of the Greeks respecting fortification in the time of Epaminondas. It appears that Mantineia was not so large as Tegea, to which last Curtius assigns a circumference of more than three miles (p. 253).

rigour of training—was the chief mental result imbibed by every pupil of Lykurgus, and hitherto ratified as legitimate by the general testimony of Greece. This was his principal recompense for the severe fatigue, the intense self-suppression, the narrow, monotonous, and unlettered routine, wherein he was born and died. As an individual, the Spartan citizen was pointed out by the finger of admiration at the Olympic and other festivals;[1] while he saw his city supplicated from the most distant regions of Greece, and obeyed almost everywhere near her own border, as Panhellenic president. On a sudden, with scarce any preparatory series of events, he now felt this proud prerogative sentiment not only robbed of its former tribute, but stung in the most mortifying manner. Agesilaus, especially, was the more open to such humiliation, since he was not only a Spartan to the core, but loaded with the consciousness of having exercised more influence than any king before him—of having succeeded to the throne at a moment when Sparta was at the maximum of her power—and of having now in his old age accompanied her, in part brought her by his misjudgements, into her present degradation.

Agesilaus had moreover incurred unpopularity among the Spartans themselves, whose chagrin took the form of religious scruple and uneasiness. It has been already stated that he was, and had been from childhood, lame; which deformity had been vehemently insisted on by his opponents (during the dispute between him and Leotychidês in 398 B.C. for the vacant throne) as disqualifying him for the regal dignity, and as being the precise calamity against which an ancient oracle —"Beware of a lame reign"—had given warning. Ingenious interpretation by Lysander, combined with superior personal merit in Agesilaus and suspicions about the legitimacy of Leotychidês, had caused the objection to be then overruled. But there had always been a party, even during the palmy days of Agesilaus, who thought that he had obtained the crown under no good auspices. And when the humiliation of Sparta arrived, every man's religion suggested to him readily the cause of it —"See what comes of having set at nought the gracious warning of the gods, and put upon ourselves a lame reign!" In spite of such untoward impression, however, the real energy and bravery

*Feeling against Agesilaus at Sparta.*

[1] Isokr. Or. vi. (Archidamus) s. 111. [2] Plutarch, Agesil. c. 30, 31, 34.

of Agesilaus, which had not deserted even an infirm body and an age of seventy years, was more than ever indispensable to his country. He was still the chief leader of her affairs, condemned to the sad necessity of submitting to this Mantineian affront, and much worse that followed it, without the least power of hindrance.

B.C. 370. Impulse among the Arcadians towards Pan-Arcadian union. Opposition from Orchomenus and Tegea.

The re-establishment of Mantineia was probably completed during the autumn and winter of B.C. 371-370. Such coalescence of villages into a town, coupled with the predominance of feelings hostile to Sparta, appears to have suggested the idea of a larger political union among all who bore the Arcadian name. As yet, no such union had ever existed; the fractions of the Arcadian name had nothing in common, apart from other Greeks, except many legendary and religious sympathies, with a belief in the same heroic lineage and indigenous antiquity.[1] But now the idea and aspiration, espoused with peculiar ardour by a leading Mantineian named Lykomedês, spread itself rapidly over the country, to form a "commune Arcadum," or central Arcadian authority, composed in certain proportions out of all the sections now autonomous—and invested with peremptory power of determining by the vote of its majority. Such central power, however, was not intended to absorb or set aside the separate governments, but only to be exercised for certain definite purposes; in maintaining unanimity at home, together with concurrent, independent, action as to foreign states.[2] This plan of a

[1] It seems however doubtful whether there were not some common Arcadian coins struck, even before the battle of Leuktra. Some such are extant; but they are referred by K. O. Müller, as well as by M. Boeckh (Metrologisch. Untersuchungen, p. 92) to a later date subsequent to the foundation of Megalopolis.
On the other hand, Ernst Curtius (Beyträge zur Aeltern Münzkunde, p. 85-90, Berlin, 1851) contends that there is a great difference in the style and execution of these coins, and that several in all probability belong to a date earlier than the battle of Leuktra. He supposes that these older coins were struck in connexion with the Pan-Arcadian sanctuary and temple of Zeus Lykæus, and probably out of a common treasury at the temple of that god for religious purposes; perhaps also in connexion with the temple of Artemis Hymnia (Pausan. viii. 5, 11) between Mantineia and Orchomenus.

[2] Xen. Hellen. vi. 5, 6. συνήγον ἐπὶ τὸ συνιέναι πᾶν τὸ Ἀρκαδικὸν, καὶ ὅ,τι νικῴη ἐν τῷ κοινῷ, τοῦτο κύριον εἶναι καὶ τῶν πόλεων, &c.
Compare Diodor. xv. 59-62.

Pan-Arcadian federation was warmly promoted by the Mantineians, who looked to it as a protection to themselves in case the Spartan power should revive; as well as by the Thebans and Argeians, from whom aid was expected in case of need. It found great favour in most parts of Arcadia, especially in the small districts bordering on Laconia, which stood most in need of union to protect themselves against the Spartans—the Mænalians, Parrhasians, Eutresians, Ægytês,[1] &c. But the jealousies among the more considerable cities made some of them adverse to any scheme emanating from Mantineia. Among these unfriendly opponents were Heræa, on the west of Arcadia bordering on Elis—Orchomenus,[2] conterminous with Mantineia to the north—and Tegea, conterminous to the south. The hold of the Spartans on Arcadia had been always maintained chiefly through Orchomenus and Tegea. The former was the place where they deposited their hostages taken from other suspected towns; the latter was ruled by Stasippus and an oligarchy devoted to their interests.[3]

Among the population of Tegea, however, a large proportion were ardent partisans of the new Pan-Arcadian movement, and desirous of breaking off their connection with Sparta. At the head of this party were Proxenus and Kallibius; while Stasippus and his friends, supported by a senate composed chiefly of their partisans, vehemently opposed any alteration of the existing system. Proxenus and his partisans resolved to appeal to the assembled people, whom accordingly they convoked in arms; pacific popular assemblies, with free discussion, forming seemingly no part of the constitution of the city. Stasippus and his friends appeared in armed numbers also; and a conflict ensued, in which each party charged the other with bad faith and with striking the first blow.[4] At first Stasippus had the

*Revolution at Tegea—the philo-Spartan party are put down or expelled. Tegea becomes anti-Spartan, and favourable to the Pan-Arcadian union.*

---

[1] See Pausanias, viii. 27, 2, 3.
[2] Xen. Hellen. vi. 5, 11.
[3] For the relations of these Arcadian cities, with Sparta and with each other, see Thucyd. iv. 134; v. 61, 64, 77.
[4] Xenophon in his account represents Stasippus and his friends as being quite in the right, and as having behaved not only with justice but with clemency. But we learn from an indirect admission, in another place, that there was also another story, totally different, which represented Stasippus as having begun unjust

advantage. Proxenus with a few of the opposite party were slain, while Kallibius with the remainder maintained himself near the town-wall, and in possession of the gate, on the side towards Mantineia. To that city he had before despatched an express, entreating aid, while he opened a parley with the opponents. Presently the Mantineian force arrived, and was admitted within the gates; upon which Stasippus, seeing that he could no longer maintain himself, escaped by another gate towards Pallantium. He took sanctuary with a few friends in a neighbouring temple of Artemis, whither he was pursued by his adversaries, who removed the roof, and began to cast the tiles down upon them. The unfortunate men were obliged to surrender. Fettered and placed on a cart, they were carried back to Tegea, and put on their trial before the united Tegeans and Mantincians, who condemned them and put them to death. Eight hundred Tegeans, of the defeated party, fled as exiles to Sparta.[1]

B.C. 370. Pan-Arcadian union is formed.
Such was the important revolution which now took place at Tegea; a struggle of force on both sides and not of discussion—as was in the nature of the Greek oligarchical governments, where scarce any serious change of policy in the state could be brought about without violence. It decided the success of the Pan-Arcadian movement, which now proceeded with redoubled enthusiasm. Both Mantineia and Tegea were cordially united in its favour; though Orchomenus, still strenuous in opposing it, hired for that purpose, as well as for her own defence, a body of mercenaries from Corinth under Polytropus. A full assembly of the Arcadian name was convoked at a small town called Asea, in the mountainous district west of Tegea. It appears to have been numerously attended; for we hear of one place, Eutæa (in the district of Mount Mænalus,[2] and near the borders of Laconia), from whence every single male adult went to the assembly. It was here that the consummation of the Pan-Arcadian confederacy was finally determined; though Orchomenus and Heræa still stood aloof.[3]

violence. Compare Hellenic. vi. 5, 7, 8 with vi. 5, 36.
The manifest partiality of Xenophon, in these latter books, greatly diminishes the value of his own belief on such a matter.
[1] Xen. Hellen. vi. 5, 8, 9, 10.
[2] Pausanias, viii. 27, 3.
[3] Xen. Hellen. vi. 5, 11, 12.

There could hardly be a more fatal blow to Sparta than this loss to herself, and transfer to her enemies, of Tegea, the most powerful of her remaining allies.[1] To assist the exiles and avenge Stasippus, as well as to arrest the Arcadian movement, she resolved on a march into the country, in spite of her present dispirited condition; while Heræa and Lepreum, but no other places, sent contingents to her aid. From Elis and Argos, on the other hand, reinforcements came to Mantineia and Tegea. Proclaiming that the Mantineians had violated the recent peace by their entry into Tegea, Agesilaus marched across the border against them. The first Arcadian town which he reached was Eutæa,[2] where he found that all the male adults had gone to the great Arcadian assembly. Though the feebler population, remaining behind, were completely in his power, he took scrupulous care to respect both person and property, and even lent aid to rebuild a decayed portion of the wall. At Eutæa he halted a day or two, thinking it prudent to wait for the junction of the mercenary force and the Bœotian exiles under Polytropus, now at Orchomenus. Against the latter place, however, the Mantineians had marched under Lykomedês, while Polytropus, coming forth from the walls to meet them, had been defeated with loss and slain.[3] Hence Agesilaus was compelled to advance onward

*Marginalia:* B.C. 370. March of Agesilaus against Mantineia. Evidence of lowered sentiment in Sparta.

---

[1] Xen. Hellen. vii. 2, 2. See the prodigious anxiety manifested by the Lacedæmonians respecting the sure adhesion of Tegea (Thucyd. v. 64).

[2] I cannot but think that Eutæa stands marked upon the maps of Kiepert at a point too far from the frontier of Laconia, and so situated in reference to Asea, that Agesilaus must have passed very near Asea in order to get to it; which is difficult to suppose, seeing that the Arcadian convocation was assembled at Asea. Xenophon calls Eutæa πόλιν ὅμορον with reference to Laconia (Hellen. vi. 5, 12); this will hardly suit with the position marked by Kiepert.

The district called Mænalia must have reached further southward than Kiepert indicates on his map. It included Oresteion, which was on the straight road from Sparta to Tegea (Thucyd. v. 64; Herodot. ix. 11). Kiepert has placed Oresteion in his map agreeably to what seems the meaning of Pausanias, viii. 44, 3. But it rather appears that the place mentioned by Pausanias must have been *Oresthasion*, and that *Oresteion* must have been a different place, though Pausanias considers them the same. See the geographical Appendix to K. O. Müller's Dorians, vol. ii. p. 449—Germ. edit.

[3] Xen. Hellen. vi. 5, 13, 14; Diodor. xv. 62.

with his own unassisted forces, through the territory of
Tegea up to the neighbourhood of Mantineia. His onward
march left the way from Asea to Tegea free, upon which the
Arcadians assembled at Asea broke up, and marched by
night to Tegea; from whence on the next day they proceeded
to Mantineia, along the mountain range eastward of the
Tegeatic plain; so that the whole Arcadian force thus
became united.

Agesilaus on his side, having ravaged the fields and
encamped within little more than two miles from the walls
of Mantineia, was agreeably surprised by the junction of
his allies from Orchomenus, who had eluded by a night-
march the vigilance of the enemy. Both on one side and
on the other, the forces were thus concentrated. Agesilaus
found himself on the first night, without intending it,
embosomed in a recess of the mountains near Mantineia,
where the Mantineians gathered on the high ground around,
in order to attack him from above the next morning. By
a well-managed retreat, he extricated himself from this inconvenient position, and regained the plain; where he
remained three days, prepared to give battle if the enemy
came forth, in order that he might "not seem (says Xenophon) to hasten his departure through fear."[1] As the
enemy kept within their walls, he marched homeward on
the fourth day to his former camp in the Tegean territory.
The enemy did not pursue, and he then pushed on his
march, though it was late in the evening, to Eutæa; "wishing (says Xenophon) to get his troops off before even the
enemies' fires could be seen, in order that no one might
say that his return was a flight. He thought that he had
raised the spirit of Sparta out of the previous discouragement, by invading Arcadia and ravaging the country
without any enemy coming forth to fight him."[2] The army
was then brought back to Sparta and disbanded.

---

[1] Xen. Hellen. vi. 5, 20. ὅπως
μὴ δοκοίη φοβούμενος σπεύδειν τὴν
ἔφοδον.
See Leake's Travels in the Morea,
vol. iii. c. xxiv. p. 74, 75. The
exact spot designated by the words
τὸν ἄκισθεν λόφον τῆς Μαντινικῆς,
seems hardly to be identified.

[2] Xen. Hellen. vi. 5, 21. βουλόμενος ἀπαγαγεῖν τοὺς ὁπλίτας, πρὶν
καὶ τὰ πυρὰ τῶν πολεμίων ἰδεῖν, ἵνα
μή τις εἴπῃ, ὡς φεύγων ἀπαγάγοι.
Ἐκ γὰρ τῆς πρόσθεν ἀθυμίας ἐδόκει
τι ἀνειληφέναι τὴν πόλιν, ὅτι καὶ
ἐμβεβλήκει εἰς τὴν Ἀρκαδίαν, καὶ
δῃοῦντι τὴν χώραν οὐδεὶς ἠθελήκει
μάχεσθαι: compare Plutarch, Agesil.
c. 30.

It had now become a matter of boast for Agesilaus (according to his own friendly historian) to keep the field for three or four days, without showing fear of Arcadians and Eleians! So fatally had Spartan pride broken down, since the day (less than eighteen months before) when the peremptory order had been sent to Kleombrotus, to march out of Phokis straight against Thebes!

Nevertheless it was not from fear of Agesilaus, but from a wise discretion, that the Arcadians and Eleians had kept within the walls of Mantineia. Epaminondas with the Theban army was approaching to their aid, and daily expected; a sum of ten talents having been lent by the Eleians to defray the cost.[1] He had been invited by them and by others of the smaller Peloponnesian states, who felt the necessity of some external protector against Sparta—and who even before they applied to Thebes for aid, had solicited the like interference from Athens (probably under the general presidency accepted by Athens, and the oaths interchanged by her with various inferior cities, since the battle of Leuktra), but had experienced a refusal.[2]

*Application by the Arcadians to Athens for aid against Sparta; it is refused; they then apply to the Thebans.*

Epaminondas had been preparing for this contingency ever since the battle of Leuktra. The first use made of his victory had been, to establish or confirm the ascendency of Thebes both over the recusant Bœotian cities and over the neighbouring Phokians and Lokrians, &c. After this had been accomplished, he must have been occupied (during the early part of 370 B.C.) in anxiously watching the movements of Jason of Pheræ; who had already announced his design of marching with an imposing force to Delphi for the celebration of the Pythian games (about August 1). Though this despot was the ally of Thebes, yet as both his power, and his aspirations towards the headship of Greece,[3] were well known, no Theban general, even of prudence inferior to Epaminondas, could venture in the face of such liabilities to conduct away the Theban force into Peloponnesus, leaving Bœotia uncovered. The assassination of Jason relieved Thebes from such appre-

*Proceedings and views of Epaminondas since the battle of Leuktra.*

[1] Xen. Hellen. vi. 5, 19.   Megalopolit. pp. 203-207. s. 13-22.
[2] Diodor. xv. 62.   [3] Diodor. xv. 60.
Compare Demosthenês, Orat. pro

hensions, and a few weeks sufficed to show that his successors were far less formidable in power as well as in ability. Accordingly, in the autumn of 370 B.C., Epaminondas had his attention free to turn to Peloponnesus, for the purpose both of maintaining the anti-Spartan revolution which had taken place in Tegea, and of seconding the pronounced impulse among the Arcadians towards federative coalition.

Plans of Epaminondas for restoring the Messenians in Peloponnesus;

But the purposes of this distinguished man went farther still; embracing long-sighted and permanent arrangements, such as should for ever disable Sparta from recovering her prominent station in the Grecian world. While with one hand he organized Arcadia, with the other he took measures for replacing the exiled Messenians on their ancient territory. To achieve this, it was necessary to dispossess the Spartans of the region once known as independent Messenia, under its own line of kings, but now, for near three centuries, the best portion of Laconia, tilled by Helots for the profit of proprietors at Sparta. While converting these Helots into free Messenians, as their forefathers had once been, Epaminondas proposed to invite back all the wanderers of the same race who were dispersed in various portions of Greece; so as at once to impoverish Sparta by loss of territory, and to plant upon her flank a neighbour bitterly hostile. It has been already mentioned, that during the Peloponnesian war, the exiled Messenians had been among the most active allies of Athens against Sparta—at Naupaktus, at Sphakteria, at Pylus, in Kephallenia, and elsewhere. Expelled at the close of that war by the triumphant Spartans,[1] not only from Peloponnesus but also from Naupaktus and Kephallenia, these exiles had since been dispersed among various Hellenic colonies; at Rhegium in Italy, at Messênê in Sicily, at Hesperidès in Libya. From 404 B.C., (the close of the war) to 373 B.C., they had remained thus without a home. At length, about the latter year (when the Athenian confederate navy again became equal or superior to the Lacedæmonian on the west coast of Peloponnesus), they began to indulge the hope of being restored to Naupaktus.[2] Probably their request may have been preferred and discussed in the synod of Athenian allies, where the Thebans sat as members. Nothing however had been done towards it by the Athe-

[1] Diodor. xiv. 34.   [2] Pausanias, iv. 26, 2.

nians—who soon became fatigued with the war, and at length made peace with Sparta—when the momentous battle of Leuktra altered, both completely and suddenly, the balance of power in Greece. A chance of protection was now opened to the Messenians from Thebes, far more promising than they had ever had from Athens. Epaminondas, well-aware of the loss as well as humiliation that he should inflict upon Sparta by restoring them to their ancient territory, entered into communication with them, and caused them to be invited to Peloponnesus from all their distant places of emigration.[1] By the time of his march into Arcadia in the late autumn of 370 B.C., many of them had already joined him, burning with all their ancient hatred of Sparta, and contributing to aggravate the same sentiment among Thebans and allies.

With the scheme of restoring the Messenians, was combined in the mind of Epaminondas another for the political consolidation of the Arcadians; both being intended as parts of one strong and self-supporting organization against Sparta on her own border. Of course he could have accomplished nothing of the kind, if there had not been a powerful spontaneous movement towards consolidation among the Arcadians themselves. But without his guidance and protection, the movement would have proved abortive, through the force of local jealousies within the country, fomented and seconded by Spartan aid from without. Though the general vote for federative coalition had been passed with enthusiasm, yet to carry out such a vote to the satisfaction of all, without quarreling on points of detail, would have required far more of public-minded sentiment as well as of intelligence, than what could be reckoned upon among the Arcadians. It was necessary to establish a new city; since the standing jealousy between Mantineia and Tegea, now for the first time embarked in one common cause, would never have permitted that either should be preferred as the centre of the new consolidation.[2] Besides fixing upon the new site required, it was indis-

*also, for consolidating the Arcadians against Sparta.*

---

[1] Diodor. xv. 66; Pausanias, iv. 26, 5, 4.

[2] To illustrate small things by great—At the first formation of the Federal Constitution of the United States of America, the rival pretensions of New York and Philadelphia were among the principal motives for creating the new federal city of Washington.

pensable also to choose between conflicting exigences, and to break up ancient habits, in a way such as could hardly have been enforced by any majority purely Arcadian. The authority here deficient was precisely supplied by Epaminondas; who brought with him a victorious army and a splendid personal name, combined with impartiality as to the local politics of Arcadia, and single-minded hostility to Sparta.

It was with a view to found these two new cities, as well as to expel Agesilaus, that Epaminondas now marched the Theban army into Arcadia; the command being voluntarily entrusted to him by Pelopidas and the other Bœotarchs present. He arrived shortly after the retirement of Agesilaus, while the Arcadians and Eleians were ravaging the lands of the recusant town of Heræa. As they speedily came back to greet his arrival, the aggregate confederate body—Argeians, Arcadians, and Eleians, united with the Thebans and their accompanying allies—is said to have amounted to 40,000, or according to some, even to 70,000 men,[1] Not merely had Epaminondas brought with him a choice body of auxiliaries—Phokians, Lokrians, Eubœans, Akarnanians, Herakleots, Malians, and Thessalian cavalry and peltasts—but the Bœotian bands themselves were so brilliant and imposing, as to excite universal admiration. The victory of Leuktra had awakened among them an enthusiastic military ardour, turned to account by the genius of Epaminondas, and made to produce a finished discipline which even the unwilling Xenophon cannot refuse to acknowledge.[2] Conscious of the might of their assembled force, within a day's march of Laconia, the Arcadians, Argeians, and Eleians pressed Epaminondas to invade that country, now that no allies could approach the frontier to its aid. At first he was unwilling to comply. He had not come prepared for the

*B.C. 370. November.*

*Epaminondas and the Theban army arrive in Arcadia. Great allied force assembled there. The allies entreat him to invade Laconia.*

---

[1] Plutarch, Agesil. c. 31; and Compar. Agesil. and Pomp. c. 4; Diodor. xv. 62. Compare Xenophon, Agesilaus, II. 24.

[2] Xen. Hellen. vl. 5, 23. Οἱ δὲ Ἀρκάδες καὶ Ἀργεῖοι καὶ Ἠλεῖοι ἐπειθον αὐτοὺς ἡγεῖσθαι ὡς τάχιστα εἰς τὴν Λακωνικήν, ἐπιδεικνύντες μὲν τὸ ἑαυτῶν πλῆθος, ὑπερκαινούντες δὲ τὸ τῶν Θηβαίων στράτευμα. Καὶ γὰρ οἱ μὲν Βοιωτοὶ ἐγυμνάζοντο πάντες περὶ τὰ ὅπλα, ἀγαλλόμενοι τῇ ἐν Λεύκτροις νίκῃ, &c.

enterprise; being well-aware, from his own journey to Sparta (when the peace congress was held there prior to the battle of Leuktra), of the impracticable nature of the intervening country, so easy to be defended, especially during the winter-season, by troops, like the Lacedæmonians, whom he believed to be in occupation of all the passes. Nor was his reluctance overcome until the instances of his allies were backed by assurances from the Arcadians on the frontier, that the passes were not all guarded; as well as by invitations from some of the discontented Periœki in Laconia. These Periœki engaged to revolt openly, if he would only show himself in the country. They told him that there was a general slackness throughout Laconia in obeying the military requisitions from Sparta; and tendered their lives as atonement if they should be found to speak falsely. By such encouragements, as well as by the general impatience of all around him to revenge upon Sparta her long career of pride and abused ascendency, Epaminondas was at length induced to give the order of invasion.[1]

That he should have hesitated in taking this responsibility, will not surprise us, if we recollect, that over and above the real difficulties of the country, invasion of Laconia by land was an unparalleled phænomenon—that the force of Sparta was most imperfectly known—that no such thought had been entertained when he left Thebes—that the legal duration of command, for himself and his colleagues, would not permit it—and that though his Peloponnesian allies were forward in the scheme, the rest of his troops and his countrymen might well censure him, if the unknown force of resistance turned out as formidable as their associations from old time led them to apprehend.

*Reluctance of Epaminondas to invade Laconia—reasonable grounds for it.*

The invading army was distributed into four portions, all penetrating by different passes. The Eleians had the westernmost and easiest road, the Argeians the easternmost;[2] while the Thebans themselves and the Arcadians formed the two central divisions. The latter alone experienced any serious resistance. More daring even than the Thebans, they encountered Ischolaus the Spartan at Ium or Oeum in the

*He marches into Laconia—four lines of invasion.*

[1] Xen. Hellen. vi. 5, 24, 25.
[2] Diodor. xv. 64.

See Colonel Leake's Travels in the Morea, vol. iii. ch. 25. p. 29.

district called Skiritis, attacked him in the village, and overpowered him by vehemence of assault, by superior numbers, and seemingly also by some favour or collusion[1] on the part of the inhabitants. After a desperate resistance, this brave Spartan with nearly all his division perished. At Karyæ, the Thebans also found and surmounted some resistance; but the victory of the Arcadians over Ischolaus operated as an encouragement to all, so that the four divisions reached Sellasia[2] and were again united in safety. Undefended and deserted (seemingly) by the Spartans, Sellasia was now burnt and destroyed by the invaders; who, continuing their march along the plain or valley towards the Eurotas, encamped in the sacred grove of Apollo. On the next day they reached the Eurotas, at the foot of the bridge which crossed that river and led to the city of Sparta.

*He crosses the Eurotas and approaches close to Sparta.*

Epaminondas found the bridge too well-guarded to attempt forcing it; a strong body of Spartan hoplites being also discernible on the other side in the sacred ground of Athênê Alea. He therefore marched down the left bank of the river burning and plundering the houses in his way, as far as Amyklæ, between two and three miles below Sparta. Here he found a ford, though the river was full, from the winter season; and accomplished the passage, defeating, after a severe contest, a body of Spartans who tried to oppose it. He was now on the same side of the river as Sparta, to which city he slowly and cautiously made his approach; taking care to keep his Theban troops always in the best battle order, and protecting them, when encamped, by felled trees; while the Arcadians and other

---

[1] Xen. Hellen. vi. 5, 26. When we read that the Arcadians got on the roofs of the houses to attack Ischolaus, this fact seems to imply that they were admitted into the houses by the villagers.

[2] Respecting the site of Sellasia, Colonel Leake thinks, and advances various grounds for supposing, that Sellasia was on the road from Sparta to the north-east, towards the Thyreatis; and that Karyæ was on the road from Sparta northward, towards Tegea. The French investigators of the Morea, as well as Professor Ross and Kiepert, hold a different opinion, and place Sellasia on the road from Sparta northward towards Tegea (Leake, Peloponnesiaca, p. 342-352; Ross, Reisen im Peloponnes. p. 187; Berlin, 1841).

Upon such a point, the authority of Colonel Leake is very high; yet the opposite opinion respecting the site of Sellasia seems to me preferable.

Peloponesian allies dispersed around to plunder the neighbouring houses and property.[1] Great was the consternation which reigned in the city; destitute of fortifications, yet hitherto inviolate in fact and unassailable even in idea. Besides their own native force, the Spartans had no auxiliaries except those mercenaries from Orchomenus who had come back with Agesilaus; nor was it certain beforehand that even these troops would remain with them, if the invasion became formidable.[2] On the first assemblage of the irresistible army on their frontier, they had despatched one of their commanders of foreign contingents (called Xenâgi) to press the instant coming of such Peloponnesian allies as remained faithful to them; and also envoys to Athens, entreating assistance from that city. Auxiliaries were obtained, and rapidly put under march, from Pellênê, Sikyon, Phlius, Corinth, Epidaurus, Trœzen, Hermionê, and Halieis.[3] But the ordinary line of march into Laconia was now impracticable to them; the whole frontier being barred by Argeians and Arcadians. Accordingly they were obliged to proceed first to the Argolic peninsula, and from thence to cross by sea (embarking probably at Halieis on the south-western coast of the peninsula to Prasiæ on the eastern coast of Laconia); from whence they made their way over the Laconian mountains to Sparta. Being poorly provided with vessels, they were forced to cross in separate detachments, and to draw lots for priority.[4] By this chance the Phliasian contingent did not come over until the last; while the xenagus, eager to reach Sparta, left them behind, and conducted the rest thither, arriving only just before the confederate enemies debouched from Sellasia. The Phliasians, on crossing to Prasiæ, found neither their comrades nor the xenagus, but were obliged to hire a guide to Sparta. Fortunately they arrived there

*Alarm at Sparta— arrival of various allies to her aid by sea.*

---

[1] Xen. Hellen. vi. 5, 30; Diodor. xv. 65.

[2] This I apprehend to be the meaning of the phrase—ἐπεὶ μέντοι ἔμεινον μὲν οἱ ἐξ Ὀρχομενοῦ μισθοφόροι, &c.

[3] Xen. Hellen. vi. 5, 29; vii. 2, 2.

[4] Xen. Hellen. vii. 2, 2. Καὶ διαβαίνειν τελευταῖοι λαχόντες (the Phliasians) εἰς Πρασιὰς τῶν συμβοηθησάντων . . . . . . οὐ γὰρ παρῆσαν ἀφίστασαν, ἀλλ' οὐδ', ἐπεὶ ὁ ξεναγὸς τοὺς προϊσταμένους λαβὼν ἀκολυθεῖν αὐτοῖς ᾤχετο, οὐδ' ὡς ἀπεστρέφησαν, ἀλλ' ἡγεμόνα μισθωσάμενοι ἐκ Πρασιῶν, ὄντων τῶν πολεμίων περὶ Ἀμύκλας, ὅπως ἐδύναντο διαδύντες εἰς Σπάρτην ἀφίκοντο.

both safely and in time, eluding the vigilance of the enemy, who were then near Amyklæ.

**Discontent in Laconia among the Periœki and Helots— danger to Sparta from that cause.**

These reinforcements were no less seasonable to Sparta, than creditable to the fidelity of the allies. For the bad feeling which habitually reigned in Laconia, between the Spartan citizens on one side, and the Periœki and Helots on the other, produced in this hour of danger its natural fruits of desertion, alarm, and weakness. Not only were the Periœki and Helots in standing discontent, but even among the Spartan citizens themselves, a privileged fraction (called Peers) had come to monopolise political honours; while the remainder—poorer men, yet ambitious and active, and known under the ordinary name of the Inferiors—were subject to a degrading exclusion, and rendered bitterly hostile. The account (given in a previous chapter) of the conspiracy of Kinadon, will have disclosed the fearful insecurity of the Spartan citizen, surrounded by so many disaffected companions; Periœki and Helots in Laconia, inferior citizens at Sparta. On the appearance of the invading enemy, indeed, a certain feeling of common interest arose, since even the disaffected might reasonably imagine that a plundering soldiery, if not repelled at the point of the sword, would make their condition worse instead of better. And accordingly, when the Ephors made public proclamation, that any Helot who would take heavy armour and serve in the ranks as an hoplite, should be manumitted —not less than 6000 Helots gave in their names to serve. But a body thus numerous, when seen in arms, became itself the object of mistrust to the Spartans; so that the arrival of their new allies from Prasiæ was welcomed as a security, not less against the armed Helots within the city, than against the Thebans without.[1] Open enmity however was not wanting. A considerable number both of Periœki and Helots actually took arms on behalf of the Thebans; others remained inactive, disregarding the urgent summons from the Ephors, which could not now be enforced[2].

---

[1] Xen. Hellen. vi. 5, 28, 29. ὥστε φόβον οὐ αὐτοὶ παρεῖχον συντεταγμένοι, καὶ λίαν ἐδόκουν πολλοὶ εἶναι, &c.

[2] Xen. Hellen. vi. 5, 25; vi. 5, 32; vii. 2, 2.

It is evident from the last of these three passages, that the number of Periœki and Helots who actually revolted was very considerable: and the contrast between the second and third passages evinces the different feelings with

Under such wide-spread feelings of disaffection, the defence even of Sparta itself against the assailing enemy was a task requiring all the energy of Agesilaus. After having vainly tried to hinder the Thebans from crossing the Eurotas, he was forced to abandon Amyklæ and to throw himself back upon the city of Sparta, towards which they immediately advanced. More than one conspiracy was on the point of breaking out, had not his vigilance forestalled the projects. Two hundred young soldiers of doubtful fidelity were marching without orders to occupy a strong post (sacred to Artemis) called the Issorium. Those around him were about to attack them, but Agesilaus, repressing their zeal, went up alone to the band, addressed them in language betokening no suspicion, yet warning them that they had mistaken his orders; their services were needed, not at the Issorium, but in another part of the city. They obeyed his orders, and moved to the spot indicated; upon which he immediately occupied the Issorium with troops whom he could trust. In the ensuing night, he seized and put to death fifteen of the leaders of the two hundred. Another conspiracy, said to have been on the point of breaking out, was repressed by seizing the conspirators in the house where they were assembled, and putting them to death untried; the first occasion (observes Plutarch) on

*Vigilant defence of Sparta by Agesilaus.*

which the two seem to have been composed by Xenophon. In the second, he is recounting the invasion of Epaminondas, with a wish to soften the magnitude of the Spartan disgrace and calamity as much as he can. Accordingly, he tells us no more than this— "there were some among the Periœki, who even took active service in the attack of Oythium, and fought along with the Thebans"— ἦσαν δέ τινες τῶν Περιοίκων, οἳ καὶ ἐπέθεντο καὶ συνεστρατεύοντο τοῖς μετὰ Θηβαίων. But in the third passage (vii. 2, 2: compare his biography called Agesilaus, ii. 24) Xenophon is extolling the fidelity of the Phliasians to Sparta, under adverse circumstances of the latter. Hence

it then suits his argument, to magnify these adverse circumstances, in order to enhance the merit of the Phliasians; and he therefore tells us—"Many of the Periœki, all the Helots, and all the allies except a few, had revolted from Sparta"—σφαλέντων δ᾽ αὐτῶν τῇ ἐν Λεύκτροις μάχῃ, καὶ ἀποστάντων μὲν πολλῶν Περιοίκων, ἀποστάντων δὲ πάντων τῶν Εἱλώτων, ἔτι δὲ τῶν συμμάχων πλὴν πάνυ ὀλίγων, ἐπιστρατευσάντων δ᾽ αὐτοῖς, ὡς εἰπεῖν πάντων τῶν Ἑλλήνων, πιστοὶ διέμειναν (the Phliasians). I apprehend that both statements depart from the reality, though in opposite directions. I have adopted in the text something between the two.

which any Spartan was ever put to death untried¹—a statement which I hesitate to believe without knowing from whom he borrowed it, but which, if true, proves that the Spartan kings and Ephors did not apply to Spartan citizens the same measure as to Periœki and Helots.

*Violent emotion of the Spartans, especially the women. Partial attack upon Sparta by Epaminondas.*

By such severe proceedings, disaffection was kept under; while the strong posts of the city were effectively occupied, and the wider approaches barricaded by heaps of stones and earth.² Though destitute of walls, Sparta was extremely defensible by position. Epaminondas marched slowly up to it from Amyklæ; the Arcadians and others in his army spreading themselves to burn and plunder the neighbourhood. On the third or fourth day his cavalry occupied the Hippodrome (probably a space of level ground near the river, under the hilly site of the town), where the Spartan cavalry, though inferior both in number and in goodness, gained an advantage over them, through the help of 300 chosen hoplites whom Agesilaus had planted in ambush hard by, in a precinct sacred to the Dioskuri. Though this action was probably of little consequence, yet Epaminondas did not dare to attempt the city by storm. Satisfied with having defied the Spartans and manifested his mastery of the field even to their own doors, he marched away southward down the Eurotas. To them, in their present depression, it was matter of consolation and even of boasting,³ that he had not dared to assail them in their last stronghold. The agony of their feelings —grief, resentment, and wounded honour—was intolerable. Many wished to go out and fight, at all hazard; but Agesilaus resisted them with the same firmness as Periklês had shown at Athens, when the Peloponnesians first invaded Attica at the beginning of the Peloponnesian war. Especially the Spartan women, who had never before beheld

---

¹ Plutarch, Agesil. c. 32; Polyænus, II. 1, 14; Ælian, V. H. xiv. 27.
² Æneas Poliorceticus, c. 2. p. 16.
³ Xen. Hellen. vi. 5, 32. Καὶ τὸ μὲν μὴ πρὸς τὴν πόλιν προσβαλεῖν ἐν ἔτι αὐτοὺς, ἤδη τι ἐδόκει ὑπέρλευκότερον εἶναι.

This passage is not very clear, nor are the commentators unanimous either as to the words or as to the meaning. Some omit μὴ, construe ἐδόκει as if it were ἐδόκει ταῖς Θηβαίοις, and translate ὑπέρλευκότερον "excessively rash."

I agree with Schneider in dissenting from this alteration and construction. I have given in the text what I believe to be the meaning.

an enemy, are said to have manifested emotions so furious and distressing, as to increase much the difficulty of defence. We are even told that Antalkidas, at that time one of the Ephors, sent his children for safety away from Sparta to the island of Kythêra. Epaminondas knew well how desperate the resistance of the Spartans would be if their city were attacked; while to himself, in the midst of a hostile and impracticable country, repulse would be absolute ruin.

On leaving Sparta, Epaminondas carried his march as far as Helos and Gythium on the sea-coast; burning and plundering the country, and trying for three days to capture Gythium, which contained the Lacedæmonian arsenal and ships. Many of the Laconian Periœki joined and took service in his army; nevertheless his attempt on Gythium did not succeed; upon which he turned back, and retraced his steps to the Arcadian frontier. It was the more necessary for him to think of quitting Laconia, since his Peloponnesian allies, the Arcadians and others, were daily stealing home with the rich

*He retires without attempting to storm Sparta: ravages Laconia down to Gythium, Its returns into Arcadia.*

---

[1] Xen. Hellen. vi. 6, 26; Aristotel. Politic. ii. 8, 8; Plutarch, Ageil. c. 32, 33; Plutarch, Comp. Agesil. and Pomp. c. 4.

[2] Aristotle (in his Politics, iv. 10, 8), discussing the opinion of those political philosophers who maintained that a city ought to have no walls, but to be defended only by the bravery of its inhabitants—gives various reasons against such opinion, and adds, "that these are old-fashioned thinkers; that the cities which made such ostentatious display of personal courage have been proved to be wrong by actual results"—λίην ἀρχαῖ ὡς ὑπολαμβάνουσι, καὶ ταῦθ᾽ ὁρῶντες ἐλεγχομένας ἔργῳ τὰς ἐκείνως κεκλωκισμένας. The commentators say (see the note of M. Barth. St. Hilaire) that Aristotle has in his view Sparta at the moment of this Theban invasion. I do not see what else he can mean; yet at the same time, if such be his meaning, the remark is difficult to admit. Epaminondas came close up to Sparta, but did not dare to attempt to carry it by assault. If the city had had walls like those of Babylon, they could not have procured for her any greater protection. To me the fact appears rather to show (contrary to the assertion of Aristotle) that Sparta was so strong by position, combined with the military character of her citizens, that she could dispense with walls.

Polyænus (ii. 2, 5) has an anecdote, I know not from whom borrowed, to the effect that Epaminondas might have taken Sparta, but designedly refrained from doing so, on the ground that the Arcadians and others would then no longer stand in need of Thebes. Neither the alleged matter of fact, nor the reason, appear to me worthy of any credit. Ælian (V. H. iv. 8) has the same story, but with a different reason assigned.

plunder which they had acquired, while his supplies were also becoming deficient.¹

Great effect of this invasion upon Grecian opinion— Epaminondas is exalted, and Sparta farther lowered.

Epaminondas had thus accomplished far more than he had projected when quitting Thebes; for the effect of the expedition on Grecian opinion was immense. The reputation of his army, as well as his own, was prodigiously exalted; and even the narrative of Xenophon, unfriendly as well as obscure, bears involuntary testimony both to the excellence of his generalship and to the good discipline of his troops. He made his Thebans keep in rank and hold front against the enemy, even while their Arcadian allies were dispersing around for plunder. Moreover, the insult and humiliation to Sparta was still greater than that inflicted by the battle of Leuktra; which had indeed shown that she was no longer invincible in the field, but had still left her with the admitted supposition of an inviolable territory and an unapproachable city.

The resistance of the Spartans indeed (except in so far as regards their city) had been far less than either friends or enemies expected; the belief in their power was thus proportionally abridged. It now remained for Epaminondas to complete their humiliation by executing those two enterprises which had formed the special purpose of his expedition; the re-establishment of Messênê, and the consolidation of the Arcadians.

Foundation of the Arcadian Megalopolis.

The recent invasion of Laconia, victorious as well as lucrative, had inspired the Arcadians with increased confidence and antipathy against Sparta, and increased disposition to listen to Epaminondas. When that eminent man proclaimed the necessity of establishing a strong frontier against Sparta on the side of Arcadia, and when he announced his intention of farther weakening Sparta by the restoration of the exiled Messenians—the general feeling of the small Arcadian communities, already tending in the direction of coalescence, became strong enough to overbear all such impediments of detail as the breaking up of ancient abode and habit involves. Respecting early Athenian history, we are told by Thucydidês,² that the legendary Theseus,

¹ Xen. Hellen. vi. 5, 50; Diodor. xv. 67. ἐβασίλευσα, γενόμενος μετὰ τοῦ ξυνετοῦ καὶ δυνατὸς, &c.
² Thucyd. ii. 15. Ἐπειδὴ δὲ Θησεὺς

"having become powerful, in addition to his great capacity," had effected the discontinuance of those numerous independent governments which once divided Attica, and had consolidated them all into one common government at Athens. Just such was the revolution now operated by Epaminondas, through the like combination of intelligence and power. A Board of Œkists or Founders was named to carry out the resolution taken by the Arcadian assemblies at Asea and Tegea, for the establishment of a Pan-Arcadian city and centre. Of this Board, two were from Tegea, two from Mantineia, two from Kleitor, two from the district of Mænalus, two from that of the Parrhasiana. A convenient site being chosen upon the river Helisson (which flowed through and divided the town in two), about twenty miles west of Tegea, well-fitted to block up the marches of Sparta in a north-westerly direction—the foundation of the new Great City (Megalopolis) was laid by the Œkists jointly with Epaminondas. Forty distinct Arcadian townships,[1] from all sides of this centre, were persuaded to join the new community. Ten were from the Mænalii, eight from the Parrhaaii, six from the Eutresii; three great sections of the Arcadian name, each an aggregate of villages. Four little townships, occupying a portion of the area intended for the new territory, yet being averse to the scheme, were constrained to join; but in one of them, Trapezus, the aversion was so strong, that most of the inhabitants preferred to emigrate and went to join the Trapezuntines in the Euxine Sea (Trebizond), who received them kindly. Some of the leading Trapezuntines were even slain by the violent temper of the Arcadian majority. The walls of the new city enclosed an area fifty stadia in circumference (more than five miles and a half); while an ample rural territory was also gathered round it, extending northward as much as twenty-four miles from the city, and conterminous on the east with Tegea, Mantineia, Orchomenus, and Kaphyæ—on the west with Messênê,[2] Phigalia, and Heræa.

---

[1] Diodor. xv. 72.
[2] Pausan. viii. 27; viii. 25, 5; Diodor. xv. 63.
See Mr. Fynes Clinton, Fasti Hellenici, Appendix, p. 416, where the facts respecting Megalopolis are brought together and discussed.
It is remarkable that though Xenophon (Hellen. v. 2, 7) observes that the capture of Mantineia by Agesipolis had made the Mantineians see the folly of having a river

The other new city—Messênê—was founded under the joint auspices of the Thebans and their allies, Argeians and others; Epitelês being especially chosen by the Argeians for that purpose.[1] The Messenian exiles, though eager and joyful at the thought of regaining their name and nationality, were averse to fix their new city either at Œchalia or Andania, which had been the scenes of their calamities in the early wars with Sparta. Moreover the site of Mount Ithômê is said to have been pointed out by the hero Kaukon, in a dream, to the Argeian general Epitelês. The local circumstances of this mountain (on which the last gallant resistance of the revolted Messenians against Sparta had been carried on, between the Persian and Peloponnesian wars) were such, that the indications of dreams, prophets, and religious signs, coincided fully with the deliberate choice of a judge like Epaminondas. In after-days, this hill, Ithômê (then bearing the town and citadel of Messênê), together with the Akrocorinthus, were marked out by Demetrius of Pharus as the two horns of Peloponnesus; whoever held these two horns, was master of the bull.[2] Ithômê was near 2500 feet above the level of the sea, having upon its summit an abundant spring of water, called Klepsydra. Upon this summit the citadel or acropolis of the new town of Messênê was built; while the town itself was situated lower down on the slope, though connected by a continuous wall with its acropolis. First, solemn sacrifices were offered, by Epaminondas, who was recognised as Œkist or Founder,[3] to Dionysus and Apollo Ismenius—by the Argeians, to the Argeian Hêrê and Zeus Nemeius—by the Messenians, to Zeus Ithomatês and the Dioskuri. Next, prayer was made to the ancient Heroes and Heroines of the Messenian nation, especially to the invincible warrior Aristomenês, that they would now come back and again take up their residence as inmates in enfranchised Messênê. After this, the ground was marked out and the building was begun, under the sound of Argeian and Bœotian flutes, playing the strains of Pronomus and Sakadas. The

Foundation of Messênê.

run through their town—yet in choosing the site of Megalopolis, this same feature was deliberately reproduced: and in this choice the Mantineians were parties concerned.

[1] Pausan. iv. 26, 6.
[2] Strabo, viii. p. 361; Polybius, vii. 11.
[3] Pausan. ix. 14, 2: compare the inscription on the statue of Epaminondas (ix. 15, 4).

best masons and architects were invited from all Greece, to lay out the streets with regularity, as well as to ensure a proper distribution and construction of the sacred edifices.[1] In respect of the fortifications, too, Epaminondas was studiously provident. Such was their excellence and solidity, that they exhibited matter for admiration even in the after-days of the traveller Pausanias.[2]

From their newly-established city on the hill of Ithômê, the Messenians enjoyed a territory extending fifteen miles southward down to the Messenian Gulf, across a plain, then as well as now, the richest and most fertile in Peloponnesus; while to the eastward, their territory was conterminous with that of Arcadia and the contemporary establishment of Megalopolis. All the newly appropriated space was land cut off from the Spartan dominion. How much was cut off in the direction south-east of Ithômê (along the north-eastern coast of the Messenian Gulf), we cannot exactly say. But it would appear that the Periœki of Thuria, situated in that neighbourhood, were converted into an independent community, and protected by the vicinity of Messênê.[3] What is of more importance to notice, however, is—that all the extensive district westward and south-westward of Ithômê—all the south-western corner of Peloponnesus, from the river Neda southward to Cape Akritas —was now also subtracted from Sparta. At the beginning of the Peloponnesian war, the Spartan Brasidas had been in garrison near Methônê[4] (not far from Cape Akritas); Pylus—where the Athenian Demosthenês erected his hostile fort, near which the important capture at Sphakteria was effected—had been a maritime point belonging to Sparta, about forty-six miles from the city;[5] Aulon (rather farther north, near the river Neda) had been at the time of the conspiracy of Kinadon a township of Spartan Periœki, of very 'doubtful fidelity.[6] Now all this wide area, from the north-eastern corner of the Messenian Gulf westward, the best half of the Spartan territory, was severed from Sparta to become the property of Periœki and Helots, converted into freemen; not only sending no rent or tribute to Sparta, as before, but bitterly hostile to

Abstraction of Western Laconia from Sparta.

[1] Pausan. iv. 27, 3.
[2] Pausan. iv. 31, 6.
[3] Pausan. iv. 31, 2.
[4] Thucyd. ii. 25.
[5] Thucyd. iv. 3.
[6] Xen. Hellen. iii. 3, 8.

her from the very nature of their tenure. It was in the ensuing year that the Arcadian army cut to pieces the Lacedæmonian garrison at Asinê,[1] killing the Spartan polemarch Geranor; and probably about the same time the other Lacedæmonian garrisons in the south-western peninsula must have been expelled. Thus liberated, the Periœki of the region welcomed the new Messênê as the guarantee of their independence. Epaminondas, besides confirming the independence of Methônê and Asinê, reconstituted some other towns,[2] which under Lacedæmonian dominion had probably been kept unfortified and had dwindled away.

In the spring of 425 B.C., when Demosthenês landed at Pylus, Thucydidês considers it a valuable acquisition for Athens, and a serious injury to Sparta, to have lodged a small garrison of Messenians in that insignificant post, as plunderers of Spartan territory and instigators of Helots to desertion[3]—especially as their dialect could not be distinguished from that of the Spartans themselves. How

*Great diminution thereby of her power, wealth, and estimation.*

---

[1] Xen. Hellen. vii. 1, 25.
[2] Pausan. iv. 27, 4. ἀνῴκιζον δὲ καὶ ἄλλα πολίσματα, &c. Pausanias, following the line of coast from the mouth of the river Pamisus in the Messenian Gulf, round Cape Akritas to the mouth of the Neda in the Western Sea—enumerates the following towns and places—Korone, Kolonides, Asinê, the Cape Akritas, the Harbour Phœnikus, Methônê or Mothônê, Pylus, Aulon (Pausan. iv. 34, 35, 36). The account given by Skylax (Periplus, c. 46, 47) of the coast of these regions, appears to me confused and unintelligible. He reckons Asinê and Mothônê as cities of Laconia; but he seems to have conceived these cities as being in the *central southern* projection of Peloponnesus (whereof Cape Tænarus forms the extremity); and not to have conceived at all the *south-western* projection, whereof Cape Akritas forms the extremity. He recognises Messênê, but he pursues the Parapius of the Messenian coast from the mouth of the river Neda to the coast of the Messenian Gulf south of Ithômê without interruption. Then, after that, he mentions Asinê, Mothônê, Achilleios Limên, and Psamathus, with Cape Tænarus between them. Besides, he introduces in Messenia two different cities—one called Messênê, the other called Ithômê; whereas there was only one Messênê situated on Mount Ithômê.

I cannot agree with Niebuhr, who resting mainly upon this account of Skylax, considers that the south-western corner of Peloponnesus remained a portion of Laconia and belonging to Sparta, long after the establishment of the city of Messênê. See the Dissertation of Niebuhr on the age of Skylax of Karyanda—in his Kleine Schriften, p. 110.

[3] Thucyd. iv. 3, 12.

prodigious must have been the impression throughout Greece, when Epaminondas, by planting the Messenian exiles and others on the strong frontier city and position of Ithômê, deprived Sparta in a short time of all the wide space between that mountain and the western sea, enfranchising the Periœki and Helots contained in it! We must recollect that the name Messênê had been from old times applied generally to this region, and that it was never bestowed upon any city before the time of Epaminondas. When therefore the Spartans complained of "the liberation of Messênê"—"the loss of Messênê"—they included in the word, not simply the city on Mount Ithômê, but all this territory besides; though it was not all comprised in the domain of the new city.

They complained yet more indignantly, that along with the genuine Messenians, now brought back from exile—a rabble of their own emancipated Periœki and Helots had been domiciled on their border.[2] Herein were included, not only such of these two classes as, having before dwelt in servitude throughout the territory westward of Ithômê, now remained there in a state of freedom —but also doubtless a number of others who deserted from other parts of Laconia. For as we know that such desertions had been not inconsiderable, even when there was no better shelter than the outlying posts of Pylus and Kythéra—so we may be sure that they became much more numerous, when the neighbouring city of Messênê was founded under adequate protection, and when there was a chance of obtaining, westward of the Messenian Gulf, free lands with a new home. Moreover, such Periœki and Helots as had actually joined the invading army of Epaminondas in Laconia, would be forced from simple

*Periœki and Helots established as freemen along with the Messenians on the Lacedæmonian border.*

---

[1] The Oration (vi.) called Arobidamus, by Isokratês, exhibits powerfully the Spartan feeling of the time, respecting this abstraction of territory, and emancipation of serfs, for the purpose of restoring Messênê. s. 50. Καὶ εἰ μὲν τοὺς ὡς ἀληθῶς Μεσσηνίους κατῆγον (the Thebans), ἢδικοῦν μὲν ἄν, ὅμως δ' εὐλογωτέρως ἂν εἰς ἡμᾶς ἐξημάρτανον· νῦν δὲ τοὺς Εἵλωτας ὁμόρους ἡμῖν καρακατοικίζουσιν, ὥστε μὴ τοῦτ' εἶναι χαλεπώτατον, εἰ τῆς χώρας στερησόμεθα παρὰ τὸ δίκαιον, ἀλλ' εἰ τοὺς δούλους ἡμετέρους ἐπιψόμεθα κυρίους αὐτῆς ὄντας.

Again—s. 101. ἦν γὰρ παρακατοικισώμεθα τοὺς Εἵλωτας, καὶ τὴν πόλιν ταύτην περιίδωμεν αὐξηθεῖσαν, εὖ ἴσμεν οἱ οὐκ οἶδεν ὅτι πάντα τὸν βίον ἐν ταραχαῖς καὶ κινδύνοις διατελοῦμεν ὄντες; compare also sections 8 and 102.

insecurity to quit the country when he retired, and would be supplied with fresh residences in the newly-enfranchised territory. All these men would pass at once, out of a state of peculiarly harsh servitude, into the dignity of free and equal Hellens,[1] sending again a solemn Messenian legation or Theôry to the Olympic festival, after an interval of more than three centuries[2]—outdoing their former masters in the magnitude of their offerings from the same soil—and requiting them for previous ill-usage by words of defiance and insult, instead of that universal deference and admiration which a Spartan had hitherto been accustomed to look upon as his due.

*The details of this re-organising process unhappily unknown.*

The enfranchisement and re-organization of all Western Laconia, the renovation of the Messenian name, the foundation of the two new cities (Messênê and Megalopolis) in immediate neighbourhood and sympathy—while they completed the degradation of Sparta, constituted in all respects the most interesting political phænomena that Greece had witnessed for many years.

To the profound mortification of the historian—he is able to recount nothing more than the bare facts, with such inferences as these facts themselves warrant. Xenophon, under whose eyes all must have passed, designedly omits

---

[1] Isokratês, Orat. vi. (Archidam.) s. 111. Ἄξιον δὲ καὶ τὴν Ὀλυμπιάδα καὶ τὰς ἄλλας πανηγύρεις, ἐν αἷς ἕκαστος ἡμῶν (Spartans) ζηλωτότερος ἦν καὶ θαυμαστότερος τῶν ἀθλητῶν τῶν ἐν τοῖς ἀγῶσι τὰς νίκας ἀναιρουμένων. Εἰς ἃς τίς ἂν ἐλθεῖν τολμήσειεν, ἀντὶ μὲν τοῦ τιμᾶσθαι καταφρονηθησόμενος—ἔτι δὲ πρὸς τούτοις ὁρώμενος μὲν τοὺς οἰκέτας ἀπὸ τῆς χώρας ἧς οἱ πατέρες ἡμῖν κατέλιπον ἀπαρχὰς καὶ θυσίας μείζους ἡμῶν ποιουμένους, ἀκουσόμενος δ᾽ αὐτῶν τοιαύταις βλασφημίαις χρωμένων, οἵαις περ εἰκὸς τοὺς χαλεπώτερον τῶν ἄλλων δεδουλευκότας, δὲ ἴσου δὲ νῦν τὰς συνθήκας τοῖς δεσπόταις πεποιημένους.

This oration, composed only five or six years after the battle of Leuktra, is exceedingly valuable as a testimony of the Spartan feeling under such severe humiliations.

[2] The freedom of the Messenians had been put down by the first Messenian war, after which they became subjects of Sparta. The second Messenian war arose from their revolt.

No free Messenian legation could therefore have visited Olympia since the termination of the first war; which is placed by Pausanias (iv. 13, 6) in 723 B.C.; though the date is not to be trusted. Pausanias (iv. 27, 3) gives 287 years between the end of the second Messenian war and the foundation of Messênê by Epaminondas. See the note of Siebelis on this passage. Exact dates of these early wars cannot be made out.

to notice them;[1] Pausanias, whom we have to thank for most of what we know, is prompted by his religious imagination to relate many divine signs and warnings, but little matter of actual occurrence. Details are altogether withheld from us. We know neither how long a time was occupied in the building of the two cities, nor who furnished the cost; though both the one and the other must have been considerable. Of the thousand new arrangements, incident to the winding up of many small townships, and the commencement of two large cities, we are unable to render any account. Yet there is no point of time wherein social phænomena are either so interesting or so instructive. In describing societies already established and ancient, we find the force of traditional routine almost omnipotent in its influence both on men's actions and on their feelings. Bad as well as good is preserved in one concrete, since the dead weight of the past stifles all constructive intelligence,

[1] The partiality towards Sparta, visible even from the beginning of Xenophon's history, becomes more and more exaggerated throughout the two latter books wherein he recounts her misfortunes; it is moreover intensified by spite against the Thebans and Epaminondas as her conquerors. But there is hardly any instance of this feeling, so glaring or so discreditable, as the case now before us. In describing the expedition of Epaminondas into Peloponnesus in the winter of 370-369 B.C., he totally omits the foundation both of Messênê and of Megalopolis; though in the after part of his history, he alludes (briefly) both to one and to the other as facts accomplished. He represents the Thebans to have come into Arcadia with their magnificent army, for the simple purpose of repelling Agesilaus and the Spartans, and to have been desirous of returning to Bœotia, as soon as it was ascertained that the latter had already returned to Sparta (vi. 5, 83). Nor does he once mention the name of Epaminondas as general of the Thebans in the expedition, any more than he mentions him at Leuktra.

Considering the momentous and striking character of these facts, and the eminence of the Theban general by whom they were achieved —such silence on the part of an historian, who professes to recount the events of the time, is an inexcuseable dereliction of his duty to state the *whole truth*. It is plain that Messênê and Megalopolis wounded to the quick the philo-Spartan sentiment of Xenophon. They stood as permanent evidences of the degradation of Sparta, even after the hostile armies had withdrawn from Laconia. He prefers to ignore them altogether. Yet he can find space to recount, with disproportionate prolixity, the two applications of the Spartans to Athens for aid, with the favourable reception which they obtained — also the exploits of the Phliasians in their devoted attachment to Sparta.

and leaves little room even for improving aspirations. But
the forty small communities which coalesced into Megalopolis, and the Messenians and other settlers who came for
the first time together on the hill of Ithômê, were in a state
in which new exigences of every kind pressed for immediate
satisfaction. There was no file to afford a precedent, nor
any resource left except to submit all the problems to discussion by those whose character and judgement was most
esteemed. Whether the problems were well or ill-solved,
there must have been now a genuine and earnest attempt
to strike out as good a solution as the lights of the time
and place permitted, with a certain latitude for conflicting
views. Arrangements must have been made for the appor-
tionment of houses and lands among the citizens, by purchase, or grant, or both together; for the political and
judicial constitution; for religious and recreative ceremonies, for military defence, for markets, for the security
and transmission of property, &c. All these and many
other social wants of a nascent community must now have
been provided for, and it would have been highly interesting
to know how. Unhappily the means are denied to us. We
can record little more than the bare fact that these two
youngest members of the Hellenic brotherhood of cities
were born at the same time, and under the auspices of the
same presiding genius, Epaminondas; destined to sustain
each other in neighbourly sympathy and in repelling all
common danger from the attacks of Sparta; a purpose,
which, even two centuries afterwards, remained engraven
on the mind of a Megalopolitan patriot like Polybius.[1]

Megalopo-
lis—the
Pan-Arca-
dian Ten
Thousand.
Megalopolis was intended not merely as a great city
in itself, but as the centre of the new confederacy;
which appears to have comprised all Arcadia,
except Orchomenus and Heræa. It was enacted
that a synod or assembly, from all the separate
members of the Arcadian name, and in which probably
every Arcadian citizen from the constituent communities
had the right of attending, should be periodically convoked
there. This assembly was called the Ten Thousand, or the
Great Number. A body of Arcadian troops, called the
Epariti, destined to uphold the federation, and receiving
pay when on service, was also provided. Assessments were

[1] See a striking passage in Polybius, iv. 32. Compare also Pausan.
v. 20, 3; and viii. 27, 2.

levied upon each city for their support, and a Pan-Arcadian general (probably also other officers) was named. The Ten Thousand, on behalf of all Arcadia, received foreign envoys —concluded war, or peace, or alliance—and tried all officers or other Arcadians brought before them on accusations of public misconduct.[1] The great Athenian orators, Kallistratus, Demosthenês, Æschinês, on various occasions pleaded before it.[2] What were its times of meeting, we are unable to say. It contributed seriously, for a certain time, to sustain a Pan-Arcadian communion of action and sentiment which had never before existed;[3] and to prevent, or soften, those dissensions which had always a tendency to break out among the separate Arcadian cities. The patriotic enthusiasm, however, out of which Megalopolis had first arisen, gradually became enfeebled. The city never attained that pre-eminence or power which its founders contemplated, and which had caused the city to be laid out on a scale too large for the population actually inhabiting it.[4]

Not only was the portion of Laconia west of the Messenian Gulf now rendered independent of Sparta, but also much of the territory which lies north of Sparta, between that city and Arcadia. Thus the Skiritæ (hardly mountaineers of Arcadian race, heretofore dependent upon Sparta, and constituting a valuable contingent to her armies[5]), with their territory forming the northern frontier of Laconia towards Arcadia, became from this time independent of and hostile to Sparta.[6] The same is the case even with a place much nearer to Sparta—Sellasia; though this latter was retaken by the Lacedæmonians four or five years afterwards.[7]

Epaminondas remained about four months beyond the legal duration of his command in Arcadia and Laconia.[8] The sufferings of a severe mid-winter were greatly mitigated to his soldiers by the Arcadians, who, full of devoted friendship,

Epaminondas and his army evacuate Peloponnesus.

[1] Xenoph. Hellen. vii. 1, 38; vii. 4, 2, 33, 31; vii. 3, 1.
[2] Demosthen. Fals. Legat. p. 344. s. 11, p. 403, s. 320; Æschinês, Fals. Leg. p. 276 c. 49; Cornel. Nepos, Epamin. c. 6.
[3] Xenoph. Hellen. vii. 1, 38; vii. 4, 83; Diodor. xv. 69; Aristotle—'Ἀρκάδων Πολιτεία—ap. Harpokration. v. Μύριοι, p. 108, ed. Neumann.
[4] Polybius, ii. 55.
[5] Thucyd. v. 66.
[6] Xen. Hellen. vii. 4, 21.
[7] Xen. Hellen. vii. 4, 12; Diodor. xv, 64.
[8] The exact number of eighty-

pressed upon them an excess of hospitality which he
could not permit consistently with their military duties.¹
He stayed long enough to settle all the preliminary debates
and difficulties, and to put in train of serious execution
the establishment of Messênê and Megalopolis. For the
completion of a work thus comprehensive, which changed
the face and character of Peloponnesus, much time was of
course necessary. Accordingly, a Theban division under
Pammenês, was left to repel all obstruction from
Sparta;² while Tegea also, from this time forward, for
some years, was occupied as a post by a Theban harmost
and garrison.³

---

five days, given by Diodorus (xv.
67) seems to show that he had
copied literally from Ephorus or
some other older author.

Plutarch, in one place (Agesil. c.
32), mentions "three entire months,"
which differs little from eighty-five
days. He expresses himself as if
Epaminondas spent all this time
in ravaging Laconia. Yet again,
in the Apophth. Reg. p. 194 B.
(compare Ælian, V. H. xiii. 42),
and in the life of Pelopidas (c. 25),
Plutarch states, that Epaminondas
and his colleagues held the command four whole months over and
above the legal time, being engaged in their operations in Laconia and Messenia. This seems to
me the more probable interpretation of the case; for the operations
seem too large to have been accomplished in either three or four
months.

¹ See a remarkable passage in
Plutarch — An Seni sit gerenda
Respublica (c. 8. p. 788 A.).

² Pausan. viii. 27, 2. Pammenês
is said to have been an earnest
friend of Epaminondas, but of
older political standing; to whom
Epaminondas partly owed his rise
(Plutarch, Reip. Ger. Præcep. p.
805 F.).

Pausanias places the foundation
of Megalopolis in the same Olympic

year as the battle of Leuktra, and
a few months after that battle,
during the archonship of Phrasikleidês at Athens; that is, between
Midsummer 371 and Midsummer
370 B.C. (Pausan. viii. 27, 6). He
places the foundation of Messênê
in the next Olympic year, under
the archonship of Dyskinêtus at
Athens; that is, between Midsummer 370 and Midsummer 369 B.C.
(iv. 27, 5).

The foundation of Megalopolis
would probably be understood to
date from the initial determination
taken by the assembled Arcadians,
soon after the revolution at Tegea,
to found a Pan-Arcadian city and
federative league. This was probably taken before Midsummer 370
B.C., and the date of Pausanias
would thus be correct.

The foundation of Messênê would
doubtless take its era from the
expedition of Epaminondas — between November and March 370-
369 B.C.; which would be during
the archonship of Dyskinêtus at
Athens, as Pausanias affirms.

What length of time was required
to complete the erection and establishment of either city, we are not
informed.

Diodorus places the foundation
of Megalopolis in 368 B.C. (xv. 72).

³ Xen. Hellen. vii. 4, 36.

Meanwhile the Athenians were profoundly affected by these proceedings of Epaminondas in Peloponnesus. The accumulation of force against Sparta was so powerful, that under a chief like him, it seemed sufficient to crush her: and though the Athenians were now neutral in the contest, such a prospect was not at all agreeable to them,[1] involving the aggrandizement of Thebes to a point inconsistent with their security. It was in the midst of the succcsses of Epaminondas that envoys came to Athens from Sparta, Corinth, and Phlius, to entreat her aid. The message was one not merely humiliating to the Lacedæmonians, who had never previously sent the like request to any Grecian city—but also difficult to handle in reference to Athens. History showed abundant acts of jealousy and hostility, little either of good feeling or consentient interest, on the part of the Lacedæmonians towards her. What little was to be found, the envoy dexterously brought forward; going back to the dethronement of the Peisistratids from Athens by Spartan help, the glorious expulsion of Xerxès from Greece by the joint efforts of both cities—and the auxiliaries sent by Athens into Laconia in 465 B.C., to assist the Spartans against the revolted Messenians on Mount Ithômê. In these times (he reminded the Athenian assembly) Thebes had betrayed the Hellenic cause by joining Xerxès, and had been an object of common hatred to both. Moreover the maritime forces of Greece had been arrayed under Athens in the Confederacy of Delos, with full sanction and recommendation from Sparta; while the headship of the latter by land had in like manner been accepted by the Athenians. He called on the assembly, in the name of these former glories, to concur with Sparta in forgetting all the deplorable hostilities which had since intervened, and to afford to her a generous relief against the old common enemy. The Thebans might even now be decimated (according to the vow said to have been taken after the repulse of Xerxès), in spite of their present menacing ascendency—if Athens and Sparta could be brought heartily to cooperate; and might be dealt with as Thebes herself had wished to deal with Athens after the Peloponnesian

---

[1] Isokratês (Archidamus), Or. vi. s. 129.

war, when Sparta refused to concur in pronouncing the sentence of utter ruin.¹

This appeal from Sparta was earnestly seconded by the envoys from Corinth and Phlius. The Corinthian speaker contended, that Epaminondas and his army, passing through the territory of Corinth, and inflicting damage upon it in their passage into Peloponnesus, had committed a glaring violation of the general peace, sworn in 371 B.C., first at Sparta and afterwards at Athens, guaranteeing universal autonomy to every Grecian city. The envoy from Phlius—while complimenting Athens on the proud position which she now held, having the fate of Sparta in her hands—dwelt on the meed of honour which she would earn in Greece, if she now generously interfered to rescue her ancient rival, forgetting past injuries and remembering only past benefits. In adopting such policy, too, she would act in accordance with her own true interests; since, should Sparta be crushed, the Thebans would become undisputed heads of Greece, and more formidable still to Athens.²

It was not among the least marks of the prostration of Sparta, that she should be compelled to send such an embassy to Athens, and to entreat an amnesty for so many untoward realities during the past. The contrast is indeed striking, when we set her present language against that which she had held respecting Athens, before and through the Peloponnesian war.

Reception of the envoys—the Athenians grant the prayer.

At first, her envoys were heard with doubtful favour; the sentiment of the Athenian assembly being apparently rather against than for them. "Such language from the Spartans (murmured the assembled citizens) is intelligible enough during their present distress; but so long as they were in good circumstances, we received nothing but ill-usage from them."³ Nor was the complaint of the Spartans, that the invasion of Laconia was contrary to the sworn peace guaranteeing universal autonomy, admitted without opposition. Some said that the Lacedæmonians had drawn the invasion upon themselves, by their previous interference

---

¹ Xen. Hellen. vi. 5, 34, 35.
² Xen. Hellen. vi. 5, 38-49.
³ Xen. Hellen. vi. 5, 35. Οἱ μέντοι Ἀθηναῖοι οὐ πάνυ ἐδέξαντο, ἀλλὰ θροῦς τις τοιοῦτος διῆλθεν, ὡς νῦν μὲν ταῦτα λέγοιεν· ὅτε δὲ εὖ ἐπράττον, ἐπέκειντο ἡμῖν.

CHAP. LXXVIII.  AID VOTED TO SPARTA.   455

with Tegea and in Arcadia; and that the intervention of
the Mantineians at Tegea had been justifiable, since Stasippus and the philo-Laconian party in that city had been
the first to begin unjust violence. On the other hand, the
appeal made by the envoys to the congress of Peloponnesian allies held in 404 B.C., after the surrender of Athens
—when the Theban deputy had proposed that Athens
should be totally destroyed, while the Spartans had strenuously protested against so cruel a sentence—made a powerful impression on the assembly, and contributed more than
anything else to determine them in favour of the proposition.[1] "As Athens was then, so Sparta is now, on the
brink of ruin, from the fiat of the same enemy: Athens
was then rescued by Sparta, and shall she now leave the
rescue unrequited?" Such was the broad and simple issue
which told upon the feelings of the assembled Athenians,
disposing them to listen with increasing favour both to the
envoys from Corinth and Phlius, and to their own speakers
on the same side.

To rescue Sparta, indeed, was prudent as well as
generous. A counterpoise would thus be main- Vote
tained against the excessive aggrandizement of passed to
Thebes, which at this moment doubtless caused aid Sparta.
serious alarm and jealousy to the Athenians. Iphikra-
And thus, after the first ebullition of resentment tes is named
against Sparta, naturally suggested by the history of the
past, the philo-Spartan view of the situation gradually
became more and more predominant in the assembly.
Kallistratus[2] the orator spoke eloquently in support of
the Lacedæmonians; while the adverse speakers were
badly listened to, as pleading in favour of Thebes, whom
no one wished to aggrandize farther. A vote, decisive and
enthusiastic, was passed for assisting the Spartans with
the full force of Athens; under the command of Iphikratês,
then residing as a private citizen[3] at Athens, since the
peace of the preceding year, which had caused him to be
recalled from Korkyra.

---

[1] Xen. Hellen. vi. 5, 35. Μήτιστον opposition to the vote for support-
δὲ τῶν λεχθέντων παρὰ Λακεδαιμο- ing Sparta (ib.).
νίων ἰδόκει εἶναι, &c. [2] Xen. Hellen. vi. 5, 49; Dionys.
[3] Demosthenês cont. Neær. p. 1353. Hal. Judic. de Lysiâ, p. 479.
Xenokleidês, a poet, spoke in

As soon as the sacrifices, offered in contemplation of this enterprise, were announced to be favourable, Iphikratês made proclamation that the citizens destined for service should equip themselves and muster in arms in the grove of Akadêmus (outside the gates), there to take their evening meal, and to march the next morning at daybreak. Such was the general ardour, that many citizens went forth from the gates even in advance of Iphikratês himself; and the total force which followed him is said to have been 12,000 men—not named under conscription by the general, but volunteers.[1] He first marched to Corinth, where he halted some days; much to the discontent of his soldiers, who were impatient to accomplish their project of carrying rescue to Sparta. But Iphikratês was well-aware that all beyond Corinth and Phlius was hostile ground, and that he had formidable enemies to deal with. After having established his position at Corinth, and obtained information regarding the enemy, he marched into Arcadia, and there made war without any important result. Epaminondas and his army had quitted Laconia, while many of the Arcadians and Eleians, had gone home with the plunder acquired; so that Sparta was for the time out of danger. Impelled in part by the recent manifestation of Athens,[2] the Theban general himself soon commenced his march of return into Bœotia, in which it was necessary for him to pass the line of Mount Oneium between Corinth and Kenchreæ. This line was composed of difficult ground, and afforded good means of resistance to the passage of an army; nevertheless Iphikratês, though he occupied its two extremities, did not attempt directly to bar the passage of the Thebans. He contented himself with sending out from Corinth all his cavalry, both Athenian and Corinthian, to harass them in their march. But Epaminondas beat them back with some loss, and pursued them to the gates of Corinth. Excited by this spectacle, the Athenian main body within the town were eager to march out and engage in general battle. Their ardour was however repressed by Iphikratês; who, refusing to go forth, suffered the Thebans to continue their retreat unmolested.[3]

*Murch of Iphikratês and his army to the Isthmus.*

---

[1] This number is stated by Diodorus (xv. 63).

[2] To this extent we may believe what is said by Cornelius Nepos (Iphicrates, c. 2).

[3] The account here given in the text coincides as to the matter of fact with Xenophon, as well as

## RETURN OF THE THEBANS.

On returning to Thebes, Epaminondas with Pelopidas and the other Bœotarchs, resigned the command. They with Plutarch; and also (in my belief) with Pausanias (Xen. Hell. vi. 5, 51; Plutarch, Pelop. c. 24; Pausan. ix. 14, 3).

But though I accept the facts of Xenophon, I cannot accept either his suppositions as to the purpose, or his criticisms on the conduct, of Iphikratês. Other modern critics appear to me not to have sufficiently distinguished Xenophon's *facts* from his *suppositions*.

Iphikratês (says Xenophon), while attempting to guard the line of Mount Oneium, in order that the Thebans might not be able to reach Bœotia—left the excellent road adjoining to Kenchreæ unguarded. Then—wishing to inform himself, whether the Thebans had as yet passed the Mount Oneium, he sent out as scouts all the Athenian and all the Corinthian cavalry. Now (observes Xenophon) a few scouts can see and report as well as a great number; while the great number find it more difficult to get back in safety. By this foolish conduct of Iphikratês, in sending out so large a body, several horsemen were lost in the retreat; which would not have happened if he had only sent out a few.

The criticism here made by Xenophon appears unfounded. It is plain, from the facts which he himself states, that Iphikratês never intended to bar the passage of the Thebans; and that he sent out his whole body of cavalry, not simply as scouts, but to harass the enemy on ground which he thought advantageous for the purpose. That so able a commander as Iphikratês should have been guilty of the gross blunders with which Xenophon here reproaches him, is in a high degree improbable; it seems to me more probable that Xenophon has misconceived his real purpose. Why indeed should Iphikratês wish to expose the whole Athenian army in a murderous conflict for the purpose of preventing the homeward march of the Thebans? His mission was, to rescue Sparta; but Sparta was now no longer in danger; and it was for the advantage of Athens that the Thebans should go back to Bœotia, rather than remain in Peloponnesus. That he should content himself with harassing the Thebans, instead of barring their retreat directly, is a policy which we should expect from him.

There is another circumstance in this retreat which has excited discussion among the commentators, and on which I dissent from their views. It is connected with the statement of Pausanias, who says —'Ὡς πρόιων τῷ στρατῷ (Epaminondas) κατὰ Λέχαιον ἐγίνετο, καὶ δυσείναι τῆς ὁδοῦ τὰ στενὰ καὶ δύσβατα ἔμελλεν, Ἰφικράτης ὁ Τιμοθέου κελτασστάς καὶ ἄλλην Ἀθηναίων ἔχων δύναμιν, ἐπιχειρεῖ τοῖς Θηβαίοις. Ἐπαμινώνδας δὲ τοὺς ἐπιθεμένους τρέπεται, καὶ πρὸς αὐτό ἀφικνόμενος Ἀθηναίων τὸ ἄστυ, ὡς ἀπεξίεναι μαχομένους τοὺς Ἀθηναίους ἐκώλυεν Ἰφικράτης, ὁ δὲ αὖθις ἐς τὰς Θήβας ἀπήλαυνε.

In this statement there are some inaccuracies, as that of calling Iphikratês "son of Timotheus;" and speaking of *Lechæum*, where Pausanias ought to have named *Kenchreæ*. For Epaminondas could not have passed Corinth on the side of Lechæum, since the Long Walls, reaching from one to the other, would prevent him; moreover the "rugged ground" was between Corinth and Kenchreæ, not between Corinth and Lechæum.

*Trial of Epaminondas at Thebes for retaining his command beyond the legal time—his honourable and easy acquittal.*

had already retained it for four months longer than the legal expiration of their term. Although, by the constitutional law of Thebes, any general who retained his functions longer than the period fixed by law was pronounced worthy of death, yet Epaminondas, while employed in his great projects for humiliating Sparta and founding the two hostile cities on her border, had taken upon himself to brave this illegality, persuading all his colleagues to concur with him. On resigning the command, all of them had to undergo that

But the words which occasion most perplexity are those which follow: ‘Epaminondas repulses the assailants, and *having come to the city itself of the Athenians*, when Iphikrates forbade the Athenians to come out and fight, he (Epaminondas) again marched away to Thebes.’

What are we to understand by the *city of the Athenians?* The natural sense of the words is certainly Athens; and so most of the commentators relate. But when the battle was fought between Corinth and Kenchreæ, can we reasonably believe that Epaminondas pursued the fugitives to Athens —through the city of Megara, which lay in the way, and which seems then (Diodor. xv. 68) to have been allied with Athens? The station of Iphikrates was *Corinth;* from thence he had marched out—and thither his cavalry, when repulsed, would go back, as the nearest shelter.

Dr. Thirlwall (Hist. Greece, vol. v. ch. 59. p. 141) understands Pausanias to mean, that Iphikrates retired with his defeated cavalry to Corinth—that Epaminondas then marched straight on to Athens— and that Iphikrates followed him. “Possibly (he says) the only mistake in this statement is, that it represents the *presence* of Iphikratês, instead of his *absence*, as the

cause which prevented the Athenians from fighting. According to Xenophon, Iphikrates must have been in the rear of Epaminondas.”

I cannot think that we obtain this from the words of Xenophon. Neither he nor Plutarch countenances the idea that Epaminondas marched to the walls of Athens, which supposition is derived solely from the words of Pausanias. Xenophon and Plutarch intimate only that Iphikratês interposed some opposition, and not very effective opposition, near Corinth, to the retreating march of Epaminondas, from Peloponnesus into Bœotia.

That Epaminondas should have marched to Athens at all, under the circumstances of the case, when he was returning to Bœotia, appears to me in itself improbable, and to be rendered still more improbable by the silence of Xenophon. Nor is it indispensable to put this construction even upon Pausanias ; who may surely have meant by the words—πρὸς αὐτὸ Ἀθηναίων τὸ ἄστυ —not Athens, but *the city then occupied by the Athenians engaged—* that is, *Corinth. The city of the Athenians*, in reference to this battle, was Corinth; it was the city out of which the troops of Iphikratês had just marched, and to which, on being defeated, they naturally retired for safety, pursued by Epaminondas to the gates.

trial of accountability which awaited every retiring magistrate, as a matter of course—but which, in the present case, was required on special ground, since all had committed an act notoriously punishable as well as of dangerous precedent. Epaminondas undertook the duty of defending his colleagues as well as himself. That he as well as Pelopidas had political enemies, likely to avail themselves of any fair pretext for accusing him—is not to be doubted. But we may well doubt, whether on the present occasion any of these enemies actually came forward to propose that the penalty legally incurred should be inflicted; not merely because this proposition, in the face of a victorious army, returning elate with their achievements and proud of their commanders, was full of danger to the mover himself—but also for another reason—because Epaminondas would hardly be imprudent enough to wait for the case to be stated by his enemies. Knowing that the illegality committed was flagrant and of hazardous example—having also the reputation of his colleagues as well as his own to protect—he would forestal accusation by coming forward himself to explain and justify the proceeding. He set forth the glorious results of the expedition just finished; the invasion and devastation of Laconia, hitherto unvisited by any enemy—the confinement of the Spartans within their walls—the liberation of all Western Laconia, and the establishment of Messênê as a city—the constitution of a strong new Arcadian city, forming, with Tegea on one flank and Messênê on the other, a line of defence on the Spartan frontier, so as to ensure the permanent depression of the great enemy of Thebes—the emancipation of Greece generally, from Spartan ascendency, now consummated.

Such justification—whether delivered in reply to a substantive accuser, or (which is more probable) tendered

---

The statement of Pausanias—that Iphikratês would not let the Athenians in the town (Corinth) go out to fight—then follows naturally. Epaminondas, finding that they would not come out, drew back his troops, and resumed his march to Thebes.

The stratagem of Iphikratês noticed by Polyænus (iii. 9, 29), can hardly be the same incident as this mentioned by Pausanias. It purports to be a nocturnal surprise planned by the Thebans against Athens; which certainly must be quite different (if it be in itself a reality) from this march of Epaminondas. And the stratagem ascribed by Polyænus to Iphikratês is of a strange and highly improbable character.

spontaneously by Epaminondas himself—was not merely satisfactory, but triumphant. He and the other generals were acquitted by acclamation; without even going through the formality of collecting the votes.¹ And it appears that both Epaminondas and Pelopidas were immediately re-appointed among the Bœotarchs of the year.²

---

¹ Plutarch, Pelopidas, c. 25; Plutarch, Apophthegm. p. 194 B.; Pausan. ix. 14, 4; Cornelius Nepos, Epaminond. c. 7, 8; Ælian, V. H. xiii. 42.

Pausanias states the fact plainly and clearly; the others, especially Nepos and Ælian, though agreeing in the main fact, surround it with colours exaggerated and false. They represent Epaminondas as in danger of being put to death by ungrateful and malignant fellow-citizens; Cornelius Nepos puts into his mouth a justificatory speech of extreme insolence (compare Arist. Or. xlvi. περὶ τοῦ παραφθέγματος—p. 385 Jebb.; p. 520 Dindorf); which, had it been really made, would have tended more than anything else to set the public against him—and which is moreover quite foreign to the character of Epaminondas. To carry the exaggeration still further, Plutarch (De Vitioso Pudore, p. 540 E.) describes Pelopidas as trembling and begging for his life.

Epaminondas had committed a grave illegality, which could not be passed over without notice in his trial of accountability. But he had a good justification. It was necessary that he should put in the justification; when put in, it passed triumphantly. What more could be required? The facts, when fairly stated, will not serve as an illustration of the alleged ingratitude of the people towards great men.

² Diodorus (xv. 81) states that Pelopidas was Bœotarch without interruption, annually re-appointed, from the revolution of Thebes down to his decease. Plutarch also (Pelopid. c. 34) affirms that when Pelopidas died, he was in his thirteenth year of the appointment; which may be understood as the same assertion in other words. Whether Epaminondas was rechosen, does not appear.

Sievers denies the re-appointment as well of Pelopidas as of Epaminondas. But I do not see upon what grounds; for, in my judgement, Epaminondas appears again as commander in Peloponnesus during this same year (369 B.C.). Sievers holds Epaminondas to have commanded without being Bœotarch; but no reason is produced for this (Sievers, Geschicht. Griech. bis zur Schlacht von Mantineia, p. 277).

END OF VOL. IX.

---

LEIPZIG: PRINTED BY W. DRUGULIN.

www.ingramcontent.com/pod-product-compliance
Lightning Source LLC
Chambersburg PA
CBHW020835020526
44114CB00040B/786